Lecture Notes in Computer Science 12400

Gillian Dobbie · Ulrich Frank ·
Gerti Kappel · Stephen W. Liddle ·
Heinrich C. Mayr (Eds.)

Conceptual Modeling

39th International Conference, ER 2020
Vienna, Austria, November 3–6, 2020
Proceedings

Editors
Gillian Dobbie ⓘ
University of Auckland
Auckland, New Zealand

Gerti Kappel ⓘ
TU Wien
Vienna, Austria

Heinrich C. Mayr ⓘ
University of Klagenfurt
Klagenfurt am Wörthersee, Austria

Ulrich Frank ⓘ
University of Duisburg-Essen
Essen, Germany

Stephen W. Liddle ⓘ
Brigham Young University
Provo, UT, USA

ISSN 0302-9743   ISSN 1611-3349 (electronic)
Lecture Notes in Computer Science
ISBN 978-3-030-62521-4   ISBN 978-3-030-62522-1 (eBook)
https://doi.org/10.1007/978-3-030-62522-1

LNCS Sublibrary: SL3 – Information Systems and Applications, incl. Internet/Web, and HCI

This Springer imprint is published by the registered company Springer Nature Switzerland AG
The registered company address is: Gewerbestrasse 11, 6330 Cham, Switzerland

Preface

This year's 39th ER conference is dedicated to a topic that represents a phenomenon unprecedented in the history of humankind. The digital transformation encompasses all areas of life and work. It is accompanied by new types of services, new forms of division of labor, interpersonal interaction, and international cooperation. It thus has a direct impact on how we see the world and what perspectives we develop for our future lives. Last but not least, we can assume that the ongoing digitalization will also have a lasting impact on scientific research. Conceptual modeling is of central importance for the successful management of the digital transformation. On the one hand, all areas of life and work are increasingly permeated by software. Conceptual models are required not only for the development of software, but also for the appropriate structuring of data. They promote reuse, integration, and integrity. Furthermore, conceptual models are also suitable for supporting the use of software. They help to open the black box as to which software often presents itself and thus contribute to transparency and user empowerment. At the same time, the digital transformation also brings with it specific challenges for modeling research. In order to support the design of software that can be adapted to profound changes of requirements, powerful abstractions are needed that are beyond the capabilities of today's prevalent modeling languages. In addition, AI research, especially in the field of machine learning, is associated with a quasi-existential challenge of modeling research. Thus, some proponents of AI research already foresee the end of traditional conceptual modeling. It would last too long and would be too expensive. It could be better handled by machines. Such daring hypotheses may be seen as a threat. But above all they are an occasion to reflect on fundamental questions of conceptual modeling, such as the difference between concepts and classifications or between human thought and data processing. Probably the central question is not whether and when machine learning can take over the human activity of conceptual modeling, but how the inductive analysis of large amounts of data and human abstraction can be synergistically combined.

Given the fascination that the digital transformation holds for conceptual modeling research, it is not surprising that we were able to quickly agree on this conference topic during last year's ER conference in Salvador, Brazil. At that time, none of us had any idea that the digital transformation would be significant for the conference in a completely different, less-than-pleasant way. The ongoing COVID-19 pandemic made it necessary for this year's conference not to take place as usual: colleagues could not meet for personal exchange and there was no opportunity to get to know a foreign city and enjoy local food. This was all the more regrettable as Vienna is one of the world's most attractive conference venues. COVID-19 also meant that many of us were burdened with additional obligations. We therefore considered it appropriate to extend the deadline for the submission of contributions. Unfortunately, this put increased time pressure on the review process. Nevertheless, we are glad that in the end the reviews were received on time.

The first-time organization of the ER as a virtual conference was associated with a number of challenges. For example, organizing the program proved to be difficult because it was almost impossible to find a schedule that would accommodate the many time zones in which the participants would be located during the conference. We were forced to make compromises here, which led to considerable limitations for individual time zones. We regret this very much and hope for the understanding of those concerned. In addition, it was not possible to foresee the impact that virtualization would have on the number of submissions. We are glad that the response to the call was considerable despite the crisis. A total of 143 contributions were submitted, of which 28 were accepted as regular papers and 16 as short papers. The papers cover a broad spectrum of innovative topics, thus underlining the great importance and attractiveness of research on conceptual modeling.

We hope that the papers will find your interest and wish you an inspiring read. Finally, we would like to thank the authors, whose contributions made the conference possible, the many reviewers for their outstanding commitment in preparing more than 400 expert opinions, and last but not least the senior editors, without whose support we would not have been able to cope with the evaluation of the expert opinions.

November 2020

Gillian Dobbie
Ulrich Frank
Gerti Kappel
Stephen W. Liddle
Heinrich C. Mayr

Organization

General Chairs

Gerti Kappel   TU Wien, Austria
Heinrich C. Mayr   Alpen-Adria University Klagenfurt, Austria

Program Committee Chairs

Gillian Dobbie   The University of Auckland, New Zealand
Ulrich Frank   University of Duisburg-Essen, Germany
Stephen W. Liddle   Brigham Young University, USA

Workshop Chairs

Georg Grossmann   University of South Australia, Australia
Sudha Ram   University of Arizona, USA

Tutorial Chairs

João Paulo A. Almeida   Federal University of Espírito Santo, Brazil
Michael Schrefl   Johannes Kepler University Linz, Austria

Panel Chairs

Micahel Grossniklaus   University of Konstanz, Germany
Maurizio Lenzerini   Università di Roma La Sapienza, Italy

Forum/Demo/Poster Chairs

Judith Michael   RWTH Aachen, Germany
Victoria Torres Bosch   Polytechnic University of Valencia, Spain

Sponsoring and Industry Chairs

Reinhold Plösch   Johannes Kepler University Linz, Austria
Manuel Wimmer   Johannes Kepler University Linz, Austria

Publicity and Social Media Chair

Dominik Bork   TU Wien, Austria

Web Chairs

Bernhard Wally   Austrian Council for Research and Technology
                          Development, Austria
Micahel Vierhauser   Johannes Kepler University Linz, Austria

ERSC Liaison

Matthias Jarke   RWTH Aachen University, Germany

Organization Chair

Claudia Habersack   TU Wien, Austria

Steering Committee

Silvana Castano   KU Leuven, Belgium
Peter P. Chen   McMaster University, Canada
Isabelle Comyn-Wattiau   Harvard University, USA
Valeria De Antonellis   Ritsumeikan University, Japan
Karen Davis   University of Porto, Portugal
Lois Delcambre   University of the Aegean, Greece
Giancarlo Guizzardi   Free University of Bozen-Bolzano, Italy
Matthias Jarke   RWTH Aachen University, Germany
Paul Johannesson   Stockholm University, Sweden
Alberto Laender   Federal University of Minas Gerais, Brazil
Stephen Liddle   Brigham Young University, USA
Tok Wang Ling   National University of Singapore, Singapore
Hui Ma   Victoria University of Wellington, New Zealand
Heinrich Mayr   Alpen-Adria University Klagenfurt, Austria
Antoni Olivé   Universitat Politécnica de Catalunya, Spain
José Palazzo Moreira   Federal University of Rio Grande do Sul, Brazil
  de Oliveira
Jeffrey Parsons   Memorial University of Newfoundland, Canada
Oscar Pastor   Universidad Polytécnica de Valencia, Spain
Sudha Ram   University of Arizona, USA
Motoshi Saeki   Tokyo Institute of Technology, Japan
Peretz Shoval   Ben-Gurion University, Israel
Il-Yeol Song   Drexel University, USA
Veda Storey   Georgia State University, USA
Juan Carlos Trujillo   University of Alicante, Spain
Yair Wand   University of British Columbia, Canada
Carson Woo   University of British Columbia, Canada
Eric Yu   University of Toronto, Canada

Program Committee

Jacky Akoka	CNAM, TEM, France
Gove Allen	Brigham Young University, USA
João Paulo Almeida	Federal University of Espirito Santo, Brazil
João Araujo	Universidade Nova de Lisboa, Portugal
Paolo Atzeni	Università Roma Tre, Italy
Claudia P. Ayala	Universitat Politècnica de Catalunya, Spain
Fatma Başak Aydemir	Utrecht University, The Netherlands
Wolf-Tilo Balke	Technische Universität Braunschweig, Germany
Ladjel Bellatreche	LIAS, ENSMA, France
Sourav S. Bhowmick	Nanyang Technological University, Singapore
Sandro Bimonte	IRSTEA, France
Mokrane Bouzeghoub	UVSQ, CNRS, France
Shawn Bowers	Gonzaga University, USA
Stephane Bressan	National University of Singapore, Singapore
Robert Andrei Buchmann	Babes-Bolyai University of Cluj Napoca, Romania
Cristina Cabanillas	Vienna University of Economics and Business, Austria
Maria Luiza Campos	Federal University of Rio de Janeiro, Brazil
Cinzia Cappiello	Politecnico di Milano, Italy
Silvana Castano	University of Milan, Italy
Stefano Ceri	Politecnico di Milano, Italy
Luca Cernuzzi	Universidad Católica, Paraguay
Samira Si-Said Cherfi	Conservatoire National des Arts et Métiers, France
Roger Chiang	University of Cincinnati, USA
Tony Clark	Aston University, UK
Isabelle Comyn-Wattiau	ESSEC Business School, France
Dolors Costal	Universitat Politècnica de Catalunya, Spain
Valeria De Antonellis	University of Brescia, Italy
Sergio de Cesare	University of Westminster, UK
Johann Eder	Alpen Adria University Klagenfurt, Austria
Vadim Ermolayev	Zaporizhzhia National University, Ukraine
Bernadette Farias Lóscio	Federal University of Pernambuco, Brazil
Michael Fellman	University of Rostock, Germany
Peter Fettke	University of Saarbrücken, Germany
Hans-Georg Fill	University of Fribourg, Switzerland
Xavier Franch	Universitat Politècnica de Catalunya, Spain
Frederik Gailly	Ghent University, Belgium
Hong Gao	Harbin Institute of Technology, China
Ming Gao	East China Normal University, China
Yunjun Gao	Zhejiang University, China
Faiez Gargouri	Institut Supèrieur d'Informatique et de Multimédia de Sfax, Tunisia
Aurona Gerber	University of Pretoria, South Africa
Mohamed Gharzouli	Constantine 2 University, Algeria
Aditya Ghose	University of Wollongong, Australia

Marcela Ruiz	Zurich University of Applied Sciences, Switzerland
Motoshi Saeki	Tokyo Institute of Technology, Japan
Melike Sah	Near East University, Cyprus
Jie Shao	University of Science and Technology of China, China
Peretz Shoval	Ben-Gurion University, Israel
Pnina Soffer	University of Haifa, Israel
Veda Storey	Georgia State University, USA
Stefan Strecker	University of Hagen, Germany
Markus Stumptner	University of South Australia, Australia
Arnon Sturm	Ben-Gurion University, Israel
David Taniar	Monash University, Australia
Ernest Teniente	Universitat Politècnica de Catalunya, Spain
Juan Trujillo	University of Alicante, Spain
Panos Vassiliadis	University of Ioannina, Greece
Gottfried Vossen	ERCIS Münster, Germany
Chaokun Wang	Tsinghua University, China
Hongzhi Wang	Harbin Institute of Technology, China
Xianzhi Wang	University of Technology Sydney, Australia
Xiaoli Wang	Xiamen University, China
Mathias Weske	University of Potsdam, Germany
Manuel Wimmer	Vienna University of Technology, Austria
Carson Woo	University of British Columbia, Canada
Robert Wrembel	Poznan University of Technology, Poland
Eric Yu	University of Toronto, Canada
Apostolos Zarras	University of Ioannina, Greece
Jelena Zdravkovic	Stockholm University, Sweden
Wenjie Zhang	The University of New South Wales, Australia
Xiangmin Zhou	RMIT University, Australia
Xuan Zhou	Renmin University of China, China

Additional Reviewers

Corina Abdelahad	Stephan Haarmann
Victorio Albani Carvalho	Felix Härer
Nabila Berkani	Chengkun He
Alessander Botti Benevides	Jelmer Jan Koorn
Marius Breitmayer	Sabine Janzen
Juan De Lara	Oussama Kamel
Marcelo Lury de Sousa Oliveira	Karamjit Kaur
Markus Fischer	Fabienne Lambusch
Jorge Galicia Auyon	Xixi Lu
Soumen Ganguly	Rosni Lumbantoruan
Antonio Garmendia	Wolfgang Mayer
Cristine Griffo	Adriatik Nikaj
Nico Grohmann	Felix Nolte

Contents

Modeling Chatbots, Narratives and Natural Language

Ontology and Conceptual Modeling

Applications of Conceptual Modeling

Conceptual Modeling of Complex and Data-Rich Systems

Foundations of Conceptual Modeling

A Refinement Calculus for Requirements Engineering Based on Argumentation Theory

Yehia ElRakaiby[1]([✉]) [iD], Alexander Borgida[2] [iD], Alessio Ferrari[3] [iD],
and John Mylopoulos[4,5] [iD]

[1] Université du Luxembourg, Luxembourg City, Luxembourg
`yehia.elrakaiby@uni.lu`
[2] Rutgers University, New Brunswick, NJ, USA
`borgida@rutgers.edu`
[3] CNR-ISTI, Pisa, Italy
`alessio.ferrari@isti.cnr.it`
[4] University of Toronto, Toronto, Canada
`jm@cs.toronto.edu`
[5] University of Trento, Trento, Italy

Abstract. The Requirements Engineering (RE) process starts with initial requirements elicited from stakeholders – however conflicting, unattainable, incomplete and ambiguous – and iteratively refines them into a specification that is consistent, complete, valid and unambiguous. We propose a novel RE process in the form of a *calculus* where the process is envisioned as an iterative application of refinement operators, with each operator removing a defect from the current requirements. Our proposal is motivated by the dialectic and incremental nature of RE activities. The calculus, which we call CaRE, casts the RE problem as an iterative argument between stakeholders, who point out defects (ambiguity, incompleteness, etc.) of existing requirements, and then propose refinements to address those defects, thus leading to the construction of a refinement graph. This graph is then *a conceptual model of an RE process enactment*. The semantics of these models is provided by Argumentation Theory, where a requirement may be attacked for having a defect, which in turn may be eliminated by a refinement.

Keywords: Requirements engineering · RE process · RE calculus · Argumentation theory

1 Introduction

The creation of software requirements is a very important initial stage of software development. The original core problem in Requirements Engineering (RE)

Electronic supplementary material The online version of this chapter (https://doi.org/10.1007/978-3-030-62522-1_1) contains supplementary material, which is available to authorized users.

consists of transforming the initial requirements R elicited from stakeholders—however informal, ambiguous, unattainable, etc.—through a systematic refinement process into a specification S that (a) consists of functional requirements, quality constraints and domain assumptions, such that (b) S is consistent, complete, and realizable, and (c) S fulfills R. Variants of this problem form the backbone of RE research, and since the late 1970's it has been recognized that the resulting requirements document contains a conceptual model of the environment and the software-to-be [1,2].

To begin with, consider two RE techniques that can be viewed as research baseline and analogues for our work. In each case, we mention 1) the basic ontology underlying the approach, 2) the refinement process by which the requirements are built, and 3) the "requirements document" resulting from the enactment of this process.

SADT (1977) [1] was the first widely known requirements specification notation and methodology. The modeling ontology of SADT consists of *data* and *activity boxes*, connected by *input/output/control arrows*. The refinement methodology is structured decomposition of non-atomic boxes into aptly named sub-boxes, which are interconnected by aptly-named arrows in appropriate ways. Therefore, the final requirements document/model consists of a number of pages, each describing the internal content of a box; all unexpanded boxes are viewed as atomic/realizable. Ross [1] explicitly stated that SADT can be used to describe not just software requirements but to communicate any idea/conceptual model, and showed how to describe the process of model building in SADT itself.

Basic Goal-Oriented RE—GORE (1993) [3,4] is one of the most influential RE paradigms, and, in its simplest form, has an ontology consisting of *goals*, connected by *reduction* and *conflict relations*. The methodology suggests refining non-realizable goals (ones that cannot be implemented directly) using AND/OR decomposition. The final requirements model then consists of the graph of goal and decomposition nodes, with operationalisable goals as leafs.

The present paper, which extends and builds on initial work in [5], proposes an approach, called **CaRE**, whose ontology consists of *goals/requirements*, *defects* and *refinements*, the latter two of various sub-types. CaRE offers a novel calculus of operators that can be used to critique goals using various defect types, and to address such defects using various kinds of refinements. The CaRE refinement methodology suggests viewing the use of the operators as a dialectic argument between stakeholders, including requirements engineers. The result of enacting this argument will be a *refinement graph*, which records goals, defects and refinements, and for which we define a notion of "acceptability". The set of defect subtypes in CaRE is inspired by the IEEE/ISO Standards on Software Requirements Specifications [6,7]. The set of refinements addressing them is gathered from the RE literature, which contains many proposals for dealing with *specific* types of problems. These include techniques for eliminating forms of conflict, such as inconsistencies [8] and obstacles [9]. For example, the **nonAtomic** defect in CaRE marks a goal as non-operationalisable (in GORE terminology), and the **reduce** operator can be used to perform AND-decomposition of the goal.

Prior RE approaches, starting with [10], viewed initial requirements R as being *satisfied* by specification S under domain assumptions A, if A and S together logically entailed R. This notion of fulfillment runs counter to requirements engineering practice, where stakeholder requirements are routinely weakened because they are unnecessarily strong (e.g., "system shall be available 7/24"), or even dropped altogether. Such refinements can't be accounted for explicitly by proposals in the literature.

The CaRE process, in contrast, results in a refinement graph with nodes corresponding to requirements: some for the initial R, some for potential specifications S, and others for intermediate refinements. Some S, consisting of leaf nodes, is said to address R if there is an *"acceptable argument"* that involves refining S from R. This renders the derivation of S from R a Hegelian dialectic process of thesis-antithesis-synthesis [11], also similar in spirit to the inquiry cycle [12], though our proposal includes more structure, technical details, and reasoning support for the RE process. Addressing a given set of requirements by offering an acceptable argument is a weaker notion of fulfillment than satisfying it, because it allows a requirement to be weakened or altogether dropped, as long as there is an acceptable argument for this. Towards this end, we adopt argumentation semantics from Dung [13].

The contributions of this work are:

- A comprehensive refinement calculus for RE, inspired by goal-oriented RE but which adds: (i) "defects" and "refinements" to its ontology, based on a full set of defect types from IEEE/ISO standards; (ii) a comprehensive set of refinement operators for defects; (iii) refinement graphs, which are conceptual models of the RE process enactment, and can serve as explanation/rationale for the specifications obtained.
- An argumentation-based semantics of what it means for a specification to address a set of stakeholder requirements The systematic process for constructing CaRE refinement graphs, inspired by its argumentation-based semantics, supports negotiation and convergence towards agreement between stakeholders. In contrast with most previous approaches, where only a requirement engineer conducts analysis, with CaRE all stakeholders are involved.
- Reasoning support that, given an initial set of requirements R and a constructed refinement graph, returns all specifications S that address R. This is implemented as a prototype tool that is available on the web.

2   CaRE Requirements Calculus

The proposed approach consists of a calculus and a systematic process for requirements elicitation, negotiation, and refinement. The calculus is based on a collection of defect types and of refinements. The defect types are inspired by the IEEE/ISO standards and represent issues that could be identified by stakeholders for one or more requirements. Refinements, on the other hand, are the means for fixing defects. By means of an iterative process of defect identification and refinement, a refinement graph is constructed and zero or more specifications are produced.

Defect Types: Defects can be found in individual requirements (single-target defects) or sets thereof (multi-target defects). The single target defects are

- **nonAtomic:** the requirement is not operationalisable. For example, $\langle g_1$: "System shall schedule a meeting upon request"$\rangle$ may not be atomic since there is no single action the system-to-be or an agent in the environment can perform to address it.
- **ambiguous:** the requirement admits many interpretations because it is vague, imprecise, or otherwise ambiguous. For example, $\langle g_2$: "The authentication process shall be easy"$\rangle$ is ambiguous since the term *easy* is vague.
- **unattainable:** the requirement is not feasible, i.e. doesn't have a realistic solution. For example, $\langle g_3$: "The system shall be available at all times"$\rangle$ is unattainable because it assumes eternal availability of power and other resources.
- **unjustified:** the requirement does not have an explicit motivation. For example, $\langle g_4$: "The system shall run on Windows operating system"$\rangle$ is missing an explicit justification why other operating systems are not considered.
- **incomplete:** the requirement is missing information. For example, $\langle g_5$: "In case of fault, the system shall send an error message"$\rangle$ is incomplete because it does not specify a recipient for the message.
- **tooStrong:** the requirement is over-restrictive. For example, $\langle g_6$: "The website shall use HTTPS protocol"$\rangle$, may be too strong if there is no sensitive data.
- **tooWeak:** the requirement is too weak. For example, $\langle g_7$: "The DB system shall process 500 transactions/sec"$\rangle$ is too weak if the expected workload for the system-to-be is 1,000 transactions/sec.
- **rejected:** the requirement is rejected. For example, in the context of an app recommending nearby restaurants to users, a requirement such as $\langle g_8$: "The app shall support chatting between user and restaurant"$\rangle$ may be deemed unacceptable.

The multitarget defects are:

- **mConflict:** the full set of requirements doesn't admit any solutions, even though subsets may do so. For example, the requirements $\langle g_9$: "The train control system shall stop the train if a red signal is missed"$\rangle$ and $\langle g_{10}$: "The train control system shall not apply brakes if the speed is below 30 km/h"$\rangle$ are conflicting, if the driver is in charge for speeds <30 km/h.
- **mMissing:** the set of requirements is incomplete. For example, a set of requirements for a social network platform is mMissing if it does not include any privacy requirement.
- **mRedundant:** here a set of requirements is too strong or redundant, as in $\langle g_{11}$: "The system shall support authentication through fingerprint recognition"$\rangle$ and $\langle g_{12}$: "The system shall support authentication through iris recognition"$\rangle$.

Refinement Operators: A refinement operator invocation, $op(D, R)$, addresses a defect D of some existing requirements, offering alternative (presumably better) requirement(s) R that address the problem. Each operator takes a (set of) defective requirements, and is applicable to one or more defect types. Each defect type has at least one refinement operator that is applicable to it, i.e., can eliminate defects of that type. Defects of type **rejected** are an exception: in this case there is no possible fix, as the rejected requirement constitutes a dead end. Although some operators behave similarly, we have chosen to keep them, to make the calculus more readily usable. The operators are as follows:

- **weaken:** introduces a weaker requirement. For example, the unattainable requirement g_3 may be weakened into $\langle g_{13}$: "The system shall be available at all times, with interruptions of ≤ 2 h"$\rangle$. **weaken** is applicable to defects of type **unattainable**, and **tooStrong**.
- **strengthen:** introduces a stronger requirement. For instance, g_7 may be strengthened into $\langle g_{14}$: "The system shall process 1,200 tps"$\rangle$. **strengthen** is applicable to defects of type **tooWeak**.
- **reduce:** decomposes a requirement into a set $g_1, ..., g_n$ using AND-refinement. **reduce** is applicable to defects of type **nonAtomic**.
- **add:** introduces new requirements, and is applicable to defects of type **mMissing**.
- **clarify:** is applicable to **incomplete** and **ambiguous** defects, and introduces a, presumably, improved requirement.
- **justify:** introduces a new requirement that represents an explicit motivation for another requirement, and is applicable to **unjustified** defects.
- **resolve:** applies to defects of type **mConflict**, typically moderating or dropping the original requirements.
- **drop:** given a set of **mRedundant** requirements, produces a proper subset not including redundant elements.

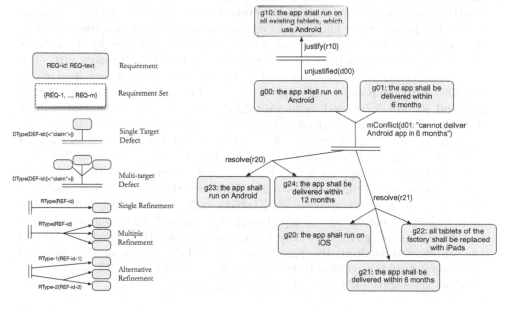

Fig. 1. Graphical notation   **Fig. 2.** Refinement graph example

2.1   Incremental Construction of a Refinement Graph

The incremental CaRE requirements acquisition process starts with an initial set of requirements. These are critiqued by stakeholders and defects in the requirements are identified. Then, requirements – or sets of requirements – that have defects are refined by applying the different refinement operators, producing new requirements. If the new requirements are acceptable, i.e. have no defects, the original (defective) requirements are accepted. Otherwise, this process is repeated until no new defects are identified. Thus, the result of the process is a *refinement graph* in which all the leaf nodes are requirements that have no defects. Therefore, in a sense, the acceptability of requirements is propagated from the leaf nodes towards the higher-level nodes. Finally, *specifications* of a refinement graph are determined by identifying minimal sets of leaf nodes that make the initial requirements acceptable.

2.2   Graphical Notation and Running Example

This section presents a simple example used to illustrate our proposal, and its graphical expression. The basic elements of the graphical notation are shown in Fig. 1, and consist of requirements, defects (single- and multi-target), and refinements. Each instance of these elements is associated with a unique id (REQ-id, DEF-id, REF-id in Fig. 1).

The example, which is based on a simple elicitation case, is represented by the refinement graph in Fig. 2. In the running example, a customer requires a new app to be installed on the tablets of factory workers, to be used for sharing workflow information. The customer requires that the app runs on Android (g00). Furthermore, the customer wants the system to be delivered within six months (g01). The requirements analyst asks why Android is required (**unjustified**(d00) defect), and the customer replies that the tablets currently used by the workers are all Android tablets (g10, introduced with the **justify** refinement r10). The requirements analyst knows that their software company has a very similar app for iOS, but that porting and adaptation would require twelve months. Hence, g00 and g01 are considered conflicting. In the refinement graph, an **mConflict** defect is specified, and a textual motivation (the optional < "claim" > in Fig. 1) is used to explain the nature of the defect: **mConflict**(d01: "cannot deliver Android app in 6 months"). To comply with the deadline, the requirements analyst suggests to develop the app for iOS (g20), so that its adaptation to the customer's needs is feasible within 6 months (g21). However, this would require replacing the tablets at the factory with iPad tablets (g22). Alternatively, the requirements analyst suggests to develop the app for Android (g23), but to deliver it in twelve months (g24). These two options aim at **resolving** conflict d01, and are represented as alternative refinements r20 and r21. Assuming that no other defects are found, according to the approach provided in Sect. 2.1, we have two possible specifications: {g20, g21, g22} and {g23, g24}.

2.3   Discussion of Design Choices

Firstly, we gained a claim of completeness with respect to the defect types of our calculus by using the IEEE/ISO standards. However, there is no claim of minimality for defect types since, e.g., **unattainable** is a form of **tooStrong**. However, there's been much research on how to recognize and deal with **unattainable** specifically – it is a special case of conflicting requirements and domain assumptions.

The set of refinement operators is not minimal since, e.g., **add** and **justify** modify the graph the same way. However, operators guide users on how to deal with defects. For example, if r is attacked as being incomplete with respect to privacy concerns, then use of **add** should introduce some privacy requirements. If, on the other hand, r is deemed unjustified, the new requirement introduced by **justify** should serve as justification for r. In short, **add** and **justify** do similar things, but for very different purposes.

CaRE might be criticized as too cumbersome for users compared to, say, GORE approaches. This may well be the case – we need empirical studies to judge this. However, as discussed above, CaRE is the only proposal in the RE literature for solving the requirements problem in its greater generality. And in any case, in addressing an open problem one may want to keep in mind Albert Einstein's dictum "Make things as simple as possible, but not simpler".

3   Argumentation Semantics

Dung [13] introduced a formal Argumentation Framework (DAF), whose basic notions are *arguments* and *attacks* (conflicts between arguments), and where the key reasoning task is the acceptability of arguments, i.e, whether and which arguments should or should not be accepted by an intelligent agent. Sets of collectively acceptable arguments are called *extensions*.

The semantics of the CaRE calculus will be given in the form of a translation from a refinement graph into an ASPIC$^+$ **argumentation theory**, a structured variant of Dung's DAF [13]. The translation leads to arguments that represent requirements, defects and refinements. Informally, attacks between these arguments correspond to (i) the identification of a defect in a requirement or set of requirements, and (ii) the application of a refinement to address a defect. More precisely, in our formalisation, an argument d that represents a defect in a requirement g attacks the argument representing g; similarly, an argument r that represents a refinement to address a defect d attacks the argument representing d, thus possibly restoring the acceptability of the attacked requirement. The specifications resulting from a refinement graph are computed by considering all possible *minimal extensions* where the initial requirements are acceptable.

The formalization of CaRE using ASPIC$^+$ is motivated by (i) the dialectic nature of requirements engineering, for which argumentation theory is a natural formal choice; (ii) the flexibility of ASPIC$^+$, being a meta-reasoning tool for reasoning over a freely chosen underlying logic, which enables us to easily consider more structured RE languages, e.g. [14], in the future; (iii) the non-monotonic nature of argumentation theories, which enables extending the framework to incorporate other important features, e.g., support of conflict and dependency relations between requirements [15].

This section first introduces the formal definition of the ASPIC$^+$ structured argumentation framework, and the formal representation of a refinement graph and its well-formedness conditions. It then describes how a refinement graph is translated into an ASPIC$^+$ argumentation theory and, thereby, into a DAF. We define how this enables determining the acceptability of requirements and computing specification sets. Finally, we conclude by describing a prototype tool implementing our calculus.

3.1   Basics of Argumentation Theory

In a DAF, arguments have an abstract representation in the form of simple propositions, e.g., the argument "It is raining today, therefore I should stay home" can be represented using a simple propositional symbol a. Conflicts between arguments are given in a relation $\mathcal{D}$ over the set of arguments. For example, consider another argument b, "I have to buy food, so I must go to the store", which obviously conflicts with a. In DAF's terminology, this conflict is called an *attack*, and is represented in the form of a tuple (a, b) in $\mathcal{D}$. Given arguments and attacks, the acceptability of arguments can be determined, informally, as follows [16]: an argument is IN (acceptable) if it is not attacked or if all its attackers are OUT (not acceptable). An argument is OUT if it is attacked by an argument that is IN. Otherwise, an argument is UNDECIDED.

Though powerful, the abstract representation of arguments in DAF makes it often less practical for modeling real-world problems. The ASPIC$^+$ framework for structured argumentation [17][1] therefore extends DAF to enable the representation of basic arguments in the form of inference rules, each having a set of premises and a conclusion. For example, argument a above can be represented using a (strict) inference rule, having a single premise "it is raining today" and a conclusion "I should stay home". One advantage of this representation is that it explicates the structure of arguments and enables the automatic construction of complex arguments by chaining inference rules. ASPIC$^+$ relies on DAF to determine *acceptability of arguments*. In particular, given an argumentation theory that includes inference rules, ASPIC$^+$ identifies the different basic and complex arguments as well as conflicts between them. Then, it constructs a DAF and uses it to determine which arguments are accepted and which are not.

---

[1] In this paper, we adapt a version of ASPIC$^+$, by simplifying and specializing it to support reasoning in our calculus. Our version is partially inspired by [18].

3.2 Formal Description of Refinement Graphs

A refinement graph RG is a tuple $\langle$Req, Defect, Ref$\rangle$ where:

- Req $\subseteq$ Id$_g$ $\times$ Text is a set of requirements. Each requirement has a unique identifier (in Id$_g$) and a natural language text description (in Text).
- Defect $\subseteq$ Id$_d$ $\times$ DType $\times$ $\mathcal{P}$(Text) $\times$ $\mathcal{P}$(Id$_g$) is a set of defects. A defect has (i) a unique identifier (in Id$_d$); (ii) a defect type; (iii) some natural language explanations of the defect's nature; and (iv) the identifier(s) of a set of requirements found to have the defect.
- Ref $\subseteq$ Id$_r$ $\times$ RType $\times$ Id$_d$ $\times$ $\mathcal{P}$(Id$_g$) is a set of refinements. A refinement has (i) a unique identifier (in Id$_r$); (ii) a refinement type; (iii) a defect that it aims at addressing, and (iv) a set of other requirements, which are meant to replace the defective one(s).

So, for example, from Fig. 2, we have the formal requirement $Req(g23, The$ $app\ shall\ run\ on\ Android)^2$. The set of identifiers Id$_g$, Id$_r$, and Id$_d$ are disjoint; henceforth, given a refinement graph RG $=$ $\langle$Req, Defect, Ref$\rangle$, the set Id$_{RG}$ is used to denote all identifiers of its elements, i.e., Id$_{RG}$ $=$ Id$_g$ $\cup$ Id$_d$ $\cup$ Id$_r$.

A refinement graph is *well-formed* iff every refinement addressing a defect matches its type, as described in Sect. 2.

In addition, to make the semantics work out more easily, we assume in this conference paper that the refinement graph is acyclic. This means that if a requirement is to be re-used it must be given a new label.

3.3 Refinement Graph Semantics by Translation to Argumentation Theory

Each refinement graph RG has a corresponding ASPIC$^+$ argumentation theory representation, denoted $\mathcal{AT}$(RG). An argumentation theory is a tuple $\langle \mathcal{L}, IR, \text{name} \rangle$ where $\mathcal{L}$ is a logical language (in our case simple propositional symbols and their negation).

IR is a set of defeasible inference rules of the form $\varphi_1, ..., \varphi_n \Rightarrow \varphi$, $n \geq 0$, where $\varphi_1, ..., \varphi_n, \varphi$ are from $\mathcal{L}$. In case $n = 0$, $\Rightarrow \varphi$ is equivalent to $true \Rightarrow \varphi$, and defeasibly asserts φ. The intended meaning of a defeasible rule is that if one accepts all antecedents/premises, then one must accept the consequent/conclusion unless there is sufficient reason to reject it. Defeasible rules with empty premises, of the form $\Rightarrow \varphi$, are called *assumptions*.

Finally, *name* is a partial function that gives names to (some) defeasible rules including assumptions. For convenience, we will write $\varphi_1, ..., \varphi_n \overset{d}{\Rightarrow} \varphi$ for a defeasible rule $\varphi_1, ..., \varphi_n \Rightarrow \varphi$ whose name is d.

---

[2] Henceforth, we will use Req, Defect and Ref as predicates in Prolog: variables (in italics) match possible values, and underscores _ are wildcards. In logical formulas, wildcards are existentially quantified anonymous variables.

Table 1. Mapping of elements of refinement graphs to ASPIC$^+$ argumentation theory.

Element type	Refinement graph element	ASPIC$^+$ representation
requirement (g)	Req(id_g, txt)	$\overset{id_g}{\Longrightarrow} txt$
defect (d)	Defect(id_d, --, --, $ID_{defective}$)	$\overset{id_d}{\Longrightarrow} \neg id_{g_i}$ for every $id_{g_i} \in ID_{defective}$
refinement (r)	Ref(id_r, --, id_d, $ID_{replace}$)	$\bigwedge_{id_{g_i} \in \text{ID}_{replace}} \wedge \text{Req}(id_{g_i}, txt_i) \overset{id_r}{\underset{txt_i}{\Longrightarrow}} \neg id_d$

Translation of Refinement Graphs to ASPIC$^+$. The argumentation theory $\mathcal{AT}(\text{RG}) = \langle \mathcal{L}_{\text{RG}}, \mathcal{IR}_{\text{RG}}, \text{name}_{\text{RG}} \rangle$ corresponding to a refinement graph RG $= \langle \text{Req}, \text{Defect}, \text{Ref} \rangle$ is constructed as follows[3]:

- The set of propositions $\mathcal{L}$ contains the elements of Text used in the graph, together with the identifiers in RG, and their negations.
- The set of defeasible rules of $\mathcal{AT}(\text{RG})$ is constructed on the basis of requirements, defects, and refinements of refinement graphs as described in Table 1.

Thus, the above formalization represents requirements and defects as antecedent-free rules, while refinements have premises which are the requirements that the refinement introduces.

Note that natural language statements of defects are not currently considered in the translation to argumentation theories. The inclusion of these elements as well as support/conflict relations between them represent future work.

Construction of Arguments and Attacks. ASPIC$^+$ constructs arguments that take the form of inference trees. In our case, complex arguments start from leaves that are rules with antecedent *true*, and are put together into larger ones by chaining with inference rules. Due to space limitations, we do not present the rules of the construction of arguments. Interested readers are referred to [17,18].

Figure 3 depicts the arguments constructed on the basis of the refinement graph shown in Fig. 2. The figure shows that all the requirements in the refinement graph correspond to arguments $\{G_0, G_1, G_2, G_3, G_4, G_5, G_6, G_7\}$ in the theory, and defects correspond to $\{D_0, D_1, D_2\}$. Refinements take the form of defeasible rules whose premises are (non-initial) requirements. These lead to inference trees where the premises are the leaves of the tree, as in $\{R_0, R_1, R_2\}$. Notice the structure of every argument: it includes a set of sub-conclusions, a (proper) conclusion, and a set of defeasible rules. For example, the sub-conclusions of argument R_1 are *The app shall run on Android, The app shall be delivered in 12 months*, and $\neg d01$; the conclusion is $\neg d01$; and it has a single defeasible rule $r01$.

---

[3] When clear from the context, we will henceforth drop the subscript RG.

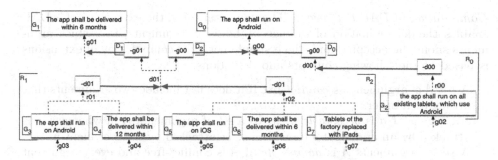

Fig. 3. Example of construction of ASPIC$^+$ arguments

Identification of Attacks. Given two ASPIC$^+$ arguments A and B, A attacks B if one of the conclusions of A conflicts with (the name of) one of the defeasible rules of B. Note that two formulas ϕ and ψ conflict if they are contradictory, i.e., if $\phi = \neg\psi$ or $\psi = \neg\phi$.

According to the previous definition, defects attack requirements that they point to, whereas refinements attack defects that they address. So, for example, Fig. 3 shows that defect D_0 attacks requirement G_0, and then the refinement R_0 attacks the defect D_0.

Construction of DAFs. The purpose of argument construction and attack identification in ASPIC$^+$ is to enable the construction of a DAF.

We present the construction process by example here (for details, see [17]): starting from the theory above, one obtains a DAF that can be represented graphically as in Fig. 4, where nodes represent arguments, and edges represent attacks. One can easily see in the graph how arguments $\{D_0, D_1, D_2\}$, representing defects, attack arguments $\{G_0, G_1, G_2\}$, representing requirements. Similarly, arguments $\{R_0, R_1, R_2\}$, denoting refinements, attack arguments $\{D_0, D_1, D_2\}$, denoting defects.

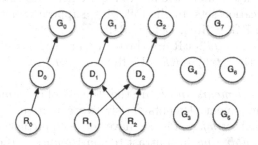

Fig. 4. DAF example

Computation of DAF Extensions. The computation of the extensions of a DAF
enables the determination of the acceptability of arguments, i.e., which arguments should be accepted and which should not. The computation of extensions
is based on the following concepts and definitions.

- A set A of arguments is *conflict-free* if it does not include two arguments that
  attack each other.
- An argument a is *acceptable* w.r.t. to a set of arguments A iff whenever a is
  attacked by an argument b then b must be attacked by some element in A.
- A set of arguments A is *admissible* iff A is conflict-free and every argument
  $a \in A$ is acceptable w.r.t. A.
- A set of arguments is *complete* iff if is admissible and includes every argument
  a that is acceptable w.r.t. to it.

In this paper, we are interested in the computation of the so-called complete
extensions. In the previous example, the only complete extension is the set
$\{G_0, G_1, G_2, G_3, G_4, G_5, G_6, G_7, R_0, R_1, R_2\}$. In general, if a DAF graph is acyclic
then it is guaranteed to have a single complete extension. To avoid the complexity of multiple extensions, we assume in this conference paper that the original
requirements graph is acyclic.

In general, the *acceptable requirements* in a refinement graph RG, denoted
by $AR(\mathcal{AT}(\mathrm{RG}))$, will be the set of requirements appearing in the conclusions
of the arguments of its complete extension.

After the identification of acceptable arguments, we determine acceptable
requirements by checking the ones that appear as conclusions of acceptable arguments. Thus, we determine that all the requirements are acceptable since they
are the conclusions of arguments $\{G_0, \dots, G_7\}$.

3.4 Identification of Specification Sets

The acceptability of requirements only indicates that either they are free of
defects or their defects have been addressed. To determine the minimal sets of
requirements necessary to make the initial requirements acceptable, we compute
the minimal specification sets. In the following, suppose we are given a specific
requirements graph RG = $\langle$Req, Defect, Ref$\rangle$.

The *initial requirements* InitR are those that are not introduced by a refine-
ment. Formally, InitR=$\{txt \mid \neg \exists RF, id \ . \ \mathrm{Ref}(\_, \_, \_, RF) \ \wedge \ id \in RF \ \wedge \mathrm{Req}(id, txt) \}$.

The *specification elements SpecE* are the "leaves" of refinement graphs. More
precisely, these requirement elements satisfy two conditions: (i) They have no
defects other than *mMissing*, and hence have not been further refined; the rationale for this is that *mMissing*, in contrast to *nonAtomic* say, is dealt with by the
add operator, which only leads to the *introduction* of other new necessary requirements as opposed to its replacement. This means that requirements found to be
mMissing can still be leaves in refinement trees, if they have no other defects.
(ii) And the leaves have not been introduced by a *justify* refinement, because
those are (higher-level) goals.

Let a *minimal set of requirements* be a (minimal) subset of the requirements Req that lead to the acceptance of the initial requirements. Formally, it is one of the sets minimal w.r.t. set inclusion of the set RR, defined as follows:

$$RR = \{R' \mid RG' = \langle R', \text{Fault}, \text{Ref} \rangle \wedge R' \subseteq \text{Req} \wedge \text{InitR} \in AR(\mathcal{AT}(RG'))\}$$

Intuitively, the set RR is the set of all subsets of the requirements proposed during refinements that lead to the acceptance of the initial requirements. In the running example, the sets $\{G_3, G_4, G_5\}$, $\{G_2, G_3, G_4, G_5\}$, and $\{G_2, G_3, G_4, G_5, G_6\}$ represent some of the elements of RR. The minimal requirements sets are $\{G_2, G_3, G_4\}$ and $\{G_2, G_5, G_6, G_7\}$. Finally, the *specification sets*, SS, are identified by taking the intersection of *specification elements* and *minimal requirements*, i.e., SS $= \{S \mid \exists R.R \in RR, S = (R \cap \text{SpecE})\}$. In the running example, the sets $\{G_3, G_4\}$ and $\{G_5, G_6, G_7\}$ represent the only specification sets.

3.5 Tool Description

We have implemented a prototype tool of the calculus. The tool aims at helping requirements engineers to systematically refine, negotiate, and document the requirements refinement process (in the form of a refinement graph). The tool also provides reasoning support by determining the acceptability of requirements and computing the minimal specifications. Due to space limitations, we only present a brief description of the tool below. The tool, as well a description of the examples in this paper and use instructions, can be downloaded at [19] (requires Java SE Development Kit 9 to run). The tool's input is a textual description of a refinement graph—a GUI is left as future work. An "Argumentation Theory Generator" module then generates an ASPIC$^+$ argumentation theory for every possible configuration of requirements. A *requirements configuration* is a subset of the requirements that could lead to the acceptance of the initial requirements. On the basis of these argumentation theories, an "ASPIC$^+$ module" identifies the ASPIC$^+$ arguments, attacks, and generates a Dung Argumentation Framework (DAF). A "DAF module" then determines the acceptability of abstract arguments by computing the complete extensions of the DAF. Finally, a "Compute Minimal Specifications" module stores all (subsets of) requirements (RR) that make the initial requirements acceptable and determines the minimal specification sets (SS) by taking the intersection of specification elements and minimal requirements (as explained in Sect. 3.4).

4 Related Work

Since requirements engineering is dialectical by nature, argumentation frameworks have been previously used to formalise and support RE activities, including elicitation [20], assessment [21–23], and regulatory compliance [24]. Some works focus on specific RE issues, such as security [21,22], or requirements conflicts [25,26]. The spirit of our work is analogous to the more comprehensive frameworks of Juret et al. [27], who support the definition of goal models through argumentation and Mirbel & Villeta [15], who manage requirements artifacts based on argumentation-theory.

Finally, RationalGRL [28,29] captures not only traditional GORE model refinement, but also arguments about design decisions (e.g., "This refinement should be OR rather than AND"), and the rationale behind them. RationalGRL also proposes argumentation patterns to point out defects in goal models. Its laudable focus is making goal models and their evolution understandable to RE users.

The main feature distinguishing our work from all of the above is the intention: CaRE is an integrated calculus for deriving specifications from stakeholder requirements. Thus the defect types used by our framework are different and comprehensive, as are refinement operators addressing each specific defect type. Moreover, CaRE proposes its own unified representation (refinement graphs), with ASPIC$^+$/AF only being used to give CaRE semantics rather than being an overt part of the framework.

The only work we know of that offers a refinement calculus for the requirements problem is the Desirée proposal [14], which generalizes GORE approaches with a rich set of operators for refinement and operationalization. The main differences between CaRE and Desirée are that CaRE (a) includes defects and defect types in its ontology, which Desiree does not, (b) casts the refinement process as a dialectic argument among stakeholders, and (c) gives a formal semantics of what does it mean for S to satisfy R based on Argumentation Theory.

5   Conclusion

This paper presents a novel calculus for RE through which initial stakeholder requirements can be refined into specifications through a dialectic process. A major advantage of our approach over existing proposals, notably GORE ones, is that it offers a *comprehensive framework* for introducing into the discussion *the full range of defects* recognized in RE standards, as opposed to the particular types considered so far. It also makes all of the stakeholders active participants in the refinement process, as opposed to traditional approaches where typically only the requirements analyst is responsible for refining the requirements and building models.

CaRE refinement graphs capture a more complete view of the RE process. Significantly, they provide a conceptual model of the enactment of our requirements engineering process. They offer excellent support for RE documentation, traceability, and change management since new defects or refinements can be added to the graph monotonically, without needing to revise its previous elements.

The semantics of the calculus is given in terms of argumentation theory, by defining a mapping from refinement graphs to constructs of the ASPIC$^+$ argumentation framework. Through this formalisation, we define what it means for a specification to make initial requirements acceptable. In our proposal, the notion of *satisfaction*, typical of earlier approaches, is replaced by the weaker notion of *acceptability*. Our contributions include a Java implementation of a prototype tool for the calculus A forthcoming paper will show the connection of the argumentation theoretic semantics here to abduction in an essentially propositional logic setting.

We have carried out a detailed scenario from the railway domain illustrating the elements of our calculus and how they can be used to derive specifications from requirements[4]. We still need a preliminary assessment of CaRE on an industrial case-study, and a consolidation assessment of domain experts using CaRE. Other future work includes adding further aspects of GORE ontologies (e.g., soft-goals, agents), and global consistency conditions on requirements graphs (e.g., can g be marked both **tooStrong** and **tooWeak** by the same person?).

References

1. Ross, D.T.: Structured analysis (SA): a language for communicating ideas. IEEE TSE **1**, 16–34 (1977)
2. Bubenko Jr, J.A.: Validation and verification aspects of information modeling. In: Proceedings of the VLDB, pp. 556–566 (1977)
3. Dardenne, A., van Lamsweerde, A., Fickas, S.: Goal-directed requirements acquisition. Sci. Comput. Program. **20**(1–2), 3–50 (1993)
4. Yu, E.S.: An organization modeling framework for information system requirements engineering. In: Proceedings of the Workshop Information Technologies and Systems, WITS 1993, p. 9 (1993)
5. Elrakaiby, Y., Ferrari, A., Mylopoulos, J.: Care: a refinement calculus for requirements engineering based on argumentation semantics. In: RE 2008, pp. 364–369 (2018)
6. IEEE Recommended Practice for Software Requirements Specifications. IEEE Std 830-1998, pp. 1–40 (1998)
7. ISO/IEC/IEEE international standard - systems and software engineering - life cycle processes - requirements engineering. ISO/IEC/IEEE 29148:2011(E) (2011)
8. Hunter, A., Nuseibeh, B.: Managing inconsistent specifications: reasoning, analysis, and action. ACM Trans. Softw. Eng. Methodol. **7**(4), 335–367 (1998)
9. van Lamsweerde, A.: Handling obstacles in goal-oriented requirements engineering. IEEE TSE **26**(10), 978–1005 (2000)
10. Jackson, M., Zave, P.: Deriving specifications from requirements: an example. In: ICSE 1995, p. 15. IEEE (1995)
11. Hegel, G.W.F.: Ph'anomenologie des Geistes (1807)
12. Potts, C., Takahashi, K., Anton, A.I.: Inquiry-based requirements analysis. IEEE Softw. **11**(2), 21–32 (1994)
13. Dung, P.M.: On the acceptability of arguments and its fundamental role in non-monotonic reasoning, logic programming and n-person games. AI J. **77**(2), 321–357 (1995)
14. Li, F.-L., Horkoff, J., Borgida, A., Guizzardi, G., Liu, L., Mylopoulos, J.: From stakeholder requirements to formal specifications through refinement. In: Fricker, S.A., Schneider, K. (eds.) REFSQ 2015. LNCS, vol. 9013, pp. 164–180. Springer, Cham (2015). https://doi.org/10.1007/978-3-319-16101-3_11

---

[4] This is available in a technical report providing further details on the application of CaRE [19].

15. Mirbel, I., Villata, S.: Enhancing goal-based requirements consistency: an argumentation-based approach. In: Fisher, M., van der Torre, L., Dastani, M., Governatori, G. (eds.) CLIMA 2012. LNCS (LNAI), vol. 7486, pp. 110–127. Springer, Heidelberg (2012). https://doi.org/10.1007/978-3-642-32897-8_9

16. Caminada, M.: On the issue of reinstatement in argumentation. In: Fisher, M., van der Hoek, W., Konev, B., Lisitsa, A. (eds.) JELIA 2006. LNCS (LNAI), vol. 4160, pp. 111–123. Springer, Heidelberg (2006). https://doi.org/10.1007/11853886_11

17. Modgil, S., Prakken, H.: The ASPIC+ framework for structured argumentation: a tutorial. Argum. Comput. 5, 31–62 (2014)

18. Caminada, M., Amgoud, L.: On the evaluation of argumentation formalisms. Artif. Intell. 171(5–6), 286–310 (2007)

19. ElRakaiby, Y., Borgida, A., Ferrari, A., Mylopoulos, J.: A Refinement Calculus for Requirements Engineering Based on Argumentation Theory: Tool and Additional Material (2020). https://doi.org/10.5281/zenodo.3958960

20. Elrakaiby, Y., Ferrari, A., Spoletini, P., Gnesi, S., Nuseibeh, B.: Using argumentation to explain ambiguity in requirements elicitation interviews. In: RE 2017, pp. 51–60. IEEE (2017)

21. Haley, C.B., Laney, R., Moffett, J.D., Nuseibeh, B.: Security requirements engineering: a framework for representation and analysis. TSE 34(1), 133–153 (2008)

22. Franqueira, V.N.L., Tun, T.T., Yu, Y., Wieringa, R., Nuseibeh, B.: Risk and argument: a risk-based argumentation method for practical security. RE 2011, 239–248 (2011)

23. Jureta, I.J., Mylopoulos, J., Faulkner, S.: Analysis of multi-party agreement in requirements validation. In: RE 2009, pp. 57–66 (2009)

24. Ingolfo, S., Siena, A., Mylopoulos, J., Susi, A., Perini, A.: Arguing regulatory compliance of software requirements. DKE 87, 279–296 (2013)

25. Bagheri, E., Ensan, F.: Consolidating multiple requirement specifications through argumentation. In: ACM SAC, pp. 659–666 (2011)

26. Murukannaiah, P.K., Kalia, A.K., Telangy, P.R., Singh, M.P.: Resolving goal conflicts via argumentation-based analysis of competing hypotheses. In: Proceedings of the RE 2015, pp. 156–165 (2015)

27. Jureta, I.J., Faulkner, S., Schobbens, P.Y.: Clear justification of modeling decisions for goal-oriented requirements engineering. Requir. Eng. 13(2), 87–115 (2008). https://doi.org/10.1007/s00766-007-0056-y

28. van Zee, M., Bex, F., Ghanavati, S.: Rationalization of goal models in GRL using formal argumentation. In: Proceedings of the RE 2015, pp. 220–225. IEEE Computer Society (2015)

29. van Zee, M., Marosin, D., Bex, F., Ghanavati, S.: RationalGRL: a framework for rationalizing goal models using argument diagrams. In: Comyn-Wattiau, I., Tanaka, K., Song, I.-Y., Yamamoto, S., Saeki, M. (eds.) ER 2016. LNCS, vol. 9974, pp. 553–560. Springer, Cham (2016). https://doi.org/10.1007/978-3-319-46397-1_43

Neo4j Keys

Sebastian Link$^{(\boxtimes)}$ (iD)

School of Computer Science,
The University of Auckland, Auckland 1010, New Zealand
s.link@auckland.ac.nz

Abstract. Keys play a fundamental role in every data model. They stipulate how real-world entities are identified in the database but also how to physically and logically organize access to data. Neo4j is currently the most popular graph database management system. We address fundamental questions about key constraints as formally defined by the Cypher language of Neo4j. Answers include axiomatic and algorithmic solutions to their implication problem.

Keywords: Integrity · Key · Neo4j · Property graph · Reasoning

1 Introduction

Keys are a core enabler for data management. They are fundamental for understanding the structure and semantics of data. Given a collection of entities, a key is a set of attributes whose values uniquely identify an entity in the collection. Keys form the primary mechanism to enforce entity integrity within database management systems (DBMS) [6]. Keys are essential to many classical areas of data management, including data modeling, database design, indexing, transaction processing, and query optimization. Knowledge about keys enables us to i) uniquely reference entities across data repositories, ii) minimize data redundancy at schema design time to process updates efficiently at run time, iii) provide better selectivity estimates in cost-based query optimization, iv) provide a query optimizer with new access paths that can lead to substantial speedups in query processing, v) allow the database administrator to improve the efficiency of data access via physical design techniques such as data partitioning or the creation of indexes and materialized views, and vi) provide new insights into application data. Keys for graphs have already been studied in academia, and the proposed notion is very expressive [10] due to its target application of entity resolution. The notion subsumes keys from XML as well as conditional constraints [10]. This expressiveness has its price, for example, the associated implication problem is NP-complete, and the associated satisfiability and validation problems are both coNP-complete [10].

While graph databases even precede the relational model of data, they have recently experienced a surge of interest due to many new areas of applications. In particular, many commercial DBMSs have emerged and are heavily used. Neo4j is the most popular graph DBMS[1]. It employs an expressive property graph model. In particular,

---

[1] https://db-engines.com/en/ranking_trend/graph+dbms.

© Springer Nature Switzerland AG 2020
G. Dobbie et al. (Eds.): ER 2020, LNCS 12400, pp. 19–33, 2020.
https://doi.org/10.1007/978-3-030-62522-1_2

objects such as vertices and edges may have properties. Properties are pairs of a property attribute and a property value, reflecting the NoSQL nature of graph databases. In this article we are interested in keys as they are used in practice and defined by Neo4j. Here, keys are expressions of the form $\ell : \mathfrak{K}$ where ℓ denotes a label and $\mathfrak{K}$ is a finite set of property attributes. A key $\ell : \mathfrak{K}$ is satisfied by a property graph whenever every vertex with label ℓ has assigned a property value to every property attribute in $\mathfrak{K}$, and there are no two distinct vertices that each have a label ℓ and every property attribute in $\mathfrak{K}$ has been assigned matching property values for these vertices. This semantics is reminiscent of candidate keys in relational databases: key attributes must not feature any null-marker occurrences and no two distinct rows can carry matching values on all attributes of the key.

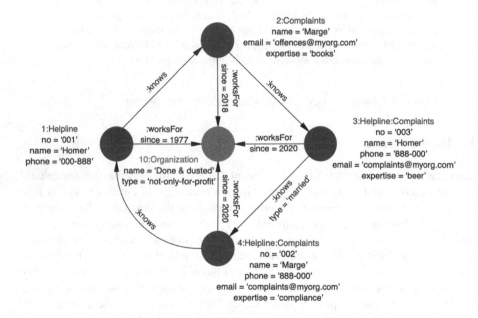

Fig. 1. Our running example of a property graph (Color figure online)

For example, Fig. 1 shows a property graph G that features some staff (blue nodes) working in the *Helpline* and *Complaints* branches of an organization (red node). The graph satisfies the keys *Helpline*:{*no*} and *Helpline*:{*name, phone*}. While the first key is unary, that is it has only a single property attribute, the second key is composite. Note that G does not satisfy the keys *Helpline*:{*no, expertise*} nor *Helpline*:{*name*} (vertex 1 and 3) nor *Helpline*:{*phone*} (3 and 4). Indeed, the key *Helpline*:{*no, expertise*} is violated by G because the vertex 1 carries the label *Helpline* but the property attribute *expertise* has not been assigned a property value. Consequently, the familiar notion of a superkey does not carry over from the relational model to the Neo4j graph model. That is, supersets of keys may not be keys. As seen on the example, the reason is that vertices may not define property values for some property attributes. Similarly, G satisfies the key *Complaints*:{*name, email*}, but violates both keys *Complaints*:{*name*} (vertex 2 and 4), and *Complaints*:{*email*} (vertex 3 and 4).

Interestingly, Neo4j property graphs can assign multiple labels to any of their vertices. For instance, the property graph in Fig. 1 shows that some staff work for both the *Helpline* and the *Complaints* branch (vertex 3 and 4). We make the interesting observation that Neo4j does not *explicitly* permit the specification of keys for multiple labels, but it does permit it *implicitly* in the sense that vertices with multiple labels inherit the keys explicitly specified on its singleton labels. For example, every property graph that satisfies the two single-label keys *Helpline*:{*no*} and *Complaints*:{*name,email*} will also satisfy the multi-label key {*Helpline,Complaints*}:{*no,email*}. Indeed, vertices that carry both labels *Helpline* and *Complaints* must have property values defined for property attributes *no* and *email*, and must have unique property value combinations assigned to *no* and *email*. Due to the semantics that Neo4j assigns to keys as well as the fact that vertices carry multiple labels, it is not clear what keys are implicitly satisfied by a property graph, given that it satisfies keys that are enforced explicitly. For instance, *G* does neither satisfy the key *Helpline*:{*no,expertise*} due to vertex 1, nor the key {*Helpline,Complaints*}:{*phone,email*} due to vertices 3 and 4, but it does satisfy the keys {*Helpline*}:{*no,phone*} and {*Helpline,Complaints*}:{*no,email*}. Hence, the fundamental question about the implication of Neo4j keys arises: Given a set Σ of Neo4j keys, which other Neo4j keys φ are implied by Σ? That is, which keys φ are guaranteed to be satisfied by a property graph *G*, whenever it satisfies all keys in Σ?

This question is important for data management in Neo4j. In particular, i) keys are strictly enforced by Neo4j under updates, meaning that existence and uniqueness of property values on the property attributes of the keys are checked for all vertices that carry the label of the key, and ii) key specification results in the automatic creation of index structures that are used for data processing, such as speeding up query evaluation by operators like `NodeUniqueIndexSeek` or `NodeUniqueIndexSeekByRange`. In particular, the ability to create index structures for object sets that carry multiple labels have the potential to speed up query evaluation more. Another motivation to study multi-label keys is the realisation of a true multi-label graph model. While multiple labels can be assigned to objects in Neo4j, the co-existence of vertex labels is not being effectively utilized by the underlying DBMS, including the lack of dedicated index structures and operators.

Contributions. We can summarize the contributions of this paper as follows. Firstly, we define multi-labels keys for Neo4j and illustrate their use by applications. Secondly, we study the implication problem associated with Neo4j keys. We derive an axiomatic characterization of the implication problem, as well as an algorithm that decides the implication problem in linear time in the input. Note that the contributions are not restricted to Neo4j, but only to the few concepts we require from the property graph model that Neo4j is based on. Indeed, property graphs in this model are rather general [2].

Organization. We comment on related work in Sect. 2, recall Neo4j's property graph model in Sect. 3, define multi-label keys in Sect. 4, highlight applications of implied keys in Sect. 5, establish axiomatic and algorithmic characterization of the implication problem associated with keys in Sect. 6, and finally conclude and comment on future work in Sect. 7.

2   Related Work

Keys form arguably the most important class of integrity constraint for any data model. For the relational model of data, a key is a set of attributes that ensures that no two different tuples in the relation can have matching values on all the attributes of the key [7, 16]. In SQL, candidate keys form minimal sets of attributes that cannot feature any null marker occurrences on any of their attributes and must have a unique combination of values on the attributes across all rows of the table. Keys enforce Codd's principle of entity integrity, which refers to the unique representation of all real-world entities of the underlying application domain within the database [6]. In addition, keys are fundamental to the most important data processing tasks. In query processing, key-foreign key relationships form the foundation for joining tables, and thus for specifying queries soundly. The primary key, which is a distinguished candidate key, determines the physical access model of the relation. Each candidate key and unique constraint gives rise to an index that accelerates query processing. As an integrity constraint, keys enforce the integrity of entities under update operations. For example, we cannot insert new rows that have missing values on some key attribute, and we cannot insert rows that have matching non-null values on the attributes of the key as an existing row in the relation. In database design, the fundamental goal is to obtain a layout of the target database in which data redundancy causing integrity constraints are transformed into keys that prohibit the occurrence of redundant data values [8].

The significance of keys carries over to other data models, in which different notions of keys arise that impact different areas of applications. This includes keys in incomplete data, such as possible and certain keys [14], key sets [11, 18], and embedded uniqueness constraints [21, 22], keys in description logics [20], keys in semantic models such as the Entity-Relationship model [5, 19], keys in object-relational models [13], keys in XML [4, 12], and keys over uncertain data such as probabilistic and possibilistic keys [1, 3].

Keys have not yet received much attention over graph data models with some noticeable differences [9, 10, 15, 17]. In [9] the authors propose a class of keys for graphs with the primary goal to perform entity matching. The associated implication problem is NP-complete, and those of satisfiability and validation are coNP-complete [10]. In [15] different ways are discussed for mapping relational databases into an RDF graph, with an emphasis on how to represent the original key and foreign key constraints in the resulting RDF graph. A new RDF namespace for the representation of keys and foreign keys is proposed as well. Finally, in [17] the authors put forward some proposals for extending the capabilities of Neo4j in specifying integrity constraints, including an extension of uniqueness constraints limited to single property attributes to uniqueness constraints with multiple property attributes. The authors have provided a simple prototype implementation and experiments.

Keys in Neo4j, in particular their implication problem or their combinatorial behavior, have not been studied in previous work. Since Neo4j is the most popular graph database in practice[2], and keys are of fundamental significance, the work in this paper starts an important line of investigation.

3   Property Graph Model

We recall the basic definitions for the property graph model [2]. For this we assume that the following sets are pairwise disjoint: $\mathcal{O}$ denotes a set of objects, $\mathcal{L}$ denotes a finite set of labels, $\mathcal{K}$ denotes a set of property attributes, and $\mathcal{N}$ denotes a set of values.

A *property graph* is a quintuple $G = (V, E, \eta, \lambda, \nu)$ where $V \subseteq \mathcal{O}$ is a finite set of objects, called *vertices*, $E \subseteq \mathcal{O}$ is a finite set of objects, called *edges*, $\eta : E \rightarrow V \times V$ is a function assigning to each edge an ordered pair of vertices, $\lambda : V \cup E \rightarrow \mathcal{P}(\mathcal{L})$ is a function assigning to each object a finite set of labels, and $\nu : (V \cup E) \times \mathcal{K} \rightarrow \mathcal{N}$ is a partial function assigning values for properties to objects, such that the set of domain values where ν is defined is finite. An example of a property graph is given in Fig. 1.

4   Key Constraints in Cypher

We formally define the syntax and semantics of key constraints. However, we do introduce multi-labelled key constraints, which strictly generalize the key constraints from Cypher that are restricted to a finite label.

According to the Cypher language[3], node key constraints ensure that, for a given label and set of properties: i) All the properties exist on all the nodes with that label, and ii) The combination of the property values is unique.

The Cypher language employs the following syntax to create a key constraint:

```
CREATE CONSTRAINT [constraint_name] ON (ℓ:LabelName)
ASSERT (ℓ.propertyAttribute_1,
     ℓ.propertyAttribute_2,..., ℓ.propertyAttribute_n)
IS NODE KEY
```

For example, in regards to Fig. 1 we may specify:

```
CREATE CONSTRAINT ON (h:Helpline)
ASSERT (h.name, h.phone) IS NODE KEY
```

as a key constraint on vertices with label *Helpline*.

We will now formally define the syntax and semantics of key constraints used by Cypher. Strictly speaking, Cypher only permits the explicit specification of keys on a single label. However, since vertices can carry multiple labels, keys on a single label implicitly also specify keys on vertices that carry multiple labels. Before the formal definition, we define the subset $V_{\mathcal{L}} \subseteq V$ of vertices in a given property graph that carry at least all the labels of given set $\mathcal{L}$ of labels, as follows: $V_{\mathcal{L}} = \{v \in V \mid \mathcal{L} \subseteq \lambda(v)\}$. For the property graph G from Fig. 1 we have $V_{\{\text{Helpline}\}} = \{1, 3, 4\}$, $V_{\{\text{Complaints}\}} = \{2, 3, 4\}$, and $V_{\{\text{Helpline, Complaints}\}} = \{3, 4\}$. Informally, $V_{\mathcal{L}}$ is the target set of vertices on which a key should hold.

---

[2] https://db-engines.com/en/ranking_trend/graph+dbms.

[3] https://neo4j.com/docs/cypher-manual/current/administration/constraints/.

Definition 1. *For a given finite set $\mathcal{L}$ of labels and a given finite set $\mathcal{K}$ of property attributes, a* key constraint *(or* key*) is an expression $\mathfrak{L} : \mathfrak{K}$ where $\mathfrak{L} \subseteq \mathcal{L}$ and $\mathfrak{K} \subseteq \mathcal{K}$. If $\mathfrak{L}$ is a singleton, we call $\mathfrak{L} : \mathfrak{K}$ a* single-labelled *key, and otherwise* multi-labelled. *For a given property graph $G = (V, E, \eta, \lambda, \nu)$ over $\mathcal{O}, \mathcal{L}, \mathcal{K},$ and $\mathcal{N}$ we say that G satisfies the key $\mathfrak{L} : \mathfrak{K}$ over $\mathcal{L}$, and $\mathcal{K}$, denoted by $\models_G \mathfrak{L} : \mathfrak{K}$, if and only if there are no vertices $v_1, v_2 \in V_{\mathfrak{L}}$ such that $v_1 \neq v_2$ and for all $A \in \mathfrak{K},$ $\nu(v_1, A)$ and $\nu(v_2, A)$ are defined and $\nu(v_1, A) = \nu(v_2, A)$.* □

Note that the key $\mathfrak{L} : \emptyset$ expresses that there is at most one vertex in a property graph that carries all the labels in $\mathfrak{L}$. In particular, if $\mathfrak{L} = \emptyset$, then there is at most one vertex in the property graph. Keys with an empty set of property attributes, even for a singleton $\mathfrak{L}$, cannot be defined in Neo4j. For illustration of the definition let us revisit the keys from the introduction.

Example 1. Some keys the property graph G of Fig. 1 satisfies are: *Helpline*:{*no*}, *Helpline*:{*name,phone*}, *Complaints*:{*name,email*}, {*Helpline,Complaints*}:{*no, email*}, and {*Helpline, Complaints*}:{*name,phone,email*}. However, some keys the property graph G of Fig. 1 does not satisfy are: *Helpline*:{*no,expertise*}, *Helpline*:{*name*}, *Helpline*:{*phone*}, *Complaints*:{*name*}, and {*Helpline, Complaints*}: {*phone, email*}.

5   Applications

We illustrate by extensions to our running example the impact of keys on the two most common data processing tasks: updates and queries.

5.1   Update Operations

Once key constraints are specified in Cypher, queries attempting to do any of the following will fail: i) Create new nodes without all the properties or where the combination of property values is not unique, ii) Remove one of the mandatory properties, and iii) Update the properties so that the combination of property values is no longer unique. The following are representative use cases illustrated on our running example:
i) Trying to create the following new node:

```
CREATE  (h:Helpline  {no:004,  name:'Bart', expertise:'pranks'})
```

will fail since no property value is specified for the property attribute *phone*, which is in violation of the key constraint on *Helpline*:{*name,phone*}.
ii) Similarly, removing the value for a key property attribute such as :

```
MATCH (h:Helpline {name:'Homer', phone:'000-888'})REMOVE  h.phone
```

will not remove this property for this vertex.
iii) Updating the values of property attributes so that the combination of property values is no longer unique, for example as in:

```
MATCH (h:Helpline {name: 'Homer', phone:'000-888'})
SET h.phone = '888-000'
RETURN h.name, h.phone
```

will not update the property since the update would violate the key constraint.

5.2 Physical Query Optimization

Furthermore, adding a key constraint for a set of property attributes will also add a composite index on those property attributes, so such an index cannot be added separately. For our example from before, such an index creation would work as follows:

```
CREATE INDEX index_Helpline FOR (h:Helpline)
ON (h.name, h.phone)
```

The index will be used when update operations are being processed to validate whether these comply with the keys or violate any of them. However, the index is also used to speed up the evaluation of queries. For instance, executing the following query without an index

```
MATCH (h:Helpline {name: 'Homer', phone:'000-888'})
RETURN h.no, h.name
```

will do a NodeByLabelScan, since the node label *Helpline* was supplied. This query would still take long on realistically-sized property graph. However, if we create an index as above, then the query optimizer will take advantage of the index and perform a NodeUniqueIndexSeek search, which is very efficient.

5.3 Logical Query Optimization and Opportunities with Multiple Labels

We illustrate how the ability to decide implication for keys will enable us to optimize queries logically, for example by rewriting them. While Neo4j does permit the assignment of multiple labels to vertices, this capability does not transfer to index creation. We will demonstrate the benefits of adding such capabilities by way of example.

Similar to SQL, the DISTINCT operator removes duplicate rows from the incoming stream of rows. To ensure only distinct elements are returned, Distinct will pull in data lazily from its source and build up state. This may lead to increased memory pressure in the system. As an example query consider the following:

```
MATCH (s:Helpline:Complaints)
RETURN DISTINCT s.no, s.email
```

Note that the query looks at returning distinct combinations of number and email of staff who work in both the Helpline and Complaints branches. If the query engine can conclude that the key *{Helpline,Complaints}:{no,email}* is implied, it becomes apparent that the DISTINCT operator becomes redundant, since by definition of the key, the combination of these values must be unique already. Hence, the query above can be rewritten by removing the DISTINCT clause.

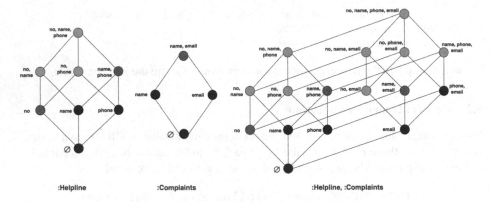

Fig. 2. Powerset Lattices of Keys Implied by Σ_1, Σ_2, and Σ_3 (the given keys are marked in magenta, implied non-given keys marked in cyan, non-implied keys marked in black) (Color figure online)

While not featured in the current Cypher language yet, the definition of multi-label keys and multi-label indices could further help speed up update and query operations. The query above, for example, would engage the single-label index on *Helpline* based on the single-label key *{Helpline}:{no}*. However, if we knew that the multi-label key *{Helpline,Complaints}:{no,email}* was implied and a multi-label index would have been created, then we could speed up the search for all query answers even more since the number of vertices that carry both labels would be smaller than the number of vertices with just the *Helpline* label.

6   Reasoning About Neo4j Keys

We formally define the implication problem associated with keys in Neo4j, illustrate it on our running example, and establish axiomatic and algorithmic solutions.

Given a set $\mathcal{L}$ of labels and a set $\mathcal{K}$ of property attributes, let $\Sigma \cup \{\varphi\}$ denote a set of keys over $\mathcal{L}$ and $\mathcal{K}$. The implication problem associated with the class of keys is to decide, given $\Sigma \cup \{\varphi\}$, whether Σ *implies* φ. In fact, Σ *implies* φ, denoted by $\Sigma \models \varphi$, if and only if every property graph G that satisfies all keys in Σ also satisfies φ.

The ability to efficiently decide whether some key constraint φ is implied by Σ is fundamental for the integrity management in Neo4j. Assume that Σ contains keys that are meaningful for the underlying application domain and have been specified, and that φ denotes another meaningful key. If φ is implied by Σ, then we do not need to specify φ because it is specified already implicitly. However, if φ is not implied, then we would need to specify it explicitly on top of all the keys in Σ. As an illustration, let us consider three different sets of keys for our running example: Σ_1 contains the keys *Helpline:{no}* and *Helpline:{name,phone}*. Σ_2 consists of the key *Complaints:{name,email}*, and Σ_3 consists of all the keys in Σ_1 and Σ_2. Figure 2 shows the powerset lattice that defines the search space for all sets of property attributes that may form a Neo4j key together with the set of labels written at the bottom of the lattice. Sets of property attributes for keys that are given by each of the three key sets are marked in magenta, while sets of property attributes for keys that are implied (but not given) by the three constraint sets are marked in cyan.

6.1 Axiomatic Characterization

We will establish an axiomatization for Neo4j keys in this section. The set $\Sigma^* = \{\varphi \mid \Sigma \models \varphi\}$ denotes the *semantic closure of* Σ, that is, the set of all keys implied by Σ. In principle, the definition of the semantic closure does not tell us whether we can compute it, nevermind how. It is a core reasoning task to investigate whether/how a semantic notion can be characterized syntactically. In fact, we determine the semantic closure Σ^* of a set Σ of keys by applying *inference rules* of the form $\frac{\text{premise}}{\text{conclusion}}$. For a set $\mathfrak{R}$ of inference rules let $\Sigma \vdash_{\mathfrak{R}} \varphi$ denote the *inference* of φ from Σ by $\mathfrak{R}$. That is, there is some sequence $\sigma_1, \ldots, \sigma_n$ such that $\sigma_n = \varphi$ and every σ_i is an element of Σ or is the conclusion that results from an application of an inference rule in $\mathfrak{R}$ to some premises in $\{\sigma_1, \ldots, \sigma_{i-1}\}$. Let $\Sigma_{\mathfrak{R}}^+ = \{\varphi \mid \Sigma \vdash_{\mathfrak{R}} \varphi\}$ be the *syntactic closure* of Σ under inferences by $\mathfrak{R}$. $\mathfrak{R}$ is *sound* (*complete*) if for every set Σ of keys we have $\Sigma_{\mathfrak{R}}^+ \subseteq \Sigma^*$ ($\Sigma^* \subseteq \Sigma_{\mathfrak{R}}^+$). The (finite) set $\mathfrak{R}$ is a (finite) *axiomatization* if $\mathfrak{R}$ is both sound and complete. Table 1 shows two inference rules for the implication of Neo4j keys, which we will show to be sound and complete. We illustrate the use of the inference rules on our running example.

Table 1. Axiomatization $\mathfrak{C}$ of Multi-label Cypher Keys

$\mathcal{L} : \mathcal{K}$	$\mathcal{L} : \mathcal{K}_1 \quad \mathcal{L} : \mathcal{K}_2 \cup \mathcal{K}_3$
$\mathcal{L} \cup \mathcal{L}' : \mathcal{K}$	$\mathcal{L} : \mathcal{K}_1 \cup \mathcal{K}_2$
(label-extension)	(attribute-extension)

Example 2. Let Σ consist of the three keys *Helpline:{no}*, *Helpline:{name,phone}*, and *Complaints:{name,email}*. A single application of the *attribute-extension* rule to the first two keys above will look as follows:

$$\frac{Helpline\!:\!\{no\} \quad Helpline\!:\!\{name,phone\}}{Helpline : \{no, name\}}$$

and derive the key *Helpline:{no, name}*. As a second example we show the following inference from Σ.

$$\frac{Helpline\!:\!\{name,phone\}}{\{Helpline,Complaints\}\!:\!\{name,phone\}} \quad \frac{Complaints\!:\!\{name,email\}}{\{Helpline,Complaints\}\!:\!\{name,email\}}$$
$$\{Helpline,Complaints\} : \{name, phone, email\}$$

Here, we infer the key *{Helpline,Complaints}:{name,phone,email}* by first apply the *label-extension* rule to the second and third input key to obtain the same label set on the left-hand side. Subsequently, we can then apply the *attribute-extension* rule to obtain the final conclusion.   □

Soundness. We show that any inference of keys by applying rules from $\mathfrak{C}$ results in keys that are implied by the given set.

Lemma 1. *Let $G = (V, E, \eta, \lambda, \nu)$ be a property graph over $\mathcal{O}$, $\mathcal{L}$, $\mathcal{K}$, and $\mathcal{N}$. For all $\mathfrak{L}, \mathfrak{L}' \subseteq \mathcal{L}$, if $\mathfrak{L} \subseteq \mathfrak{L}'$, then $V_{\mathfrak{L}'} \subseteq V_{\mathfrak{L}}$.*

Proof. Let $v \in V$ such that $v \in V_{\mathfrak{L}'}$. Then $\mathfrak{L}' \subseteq \lambda(v)$. Since $\mathfrak{L} \subseteq \mathfrak{L}'$ it follows that $\mathfrak{L} \subseteq \lambda(v)$, too. Hence, $v \in V_{\mathfrak{L}}$. Consequently, $V_{\mathfrak{L}'} \subseteq V_{\mathfrak{L}}$.   □

Lemma 2. *The inference rules in $\mathfrak{C}$ are sound for the implication of Neo4j keys.*

Proof. We show the soundness of the *label-extension* rule first. For that purpose we assume that there is a property graph $G = (V, E, \eta, \lambda, \nu)$ that violates the Cypher key $\mathfrak{L} \cup \mathfrak{L}' : \mathfrak{K}$. This means that i) there is some $v \in V_{\mathfrak{L} \cup \mathfrak{L}'}$ and some $A \in \mathfrak{K}$ such that $\nu(v, A)$ is undefined, or ii) there are $v_1, v_2 \in V_{\mathfrak{L} \cup \mathfrak{L}'}$ such that $v_1 \neq v_2$ and $\nu(v_1, \mathfrak{K}) = \nu(v_2, \mathfrak{K})$. From i) and Lemma 1 it would follow that there is some $v \in V_{\mathfrak{L}}$ and some $A \in \mathfrak{K}$ such that $\nu(v, A)$ is undefined. This means that G would also violate $\mathfrak{L} : \mathfrak{K}$. From ii) and Lemma 1 it would follow that there are $v_1, v_2 \in V_{\mathfrak{L}}$ such that $v_1 \neq v_2$ and $\nu(v_1, \mathfrak{K}) = \nu(v_2, \mathfrak{K})$. This means that G would also violate $\mathfrak{L} : \mathfrak{K}$. Hence, we conclude that G would also violate the Cypher key $\mathfrak{L} : \mathfrak{K}$. This proves the soundness of the *label-extension* rule.

It remains to show the soundness of the *attribute-extension* rule. For that purpose we assume that there is a property graph $G = (V, E, \eta, \lambda, \nu)$ that violates the Cypher key $\mathfrak{L} : \mathfrak{K}_1 \cup \mathfrak{K}_2$. Then it follows that either i) there is some $v \in V_{\mathfrak{L}}$ and some $A \in \mathfrak{K}_1 \cup \mathfrak{K}_2$ such that $\nu(v, A)$ is undefined, or ii), for all $v \in V_{\mathfrak{L}}$ and all $A \in \mathfrak{K}_1 \cup \mathfrak{K}_2$, $\nu(v, A)$ is defined, and there are $v_1, v_2 \in V_{\mathfrak{L}}$ such that $v_1 \neq v_2$ and $\nu(v_1, \mathfrak{K}_1 \cup \mathfrak{K}_2) = \nu(v_2, \mathfrak{K}_1 \cup \mathfrak{K}_2)$. From i) it follows that $A \in \mathfrak{K}_1$ or $A \in \mathfrak{K}_2$ such that $\nu(v, A)$ is undefined. Hence, G violates $\mathfrak{L} : \mathfrak{K}_1$ or G violates $\mathfrak{L} : \mathfrak{K}_2 \cup \mathfrak{K}_3$. It remains to consider case ii) above. That is, for all $v \in V_{\mathfrak{L}}$ and for all $A \in \mathfrak{K}_1 \cup \mathfrak{K}_2$, $\nu(v, A)$ is defined, and there are $v_1, v_2 \in V_{\mathfrak{L}}$ such that $v_1 \neq v_2$ and $\nu(v_1, \mathfrak{K}_1 \cup \mathfrak{K}_2) = \nu(v_2, \mathfrak{K}_1 \cup \mathfrak{K}_2)$. In particular, this means that $\nu(v_1, \mathfrak{K}_1) = \nu(v_2, \mathfrak{K}_1)$. Consequently, G violates $\mathfrak{L} : \mathfrak{K}_1$. In summary, we have shown that any property graph that violates $\mathfrak{L} : \mathfrak{K}_1 \cup \mathfrak{K}_2$ will also violate $\mathfrak{L} : \mathfrak{K}_1$ or $\mathfrak{L} : \mathfrak{K}_2 \cup \mathfrak{K}_3$. This proves the soundness of the *attribute-extension* rule.

Example 3. We have seen in Example 2 how the keys

$$Helpline:\{no,name\} \text{ and } \{Helpline,Complaints\}:\{name,phone,email\}$$

can be inferred from the set Σ with *Helpline:{no}*, *Helpline:{name,phone}*, and *Complaints:{name,email}*, by using the inference rules in $\mathfrak{C}$. Due to the soundness of the rules it follows that these keys are also implied by Σ.   □

Completeness. Before we establish the completeness of our inference rules for Neo4j keys, we introduce some useful notation.

Definition 2. *For a given set Σ of Neo4j keys over $\mathcal{L}$ and $\mathcal{K}$, and a given set $\mathfrak{L} \subseteq \mathcal{L}$ of labels and a given set $\mathfrak{K} \subseteq \mathcal{K}$ of property attributes, let $\Sigma_{\mathfrak{L}} = \{\mathfrak{L}' : \mathfrak{K}' \in \Sigma \mid \mathfrak{L}' \subseteq \mathfrak{L}\}$ denote the set of keys from Σ that are only labelled by labels in $\mathfrak{L}$. Furthermore, let $\mathfrak{K}_{\mathfrak{L},\Sigma} := \bigcup_{\mathfrak{L}':\mathfrak{K}' \in \Sigma_{\mathfrak{L}}} \mathfrak{K}'$ denote the set of property attributes that must be specified by any nodes labelled by labels in $\mathfrak{L}$.*   □

We illustrate these new notions by our running example.

Example 4. Let Σ denote the set with *Helpline:*$\{no\}$, *Helpline:*$\{name,phone\}$, and *Complaints:*$\{name,email\}$. Then we have $\Sigma_{\{Complaints\}} = \{Complaints:\{name,email\}\}$, $\Sigma_{\{Helpline\}} = \{Helpline:\{no\}, Helpline:\{name,phone\}\}$, and $\Sigma_{\{Helpline, Complaints\}} = \Sigma$. Also, we get $\mathfrak{K}_{\{Helpline\},\Sigma} = \{no,name,phone\}$, $\mathfrak{K}_{\{Complaints\},\Sigma} = \{name,email\}$, and $\mathfrak{K}_{\{Helpline,Complaints\},\Sigma} = \{no,name,phone,email\}$. $\qquad\square$

Lemma 3. *Let Σ denote a set of Neo4j keys over $\mathcal{L}$ and $\mathcal{K}$. Then the following hold:*

1. *If $\Sigma_\mathcal{L} \neq \emptyset$, then $\mathcal{L} : \mathcal{K}_\mathcal{L} \in \Sigma^+$.*
2. *For every $\mathcal{L}' : \mathcal{K}' \in \Sigma_\mathcal{L}$ and for all $\mathfrak{K} \subseteq \mathcal{K}$ such that $\mathfrak{K}' \subseteq \mathfrak{K} \subseteq \mathfrak{K}_{\mathcal{L},\Sigma}$, we have $\mathcal{L} : \mathfrak{K} \in \Sigma^+$.*

Proof. 1. Let $\Sigma_\mathcal{L} = \{\mathcal{L}_1 : \mathfrak{K}_1, \ldots, \mathcal{L}_n : \mathfrak{K}_n\}$ for some non-negative integer n. Since $\Sigma_\mathcal{L}$ is non-empty, it follows that n is a positive integer $n > 0$. Due to the soundness of the label-extension rule it follows that for all $i = 1, \ldots, n$, $\mathcal{L} : \mathfrak{K}_i \in \Sigma^+$. Due to the soundness of the attribute-extension rule we derive $\mathcal{L} : \bigcup_{i=1}^{n} \mathfrak{K}_i \in \Sigma^+$, but $\bigcup_{i=1}^{n} \mathfrak{K}_i = \mathfrak{K}_{\mathcal{L},\Sigma}$. Consequently, $\mathcal{L} : \mathfrak{K}_{\mathcal{L},\Sigma} \in \Sigma^+$.

2. Let $\mathcal{L}' : \mathfrak{K}' \in \Sigma_\mathcal{L}$, and $\mathfrak{K} \subseteq \mathcal{K}$ such that $\mathfrak{K}' \subseteq \mathfrak{K} \subseteq \mathfrak{K}_{\mathcal{L},\Sigma}$. Since $\mathcal{L}' : \mathfrak{K}' \in \Sigma_\mathcal{L}$, it follows that $\Sigma_\mathcal{L} \neq \emptyset$. Hence, property *1.* of Lemma 3 implies that $\mathcal{L} : \mathfrak{K}_{\mathcal{L},\Sigma} \in \Sigma^+$. Since $\mathfrak{K} \subseteq \mathfrak{K}_{\mathcal{L},\Sigma}$, it follows that $\mathfrak{K} \cup \mathfrak{K}_{\mathcal{L},\Sigma} = \mathfrak{K}_{\mathcal{L},\Sigma}$. Consequently, we have $\mathcal{L} : \mathfrak{K} \cup \mathfrak{K}_{\mathcal{L},\Sigma} \in \Sigma^+$. We apply the label-extension rule to $\mathcal{L}' : \mathfrak{K}' \in \Sigma$ to derive $\mathcal{L} : \mathfrak{K}' \in \Sigma^+$. We can then apply the *attribute-extension* rule to $\mathcal{L} : \mathfrak{K}'$ and $\mathcal{L} : \mathfrak{K} \cup \mathfrak{K}_{\mathcal{L},\Sigma}$ to derive $\mathcal{L} : \mathfrak{K}' \cup \mathfrak{K} \in \Sigma^+$. Since $\mathfrak{K}' \subseteq \mathfrak{K}$ it follows that $\mathcal{L} : \mathfrak{K} \in \Sigma^+$. $\qquad\square$

Note that property *1.* of Lemma 3 does not hold when $\Sigma_\mathcal{L} = \emptyset$. In this case, $\mathfrak{K}_\mathcal{L} = \emptyset$, but the Neo4j key $\mathcal{L} : \emptyset$ is satisfied by a property graph $G = (V, E, \eta, \lambda, \nu)$ if and only if $|V_\mathcal{L}| \leq 1$, that is, if there is at most one vertex in V that carries all the labels of $\mathcal{L}$.

Theorem 1. *The set $\mathfrak{C}$ forms a finite axiomatization for the implication of Neo4j keys.*

Proof. The soundness of $\mathfrak{C}$ has been established in Lemma 2. It remains to show the completeness. Let $\Sigma \cup \{\mathcal{L} : \mathfrak{K}\}$ denote a set of Neo4j keys over $\mathcal{L}$ and $\mathcal{K}$ such that $\mathcal{L} : \mathfrak{K} \notin \Sigma^+$. We need to show that Σ does not imply $\mathcal{L} : \mathfrak{K}$.

We distinguish between two main cases. In the first main case we assume that $\mathfrak{K} \not\subseteq \mathfrak{K}_{\mathcal{L},\Sigma}$. That is, there is some property attribute $A \in \mathfrak{K} - \mathfrak{K}_{\mathcal{L},\Sigma}$. Let us define the property graph $G = (V, E, \eta, \lambda, \nu)$ as follows: $V = \{v\}$, $E = \emptyset$, and therefore there is nothing to define for η, $\lambda(v) = \mathcal{L}$, and for all $B \in \mathfrak{K}_{\mathcal{L},\Sigma}$ we define $\nu(v, B) := 0$ and $\nu(v, B)$ remains undefined on other property attributes. For this first main case it follows that G violates the key $\mathcal{L} : \mathfrak{K}$ since $v \in V_\mathcal{L}$ and $\nu(v, A)$ is undefined since $A \in \mathfrak{K} - \mathfrak{K}_{\mathcal{L},\Sigma}$. It remains to show in this case that G satisfies $\mathcal{L}' : \mathfrak{K}'$ for all $\mathcal{L}' : \mathfrak{K}' \in \Sigma$. If $\mathcal{L}' : \mathfrak{K}' \in \Sigma_\mathcal{L}$, then we have $\mathfrak{K}' \subseteq \mathfrak{K}_{\mathcal{L},\Sigma}$. It follows that for all $v \in V_{\mathcal{L}'}$ and for all $B \in \mathfrak{K}'$, $\nu(v, B)$ is defined. Since there is only one vertex in V, it follows that G must satisfy $\mathcal{L}' : \mathfrak{K}' \in \Sigma_\mathcal{L}$. Otherwise, $\mathcal{L}' : \mathfrak{K}' \notin \Sigma_\mathcal{L}$, which means that $\mathcal{L}' \not\subseteq \mathcal{L}$. Consequently, $V_{\mathcal{L}'} = \emptyset$ and G must satisfy $\mathcal{L}' : \mathfrak{K}' \notin \Sigma_\mathcal{L}$. Hence, we have shown that Σ does not imply $\mathcal{L} : \mathfrak{K}$ in the first main case.

In the second main case we assume the opposite, that is, $\mathfrak{K} \subseteq \mathfrak{K}_{\mathfrak{L},\Sigma}$. Let us define the property graph $G = (V, E, \eta, \lambda, \nu)$ as follows: $V = \{v_1, v_2\}$, $E = \emptyset$, and therefore there is nothing to define for η, $\lambda(v_1) = \mathfrak{L} = \lambda(v_2)$, for all $B \in \mathfrak{K}$ we define $\nu(v_1, B) = 0 = \nu(v_2, B)$, for all $B \in \mathfrak{K}_{\mathfrak{L},\Sigma} - \mathfrak{K}$ we define $\nu(v_1, B) = 0$ and $\nu(v_2, B) = 1$, and $\nu(v, B)$ and $\nu(v, B)$ remains undefined on other property attributes. It follows that G violates $\mathfrak{L} : \mathfrak{K}$ since there are $v_1, v_2 \in V_{\mathfrak{L}}$ such that $v_1 \neq v_2$ and $\nu(v_1, \mathfrak{K}) = \nu(v_2, \mathfrak{K})$. It remains to show that G satisfies every $\mathfrak{L}' : \mathfrak{K}' \in \Sigma$. In case $a)$ we assume $\mathfrak{L}' : \mathfrak{K}' \notin \Sigma_{\mathfrak{L}}$, which means that $\mathfrak{L}' \not\subseteq \mathfrak{L}$. Consequently, $V_{\mathfrak{L}'} = \emptyset$ and G must satisfy $\mathfrak{L}' : \mathfrak{K}' \notin \Sigma_{\mathfrak{L}}$. In case $b)$ we assume $\mathfrak{L}' : \mathfrak{K}' \in \Sigma_{\mathfrak{L}}$. Hence, $\Sigma_{\mathfrak{L}} \neq \emptyset$ and $\mathfrak{L} : \mathfrak{K}_{\mathfrak{L},\Sigma} \in \Sigma^+$ by Property 1. of Lemma 3. In particular, $\mathfrak{K}' \subseteq \mathfrak{K}_{\mathfrak{L},\Sigma}$. Consequently, for all $v \in V_{\mathfrak{L}'}$ and for all $B \in \mathfrak{K}'$ it follows that $\nu(v, B)$ is defined. In case $b.1)$ we assume that $\mathfrak{K}' \not\subseteq \mathfrak{K}$. Hence, there is some $A \in \mathfrak{K}' - \mathfrak{K}$ such that $\nu(v_1, A) = 0 \neq 1 = \nu(v_2, A)$ holds. That is, $\mathfrak{L}' : \mathfrak{K}'$ is satisfied by G. Finally, in case $b.2)$ we assume that $\mathfrak{K}' \subseteq \mathfrak{K}$. Hence, in this case we have $\mathfrak{K}' \subseteq \mathfrak{K} \subseteq \mathfrak{K}_{\mathfrak{L},\Sigma}$ with $\mathfrak{L}' : \mathfrak{K}' \in \Sigma_{\mathfrak{L}}$. Hence, Property 2. of Lemma 3 would imply that $\mathfrak{L} : \mathfrak{K} \in \Sigma^+$. This would be a contradiction to our original assumption that $\mathfrak{L} : \mathfrak{K} \notin \Sigma^+$, so case $b.2)$ cannot occur. We have just shown that in all possible cases, Σ does not imply $\mathfrak{L} : \mathfrak{K}$. This shows the completeness of $\mathfrak{C}$.   □

The proof of Theorem 1 contains a general construction of property graphs showing that a key is not implied by a given set of keys, as illustrated on our running example.

Example 5. Let Σ consist of the keys: *Helpline:{no}*, *Helpline:{name,phone}*, and *Complaints:{name,email}*. The key *Helpline:{no,expertise}* is not implied by Σ. Following the construction of Theorem 1 we would create a property graph G_1 with one vertex v, label $\lambda(v) = $ *:Helpline* and properties $\nu(v, no) = \nu(v, name) = \nu(v, phone) = 0$. In particular, $\mathfrak{K}_{Helpline,\Sigma} = \{no, name, phone\}$. Indeed, the property graph G_1 satisfies all keys in Σ, but violates the key *Helpline:{no,expertise}* since the value $\nu(v, expertise)$ has remained undefined. As observed before, *{Helpline,Complaints}:{phone,email}* is not implied by Σ. Following the construction of Theorem 1 we would create a property graph G_2 with two vertices v_1 and v_2, labels $\lambda(v_1) = $ *{:Helpline,:Complaints}* and properties $\nu(v_1, phone) = \nu(v_2, phone) = \nu(v_1, email) = \nu(v_2, email) = 0$, and $\nu(v_1, name) = \nu(v_1, no) = 0 \neq 1 = \nu(v_2, name) = \nu(v_2, no)$. In particular, $\mathfrak{K}_{\{Helpline,Complaints\},\Sigma} = \{no, name, phone, email\}$, and $\mathfrak{K} = \{phone, email\}$. Indeed, G_2 satisfies all keys in Σ, but violates the key *{Helpline,Complaints}:{phone,email}* since the two distinct vertices v_1 and v_2 both have labels *:Helpline* and *:Complaints*, and have matching property values on both *phone* and *email*.   □

6.2 Algorithmic Characterization

The axiomatization of keys enables us to establish an algorithm that decides the associated implication problem. In fact, we can derive the following characterization for the implication problem, from which we will derive such an algorithm.

Theorem 2. *Let* $\Sigma \cup \{\mathfrak{L} : \mathfrak{K}\}$ *denote a set of Neo4j keys over* $\mathcal{L}$ *and* $\mathcal{K}$. *Then* $\Sigma \models \mathfrak{L} : \mathfrak{K}$ *if and only if* $\mathfrak{K} \subseteq \mathfrak{K}_{\mathfrak{L},\Sigma}$ *and there is some* $\mathfrak{L}' : \mathfrak{K}' \in \Sigma_{\mathfrak{L}}$ *such that* $\mathfrak{K}' \subseteq \mathfrak{K}$.

Proof. **Sufficiency.** If $\mathfrak{K} \subseteq \mathfrak{K}_{\mathfrak{L},\Sigma}$ and there is some $\mathfrak{L}' : \mathfrak{K}' \in \Sigma_{\mathfrak{L}}$ such that $\mathfrak{K}' \subseteq \mathfrak{K}$, then the second property of Lemma 3 shows that $\mathfrak{L} : \mathfrak{K} \in \Sigma_{\mathfrak{C}}^{+}$. The soundness of $\mathfrak{C}$ means that $\mathfrak{L} : \mathfrak{K}$ is implied by Σ.

Necessity. Suppose that $\mathfrak{K} \not\subseteq \mathfrak{K}_{\mathfrak{L},\Sigma}$. This constitutes the first main case in the proof of Theorem 1. Hence, the property graph created in that case satisfies Σ and violates $\mathfrak{L} : \mathfrak{K}$. Consequently, $\mathfrak{L} : \mathfrak{K}$ is not implied by Σ.

Suppose now that for all $\mathfrak{L}' : \mathfrak{K}' \in \Sigma_{\mathfrak{L}}$ we have that $\mathfrak{K}' \cap (\mathfrak{K}_{\mathfrak{L},\Sigma} - \mathfrak{K}) \neq \emptyset$. Then the property graph from the second main case in the proof of Theorem 1 satisfies Σ and violates $\mathfrak{L} : \mathfrak{K}$. Consequently, $\mathfrak{L} : \mathfrak{K}$ is not implied by Σ. □

Algorithm 1 is based on the characterization of key implication in Theorem 2.

Theorem 3. *Algorithm 1 decides the implication problem* $\Sigma \models \mathfrak{L} : \mathfrak{K}$ *for the class of keys in* $\mathcal{O}(\|\Sigma \cup \{\mathfrak{L} : \mathfrak{K}\}\|)$ *time.*

Proof. The soundness of Algorithm 1 follows from Theorem 2. The upper time bound follows straight from the loop between steps 4–8. □

Example 6. On the input where Σ consist of *Helpline:*$\{no\}$, *Helpline:*$\{name,phone\}$, and *Complaints:*$\{name,email\}$, and φ denotes *Helpline:*$\{no,expertise\}$, Algorithm 1 returns *FALSE* due to *expertise* $\notin \{no,name,phone\} = \mathfrak{K}_{\{Helpline\},\Sigma}$ in line 9. On input Σ and $\{Helpline,Complaints\}$:$\{no,email\}$, Algorithm 1 returns *TRUE* since $\{no,email\} \subseteq \{no,name,phone,email\} = \mathfrak{K}_{\{Helpline,Complaints\},\Sigma}$, *Helpline:*$\{no\} \in \Sigma_{\{Helpline,Complaints\}}$ and $\{no\} \subseteq \{no,email\}$. □

Algorithm 1. Implication of Neo4j Keys

Require: Neo4j Key Set $\Sigma \cup \{\mathfrak{L} : \mathfrak{K}\}$
Ensure: *TRUE*, if $\Sigma \models \mathfrak{L} : \mathfrak{K}$, and *FALSE*, otherwise
 1: Unique ← *FALSE*;
 2: Exists ← *FALSE*;
 3: $\mathfrak{K}_{\mathfrak{L},\Sigma} \leftarrow \emptyset$;
 4: **for all** $\mathfrak{L}' : \mathfrak{K}' \in \Sigma$ **do**
 5:     **if** $\mathfrak{L}' \subseteq \mathfrak{L}$ **then**   ▷ This means $\mathfrak{L}' : \mathfrak{K}' \in \Sigma_{\mathfrak{L}}$
 6:         $\mathfrak{K}_{\mathfrak{L},\Sigma} \leftarrow \mathfrak{K}_{\mathfrak{L},\Sigma} \cup \mathfrak{K}'$;   ▷ All properties of this key exist
 7:     **if** (NOT(Unique) AND $\mathfrak{K}' \subseteq \mathfrak{K}$) **then**
 8:         Unique ← *TRUE*;   ▷ Found an input key that makes our candidate unique
 9: **if** $\mathfrak{K} \subseteq \mathfrak{K}_{\mathfrak{L},\Sigma}$ **then return** Exists ← *TRUE*;   ▷ All required properties exist
10: **if** (Exists AND Unique) **then return** *TRUE*   ▷ Properties exist and are unique
11: **else return** *FALSE*

---

7 Conclusion and Future Work

We have established that Neo4j keys can be reasoned about efficiently, which is beneficial to update and query operations on property graphs. In particular, multiple labels offer new opportunities for physical and logical data management. In the future, we will study the interaction of Neo4j keys with existence and uniqueness constraints that are also part of the Cypher language. In addition, we will also investigate different semantics and different sets of constraints. An interesting proposal might be to combine Neo4j keys with recently investigated embedded uniqueness constraints [21,22]. These would be expressions of the form $\mathfrak{L} : E : X$ with the semantics that for the set of vertices v that carry all labels in $\mathfrak{L}$ and for which $\nu(v, A)$ is defined for all $A \in E$, the combination of property values over the property attributes in X is unique.

References

1. Balamuralikrishna, N., Jiang, Y., Koehler, H., Leck, U., Link, S., Prade, H.: Possibilistic keys. Fuzzy Sets Syst. **376**, 1–36 (2019)
2. Bonifati, A., Fletcher, G.H.L., Voigt, H., Yakovets, N.: Querying Graphs. Synthesis Lectures on Data Management. Morgan & Claypool Publishers, San Rafael (2018)
3. Brown, P., Link, S.: Probabilistic keys. IEEE Trans. Knowl. Data Eng. **29**(3), 670–682 (2017)
4. Buneman, P., Davidson, S.B., Fan, W., Hara, C.S., Tan, W.C.: Keys for XML. Comput. Netw. **39**(5), 473–487 (2002)
5. Chen, P.P.: The entity-relationship model - toward a unified view of data. ACM Trans. Database Syst. **1**(1), 9–36 (1976)
6. Codd, E.F.: A relational model of data for large shared data banks. Commun. ACM **13**(6), 377–387 (1970)
7. Demetrovics, J.: On the number of candidate keys. Inf. Process. Lett. **7**(6), 266–269 (1978)
8. Fagin, R.: A normal form for relational databases that is based on domains and keys. ACM Trans. Database Syst. **6**(3), 387–415 (1981)
9. Fan, W., Fan, Z., Tian, C., Dong, X.L.: Keys for graphs. PVLDB **8**(12), 1590–1601 (2015)
10. Fan, W., Lu, P.: Dependencies for graphs. ACM Trans. Database Syst. **44**(2), 5:1–5:40 (2019)
11. Hannula, M., Link, S.: Automated reasoning about key sets. In: Galmiche, D., Schulz, S., Sebastiani, R. (eds.) IJCAR 2018. LNCS (LNAI), vol. 10900, pp. 47–63. Springer, Cham (2018). https://doi.org/10.1007/978-3-319-94205-6_4
12. Hartmann, S., Link, S.: Efficient reasoning about a robust XML key fragment. ACM Trans. Database Syst. **34**(2), 1–33 (2009)
13. Khizder, V.L., Weddell, G.E.: Reasoning about uniqueness constraints in object relational databases. IEEE Trans. Knowl. Data Eng. **15**(5), 1295–1306 (2003)
14. Köhler, H., Leck, U., Link, S., Zhou, X.: Possible and certain keys for SQL. VLDB J. **25**(4), 571–596 (2016). https://doi.org/10.1007/s00778-016-0430-9
15. Lausen, G.: Relational databases in RDF: keys and foreign keys. In: Christophides, V., Collard, M., Gutierrez, C. (eds.) ODBIS/SWDB -2007. LNCS, vol. 5005, pp. 43–56. Springer, Heidelberg (2008). https://doi.org/10.1007/978-3-540-70960-2_3
16. Lucchesi, C.L., Osborn, S.L.: Candidate keys for relations. J. Comput. Syst. Sci. **17**(2), 270–279 (1978)
17. Pokorný, J., Valenta, M., Kovacic, J.: Integrity constraints in graph databases. In: The 8th International Conference on Ambient Systems, Networks and Technologies, ANT 2017/The 7th International Conference on Sustainable Energy Information Technology, SEIT 2017, Madeira, Portugal, 16–19 May 2017, vol. 109, pp. 975–981. Elsevier (2017). Procedia Computer Science
18. Thalheim, B.: On semantic issues connected with keys in relational databases permitting null values. Elektronische Informationsverarbeitung und Kybernetik **25**(1/2), 11–20 (1989)

19. Thalheim, B.: Entity-Relationship Modeling - Foundations of Database Technology. Springer, Heidelberg (2000). https://doi.org/10.1007/978-3-662-04058-4
20. Toman, D., Weddell, G.E.: On keys and functional dependencies as first-class citizens in description logics. J. Autom. Reason. **40**(2–3), 117–132 (2008). https://doi.org/10.1007/s10817-007-9092-z
21. Wei, Z., Leck, U., Link, S.: Discovery and ranking of embedded uniqueness constraints. PVLDB **12**(13), 2339–2352 (2019)
22. Wei, Z., Link, S., Liu, J.: Contextual keys. In: Mayr, H.C., Guizzardi, G., Ma, H., Pastor, O. (eds.) ER 2017. LNCS, vol. 10650, pp. 266–279. Springer, Cham (2017). https://doi.org/10.1007/978-3-319-69904-2_22

Past Trends and Future Prospects in Conceptual Modeling - A Bibliometric Analysis

Felix Härer[(✉)] and Hans-Georg Fill

Digitalization and Information Systems Group,
University of Fribourg, 1700 Fribourg, Switzerland
{felix.haerer,hans-georg.fill}@unifr.ch
https://www.unifr.ch/inf/digits/en/

Abstract. Research in conceptual modeling is today undertaken in a large number of fields. We describe the results from a bibliometric analysis of major outlets for conceptual modeling research for investigating the evolution of research topics. As a basis for the study we used the openly accessible DBLP dataset which we enriched with data from related publisher's websites and databases. Besides a descriptive analysis of the publication data, we conducted a content-based analysis of more than 3.200 papers using Latent Dirichlet Allocation. This permits to gain insights into the past trends in conceptual modeling research and derive future prospects for the community.

Keywords: Conceptual modeling · Research communities · Bibliometric analysis

1 Introduction

The benefits of conceptual modeling for digital transformation as implied by this year's conference theme seem to be largely undisputed within the conceptual modeling community itself [2,3,12,14,23]. However, from the viewpoint of other disciplines, practitioners and newcomers it is often not so obvious what conceptual modeling stands for, which topics are investigated and where according research takes place, cf. [8]. And even for a scientific community itself it is from times to times beneficial to reflect on its past achievements, on the evolution of topics and the identification of visions and future directions [21].

The initial impulse for our investigation was a statement by an anonymous reviewer in an evaluation report, who stated that some geographical regions would dominate certain areas in conceptual modeling. Whereas any member of the community might have some gut feelings of whether this may be true or not, we could not find previous analyses that would have permitted us to verify or counter this statement. Some indication exists that there is a dependency between organizational and educational cultures and the use of certain diagrams

G. Dobbie et al. (Eds.): ER 2020, LNCS 12400, pp. 34–47, 2020.
https://doi.org/10.1007/978-3-030-62522-1_3

[13]. To the best of our knowledge, the only bibliometric analysis available so far is the paper by Chen et al. who had looked at papers from the ER conference from 1979–2005 with a focus on authors and citation counts [7]. As conceptual modeling is however today spread across many different outlets, we decided to conduct a more comprehensive analysis. The research questions we defined for this undertaking were as follows:

- RQ 1: In which geographical regions is conceptual modeling research conducted?
- RQ 2: How has the quantity of conceptual modeling papers evolved over time, taking into account specific regions and the communities of specific outlets?
- RQ 3: How many authors are active in conceptual modeling and what is their typical number of papers?
- RQ 4: What are the major conceptual modeling topics in terms of published research, how do they differ per outlet and how did they evolve over time?
- RQ 5: With the topical evolution, where is conceptual modeling positioned now and are there indications of research gaps or opportunities?
- RQ 6: Is there an indication of prospective topics, application areas, or domains where conceptual modeling might be used in the future?

For answering these questions we will report in the following results from a bibliometric analysis that we have conducted based on the openly accessible DBLP dataset as the main source. Due to several manual steps that were required for the analysis, we restricted the outlets to nine core outlets in conceptual modeling: the International Symposium on Business Modeling and Software Design (BMSD), the joint publication of Business Process Modeling, Development and Support in conjunction with Evaluation and Modelling Methods for Systems Analysis and Development (BPMDS/EMMSAD), the International Conference on Conceptual Modeling (ER), the International Conference on Model Driven Engineering Languages and Systems (MoDELS), and the Practice of Enterprise Modeling (PoEM) conference as well as the Complex Systems Informatics and Modeling Quarterly (CISMQ), the Enterprise Modelling and Information Systems Architectures - International Journal of Conceptual Modeling (EMISAJ), the International Journal of Information System Modeling and Design (IJISMD), and the Software and Systems Modeling (SoSyM) journal. We further enriched the data of the time span from 2005–2019 with information from publishers' websites for adding further author attributes, e.g. for determining their geographical origin and institution. In addition, we retrieved the full-texts of approx. 3.200 papers to conduct content-based analyses.

The remainder of the paper is structured as follows: in Sect. 2 we describe the data collection and analysis process in detail, followed by a descriptive analysis in Sect. 3 and a content-based analysis in Sect. 4. The results are discussed in Sect. 5 and conclusions are drawn in Sect. 6.

2 Data Collection and Analysis Process

For the data collection and analysis process we reverted to the well-known KDD process commonly used in data mining [10]. It contains the steps *data selection, preprocessing, transformation,* and *data mining* and applies the Extract-Transform-Load (ETL) procedure [1]. The data collection and analysis process is outlined in Fig. 1.

2.1 Data Collection Process

By using the DBLP database dump from 2019-10-11[1] as a starting point, nine major English-language conference and journal outlets for conceptual modeling were selected. For each of the 4.131 entries matching the relevant identifiers of the outlets, metadata in the form of *Title, Authors, Year, Outlet, URL,* and *DOI* in most cases, was collected in a JSON file. For further enrichment, data was retrieved from the publishers' websites, e.g. IEEE, and included metadata on DOI, affiliation, and country, with additional manual extractions of countries from the affiliation in case of known and exact matches.

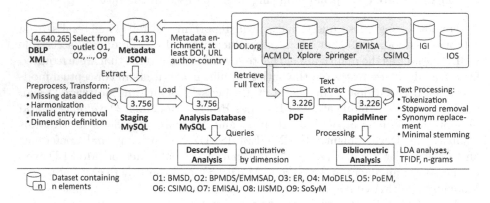

Fig. 1. Data collection and analysis process based on the DBLP XML dataset

Metadata was extracted into a staging database while cleaning operations were applied regarding the addition of missing data for DOI and authors, the manual harmonization of all names, countries, and outlets, as well as the removal of invalid entries including non-paper articles such as editorials and placeholders with missing authors. For an analysis along multiple dimensions, the 3.756 remaining entries were transformed into the star schema shown in Fig. 2 with partially normalized dimensions or "snowflaking". With this standard practice in data warehousing, redundancy is accepted for never-changing historized data to minimize query latency [15, p. 55]. Finally, we loaded 3.756 entries for analysis[2].

---

[1] https://dblp.uni-trier.de/xml/.
[2] For all publications see https://zenodo.org/record/3982628.

Full text documents were available to us from all publishers except IGI and IOS. The 3.226 available full texts of the publishers indicated in Fig. 1 were retrieved using Node.js scraping scripts. Subsequently, the documents were loaded into RapidMiner Studio 9.5. There, NLP operations were applied such as tokenization, stopword removal, synonym replacement and some minimal stemming for the normalization of plural and common inflected forms[3].

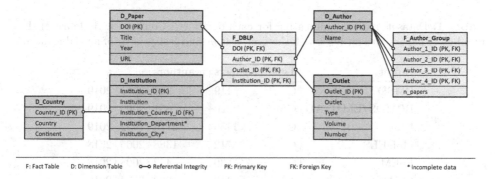

F: Fact Table   D: Dimension Table   o—o Referential Integrity   PK: Primary Key   FK: Foreign Key   * incomplete data

Fig. 2. Schema of the analysis database. Fact tables (prefix F) for the storage of DBLP publications and author groups reference according dimension tables (prefix D).

2.2 Data Analysis Process

The analysis database served as a source for descriptive statistics. By using queries over the dimensions, the quantitative analysis yielded exact answers such as the absolute frequencies of publications. The database architecture proved to be useful for multi-dimensional queries, e.g. authors affiliated with institutions from countries at varying levels of granularity such as specific countries, continents or all countries. A second analysis of bibliographic data was based on the full texts of the documents. Latent Dirichlet Allocation (LDA) was applied, which is a statistical method for the identification of topics in documents [4,5]. Further operations for TF-IDF, n-gram occurrences, and clustering were deferred to the future analysis of the dataset and will not be regarded here.

3   Descriptive Analysis of the Dataset

For a first descriptive analysis, Table 1 outlines the properties of the dataset, showing the contained outlets with publications, author figures and availability. For the following analysis, the time period 2005 to 2019 is considered and

---

[3] The NLP and analysis processes for RapidMiner as well as stopwords and synonyms are available at https://zenodo.org/record/3982628.

grouped into time frames where appropriate. The interpretation of these results will be discussed in Sect. 5.

For investigating the worldwide distribution of conceptual modeling research as described in RQ1, we conducted a quantitative analysis by querying the affiliations of each paper with their known geographical locations. As shown in Table 2, 2.466 or 66% of publications originated from Europe, 603 or 16% from North America, and 10% or 359 from Asia.

Table 1. Dataset overview indicating for each outlet (C: Conference, J: Journal) the number of papers and authors with the first year y_1 and last year y_2 of available data.

Outlet	Type	n papers	n authors	y_1	y_2
BMSD	C	119	214	2011	2019
BPMDS/EMMSAD	C	320	651	2009	2019
ER	C	1155	2115	1992	2019
MoDELS	C	712	1388	2005	2018
PoEM	C	230	442	2008	2018
CSIMQ	J	112	262	2014	2019
EMISAJ	J	131	303	2005	2018
IJISMD	J	161	411	2010	2019
SoSyM	J	816	1703	2002	2019
Σ		3756			

Concerning the evolution of the number of publications over time (RQ2), it can be stated that from the total of 3.199 publications, most publications fall into the period 2015–2019, i.e. 1.347 (42%), compared to 1.101 (34%) in the timeframe 2010–2014 and 751 (23%) in 2005–2009 as shown in Table 2 per continent and in Table 3[4] per outlet. Considering specific outlets, most publications in the dataset are from SoSyM, i.e. 762 papers, followed by 712 papers in MoDELS and 652 papers in ER.

In RQ3 we considered the number of authors who are active in conceptual modeling and their typical number of papers. In our dataset we identified $n = 5.141$ authors, indicated per outlet in Table 1. For the typical number of publications, a skew has been observed in that 69% of authors have exactly one publication while 31% have between 2 and 61 publications. Considering percentile measures, 80% of the observed authors have less than $P_{80} = 2$ publications. Furthermore the progression $P_{85} = 3$, $P_{90} = 4$, $P_{95} = 6$ indicates authors with several publications. The indication is a power law distribution, sometimes observed in social networks [6], as the steep increase to $P_{96} = 6$, $P_{97} = 7$, $P_{98} = 10$, $P_{99} = 14$ shows. It can be concluded that most of the interactions or publications are from a relatively small community of authors. One

---

[4] Note that countries located on multiple continents cause the total sum of publications in Table 2 to exceed the one of Table 3.

Table 2. Publications originating from authors affiliated with institutions in the given continents over time frames of five years.

Continent	Year			Σ
	2005–2009	2010–2014	2015–2019	
Africa	3	17	26	46
Asia	58	104	197	359
Europe	532	882	1052	2466
North America	202	199	202	603
Oceania	37	44	46	127
South America	26	45	75	146

first interpretation is that many of the 5.141 authors might not be from the core conceptual modeling community but rather from collaborating fields.

4 Content-Based Analysis of Publications

In a second step, we analyzed the contents of the papers contained in our dataset. For this we used the LDA implementation of MALLET (MAchine Learning for LanguagE Toolkit[5]) that is part of RapidMiner 9.5[6]. In comparison to simpler methods such as term frequency and n-gram analysis, LDA is a topic modeling approach operating on the level of documents with the goal of identifying their topics. Thereby, LDA assumes that several topics are present in each document. Given a document collection, any document d is described by a statistical distribution θ_d over its topics. That is, each topic has a particular probability or weight for d, and a distribution of words $\theta_{d,k}$ for any topic k [4]. Each topic k therefore is represented by the top n words according to their probability or weight. The particular weights can be considered hidden variables, determined with the Gibbs sampling scheme, which is carried out iteratively for each word such that its likelihood of appearing in a particular topic is maximized [20].

For all LDA analyses that we performed, we show the top eight topics inferred from the top five words according to their weight (cf. [4,22]). In addition, the topics are ordered by the cumulative weight of the top five words, where a weight of topic k and word w is an absolute measure of the occurrences for w assigned to k in all documents[7]. The LDA analysis of full-text documents between 2005 and 2019 was performed for the top eight topics in the whole data set, in each outlet, over each continent and over consecutive time-frames of five years. In the following we will only discuss a subset of the results due to limitations of space.

---

[5] http://mallet.cs.umass.edu/topics.php.

[6] Specifically, a concurrent implementation for the detection of topics [24] was used in combination with a specialized sampling scheme based on Gibbs sampling [20].

[7] Note that the ordering is solely for presentation as it can only consider known weights. Weights beyond the top words possibly involve all words of all documents.

Table 3. Publications of individual outlets over time frames of five years.

Outlet	Year			Σ
	2005–2009	2010–2014	2015–2019	
BMSD	0	30	89	119
BPMDS/EMMSAD	33	161	126	320
ER	214	217	221	652
MoDELS	286	248	178	712
PoEM	36	92	102	230
CSIMQ	0	4	108	112
EMISAJ	30	45	56	131
IJISMD	0	82	79	161
SoSyM	152	222	388	762
Σ	751	1101	1347	3199

The results for the LDA analyses are shown in the following tables, with Table 4 demonstrating overall results and Table 5 an analysis of an outlet dimension by using the ER conference as example. We can observe for the topics of the ER conference that the word *model* occurs in all topics except for Topics 2, 7, and 8. In Topic 2 *schema* is obviously prominent. Most weight is accumulated by Topic 1 with the highest-weighted words *model* and *conceptual, system, design*, and *information*. This is followed by Topic 2 in the context of schemas and databases, Topic 3 in the context of processes and services, and Topic 4 in the context of goals and requirements[8]. The remaining topics cover additional themes typically considered for the ER conference, probably with the exception of Topic 7 that leaves room for interpretation.

Table 4. LDA analysis of papers from 2005–2019 ordered by cumulative topic weight.

Topic 1		Topic 2		Topic 3		Topic 4	
Word	Weight	Word	Weight	Word	Weight	Word	Weight
process	83634	model	84526	model	59466	model	33915
model	56049	language	29097	transformation	41565	system	28213
business	47149	tool	18822	rule	27674	test	17407
service	30829	metamodel	16466	graph	18114	software	17176
system	23810	uml	16429	element	13825	feature	15532

Topic 5		Topic 6		Topic 7		Topic 8	
Word	Weight	Word	Weight	Word	Weight	Word	Weight
model	58638	state	32081	class	21079	data	28064
use	14060	event	24238	constraint	21019	schema	10742
case	12277	model	16437	model	19568	database	10260
software	12206	transition	13856	type	14748	query	8659
tool	10573	system	13477	object	13784	set	8190

---

[8] Note the absence of the term *ER* that is part of the stop word list described in Sect. 2.1 due to frequent mentions of the conference name.

Table 5. LDA analysis of papers published at the ER conference between 2005 and 2019 ordered by cumulative topic weight

Topic 1		Topic 2		Topic 3		Topic 4	
Word	Weight	Word	Weight	Word	Weight	Word	Weight
model	16398	schema	5967	process	7853	goal	6068
conceptual	4162	data	4344	model	3571	model	4222
system	3748	node	3423	service	3017	requirement	3058
design	3207	database	3215	data	2993	value	2085
information	2864	query	3200	event	2256	system	2082

Topic 5		Topic 6		Topic 7		Topic 8	
Word	Weight	Word	Weight	Word	Weight	Word	Weight
model	3820	ontology	4668	data	5482	set	2987
type	3530	model	2782	user	2713	constraint	2115
class	3253	type	2356	concept	1718	relation	1890
relationship	2962	concept	2018	web	1714	data	1601
object	2406	relation	1840	result	1702	tuple	1498

Excerpts from the LDA analysis results per continent are shown in Table 6 for Europe and in Table 7 for North America. The topic with the most cumulative weight for publications with authors from European institutions contains the terms *model* and *language*, which are also found in the first topic for North America. There, *tool* and *software* seem to be more prominent than *language*, whereas *UML* and *metamodel* are prominently observed in Europe. A further observation is that the terms contained in Topic 8 for Europe around databases do not occur in a similar way in any of the top topics for North America. Conversely, topics related to *goal* and *requirement* are absent in the top European topics. Topics around business processes are strongly represented in Europe through Topic 2 and Topic 4 and only considered in Topic 5 in North America.

Table 6. LDA analysis of papers by authors affiliated with institutions in Europe between 2005 and 2019 ordered by cumulative topic weight

Topic 1		Topic 2		Topic 3		Topic 4	
Word	Weight	Word	Weight	Word	Weight	Word	Weight
model	70196	model	48435	model	47688	process	60317
language	27875	business	24000	transformation	35420	model	28576
class	16830	process	21852	rule	22523	business	15904
uml	14970	system	19973	graph	15231	event	9714
metamodel	14570	information	18395	element	11086	activity	9536

Topic 5		Topic 6		Topic 7		Topic 8	
Word	Weight	Word	Weight	Word	Weight	Word	Weight
model	41349	system	22905	state	24032	data	18289
test	15518	model	22082	set	11431	schema	9311
software	14148	service	14566	system	10664	set	7180
feature	13442	component	13142	event	10508	database	7134
case	11564	time	12182	model	9555	ontology	6331

Table 7. LDA analysis of papers by authors affiliated with institutions in North America between 2005 and 2019 ordered by cumulative topic weight

Topic 1		Topic 2		Topic 3		Topic 4	
Word	Weight	Word	Weight	Word	Weight	Word	Weight
model	19129	transformation	9864	state	5663	model	10141
tool	5872	model	9814	model	5598	feature	4989
software	4951	rule	6553	system	4567	product	2472
language	3641	metamodel	3604	time	3721	element	2138
system	3171	graph	3444	event	2798	change	1959

Topic 5		Topic 6		Topic 7		Topic 8	
Word	Weight	Word	Weight	Word	Weight	Word	Weight
process	7551	model	4869	goal	5776	data	3806
business	4085	system	4017	model	5648	type	2195
service	3318	test	3448	requirement	3012	attribute	2142
model	2395	uml	3110	system	1797	conceptual	2102
system	2359	case	2799	analysis	1656	relationship	2011

In Table 8 and Table 9 the results from the LDA analysis of two time frames are shown. It can be observed that the predominant topic in the earlier time frame (2010–2014) includes the terms *model, transformation, rule, element,* and *graph*. In the more recent time frame (2015–2019), the predominant topic contains the terms *model, transformation, language, element,* and *metamodel*.

5   Discussion

The discussion of the results of our analysis will be divided into *a.* the discussion of the descriptive analysis results of the retrieved data and *b.* the discussion of the content-based analysis results through the application of LDA to the contents of the retrieved papers.

Table 8. LDA of papers in 2010–2014 ordered by cumulative topic weight

Topic 1		Topic 2		Topic 3		Topic 4	
Word	Weight	Word	Weight	Word	Weight	Word	Weight
model	23689	model	27849	process	26140	model	24810
transformation	14645	software	8282	model	10824	process	5977
rule	9910	tool	7229	business	7740	system	5492
element	5783	language	7227	activity	5153	design	5129
graph	5688	feature	6932	event	3965	information	4766

Topic 5		Topic 6		Topic 7		Topic 8	
Word	Weight	Word	Weight	Word	Weight	Word	Weight
service	12192	model	9312	constraint	7639	data	8192
business	9311	system	7684	model	5512	schema	4331
model	7703	state	6073	semantic	5150	query	3618
goal	6756	test	5423	class	5065	database	3028
system	5717	time	5055	set	4477	user	2886

The development of the overall numbers of publications as shown in Table 3 shows the positive development of the conceptual modeling community in general. With regard to the three time periods 2005–2009, 2010–2014, and 2015–2019, most outlets show increasing numbers of publications. The only exceptions being here the MoDELS conference that shows a decline of approx. −13% and −28%, the BPMDS/EMMSAD conference with a decline of −22% in the last period and the IJISMD journal with a slight decline of −4%.

A closer inspection for the MoDELS conference revealed that this decline is primarily not due to a decrease in the acceptance rate but rather due to lower submission numbers, i.e. for example 172 submissions and 35 accepted full papers in the foundations track in 2015 compared to 89 submissions and 18 full papers in 2019 [19, 25].

Table 9. LDA of papers in 2015–2019 ordered by cumulative topic weight

Topic 1		Topic 2		Topic 3		Topic 4	
Word	Weight	Word	Weight	Word	Weight	Word	Weight
model	43627	process	39247	model	20638	model	25545
transformation	20563	model	20585	system	12527	software	9678
language	11544	business	10396	business	11773	feature	9389
element	10093	event	5792	information	10395	case	8671
metamodel	8930	task	5171	service	9866	use	8267

Topic 5		Topic 6		Topic 7		Topic 8	
Word	Weight	Word	Weight	Word	Weight	Word	Weight
model	19817	model	19027	state	9975	data	13071
system	15845	type	7502	set	8150	database	4640
component	6957	class	7203	model	6258	time	4554
time	6507	level	6502	constraint	5998	set	4125
state	6377	instance	5349	rule	5231	value	4093

At the same time, the MoDELS conference hosted 18 workshops in 2019, which may outweigh the decline in submissions to the main conference and which are not part of our analysis. The reasons for such a shift would need to be investigated more closely, e.g. through expert interviews with authors and organizers. One reason could be the generally higher acceptance rate of workshops and the increasing pressure to publish results that has been reported for many fields [18], which could make submissions to workshops more attractive.

Overall, the top three outlets in terms of publication numbers in 2005–2019 are the SoSyM journal, the MoDELS conference, and the ER conference. Several smaller outlets such as BMSD, PoEM, CSIMQ, and EMISAJ started to make good progress. It has to be noted that some outlets were not yet present in all time periods, i.e. BMSD, CSIMQ, and IJISMD began their activities only after 2009.

When analyzing the origins of the authors of the respective papers across geographical regions, the strong predominance of researchers with a European affiliation stands out. Whereas the number of contributions from authors in

North America stayed relatively constant, conceptual modeling research is clearly on the rise in the last two time periods (2010–2014/2015–2019) in Europe (+19%/+134%), Asia (+89%/+82%), and South America (+67%/+95%). Though the overall increase in publications can be witnessed across disciplines[9], the relative increases per region should be considered by editors and conference organizers.

In terms of the content-based analysis using LDA, the results for the whole data set over all periods show the broad range of topics that have been investigated by the conceptual modeling community in the past – see Table 4. We can make two major observations here: first, several topics are related to technical, fundamental aspects of modeling and schemas, e.g. in terms of metamodels, languages, transformation, constraints, and schemas (Topics 2, 3, 7, 8), which one would expect in such a research community. Second however, the application domains seem to be centered so far mostly around business/business process models, software and data models, with process and business modeling topics on the forefront. Other domains such as the humanities, e.g. [17], the legal domain, e.g. [11] or natural and exact sciences, e.g. [9], have not yet gained high visibility - at least in the investigated outlets. It could be an opportunity for the future orientation of the conceptual modeling community to broaden its scope to further domains and thus increase its relevance and impact.

The results of the LDA analysis per outlet permit to assess the scope of topics that have been primarily published in a particular publication source and also give an estimation of the importance of topics within this source. The topics in Table 5 nicely show the primary topics for the ER conference in the past. Although we were not able to integrate the results from the analysis of other outlets due to space restrictions, we can conclude that such insights can serve well in guiding potential authors in choosing an outlet for publishing their research and they support our understanding based on our own experience with these outlets. The results may be further used to assess the strategies of the different outlets, e.g. of journals publishing conceptual modeling research to decide which audiences they want to address and for conference organizers to decide about the tracks and workshops.

The LDA analysis per continents as shown for Europe and North America revealed that process modeling and business information systems are discussed to a higher extent in Europe than in North America as shown by Topics 2 and 4. As we had already noted in the descriptive analysis, goal and requirements modeling seems to have a stronger standing in North America than in Europe, whereas a topic around databases and data schemas is only present among the first eight topics in Europe but not in North America.

Finally, the LDA analysis per time periods as shown here for 2010–2014 and 2015–2019 can aid in tracking the importance of topics over time. Based on the cumulative weights of the topics and the resulting ordering, it can be derived that model transformation has been of constant interest and less papers have

---

[9] See the large increases in the number of publications recorded in DBLP https://dblp.uni-trier.de/statistics/newrecordsperyear.

recently focused on software models while more papers have been published on process and business information systems modeling. Interpretations for these shifts have to be made carefully as we did not investigate the reasons for these shifts. Together with the results shown for the distribution of papers across outlets and the topics discussed for each outlet, one interpretation would be that this is linked to the decrease of papers in our dataset for the MoDELS conference, which is strongly positioned in software modeling and UML.

There are several limitations of this study that need to be noted. This concerns foremost the selection of only a subset of outlets for publishing research on conceptual modeling. Due to the highly inter-disciplinary nature of the field, results of conceptual modeling research are often published in other, domain-oriented outlets apart from the traditional modeling outlets. Furthermore, the investigated conferences typically host a large number of workshops that also publish high volumes of papers, which have not been considered. This also applies to conferences and journals that are not published in English - e.g. the German Modellierung conference[10] - that have a long tradition of conceptual modeling research and have neither been included. This may change some results of the analysis. On the other hand, we believe that we have based our analysis on a good sample of conferences and journals that are relevant for the community.

6   Conclusion and Future Prospects

In summary we can draw the following conclusions: conceptual modeling research is well-established and shows a positive development in terms of the number of publications as well as the number of outlets available for presenting results. Despite these good news, it should be considered to widen the scope of traditional conceptual modeling outlets or to create new outlets for investigating novel applications of conceptual modeling to further domains. Whereas topics related to conceptual modeling and databases, business and information systems have been well covered, other domains seem to be underrepresented so far. Although workshops, which are traditionally held in conjunction with the major conferences, may serve this purpose, many of them only take up specialized topics in the traditional domains. With these results, our next steps encompass the design of tests on available and ongoing data to complete the cycle of hypothesis testing and hypothesis generation [16] for informing future analyses.

Based on the insights we have gained during our analysis, we see future prospects for conceptual modeling in a multitude of new domains, which would increase the overall relevance and impact. Potential candidates for such domains are the humanities, the legal domain or natural sciences. First indications for such directions are the 1st International Workshop on Conceptual Modeling for Life Sciences initiated by Bernasconi, Canakoglu, Palacio, and Román, which is hosted at this year's ER conference[11] as well as the ongoing workshops on

---

[10] See https://dblp.uni-trier.de/db/conf/modellierung/.
[11] http://www.bioinformatics.deib.polimi.it/cmls/.

Characterizing the Field of Conceptual Modeling initiated by Delcambre, Pastor, Liddle, and Storey[12].

References

1. Ali, S.M.F., Wrembel, R.: From conceptual design to performance optimization of ETL workflows: current state of research and open problems. VLDB J. **26**(6), 777–801 (2017). https://doi.org/10.1007/s00778-017-0477-2
2. Babar, Z., Yu, E.S.K.: Digital transformation - implications for enterprise modeling and analysis. In: 23rd IEEE International Enterprise Distributed Object Computing Workshop, EDOC Workshops 2019, Paris, France, 28–31 October 2019, pp. 1–8. IEEE (2019). https://doi.org/10.1109/EDOCW.2019.00015
3. Bērziša, S., et al.: Capability driven development: an approach to designing digital enterprises. Bus. Inf. Syst. Eng. **57**(1), 15–25 (2015). https://doi.org/10.1007/s12599-014-0362-0
4. Blei, D.M.: Probabilistic topic models. Commun. ACM **55**(4), 77–84 (2012). https://doi.org/10.1145/2133806.2133826
5. Blei, D.M., Ng, A.Y., Jordan, M.I.: Latent Dirichlet allocation. J. Mach. Learn. Res. **3**, 993–1022 (2003)
6. Broido, A.D., Clauset, A.: Scale-free networks are rare. Nat. Commun. **10**(1), 1–10 (2019). https://doi.org/10.1038/s41467-019-08746-5
7. Chen, C., Song, I.Y., Zhu, W.: Trends in conceptual modeling: citation analysis of the ER conference papers (1979–2005). In: Proceedings of the 11th International Conference on the International Society for Scientometrics and Informatrics, pp. 189–200. CSIC (2007)
8. Delcambre, L.M.L., Liddle, S.W., Pastor, O., Storey, V.C.: A reference framework for conceptual modeling. In: Trujillo, J.C., et al. (eds.) ER 2018. LNCS, vol. 11157, pp. 27–42. Springer, Cham (2018). https://doi.org/10.1007/978-3-030-00847-5_4
9. Döller, V.: ProVis - probability visualized: a modeling tool for teaching stochastics. In: Companion Proceedings of Modellierung 2020 Short, Workshop and Tools & Demo Papers. CEUR Workshop Proceedings, vol. 2542, pp. 222–226. CEUR-WS.org (2020)
10. Fayyad, U.M., Piatetsky-Shapiro, G., Smyth, P.: From data mining to knowledge discovery: an overview. In: Advances in Knowledge Discovery and Data Mining, pp. 1–34. American Association for Artificial Intelligence, USA (1996)
11. Fill, H.G.: Towards requirements for a meta modeling formalism to support visual law representations. In: Schweighofer, E., Kummer, F., Hoetzendorfer, W. (eds.) Internationales Rechtsinformatik Symposium 2012, Salzburg (2012)
12. Gray, J., Rumpe, B.: Models for the digital transformation. Softw. Syst. Model. **16**(2), 307–308 (2017). https://doi.org/10.1007/s10270-017-0596-7
13. Jaakkola, H., Thalheim, B.: Culture-adaptable web information systems. In: Information Modelling and Knowledge Bases XXVII. Frontiers in Artificial Intelligence and Applications, vol. 280 (2016)
14. Karagiannis, D., Mayr, H.C., Mylopoulos, J.: Domain-Specific Conceptual Modeling. Springer, Cham (2016). https://doi.org/10.1007/978-3-319-39417-6
15. Kimball, R., Ross, M.: The Data Warehouse Toolkit: The Definitive Guide to Dimensional Modeling, 3rd edn. Wiley Publishing, Hoboken (2013)

---

[12] http://www.nwpu-bioinformatics.com/ER2018/file/ccm.pdf.

16. Knobloch, B.: A framework for organizational data analysis and organizational data mining. In: Data Warehousing and Mining: Concepts, Methodologies, Tools, and Applications: Concepts, Methodologies, Tools, and Applications, pp. 449–462. IGI Global (2008)
17. Kropp, Y.O., Thalheim, B.: Conceptual modelling and humanities. In: Michael, J., et al. (eds.) Companion Proceedings of Modellierung 2020 Short, Workshop and Tools & Demo Papers co-located with Modellierung 2020, Vienna, Austria, 19–21 February 2020. CEUR Workshop Proceedings, vol. 2542, pp. 13–21. CEUR-WS.org (2020)
18. Kun, Á.: Publish and who should perish: you or science? Publications **6**(2), 18 (2018). https://doi.org/10.3390/publications6020018
19. Lethbridge, T., Cabot, J., Egyed, A.: Message from the chairs. In: 2015 ACM/IEEE 18th International Conference on Model Driven Engineering Languages and Systems (MODELS), p. iii (2015)
20. Newman, D., Asuncion, A., Smyth, P., Welling, M.: Distributed algorithms for topic models. J. Mach. Learn. Res. **10**, 1801–1828 (2009)
21. Pastor, O.: Conceptual modeling of life: beyond the homo sapiens. In: Comyn-Wattiau, I., Tanaka, K., Song, I.-Y., Yamamoto, S., Saeki, M. (eds.) ER 2016. LNCS, vol. 9974, pp. 18–31. Springer, Cham (2016). https://doi.org/10.1007/978-3-319-46397-1_2
22. Rosen-Zvi, M., Griffiths, T.L., Steyvers, M., Smyth, P.: The author-topic model for authors and documents. In: UAI 2004, Proceedings of the 20th Conference in Uncertainty in Artificial Intelligence, Banff, Canada, 7–11 July 2004, pp. 487–494 (2004)
23. Sandkuhl, K., et al.: From expert discipline to common practice: a vision and research agenda for extending the reach of enterprise modeling. Bus. Inf. Syst. Eng. **60**(1), 69 80 (2018). https://doi.org/10.1007/s12599-017-0516-y
24. Yao, L., Mimno, D., McCallum, A.: Efficient methods for topic model inference on streaming document collections. In: Proceedings of the 15th ACM SIGKDD International Conference on Knowledge Discovery and Data Mining, KDD 2009, pp. 937–946. Association for Computing Machinery, New York (2009)
25. Yue, T., Kessentini, M., Pretschner, A., Voss, S.: Preface. In: 2019 ACM/IEEE 22nd International Conference on Model Driven Engineering Languages and Systems (MODELS), pp. 10–11 (2019)

Process Mining and Conceptual Modeling

Bot Log Mining: Using Logs from Robotic Process Automation for Process Mining

Andreas Egger[1]([✉])[iD], Arthur H. M. ter Hofstede[3][iD], Wolfgang Kratsch[2][iD],
Sander J. J. Leemans[3][iD], Maximilian Röglinger[2][iD],
and Moe Thandar Wynn[3][iD]

[1] FIM Research Center, University of Augsburg, Project Group Business and
Information Systems Engineering of the Fraunhofer FIT, Augsburg, Germany
andreas.egger@fim-rc.de
[2] FIM Research Center, University of Bayreuth, Project Group Business and
Information Systems Engineering of the Fraunhofer FIT, Bayreuth, Germany
{wolfgang.kratsch,maximilian.roeglinger}@fim-rc.de
[3] Queensland University of Technology, Brisbane, Australia
{a.terhofstede,s.leemans,m.wynn}@qut.edu.au

Abstract. Robotic Process Automation (RPA) is an emerging technology for automating tasks using bots that can mimic human actions on computer systems. Most existing research focuses on the earlier phases of RPA implementations, e.g. the discovery of tasks that are suitable for automation. To detect exceptions and explore opportunities for bot and process redesign, historical data from RPA-enabled processes in the form of bot logs or process logs can be utilized. However, the isolated use of bot logs or process logs provides only limited insights and not a good understanding of an overall process. Therefore, we develop an approach that merges bot logs with process logs for process mining. A merged log enables an integrated view on the role and effects of bots in an RPA-enabled process. We first develop an integrated data model describing the structure and relation of bots and business processes. We then specify and instantiate a 'bot log parser' translating bot logs of three leading RPA vendors into the XES format. Further, we develop the 'log merger' functionality that merges bot logs with logs of the underlying business processes. We further introduce process mining measures allowing the analysis of a merged log.

Keywords: Robotic Process Automation · Process mining · Business process management

1 Introduction

Robotic Process Automation (RPA) is an emerging technology that refers to tools that mimic human actions on computer systems by interacting with the user interface or by connecting to APIs [3,28]. Applied for repetitive tasks, RPA can replace or even outperform humans regarding time, costs and quality [14,29]. It can be seen as the administrative counterpart of manufacturing robots [16].

© Springer Nature Switzerland AG 2020
G. Dobbie et al. (Eds.): ER 2020, LNCS 12400, pp. 51–61, 2020.
https://doi.org/10.1007/978-3-030-62522-1_4

For example, with the help of RPA, Telefónica O2 improved 15 core processes in 2015 and achieved a three-year return on investment of 650%–800% [17]. Further benefits of RPA, like increased productivity, consistency and reliability, have been shown in literature [17,24,26,29]. RPA technology is already used by many organizations and the usage is expected to rise [7,18].

In the relatively new research field around RPA, some approaches combine techniques from process mining with RPA [20]. Process mining uses event logs recorded in information systems to discover, monitor, and improve business processes [2]. In the literature combining RPA and process mining, methods are proposed that discover the business processes that are best suited for automation [20,22]. Other concepts support the development phase of bots, e.g. by recording user actions to derive process models [21,23]. However, the post-implementation phase, i.e. when bots are already deployed in an organization, plays a crucial role in increasing bot efficiencies. After bots are implemented and run live, their actions and performance have to be continuously observed to detect exceptions and opportunities for further development or bot redesign. A failing bot can have effects on underlying business processes, e.g. a bot exception can lead to a longer process duration or even an abortion of the whole business process [16]. Therefore, an integrated view of steps performed by bots in the context of existing business processes is needed to analyze these effects and the role of bots in business processes.

On the one hand, leading RPA software can be configured to record logs of the executed steps of bots (bot logs). On the other hand, process mining offers a wide range of tools and techniques to discover process inefficiencies from process logs. Therefore, an integrated analysis using bot and process logs could provide new insights in bot-human interaction, show effects of bots on business processes, show how exceptions of bots are handled and benefit the redesign of bots used in business processes. In this paper, we investigate the following research question: *How can bot logs and process logs be used for process mining to get a better understanding of the behaviors of bots in RPA-enabled business processes?*

To answer this question we first develop an integrated conceptual data model visualized as an ORM diagram describing the relations between bots and business processes. We then specify and instantiate the bot log parser that brings bot logs of the three leading RPA vendors software into the XES format, which is an IEEE standard format for event logs [12]. Moreover, we introduce the log merger that merges bot logs with process logs of the underlying business processes. Next, we propose some process mining measures that help to analyze the merged log. There are many possibilities for new measures, however for this paper we developed two exemplary measures, to illustrate the concept of our approach.

The remainder of this paper is structured as follows: Section 2 introduces a running example. Section 3 summarizes the related work on RPA and process mining. In Sect. 4 we present the proposed data model, provide a conceptual overview of the approach and develop the bot log parser, the log merger and the exemplary process mining measures. Section 5 concludes the paper and discusses ideas for future work.

2   Running Example

The following exemplary process serves as running example throughout this paper. A visualization of the process can be found in our repository: https:// bit.ly/2Q4CbYr. Consider an organization with a simplified business process 'Monthly Payroll' which consists of the two activities 'Calculation' and 'Prepare Documents'. Imagine that a bot process 'Auto Calculation', which consists of the three activities 'Open Payroll Spreadsheet', 'Sum up Working Hours' and 'Save and Close Spreadsheet', now automates the so far manual activity 'Calculation'.

Let's assume that process activity 'Calculation' fails in 80% of the cases because bot activity 'Open Payroll Spreadsheet' encounters exceptions when opening the spreadsheet. The failure of 'Calculation' has negative effects on the whole process 'Monthly Payroll'. If we solely analyze the process log, the failures of 'Calculation' and the resulting effects on the rest of the process can be detected. However, the exact reasons of these failures remain unclear. On the other hand, by solely looking at the bot log, the exact reason for the fails, namely the bot activity 'Open Payroll Spreadsheet', can be observed with all relevant variables, however the resulting effects on the business process 'Monthly Payroll' can not. By combining the bot log with the process log, however, the exact causes and the effects of exceptions are observable in an integrated analysis. This exemplary case shows how integrating bot logs in process logs enables new opportunities for process mining and the redesign of bot and business processes.

3   Background

RPA tools mimic human actions on computer systems by interacting with the user interface or by connecting to APIs [3, 28]. In the literature, there are various definitions of RPA [14]. RPA is mostly used on rule-based and repetitive tasks and has the potential to replace humans [14, 29]. As a result, employees can tackle more complex tasks instead of executing repetitive actions.

Organizations can benefit from using RPA in several ways, e.g. by increasing productivity, by using human resources more effectively as well as a by a more consistent and accurate execution of repetitive tasks by bots [24, 26]. Combining RPA with other technologies, such as machine learning, could enable the automation of more complex tasks and provide even more benefits [3, 10]. However, there are also challenges when implementing RPA [4, 27]. Bots follow the rules written in their code, therefore poorly defined rules can lead to unwanted results [16]. Furthermore, it is important to question the business processes that are automated and to not just blindly automate them, for which an integrated view on bots and the underlying processes is key [16].

UiPath, Automation Anywhere, and Blue Prism are the three leading vendors of RPA solutions [18]. Most RPA tools provide logs that report on bot-executed steps. These bot logs also contain additional payload attributes, such as used input variables and success states. For analytic purposes, some basic bot-related performance measures are provided by RPA tools, e.g. the total number of executions or how many errors occurred [9].

Process mining is based on process logs and allows for discovering as-is models, enhancing existing process models with new insights as well as checking conformance of process enactments [1]. Process logs describe occurrences of historic events and can be extracted from organizations' information systems [5]. By standardizing events along traces, XES is an IEEE format for process logs [12]. The research streams of RPA and process mining already are growing together [20]. Current research predominantly covers the early stages of RPA [15], e.g. by identifying the most suitable processes for RPA [11,22] or desktop activity mining to help constructing bots [21,23]. However, to the best of our knowledge, there is no approach that systematically uses bot logs for applying integrated process mining analysis on automated as well as non-automated process parts.

4   Using Bot and Process Logs for Process Mining

Figure 1 visualizes the conceptual overview of our approach. As a first step we developed a data model that describes the structure and relation of bot processes and business processes along with the required attributes for using bot logs for process mining (Sect. 4.1). Second, we introduce the bot log parser, bringing bot logs of the three leading RPA vendors into XES format (Sect. 4.2). Third, we specify the log merger that combines XES-parsed bot logs with process logs to one aggregated merged log (Sect. 4.3). Fourth, the resulting merged log can be used to gain new insights regarding the role of bots in business processes. For this purpose we suggest exemplary measures as well as develop a concept for visualizing results (Sect. 4.4). We implemented the bot log parser and the log merger in Java as well as the suggested measures as an extension for the Directly Follows visual Miner (DFvM) [19] in the open-source ProM framework [8]. For more details on this open-source implementation please refer to our repository: https://svn.win.tue.nl/repos/prom/Packages/BotLogMining/Trunk/src/.

4.1   Conceptual Mapping of Bot Logs and Process Logs

To describe the basic structure of bot logs and develop an approach that enables using them for process mining, we examined the software of the three leading RPA vendors. The tools of all three vendors allow modification of the level of logging, i.e. to which extent bot actions are logged, or to even insert customized logging commands. Therefore, the actual attributes provided in the bot logs can vary from just basic information (e.g., start/end of an action) to detailed payload data (e.g., the accessed URL for bot activity 'Open Browser').

In Fig. 2, we describe the structure of bot and business processes along with attributes that are needed to effectively merge bot logs and process logs in Object Role Modeling (ORM) 2 notation [13]. In the following, we describe the key elements of this model:

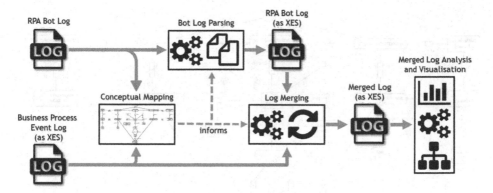

Fig. 1. Conceptual overview of our approach. (Color figure online)

- A **bot process** is identified by a name and has a **version**, identified by a number. A bot process (e.g. 'Auto Calculation' in the running example) is an algorithm created with RPA software, including the actions a bot performs.
- A bot process consists of **bot activities**, identified by a name. One bot activity for the bot process 'Auto Calculation' is 'Open Payroll Spreadsheet'.
- An instance of a bot process is a **bot process instance**, executed by a **bot**, with an identifying Id. A bot is a resource and can be allocated to bot processes. A bot process instance is a subtype of a process instance and is identified by a case Id which in turn is executed during a period that consists of a start and an end timestamp.
- A bot process instance consists of **bot activity instances** which are the instances of corresponding bot activities and subtypes of activity instances.
- An activity instance consists of **events** with an identifying Id, recorded at a specific timestamp, going through a lifecycle like 'start' or 'complete', being performed by a bot or not and either failing (because of a reason) or not.

On the right side of Fig. 2 a similar structure for business processes as for bot processes is described. In our running example, the business process has the name 'Monthly Payroll' and consists of the business process activities 'Calculation' and 'Prepare Documents'. A bot activity instance is always related to a business process activity instance. In the running example, the instances of the bot activities 'Open Payroll Spreadsheet', 'Sum up Working Hours' and 'Save and Close Spreadsheet' relate to the instances of the business process activity 'Calculation'.

4.2   Bot Log Parsing

To bring bot logs into XES format, relevant attributes have to be extracted from the bot log and standardized according to the specification in Fig. 2 to conform to established attribute definitions of the XES standard. Since the bot logs can be customized or the level of logging can be set to different levels, we need to answer the question, which attributes (as a minimum) should be included in a bot log in order to successfully merge it with process logs.

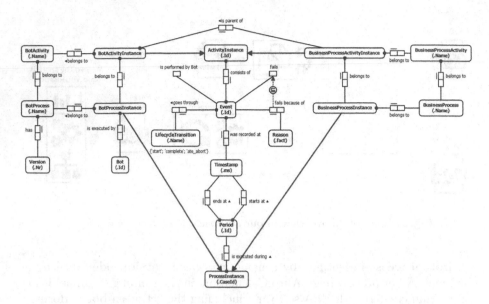

Fig. 2. Structure of bot processes and business processes with relevant attributes.

We define the following standardized attributes for every event in a bot log (i.e. for every action performed by the bot): concept:name, time:timestamp, life-cycle:transition, eventId, caseId, org:resource, botProcessName, botProcessVersionNumber, success and a connecting attribute. Table 1 shows the standardized attributes that can be extracted from various attributes of bot logs, depending on the RPA software used. The notion 'customized' in the table indicates, that the logging can be customized in different ways, depending on the underlying process and therefore the extraction of the standardized attribute can be done in different ways. The connecting attribute will be further explained in Sect. 4.3.

Table 1. Standardizing bot logs to the XES format.

XES Attribute	UiPath	Blue Prism	Automation Anywhere	Attribute in ORM diagram
concept:name	DisplayName	StageName	customized	BotActivityName
time:timestamp	timeStamp	Resource Start+End	first attribute	Timestamp
lifecycle:transition	State	Resource Start+End	customized	LifecycleTransition
eventId	fingerprint	StageID	customized	EventId
caseId	jobId	customized	customized	CaseId
org:resource	robotName	customized	customized	BotId
botProcessName	processName	Process	customized	BotProcessName
botProcessVersionNumber	processVersion	customized	customized	VersionNr
success	State	Result	customized	fails
connectingAttribute	customized	customized	customized	customized

UiPath provides bot logs in a JSON like format with many different attributes. A figure of the parsing of an exemplary UiPath bot log of the running example can be found in our repository: https://bit.ly/319wKxM. The bot log parser extracts the 'Trace Level' logs and uses the provided attributes, according to Table 1, to create a log in XES format. Blue Prism provides logs in a line-by-line format, where several lines can have information about the same action performed by a bot. The bot log parser extracts relevant attributes of an action from different lines and creates a corresponding XES log. In Automation Anywhere the attributes of a bot log can be customized to a high degree. The 'Log-to-File' command can be built into the robotic process algorithm and the exact attributes that are logged for specific bot actions can be defined in this command. According to our conceptual model, we suggest to log at least the attributes provided in Table 1 and we created a corresponding parser for Automation Anywhere bot logs that includes these attributes. However, the code for the parser can easily be adapted to other customized Automation Anywhere bot log structures.

4.3 Log Merging

The goal of the log merger is to create a merged log in XES format by combining a bot log with a process log. As input, the merger takes the process log, the bot log, and the name of the connecting attribute in the process log and in the bot log, respectively. The log merger iterates over the events in the process log and checks the value of the connecting attribute. It then compares this value with the values of the connecting attribute of all events in the bot log. If the values match, the bot event is put at the correct position in the process log, depending on the lifecycle attribute of the process event: If it is in the 'start' lifecycle, the bot event is put after the process event, if it is in the 'complete' lifecycle, the bot event is put before the process event.

In the running example (see Sect. 2) the instances of the bot activities 'Open Payroll Spreadsheet', 'Sum up Working Hours' and 'Save and Close Spreadsheet' would log a connecting attribute which is also logged by the business process activity instance 'Calculation' (e.g. a common documentId). The 'start' and 'complete' events of the three bot activities would then be placed before the 'complete' event of 'Calculation'. The log merger also puts a new 'bot' attribute to every bot event, which is set to true. This ensures that in the merged log, bot activities can be spotted by looking at this attribute.

The ORM diagram in Fig. 2 showed, that every bot activity instance has to belong to a business process activity instance. The connecting attribute includes information about the underlying business process activity the current bot activity belongs to and can vary depending on the use case. It can for example be a document Id, i.e when a bot performs an action the Id of the document the bot is working on is recorded in the bot log. The document Id can then also be found in the process log and thus the connection between bot events and business process events can be observed. If such a connecting attribute is missing, approaches from event correlation could be used to map bot events to corresponding process events (e.g. [25] or [6]).

4.4   Merged Log Analysis and Visualization

A merged log provides opportunities for a more detailed analysis of the underlying processes. The idea is to create new measures and visualizations for process mining that use a merged log as input and provide useful information on the underlying partly automated processes as output. There are many possibilities for new measures, however for this paper we developed two exemplary measures, 'Exception Time Impact' (ETI) and 'Relative Fails' (RF), to illustrate the concept of our approach.

$$ETI_A = \frac{\sum Trace\ rem.Dur.\ (A\ failed)}{\#traces(A\ failed)} - \frac{\sum Trace\ rem.Dur.\ (A\ success)}{\#traces(A\ success)} \qquad (1)$$

$$RF_A = \frac{\#events(A\ failed)}{\#events(A)} \qquad (2)$$

Equation 1 depicts the ETI measure, that calculates the average impact (in terms of time) which an activity (A) has on the process, if A fails. It compares the average remaining duration of the whole process in cases where A failed to the average remaining duration of the whole process in cases where A did not fail. An interpretation of the measure for the running example could be for example: When the bot activity 'Open Payroll Spreadsheet' fails, the business process 'Monthly Payroll' on average takes 5 h longer to end. In the visualization of the measure, activities are then colored based on the average time impact in case of failure and based on if they were performed manually or by a bot. This view enables the discovery of critical parts in the process as well as possible effects between bot and human activities. Following the exemplary interpretation of our running example, this could lead to a redesign of the bot process, especially of the bot activity 'Open Payroll Spreadsheet', since this activity on average delays the whole process by 5 h if it fails.

Equation 2 depicts the RF measure, that calculates the relative exception rate of A by dividing the number of events of A that have the success attribute value 'false' by the total number of occurrences of A in the merged log. In the visualization A is then colored based on the result of that division and based on by whom it was performed. This coloring enables the discovery of often failing activities by bots and humans and possible connections of fail rates of different activities. Further, the fail rates at points of bot-human interaction can be observed and checked for possible patterns.

5   Conclusion and Future Work

In this paper we presented an approach that uses bot logs for process mining, in order to get a better understanding of the behavior of bots in business processes.

We first developed an integrated data model, visualized as an ORM diagram, that describes the structure of bot processes and their relation with business processes. On this basis, we introduced the bot log parser that brings bot logs into the XES format. Furthermore, we introduced the concept of a merged log, and a log merger that combines bot logs with underlying process logs. We then introduced two process mining measures that help analyze merged logs.

We already conducted a first evaluation by parsing a real-life and three artificial bot logs, merging the resulting log with a real-life process log and analyzing the resulting merged log with the two created measures. All datasets and results can be found in our repository. We extend existing knowledge by describing the structure and relation of bot and business processes and by enabling the use of bot logs for process mining.

Our work has some limitations that raise opportunities for future work. First, the basic inputs for the approach are bot logs, which assumes that RPA users have set their logging level accordingly. A more detailed logging can result in more data, which may not always be favored in practice. Second, our approach requires a connecting attribute that allows linking bot actions and business process actions. If there is no such attribute, event correlation techniques have to be applied (e.g. [6] or [25]). Third, more measures are needed to analyze merged logs. We provided two measures to illustrate how new information can be gained from analyzing merged logs. However, there are more opportunities to extract useful information from merged logs, and thus more complex measures are needed.

A possible avenue for future work is to develop an event correlation approach specific for the RPA context. This can help merging bot logs and process logs when connecting attributes are missing, and thus provides further opportunities for generating merged logs. Additional to the two sample measures, more complex measures can be implemented in future work. One idea is to analyze failing bot activities and search for patterns in the corresponding bot log attributes. This measure could be used for mapping exact causes of bot exceptions and exact effects on business processes and thus could benefit bot and process redesign. Moreover, we plan to extend the evaluation with more real-world and artificial data. A further idea is to use more sophisticated techniques like machine learning on merged logs. Bot behavior in new business processes could be predicted and thus possible effects can be derived prior to bot implementation.

References

1. van der Aalst, W.: Process Mining: Discovery, Conformance and Enhancement of Business Processes, vol. 2. Springer, Heidelberg (2011). https://doi.org/10.1007/978-3-642-19345-3
2. van der Aalst, W., et al.: Process mining manifesto. In: Daniel, F., Barkaoui, K., Dustdar, S. (eds.) BPM 2011. LNBIP, vol. 99, pp. 169–194. Springer, Heidelberg (2012). https://doi.org/10.1007/978-3-642-28108-2_19
3. van der Aalst, W.M., Bichler, M., Heinzl, A.: Robotic process automation. Bus. Inf. Syst. Eng. **60**, 269–272 (2018). https://doi.org/10.1007/s12599-018-0542-4

4. Agostinelli, S., Marrella, A., Mecella, M.: Towards intelligent robotic process automation for BPMers. arXiv preprint arXiv:2001.00804 (2020)
5. Andrews, R., et al.: Quality-informed semi-automated event log generation for process mining. In: DSS, p. 113265 (2020)
6. Bayomie, D., Di Ciccio, C., La Rosa, M., Mendling, J.: A probabilistic approach to event-case correlation for process mining. In: Laender, A.H.F., Pernici, B., Lim, E.-P., de Oliveira, J.P.M. (eds.) ER 2019. LNCS, vol. 11788, pp. 136–152. Springer, Cham (2019). https://doi.org/10.1007/978-3-030-33223-5_12
7. Deloitte: The robots are ready. are you? Untapped advantage in your digital workforce (2017). https://www2.deloitte.com/content/dam/Deloitte/tr/Documents/technology/deloitte-robots-are-ready.pdf
8. van Dongen, B.F., de Medeiros, A.K.A., Verbeek, H.M.W., Weijters, A.J.M.M., van der Aalst, W.M.P.: The ProM framework: a new era in process mining tool support. In: Ciardo, G., Darondeau, P. (eds.) ICATPN 2005. LNCS, vol. 3536, pp. 444–454. Springer, Heidelberg (2005). https://doi.org/10.1007/11494744_25
9. Enríquez, J., et al.: Robotic process automation: a scientific and industrial systematic mapping study. IEEE Access 8, 39113–39129 (2020)
10. Gao, J., van Zelst, S.J., Lu, X., van der Aalst, W.M.P.: Automated robotic process automation: a self-learning approach. In: Panetto, H., Debruyne, C., Hepp, M., Lewis, D., Ardagna, C.A., Meersman, R. (eds.) OTM 2019. LNCS, vol. 11877, pp. 95–112. Springer, Cham (2019). https://doi.org/10.1007/978-3-030-33246-4_6
11. Geyer-Klingeberg, J., Nakladal, J., Baldauf, F., Veit, F.: Process mining and robotic process automation: a perfect match. In: BPM (Dissertation/Demos/Industry), pp. 124–131 (2018)
12. Günther, C., Verbeek, H.: XES v2.0 (2014). http://www.xes-standard.org/
13. Halpin, T.: ORM 2 graphical notation. Technical Report ORM2-02 (2005)
14. Ivančić, L., Vugec, D.S., Vukšić, V.B.: Robotic process automation: systematic literature review. In: Di Ciccio, C., et al. (eds.) BPM 2019. LNBIP, vol. 361, pp. 280–295. Springer, Cham (2019). https://doi.org/10.1007/978-3-030-30429-4_19
15. Jimenez-Ramirez, A., Reijers, H.A., Barba, I., Del Valle, C.: A method to improve the early stages of the robotic process automation lifecycle. In: Giorgini, P., Weber, B. (eds.) CAiSE 2019. LNCS, vol. 11483, pp. 446–461. Springer, Cham (2019). https://doi.org/10.1007/978-3-030-21290-2_28
16. Kirchmer, M., Franz, P.: Value-driven robotic process automation (RPA). In: Shishkov, B. (ed.) BMSD 2019. LNBIP, vol. 356, pp. 31–46. Springer, Cham (2019). https://doi.org/10.1007/978-3-030-24854-3_3
17. Lacity, M., Willcocks, L.P., Craig, A.: Robotic process automation at Telefonica O2 (2015)
18. Le Clair, C., UiPath, A.A., Prism, B.: The Forrester wave^{TM}: robotic process automation, Q2 2018. Forrester Research (2018)
19. Leemans, S.J., Poppe, E., Wynn, M.T.: Directly follows-based process mining: exploration & a case study. In: ICPM, pp. 25–32 (2019)
20. Leno, V., Polyvyanyy, A., Dumas, M., La Rosa, M., Maggi, F.M.: Robotic process mining: vision and challenges. In: BISE, pp. 1–14 (2020)
21. Leno, V., et al.: Action logger: enabling process mining for robotic process automation. In: BPM Demos, pp. 124–128 (2019)
22. Leopold, H., van der Aa, H., Reijers, H.A.: Identifying candidate tasks for robotic process automation in textual process descriptions. In: Gulden, J., Reinhartz-Berger, I., Schmidt, R., Guerreiro, S., Guédria, W., Bera, P. (eds.) BPMDS/EMMSAD -2018. LNBIP, vol. 318, pp. 67–81. Springer, Cham (2018). https://doi.org/10.1007/978-3-319-91704-7_5

23. Linn, C., Zimmermann, P., Werth, D.: Desktop activity mining-a new level of detail in mining business processes. In: APSN Workshops (2018)
24. Madakam, S., Holmukhe, R.M., Jaiswal, D.K.: The future digital work force: robotic process automation (RPA). JISTEM **16**, 1–17 (2019)
25. Pourmirza, S., et al.: Correlation miner: mining business process models and event correlations without case identifiers. IJCIS **26**(02), 1742002 (2017)
26. Slaby, J.R.: Robotic automation emerges as a threat to traditional low-cost outsourcing. HfS Res. Ltd **1**(1), 3 (2012)
27. Syed, R., et al.: Robotic process automation: contemporary themes and challenges. CI **115**, 103162 (2020)
28. Tornbohm, C., Dunie, R.: Gartner market guide for robotic process automation software. Report G00319864. Gartner (2017)
29. Willcocks, L.P., Lacity, M., Craig, A.: Robotic process automation at Xchanging (2015)

Discovering Data Models from Event Logs

Dorina Bano$^{(\boxtimes)}$ and Mathias Weske

Hasso Plattner Institute, University of Potsdam, Potsdam, Germany
{Dorina.Bano,Mathias.Weske}@hpi.de

Abstract. Business process mining is becoming an increasingly important field for understanding the behavioral perspective of any given organization. In a process mining project, process experts are tasked with discovering or improving the operational business processes. They do so by analyzing event logs, the starting point of any process mining endeavor. Despite event logs capturing behavioral information, we argue that they are also a rich source of domain specific information. This information is not represented explicitly in a process model but, nevertheless, it provides valuable contextual information. To this end, we propose a semi-automatic approach to discover a data model that complements traditional process mining techniques with domain specific information. The approach is evaluated in terms of feasibility by being applied to two real-life event logs.

Keywords: Process mining · Event log · Data model

1 Introduction

Process mining is an area of business process management that has taken increased attention from scholars and practitioners in different domains. Some examples of process mining techniques include: process discovery, which aims at discover a process model from the recorded executions of a process; conformance checking, which intends to compare event data with a given process model in order to find deviations; and process improvement, where a business process model is enriched with additional details about its performance [1].

The starting point of any process mining technique is an event log, which is purely a collection of events [2]. In many real-world scenarios such event logs are extracted from data warehouses of a given organizations [3]. After the extraction process takes place the event logs are made available to business process mining experts. Since the log is tailored to discovering and improving a business process the data perspective is usually overlooked. Therefore the process mining experts are left with an event log that does not provide explicit information about the context the data it was extracted from. We argue that the data perspective is an important aspects that complements the process mining procedure with useful information. It plays an important role in the understandability of the event logs and consecutively the process model.

G. Dobbie et al. (Eds.): ER 2020, LNCS 12400, pp. 62–76, 2020.
https://doi.org/10.1007/978-3-030-62522-1_5

In this paper, we introduce a semi-automatic two-step approach for discovering a complementary UML data model from an event log which is tailored for process mining. The discovered data model provides additional insights regarding the domain specific information in the log. In addition, it can be used to enrich the mined process with data objects, therefore, improving its readability.

The reminder of this paper is organized as follows. Section 2 briefly discusses the basic notions needed to understand the rest of the paper. An overview of our two-steps approach is described and illustrated in Sect. 3. Deriving an intermediate representation called activity-attribute relationship diagram (A2A diagram) from an event log is explained in Sect. 4. While the second step of our approach, which discovers a data model from the A2A diagram is depicted in Sect. 5. Section 6 briefly discussed related work. Consecutively, Sect. 7 provides an evaluation of the approach before Sect. 8 concludes the paper.

2 Preliminaries

This section introduces the basic notions and concepts regarding the event log and data model, which we refer to throughout this paper.

2.1 Event Log

Event logs can be extracted from different information systems. Each event log consists of a set of cases. A case is defined as a set of events. Each event involves several attributes such as: the case identifier; the activity name; the timestamp representing the time when the event occurs (i.e., all illustrated in Fig. 1); the resource, i.e. the person or device who executes the activity; the department in which the resource belongs to etc. The first three attributes above are meta-attributes and are mandatory for any event log that is subject to process mining. Let us denote the set of the mandatory meta-attributes with $M_{att} = \{Case, Act, Time\}$. The following definition of event log is based on [1]:

Case	Act	Time	Att1	Att2	Att3	Att4
1	A	24.02.2007	10		1	0
2	A	27.03.2007	7		1	0
2	B	28.05.2007	6	8		0
3	A	01.06.2007	3			0
3	B	19.06.2007	23	2		0

Fig. 1. An example of the event log

Definition 1. *(Event, event log) An event e over a set of attributes Att is defined as $e = (\#_{att_1}, \#_{att_2}, ..., \#_{att_n})$ where $\#_{att_i}$ is the value of attribute $att_i \in Att$ for $i = 1..n$. An event log El is defined as $El = \{e_1, e_2, ..., e_m\}$ where $m \in \mathbb{N}$ is the number of events.*

Definition 2. *(Activity-attribute access relation)*

Let El be an event log and A the set of all unique activities. We define $\#_{att}(e)$, where $att \in Att$, the value of attribute att for event e. We say an activity $a \in A$ accesses an attribute $att \in Att \setminus M_{att}$ iff $\exists e \in El \mid \#_{act}(e) = a \wedge \#_{att}(e) \neq \bot$. Let us denote $r = (a, att, n)$ the access relation between an activity $a \in A$ and an attribute $att \in Att$ in the event log, where $n \in \mathbb{N}$ is the occurrence of the relation in a log. The set of all access relations in the event log is defined as R.

Definition 3. *(No access relation) An activity $a \in A$ does not access an attribute $att \in Att$ iff $\forall e \in El, \#_{act}(e) = a \Rightarrow \#_{att}(e) = \bot$.*

2.2 Data Model

Data model is a fundamental concept for designing and documenting software application. Because of its simplicity, mainly during the design phase, it is used as a mean for communication between the team members. As a target of our approach, the data model is used as a complementary view of the mined business process model to enhance understandability of the use-case scenario.

Below, it is provided a definition of data model withing the scope of this paper:

Definition 4. *A data model is a tuple*
$D = (C, Att, Aso, member, attrmulti, asomulti)$ where:

- *C is a non-empty set of classes*
- *Att is a set of attributes*
- *$Aso \subseteq C \times C$ is a set of associations between classes*
- *$member : C \to 2^{Att}$ assigns attributes to classes*
- *$attrmulti : Att \to \mathbb{N}_0 \times \mathbb{N}$ defines the multiplicity of any attribute in a class*
- *$asomulti : Aso \to \mathbb{N}_0 \times \mathbb{N}$ defines the multiplicity of any association in the data model*

3 Overview of the Data Model Discovering Approach

Before explaining our data model discovery approach let us shortly state the assumptions. We assume that the attribute write access is explicitly represented in the event log, in that for each event it is clear which attributes are written by which activity. For simplicity purpose, we will refer to "write access" as simply "access" for the rest of this paper. In existing event logs, like [4] and [5], the access is represented by concrete values in the accessed attributes and empty values for the rest of attributes that are not accessed. For example, as it shown in the event log illustrated in Fig. 1, activity A access attribute $Att1$ three times while activity B access the same attribute two times. Meanwhile, $Att2$ is accessed only two times by activity B. In contrast, $Att2$ is only accessed by activity A and never by B.

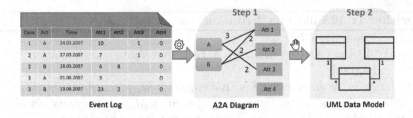

Fig. 2. Overview of the data model discovering approach.

As a pre-processing phase, the event log is cleaned from *null* or *0* values. This implies that we look at activities that in all cases write a certain attribute with null or 0 value. In this case, the activity is considered to not access the given attribute. For example, in the log file shown in Fig. 2 $Att4$ is always accessed by both activities with value 0. In this case, we assume that $Att4$ is not accessed by any activity as the value 0 may represents an initialization of this attribute or an software error (e.g., default value).

Deriving a data model from the event log implies systematically deriving the individual UML language [6] (our language of choice) constructs: classes, class attributes, and the associations between classes. To this end, we will follow a two-step approach as depicted in Fig. 2. In the first automatic step we introduce a intermediate representation that captures the access relation between all activities and all attributes from the event log. This representation is called Activity-Attribute relationship (A2A) diagram, which is inspired from [7]. In the second step, a set of generic rules are applied to the A2A diagram resulting in the target data model. Afterwards, we leave the choice to the user of the approach to review the generated data model. A detailed explanation of each step is given in the following sections respectively.

4   Derivation of the A2A Diagram

The most prominent information that we have from the event log is the relation of attributes with the activities. To that end, the A2A diagram is derived based on Algorithm 1 as an intermediate step and it is used as input for the data model generation. The starting step for construction such diagram is to identify the activities and attributes from the event log. Therefore, we first derive the set of all activities (at the model level). Second, all attributes, except the meta-attributes (like case identifier, activity name and timestamp), are identified.

The next step for construction of the A2A diagram is to identify the access relation between activities and attributes. Based on Definition 2, if an activity A writes a value to an attribute $Att1$, then there is an access relation between activity A and attribute $Att1$ (see Fig. 2). The access occurrence number (depicted over the access arrow in Fig. 2, Step2) represent the number of times an access relation between an activity and attribute holds in the event log independently of the case.

Algorithm 1: A2A diagram derivation from an event log

---

input : Event log El

output: $A2A = (A, Att \setminus M_{att}, R)$ Activity-Attribute access relation
         diagram

initialization A: empty set of activities, $Att \setminus M_{att}$: set of attributes
         without the meta-attributes, $R \subseteq A \times Att \setminus M_{att} \times \mathbb{N}$: empty set of
         access relations // create a unique set of activities

[!ht] **for** e *in* El **do**
     if $\#_{act}(e) \notin A$ **then**
         | *add* $\#_{act}(e)$ in A ;
     end
end

// populate the set R

for a *in* A **do**
     for att *in* Att **do**
         int $n = 0$ // n represents the access relation occurrence
         for e *in* El **do**
             if $\#_{act}(e) = a \wedge \#_{att}(e) \neq \emptyset$ **then**
             | $n = n + 1$
             end
         end
         add $r = (a, att, n)$ in R
     end
end
print(A2A)

---

5   Data Model Discovery Approach

The data model generation consist in generating the data model classes with their attributes and the associations between the classes. For the data model classes generation we look at the relations between two or more attributes in the A2A diagram and consider whether they belong to the same data model class. After exhaustively going through all the attributes and grouping them into UML classes, we identify the UML associations between those classes. Defining the UML associations entails specifying their multiplicity.

Below we provide a set of rules (see Fig. 3) that are applied to the A2A diagram for grouping the attributes into data model classes. These rules are organized based on two aspects: not/isolated attributes and not/isolated activities. An attribute is called isolated if all the activity that access it do not access other attributes. Likewise, an activity is isolated if all the attributes it accesses are not accessed by any other activity.

Rule 1: Isolated Attributes, Isolated Activities
We identify the isolated access relations in the A2A diagram, in that an attribute is accessed only by a single activity and the activity accesses only the said attribute. In this case, the rule is to assign all isolated attributes to separate independent UML classes. At this stage, there is no other information in the A2A diagram that can give insights about how the generated UML classes could be related.

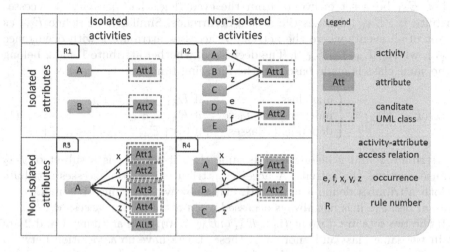

Fig. 3. Rules for deriving data model classes

An example is illustrated in Fig. 3 R1, where activity *A* and attribute *Att1* are isolated because *A* access only *Att1* and *Att1* is accessed by said activity. The same holds for activity *B* and *Att2*. The *Att1* and *Att2* are assigned to a separate UML classes (represented in Fig. 3 by a dashed-line rectangle).

Last, the isolated attributes assigned to the UML class together with their accessing activities are removed from the A2A diagram. This action takes place at the end of each rule.

Rule 2: Isolated Attributes, Non-isolated Activity
In this case, we search the A2A diagram for isolated attributes that are accessed by non-isolated activities. Similar to rule R1, the attributes are isolated and, thus, there is no additional information on how they can be grouped into classes. Hence, the isolated attributes will be each assigned to a separated class.

As it is illustrated in Fig. 3 R2, activity *A*, *B* and *C* are accessing *Att1* with the different cardinalities. The same hold for *Att2*, which is accessed by *D* and *E*. Based on this rule, *Att1* and *Att2* are placed in two independent UML classes.

Rule 3: Non-isolated Attributes, Isolated Activities

If at least one common activity accesses two or more attributes, then the attributes are said to be related. We are looking specifically for related attributes that may belong to the same class. We argue that if an activity accesses two or more attributes with the same occurrence then these attributes are highly likely to be contained in a single class. Therefore, we group these attributes based on common occurrences. However, we cannot deduce from the A2A diagram alone whether the attributes are accessed simultaneously by the activity. It may happen that in total these attributes are accessed the same amount of time by the activity but never in the same event. This means that the attributes are highly likely to not belong to the same class as they seem to be accessed independently. To counter this problem we offer the following solution.

Let E_{A1} be a set of events from the event log where activity A accesses attribute 1. $\mid E_{A1} \mid$ denotes the access occurrence. Similarly, we define E_{A2} as the set of all events where the activity A accesses attribute 2 with occurrence $\mid E_{A2} \mid$, where $\mid E_{A2} \mid \geq \mid E_{A1} \mid$. The decision of whether attribute 1 and 2 belong to the same class is made based on the following function:

$$rel(E_{A1}, E_{A2}) = \begin{cases} \text{one class} & \text{, if } E_{A1} \cap E_{A2} = E_{A1} \\ \text{independent classes} & \text{, if } E_{A1} \cap E_{A2} = \emptyset \\ \text{dependent classes} & \text{, if } 0 <\mid E_{A1} \cap E_{A2} \mid<\mid E_{A1} \mid \end{cases} \tag{1}$$

Attribute 1 and 2 belong to the same class if set E_{A1} is a subset of E_{A2} because anytime the activity A accesses attribute 1 it also accesses attribute 2. Both attributes define a new UML class, however, attribute 1 is marked as optional because it is not always accessed when attribute 2 is accessed.

If the two sets are disjoint (i.e., $E_{A1} \cap E_{A2} = \emptyset$), then attribute 1 and 2 are not in the same class and, moreover, these classes have no association between them. This is due to attribute 1 and 2 happening independently of each other.

Finally, there are events in which attribute 1 and attribute 2 are accessed simultaneously except the first case. This means that there are some events where the attribute 1 and 2 are accessed by the same activity A but this number of events is not the same as $\mid E_{A1} \mid$. In this case, the attributes are placed in different classes, but the classes are still related via an bidirectional association. The multiplicity of the association is 0..1 to * from the class containing attribute 1 to the class containing attribute 2.

In a more general case, where the number of attributes which share the same activity with the same occurrence is more than two, we apply the above function for every pair of attributes to determine the resulting classes.

This rule is illustrated in Fig. 3 R3. Activity A access *Att1* and *Att2* with the occurrence x, *Att3* and *Att4* with the occurrence y and *Att5* with occurrence z. The decision of *Att1* and *Att2* belonging to the same UML class or not depends on whether the events where the activity A access the *Att1* are the same events where the same activity access *Att2*. The same holds for the *Att3* and *Att4* accessed with cardinality y by the same activity.

At last, the attribute assigned to the corresponding classes are removed from the A2A diagram. If their accessing activities do not access other non-isolated attributes, they are removed as well.

Rule 4: Non-isolated Attributes, Non-isolated Activities

Every relation that cannot be expressed by the previous rules is captured by this rule. Activities and attributes are non-isolated, which mean that an attribute is accessed by several activities and each activity accesses several attributes.

After removing the attributes and activities that satisfied the previous three rules we are left with an A2A diagram that contains one or more disconnected subgraphs (i.e., interconnected activities and attributes) which we are referring to as islands. In Fig. 3 R4, there is only one island, but it can happen that another set of non-isolated activities and attributes, which has no relation with the first set, can be left in the A2A diagram. That is why we call these sets islands.

To group the attributes into UML classes each island is decomposed into smaller A2A diagram fragments for each activity. This means that the number of the fragments is the same with the number of activities in an island. The attributes that are accessed by the activity are represented in the respective fragment. Hence, an attribute may appear in one or more fragments (see Fig. 4).

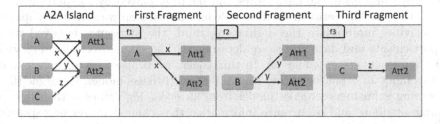

Fig. 4. Decomposed A2A diagram into three fragments after applying the fourth rule

The resulting fragments can satisfy either rule 1 or rule 3 but not rule 2 because the fragments contain only isolated activities. The grouping of the attributes, then, follows the rule 1 or 3. However, since attributes may belong to two or more distinct fragments there is a conflicts that needs to be resolved. For example, it might happen that the same attribute is grouped either in a standalone UML class or in a class with some other attributes depending on the grouping results from each fragment. In this case, we leave the choice to the user of the approach to make a decision that better fits the overall result.

Figure 4 shows an island fragmentation example. Activity A accesses attributes $Att1$ and $Att2$ with occurrence x. The same holds for activity B except the occurrence, which is y. Last, activity C accesses attribute $Att2$ with occurrence z. Based on this rule the A2A diagram is decomposed in three other A2A fragments, one for each activity.

In the first and the second fragment we are dealing with non-isolated attributes and isolated activities. Therefore, rule 3 is applied to derive the classes. In the third fragment, rule 1 is applied because activity C and attribute $Att2$ are both isolated.

After all the classes are created, the classes can be named based on the activity they were generated from. Finally, we have to consider the associations between the remaining independent classes. To this end, we will consider the most frequently accessed class as the root class, which has the highest potential to represent the business process case notion. Then, we introduce an association between the remaining classes and the root class. Their multiplicities are set based on the occurrences from the A2A diagram.

6   Related Work

In [8] the authors present an approach to obtain a data model from the BPM model, which is then useful for the design phase of the software development process. The authors emphasize that during this phase it is important to use the data model as a common language between the business process analysts and software developers. The focus is on the persistent data rather then the processes' data objects. The authors use a three phase-approach: first, the entities are defined by considering the data stores and the roles played by the participants; second, the relation between entities is deducted based on way the participants and activities manipulate the data store; third, the attributes involved with the participants and data stores are determined. The same direction is followed in the approach presented in [9]. In this paper, we propose an approach that takes as input an event log rather than a business process model. We argue that discovering a business process model from an event log comes with losses in valuable attribute and occurrence information that cannot always be captured by the process model.

Breitmayer et al., [10] propose the discovers of the data model as an intermediate step for discovering object-aware processes. Each table in the database belongs to an object in the data model whereas the database columns represents object attributes. By considering the primary keys and the relation between tables in the database the relations between data objects are defined. The discovered data model is a crucial step for the discovery of the process model. In contrast, our approach relies only in the event log to discover the data model and the data model serves as a complementary artifact to understand the process model.

In [11], the author provides a richer event log, compared to XES, called eXtensible Object-Centric (XOC) by considering multiple case notions called object types. Each event may refer to any number of objects in contrast to the traditional XES format where a single case notion is consider and every event belongs to exactly one case. Constructing a data model from an XES event log is more complicated than deriving it from the XOC format because of the single case notion perspective of XES. XOC holds more information about the data model because the object relations can be derived from the global perspective (rather than the case perspective) of the events.

There are other approaches, like in [12], that make use of Natural Language Processing (NLP) for deriving a data model from natural language descriptions. The authors argue that such a model is important for the system understand-ability as it significantly decreases the time needed by a human to understand the system. In this paper, we are introducing a two-step approach by following a set of rules rather than an NLP-based approach, although, the approaches are not mutually exclusive and could be combined to achieve better results.

7   Evaluation

The approach presented in this paper is evaluated based on two real-life event logs, namely: Road Traffic Fine Management (RTFM) [5]; and Sepsis event log [4]. However, for sake of writing space, we describe the evaluation of our app-roach based on RTFM event log, which is taken from the information systems of the Italian police. The event log contains information regarding the road-traffic fines and includes 150.370 cases (561.470 events) that are processed by the municipality over a three-years time period (January 2010–June 2013). To provide a behavioral overview of the event log, we show in Fig. 5 the process model (represented as BPMN [13]) that is discovered by applying the Induc-tive Miner algorithm [14]. Some activities that do not access any attribute are excluded from the process model without breaking its meaning.

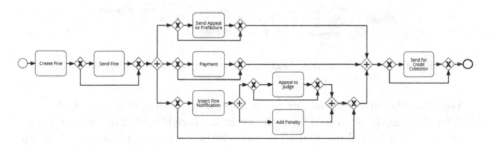

Fig. 5. BPMN model discovered from the RTFM event log

The process starts with *Create Fine* activity. After the fine is created it can be send to the offender via *Send Fine*. The offender has the option to pay the fine immediately after it is handed over to him (*Payment*). If this is not the case, the date when the offender receives the fine is registered (*Insert Fine Notification*). If the payment will not take place (i.e., within 60 days) then a penalty (*Add Penalty*) is added to the fine. The offender has the option to appeal against the fine through the Judge (*Appeal to Judge*) or Prefecture (*Send Appeal to Prefecture*). If the appeal is successful then the process ends. Otherwise the fine is sent for credit collection (*Send for Credit Collection*) marking the process terminations.

Before generating the A2A diagram the RTFM event log is cleaned from the activity-attribute access relations with the value 0 (i.e., the activity always access the attribute the value 0). For example, *Create Fine* activity access the *Total Payment Amount* always with the value 0. The same holds for *Matricola* and *Resource* attributes accessed by *Appeal to Judge* activity.

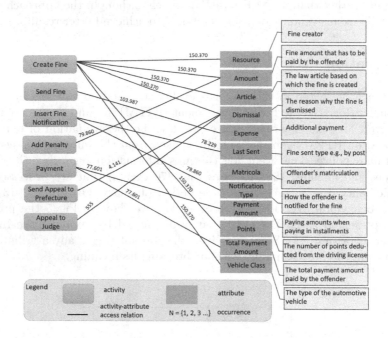

Fig. 6. The RTFM A2A diagram derived by applying Algorithm 1

Applying the first step of our main approach, as that described in Sect. 4, the A2A diagram is generated from the event log (see Fig. 6). The activities that do not access any attribute and all access relations discarded from the clean-up phase are not shown in the A2A diagram. For example, *Matricola* is represented as a stand-alone attribute in Fig. 6 as it is always accessed with value 0.

In the second step, the A2A diagram generated from the event log is used as an input for discovering the data model. Figure 7 depicts the application of the rules from the second step of the approach to the generated A2A diagram. The rules are applied following the defined order (R1 to R4). If a rule is satisfied, all activities and attributes related to that rule are excluded from A2A diagram and the attributes are added in the respective classes. This is repeated until all attributes are grouped into UML classes and there are no attributes left in A2A diagram.

As it is shown in Fig. 7, rule R1 is fulfilled by *Send Fine* activity and *Expense* attribute both represented as isolated in the A2A diagram. Therefore, *Expense*

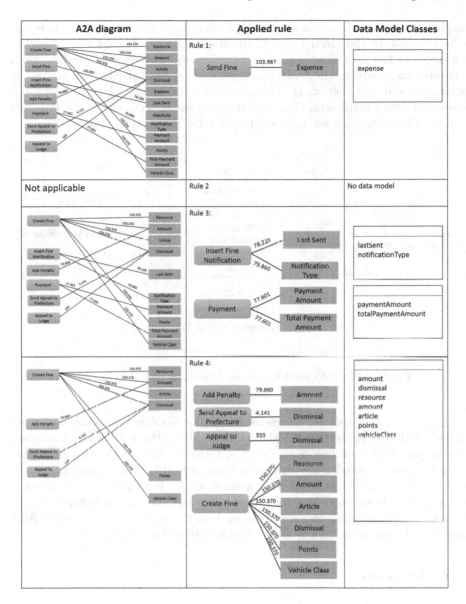

Fig. 7. The approach rules applied to the RTFM A2A diagram

attribute is assigned in separate independent UML classes. Since there is no case of isolated attributes and not-isolated activities in the A2A diagram rule number two does not apply. Subsequently, we check for isolated activities and non-isolated attributes. There are two activities that satisfy the rule R3. First, *Insert Fine Notification* accesses the *Last Sent* and *Notification Type* with different occurrence. In this case, Function 1 is applied to check whether *Insert Fine*

Notification activity is accessing simultaneously both attributes. This happens to be the case in the given log, i.e., in all events where *Insert Fine Notification* accesses the *Last Sent* it also accesses *Notification Type*. Therefore, both attributes are stored in one UML class, where *Last Sent* attribute is marked as optional (based on Function 1). The same holds for *paymentAmount* and *total-PaymentAmount* attributes. Both are simultaneously accessed by the *Payment* activity. Therefore, they are grouped to the same data model class.

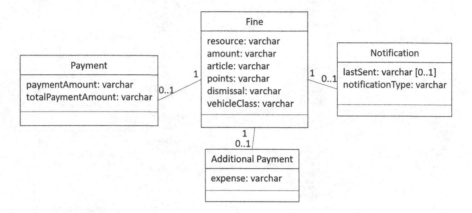

Fig. 8. UML data model generated from the RTFM event log

Lastly, based on rule R4 we check for the non-isolated activities and non-isolated attributes in the derived islands. By applying this rule the A2A diagram is decomposed into four fragments (see Fig. 7, rule 4). In the first three fragments rule R1 can be applied while in the last one rule R3. In this case, the user's choice is to group the attributes in a single class. Fine is the most frequent class therefore is assigned as a root class. After the association between classes are defined the multiplicities are set based on the occurrences from the A2A diagram. The resulting RTFM UML class is depicted in Fig. 8.

8   Conclusion

This paper presents a two-step semi-automatic approach to discover a UML data model from an event log that is purposely designed for process mining. The proposed approach is useful for discovering a data model that complements and increases the understandability of the discoverable process model. The data model contains classes with their attribute, which represent the main entities involved in the process model, and the associations between classes (the relationships between those entities). To achieve this, we consider the relations between activities and attributes in the event log and represent them via an A2A diagram, which is an interim artifact of our approach.

We argue that the discovered data model provides additional insights regarding the domain specific information in the event log. The data model provides complementary information about the entities that are subject to and cannot be captured by a process model.

In future work we plan to extend the approach with NLP solutions to ground the resulting model into a domain specific terminology. In addition, more than one event log from the same organization can be considered to derive a common data model that spans many discoverable business processes.

References

1. van der Aalst, W.M.P.: Process Mining: Data Science in Action, 2nd edn. Springer, Heidelberg (2016). https://doi.org/10.1007/978-3-662-49851-4
2. Aalst, W.M.P.: Process mining in the large: a tutorial. In: Zimányi, E. (ed.) eBISS 2013. LNBIP, vol. 172, pp. 33–76. Springer, Cham (2014). https://doi.org/10.1007/978-3-319-05461-2_2
3. Diba, K., Batoulis, K., Weidlich, M., Weske, M.: Extraction, correlation, and abstraction of event data for process mining. Wiley Interdisc. Rev. Data Min. Knowl. Discov. **10**(3) (2020)
4. Mannhardt, F.: Sepsis cases-event log. Eindhoven University of Technology, Eindhoven (2016). https://doi.org/10.4121/uuid:915d2bfb-7e84-49ad-a286-dc35f063a460
5. Mannhardt, F., de Leoni, M.: Road traffic fine management process. Eindhoven University of Technology, Eindhoven (2015). https://doi.org/10.4121/uuid:270fd440-1057-4fb9-89a9-b699b47990f5
6. Rumbaugh, J., Jacobson, I., Booch, G.: Unified Modeling Language Reference Manual, The (2nd Edition). Pearson Higher Education, London (2004)
7. van der Aalst, W.M.P.: Object-centric process mining: dealing with divergence and convergence in event data. EasyChair Preprint no. 2301. EasyChair 2020)
8. Cruz, E.F., Machado, R.J., Santos, M.Y.: From business process modeling to data model: a systematic approach. In: Proceedings of the 8th International Conference on the Quality of Information and Communications Technology, QUATIC 2012, Lisbon, Portugal, 2–6 September 2012, pp. 205–210. IEEE Computer Society (2012)
9. Brdjanin, D., Banjac, D., Banjac, G., Maric, S.: An online business process model-driven generator of the conceptual database model. In: Proceedings of the 8th International Conference on Web Intelligence, Mining and Semantics, WIMS 2018, Novi Sad, Serbia, 25–27 June 2018, pp. 16:1–16:9. ACM (2018)
10. Breitmayer, M., Reichert, M.: Towards the discovery of object-aware processes. In: Manner, J., Haarmann, S., Kolb, S., Kopp, O., (eds.) Proceedings of the 12th ZEUS Workshop on Services and their Composition, Potsdam, Germany, 20–21 February 2020. Volume 2575 of CEUR Workshop Proceedings, pp. 1–4. CEUR-WS.org (2020)
11. Li, G., de Murillas, E.G.L., de Carvalho, R.M., van der Aalst, W.M.P.: Extracting object-centric event logs to support process mining on databases. In: Mendling, J., Mouratidis, H. (eds.) CAiSE 2018. LNBIP, vol. 317, pp. 182–199. Springer, Cham (2018). https://doi.org/10.1007/978-3-319-92901-9_16

12. Meziane, F., Athanasakis, N., Ananiadou, S.: Generating natural language specifications from UML class diagrams. Requir. Eng. **13**(1), 1–18 (2008). https://doi.org/10.1007/s00766-007-0054-0
13. Weske, M.: Business Process Management - Concepts, Languages, Architectures, 3rd edn. Springer, Heidelberg (2019). https://doi.org/10.1007/978-3-662-59432-2
14. Leemans, S.J.J., Fahland, D., van der Aalst, W.M.P.: Process and deviation exploration with inductive visual miner. In: Proceedings of the BPM Demo Sessions 2014 Co-located with the 12th International Conference on Business Process Management, BPM 2014. CEUR-WS.org (2014)

Semi-automated Time-Granularity Detection for Data-Driven Simulation Using Process Mining and System Dynamics

Mahsa Pourbafrani[1(✉)], Sebastiaan J. van Zelst[1,2],
and Wil M. P. van der Aalst[1,2]

[1] Process and Data Science, RWTH Aachen University, Aachen, Germany
{mahsa.bafrani,s.j.v.zelst,wvdaalst}@pads.rwth-aachen.de
[2] Fraunhofer Institute for Applied Information Technology (FIT),
Erlangen, Germany
{sebastiaan.van.zelst,wil.van.der.aalst}@fit.fraunhofer.de

Abstract. Most information systems supporting operational processes also record event logs. These can be used to diagnose performance and compliance problems. The majority of process mining techniques extract models that are descriptive and describe what happened in the past. Few process mining techniques discover models that allow us to "look into the future" and perform predictive analyses. Recently, novel approaches have been developed for scenario-based prediction, i.e., predicting the effects of process changes on process performance, e.g., investing in an additional resource. To work accurately, the techniques need an appropriate time step-size, the selection of which, thus far, has been an ad-hoc and manual endeavor. Therefore, in this paper, building upon time-series analysis and forecasting techniques, we propose a novel semi-automated time-granularity detection framework. Our framework detects the best possible time-granularity to be used, whilst taking user preferences into account. Our evaluation, using both real and synthetic data, confirms the feasibility of our approach and highlights the importance of using accurate granularity in time step selection.

Keywords: Process mining · Scenario-based predictions · System dynamics · What-if analysis · Simulation · Time-series analysis

1 Introduction

Process Mining [1] techniques derive knowledge of the execution of processes, by means of analyzing the data generated during their execution, which are stored in *event logs*. Several techniques exist, e.g., discovering a process model describing the process (*process discovery techniques* [7]), examining to what degree reality, captured in the data, conforms to a given process model (*conformance checking* techniques [10]), etc. Most techniques, extract models and insights that are

© Springer Nature Switzerland AG 2020
G. Dobbie et al. (Eds.): ER 2020, LNCS 12400, pp. 77–91, 2020.
https://doi.org/10.1007/978-3-030-62522-1_6

descriptive. Few approaches focus on prescriptive/predictive models, i.e., models that allow us to "look into the future". Yet, at the same time, such techniques allow us to effectively *improve* the process, rather than just understanding its past performance.

In [16], we proposed a new process mining approach, i.e., *scenario-based prediction* of future process performance, using *System Dynamics* (SD) [21] as a prediction technique. The approach transforms an event log into a sequence of continuous variable values (e.g., process instance arrival rate), referred to as a *System Dynamics Log (SD-Log)*. The SD-Log forms the basis for simulation and prediction. Consider Fig. 1, in which we depict the general framework of the presented approach in [16]. First, we construct an SD-Log (Preprocessing step), and use it, together with a constructed model, to run a sample simulation ("as-is situation"). The quality of the simulations, i.e., both terms of validation and prediction, depends on the stability of the simulation model. In particular, the window-size of the time steps being used to generate the SD-Log highly affects the stability. Thus far, selecting such a window-size has been an ad-hoc/manual endeavor having negative effects on the prediction results.

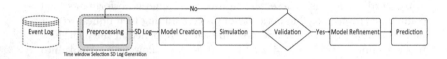

Fig. 1. The proposed framework for scenario-based process prediction, using system dynamics [16]. This paper focuses on *preprocessing* (highlighted), in particular, discovering the best time window for generating system dynamics logs.

Therefore, in this paper, we propose an approach that semi-automatically *identifies the best window-size* to be used in order to generate an SD-Log. Initially, the user provides a set of logical units (hours/days) based on domain knowledge that she/he wants to use in prediction. Subsequently, using the input event log, the proposed approach generates SD-Logs, based on several derivatives of the provided units. Subsequently, trend and pattern detection is applied to the different time-series, and correspondingly, the best step-size is selected. Within the trend and pattern detection, our approach is able to remove regular inactive time in the process. Using different real event logs, we assess the proposed approach including finding periodic behavior of the process including inactive steps. Then, we train different models and show the effect of the approach on reducing the prediction error. Furthermore, we use synthetic event logs with known patterns, including artificial noise/infrequent behavior, to test the feasibility of our approach. Our obtained results discover hidden patterns in the process variables and highlight the importance of selecting a suitable time step granularity.

The remainder of this paper is organized as follows. In Sect. 2, we present a running example. In Sect. 3, we introduce background concepts and notation. In

Sect. 4, we present our main approach, which we evaluate in Sect. 5. In Sect. 6, we present related work. Section 7 concludes this work.

2   Running Example

In order to clearly demonstrate each step of our approach, we use a running example. We consider a simple, fictional process of a *car rental company*, i.e., called CARZ. Working days at CARZ are from Monday to Friday. The working hours are from 8:00 am to 5:00 pm (including 1 h lunchtime). Requests for a rental car are received by phone. A different process is executed to handle the different types of requests, e.g., *rent a car* or *rent a car with a driver*. In the model, the time of the next call is derived from a normal distribution with 5 mins average. The hours of the days affect the probability of generating new calls, e.g., the intensity of receiving calls at 10:00 am is 3 times higher than 8:00 am. If the number of callers in the queue is more than 20, new calls get rejected.

For each type of request, we use a (different) normal distribution to generate service times. The service time also gets affected by the number of requests in the queue. On average, the duration of handling *a car with a driver* request is 10 mins higher than handling *rent a car* requests. We designed the model, such that operators perform the process of the calls faster if the number of calls in the line is higher. This effect, the queue length on time of processing calls, is modeled as an exponential nonlinear relation. We modeled the request handling process of CARZ, using CPN Tools [13].

3   Preliminaries

Here, we introduce background concepts and basic notation. We briefly cover common notions from the field of process mining, as well as system dynamics.

Process Mining. Process mining techniques analyze the historical execution of processes, i.e., captured in the form of event logs, [1]. An event log captures what activity has been performed, at what time, for which instance of the process.

Definition 1 (Event Log). *Let ξ denote the universe of events. Furthermore, let C, A, R and T denote the universe of case identifiers, activities, resources, and the time universe, respectively. We define projections $\pi_C\colon \xi \to C$, $\pi_A\colon \xi \to A$, $\pi_R\colon \xi \to R$ and $\pi_T\colon \xi \to T \times T$, s.t., given $e \in \xi$, we have $\pi_C(e)=c$, $\pi_A(e)=a$, $\pi_R(e) = r$, and $\pi_T(e)=(t_s, t_c)$, indicating that event $e \in \xi$ captures the execution of an activity $a \in A$, in the context of case $c \in C$ by resource $r \in R$, started at time $t_s \in T$, and completed at time $t_c \in T$. An event log L is a set of events, i.e., $L \subseteq \xi$.*

Table 1 depicts a snippet of a generated event log for the running example. The first row describes an event for which the activity *Process next Car Req* is executed by *Monika* for a request with *case ID* 10. An event log may include more data attributes, e.g., here type of requests is also logged (`CarRequest` or `DriverRequest`), but, for simplicity, we abstract from such additional attributes.

Table 1. Sample event log, generated for the CARZ running example. Each row is an event in which for each unique customer (case) in the process, a specific activity at a specific time is performed by a specific resource.

Case ID	Activity	Request Type	Timestamp	Complete Timestamp	Resource
10	Next Call	CarRequest	1/1/2018 10:29	1/1/2018 10:47	Monika
11	Next Call	DriverRequest	1/1/2018 10:29	1/1/2018 10:29	System
8	Process Next Driver Req	DriverRequest	1/1/2018 10:30	1/1/2018 10:50	Pheobi
10	Process Next CarReq	CarRequest	1/1/2018 10:31	1/1/2018 10:49	Chandler
13	Next Call	DriverRequest	1/1/2018 10:31	1/1/2018 10:31	System
10	Processed CarReq	CarRequest	1/1/2018 10:32	1/1/2018 10:32	System
⋮	⋮	⋮	⋮	⋮	⋮

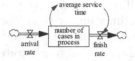

Fig. 2. Simple stock-flow diagram. The value of the stock *number of cases in process* is calculated based on the *arrival rate* and *finish rate* flows (per time step). The value of *finish rate* is affected by the *average service time*.

System Dynamics. System dynamics techniques are used to model dynamic systems and their relations with their environment [21]. One of the main modeling notations in system dynamics is the stock-flow diagram, which models the system w.r.t. three different elements, i.e., stocks, flows and variables [19]. Stocks are accumulative variables over time, flows manipulate the stock values and variables influence the values of flows and other variables over time. Figure 2 shows a simple stock-flow diagram for the example in which *arrival rate* and *finish rate* as flows add/remove to/from the values of *number of cases in the process* as stock, also, *average service time* as a variable affects the finish rate based on the number of cases in the process.

System Dynamics Logs. Event logs do not suffice to populate a given system dynamics model with values for stocks, flows, and variables, therefore, they should be transformed into an actionable form, i.e., numerical values. Hence, we define the notion of a *System Dynamics Log (SD-Log)*, i.e., a sequence of continuous variable values, capturing the numerical values for a set of variables of interest over time, as described by the event log. Assume that, the first event in an event log starts at time t_s, and, the last event is completed at time t_C. Given time window $\delta \in \mathbb{N}_{\geq 0}$, there are $k = \lceil (t_C - t_S)/\delta \rceil$ subsequent time steps in the event log for time window δ. An SD-Log captures all the values for the variables of interest, in each time-window.

Definition 2 (SD-Log). *Let $L \subseteq \xi$ be an event log, let $\mathcal{V}$ be a set of process variables, and let $\delta \in \mathbb{N}_{\geq 0}$ be the selected time window. Let t_S denote the minimal start timestamp in L, let t_C denote the maximal end timestamp in L and let $k = \lceil (t_C - t_S)/\delta \rceil$. An SD-Log of L, given δ, $sd_{L,\delta}$, is a multivariate time-series, i.e., $sd_{L,\delta} \in \{1, ..., k\} \times \mathcal{V} \to \mathbb{R}$, s.t., $sd_{L,\delta}(i, v)$ represents the value of process variable $v \in \mathcal{V}$ in the ith-time window $(1 \leq i \leq k)$.*

Given an event log L, a set of variables $\mathcal{V}$, and window δ, the event log is transformed log into an SD-Log. If L is clear from the context, we omit it and write sd_δ. Given sd_δ and $v \in \mathcal{V}$, we write $\Pi_v(sd_\delta) \in \mathbb{R}^*$, returning the sequence of values $\langle x_1, ..., x_k \rangle$ for variable v. Furthermore, π_i returns the ith value in a sequence, for instance, $\pi_i(\Pi_v(sd_\delta)) = x_i$.

Table 2. Example derived SD-Log for the running example with a time window of 1 day and 6 different process variables. Each row shows a time step, here 1 day, cell-values represented aggregated variable values.

Time Window Daily	Arrival rate	Finish rate	Num of unique resources	Avg service time	Avg time in process	Avg waiting time in process
1	180	180	6	0.3590	0.9689	0.6099
2	147	147	6	0.4156	0.9565	0.5409
3	160	160	6	0.4011	0.9972	0.5961
4	116	116	6	0.4455	0.9363	0.4908
5	94	94	6	0.5024	0.8258	0.3234
6	0	0	0	0	0	0
7	0	0	0	0	0	0
8	147	147	6	0.4421	0.9898	0.5477
⋮	⋮	⋮	⋮	⋮	⋮	⋮

In the running example, consider the set of variables $\mathcal{V} = \{arrival\ rate,\ average\ service\ time, number\ of\ people\ in\ the\ process\}$, for a duration of 14 days with $\delta = 1\ day$, i.e., the corresponding SD-Log includes 14 time steps. Consider Table 2, in the first time window (day) 180 cases were arrived at the process and 6 unique resources were performing the tasks. $\Pi_v(sd_\delta) = \langle x_1, ..., x_k \rangle$ is a series of values over steps of time with length k, which is in the form of time-series data.

Time-Series. The analysis of sequences of real values and/or sequences of tuples of real values is often referred to as *time-series analysis* [12]. Several models exist that, given a sequence of values and/or tuples of values, predict the next (sequence of) number(s). Examples include *Moving Average models* (MA), *Auto-Regressive models* (AR), and *Auto Regressive Integrated Moving Average models* (ARIMA). The exact type of model used to predict the next likely values is not relevant for our approach, i.e., any method that allows us to do so suffices. Hence, in Definition 3, we propose a generic definition of a *time-series model*.

Definition 3 (Time-Series Model). *Let $\sigma = \langle x_1, ..., x_k \rangle \in \mathbb{R}^*$ be a sequence of real values (a time-series). A time-series model θ is a function $\theta : \mathbb{R}^* \to \mathbb{R}^*$. Given $\sigma = \langle x_1, ..., x_k \rangle$, $\theta(\sigma) = \langle \hat{x}_1, ..., \hat{x}_k \rangle$, s.t., for $1 \le i \le k$: $\hat{x}_i$ is the expected value for x_i.*

Observe that Definition 3 covers *univariate time-series*. For predicting the first value (x_1), we use random initial values. To measure the accuracy of the time-series model (θ), we use *Mean Absolute Percentage Error* ($MAPE = \frac{100\%}{k} \sum_{i=1}^{k} |\frac{x_i - \hat{x}_i}{x_i}|$).

4   Proposed Approach

Consider Fig. 3, in which we depict an overview of the approach. The approach starts with an event log and logical units of time, as shown in the top left side of Fig. 3. The logical units can be minutes, hours, days, etc. Furthermore, units are related to one-an-other, e.g., days consist of 24 h, weeks are 7 days, etc. Our approach starts with a set of initial sizes of time steps, Δ, provided by the user. Given a set of process variables $\mathcal{V}$ and the set of different sizes Δ, for each $\delta \in \Delta$ by the user, a corresponding SD-Log sd_δ is calculated. The derived values in the SD-Logs are tested for repetitive patterns over time, i.e., regular behavior (*Process Behavior Verification* step). Inactive steps are removed using the discovered regular inactive patterns (*SD-Logs Post processing*). If the SD-Log shows patterns of inactivity, then all the corresponding inactive steps are removed. The last step is to find the best time window for extracting the values for simulation models by training time-series models as explained in Sect. 4.3.

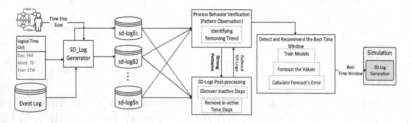

Fig. 3. Proposed approach for discovering the best time window, generating/analyzing time-series data from event logs, investigating the effect of business processes inactivity and detecting strong patterns in the processes over time.

4.1   Process Behavior Observation

Observing the process behavior over time makes it possible to see and discover periodic patterns. We define function *Test Time Step (TTS)* to discover strong patterns for process variables that show repetitive behavior in the context of the process environment over time, e.g., *arrival rate*. We use the partial auto-correlation function [20] to find the possible existing patterns in $\Pi_v(sd_\delta)$ for variable $v \in \mathcal{V}$, for each derived sd_δ, $\delta \in \Delta$, where Δ is provided by the user. In real event logs, process variables over time, e.g., arrival rate, can be highly correlated to the previous values of themselves, hence, computing the partial auto-correlation allows us to remove such internal dependencies. By doing so, we only consider the correlation between two lagged-values, aim in finding clear patterns inside the data. The *lag-value* shows that the correlation between which pair of values should be calculated.

Definition 4 (Test Time Step). *Let $\sigma \in \mathbb{R}^*$ and $T \subseteq \mathbb{N}$ be the set of possible lag-values. $PAC_\tau : \mathbb{R}^* \rightarrow [-1, 1]$ defines the partial auto-correlation of given lag-value $\tau \in T$. Function TestTimeStep is defined as $TTS_\rho : \mathbb{R}^* \rightarrow 2^T$, where $\rho \in \mathbb{R}_{\geq 0}$. For $\sigma \in \mathbb{R}^*$ and threshold ρ, $TTS_\rho(\sigma) = \{\tau \in T | abs(PAC_\tau(\sigma)) \geq \rho\}$.*

By definition, the value of the partial auto-correlation function is always 1 for lag 0. Figure 4 shows the partial auto-correlation values as a sample for the process arrival rate in an hourly and daily manner. For the running example, consider sd_{hour} as the derived SD-Log and *arrival rate* as a process variable $v \in \mathcal{V}$, $\Pi_{arrival\ rate}(sd_{hour})$ returns a sequence of values for arrival rate per hour. For $\rho = 0.5$, the function TTS_ρ over the derived sequence, returns $\{24\}$, i.e., the process shows similar/stable behavior every 24 h.

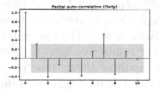 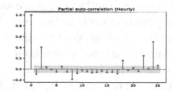

Fig. 4. The partial auto-correlations for the process arrival rate. Daily (left) and hourly (right) time windows (left).

4.2   SD-Log Post-Processing

In addition to the patterns inside the process variables for different sizes of time steps, the *inactivity* of the process in each step is also important. There are time steps in which the process is inactive. Such inactivity can either be planned/intentional or, unexpected. Differentiating different types of inactivity is required in order to capture the most stable behavior of the process. This behavior is directly affecting the simulation results. In this step, first, we need to discover the inactive steps in the process and then, using the previous step, TTS function result, remove periodic and regular inactive steps. Function *Detect Inactivity* (Definition 5) discovers the inactive steps of time for the process. The function maps each step of time in the SD-Log into a boolean value, indicating whether or not there are reasons to believe that the process was inactive, in that time step. Inactivity is measured on the basis of all the process variables $\mathcal{V}$ combined, i.e., there has to be a significant amount of variables that show inactivity to classify the step as an inactive step.

Definition 5 (Detect Inactivity). *Let $\mathcal{V}$ be the set of process variables and $|\mathcal{V}| = n$, let $\gamma \in \mathbb{R}_{>0}$, and let $\kappa \in \mathbb{R}^n$ denote a vector of thresholds for considering a variable as active. $DIA_\kappa : \mathbb{R}^n \rightarrow \{0,1\}$ is a function describing the relative inactivity of a given $\mathbf{x} \in \mathbb{R}^n$, subject to activity threshold κ, i.e.,:*

$$DIA_{\kappa,\gamma}(\mathbf{x}) = \begin{cases} 0 & if \ \frac{|\{i \in \{1,...,n\}|\mathbf{x}(i) \geq \kappa(i)\}|}{n} \geq \gamma \\ 1 & if \ \frac{|\{i \in \{1,...,n\}|\mathbf{x}(i) \geq \kappa(i)\}|}{n} < \gamma \end{cases}$$

For instance, given SD-Log sd_δ and the set of variables $\mathcal{V}$, function $DIA_{\kappa,\gamma}$ returns 0 if the relative number of values in each time step is above γ, otherwise it returns 1. The function indicates whether a time step in the process is active or inactive. The output of the DIA function, is used as input of TTS function. By applying TTS function on the result of the DIA which is a sequence over time, we discover whether there are any strong patterns inside the inactive steps. The strong patterns reveal the periodic inactivity, then we remove the inactive steps from the SD-Log. We call the new refined SD-Log sd'_δ. The option for users with domain knowledge is available here to either remove or keep the detected inactive time steps. In the running example, the result of *Detect inactivity function* DIA for all the steps is $\langle 1,1,1,1,1,0,0,1,1,1,1,1,0,0...\rangle$, where 0-values are weekends. Applying the TTS function, again returns 7 days as a strong pattern in the data, hence, the inactive time steps, i.e., weekends, are removed. Figure. 5 shows the hourly arrival rate of the process for 3 weeks before and after removing regular inactivity. The removed hours are nights and weekends. Note that in Fig. 5, the minimum value in the active steps is 1. Furthermore, applying TTS after removing the regular inactive steps, make it possible to discover whether there are interesting patterns inside the active steps of the process.

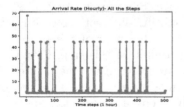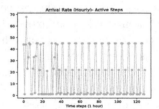

Fig. 5. The arrival rate of the running example in 1 h steps for 3 weeks before (left) and after (right) removing regular inactivity. In the active steps, the minimum values are 1. The weekends and night hours have been removed.

4.3   Detect the Best Time Window

After pattern detection and removing inactive time steps, we aim to find the best window of time, in order to generate the SD-Logs and perform simulations.

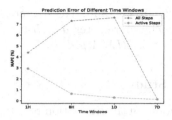

Fig. 6. The prediction errors of the models (ARIMA [9]) for different time windows. The models are trained based on the values of arrival rate, before (blue) and after (red) applying the proposed approach on the SD-Logs (Color figure online).

Using *TTS* and *DIA* functions, we transform the values of process variables in the SD-Logs into the steady time series values, which the frequent patterns and inactivity have been removed. We are looking for the time step size that displays the most stable behavior of the process. We use a time-series prediction model θ, to predict the expected values of a process variable (Definition 3). By *differencing* the values of the generated time-series data for the process variables, i.e., computing the differences between consecutive observations, the data becomes stationary and can be used in time-series models, e.g., *ARIMA*. The accuracy of the models, for each of the selected time windows, shows the best time window to be used in prediction. For each time window $\delta \in \Delta$ provided by the user and corresponding SD-Log after removing inactivity sd'_δ, the values for v is $\Pi_v(sd'_\delta)=\langle x_1, ...x_k \rangle$. After training the models, we calculate the *Mean Absolute Percentage Error* (MAPE). Among all the tested sizes of the time step, the one with the minimal MAPE value indicates the best time window to be used for extracting SD-Log and performing the simulation. Variable *arrival rate* often is the only variable that shows the influence of the environment directly on the process. However, in the case of more variables, the average MAPE value is considered.

In the example, if $\Lambda = \{hour, 8h, day, 7 days\}$, the SD-Logs are sd_{hour}, sd_{8h}, sd_{day}, and $sd_{7 days}$. For the process variable $v = arrival\ rate$, *TTS* and *DIA* are performed on the results of the projection function Π_v. In this step, ARIMA models are trained with different parameters and the prediction error for each δ is shown in Fig. 6 (red). The errors indicate that for the time window of 1 day or 7 days the values of arrival rate are more stable. Figure 6 also demonstrates the errors of the trained models before applying the steps of our approach (blue). Since there is no inactive week, the error for 7 days is the same, however, for other steps, after removing the inactivity, the error has reduced, e.g., removing weekends from daily time step, resulted in more stable and predictable behavior in the process.

5   Evaluation

To evaluate the approach, we use both synthetic and real event logs. Using the synthetic event log, we assess the effect of choosing time windows on the simulation accuracy. We discover the strong patterns in the real event logs.

Implementation. The experiments are conducted with an implementation of the framework in the *PMSD* tool [15]. For time-series prediction, used in best time window detection (Sect. 4.3), we use ARIMA [9]. To compute ARIMA models, we need to set three parameters, i.e., differencing-parameter d, AR-term $p \geq 1$ and MA-term $q \geq 1$. In the remainder, we write $ARIMA(p, d, q)$.

5.1 Synthetic Event Log: Simulation Case Study

In order to assess the effect of the selected time window on the simulation results, we use the results of the performed steps on the running example through the sections to generate a system dynamic simulation model. Consider that businesses might be interested in a smaller window of time for prediction, e.g., a daily manner is more useful for decreasing the average daily waiting time rather than a weekly manner in the process. Therefore, the time window with the minimum error is not always the best option for the businesses. We generate the system dynamic models using the technique presented in [17].

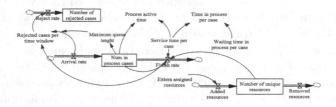

Fig. 7. System dynamics model for the running example. What-if analysis for the number of rejected cases per time window and the number of resources.

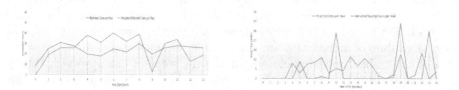

Fig. 8. The actual (blue) and simulated (red) number of rejected cases using daily (left) and hourly (right) time windows using the model in Fig. 7. (Color figure online)

The designed model in Fig. 7 is populated with two different SD-Logs, sd_{day} and sd_{hour}, after applying the approach. The target scenario is to simulate the number of rejected people in the process per time window and the effect of the number of resources to decrease the rejected cases.

Figure. 8 shows the results of the simulation for two selected time windows and the actual values from the event logs. The simulation results using the 1 day time window is close to reality behavior over 1 h time window. As expected from the results of the approach, the time windows with lower errors provide more accurate simulation results. Note that, we designed the process in Sect. 2 such that the number of requests is higher for the specific time of the days, e.g., at 10:00 am the number of requests is more than 8:00 am. Therefore, even after removing regular inactive hours from sd_{hour}, the variation between the values in high. The results illustrate that selecting a proper time window to extract the values of variables highly affects the accuracy of the predictions and our approach is able to provide the information needed to pick the best time window.

5.2 Feasibility Test on Real Event Data

We use two real event logs, BPI Challenge 2012 [24] and BPI Challenge 2017 [25], to evaluate our work. The errors of the models for predicting the values of variables in different time windows, before and after performing the steps of the approach show the effect of the approach on selecting the best time window.

BPI Challenge 2012. We start with four time window sizes, *2 h, 8 h, 1 day and 7 days* and extract the SD-Logs for each time window. Using the function *TTS* in the *process behavior observation* step, the strong patterns in the values of arrival rate are discovered, e.g., with threshold 0.5, there are strong patterns in every 2 h (lag 1 for 2 h time window in Fig. 9 (right)) and 7 days for the daily time window. *Post processing* step and *DIA* function result in the refined SD-Logs for the selected time windows by removing possible periodic inactive steps. In Fig. 9 (left), we present the error of the training ARIMA model with different parameters before (blue) and after (red) removing inactive steps. For instance, the best one for the hourly window after removing the inactive steps is $ARIMA(2, 0, 1)$ and for 1 day window is $ARIMA(1, 0, 1)$. Since in the process, there is no inactive week, day and 8 h, therefore the prediction errors are the same for including all the steps and active steps. However, the error of the 2 h time window has decreased. The reduction shows that in the process there were periodically inactive steps between each 2 h.

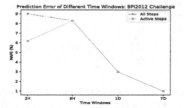
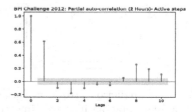

Fig. 9. The prediction errors of the trained models for time windows before and after removing inactive steps, BPI 2012 (left). The partial auto-correlation after removing inactive periods for 2 h time window (right).

As expected, the strongest pattern inside the process w.r.t. its environment, i.e., the arrival rate of cases, is *7 days*. Furthermore, the time window sizes based on the domain knowledge can be changed, e.g., 8 h is tested to see whether the process follows the common working hours.

BPI Challenge 2017. In the process, there are different types of activities. We focus on activities which are triggered by the employees, (activities with a W_- prefix). We also use *8 h, 1 day* and *7 days* as time windows with respect to the employees' working hours. Figure 10 represents the partial auto-correlation of the arrival rate (daily and 8 h) in *behavior observation* step. As expected, the strongest pattern is every 7 days (weekly). Also, in 8 h time window, lag 3 shows a strong pattern.

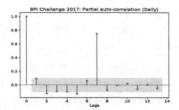 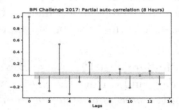

Fig. 10. The partial auto-correlation before removing inactivity in 1 day window (left) and 8 h time window (right) for the BPI challenge 2017.

DIA function is applied on the SD-Logs to indicate the inactive steps and using results of TTS to remove the regular inactive steps, the process shows more stable behavior. For instance, Fig. 11 (right) is the TTS result on the daily arrival rate after removing weekends, hence there is no more strong pattern. This information helps in analyzing the process behavior and have more accurate simulation models.

 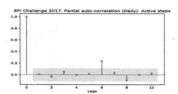

Fig. 11. The prediction errors of the arrival rate in the BPI 2017 event log before and after removing the inactive time steps (left). The partial auto-correlation after removing inactive time steps (right).

The prediction errors of the trained models for predicting the values of the arrival rate for three selected time windows are presented in Fig. 11 for the derived SD-Logs and the refined SD-Logs using our approach. Same as the BPI Challenge 2012, there are no regular inactive weeks in the process, therefore the error has not changed before and after applying the approach. However, in both 8 h and 1 day time windows, there are considerable reductions in the prediction errors. The evaluation using real event logs indicates that the approach is able to find a better time window among the possible time step sizes to have the most stable behavior of the processes.

6 Related Work

Process mining techniques implicitly use time-series data for different purposes such as performance analysis [3], bottleneck analysis, prediction [2] and the enhancement of the processes, e.g., providing recommendations [5]. Process mining techniques mostly focus on the current state of processes. At the same time, in simulation, the current state is employed to generate similar behavior of the processes. Therefore, the combination of these two fields is a promising direction for the enhancement of processes [2].

Prediction and simulation techniques in process mining focus mostly on instances of the process, e.g., the execution/ waiting time for a specific case in the process [22]. Moreover, in [6] a configurable approach is proposed to construct a process model enhanced with time information from previous instances, and use the model for prediction, for example, the completion time. However, most of the mentioned techniques are at a detailed level and missing the effect of external factors [4]. Furthermore, in [23] a survey of prediction techniques in process mining is presented in which most of the techniques use a predefined unit of time such as days or hour. In the context of simulation and prediction in process mining, there is not enough focus on the effect of the size of time windows on the result of simulation and prediction techniques. Work such as [11] explains the possibility of using time-series analysis in data analysis. Two main types of time-series analysis exist including univariate and multi-variate. Box et al. introduced the ARIMA method [8]. This method now represents one of the most frequently used univariate time-series modeling tools. In [14], techniques such as the ARIMA technique are shown to be more effective than LSTM techniques in univariate time-series data [22].

In most of the techniques in process mining, the selection of the time window for generating data either has not been mentioned explicitly or they used the predefined logical unit of time. The techniques at the aggregated level use the current state of the processes over time. Techniques such as [16] are proposed which employ different time windows. This approach can be used with domain knowledge about the working hours of the processes, e.g., a production line process is running 8 h per day [18].

7 Conclusion

In this paper, we proposed an approach to discover the best window of time for capturing the most stable behavior of processes over time. The discovered time window is used for extracting values of process variables from event logs.

Since these values are an aggregated value for each time window, they behave like time-series data. We used the derived time-series data to discover strong patterns inside the process variables related to the process environment, e.g., arrival rate. Moreover, in the approach, inactive time windows are distinguished and removed. A time-series prediction approach (ARIMA) is used to find the best models that predict the next values accurately and their parameters. The proposed approach is effective in picking the size of the time window to generate the performance variables in business processes. The generated values for process variables over time that represent the process behavior, i.e., SD-Log, are exploited for simulation and prediction purpose. The evaluation section shows that our approach provides business owners with actionable insights into the current situation of the processes to be used in simulation as system dynamics.

Acknowledgments. Funded by the Deutsche Forschungsgemeinschaft (DFG, German Research Foundation) under Germany's Excellence Strategy–EXC-2023 Internet of Production – 390621612. We also thank the Alexander von Humboldt (AvH) Stiftung for supporting our research.

References

1. van der Aalst, W.M.P.: Process Mining - Data Science in Action, 2nd edn. Springer, Heidelberg (2016). https://doi.org/10.1007/978-3-662-49851-4
2. van der Aalst, W.M.P.: Process mining and simulation: a match made in heaven! In: D'Ambrogio, A., Zacharewicz, G. (eds.) Computer Simulation Conference (SummerSim 2018), pp. 1–12. ACM Press (2018)
3. van der Aalst, W.M.P., Adriansyah, A., van Dongen, B.F.: Replaying history on process models for conformance checking and performance analysis. Wiley Interdiscip. Rev. Data Min. Knowl. Discov. **2**(2), 182–192 (2012)
4. van der Aalst, W.M.P., Dustdar, S.: Process mining put into context. IEEE Internet Comput. **16**, 82–86 (2012)
5. van der Aalst, W.M.P., Pesic, M., Song, M.: Beyond process mining: from the past to present and future. In: Pernici, B. (ed.) CAiSE 2010. LNCS, vol. 6051, pp. 38–52. Springer, Heidelberg (2010). https://doi.org/10.1007/978-3-642-13094-6_5
6. van der Aalst, W.M.P., Schonenberg, M.H., Song, M.: Time prediction based on process mining. Inf. Syst. **36**(2), 450–475 (2011)
7. Augusto, A., Conforti, R., Dumas, M., Rosa, M.L., Maggi, F.M., Marrella, A., Mecella, M., Soo, A.: Automated discovery of process models from event logs: review and benchmark. IEEE Trans. Knowl. Data Eng. **31**(4), 686–705 (2019)
8. Box, G.E.P., Jenkins, G.: Time Series Analysis. Forecasting and Control. Holden-Day Inc, USA (1990)
9. Box, G.E., Jenkins, G.M., Reinsel, G.C., Ljung, G.M.: Time Series Analysis: Forecasting and Control. Wiley, Hoboken (2015)
10. Carmona, J., van Dongen, B.F., Solti, A., Weidlich, M.: Conformance Checking - Relating Processes and Models. Springer, Cham (2018). https://doi.org/10.1007/978-3-319-99414-7
11. Esling, P., Agón, C.: Time-series data mining. ACM Comput. Surv. **45**(1), 12:1–12:34 (2012). https://doi.org/10.1145/2379776.2379788
12. Hamilton, J.D.: Time Series Analysis, vol. 2. Princeton, New Jersey (1994)

13. Coloured Petri Nets. Lecture Notes in Computer Science. Springer, Heidelberg (2009). https://doi.org/10.1007/b95112
14. Makridakis, S., Spiliotis, E., Assimakopoulos, V.: Statistical and machine learning forecasting methods: Concerns and ways forward. PLoS ONE **13**(3), 31 (2018)
15. Pourbafrani, M., van der Aalst, W.M.P.: PMSD: data-driven simulation using system dynamics and process mining. In: Proceedings of the Best Dissertation Award, Doctoral Consortium, and Demonstration & Resources Track, pp. 77–81 (2020). http://ceur-ws.org/Vol-2673/paperDR03.pdf
16. Pourbafrani, M., van Zelst, S.J., van der Aalst, W.M.P.: Scenario-based prediction of business processes using system dynamics. In: OTM 2019 Conferences, 2019. pp. 422–439 (2019). https://doi.org/10.1007/978-3-030-33246-4_27
17. Pourbafrani, M., van Zelst, S.J., van der Aalst, W.M.P.: Supporting automatic system dynamics model generation for simulation in the context of process mining. In: BIS 2020, Colorado Springs, CO, USA, June 8–10, 2020, Proceedings, pp. 249–263 (2020). https://doi.org/10.1007/978-3-030-53337-3_19
18. Pourbafrani, M., van Zelst, S.J., van der Aalst, W.M.P.: Supporting decisions in production line processes by combining process mining and system dynamics. In: Intelligent Human Systems Integration 2020 - Proceedings of the 3rd International Conference on Intelligent Human Systems Integration, pp. 461–467 (2020). https://doi.org/10.1007/978-3-030-39512-4_72
19. Pruyt, E.: Small System Dynamics Models for Big Issues: Triple Jump towards Real-World Dynamic Complexity. TU Delft Library (2013)
20. Ramsey, F.L., et al.: Characterization of the partial autocorrelation function. Ann. Stat. **2**(6), 1296–1301 (1974)
21. Sterman, J.: System Dynamics: Systems Thinking and Modeling for a Complex World (2002)
22. Tax, N., Verenich, I., Rosa, M.L., Dumas, M.: Predictive business process monitoring with LSTM neural networks. CoRR abs/1612.02130 (2016)
23. Teinemaa, I., Dumas, M., Rosa, M.L., Maggi, F.M.: Outcome-oriented predictive process monitoring: review and benchmark. TKDD **13**(2), 17:1–17:57 (2019)
24. van Dongen, B.F.: BPIC 2012. Eindhoven University of Technology (2012)
25. van Dongen, B.F.: BPIC 2017. Eindhoven University of Technology (2017)

Identifying Cohorts: Recommending Drill-Downs Based on Differences in Behaviour for Process Mining

Sander J. J. Leemans[1]([✉]), Shiva Shabaninejad[2], Kanika Goel[1], Hassan Khosravi[2], Shazia Sadiq[2], and Moe Thandar Wynn[1]

[1] Queensland University of Technology, Brisbane, Australia
{s.leemans,k.goel,m.wynn}@qut.edu.au
[2] University of Queensland, Brisbane, Australia
{h.khosravi,s.shabaninejad}@uq.edu.au
shazia@itee.uq.edu.au

Abstract. Process mining aims to obtain insights from event logs to improve business processes. In complex environments with large variances in process behaviour, analysing and making sense of such complex processes becomes challenging. Insights in such processes can be obtained by identifying sub-groups of traces (cohorts) and studying their differences. In this paper, we introduce a new framework that elicits features from trace attributes, measures the stochastic distance between cohorts defined by sets of these features, and presents this landscape of sets of features and their influence on process behaviour to users. Our framework differs from existing work in that it can take many aspects of behaviour into account, including the ordering of activities in traces (control flow), the relative frequency of traces (stochastic perspective), and cost. The framework has been instantiated and implemented, has been evaluated for feasibility on multiple publicly available real-life event logs, and evaluated on real-life case studies in two Australian universities.

Keywords: Process mining · Drill-down recommendation · Filter recommendation · Stochastic comparative process mining

1 Introduction

In organisational processes, users and computers interact with information systems to handle cases such as orders, claims and applications. These interactions are logged as events, and process mining utilises such event data in the form of an event log to gain evidence-based insights in the structure and performance of organisational processes. In order to gain insights in a process, typically first a process model is discovered from a log, then this model is evaluated and finally additional perspectives such as performance, costs or resources are projected on the process model such that analysts can identify potential problems and

© Springer Nature Switzerland AG 2020
G. Dobbie et al. (Eds.): ER 2020, LNCS 12400, pp. 92–102, 2020.
https://doi.org/10.1007/978-3-030-62522-1_7

gain insights [8]. Many processes are highly variable, which may be due to geographically different entities executing the process, different customers interacting with it, or different backgrounds of students being involved in it. Analysing highly variable processes challenges analysts, as conclusions and insights might get watered down or might not hold in all variants [5,7].

To address high variability in processes, in a typical process mining project, discussions with stakeholders would be required to identify a set of key attributes, after which these attributes and their values (*trace features*) can be used to split the log into *cohorts*. For instance, the trace $\langle$receive claim, decide claim $\rangle [\begin{smallmatrix} ID & 1234 \\ amount & 10000 \end{smallmatrix}]$ has two trace attributes, and a trace feature of amount ≥ 5000 applies to this trace. These cohorts can then be analysed separately (*drill down*) or compared to one another [7,21]. To reduce variability, trace features should be chosen such that behavioural variability within cohorts is minimised, while between cohorts it is maximised. We refer to this technique as *cohort identification*, and automation makes it more objective, enables explorative approaches that might reveal yet-unknown cohorts, and increases feasibility. To the best of our knowledge, cf. data mining [9], no process mining techniques were published that recommend trace features for drill downs based on behaviour.

In this paper, we introduce a new framework called Cohort Identification (CI) that takes a log as input and outputs a landscape of sets of trace features which maximise between-cohort behavioural variability. Figure 1 shows an overview of the framework: first, CI elicits trace features from the log. Second, CI combines them into feature sets exhaustively and, for each set, quantifies the differences between the cohort defined by the feature set and the other traces in the log. CI can take many aspects of behaviour into account, such as the ordering of activities in traces (control flow), cost of executions, and relative frequency of traces (stochastic perspective [12]). We evaluate CI on feasibility using real-life public event logs, and we illustrate its applicability using two case studies.

The remainder of this paper discusses related work in Sect. 2, introduces existing concepts in Sect. 3, introduces the framework and an open source implementation in Sect. 4; evaluates our approach using 21 publicly available logs and two illustrative case studies in Sect. 5, and concludes in Sect. 6.

2 Related Work

In this section, we first discuss three types of techniques (trace clustering, concept drift detection, cohort identification) to reduce variance in logs. Second, we discuss how our approach complements process comparison techniques.

Trace Clustering aims to find groups of structurally similar traces, such that these groups can be studied in isolation [6,21,23]. Secondary, the relation between these groups and trace attributes can be analysed using standard data mining techniques. For instance, a recent trace clustering approach [17] clusters traces based on control flow and performance patterns, and recommends clusters of traces to users, after which users can inspect KPIs of selected clusters. While trace clustering techniques take similar behaviour and search for relations with trace features, our approach does the opposite: it takes trace features and searches for relations with behaviour. Trace clustering inherently cannot consider the frequency of trace variants within groups, typically do not provide an explanation to justify their grouping ("black box"), provide little additional insights into the log, and are challenging to use for drill-down recommendations.

Concept Drift Detection aims to identify points in time where the process changed. The behaviour before and after the drift point might have a lower variance, and the changes can be studied comparatively (e.g. [15]). CI could be seen as a generalisation of concept drift techniques as it can detects changes in behaviour related to trace features, including when traces happened.

Cohort Identification [2] uses decision points in a process model and event attribute clustering to identify groups of traces, and performs significance tests to limit the reported groups. In contrast with our approach, this technique requires a process model and operates on event features (rather than trace features), however it would be interesting to extend CI with similar significance tests in future work.

Attribute clustering techniques first cluster the features of traces, after which the corresponding groups of traces can be studied in isolation. For instance, in [14], an extensive framework for correlating, predicting and clustering is proposed. This framework supports the splitting of logs based on extensive analyses on event features, however has a different focus than CI: event vs trace features and clustering rather than recommending drill downs.

To the best of our knowledge, no techniques have been published that recommend trace features for drill downs in process mining, based on behaviour. In addition: none of the mentioned techniques considers the relative frequency of behaviour (i.e. the stochastic behaviour recorded in logs) as a source of behavioural differences.

Complementing: Process Comparison. The CI framework recommends feature sets that relate to differences in stochastic behaviour, however does not explain what these differences are, for which a process comparison technique can be used. In a recent literature review of such techniques [22], three types of techniques were identified: discriminative (pattern extraction), generative (comparison through process models) [21] and hybrid (a combination of both). For

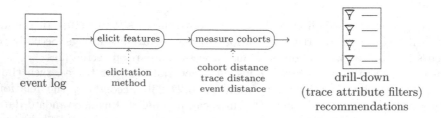

Fig. 1. Overview of the Cohort Identification (CI) framework.

instance, differences between logs have been visualised on their transition systems [3] or compared simply by hand [20].

Process cubes provide skeletons for process comparison by selections (cells) of traces based on trace features, and enable slicing and dicing the log to find cohorts of interests. For instance, in [1,4], process cubes were used to study differences in students' online learning activities (similar to one of our case studies). CI recommends *which* cells might be of interest, based on their behaviour, without having to resort to process discovery techniques.

CI acts as an enabler for these techniques, making them applicable to a single log cf. at least two logs. Finally, these techniques could *also* be used within CI, if they return a number expressing the equivalence between logs.

3   Preliminaries

In this section, we introduce existing concepts.

3.1   Event Logs

An *event log* or *log* L is a collection of traces. A *trace* represents a case handled by the business process, and is a sequence of events. A trace is annotated with *trace attributes*, which represent properties of the trace. An *event* represents the execution of a process step (an *activity*). An event is annotated with *event attributes* that denote properties of the event. For instance, the trace

$$\langle \text{receive claim}\begin{bmatrix} date & 20\text{-}02\text{-}20 \\ resource & online \end{bmatrix}, \text{decide claim}\begin{bmatrix} date & 21\text{-}02\text{-}20 \\ resource & Dave \\ decision & approved \end{bmatrix}\rangle\begin{bmatrix} ID & 1234 \\ amount & 10000 \\ gender & F \end{bmatrix}$$

consists of a single trace, which consists of two events, indicating the execution of two process steps ("receive claim" and "decide claim"). This trace has three trace attributes: an ID, a claim amount and the gender of the claimant. The first event has two event attributes: a date that it was executed and the resource that executed it. Given an event $e\begin{bmatrix} a_1 & v_1 \\ \dots & \dots \\ a_n & v_n \end{bmatrix}$, we write $e^{a_1} = v_1$ to retrieve the value of an attribute that e is annotated with. If e is not annotated with an attribute x, then we define $e^x = \bot$. Retrieving trace attributes is similar.

3.2   Cohorts

Let L be a log, and let a be a trace attribute. Then, let $\mathcal{F}^a$ denote all the values of a in L: $\mathcal{F}^a = \{v = t^a \mid t \in L \land v \neq \bot\}$. We refer to the combination of a trace attribute a and a range of its values $F \subseteq \mathcal{F}^f$ as a *trace feature* a^F. Given a log L, we refer to the sub-log of traces that have trace feature a^F as the *projection* $L|_{a^F}$. For instance, let $L = [\langle g_1, \dots g_n\rangle^{[amount\ 100]}, \langle h_1 \dots h_m\rangle^{[amount\ 50]}]$ be a log. Then, $L|_{amount \geq 70} = [\langle g_1, \dots g_n\rangle^{[amount\ 100]}]$. We refer to such a sub-log of L as a *cohort* of L.

4   A Framework for Cohort Identification (CI)

Given a log, CI aims to recommend trace features to drill down on, that is, to identify cohorts whose behaviour differs considerably from the other traces in the log in terms of process, frequency of paths and event attributes. The main input of CI is a log, and its output is list of recommendations (that is, a list of feature sets with their cohort distances).

Figure 1 shows an overview of the framework, while Algorithm 1 shows its pseudocode. First, trace features are elicited from the log using an elicitation method E. Second, for each sub-set of features of size at most k and of which the corresponding sub-logs are large enough (according to a cohort imbalance threshold α), a distance between the cohorts is computed, using a cohort distance δ_c parameterised with a trace distance δ_t, which in turn is parameterised with an event distance δ_e. Instantiating the framework requires the mentioned functions E, δ_e, δ_t, δ_c and D. In the remainder of this section, we discuss the steps of CI in more detail and we introduce an instantiation.

Algorithm 1. Cohort Identification framework

1: **procedure** $\text{CI}_{E,\delta_c,\delta_t,\delta_e,D}$(log L, cohort imbalance threshold α, max feature set size
   k, correction repetition φ)
2:     $F \leftarrow E(L)$ ▷ elicit features
3:     $M \leftarrow \emptyset$
4:     **for** $S \subseteq F^*$ such that $|S| \leq k$ **do**   ▷ for each feature set
5:         $L_1, L_2 \leftarrow L|_S, L \setminus L|_S$
6:         **if** $\min(|L_1|, |L_2|) \geq \alpha \times |L|$ **then**   ▷ prune too-small cohorts
7:             $d \leftarrow \dfrac{\delta_{c(\delta_{t(\delta_e)})}(L_1, L_2)}{\frac{1}{\varphi}\sum_{L'_1, L'_2 \, \varphi \text{ randomly from} Ls.t. \, |L'_1| \approx |L_1|} \delta_{c(\delta_{t(\delta_e)})}(L'_1, L'_2)}$
8:   ▷ compute corrected cohort distance
9:             $M \leftarrow M \cup \{(S, d)\}$
10:        **end if**
11:    **end for**
12:    **return** M
13: **end procedure**

4.1   Feature Elicitation

The first step of CI is to obtain a collection of features from the log. Trace attributes with literal values straightforwardly yield one feature for each value, or could be clustered for reduced complexity. Numerical trace attributes need to be discretised, after which a feature can be added for each discrete value. The framework supports any discretisation, for instance using numerical value clustering or by using quartiles, though it is important that sufficiently large groups of traces remain.

Our instantiation elicits features for numerical attributes by discretising them in two bins, separated by the median. That is, let L be a log and let a be a numerical trace attribute in L. Then, two features are added: $a^{\geq m}$ and $a^{<m}$, in which m is the median of $\mathcal{F}^a$. Finally, for any typed attribute a, a feature $a^{\perp}$ is added, which expresses that a is missing.

4.2   Measure Cohorts

Second, CI aims to find the cohorts that differ the most from the other traces in the log, in terms of process, frequency of paths and other event attributes. To this end, it considers all possible feature sets S that can be made of combinations of the elicited features. Each such feature set S defines two cohorts: one cohort of traces that possess each feature in S ($L_1 = L|_S$) and the other cohort of traces that do not possess any feature ($L_2 = L \setminus L_1$).

In the cohort measuring step, CI measures the distance between pairs of such L_1 and L_2, using event and trace distance measures:

Definition 1 (Distance measures). *Let δ_e be an* event distance *measure, such that for all events v, v' it holds that $0 \leq \delta_e(v, v') \leq 1$. Let $\delta_{t(\delta_e)}$ be a* trace distance *measure, such that for all traces u, u' it holds that $0 \leq \delta_{t(\delta_e)}(u, u') \leq 1$. Let L, L' be logs. Then, $0 \leq \delta_{c(\delta_{t(\delta_e)})}(L, L') \leq 1$ is a* cohort distance *measure.*

These measures are parameters to CI, and can take any event attribute into account, which makes the CI flexible. Thus, any event, trace and (aggregated) log attribute could contribute to the cohort distance measure given appropriate distance measures. Still, instantiations can opt not to if desired.

On small cohorts, distance measures may be meaningless, as too-small cohorts merely represent outliers. Also, as the number of possible feature sets is exponential in the number of features, CI takes a cohort imbalance threshold $0 \leq \alpha \leq \frac{1}{2}$, which sets the maximum imbalance in the two cohorts: if either $|L_1| < \alpha \times |L|$ or $|L_2| < \alpha \times |L|$, then the feature set S is discarded.

In our instantiation, we use the Earth Movers' Stochastic Conformance (EMSC) [12] as the cohort distance measure. EMSC considers both logs as piles of earth, and computes the effort to transform one pile into the other, in terms of the number of traces to be transformed into other traces times the trace distances of these transformations. Thus, the stochastic perspective is inherently taken into account by EMSC. Another option for δ_c could be to discover two process models, and cross-evaluating these models with the cohorts [21], although this has the downsides of incorporating model discovery trade-offs, asymmetry of the cohort distance measure, and the inability to include the stochastic perspective.

For the trace distance, as in [12], our instantiation uses the normalised Levenshtein distance, which expresses the minimum cost in terms of insertions, deletions and swaps of events to transform one trace into the other. Normalisation is achieved by dividing the minimum cost by the maximum possible cost, which is the length of the longest trace. The cost of insertions, deletions and swaps of events is determined by the event distance. Where EMSC uses unit event distances, we generalise this to any event distance measure δ_e, thus enabling analysts to compare traces based on any event attribute. Our instantiation allows a user to choose several event attributes, and uses a generic event distance measure for each attribute, based on whether the attribute is textual or numerical.

For a textual attribute a (δ_{e_T}) and a numerical attribute b (δ_{e_N}), in which m is the difference of the minimum and maximum of b over the entire log:

$$\delta_{e_T}(v, v') = \begin{cases} 0 & \text{if } v^a = v'^a \\ 1 & \text{otherwise} \end{cases} \qquad \delta_{e_N}(v, v') = \begin{cases} \frac{|v^b - v'^b|}{m} & \text{if } v^b \neq \bot \wedge v'^b \neq \bot \\ 0 & \text{if } v^b = \bot \wedge v'^b = \bot \\ 1 & \text{otherwise} \end{cases}$$

An extension would be to choose multiple attributes and taking their weighted average. Even though any event attribute can be used, one should be careful to avoid the curse of dimensionality: when the number of involved attributes increases, the expected overall distance between arbitrary events approaches 0, which could render the comparison less useful.

4.3 Corrected Cohort Distance

For each feature set S and cohorts L_1, L_2 of log L, a cohort distance measure $\delta_{c(\delta_{t(\delta_e)})}(L_1, L_2)$ is computed, which is parameterised with a trace measure function δ_t, which in turn is parameterised with an event measure function δ_e.

A log with a high variety of traces will in general have higher cohort distances than a log with a low variety of traces, as cohorts of the first will inherently differ more than cohorts of the second. To correct for this, CI scales the computed cohort distance for variance in the log as follows: the traces of L are randomly divided over sub-logs L_1' and L_2', such that $|L_1'| \approx |L_1|$. The distance $\delta_{c(\delta_{t(\delta_e)})}(L_1', L_2')$ between these sub-logs is measured, the procedure is repeated φ times and the average cohort distance is taken as the *corrected cohort distance* (see line 8 of Algorithm 1). Intuitively, the corrected cohort distance shows the *gain in information* about process behaviour of a feature set S: given L, a value of 0 indicates that S provides no extra information over a random division of L, while a value of 1 indicates that S fully distinguishes all behaviour of L.

The output of the cohort measuring step is a list of feature sets annotated with their corresponding corrected cohort distance, sorted on this distance. That is, the feature set that relates the most to differences in stochastic behaviour, thus providing the most information, is on top (see an example in Sect. 5).

4.4 Implementation

CI and our instantiation of it have been implemented as a plug-in of the ProM framework (see http://promtools.org), and are open source https://svn.win.tue. nl/repos/prom/Packages/CohortAnalysis/Trunk, SVN revision 43272. On top of the trace attributes present in the log, CI considers the total trace duration as well. To save time computing the corrected cohort distance $\delta_{c'}$, our implementation caches the cohort distance between randomly divided sub-logs of 10 sub-log sizes, rather than for each feature set separately.

5 Evaluation

We evaluate CI and our instantiation threefold. First, we illustrate its feasibility and use on publicly available logs. Second, we study its explorative and question-driven capabilities, and its embedding in process mining projects in two case studies, with a brief empirical evaluation with stakeholder feedback.

5.1 Public Logs

To illustrate our instantiation, we applied it to 21 real-life publicly available event logs. We applied CI to each of them with the maximum feature set size (k) ranging from 1 to 5. The results show that our implementation of CI is feasible on real-life logs for small k (for $k = 1$, 18/21 logs finished in 74 s or less, with a maximum of 36 h; the maximum feasible number of feature sets was around 10^7). The experimental results indicate that while the number of activities does not seem to have an influence on the run time, an exponentially increasing number of feature sets does. Hence, it suggests that our instantiation of CI could be used to derive initial insights into logs without analysts having to consider models with hundreds of activities. For more details, please refer to [13].

5.2 Case Study I: Digital Learning Environment Interactions

Course Insights is a learning analytics dashboard (LAD) that provides comparative visualisations of students interacting with a digital learning environment [18], by filtering on trace attributes such as residential status, gender, program or assessment grade. Drill-downs has been under-utilised: rarely more than one feature is filtered for [18]. We applied CI to a log from a calculus and linear algebra course offered to 736 undergraduate students at the University of Queensland, containing 18,883 events, 51 activities (per chapter: read material, submit quiz and review solutions), and 2,447 trace feature sets ($k = 4$). In collaboration with the instructor, who was not otherwise involved in this study, we selected a cohort with a high distance: international students with a high exam grade (9% of the traces, 0.16 distance, IH), and compared it with the other students (¬IH). We found clear differences in their process: while IH alternates between the types of activities troughout the semester, ¬IH mainly performs quizzes sequentially at the end of the semester. To verify that these patterns are not also present in IH's super-cohorts of international students (I) or students with high exam grades (H) (to avoid a drill-down fallacy [10]), we repeated the analysis on I and H, and did not find these patterns.

The feedback of the instructor can be summarised as follows: (1) the recommendation of filters enables finding the differences between students' cohorts, while the current number of filtering choices in the LAD is too overwhelming to use; (2) the findings of learning behaviour that have led to successful outcome can be used for positive deviance [16] purposes. The instructor showed interest in sharing the findings about IH's learning process as a successful learning pattern with students to encourage early engagement; (3) getting notified (by the system) during the semester of any deviation of cohorts which might lead to learning failure could help with supporting students in-time. Thus, the integration of CI in the LAD has been considered [19]. This case study illustrates that certain insights might only be found using $k > 1$.

5.3   Case Study II: Research Student Journeys

The Queensland University of Technology utilises electronic forms (e-forms) to support higher degree research students with milestones. A log was extracted of 1,520 traces (students), 42,426 events, 15 activities (submission of forms, checks, approvals, ...) and 4 trace attributes: faculty, scholarship, study mode (full/part time), and residency. Stakeholders' questions were whether processing was consistent across (q1) faculties and (q2) other student groups. To answer these questions, we applied CI with $k = 1$. The results showed that faculty B had the highest distance (0.19). In answer to q1, process models [11] of B and the other traces ($\neg B$) are similar, indicating little difference in control flow. However, the likelihoods of choices and rework were different. Second, the results conveyed that there was minimal variation related to other demographic factors such as mode of study or domestic and international students: their distances were close to 0, which indicates that these features contribute no more to behaviour than randomly selected cohorts.

As a brief empirical evaluation, we presented key findings to stakeholders who were otherwise not involved in this study. The results were well-received: (1) insights regarding high variations across faculties were used to propose standardisation of e-forms processing, and (2) objective evidence was found that student demographic factors had no influence on the stochastic behaviour of processing e-forms. In summary, this case study demonstrates the utility of CI in a question-driven context in which its outputs were used to directly answer stakeholders' questions and can lead to actionable insights.

5.4   Discussion and Limitations

In Sect. 5.1, we showed that CI is feasible on real-life logs, however for higher k, its exponential nature kicks in. Further pruning steps could use monotonicity, which however does not hold for our current instantiation with EMSC: a cohort's distance is not a bound for the distance of including additional features. Our instantiation could be extended to include smarter elicitation of numerical ranges using e.g. clustering, and to include more elaborate ways to combine several event-distance measures into δ_e without hitting the curse of dimensionality.

The two case studies showed that CI can lead to insights by itself, and that CI can assist explorative and question-driven process mining efforts as a first step before existing process comparison techniques are applied (for which the case studies provided examples). Furthermore, the case studies highlight that the recommended cohorts cannot be identified by existing techniques: trace clustering techniques (e.g. [17]) would not be able to provide clear-cut trace feature drill-down recommendations, and existing cohort identification techniques either require a process model and operate on event features only [2], or do not provide trace feature recommendations at all [14]. While there are currently no published techniques to recommend trace attributes for filtering based on behaviour, it would be interesting to compare CI with existing approaches of log variance reduction (using e.g. variance metrics), or commercial feature recommendations (using e.g. user studies) , all of which we leave as future work.

6   Conclusion

Applying process mining techniques to event logs with high variance is challenging, which can be addressed by filtering sub-logs of traces (*cohorts*) defined by trace attribute value ranges (*features*), in order to compare behavioural differences between cohorts or to drill down into a particular cohort. To the best of our knowledge, no *cohort identification* techniques have been published, that is, techniques that recommend feature sets for logs, based on behavioural differences, which may include control flow and frequency of trace variants. In this paper, we proposed the Cohort Identification (CI) framework to automatically recommend feature sets that correspond to the largest differences in behaviour, where users can select what data or information constitutes behaviour. The framework was instantiated and implemented as a plug-in of the ProM framework.

Our evaluation found that CI can be applied in reasonable time to public real-life logs. Furthermore, we reported on two case studies in two Australian universities, showing that question-driven application led to addressing questions from stakeholders that could only be answered using stochastic-aware techniques. Stakeholders who were not otherwise involved in this work verified the findings.

Future extensions of CI could include clustering of numerical values in the feature elicitation step, and further heuristics to prune the feature sets to be considered. Second, it would be interesting to integrate CI in process mining methodologies such as [8] to assist in drill-down cycles. Third, stochastic log-log comparison techniques could be used to highlight differences in the stochastic behaviour of cohorts. Finally, we intend to perform elaborate user studies into the usefulness of the recommendations, similar to [17], in combination with an evaluation of, potentially new, log-log comparison techniques.

References

1. van der Aalst, W.M.P., et al.: Comparative process mining in education: an approach based on process cubes. SIMPDA **203**, 110–134 (2013)
2. Bolt, A., van der Aalst, W.M.P., de Leoni, M.: Finding process variants in event logs. In: Panetto, H., et al. (eds.) OTM 2017. LNCS, vol. 10573, pp. 45–52. Springer, Cham (2017). https://doi.org/10.1007/978-3-319-69462-7_4

3. Bolt, A., de Leoni, M., van der Aalst, W.M.P.: Process variant comparison: using event logs to detect differences in behavior and business rules. IS **74**, 53–66 (2018)
4. Bolt, A., et al.: Exploiting process cubes, analytic workflows and process mining for business process reporting: a case study in education. SIMPDA **1527**, 33–47 (2015)
5. Bolt, A., de Leoni, M., van der Aalst, W.M.P.: A visual approach to spot statistically-significant differences in event logs based on process metrics. In: Nurcan, S., Soffer, P., Bajec, M., Eder, J. (eds.) CAiSE 2016. LNCS, vol. 9694, pp. 151–166. Springer, Cham (2016). https://doi.org/10.1007/978-3-319-39696-5_10
6. Bose, R.P.J.C., van der Aalst, W.M.P.: Context aware trace clustering: towards improving process mining results. In: SDM, pp. 401–412 (2009)
7. Buijs, J.C.A.M., Reijers, H.A.: Comparing business process variants using models and event logs, In: BPMDS. pp. 154–168 (2014)
8. van Eck, M.L., Lu, X., Leemans, S.J.J., van der Aalst, W.M.P.: PM^2: a process mining project methodology. In: CAiSE, pp. 297–313 (2015)
9. Joglekar, M., Garcia-Molina, H., Parameswaran, A.G.: Interactive data exploration with smart drill-down. TKDE **31**(1), 46–60 (2019)
10. Lee, D.J.L., et al.: Avoiding drill-down fallacies with VisPilot: assisted exploration of data subsets. In: IUI, pp. 186–196. ACM (2019)
11. Leemans, S.J.J., Poppe, E., Wynn, M.T.: Directly follows-based process mining: exploration & a case study. In: ICPM, pp. 25–32 (2019)
12. Leemans, S.J.J., Syring, A.F., van der Aalst, W.M.P.: Earth movers' stochastic conformance checking. In: BPM Forum, pp. 127–143 (2019)
13. Leemans, S.J.J., et al.: Results with identifying cohorts: Recommending drill-downs based on differences in behaviour for process mining. Queensland University of Technology, Technical report (2020)
14. de Leoni, M., et al.: A general process mining framework for correlating, predicting and clustering dynamic behavior based on event logs. Inf. Syst. **56**, 235–257 (2016)
15. Maaradji, A., Dumas, M., Rosa, M.L., Ostovar, A.: Detecting sudden and gradual drifts in business processes from execution traces. TKDE **29**(10), 2140–2154 (2017)
16. Marsh, D.R., Schroeder, D.G., Dearden, K.A., Sternin, J., Sternin, M.: The power of positive deviance. BMJ **329**(7475), 1177–1179 (2004)
17. Seeliger, A., Sánchez Guinea, A., Nolle, T., Mühlhäuser, M.: ProcessExplorer: intelligent process mining guidance. In: Hildebrandt, T., van Dongen, B.F., Röglinger, M., Mendling, J. (eds.) BPM 2019. LNCS, vol. 11675, pp. 216–231. Springer, Cham (2019). https://doi.org/10.1007/978-3-030-26619-6_15
18. Shabaninejad, S., et al.: Automated insightful drill-down recommendations for learning analytics dashboards. In: LAK, p. 41–46 (2020)
19. Shabaninejad, S., et al.: Recommending insightful drill-downs based on learning processes for learning analytics dashboards. In: AIED, pp. 486–499 (2020)
20. Suriadi, S., Mans, R.S., Wynn, M.T., Partington, A., Karnon, J.: Measuring patient flow variations: a cross-organisational process mining approach. In: Ouyang, C., Jung, J.-Y. (eds.) AP-BPM 2014. LNBIP, vol. 181, pp. 43–58. Springer, Cham (2014). https://doi.org/10.1007/978-3-319-08222-6_4
21. Syamsiyah, A., et al.: Business process comparison: a methodology and case study. In: Abramowicz, W. (ed.) BIS 2017. LNBIP, vol. 288, pp. 253–267. Springer, Cham (2017). https://doi.org/10.1007/978-3-319-59336-4_18
22. Taymouri, F., Rosa, M.L., Dumas, M., Maggi, F.M.: Business process variant analysis: Survey and classification. CoRR abs/1911.07582 (2019)
23. Weerdt, J.D., vanden Broucke, S.K.L.M., Vanthienen, J., Baesens, B., : Active trace clustering for improved process discovery. TKDE **25**(12), 2708–2720 (2013)

Conceptual Modeling of Business Rules and Processes

Sensemaking in Dual Artefact Tasks – The Case of Business Process Models and Business Rules

Tianwa Chen[1]([⊠]) [iD], Shazia Sadiq[1] [iD], and Marta Indulska[2] [iD]

[1] School of Information Technology and Electrical Engineering, The University of Queensland, Brisbane, Australia
tianwa.chen@uq.edu.au, shazia@itee.uq.edu.au
[2] Business School, The University of Queensland, Brisbane, Australia
m.indulska@business.uq.edu.au

Abstract. Knowledge workers often have to navigate through multiple information artefacts to complete their tasks. Business process models and business rule repositories are two such artefacts, which when presented separately are known to cause a lack of shared understanding, conflicts and redundancies that can lead to inefficiencies and even compliance breaches. Although a number of integrated modeling approaches for business processes and rules have been proposed, there is a limited knowledge on how these approaches affect worker behavior and task performance. In this paper, we present the outcomes of an exploratory study undertaken to investigate the behavior of workers performing tasks that require dual artefacts namely business processes and rules. By using a sensemaking lens, our study reveals insights into worker behavior when the representation approach and task complexity is varied. Our results contribute to a better understanding of the sense making processes in various settings and inform modeling practice.

Keywords: Sensemaking · BPMN · Business process modeling · Business rules · Eye tracking

1 Introduction

The widespread problem of information silos in organizations has resulted in knowledge workers having to navigate multiple information artefacts to complete their tasks. Such artefacts are often presented in different modalities and additionally may present overlapping, redundant or even conflicting information. Two commonly used artefacts are business process models and business rule repositories. A knowledge worker's understanding of a task will be based on both the business process model and any related business rules, which may or may not be part of the model [31]. The understanding extracted from graphical process models is focused on the temporal or logical relationships between business activities, whereas the understanding of business rules may be embedded in constraints and policies to control the behavior of the process and its activities [36]. When these two artefacts are not integrated, which is often the case, the risk of incomplete understanding is increased, resulting in compromised efficiency and potential compliance breeches.

© Springer Nature Switzerland AG 2020
G. Dobbie et al. (Eds.): ER 2020, LNCS 12400, pp. 105–118, 2020.
https://doi.org/10.1007/978-3-030-62522-1_8

To overcome such problems, prior studies have advocated integration of business rules into business process model [e.g. 15, 31, 32], and various forms of integration have been proposed, namely diagrammatic integration, integration through text annotation, and linked rules [3, 31]. Further studies have also outlined when it may not be desirable to represent related business rules within process models [e.g. 9, 32]. Despite these previous works, there is limited knowledge on how knowledge workers make sense of the various representations and what effect these approaches have on the efficacy of accomplishing a task, including quality of the task performance as well as time and effort efficiency.

In this paper, we present the outcomes of an exploratory study undertaken to investigate the behavior of workers in tasks that require dual artefacts, namely business process models and business rules. We have approached the design of the study through a sensemaking lens. Sensemaking is defined as "the process of searching for a representation and encoding data in that representation to answer task-specific questions" [25]. Although extant literature on sensemaking [33] was primarily focused on the collective construction of meaning, later studies [14] expanded the role of sensemaking to individual cognitive processes, typically separated into two distinct phases, *viz.* information foraging and task specific information processing. In the context of business process and business rule integration, the current body of knowledge does not provide an adequate explanation of sensemaking behavior as knowledge workers navigate the two artefacts with various forms of representation integration, namely text, diagrammatic and linked integration. To explore this, we consider foundational sensemaking constructs of attention (search and encoding) and memory (performance on task-specific questions), and use a number of behavioral and performance measures to operationalize these constructs through the use of eye-tracking devices in a controlled experiment. Our objective is to unpack the mechanisms by which sensemaking behavior occurs when the form of integrated representation and task complexity changes. The results of our analysis show specific behaviors with respect to the three representations for integrated business process and rule modeling and provide insights to inform modeling practice with respect to representation approach and task complexity.

2   Related Work

2.1   Sensemaking

Sensemaking has been an active area of study from different perspectives, including Human Computer Interaction (HCI) [e.g. 25], Cognitive Systems [e.g. 14], Organizational Communication [e.g. 33] and Library and Information Science [e.g. 4, 17]. These studies have contributed to the understanding of sensemaking behavior in the context of information search, learning of new domains, problem solving, situation awareness, and participation in social exchange [14, 23, 26]. A number of models capture sensemaking as multiple loops. For example, the Representation Construction Model [22] has two major loops of sensemaking. The first is the information foraging loop, which includes seeking, filtering, reading and extracting information processes, and the second is the sensemaking loop which includes iterative development of representational schemas to provide a basis for understanding and performance.

Sensemaking is also classified across collective and individual perspectives. In collective settings, the focus is on collective construction of meaning and various studies have analyzed it through organizational [33], strategic [16], entrepreneurial [7] and team structures perspective [28]. In individual settings, which is more relevant for our work, the focus is on cognitive mechanisms [14, 35] that underpin individual sensemaking. Cognitive constructs of attention and memory have a natural and strong affinity to the two phases in sensemaking models. A large body of knowledge on cognitive load theory [2, 19, 27] provides proven mechanisms through which these constructs can be operationalized. For example, measurement of attention and search behavior has been undertaken through eye tracking devices, which can capture data on visual attention, scans and fixations [6], which in turn can be used for various behavioral measurements such as cognitive load, visual association, visual cognition efficiency and intensity [24]. Similarly measurement of memory is often undertaken through performance-based measures, such as task completion time, answer correctness, and task complexity [34].

2.2 Business Process and Rule Integration

Our study considers the specific context of business process and business rule modeling – two complementary approaches for modeling business activities, which have multiple integration methods [15] to improve their individual representational capacity. In summary, the integration methods can be categorized into three approaches with distinct format and construction, namely: text annotation, diagrammatic integration and link integration [3], as shown in Fig. 1. Text annotation and link integration both use a textual expression to describe the business rules and connect them with the corresponding section of the process model. With link integration, visual links can explicitly connect corresponding rules with the relevant process section. Diagrammatic integration relies on graphical process model construction, such as, sequence flows and gateways, to represent business rules in the process model.

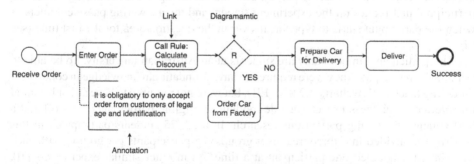

Fig. 1. Business rules integration approaches [31]

Each of these methods has strengths and weaknesses, as summarized in [3, 31], and thus a potential impact on a knowledge worker's understanding of a process.

2.3 Process Model Understanding

Prior research has shown that a variety of factors can affect the understanding of a process, including both process model factors, as well as human factors [29]. Cognitive load [27], and visual cognition [5] have been used as measures of process model understanding. Eye activity is one of the physiological variables that can be used as a technique to reflect the changes in cognition [5, 19]. Through the use of eye tracking technology, one can directly collect eye movement data and capture objective metrics such as pupillary response and fixation durations to indicate the correlation with cognitive function [2], and use indicators such as fixation in each area of interest (AOI), to identify the exact area that draws the attention of the participant. Although there is a long history on the use of eye tracking technology in medical and psychological studies [13], the use of such technology in the business process modeling context is quite recent. To exemplify a few, [21] defined the notion of Relevant Region and Scan-path to prove that Relevant Region is correlated to the answer during question comprehension. In [11], researchers used eye tracking technology to measure and assess user satisfaction in process model understanding. In [20], the use of eye tracking technology enabled researchers to identify the visual cues of coloring and layout that can improve performance in process model understanding. Recent work has also explored reading patterns in hybrid processes of DCR-HR [1], as well as on domain and code understanding tasks [12]. Our work builds on these works in the use of eye tracking data to study sense-making behaviour in dual-aretefact tasks.

3 Study Design

In this study, we use an experimental research design. In line with sensemaking foundations, we segment the experiment into two phases, namely a searching and encoding phase (we term this as the *understanding* phase) and a task specific information processing phase (termed the *answering* phase). The understanding phase commences when the participant first fixates on the experiment screen, and the answering phase commences when the participant starts to type the answer in the question area for the first time (see Fig. 2).

The participants in our study are students at an Australian university. To be able to voluntarily participate, they were required to have foundational knowledge in conceptual modeling (such as flowcharts, UML or ER), but were not required to have any substantial knowledge of business process or rule modeling. Eligible participants were offered a $30 voucher for taking part in this research. In total, 75 students participated in this experiment, divided into three treatment groups (25 participants per group), with each experiment conducted one participant at a time. As in other similar experiments [10, 18], a sample size of 20 to 30 participants per group is considered adequate.

The experiment data consists of a pre-experiment questionnaire, eye tracking log data and task performance data. The eye tracking data was collected through a Tobii Pro TX300 eye tracker[1], which captures data on fixations, gaze, saccades, etc., with

---

[1] For more specifications of eye tracker, please visit https://www.tobiipro.com/product-listing/tobii-pro-tx300/

timestamps. To capture sensemaking behavior we used measurements related to fixation durations and frequencies to study the searching and encoding behavior in the *understanding* phase. To study the behavior related to task specific information processing behavior in the *answering* phase, we included task performance data in the analysis and used measurements related to AOI specific fixations, as well as transitions between AOIs.

3.1 Instruments

The experiment instruments included a tutorial, the treatments and a questionnaire. Each group of participants was first provided a BPMN tutorial and was then offered a model using one of the three different rule integration approaches. Our business process modeling language of choice was BPMN 2.0, due to its wide adoption and standing as an international standard. We encouraged each participant to ask questions during the tutorial session, to ensure their readiness for the experiment.

To ensure group balance, we used a pre-experiment questionnaire to capture participants' prior knowledge and basic demographics, which we used to distribute participants across groups to avoid accidental homogeneity. The data of three participants whose eye movements failed to be properly recorded by Tobii eye tracker was discarded. We collected initial participant data including BPMN familiarity (1-3, from most unfamiliar to most familiar), Study major (0 and 1, Engineering and Science related majors were coded as 1, Business and Humanities related majors coded as 0), Language (0 and 1, first language is English being 1), Gender (0 and 1, female being 1, male being 0). Our results based on the Kruskal-Wallis[2] test indicate that there were no significant differences between the three groups in any aspect, that is identified gaze ($p = 0.694$), tutorial time ($p = 0.375$), BPMN familiarity ($p = 0.929$) and study major ($p = 0.933$).

In the treatment, we used the three integration approaches (one per each treatment group). The scenarios of the model and rules originated from a travel booking diagram included in OMG's BPMN 2.0 documentation[3]. We ensured, through multiple revisions, that we created informationally equivalent models for all three integration approaches. Due to space limitations, the models cannot be included in the paper, but the complete experiment instruments are available for download[4]. We ensured all confounding factors were constant, including same eye-tracking lab equipment and tutorial content. We did not set a limit on the experiment duration nor a word count limit on participants' answers. The model was adjusted to ensure consistency of format for each of the integration approaches, while providing some diversity in terms of constructs and coverage, as summarized in Table 1, which indicates the types of constructs a participant will have to review to answer each question and the span of the question (a participant may have to navigate only a specific section of the process model to answer the question (local), or the whole process (global)). This diversity allowed us to gain further insights into

---

[2] Kruskal-Wallis test is a non-parametric method when there are more than two groups.

[3] Model originated from a travel booking diagram in OMG's BPMN 2.0 examples can be viewed in http://www.omg.org/cgi-bin/doc?dtc/10-06-02

[4] The experiment materials can be downloaded from https://www.dropbox.com/sh/zfw5uq0jyja8 tt6/AADx2fm8Y9SSqAkGwTDKD7ITa?dl=0

the relationship between integration approaches and task complexity (reflected by the coverage of the model required to answer a particular question).

Table 1. Comparison of questions

Question	Model Constructs	Model Coverage
Q1	Sequence, AND gateways	Local area
Q2	Sequence, AND gateways	Local area
Q3	Sequence, AND gateways, XOR gateways	Global and local areas

3.2 Setting

The experiment was conducted in full screen mode and complete models were displayed without the function of zooming in or scrolling. The visibility of the experiment text and diagrams were examined carefully, with all text and diagrams being clear from a distance of 1.2 m. All experiments were conducted in the same lab with the same eye tracker.

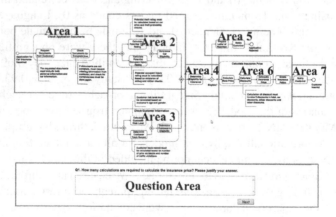

Fig. 2. Visual experiment design

We used multiple Areas of Interest (AOI) to capture eye movements (these were used for analysis and were invisible to participants). As shown in Fig. 2, for models featuring text annotation and diagrammatic integration, the screen was divided into 8 areas: seven different process model areas and a question area (which showed one question at a time). For models featuring link integration, there was an additional ninth area for rules, which displayed the corresponding business rules when participants clicked on each "R" icon in the model. Each question answer is related to different process areas. For local questions Q1 and Q2, the answer is related to area 6 and area 2, respectively. For Q3 (global question), the answer is related to areas 1, 5 and 7.

4 Results

4.1 Scanning and Attention

We note that, overall, the differences in fixation and visit durations of participants between the three groups is not significant ($p = 0.946$ and $p = 0.884$ respectively based on Kruskal-Wallis tests). However, by using mean fixation duration as a measure, a question wise analysis indicates that there is some fluctuation in attention between the three groups, as shown in Fig. 3.

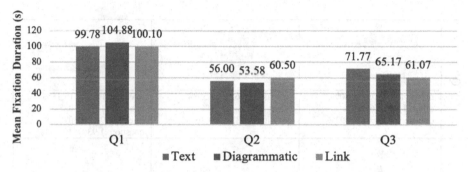

Fig. 3. Mean fixation duration of each question for all participants

The mean fixation durations for Q1 are the highest among the three questions for all groups, followed by a reduced mean fixation for Q2, and a less increase in mean fixation for link group compared with text and diagrammatic groups for Q3. While mean fixation durations are limited in the insights they offer, heat maps can effectively reveal the focus of visual attention for multiple participants, especially for specific AOIs. Such maps show how participants' gaze is distributed over the stimulus, although they cannot present the sequence of their gaze. In order to provide a snapshot in limited space, in Fig. 4 we show the respective heat maps in the understanding phase (phase 1) for participants who answered all questions correctly, i.e., best performers. The heat maps are generated on the basis of absolute fixation durations. The radius is 50px, with an adjusted scale to 0.5 s maximum (corresponding to deep red) in line with the threshold of deep processing [8]. The mean fixation duration and percentage proportion of fixation count for the area relevant to the question, other areas i.e., AOIs not relevant to the question, and the question area AOI is also shown in Fig. 4. For link representation the measurements for the rule area are also provided.

To uncover the significant differences in scanning and attention behavior between the three representations we conducted a series of statistical tests, contrasting specifically the differences as task complexity changes, where Q1 and Q2 represent local questions and Q3 represents a more complex global question. We conducted the tests for best performers (also shown in the heat maps in Fig. 4) as well as all performers. For numerical data (mean fixation duration and proportion of transition of frequency), we used the Shapiro-Wilk test[5] to check whether it is normally distributed. For non-parametric data,

---

[5] The Shapiro-Wilk test is a test of normality.

we used the Kruskal-Wallis test for our analysis. If the result was significant, we used pairwise comparisons of Dunn's test[6] to rank the groups in a pair-wise comparison. For parametric data, we used Levene's test[7] for homogeneity of variance to check the assumption of equal variance. If the condition was met, we used one-way analysis of variance (ANOVA) to further test the difference of means. If the test result was significant, we used the Tukey's HSD test[8] to further compare the difference in each pair of groups. For ordinal data (number of correct answers of each participant), we used Kruskal-Wallis test. If the result was significant, we used the same post hoc test to rank the groups in pair-wise comparison. We used 0.05 as the significance threshold for all tests.

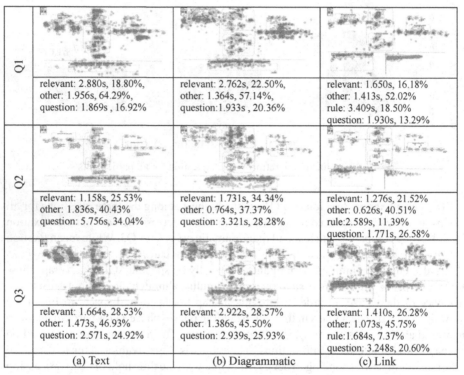

	(a) Text	(b) Diagrammatic	(c) Link
Q1	relevant: 2.880s, 18.80%, other: 1.956s, 64.29%, question: 1.869s , 16.92%	relevant: 2.762s, 22.50%, other: 1.364s, 57.14%, question:1.933s , 20.36%	relevant: 1.650s, 16.18% other: 1.413s, 52.02% rule: 3.409s, 18.50% question: 1.930s, 13.29%
Q2	relevant: 1.158s, 25.53% other: 1.836s, 40.43% question: 5.756s, 34.04%	relevant: 1.731s, 34.34% other: 0.764s, 37.37% question: 3.321s, 28.28%	relevant: 1.276s, 21.52% other: 0.626s, 40.51% rule:2.589s, 11.39% question: 1.771s, 26.58%
Q3	relevant: 1.664s, 28.53% other: 1.473s, 46.93% question: 2.571s, 24.92%	relevant: 2.922s, 28.57% other: 1.386s, 45.50% question: 2.939s, 25.93%	relevant: 1.410s, 26.28% other: 1.073s, 45.75% rule:1.684s, 7.37% question: 3.248s, 20.60%

Fig. 4. Heat maps and AOI measures in phase 1 for best performers. Larger and clear version can be downloaded from https://www.dropbox.com/sh/zfw5uq0jyja8tt6/AADx2fm8Y9SSqAkGwT DKD7ITa?dl=0

For best performers, there is no significant difference in the mean fixation duration in model area across groups for local questions ($p = 0.195$ and $p = 0.109$ for Q1 and Q2 respectively; Kruskal-Wallis test). The model area includes all AOIs except the question

---

[6] Dunn's test is a non-parametric multiple comparison post-hoc test of Kruskal-Wallis test.

[7] Levene's test is an inferential statistic used to assess the equality of variances for a variable calculated for two or more groups.

[8] Tukey's HSD is a post-hoc analysis of ANOVA that can be used to find means that are significantly different from each other.

area (for link representation it also includes the rule area). For the global Q3, compared with text and diagrammatic groups, the results indicate that best performers in the link group have the lowest mean fixation duration on the model area ($p = 0.014$; Kruskal-Wallis test). Further, using post-hoc pairwise comparisons of Dunn's test, the link group shows a significantly lower mean fixation duration than the text ($p = 0.036$) as well as the diagrammatic group ($p = 0.009$), but text and diagrammatic group results do not differ significantly ($p = 0.434$). In other words, participants in the link group require less effort to interpret the model, even when question complexity increases.

For all participants, not just the best performers, there is significant difference in the mean fixation durations in the model area across groups for Q1 and Q3 in phase 1. On local question Q1, link group has the lowest mean fixation duration in the model area ($p = 0.000$; Kruskal-Wallis test). Given the result of post-hoc pairwise comparisons of Dunn's test, the link group has a significantly lower mean fixation duration than text annotation ($p = 0.000$) and diagrammatic integration ($p = 0.000$), but text annotation and diagrammatic integration do not differ significantly ($p = 0.436$). However, there is no significant difference found for local question Q2 ($p = 0.890$). On global question Q3, there is a significant difference on mean fixation duration in the model area across groups ($p = 0.010$). Given the result of post-hoc pairwise comparisons of Dunn's test, link group has a significantly lower mean fixation duration than diagrammatic group ($p = 0.003$), but no significant difference was found between link and text groups ($p = 0.051$), or between text and diagrammatic groups ($p = 0.306$).

From the above results we note that link representation requires less attention, as measured through mean fixation duration, indicating favorable performance from a scanning and attention perspective. For all participants this is observed in the initial question (Q1) and again as task complexity increases in the global question (Q3). For best performers, the lower level of attention required is again noted as task complexity increases, reflected through global question (Q3).

In addition to fixation behavior, the gaze paths of participants also provide insights into scanning and attention behavior, in particular how the movement across AOIs occurs in the different groups. However, the limitation of gaze plots is that it is hard to compare aggregated gaze plots across groups. We use process diagrams created with a process mining tool[9] to expose sequences of fixations and saccades. Although these diagrams for phase 1 are not included in the paper due to space limitations (see phase 2 diagrams in the next section), we provide some summary observations here. First, we noted that the transitions in Q1 have large loops across the other, relevant, and question areas, indicating that even the best performers need to reinspect areas they have already scanned as they develop an understanding of the model. In comparison, in Q2, the proportion of transition frequency was largest between the *question and relevant area* for all groups, possibly indicating an improvement in attention and hence a reduction in mental effort, although our data did not show a statistically significant difference. In Q3, we observe an increase in transition loops overall. In particular, we note that the transition loops are diverse in the text and link group compared with the diagrammatic group, which has the highest transition frequency between *relevant area and question area*. This might imply that the

---

[9] Process Mining and Automated Process Discovery Software for Professionals – Fluxicon Disco. https://fluxicon.com/disco/

separation in text and link approaches (through annotations and rule area respectively) may afford some reduction in mental effort, compared to the diagrammatic integration approach. Despite these observations, no statistically significant difference was observed in the transition frequencies between the groups.

4.2 Task Specific Information Processing

The question answering phase in our study commences when the participant starts to type in the question area. This phase represents task specific information processing behavior – i.e. the sensemaking loop. To distinguish behavior between various levels of task performance (i.e. correctness of the answers provided), we categorize answers based on completeness of activities and rules (no missing content) and minimality (no redundancy). Figure 5 (a) shows the number of correct answers. Overall, our results indicate there is no significant difference between the three groups in terms of understanding accuracy ($p = 0.579$; Kruskal-Wallis test).

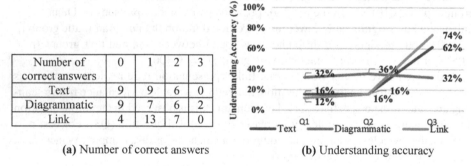

Number of correct answers	0	1	2	3
Text	9	9	6	0
Diagrammatic	9	7	6	2
Link	4	13	7	0

(a) Number of correct answers   **(b)** Understanding accuracy

Fig. 5. Task performance

However, as per Fig. 5 (b), we observe an increase in the percentage of questions answered correctly for the text and link treatment group, while understanding accuracy in diagrammatic treatment group remains relatively stable. While task performance results provide an important perspective, we further investigated the answering phase (with respect to fixations as well as transitions) to reveal the sensemaking behavior that resulted in the respective task performance. We illustrate our results with the help of process diagrams (Fig. 6), where we have aggregated all the *other* areas for the purpose of illustration. The transition values indicate transition frequency proportion and the activity values indicate visit frequency proportion. For the global question Q3, the relevant areas include area 1, 5 and 7, hence we aggregated the proportion of the frequency of transitions on all relevant areas for Q3.

Our results indicate that on global question Q3 (phase 2), compared with text and diagrammatic groups, the link group has the lowest mean fixation duration on the model area ($p = 0.016$; Kruskal-Wallis test). The link group has a lower mean fixation duration than text annotation ($p = 0.005$; post-hoc pairwise comparisons of Dunn's test), but link and diagrammatic integration and text annotation and diagrammatic integration do

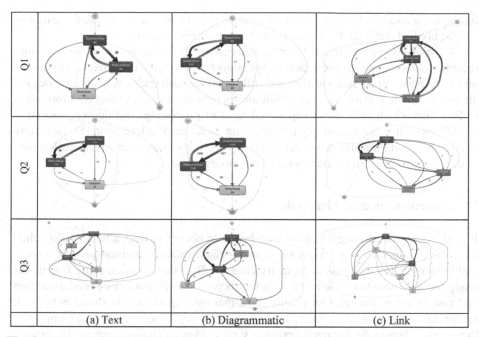

| | (a) Text | (b) Diagrammatic | (c) Link |

Fig. 6. Sequence of fixations in answering phase for best performers. Larger and clear version can be downloaded from https://www.dropbox.com/sh/zfw5uq0jyja8tt6/AADx2fm8Y9SSqAkGwT DKD7ITa?dl=0

not differ significantly ($p = 0.118$ and $p = 0.440$, respectively). Hence, link representation requires the least attention, indicating favorable performance from a task specific information processing perspective as task complexity increases.

For all groups, we observe reduced transitions (proportion of transition frequency count) in the answering phase as compared to the understanding phase, between *relevant and other* area[10]. Similarly, the transitions between *question and other* area is reduced for all groups[11]. It is important to note the presence of an additional rule area in the link group. All questions in the link group show reduced transitions between *rule and other* area[12] and reduced transitions between *rule and relevant* area.[13] We further note that the link group showed the best accuracy in Q3 (Fig. 5 (b)). We would expect such transition

---

[10] The differences between the two phases for Q1, Q2 and Q3 are: text group: 27.57%, 17.86%, and 12% respectively; diagrammatic group: 29.18%, 22.67% and 7.38%; link group: 2.24%, 3.87% and 8.91%.

[11] The differences between the two phases for Q1 and Q2 are: text group: 19.06% and 30.18% respectively; diagrammatic group: 12.60% and 7.18% respectively; link group: 23.49% and 18.74% respectively. In Q3, the reduction is not observed for text and link groups (−2% and − 4.49%, respectively), while the diagrammatic group has a slight reduction (0.84%).

[12] The difference of reduced transition between *rule and other* area is 22.75%, 1.32%, and 1.9% for Q1, Q2 and Q3 respectively.

[13] The difference of reduced transition between *rule and relevant* area is 0.99%, 0.98%, and 4.12% for Q1, Q2 and Q3 respectively.

frequency reductions to occur if efficiency gains were being made. Despite these trends, we did not find statistically significant differences across the groups.

Additionally, we note that the represented best performers undertake deep processing (number of long fixations above 500 ms) in both phases (i.e., the mean fixation durations on the relevant, other, and question and (rule area) for each question in both phases are all above 500 ms). Prior research differentiates between mere scanning of information (<500 ms), which indicates a superficial level of processing, and deeper processing (>500 ms) that is connected to purposeful consideration of information [8]. Our study results show that even after the understanding phase is complete, participants still engage in deep processing of information in the answering phase.

5   Conclusions and Outlook

In this paper we investigated how user behavior occurs in dual artefact tasks when the form of integrated representation of the artefacts (namely business process models and business rules) and task complexity changes. By using a sensemaking lens in our study we were able to delineate the behavior between developing model understanding and task accomplishment. Our results show that link representation shows better task performance in terms of accuracy as well as efficiency, especially as task complexity increases. Additionally our results provide some evidence that diagrammatic integration has better task performance on local questions in terms of accuracy, but also requires the most effort in the initial information foraging (understanding) phase. As task complexity increases, diagrammatic representation arguably requires the most effort indicated by the highest transition frequency between question and relevant areas. These results have implications for business process and rule integrated modeling frameworks, and may also provide guidance for users' training and work allocation decisions. In addition, our study provides a methodological contribution by offering an approach to visualize the different behaviors inherent in the two phases of sensemaking.

Our study is not without limitations. We only considered basic constructs in business process models whereas advanced loop and nesting structures may introduce further complexities in sensemaking. The limitation of the eye tracking software limits the granularity of the AOI which causes some level of imprecision in AOI level metrics. Complementary approaches such as cued retrospective 'thinking-out-loud' [30] could also help to provide further explanations on the sensemaking behavior. In this paper, we have mostly analyzed and presented the results of performers who answered the questions correctly. Analysis of behavior of other participants as well as change in behavior over longer tasks with greater variability in task complexity will help further reveal insights into sensemaking, and may especially be valuable for training and work allocation purposes.

References

1. Abbad Andaloussi, A., Burattin, A., Slaats, T., Petersen, A.C., Hildebrandt, T.T., Weber, B.: Exploring the understandability of a hybrid process design artifact based on DCR graphs. In: Reinhartz-Berger, I., Zdravkovic, J., Gulden, J., Schmidt, R. (eds.) BPMDS/EMMSAD -2019. LNBIP, vol. 352, pp. 69–84. Springer, Cham (2019). https://doi.org/10.1007/978-3-030-20618-5_5
2. Chen, F., Zhou, J., Wang, Y., Yu, K., Arshad, S.Z., Khawaji, A., Conway, D.: Robust Multimodal Cognitive Load Measurement. HIS. Springer, Cham (2016). https://doi.org/10.1007/978-3-319-31700-7
3. Chen, T., Wang, W., Indulska, M., Sadiq, S.: Business process and rule integration approaches - an empirical analysis. In: Weske, M., Montali, M., Weber, I., vom Brocke, J. (eds.) BPM 2018. LNBIP, vol. 329, pp. 37–52. Springer, Cham (2018). https://doi.org/10.1007/978-3-319-98651-7_3
4. Dervin, B.: Sense-making theory and practice: an overview of user interests in knowledge seeking and use. J. Knowl. Manage. 2(2), 36–46 (1998)
5. Duchowski, A.T.: Eye tracking methodology. Theory Pract. 328(614), 2–3 (2007)
6. Duchowski, A.T.: Gaze-based interaction: a 30 year retrospective. Comput. Graph. 73, 59–69 (2018)
7. Ganzin, M., Islam, G., Suddaby, R.: Spirituality and entrepreneurship: the role of magical thinking in future-oriented sensemaking. Organ. Stud. 41(1), 77–102 (2020)
8. Glöckner, A., Herbold, A.K.: An eye-tracking study on information processing in risky decisions: evidence for compensatory strategies based on automatic processes. J. Behav. Decision Making 24(1), 71–98 (2011)
9. Governatori, G., Shek, S.: Rule based business process compliance. In: Proceedings of the RuleML2012@ECAI challenge, CEUR workshop proceedings, p. 874 (2012)
10. Haji, F.A., Rojas, D., Childs, R., de Ribaupierre, S., Dubrowski, A.: Measuring cognitive load: performance, mental effort and simulation task complexity. Med. Educ. 49(8), 815–827 (2015)
11. Hogrebe, F., Gehrke, N., Nüttgens, M.: Eye tracking experiments in business process modeling: agenda setting and proof of concept. Enterprise modelling and in-formation systems architectures (EMISA 2011) (2011)
12. Ioannou, C., Nurdiani, I., Burattin, A., Weber, B.: Mining reading patterns from eye-tracking data: method and demonstration. Software Syst. Model. 19(2), 345–369 (2019). https://doi.org/10.1007/s10270-019-00759-4
13. Just, M.A., Carpenter, P.A.: Eye fixations and cognitive processes. Cogn. Psychol. 8(4), 441–480 (1976)
14. Klein, G., Moon, B., Hoffman, R.R.: Making sense of sensemaking 2: a macrocognitive model. IEEE Intell. Syst. 21(5), 88–92 (2006)
15. Knolmayer, Gerhard., Endl, Rainer, Pfahrer, M.: Modeling processes and workflows by business rules. In: van der Aalst, W., Desel, J., Oberweis, A. (eds.) Business Process Management. LNCS, vol. 1806, pp. 16–29. Springer, Heidelberg (2000). https://doi.org/10.1007/3-540-45594-9_2
16. Kurtz, C.F., Snowden, D.J.: The new dynamics of strategy: sense-making in a complex and complicated world. IBM Syst. J. 42(3), 462–483 (2003)
17. Marchionini, G.: Search, sense making and learning: closing gaps. Information and Learning Sciences (2019)
18. Meghanathan, R.N., van Leeuwen, C., Nikolaev, A.R.: Fixation duration surpasses pupil size as a measure of memory load in free viewing. Front. Hum. Neuro-sci. 8, 1063 (2015)

19. Paas, F., Tuovinen, J.E., Tabbers, H., Van Gerven, P.W.: Cognitive load measurement as a means to advance cognitive load theory. Educ. Psychologist **38**(1), 63–71 (2003)
20. Petrusel, R., Mendling, J., Reijers, H.A.: Task-specific visual cues for improving process model understanding. Inf. Software Technol. **79**, 63–78 (2016)
21. Petrusel, R., Mendling, J.: Eye-tracking the factors of process model comprehension tasks. In: Salinesi, C., Norrie, M.C., Pastor, O. (eds.) CAiSE 2013. LNCS, vol. 7908, pp. 224–239. Springer, Heidelberg (2013). https://doi.org/10.1007/978-3-642-38709-8_15
22. Pirolli, P., Card, S.: The sensemaking process and leverage points for analyst technology as identified through cognitive task analysis. In: Proceedings of International Conference on Intelligence Analysis, vol. 5, pp. 2–4. McLean, VA, USA (2005)
23. Pirolli, P., Russell, D.: Introduction to this special issue on sensemaking. Hum. Comput. Interact. **26**(1), 1–8 (2011)
24. Rayner, K.: Eye movements in reading and information processing: 20 years of research. Psychol. Bulletin **124**(3), 372 (1998)
25. Russell, D.M., Stefik, M.J., Pirolli, P., Card, S.K.: The cost structure of sensemaking. In: Proceedings of the INTERACT 1993 and CHI 1993 Conference on Human Factors in Computing Systems, pp. 269–276 (1993)
26. Stefik, M., et al.: The knowledge sharing challenge: the sensemaking white paper: Parc (1999)
27. Sweller, J.: Cognitive load theory. In: Psychology of Learning and Motivation, vol. 55, pp. 37–76. Elsevier (2011)
28. Talat, A., Riaz, Z.: An integrated model of team resilience: exploring the roles of team sensemaking, team bricolage and task interdependence. Personnel Review (2020)
29. Turetken, O., Rompen, T., Vanderfeesten, I., Dikici, A., van Moll, J.: The effect of modularity representation and presentation medium on the understandability of business process models in BPMN. In: La Rosa, M., Loos, P., Pastor, O. (eds.) BPM 2016. LNCS, vol. 9850, pp. 289–307. Springer, Cham (2016). https://doi.org/10.1007/978-3-319-45348-4_17
30. Van Gog, T., et al.: Uncovering the problem-solving process: cued retrospective reporting versus concurrent and retrospective reporting. J. Exper. Psychol. Appl. **11**(4), 237–244 (2005). https://doi.org/10.1037/1076-898X.11.4.237
31. Wang, W., Indulska, M., Sadiq, S.W.: Cognitive efforts in using integrated models of business processes and rules. In: CAiSE Forum, pp. 33–40 (2016)
32. Wang, W., Indulska, M., Sadiq, S., Weber, B.: Effect of linked rules on business process model understanding. In: Carmona, J., Engels, G., Kumar, A. (eds.) BPM 2017. LNCS, vol. 10445, pp. 200–215. Springer, Cham (2017). https://doi.org/10.1007/978-3-319-65000-5_12
33. Weick, K.E.: Sensemaking in Organizations, vol. 3. Sage (1995)
34. Wood, R.E.: Task complexity: definition of the construct. Organizational Behav. Hum. Decision Processes **37**(1), 60–82 (1986)
35. Zhang, P., Soergel, D.: Cognitive mechanisms in sensemaking: a qualitative user study. J. Assoc. Inf. Sci. Technol. (2020)
36. Zur Muehlen, M., Indulska, M., Kittel, K.: Towards integrated modeling of business processes and business rules. In: ACIS 2008 Proceedings, p. 108 (2008)

Do Declarative Process Models Help to Reduce Cognitive Biases Related to Business Rules?

Kathrin Figl[1] (✉) ⓘ, Claudio Di Ciccio[2] ⓘ, and Hajo A. Reijers[3] ⓘ

[1] University of Innsbruck, Innsbruck, Austria
kathrin.figl@uibk.ac.at
[2] Sapienza University of Rome, Rome, Italy
diciccio@di.uniroma1.it
[3] Utrecht University, Utrecht, The Netherlands
h.a.reijers@uu.nl

Abstract. Declarative process modeling languages, such as DECLARE, represent processes by means of temporal rules, namely constraints. Those languages typically come endowed with a graphical notation to draw such models diagrammatically. In this paper, we explore the effects of diagrammatic representation on humans' deductive reasoning involved in the analysis and compliance checking of declarative process models. In an experiment, we compared textual descriptions of business rules against textual descriptions that were supplemented with declarative models. Results based on a sample of 75 subjects indicate that the declarative process models did not improve but rather lowered reasoning performance. Thus, for novice users, using the graphical notation of DECLARE may not help readers properly understand business rules: they may confuse them in comparison to textual descriptions. A likely explanation of the negative effect of graphical declarative models on human reasoning is that readers interpret edges wrongly. This has implications for the practical use of business rules on the one hand and the design of declarative process modeling languages on the other.

Keywords: Business rule representation · Declarative process modeling · Reasoning · Diagrams · Cognition

1 Introduction

Visual diagrammatic process models are widely used to analyze, design, and improve business processes. As process orientation and process awareness are guiding paradigms for organizational innovation, standardization, and information systems design, they attract high attention in research and practice. Against this background, human comprehensibility of diagrammatic process models is a highly relevant issue. Many researchers have recently turned to empirically investigate factors that influence their comprehensibility with the final goal to optimize the fit between process model design and human cognitive capabilities [1].

In the last decade, a paradigm to represent processes has gained momentum, which is an alternative to the classical, state-transition based one: the declarative specification

© Springer Nature Switzerland AG 2020
G. Dobbie et al. (Eds.): ER 2020, LNCS 12400, pp. 119–133, 2020.
https://doi.org/10.1007/978-3-030-62522-1_9

of processes. Declarative process models dictate the business rules that the process must comply with in the form of constraints. In comparison with procedural approaches, which consist of "closed" representations (i.e., only the represented process runs are allowed), declarative approaches yield "open" representations (i.e., every run is allowed, unless it violates a constraint). Declarative languages such as DECLARE provide a repertoire of constraint templates that come bundled with a graphical representation [2, 3]. The understandability of declarative process models, however, is still a matter of debate [4].

The main aim of this paper is to investigate the effect that declarative process models have on the way humans reason. To that extent, we report in this paper on our controlled experiment in which we compare textual descriptions of business rules against textual descriptions supplemented with DECLARE models. Interestingly, our results indicate that the DECLARE models do not improve but rather decrease the reasoning performance of participants. In fact, the use of supplementary DECLARE models did not help novice users understand business rules better, but seemed to have confused them in comparison to textual descriptions alone. The evidence from this study points at the difficulty of novice users to master the meaning of such models and use these effectively. This motivates further research into more intuitive notations for declarative constraints.

2 Related Work

Considerable research work has been conducted on the comprehension of process models [5], However, relatively limited research has taken place to investigate the effect of process models on *deductive reasoning*. In such an approach, the "mental process of making inferences that are logical" [6, p. 8] based on process models is compared against a baseline (such as, for instance, a textual narrative of the process). One of the few examples of this type of research is the work of Boritz et al. [7], who report the superiority of a narrative process version over a process model for deductive reasoning tasks while identifying and assessing control risks of the process. Our work can be placed in this tradition.

Relevant from the viewpoint of investigating declarative process models more generally is the work by Haisjackl and Zugal [8]. They compared graphical and textual declarative process models and reported lower comprehension performance for the textual representation. However, the textual notation they used was not a natural language narrative version of the declarative process model, but a domain-specific textual language. More recently, López et al. [9] introduced a tool that allows users to highlight in a process textual description the passages that describe constraints. The tool automatically generates the corresponding visual elements of the DCR Graphs declarative notation. To improve the comprehensibility of declarative process models, De Smedt et al. [10] introduced an approach to uncover "hidden" behavioral restrictions, which are not explicitly visible when reading a declarative model yet are entailed by the interplay of the rules. Other research efforts have been made to investigate the effect of using gateway symbols in process models on human reasoning [11]. Further studies have identified specific difficulties of reasoning on the basis of process models, e.g., high interactivity of model elements and the presence of control-flow patterns as loops heighten the cognitive difficulty and error-proneness of reasoning tasks [12].

The present study differs from prior experiments in that we compare textual narratives with textual narratives that are supplemented with declarative process models. More specifically, we address the research question whether DECLARE models, when used in addition to if-then clauses in written language, help humans understand conditional if-then arguments in business rules. The idea, here, is that a graphical, declarative process model may serve as a cognitive short-hand for processing the textual clauses. From a cognitive research viewpoint, it is already known that typical logical fallacies may occur in conditional reasoning with text [6]. However, it is not known whether the same fallacies do occur when using DECLARE models or whether these visual representations actually help readers to understand business rules avoiding cognitive fallacies. Answering this question is relevant for a variety of tasks in which humans use process models, e.g., for checking compliance of process execution traces with a process model.

3 Theoretical Background

Business Rules and Deductive Reasoning. Business rules are generally defined as "statements that aim to influence or guide behavior and information in the organization." [13, p. 52] Documentation of business rules is relevant to make them transparent and to avoid rule conflicts. In practice, when using natural language to document business rules, conditional if-then statements (if *cause*, then *effect*) are made to describe causal relationships [14]. Formal logics define whether a conditional inference based on given premises is true. A deduction is valid "if its conclusion must be true given that its premises are true" [15, p. 372]. Table 1 gives an example of the four standard conditional inferences based on a business rule [16].

Table 1. Examples of valid and invalid conditional inferences.

	Affirmative	Negative
Valid	If a rental car is returned late, then a penalty is charged The rental car is returned late Therefore, a penalty was charged **"Modus ponens"**	If a rental car is returned late, then a penalty is charged A penalty is not charged Therefore, the rental car was not returned late **"Modus tollens"**
Invalid	If a rental car is returned late, then a penalty is charged A penalty is charged Therefore, the rental car was returned late **"Affirmation of the consequent"**	If a rental car is returned late, then a penalty is charged The rental car is not returned late Therefore, a penalty was not charged **"Denial of the antecedent"**

However, "natural" human reasoning may not always be sound. Humans are prone to typical misinterpretations of if-then statements. For instance, they may interpret the business rule "If the product is deliverable in less than two days, then the product is ordered from the supplier" in a probabilistic way (it is usually this way, but not always). They may also re-interpret the rule biconditionally as "If the product is ordered from the supplier that means the product has been deliverable in less than two days." From a logical standpoint, these are both logical fallacies. If we take an example from everyday life with the two premises "If it's raining then the streets are wet," then the commutation of conditionals "If the streets are wet then it's raining" would also be logically incorrect. People are still likely to make this logical error, because in reality it might be a good rule of thumb since wet streets dry fast after rain. Depending on content-effects, people are likely to misinterpret conditional relationships [17]. A biconditional misunderstanding leads to the logical fallacy known as *"affirmation of the consequent."*

Representation of Business Rules. Business rules may be found as tacit knowledge in the heads of employees (unwritten), may be part of guidelines (varying from informal to formal), part of enterprise models, are implemented in an information system, or are part of a rules engine (highly formalized) [18]. As most organizations use text and graphical languages to document their processes, business rules are likely to be found in practice in textual descriptions as well as in diagrams.

The Business Rules Manifesto [19] advises to separate business models from processes and states: "Rules should be expressed declaratively in natural-language sentences for the business audience." However, natural language may be ambiguous and not precise enough to document business rules. Traditional means to document business rules are structured English (a subset of natural language), decision tables, and decision trees [20]. Process modeling languages focus on representing the control flow of activities, including decisions. It is possible to implicitly model business rules in a process model embedded in the control flow logic. In a procedural approach, a business rule on, for example, a credit limit may be included in various processes (e.g., new order, change order, change costumer credit limit), while in the business rule approach it might be defined in a rulebase of a rule management system, which all processes can then use [18]. As process models are typically procedural, they do not offer the same modeling convenience for documenting business rules as declarative rule specification languages do. Therefore, research efforts have been undertaken to integrate and combine process models and rule modeling languages [21]. In recent years, researchers have proposed approaches to visually model business rules as an extension to existing process modeling languages [22].

In this paper, we focus on the expression of business rules in declarative process models. A primary goal of this paper is to assess whether declarative process models help humans to better understand business rules in comparison to natural language if-then statements. In particular, we like to understand how a declarative process model as a visual aid influences human cognitive processes.

In general, the cognitive fit between an information representation and the specific task is necessary—a representation may never be optimal in all cases but should relate to the task at hand [23]. While researchers have argued that "once the logical form of the problem has been extracted from a diagram, the same chain of deductions based on the same rules of inference [in mind] should unfold" [15, p. 372]. There are also a variety of theoretical perspectives that suggest superiority of diagrams over narrative text for human reasoning. For instance, externalizations in the form of diagrams can reduce working memory overload due to computational off-loading [24]. Knowledge put down in a diagram as "external storage" need not be maintained in the working memory. Also, both the visual and verbal working memory subsystem can be used when working with process models [25]. There are also hints that the visual structure of process models is closer to human mental models than text [26]. Based on the high importance of mental models for reasoning [27], this may also lead to easier reasoning with process models than with text. We expect similar effects for representing rules in the context of business process models.

Constraints for Declarative Process Models. Declarative process models define the behavior of a process by means of constraints, i.e., temporal rules that specify the conditions under which activities may, must, or cannot be executed. A well-known declarative process modeling language is DECLARE [2]. This language provides a repertoire of (constraint) *templates*, i.e., parametrized rules. The major benefit of using templates is that analysts do not have to be aware of the underlying logic-based formalization to understand the models. They work with the graphical or textual representation of templates, while the underlying formulae remain hidden. The repertoire of templates of DECLARE is based upon the seminal work of Dwyer, Avrunin, and Corbett [28] on the most recurring property specification patterns for the verification of finite-state systems in software engineering. Typical examples of DECLARE templates are *Participation* (x) and *Precedence* (x,y). The former applies the *Participation* template on the parametric activity x (the *target*) and states that x must occur in every run of the process. The latter applies the *Precedence* relation template on activities y (*activation*) and x (*target*), imposing that if y occurs, then x must have occurred earlier in the same run. Intuitively, activations determine the circumstances triggering the constraint (the *if* part of an if-then statement); targets are the consequential conditions being imposed upon the occurrence of the activations (the *then* part of an if-then statement).

A declarative process model is a set of constraints that must all be satisfied during the process run. The graph built from the network of graphical elements denoting the DECLARE constraints is called a DECLARE model [3]. Table 2 illustrates the list of DECLARE templates that will be considered in the context of this paper. For the sake of clarity, we adopt the abbreviated names *Participation*(x) and *AtMostOne*(x), introduced in [29], to indicate the *Existence*$(1, x)$ and *Absence*$(2, x)$ templates, respectively. In particular, we consider in this paper at least a DECLARE template for each of the categories illustrated in [29]: *Participation* and *AtMostOne* (predicating on the number of activity occurrences); *Init* and *Last* (on the position of activity occurrences); *Response* (imposing a temporal order between activation and target); *ChainResponse* (forcing an immediate occurrence of the target after the activation); *Precedence* (reverting the temporal order imposed by *Precedence*); *AlternatePrecedence* (which enforces *Precedence* by avoiding the recurrence of the activation); *ChainPrecedence* (forcing an immediate occurrence of the target before the activation); *Succession* (assigning both activities the role of activation and target, as it stems from the conjunction of *Response* and *Precedence*); *NotCoExistence* (dictating the mutual absence of activities, rather than their co-occurrence). Notice that templates like *Succession*(x, y) and *NotCoExistence*(x, y) are biconditional; therefore, both parameters x and y play the role of activation and target.

Table 2. Some DECLARE templates.

Template	Act.	Tar.	Description	Graphical notation
AtMostOne(x)		x	Activity x occurs at most once	
Participation(x)		x	Activity x occurs at least once	
Init(x)		x	Activity x always occurs first	
Last(x)		x	Activity x always occurs last	
Responded Existence(x,y)	x	y	If x occurs, then y must occur, too	
Response(x,y)	x	y	If x occurs, then y must occur afterwards	
ChainResponse(x,y)	x	y	If x occurs, then y must occur immediately afterwards	
Precedence(x,y)	y	x	If y occurs, then x must have occurred beforehand	
Alternate Precedence(x,y)	y	x	If y occurs, then x must have occurred beforehand, and no other y can have recurred in between	
ChainPrecedence(x,y)	y	x	If y occurs, then x must have occurred immediately beforehand	
Succession(x,y)	x, y	x, y	If x occurs, then y must occur afterwards; if y occurs, then x must have occurred beforehand	
NotCoExistence(x,y)	x, y	x, y	If x occurs, then y cannot occur; if y occurs, then x cannot occur	

4   Research Model and Hypotheses

Having laid out the relevant theoretical foundation to examine textual and diagrammatic representations of business rules, we present our research model in Fig. 1. We expect the *process rule representation* to influence *deductive reasoning performance* of a person (as measured in terms of the percentage of correctly solved reasoning tasks, the time taken to solve those tasks, and the occurrence of reasoning fallacies).

In detail, we advance the following hypotheses concerning business rules in an if-then form. We hypothesize that reasoning based on text and supplementary graphical process models, i.e., a mixed model, may deviate from reasoning based on natural text alone. Based on the fact that rules are made *explicit* within the declarative process model that is part of the mixed model, one can assume that people are less likely to misinterpret the underlying logic than in the setting of having to rely purely on text. Therefore, we first propose that: Declarative process models in combination with textual representations support higher reasoning performance compared to the use of textual representations on their own (**H1**).

We do think that the positive effects of using a declarative process model as part of a mixed model should be qualified. It is conceivable that opposing effects may also occur

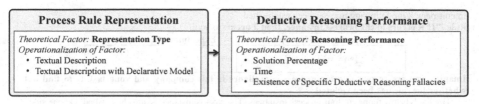

Fig. 1. Research model.

for the use of certain model structures. According to Britton and Jones [30], uni-directed arrow symbols (as the directed edges used in declarative process models) are mostly interpreted as "if... and only if", while bidirectional arrow symbols are interpreted as "if... then". Therefore, it may happen that directed edges – which occur in DECLARE models – are perceived as "semantically perverse", i.e., "a novice reader would be likely to infer a different (or even opposite) meaning from its appearance" [31, p. 764]. Such a misunderstanding would increase the probability of a biconditional misinterpretation of rules in declarative process models. Thus, we propose that: Rules in declarative process models with directed edges that are combined with a textual representation are more likely to be misinterpreted as biconditional than rules as textual representation alone (**H2**).

5 Research Method

To test the hypotheses, we conducted a fully randomized, controlled laboratory experiment. The research design included one between-group factor business rule representation with two levels: textual vs. text with a diagram. In particular, we compare the results yielded by textual representations with those achieved with *mixed* text-diagram representation. Our rationale is that comparing pure text with declarative models alone (without additional descriptions) would bias our results with factors that are out of scope. Specifically, these factors are (1) the efficacy with which users were trained with the graphical notation of DECLARE, and (2) the personal inclination of users towards textual or visual means. Instead, we aim at investigating whether the graphical notation of rules adds value over the use of pure text. Therefore, we resort to declarative process models that are enriched with textual descriptions. This representation style is well-known; its benefits are described, for example, by Recker et al. [32].

Materials and Procedures. We employed business rules from different scenarios in two different types of reasoning tasks: card-based Wason selection tasks and model-based comprehension tasks. Experimental materials are available under the following link: http://kathrinfigl.com/declare-questionnaire/. The first type of reasoning tasks for participants were Wason selection tasks [33, 34]. The Wason selection task is a famous puzzle often used in deductive reasoning research. The participants are confronted with a business rule in the form "if P then Q." They get cards (with "P"/"not-P" on one side and "Q"/"not Q" on the other side) and have to select all cards that need to be turned over to test the business rule and to find out whether the business rule is verified or not. Figure 2 shows the Wason selection task for the *RespondedExistence* template.

In company X the following rule has been established: Rule: "**If K occurs in the process instance, then J occurs as well.**"	
Experimental Group 1	**Experimental Group 2**
[no visual model]	K ●——— J

Imagine you are responsible for process compliance in this company and your task is to find out whether the rule has been violated.

The cards below represent four process instances. The process instance is already finished. On one side of each card is written whether or not the K did occur, on the other side whether or not J did occur.

Your task: Please select all the cards that you have to turn over (i.e., all of which you need to know the information on the back) in order to find out whether the rule was violated.

Not Selected:	Selected Cards:
K did occur *[Modus ponens (valid); card should be selected]*	chosen
J did occur *[Affirming the consequent (invalid); card should not be selected]*	chosen
K did not occur *[Denying the antecedent (invalid); card should not be selected]*	chosen
J did not occur *[Modus tollens (valid); card should be selected]*	chosen

Fig. 2. Wason selection task for the compliance check of DECLARE constraints.

In the Wason selection tasks, we could focus on an isolated representation of single constraints. We chose those five constraints having defined activation (if) and target (then), regardless of the temporal perspective (*RespondedExistence*), or containing ordering criteria (*Response* and *Precedence*), also including immediate sequencing (*ChainResponse, ChainPrecedence*).

In addition to the five Wason selection tasks, we used two declarative process models with comprehension tasks: one dealt with the issue of handling orders (Fig. 3), the other with handling invoices (Fig. 4). For the "order handling" and "invoice handling" process models we asked 9 and 14 questions respectively, requiring the participants to classify process runs as "correct" or "incorrect" (or select "I don't know"). Although we used an online survey tool, we also provided the two models on paper to ensure readability. Figure 3 and Fig. 4 show the mixed text-diagram representation. In the textual experimental group, we left out the DECLARE models; we only gave the remaining textual parts to the participants. In the following, we present some examples of process runs for the "order handling" process model, which we will henceforth represent as finite sequences delimited by angular brackets. For instance, ⟨"Receive order", "Locate ordered goods", "Dispatch ordered good", "Mark order as completed"⟩ is a correct process run. By contrast, ⟨"Receive order", "Dispatch ordered good", "Mark order as 'out of stock'", "Mark order as completed"⟩ is incorrect because *NotCoExistence*("Dispatch ordered good", "Mark order as 'out of stock'") is violated. Also, ⟨"Locate ordered goods", "Dispatch ordered good", "Mark order as completed"⟩ is incorrect too, because *Init*("Receive order") is violated.

Participants. In this study, 74 information systems students from the Vienna University of Business and Economics participated voluntarily in the context of course units. We

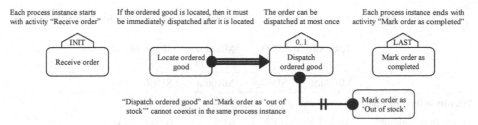

Fig. 3. DECLARE model of an order handling process mixed with textual descriptions.

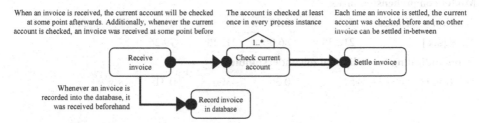

Fig. 4. DECLARE model of an invoice handling process mixed with textual descriptions.

chose to involve information systems students as they serve as an adequate proxy for novice corporate users of business process models. Therefore, they are good target users of declarative process modeling notations. We recruited students from a Bachelor course on enterprise modeling and a Masters course in Business Process Management. This helped to ensure that the students that participated would already have some experience on the use of conceptual, graphical models, in particular event-driven process chains or BPMN models.

6 Results

To compare the experimental groups, we performed analyses of variance. Table 3 illustrates the results. We can see that no differences between experimental groups could be found concerning solution percentages in the Wason selection tasks. Yet there was a significant effect of the presence of DECLARE models (in addition to the textual description) on the solution percentage in the model comprehension tasks. In contrast to the expectation behind H1, participants could answer more model comprehension tasks correctly in the text-only setting (71%) than with an additional DECLARE model (64%). Time did not differ significantly between the groups in both task types.

We also tested for differences between the text-only and mixed text-diagram condition of the solution percentage of the four standard conditional inferences (modus ponens, modus tollens, affirmation of the consequent and denial of the antecedent). No significant differences could be detected either. In general, 'modus ponens' and 'denial of the antecedent' were easiest (correctly identified by 74% and 63% of participants); 'affirmation of the consequent' (55% of participants did solve this task correctly; thus, 45% committed this fallacy) and modus tollens were most difficult (53% solution percentage).

Table 3. Influence of DECLARE models on deductive reasoning.

	Text only (n = 38)		Mixed text + diagram (n = 37)		Stat. test
	M/count	SD/%	M/count	SD/%	
Wason selection tasks					
Solution percentage	61%	0.17	61%	0.16	*n.s.*
Time [sec]	59.73	25.1	77.01	76.64	*n.s.*
Model comprehension tasks					
Solution percentage	71%	0.17	64%	0.16	F = 4.03, p = 0.05
Time [sec]	212.38	86.06	212.10	79.26	
Items indicating biconditional misunderstanding					
Solution percentage	51%	0.38	43%	0.31	*n.s.*

The DECLARE models that were part of the mixed representations did not help to prevent any of the logical errors. However, since absence of evidence is not evidence of absence, an additional graphical representation could have qualitatively altered the reasoning of participants. To avoid a Type II error (i.e. failing to reject an erroneous null hypothesis), we calculated a post hoc power analysis with the G*Power tool [35]. The power $(1-\beta)$ of a statistical test "is the complement of β, which denotes the Type II or beta error probability of falsely retaining an incorrect H0" [35, p. 176]. In the case of a one-sided t-test for two independent means, the samples sizes (group 1 = 38, group 2 = 37), an error probability of $\alpha = 0.05$ and medium effect size $d = 0.5$, the power $(1-\beta) = 0.69$. Since conventionally a power of $1-\beta = 0.8$ should be reached [36], a higher sample size might be needed to detect a medium effect that might be relevant to practice.

To test hypothesis **H2**, we identified four items in which biconditional misunderstanding could occur due to process model parts with directed edges. Table 3 illustrates the mean solution percentage for these three items alone (but does not report time, because times were not recorded item-wise). **H2** had to be rejected since the mean solution percentage was not significantly different. Still, we want to discuss results for one item of the "order handling" process model. It is interesting to note that the process run ⟨"Receive order," "Dispatch ordered good," "Mark order as completed"⟩ was identified for the "order handling" process model as correct by only 32% of participants. Thus, 67% of participants answered this question wrongly. A likely explanation for this misunderstanding in our opinion is the biconditional misinterpretation of the business rule "If the ordered good is located, then it must be immediately dispatched after it is located." This item was significantly (F = 4.29, p = 0.03) answered correctly more often by participants in the text-only group (42%) than in the group having text and a DECLARE model at hand (19%). Thus, the DECLARE model was in this case even more misleading than the textual if-then statement.

A more detailed analysis of the items in which the two groups differed suggests that DECLARE models were probably read as if they were procedural process models, especially if directed edges were used. Notice that all participants already had experience with procedural process models. Table 4 reports some examples of reasoning tasks based on the "invoice handling" process model (Fig. 4). Visual elements used in procedural process models to depict control flow – directed edges/arrows – can easily be associated with a causal meaning [37] and look similar to directed edges used in DECLARE models. This could explain why participants were confused in the text + DECLARE condition and performed worse than those who only received the textual description.

Table 4. Influence of DECLARE models on selected reasoning tasks.

Process runs for reasoning tasks	Verif.	Text only (n = 38)		Text + DECLARE model (n = 37)		Stat. test
		Mean	SD	Mean	SD	
("Receive invoice", "Record invoice in database", "Check current account")	valid	82%	0.39	51%	0.51	t = 2.88, p = 0.005
("Receive invoice", "Record invoice in database")	invalid	71%	0.46	49%	0.51	t = 2.00, p = 0.05
("Receive invoice", "Check current account", "Record invoice in database")	valid	74%	0.45	38%	0.49	t = 3.30, p = 0.001

7 Discussion and Limitations

Our study set out to empirically evaluate the effect of a declarative process model on human reasoning, focusing in particular on common reasoning fallacies regarding if-then constructs. Our results, while preliminary, suggest that DECLARE models do not help readers to better understand given textual business rules. Rather, they lead to more reasoning mistakes.

Boekelder et al. [38] have compared similar representations of if-then statements in their experiment on operating control panels. Contrary to our results, they found that participants took more time for reading and solving the tasks when using lists (comparable to our textual condition) than when using flowcharts (comparable to a procedural process model), but no significant performance differences were found. A possible explanation for the contrasting results might be that they compared if-then-else statements instead of if-then statements and procedural instead of declarative visual representations. This conjecture finds support in the experimental results described by Haisjackl et al. [39], which indicate that the graphical notation elements that are similar in both procedural and declarative process modeling languages, though different semantics, cause considerable confusion.

As this was the first study addressing the effect of declarative process models on deductive reasoning, we deemed internal validity more important than external validity [40]. We used artificially created snippets of declarative process models and relatively small and straightforward process models to isolate the factor of interest. External validity in the sense of generalizing the findings to more complex process scenarios will thus be limited. Additionally, our choice of a student sample limits generalizability as, e.g., results are not generalizable to users who are already experts in using the DECLARE graphical notation. The main reason to use a student sample was to avoid an experimental bias of prior experience with process modeling. Although students had prior experience with event-driven process chains or BPMN models, we do not think that it would have been advantageous to take participants without any experience with process models to avoid misinterpretations of directed edges in DECLARE models. After all, the semantic association of directed edges with sequence/causality and their interpretation as "if...and only if" is naturally and culturally shaped [31]. Similarly, participants have been familiar with ER modelling and, therefore, might have recognized the use of cardinalities in the symbols for *AtMostOne* and *Participation* more easily than participants without any prior modeling experience.

8   Implications for Research and Practice

The presented work contributes to the advancement of modeling language evaluation methods. It demonstrated how data collection methods from the cognitive science field of deductive reasoning research as the Wason selection task could be used to assess model comprehension empirically.

The research design and the preliminary results presented in this paper serve as a contribution to further open the black box of human understanding of process models. It adds to the growing body of empirical work on process model comprehension. An implication of the results for practitioners includes exercising caution when tasks involve reasoning on the basis of business rules, and formal correctness of human inferences is important. There is a variety of real, practical situations in which human reasoning based on business rules is relevant and cannot or should not be automated. For instance, employees may need to analyze or check conditions for decision points, and they may give instructions on how to enforce specific business rules. Similarly, business process analysts may assess and evaluate differences between rules in existing process models and their application in real-world process instances. However, human actors might use rules of thumb and, as the low solution percentages demonstrated, logical errors do occur. The evidence from this study further emphasizes the importance of developing understandable visual modeling approaches to business rules, to support enterprise modeling practice.

The results gave a hint that readers of a process model tend to misinterpret declarative process models as procedural models, and are less likely to look at the embedded business rules in isolation. Such results support the idea to further separate business decision and process logic to avoid human reasoning fallacies.

9 Conclusion

The present study was designed to determine the effect of declarative process models on human reasoning. By taking a look at various potential deductive reasoning fallacies, this work denotes an essential extension to the literature on process model comprehensibility. Overall, our preliminary findings suggest that declarative process models do not qualitatively alter human reasoning and visual process models do not outperform written language in supporting humans to understand conditional if-then arguments. Rather, they may even confuse readers. As business rules can help organizations to achieve their goals, e.g., by reducing costs or improving communication, their proper understanding by all human actors involved is crucial.

References

1. Houy, C., Fettke, P., Loos, P.: On the theoretical foundations of research into the understandability of business process models. In: European Conference on Information Systems, Tel Aviv (2014)
2. van der Aalst, W.M.P., Pesic, M.: DecSerFlow: towards a truly declarative service flow language. In: Bravetti, M., Núñez, M., Zavattaro, G. (eds.) WS-FM 2006. LNCS, vol. 4184, pp. 1–23. Springer, Heidelberg (2006). https://doi.org/10.1007/11841197_1
3. Bose, R.P.J.C., Maggi, F.M., van der Aalst, W.M.P.: enhancing declare maps based on event correlations. In: Daniel, F., Wang, J., Weber, B. (eds.) BPM 2013. LNCS, vol. 8094, pp. 97–112. Springer, Heidelberg (2013). https://doi.org/10.1007/978-3-642-40176-3_9
4. Fahland, D., et al.: Declarative versus imperative process modeling languages: the issue of understandability. In: International Workshop BPMDS and International Conference EMMSAD, pp. 353–366 (2009)
5. Figl, K.: Comprehension of procedural visual business process models. Bus. Inf. Syst. Eng. **59**, 41–67 (2017)
6. Johnson-Laird, P.N.: Deductive reasoning. Wiley Interdisciplinary Rev. Cogn. Sci. **1**, 8–17 (2010)
7. Boritz, J.E., Borthick, A.F., Presslee, A.: The effect of business process representation type on assessment of business and control risks: diagrams versus narratives. Issues Account. Educ. **27**, 895–915 (2012)
8. Haisjackl, C., Zugal, S.: Investigating differences between graphical and textual declarative process models. In: Iliadis, L., Papazoglou, M., Pohl, K. (eds.) CAiSE 2014. LNBIP, vol. 178, pp. 194–206. Springer, Cham (2014). https://doi.org/10.1007/978-3-319-07869-4_17
9. López, H.A., Debois, S., Hildebrandt, T.T., Marquard, M.: The process highlighter: from texts to declarative processes and back. BPM (Dissertation/Demos/Industry) **2196**, 66–70 (2018)
10. De Smedt, J., De Weerdt, J., Serral, E., Vanthienen, J.: Discovering hidden dependencies in constraint-based declarative process models for improving understandability. Inf. Syst. **74**, 40–52 (2018)
11. Recker, J.: Empirical investigation of the usefulness of gateway constructs in process models. European J. Inf. Syst. **22**, 673–689 (2013)
12. Figl, K., Laue, R.: Influence factors for local comprehensibility of process models. Int. J. Hum Comput Stud. **82**, 96–110 (2015)
13. Steinke, G., Nickolette, C.: Business rules as the basis of an organization's information systems. Ind. Manage. Data Syst. **103**, 52–63 (2003)
14. Ross, R.G.: What's wrong with if-then syntax for expressing business rules ~ one size doesn't fit all. Bus. Rules J. **8** (2007)

15. Bauer, M.I., Johnson-Laird, P.N.: How diagrams can improve reasoning. Psychol. Sci. **4**, 372–378 (1993)
16. Byrne, R.M.J., Johnson-Laird, P.N.: If and the problems of conditional reasoning. Trends Cogn. Sci. **13**, 282–287 (2009)
17. Cummins, D., Lubart, T., Alksnis, O., Rist, R.: Conditional reasoning and causation. Memory Cogn. **19**, 274–282 (1991)
18. Object Management Group: How Business Rules Relate to Business processes from a business person's point of view. Business Rules Symposium, Minneapolis (2010)
19. Ross, R.G.: The Business Rules Manifesto. Business Rules Group (2003)
20. Vessey, I.: Cognitive fit: a theory-based analysis of the graphs versus tables literature. Decision Sci. **22**, 219–240 (1991)
21. Zur Muehlen, M., Indulska, M.: Modeling languages for business processes and business rules: a representational analysis. Inf. Syst. **35**, 379–390 (2010)
22. Knuplesch, D., Reichert, M., Ly, L.T., Kumar, A., Rinderle-Ma, S.: Visual modeling of business process compliance rules with the support of multiple perspectives. In: Ng, W., Storey, V.C., Trujillo, J.C. (eds.) ER 2013. LNCS, vol. 8217, pp. 106–120. Springer, Heidelberg (2013). https://doi.org/10.1007/978-3-642-41924-9_10
23. Vessey, I., Galletta, D.: Cognitive fit: An empirical study of information acquisition. Information Systems Research **2**, 63–84 (1991)
24. Scaife, M., Rogers, Y.: External cognition: How do graphical representations work? Int. J. Hum.-Comput. Stud. **45**, 185–213 (1996)
25. Baddeley, A.D.: Working memory. Science **255**, 556–559 (1992)
26. Glenberg, A.M., Langston, W.E.: Comprehension of illustrated text: Pictures help to build mental models. J. Memory Lang. **31**, 129–151 (1992)
27. Johnson-Laird, P.N.: Mental models and human reasoning. Proc. Nat. Acad. Sci. **107**, 18243–18250 (2010)
28. Dwyer, M.B., Avrunin, G.S., Corbett, J.C.: Patterns in property specifications for finite-state verification. In: International Conference on Software Engineering, pp. 411–420. IEEE (1999)
29. Di Ciccio, C., Maggi, F.M., Montali, M., Mendling, J.: Resolving inconsistencies and redundancies in declarative process models. Inf. Syst. **64**, 425–446 (2017)
30. Britton, C., Jones, S.: The untrained eye: How languages for software specification support understanding in untrained users. Hum.-Comput. Interact. **14**, 191–244 (1999)
31. Moody, D.L.: The "physics" of notations: towards a scientific basis for constructing visual notations in software engineering. IEEE Trans. Software Eng. **35**, 756–779 (2009)
32. Recker, J., Green, P.: How do individuals interpret multiple conceptual models? a theory of combined ontological completeness and overlap. J. Assoc. Inf. Syst. **20**, 1 (2019)
33. Liberman, N., Klar, Y.: Hypothesis testing in wason's selection task: social exchange cheating detection or task understanding. Cognition **58**, 127–156 (1996)
34. Wason, P.C.: Reasoning. In: Foss, B. (ed.) New Horizons in Psychology. Penguin, London (1966)
35. Faul, F., Erdfelder, E., Lang, A.-G., Buchner, A.: G* power 3: a flexible statistical power analysis program for the social, behavioral, and biomedical sciences. Behav. Res. Methods **39**, 175–191 (2007)
36. Fox, N., Mathers, N.: Empowering research: statistical power in general practice research. Family Pract. **14**, 324–329 (1997)
37. Tversky, B., Zacks, J., Lee, P., Heiser, J.: Lines, blobs, crosses and arrows: diagrammatic communication with schematic figures. In: Anderson, M., Cheng, _.P., Haarslev, V. (eds.) Diagrams 2000. LNCS (LNAI), vol. 1889, pp. 221–230. Springer, Heidelberg (2000). https://doi.org/10.1007/3-540-44590-0_21

38. Boekelder, A., Steehouder, M.: Selecting and switching: some advantages of diagrams over tables and lists for presenting instructions. IEEE Trans. Professional Commun. **41**, 229–241 (1998)
39. Haisjackl, C., et al.: Understanding declare models: Strategies, pitfalls, empirical results. Software Syst. Model. **15**, 325–352 (2016)
40. Straub, D.W., Boudreau, M.-C., Gefen, D.: Validation guidelines for is positivist research. Commun. Assoc. Inf. Syst. **13**, 380–427 (2004)

Modeling Behavioral Deontic Constraints Using UML and OCL

Antonio Vallecillo[1]([✉])[iD] and Martin Gogolla[2][iD]

[1] ITIS Software, Universidad de Málaga, Málaga, Spain
av@lcc.uma.es
[2] University of Bremen, Bremen, Germany
gogolla@uni-bremen.de

Abstract. Business rules specify the required or desirable states of affairs or behavior of IT systems, and typically involve deontic constraints that must be adequately specified to enable their appropriate representation and effective analysis. Such deontic constraints focus on the permitted actions and obligations of the agents to carry them out. In this paper we present a proposal to explicitly specify dynamic deontic constraints in UML and OCL so that, on the one hand, they can guide and restrict the system behavior and, on the other hand, allow us to reason about such deontic behavior, including accountability analysis.

Keywords: Business rules · Deontic constraints · UML · OCL

1 Introduction

The digital world confronts us with a multitude of computer systems for everyday tasks like paying a hotel bill, delivering a parcel or booking a hotel room. In this context, the need for explicitly formulating and managing moral obligations seems to be more necessary than ever [11]; for example, when ordering commercial products with the help of virtual assistants like Alexa, or reviewing a scientific report for a close colleague or student. According to the Webster's dictionary, the term *deontic* means "of or relating to moral obligation," while *deontic reasoning* refers to the ability to recognize and understand social or business rules and what happens when the rules are transgressed. In this context, we understand a *deontic constraint* as a requirement on how a part of the real world (the universe of discourse) and a digital system are related to each other, as well as what obligations are induced from the real world on the digital system, and the other way around. In particular, we understand such deontic constraints as ways of expressing how a digital system is used and applied in the real world so that moral or business obligations are respected.

In the IT domain, business rules specify the required or desirable states of affairs or behavior of an IT system, and typically include constraints of *alethic* and *deontic* modalities [21]. Alethic rules impose *necessities*, which cannot be violated (e.g., the age of a person cannot be negative). Deontic rules impose

G. Dobbie et al. (Eds.): ER 2020, LNCS 12400, pp. 134–148, 2020.
https://doi.org/10.1007/978-3-030-62522-1_10

obligations, which might be violated even though they should not (e.g., borrowed books must be returned within one week). In practice, many business rules are of a deontic rather than alethic nature [7], and normally involve moral obligations.

Deontic constraints are closely related to the concept of *accountability*, too, whereby objects representing actors in the system are responsible for what they do (or don't do) and must be able to give a satisfactory reason for it. In other words, actors are liable for both their actions and inactions, in case they do not fulfil one of their obligations, or transgress the system rules. In this context, the actions of the objects must respond to their *duties*, and the actors must be *permitted* to accomplish them. Accountability enables that system actions can be traced back to the legally accountable parties concerned.

Some conceptual modeling approaches such as SBVR [21], ORM [8] or the RM-ODP [12] provide powerful representations of deontic constraints, and even define mappings to their corresponding UML representations. They have successfully been used to specify policies and other deontic constraints in several domains, such as eHealth [19,20]. However, most of these notations are based on modal logics, which require specialized knowledge and dedicated analysis toolkits, mainly due to their declarative nature.

In this paper we present a proposal to explicitly specify dynamic (i.e., behavioral) deontic constraints in UML and OCL so that, on the one hand, they can guide and restrict the behavior of the system, and on the other hand, allow deontic reasoning about such a behavior, including accountability analysis. For this we use an operational style of specification, based on (*a*) *deontic tokens*, which reify deontic permissions and obligations as objects that can be explicitly handled in pre- and postconditions of operations [13,16], and (*b*) *filmstrip models*, which reify the system actions as objects that enable the representation of the system behavior as a sequence of *snapshots*, each one describing a particular state of the system [3]. The proposal is illustrated with an exemplary case study of a student grading system.

The structure of this paper is as follows. After this introduction, Sect. 2 presents the running example, and briefly describes the related concepts and technologies used in this work. Then, Sect. 3 presents our proposal and how it has been implemented, as well as the kinds of analyses that are possible for deontic reasoning and accountability analysis of the system. Finally, Sect. 4 discusses related work, and Sect. 5 concludes with an outline on future works.

2   Background

2.1   Running Example

Suppose a student grading system, in which *teachers* grade the *reports* delivered by *students*. A student must first register with a teacher, who assigns a report to the student. Once the student completes the report, it is delivered to the teacher, who will grade it giving a mark between 1 and 5. Once marked, both the student and the teacher can consult the mark as many times as they wish. The metamodel of that system is shown in the center of Fig. 1. It is composed of three main classes: **Student**, **Teacher** and **Report**. The actions that can be carried out by students are specified by the operations **register()**, **deliver()** and **viewMark()**. In turn, operations **grade()** and **viewMark()** represent the possible actions of teachers.

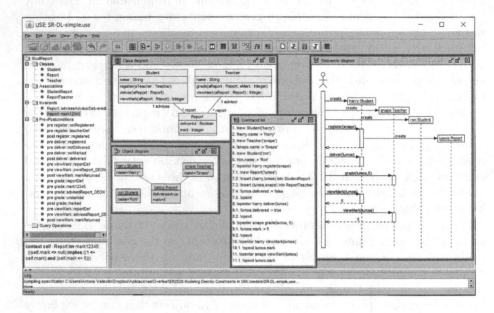

Fig. 1. The student grading system example.

Figure 1 shows a screenshot of the environment provided by the USE (UML-based Specification Environment) modeling tool [14]. The left column displays the model containment tree. The canvas contains a class diagram with the system model; an object diagram (below the class diagram) with the state of the system at one moment in time, with 4 instances; the command list that has been carried out to achieve this state (expressed in the language SOIL [1]), and a sequence diagram showing the execution of these commands.

The following list describes some examples of deontic constraints that can apply to that system:

1. Students are permitted to register with any teacher who does not have a report from them that is still pending to grade.
2. Students registered with a teacher have the permission, and the obligation, to deliver the report to that teacher.
3. Teachers have the permission, and the obligation, to grade all reports that they advise and that are delivered to them.
4. Students are permitted to view only the marks of their reports, but only once these have been graded.
5. Teachers are permitted to view only the marks of the reports they have graded, but only once they have given the mark.

2.2   Deontic Logic

Deontic logic [23] is a branch of modal logic that refers to the *permitted, obligatory*, and *forbidden* actions in a system.

Deontic constraints on logic propositions ϕ are normally expressed by means of modal operators $\mathbf{O}(\phi)$ and $\mathbf{P}(\phi)$, which can be read, respectively, as "It is obligatory that ϕ" and "It is permitted that ϕ". These two deontic operators complement their alethic counterparts, the traditional temporal logic operators *always* ($\square$), which implies necessity, and *eventually* ($\lozenge$), which refers to possibility. Alethic rules cannot be violated, while deontic ones could, even although they ought not. Modal negation rules also apply to deontic operators, namely, $\neg\mathbf{O}(\phi) \equiv \mathbf{P}(\neg\phi)$ and $\neg\mathbf{P}(\phi) \equiv \mathbf{O}(\neg\phi)$. Prohibitions are sometimes considered, too, although they are just the negation of permissions.

An alternative specification of deontic constraints, in particular those that refer to the dynamics of the system, uses *deontic tokens* [12,13,16,17]. Following an object-oriented style of specification, tokens are associated to the system objects that are capable of executing behavior. These objects become responsible for carrying out the appropriate actions to fulfil the corresponding obligations. Similarly, agents can also have associated permissions or prohibitions.

One of the advantages of Deontic logic is that it can also be used to represent and reason about the *accountability* of the different parties of a system, since we should be able to assign responsibility to objects and, more importantly, to know who to blame when problems or contract violations occur. Thus we are able to verify if the behavior of the system conforms to the deontic constraints, i.e., that no forbidden actions occur, and that all obligations are eventually discharged. *Liability* can be traced in case of problems, and parties become *accountable* for their actions — and also for their inactions.

2.3   Filmstrip Models

Filmstrip models [3] enable the explicit representation of the behavior of a set of objects as a sequence of *snapshots*, each one describing a particular state of the system. Snapshots are connected through other objects (*operation calls*) that represent the execution of the operation that causes the state change, i.e., that makes the state of the system transit from one snapshot to the next one.

The idea behind this materialization of filmstrip models is the *reification* of the operation calls, so they become objects that can be subject to explicit representation and analysis. This way, any UML model that describes the structure of the system in terms of class diagrams and OCL invariants, and the behavior of the system by means of operations and pre- and postconditions on them, can be transformed into an equivalent "filmstrip model" that only involves structural aspects (class diagrams and invariants). This transformation is fully automated by the USE tool [10], and enables the use of analysis to reason about the behavioral aspects of the system [5,9].

Figure 2 shows the metamodel of the student grading system enriched with the appropriate classes and associations. Basically, each operation is transformed

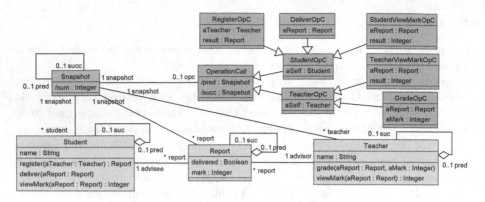

Fig. 2. The Filmstrip Specification of the Student Grading system.

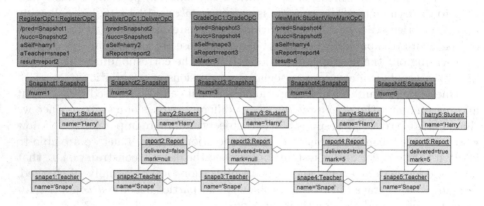

Fig. 3. A sequence of operation calls described by a filmstrip.

into a class of kind `OperationCall`, which has an attribute `aSelf` that describes the object on which the operation is called, and the rest of the operation parameters. The states through which the system goes during its execution are represented by objects of class `Snapshot`, which are linked to the relevant system objects in the state represented by the snapshot. State transitions are described by `OperationCall` objects, which relate pairs of snapshots: the one that describes the state of the system when the operation is invoked (directly linked to the `OperationCall` object, and also pointed to by derived attribute `pred` of the operation call), and the snapshot that describes the state of the system after the operation, i.e., the effect of the operation. This latter snapshot corresponds to the successor snapshot of the initial one, which is also pointed to by derived attribute `succ` of the operation call object. Although other representations of filmstrip models are possible, this has proved to be the most effective one [2].

Figure 3 shows one possible execution of the student grading system using the corresponding filmstrip model, where a student registers with a teacher, delivers a report, the teacher grades it, and the student consults the mark. This is the same behavior that was described by the sequence diagram represented in Fig. 1. Note how the reflexive aggregations added in the filmstrip model to classes Student, Report and Teacher, are used to relate the instances that represent the same objects but in different snapshots.

3   Dynamic Deontic Constraints and Their Accountability

This section describes our proposal, which is based on the reification of deontic tokens, the use of pre- and postcondition of operations to specify deontic rules, and the use of filmstrip models to reason about the system.

3.1   Reification of Deontic Concepts

To represent deontic concepts we will follow the approach described in [16,17], which proposes an object-oriented treatment of deontic rules in which obligations and permissions are *reified* as *deontic tokens*, which are first-class objects held by agents in the system. Tokens can be used in expressing Obligations, i.e., what must be done (*Burdens*), and Permissions, i.e., what can be done (*Permits*). If an object holds a Permit, it has the corresponding permission, and if it holds a Burden, it has the corresponding obligation. Burdens are discharged, and cease to exist if the associated conditions are satisfied. This approach was the one adopted by ISO to represent deontic concepts in the RM-ODP Enterprise Language [12] and its specification in UML [13,15].

Deontic tokens can be used in pre- and postconditions of operations to check that the appropriate agents hold the permissions to carry them out, and to discharge the appropriate burdens when the operations are accomplished.

One of the advantages of USE is that it provides a high-level textual action language, called SOIL [1] that enables the behavioral specification of UML models. SOIL extends the OCL notation with imperative constructs, including the creation of instances and links, the assignment of values to attributes, and the imperative specification of bodies of operations. SOIL specifications are executable, which enables the system analysis by means of simulations.

In addition to the execution of sequences of operations, the explicit representation of obligations and permissions as tokens enables a different style of specification where the focus is not only on the concrete steps and processes, but on discharging the objects' obligations. In other words, there is a shift from concentrating purely on behavior, towards concern with system state and future behavior, focusing on the obligations that must be discharged; who is responsible for discharging them, and who is allowed to do that and when [16]. We will discuss this type of behavioral specification later in Sect. 3.3.

3.2   Modeling Deontic Behavior with Pre- and Postconditions

In order to model the behaviour of objects taking into account deontic constraints, we will model system actions by means of operation calls, and deontic

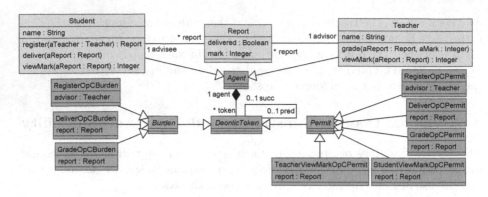

Fig. 4. The specification of the *Student Grading* system, with deontic tokens.

constraints by means of pre- and postconditions on these operations. For example, Fig. 4 shows a UML class diagram for the specification of the *Student Grading* system, with deontic tokens. Permits and burdens can be defined for every possible operation of the system agents.

The following listing shows how tokens are used to specify the behavior of the system operations, indicating the permissions that the corresponding agents are required to have in order to execute them, and how the operations change the permissions and burdens of the agents participating in the action after their execution. This required behavior is naturally expressed in terms of pre- and postconditions.

```
register(aTeacher:Teacher) : Report
  pre   notRegistered: not Report.allInstances->exists(r|
          r.advisee=self and r.advisor=aTeacher)
  pre   teacherDef: aTeacher<>null
  post  registered: Report.allInstances->one(r| r.advisee=self and
          r.advisor=aTeacher and not r.delivered and
          r.mark=null and result=r)
-- DEONTIC pre- and post conditions:
-- PRE: the student has the permission to register (no burden required):
  pre   canRegister : self.token->select(p |
          p.oclIsKindOf(RegisterOpCPermit) and
          p.oclAsType(RegisterOpCPermit).advisor=aTeacher)->notEmpty()
-- POST: The student is relieved from the burden to register,
--   but she adquires the burden to deliver, and the permit to do so
--   Moreover, the student permission to register a report to the same
--   teacher is revoked until the report is marked
  post  burdenToRegisterReleased: self.token->select(p |
          p.oclIsKindOf(RegisterOpCBurden) and
          p.oclAsType(RegisterOpCBurden).advisor=aTeacher)->isEmpty()
  post  mustDeliver: self.token->select(p |
          p.oclIsKindOf(DeliverOpCBurden) and
          p.oclAsType(DeliverOpCBurden).report=result)->notEmpty()
  post  canDeliver: self.token->select(p |
          p.oclIsKindOf(DeliverOpCPermit) and
          p.oclAsType(DeliverOpCPermit).report=result)->notEmpty()
  post  canNotRegister: self.token->select(p |
          p.oclIsKindOf(RegisterOpCPermit) and
          p.oclAsType(RegisterOpCPermit).advisor=aTeacher)->isEmpty()
```

We can see how the student has to have the permission to register the report (although the student may have the burden to do so, this is not compulsory for executing this action). As a result of the `register()` operation, the student is relieved from the burden to register the report, in case she held that burden, but she now acquires the burden to deliver the report, together with the permission to do so. In addition, the student permission to register another report to the same teacher is revoked. This latter permission will be reinstated when the registered report is finally graded.

This way, we are able to check that all the agents that intervene in an action have the appropriate permissions to participate, and that their corresponding burdens are discharged after the action. Moreover, new burdens (and the corresponding permissions, when applicable) are associated to the corresponding agents to continue the process.

Further deontic properties can be specified using invariants on deontic tokens. For example, the fact that no agent can grade a report prepared by itself can be stated by simply disallowing any agent to acquire a permission to do so:

```
context Agent inv noSelfAssessment:
  self.token->select(t|t.oclIsKindOf(GradeOpCPermit) and
          t.oclAsType(GradeOpCPermit).report.advisee=self)->isEmpty()
```

Note how this mechanism could be used to specify the *static* deontic constraints on the system, with the advantage that it enables the required traceability to the objects that might transgress these types of constraints.

3.3   Modeling Deontic-Constrained Behavior

As mentioned above, with our proposal we could decide to implement two behavioral styles. The first one is based on strict processes that define the order in which the system actions are executed — see, e.g., the sequence diagram shown in Fig. 1. The second style chooses the next action whose owner has the burden to perform it and whose participating agents (including the caller) all have the necessary permissions to carry it out. In this second style, system execution will continue until all burdens have been removed, or no further burden can be discharged because of lack of permissions.

To achieve this execution mechanism, an additional object (the so-called `scheduler`) would be introduced in the system. It is in charge of deciding, from the list of possible actions, the set of actions that currently satisfy their preconditions, and selecting one from this set. The execution of that object will continue until no further action can be executed. The implementation of the scheduler can be greatly simplified by the use of filmstrip objects, which are discussed next.

3.4   Combining Filmstripping and Deontic Tokens

Using deontic tokens for pre- and postconditions of operations provides a powerful mechanism to check that the behavior of the system objects respect the

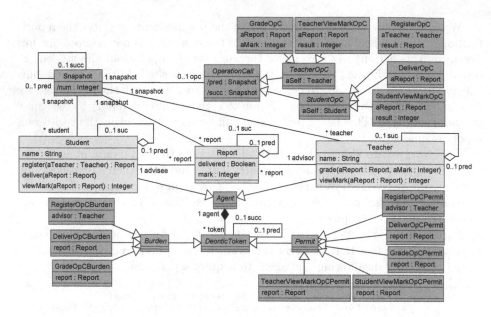

Fig. 5. The *Student Grading* system, with deontic tokens and filmstrip items.

deontic constraints. However, in many occasions we are more interested in performing static analysis on these behaviors. This is where filmstrip models can be very useful, as we shall see later in Sect. 3.5.

Figure 5 shows a class diagram of the student grading system that combines filmstrips and deontic tokens. Basically, this model reifies both the system operations, which represent the system actions, and the deontic tokens, which represent the corresponding permissions and obligations.

A filmstrip object model that uses the class diagram of Fig. 5 is shown in Fig. 6. It corresponds to the sequence of operations initially described in Fig. 1, where a student `registers` a report, `delivers` it, the advisor `grades` the report, and the student `views` the mark. Figure 6 shows how the deontic tokens associated to each agent evolve.

3.5 Dynamic Analysis with Filmstrip Models

This section discusses some of the dynamic analysis that can be performed with our proposal and how filmstrip models can be used for deontic reasoning about the system. One of the main advantages of filmstrip models is that dynamic analysis on the system can be accomplished by means of static analysis on the filmstrip models, including model consistency, property satisfiability, constraint implication, and partial model completion [4]. Let us describe here some of the behavioral properties of the system and how they can be analysed with USE.

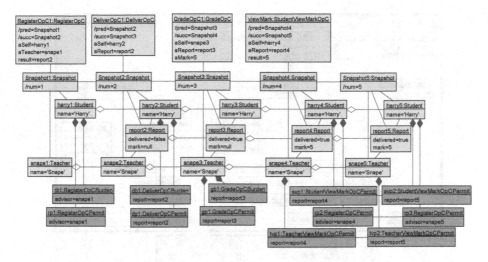

Fig. 6. A sequence of operation calls specified by a filmstrip, showing how the agents' tokens evolve.

Temporal Properties. Filmstrip models can cover complete development stories, i.e., temporal properties can be monitored. Thus it is possible to check, e.g., that only certain patterns of operation calls can occur. In the running example, we can check that the pattern Student::register; Student::deliver; Teacher::grade; [Student::viewMark | Teacher::viewMark]+ must be respected. This can be accomplished by defining an OCL invariant on the filmstrip model:

```
context Report inv correctChoreography
    (self.snapshot.pred.opc.oclIsTypeOf(RegisterOpC) implies
        self.pred=null)
and (self.snapshot.pred.opc.oclIsTypeOf(DeliverOpC) implies
        self.pred.snapshot.pred.opc.oclIsTypeOf(RegisterOpC))
and (self.snapshot.pred.opc.oclIsTypeOf(GradeOpC) implies
        self.pred.snapshot.pred.opc.oclIsTypeOf(DeliverOpC))
and (self.snapshot.opc.oclIsTypeOf(GradeOpC) implies
        self.suc->asSet()->closure(suc)->forAll(r |
            r<>null and r.snapshot.opc<>null implies
            r.snapshot.opc.oclIsTypeOf(StudentViewMarkOpC) or
            r.snapshot.opc.oclIsTypeOf(TeacherViewMarkOpC)))
```

Fairness. Tokens allow reasoning about interesting properties of agent burdens. For example, we could easily check if the grading workload is fairly distributed among teachers. This could be regulated by a deontic constraint that establishes that the number of grading burdens that all teachers hold is always similar.

```
context t1,t2:Teacher inv sameNumReports:
    (t1.token->select(oclIsTypeOf(GradeOpC)->size()) -
    t2.token->select(oclIsTypeOf(GradeOpC)->size())).abs() <= 1
```

Note how the use of tokens also allows us to identify the teachers with a heavier workload at that moment in time.

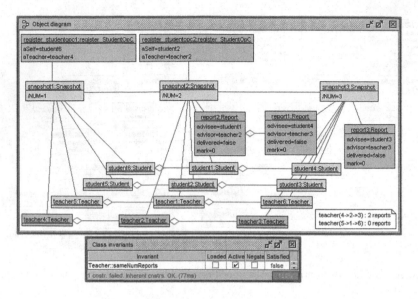

Fig. 7. Generated Filmstrip by negating invariant `Teacher::sameNumReports`.

Model Completion. The USE model validator [6] can be applied to complete a partially specified filmstrip object model in order to check whether a certain behavior satisfying all deontic constraints can be constructed or not. This can be used to perform **reachability analysis**, whereby starting from a filmstrip object model that represents the state of the system at a specific moment in time, and the behavior that led to it, we could add an invariant that represents a future state and ask the model validator to find a behavior that leads to such a future state. For example, find a behavior that ends up in a state where three students are waiting to be graded by the same teacher.

In this context, reachability analysis is very useful when the future state represents an undesirable situation, and we need to look for potential behaviors that can lead to it. For example, suppose that, in addition to the previous invariant about the fair grading workload of teachers, we want to control that even the number of registered reports in each one is always similar (and not only that of delivered reports). One way of looking for situations that violate such a constraint is to define an OCL invariant for it, and let the model validator construct an example filmstrip where that invariant is violated. Figure 7 shows the filmstrip found by the model validator in this case (deontic tokens excluded).

Note that system pre- and postconditions of operations are also taken into account when building these examples of behaviors, because pre- and postconditions become invariants in the filmstrip models, and thus they can be handled by the model validator and considered when generating the filmstrip object models.

Deontic Constraint Independence. Another application of the USE model validator in this context is the analysis of the set of deontic constraints. For example, the minimality of the deontic constraint set can be checked by showing the independence and necessity of single constraints. This can be proved by systematically negating exactly one constraint, and letting the model validator construct an example filmstrip where exactly that constraint is violated [4].

Again, one advantage of this approach is that the model validator is not only able to find whether a constraint expressing a deontic rule can be transgressed or not, but also the concrete behavior that leads to the violation of the rule.

Accountability Analysis. A further interesting application of our proposal is the identification of situations where one of more agents have burdens to discharge, but they cannot carry out the required actions because they do not have the necessary permissions. Although this can be a common situation during the execution of the system, there are cases of special interest. For example, the system may be in a deadlock state if no more actions can be executed but still some agents hold burdens that need to be discharged (see Sect. 3.3). In these cases, it is important to identify the objects accountable for holding undischarged burdens. In our proposal, checking that the set of these agents is empty can be specified using a simple OCL expression:

```
Agent.allInstances->select(a |
    a.token->select(t|t.oclIsKindOf(Burden)))->isEmpty()
```

4 Related Work

Conceptual modeling approaches such as the OMG's Semantics of Business Vocabulary and Business Rules (SBVR) [7,21], and Object Role Modeling (ORM) [8] already provide powerful representations of deontic constraints, and even define mappings to their corresponding UML representations. However, they are of a declarative nature, and mostly based on modal logics that are some times too abstract for our analyses, because they abstract from the particular sequence of actions executed by a system, and instead make general statements about temporal or deontic properties of those actions [25].

Other authors propose UML representations of deontic constraints. For example, the work [22] deals with the partial fulfilment of constraints in UML models, especially those constraints that represent obligations. The author propose to relax these constraints (along the same lines as in [6]) and how to map them to SQL, but no behavioral aspects are considered.

A different approach is followed by Deontic STAIRS [24], which proposes an extension of the UML sequence diagram notation with customized constructs for policy specification. Deontic STAIRS is underpinned by a denotational semantics, and provides a powerful framework for reasoning about some deontic properties of policy specifications, such as policy consistency, adherence and refinement. However, the use of sequence diagrams limits the range of analyses, and in particular dealing with modal properties of the system is not easy.

To address some of these issues, other operational approaches to specify deontic constraints use the reification of deontic concepts as other system objects [17].

These ideas were later adopted by ISO and ITU-T in the ODP Reference Model [15], particularly in the ODP Enterprise Language [12,13,16]. However, reasoning about these specifications is not easy either, because specifying and proving modal properties on them is not obvious.

This is why our proposal combines this operational approach for the specification of deontic concepts with the use of filmstrip models, which allow the reification of the system actions as objects, too, in order to enable behavioral analysis using static mechanisms and tools. Although there are several authors who also use this behavioral specification technique, to the best of our knowledge no one has dealt with the specification and analysis of deontic constraints.

5   Conclusions and Future Work

The need to deal with deontic concerns in information systems has been claimed for a long time by different authors, who highlight the importance of dealing with moral obligations in a digital world [7,11,18].

In this paper we have presented a proposal to explicitly specify dynamic deontic constraints in UML and OCL, using the reification of deontic concepts as other system objects (deontic tokens), as well as the reification of the system actions as objects too, so that we can deal explicitly with them to analyze the modal properties of the system. In addition, the accountability of agents can be analyzed with the use of deontic tokens. The proposal employs the tool USE and its model validator to support not only the simulation, but more importantly the automated analysis of some of the system properties of interest.

The main advantages of our proposal include, among others, the explicit representation of the deontic rules and tokens, instead of their implicit representation as formulas in any modal logic, which might be more difficult to debug, implement and maintain. UML models with deontic tokens and rules can also be simulated to detect undesirable situations ranging from constraint violations to deadlocks or starvation, due to lack of permissions or non-dischargeable burdens. Finally, we achieve the necessary separation of concerns that allows decoupling the functional specifications of a system from the deontic rules that are applicable to it at a given moment, since the latter can evolve over time, for example when fiscal or tax laws change, or when new government regulations are approved.

Although our approach seems to be flexible and expressive enough for conducting deontic reasoning of IT systems, this is just an initial proposal and we would still need to validate the proposal with more case studies. Furthermore, in this paper we have just considered the basic deontic aspects, but there are many other issues of interest still to be addressed as part of our future research. For example, the specification of *delegation* of obligations and permissions is not simple, because it may require further permissions, too, and makes accountability more difficult to trace. Second, in addition to individual tokens for particular actions we may also consider *global tokens* for types of actions (e.g., permission to view one report vs. permission to view all reports in a given department). Third, we have used explicit permissions to enable the occurrence of actions, implementing the so-called pessimistic enforcement model where actions are forbidden unless they are explicitly permitted. An optimistic enforcement model would allow all actions to be executed unless explicitly prohibited. We can model different strategies depending on the system we want to specify, and therefore a study on the appropriateness of the use of each enforcement model would be interesting. The use of one or the other has, overall, impact on the usability and readability of the specifications and on the economy of the language, and are essential for the development and maintainability of the UML specifications. Finally, mappings between SBVR and ORM representations and our proposal would be of interest, so that these specifications can be translated to our proposal and simulated with it, and vice-versa.

Acknowledgment. We would like to thank the reviewers for their constructive and helpful comments on previous versions of this paper. This work has been partially supported by Spanish Research Project PGC2018-094905-B-I00.

References

1. Büttner, F., Gogolla, M.: On OCL-based imperative languages. Sci. Comput. Program. **92**, 162–178 (2014). https://doi.org/10.1016/j.scico.2013.10.003
2. Desai, N., Gogolla, M., Hilken, F.: Executing models by filmstripping: enhancing validation by filmstrip templates and transformation alternatives. In: Proceedings of MODELS 2017 Workshops. CEUR Workshop Proceedings, vol. 2019, pp. 88–94. CEUR-WS.org (2017). http://ceur-ws.org/Vol-2019/exe_2.pdf
3. Gogolla, M., Hamann, L., Hilken, F., Kuhlmann, M., France, R.B.: From application models to filmstrip models: an approach to automatic validation of model dynamics. In: Proceedings of Modellierung 2014. LNI, vol. 225, pp. 273–288. GI (2014)
4. Gogolla, M., Hilken, F., Doan, K.H.: Achieving model quality through model validation, verification and exploration. Comput. Lang. Syst. Struct. **54**, 474–511 (2018). https://doi.org/10.1016/j.cl.2017.10.001
5. Gogolla, M., Hilken, F., Doan, K., Desai, N.: Checking UML and OCL model behavior with filmstripping and classifying terms. In: Proceedings of TAP 2017. LNCS, vol. 10375, pp. 119–128. Springer, Cham (2017). https://doi.org/10.1007/978-3-319-61467-0_7
6. Gogolla, M., Vallecillo, A.: On softening OCL invariants. J. Object Technol. **18**(2), 6:1–6:22 (2019). https://doi.org/10.5381/jot.2019.18.2.a6
7. Halpin, T.: Business rule modality (2008). http://www.orm.net/pdf/RuleModality.pdf
8. Halpin, T.: Object-Role Modeling Fundamentals. Technics Publications (2015)
9. Hilken, F., Gogolla, M.: Verifying linear temporal logic properties in UML/OCL class diagrams using filmstripping. In: Proceedings of DSD 2016, pp. 708–713. IEEE Computer Society (2016). https://doi.org/10.1109/DSD.2016.42
10. Hilken, F., Hamann, L., Gogolla, M.: Transformation of UML and OCL models into filmstrip models. In: Proceedings of ICMT 2014. LNCS, vol. 8568, pp. 170–185. Springer, Heidelberg (2014). https://doi.org/10.1007/978-3-319-08789-4_13
11. van den Hoven, J.: Ethics for the digital age: where are the moral specs? In: Proceedings of ECSS 2015 Informatics in the Future, pp. 65–76 (2015). https://doi.org/10.1007/978-3-319-55735-9_6

12. ISO/IEC 15414, ITU-T Rec. X.911: Information technology - Open distributed processing - Reference model - Enterprise language. ISO/IEC and ITU-T (2015)
13. ISO/IEC 19793, ITU-T Rec. X.906: Information technology - Open distributed processing - Use of UML for ODP system specifications. ISO/IEC, ITU-T (2015)
14. Kuhlmann, M., Hamann, L., Gogolla, M.: Extensive validation of OCL models by integrating SAT solving into USE. In: Bishop, J., Vallecillo, A. (eds.) TOOLS 2011. LNCS, vol. 6705, pp. 290–306. Springer, Heidelberg (2011). https://doi.org/10.1007/978-3-642-21952-8_21
15. Linington, P.F., Milosevic, Z., Tanaka, A., Vallecillo, A.: Building Enterprise Systems with ODP – An Introduction to Open Distributed Processing. Chapman & Hall/CRC Press (2012)
16. Linington, P.F., Miyazaki, H., Vallecillo, A.: Obligations and delegation in the ODP enterprise language. In: Proceedings of VORTE 2012 (EDOC Workshops), pp. 146–155. IEEE Computer Society (2012). https://doi.org/10.1109/EDOCW.2012.28
17. Linington, P.F., Neal, S.: Using policies in the checking of business to business contracts. In: Proceedings of POLICY 2003, pp. 207–218. IEEE Computer Society (2003). https://doi.org/10.1109/POLICY.2003.1206975
18. Meyer, J.C., Weigand, H., Wieringa, R.J.: A specification language for static, dynamic and deontic integrity constraints. In: Proceedings of MFDBS 1989. LNCS, vol. 364, pp. 347–366. Springer, Jeidelberg (1989). https://doi.org/10.1007/3-540-51251-9_23
19. Milosevic, Z.: Ethics in digital health: a deontic accountability framework. In: Proceedings of EDOC 2019, pp. 105–111. IEEE (2019). https://doi.org/10.1109/EDOC.2019.00022
20. Milosevic, Z.: Enacting policies in digital health: a case for smart legal contracts and distributed ledgers? Knowl. Eng. Rev. **35**, e6 (2020). https://doi.org/10.1017/S0269888920000089
21. Object Management Group: Semantics Of Business Vocabulary And Rules. Version 1.5 (Dec 2019), OMG document formal/19-10-02
22. Ramos, P.N.: Deontic database constraints - from UML to SQL. In: Proceedings of ICEIS 2013, pp. 102–109. SciTePress (2013). https://doi.org/10.5220/0004415801020109
23. Rönnedal, D.: An Introduction to Deontic Logic. CreateSpace (2010)
24. Solhaug, B., Stølen, K.: Compositional refinement of policies in UML - exemplified for access control. In: Proceedings of ESORICS 2008. LNCS, vol. 5283, pp. 300–316. Springer, Cham (2008). https://doi.org/10.1007/978-3-540-88313-5_20
25. Wieringa, R.J., Meyer, J.C., Weigand, H.: Specifying dynamic and deontic integrity constraints. Data Knowl. Eng. **4**, 157–189 (1989). https://doi.org/10.1016/0169-023X(89)90038-4

Defining Instance Spanning Constraint Patterns for Business Processes Based on Proclets

Karolin Winter[✉] and Stefanie Rinderle-Ma

Faculty of Computer Science, University of Vienna, Vienna, Austria
{karolin.winter,stefanie.rinderle-ma}@univie.ac.at

Abstract. Instance Spanning Constraints (ISC) establish controls across multiple instances of one or several business process types. Consider, e.g., medical treatments during which drug-drug interactions might occur. Different treatments are likely to be modeled in separate processes, but yet have to be coordinated in order to avoid harm for patients. ISC typically stem from regulatory documents and must be integrated into business processes. In order to facilitate ISC integration, we provide six ISC patterns which are based on a real-world ISC collection as well as a categorization of ISC. The presented ISC patterns are formalized using Proclets based on timed colored workflow nets. This formalization choice results from an elaborated requirements analysis and enables the synchronization of instances of one or several process types while employing well-known process modeling approaches. The ISC patterns are evaluated through their application to i) selected business processes and ii) existing approaches for batching and security in business processes.

Keywords: Patterns and reuse · Business process modeling · Business process compliance · Instance spanning constraints

1 Introduction

Today's highly flexible and interconnected business environments require the coordination of their business processes based on so called Instance Spanning Constraints (ISC) which span multiple instances of one or several process types. Figure 1 depicts a process model describing process type *laboratory process*. During runtime, for each lab sample a corresponding process instance is created and executed based on the process model. Assume that resource *centrifuge* employed is limited. An ISC *Wait until centrifuge is filled* can be employed to coordinate the efficient usage of the *centrifuge*. More precisely, if *centrifuge* offers n slots, the ISC realizes a synchronization of n process instances in order to execute the task `centrifugation` simultaneously.

ISC are present throughout many applications (e.g., security, batching, queueing) and domains (e.g., manufacturing, medicine). Various aspects connected with ISC, including modeling, enactment, and mining of ISC have been

© Springer Nature Switzerland AG 2020
G. Dobbie et al. (Eds.): ER 2020, LNCS 12400, pp. 149–163, 2020.
https://doi.org/10.1007/978-3-030-62522-1_11

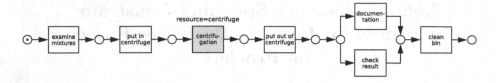

Fig. 1. Example of a laboratory process modeled as Petri net adapted from [18]

addressed by literature, e.g., [3,7,9,10,12,19]. However, a "common ground" for the different approaches, applications, and domains is still missing, though this would foster the understanding, transparency, reuse, and sharing of ISC.

In business process management, patterns have already proven useful for creating "common ground", including workflow patterns [1], change patterns [16], compliance monitoring functionalities [6], and compliance patterns [15]. In this spirit, we think that a set of ISC patterns will be useful and support the usage, transparency, and understandability of ISC across various approaches, applications, and domains. Hence, this work raises the following research questions:

1. Which ISC patterns are useful for establishing controls that span multiple process instances of one or several process types?
2. How to formalize ISC patterns?
3. How to realize ISC patterns?

When addressing RQ1, RQ2, and RQ3, the paper follows the methodology depicted in Fig. 2. The elicitation of ISC patterns is based on the ISC categorization elaborated in [19] which rests on the ISC collection presented in [3]. The ISC categorization [19] comprises *Category I: simultaneous execution of activities, Category II: constrained activity execution, Category III: order of activities,* and *Category IV: non-concurrent execution of activities* accounting for around 85.9% of the examples from the 114 ISC examples in [3]. The remaining 14.1% of the examples refer to ISC handling exceptions in process executions. This work will elaborate on Categories I–IV for ISC pattern formalization. In particular, the ISC patterns distinguish between ISC patterns for multiple instances of one process type and ISC patterns for multiple instances of multiple process types.

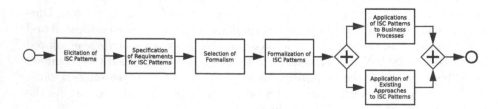

Fig. 2. Methodology adapted from [6]

The ISC pattern formalization poses several challenges, for example, the representation of an instance-spanning attribute such as the *centrifuge* in Fig. 1. Especially interesting is that ISC introduce virtual decision points between process instances and/or process types as shown in [18]. How can they be formalized, but without allowing any undesired exchange of data between process instances or types? This is a differentiation to approaches for modeling interorganizational processes that are established based on the desired exchange of messages. Hence, Sect. 2 states requirements on ISC pattern formalization and discusses timed colored Workflow Nets and Proclets as formalization of choice. The formalized ISC patterns are presented in Sect. 3. The evaluation focuses on ISC realization based on the application to two business processes as well as to existing approaches followed by a discussion (cf. Sect. 4). The application to existing approaches also serves as related work discourse. The paper concludes in Sect. 5.

2 Formalism Choice and Fundamentals

Overarchingly, the selection of a formalism for defining ISC patterns shall rest on well established concepts in business process management. This facilitates the understanding and sharing of ISC patterns for different business process scenarios. In literature, there is a debate on how to treat compliance constraints and business processes, i.e., keeping them separated as mostly the case for imperative approaches or "mixing" them as mostly the case for declarative approaches. With choosing an imperative formalism the definition of the ISC patterns becomes close to the business process definition (keeping the mental map) and ISC patterns can be directly used within the processes. This way it becomes transparent how the ISC are executed during runtime. Therefore, we opt for an imperative approach. Further on, the formalism should have a well-defined formal execution semantics in order to enable the smooth transformation into executable process code. Finally, we aim at a formalism that enables the formal analysis of ISC and related process types/instances.

Besides these general considerations, we postulate four requirements that result from an analysis of the ISC categories from [19] based on ISC examples from [3]. Let in the following, $ISC_S \subseteq ISC$ denote ISC that span one process type and $ISC_P \subseteq ISC$ denote ISC that span multiple process types.

Category I. ISC of this category refer to the simultaneous execution of events, e.g., that *Task* centrifugation *must be executed for five instances simultaneously.* An example of an ISC_P could be that *When the centrifugation is started a protocol must be created simultaneously.* In this case the two tasks, centrifugation and write protocol would be present in two separate processes but must be coordinated and started simultaneously. Simultaneous execution of tasks is crucial for an ISC pattern formalism.

Category II. ISC of this category refer to the constrained execution of events which can either refer to time or data constraints but also the absolute number of executions of a task or process. An example for the first case is *Loans may* *only be approved as long as the amount is below $1M per day.* This ISC depends on the data element *amount* and the timespan *day* for a task `approve loan`. An example for the latter is *Two tasks B and B' may only executed in sum 100 times a day.* Not only the absolute number but also the timespan *day* is of importance. If B and B' are located in different processes, this is an ISC$_P$.

Category III. ISC of this category refer to the order of event executions and only appear in the form of ISC$_P$ since for ISC$_S$ this would correspond to intra instance constraints. Consider for example *Before the centrifugation can be started, the blood sample must have been taken.* The corresponding tasks `centrifugation` and `take blood sample`, though located in separate processes, must be executed in a specific order.

Category IV. ISC of this category are also of type ISC$_P$ and describe the non-concurrent execution of events, e.g., *Tasks* `take blood sample` *and* `administer inoculation` *may not be executed concurrently for one patient.*, whereas the two tasks are present in different processes.

In order to cover Categories I–IV for multiple instances of one, but also multiple process types, a formalism for defining ISC patterns should

- support instance correlation through an instance unique identifier (uid) in case of multiple process types ($\mapsto$ Rq1).
- represent attributes shared by multiple instances/processes (e.g., centrifuge) ($\mapsto$ Rq2).
- support the synchronization of instances at well-defined points such as tasks ($\mapsto$ Rq3).
- support the simultaneous execution of tasks across multiple instances for one or several process types ($\mapsto$ Rq4).

Rq1 refers to instance correlation. Consider, e.g., a patient being subject to multiple different treatment processes. If one examination has already been carried out within one process, the other processes should skip this task. In order to recognize for which instance, i.e., patient this task must be skipped, patient instances must be identifiable via, e.g., a unique patient id (cf. [19]). According to [3], an ISC is linked to event attributes, so-called *instance spanning attributes* which are time, resource and data. ISC can refer to multiple instance spanning attributes at once. Consider, e.g., an ISC stating *A user is not allowed to do event* `approve loan` *if the total loan amount per day and clerk exceeds $1M* (cf. [18]). In this case, the ISC refers to three event attributes, i.e., the clerk (resource), the same day (time) and the current loan amount (data). Therefore, instance spanning attributes must be representable by an ISC pattern formalism (*Rq2*). Moreover, instances must synchronize like in the centrifuge example where $n - 1$ instances have to wait before the `centrifugation` task until the n-th instance has arrived (*Rq3*). *Rq4* results from Category I. Note that *Rq1–Rq4* also respect the requirements for a visual ISC modeling notation as stated in [4].

In summary, we are looking for a well-established, imperative design formalism with formal execution semantics and strong support of formal analysis.

Workflow nets (WF-nets) and suitable extensions are good candidates for an initial selection. Table 1 evaluates this selection along requirements $Rq1$–$Rq4$.

Table 1. Assessment of WF-nets and suitable extensions

Formalism	$Rq1$	$Rq2$	$Rq3$	$Rq4$
WF-net	−	−	$+\backslash-$	−
Colored WF-net	$+\backslash-$	+	$+\backslash-$	−
Timed WF-net	−	−	$+\backslash-$	+
Proclets based on timed colored WF-nets	+	+	+	+

+ fulfilled, − not fulfilled, $+\backslash-$ partly fulfilled

Colored WF-nets support the representation of event attributes and hence meet $Rq1$ and $Rq2$. In order to enable the synchronization of instances of different process types ($Rq3$) Proclets (cf. [14]), which allow for modeling interactions of processes, were identified as potential formalism candidate. An alternative would be *Workflow Modules* which are often employed in process choreography design (cf., e.g., [17]) and exchange information via incoming and outgoing places. In particular, exchange of instance specific information via colored tokens is enabled which is not a desirable behaviour for ISC patterns since execution of processes should just be coordinated without direct information exchange on running instances. For satisfying $Rq4$ the formalism must be able to deal with time aspects which is only the case for timed WF-nets. Consequently, just the combination of timed colored WF-nets and Proclets fulfills all requirements. Proclet instances relying on timed colored WF-nets have a state, support the notion of a task and timed colored WF-nets are a graphical process notation providing soundness which is a prerequisite for a Proclet [8]. Definitions and concepts of the chosen formalism are described in the following.

Definition 1 (Petri/Workflow Net, [13]). *A Petri net is a triplet* (P, T, A) *where*

- *P is a finite set of places*
- *T is a finite set of transitions, such that $P \cap T = \emptyset$*
- *$A \subseteq (P \times T) \cup (T \times P)$ is a set of directed arcs.*

A Petri net is called Workflow Net (WF-net) *if and only if*

- *there is a dedicated source place where the process starts and that has no incoming edge*
- *there is a dedicated sink place where the process ends and that has no outgoing edge*
- *all nodes are on a path from the source place to the sink place.*

The current state of a WF-net is determined by its markings.

Definition 2 (Marked Labeled WF-net, [13]). *A* marked WF-net *is a pair* $((P, T, A), M)$, *where* (P, T, A) *is a WF-net and* $M \in \mathbb{B}(P)$ *is a multiset over* P *denoting the marking of the net.*

Running Example: Figure 3 depicts two processes in terms of marked labeled WF-nets. Based on Definition 2, process $\mathcal{P}1$ depicted in Fig. 3 is then given as $((P_{\mathcal{P}1}, T_{\mathcal{P}1}, A_{\mathcal{P}1}), [s])$ with $P_{\mathcal{P}1} = \{s, p_1, p_2, e\}$, $T_{\mathcal{P}1} = \{A, B, C\}, A_{\mathcal{P}1} = \{a_1, a_2, ..., a_6\}$,

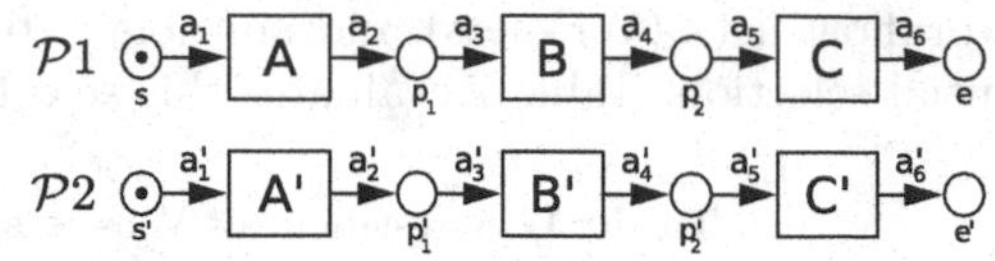

Fig. 3. Running example, cf. [19]

whereas $a_1 = (s, A), a_2 = (A, p_1), a_3 = (p_1, B), a_4 = (B, p_2), a_5 = (p_2, C), a_6 = (C, e)$. The initial marking has one token in s. Process $\mathcal{P}2$ is given analogously.

Since the requirements for ISC patterns demand the display of event attributes as well as consumption times of tokens, we formalize the ISC patterns through so called *timed colored Workflow nets* which are capable of dealing with data- and time-related aspects [13].

Definition 3 ((Timed) Colored WF-net, [5,17]). *A Colored WF-net is a nine-tuple $(P, T, A, \Sigma, V, C, G, E, I)$ with*

- *(P, T, A) being a WF-net as described in Definition 1*
- *Σ is a finite set of nonempty types, called color sets*
- *$V: A \to (P \times T) \cup (T \times P)$ is a node function that maps each arc identifier to a pair (start node, end node) of the arc*
- *$C: P \to \Sigma$ is a color function that associates each place with a color set*
- *$G: T \to BooleanExpr$ is a guard function that maps each transition to a predicate*
- *$E: A \to Expr$ is an arc expression that evaluates to a multi-set over the color set of the place*
- *I is an initial marking of the colored WF-net.*

Timed colored WF-nets *carry in addition to the token colors a non-negative integer value called* timestamp *determining the time when the token can be consumed by a transition [5]. Markings of places having timestamps correspond to timed multisets and each colored WF-net also has a global clock which represents model time [5].*

For enabling the coordination across instances in the ISC pattern formalism, *Proclets* based on timed colored WF-nets are used which are defined as follows.

Definition 4 (Proclet, Proclet Instance, Proclet System, [2,8,14]).

- *A Proclet is a tuple $Pr = (N, ports)$ consisting of a timed colored WF-net N, a set of ports, $ports \subseteq 2^T \times \{in, out\} \times \{?, 1, *, +\} \times \{?, 1, *, +\}^1$ where each port $pr = (T_{pr}, dir_{pr}, card_{pr}, mult_{pr})$*
  - *is associated to a set $T_{pr} \subseteq T$ of transitions, s.t. $\forall t_1, t_2 \in T_{pr}$ holds: $l(t_1) = l(t_2)$*
  - *has a direction of communication $dir_{pr} \in \{in, out\}$*
  - *has a cardinality $card_{pr} \in \{?, 1, *, +\}$ specifying how many performatives may or have to be sent or received upon an occurence of one $t \in T_{pr}$*
  - *has a multiplicity $mult_{pr} \in \{?, 1, *, +\}$ specifying how often all transitions T_{pr} may occur together during the lifetime of an instance of Pr*

---

[1] ? means 0 or 1, 1 exactly one, ∗ arbitrary number, + at least one.

- *no two ports share a transition, $T_{pr} \cap T_{pr'} = \emptyset, \forall pr, pr' \in ports, pr \neq pr'$.*
  and has a unique transition with no incoming arcs, and a unique transition
  with no outgoing arcs. These transitions denote actions to create and finish
  an instance of Pr respectively.
- A Proclet instance *corresponds to an instance of the process definition. Ports*
  exchange performatives, *which have at least six attributes (time, channel,*
  sender, set of recipients, action and content) and are stored in the knowledge
  base *of a Proclet instance. The knowledge base can be queried by tasks and con-*
  tains public as well as private parts. The public part is identical for all instances
  of the class, i.e. this part resides at the class level even though it holds informa-
  tion about instances. The private part resides exclusively at the instance level.
  A task may have a precondition based on the knowledge base. A task is enabled
  if i) the corresponding transition in the WF-net is enabled, ii) the precondition
  evaluates to true, and iii) each input port contains a performative.
- A Proclet System *consists of a finite set of Proclets together with a set of*
  channels via which a Proclet can interact with other Proclets. A naming ser-
  vice keeps track of all Proclet instances.

3   Formalization of ISC Patterns

In the following, 6 ISC patterns are formalized, two for Cat. I and II, whereas
the distinction is made between one or multiple process types, and one for Cat.
III and IV. The ISC patterns are exemplary illustrated for two Proclets.

Figure 4 depicts the basic
building blocks for ISC patterns which are similar, in
the case of Category I
and II for ISC$_S$ as well
as ISC$_P$. These ISC patterns are just distinguish-
able based on the underlying timed colored WF-net.
In case of Category III, the
ISC pattern requires only
a onedirectional information
exchange. Consider, e.g., B
must be executed before C'
(cf. Fig. 3). The further execution of process $\mathcal{P}_1$ containing B is independent of
whether C' has been exe-
cuted or not. Categories I
and II in contrast require a

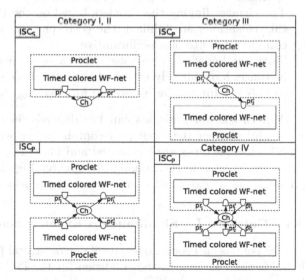

Fig. 4. Building blocks for ISC patterns

bidirectional information exchange. For Category IV two output ports and one
input port are necessary to formalize the ISC pattern.

Let $\mathcal{N} = \{N_i\}_{i=1,...,n}$ be a set of timed colored WF-nets with $N_i = (P_i, T_i, A_i, \Sigma_i, V_i, C_i, G_i, E_i, I_i)$ as defined in Definition 3 with $\bigcap_i P_i = \emptyset, \bigcap_i T_i = \emptyset, \bigcap_i A_i = \emptyset$.

- The set of ISC transitions is given as $T_{ISC} \subseteq \bigcup_i T_i$. ISC transitions are those tasks affected by the ISC.
- The set of transitions preceding the ISC transition is given as $T_{pre} \subseteq \bigcup_i T_i$. For Category IV, the set of transitions succeeding the ISC transition is defined analogously $T_{post} \subseteq \bigcup_i T_i$.
- The set containing all colors representing the instance spanning attributes is denoted as $\Sigma_{ISC} \subseteq \bigcup_i \Sigma_i$.

Further, let PS be a Proclet system as defined in Definition 4. For modeling ISC the following must be at least fulfilled

- Each Proclet in PS consists of one element in $\mathcal{N}$ and up to three ports. The port connected to the ISC transition is always an input port, the others are output ports. The output ports send performatives, holding information on ISC colors in their content attributes. This enables to check ISC.
- If PS consists of more than one Proclet, Σ_{ISC} must, based on $Rq1$, contain at least one element. This element represents the corresponding instance uid and is defined as type *string*, i.e., *colset* $ID = string; \Sigma_{ISC} = \{ID\}, var\ iscid : ID$.
- Each Proclet instance, corresponding to a process instance, has a $proc_{id}$ which serves for identifying instances within the WF-net, i.e., there exists a corresponding variable $var\ proc_{id} : ID$. Each Σ_i is therefore not empty.
- The channel linking the Proclets based on the ISC is denoted as Ch. If the ISC conditions are fulfilled, the corresponding $proc_{id}$(s) are handed to the content attribute of a performative.
- Since the knowledge base keeps track of all performatives we know which instances have already executed their ISC task(s). Instances that have done so may not further be considered for checking the ISC condition.

Whether ISC transitions can fire depends on the tokens in the preceding place and whether the input port contains a performative.

The ISC patterns are formalized and illustrated based on the timed colored WF-nets depicted in the running example (cf. Fig. 3, Sect. 2). Note that the ISC patterns can be extended to more than two processes as well.

3.1 Category I – Simultaneous Event Execution

For ISC of this category, no matter if one or several process types are considered, it holds that, as long as the condition for the ISC is not fulfilled, all instances have to wait before the ISC transition(s). As soon as the condition is fulfilled, all tokens have to be consumed simultaneously by the ISC transition(s). Therefore, all tokens have a suitable timestamp indicating that they need to be consumed without delay. This timestamp corresponds to the timestamp of the global glock when the transition preceding the ISC transition fires. By that, we ensure that the timestamp is "old enough" such that the ISC transition can always fire. Moreover, we demand that transitions fire as soon as the enablement conditions according to Definition 4 are fulfilled. In the case of multiple process types, all global clocks start with 0. We assign the timestamp to the color set representing the $proc_{id}$, i.e., this becomes a timed color set with initial timestamp 0.

Simultaneous ISC Pattern (one process type)
Description: As long as the ISC is not fulfilled, all instances have to wait before the ISC transition. As soon as the ISC condition is fulfilled, all affected instances must execute the ISC transition simultaneously.
Formalization: Let $A \in T_{pre}, B \in T_{ISC}, pr = (\{A\}, out, +, 1)$ and $pr' = (\{B\}, in, 1, +)$. The guard function G for B must identify the correct tokens based on the $proc_{id}$, i.e., transition B may only consume the tokens having the correct $proc_{id}$. This information is encoded in the content attribute of the performative received via pr'. All tokens must be consumed by B simultaneously.

Simultaneous ISC Pattern (multiple process types)
Description: Until the ISC condition is not fulfilled, all instances have to wait before the ISC transitions. As soon as the ISC condition is fulfilled, all affected instances must execute the ISC transitions simultaneously.
Formalization: Let $A, A' \in T_{pre}, B, B,' \in T_{ISC}, pr_1 = (\{A\}, out, +, 1), pr_2 = (\{A'\}, out, +, 1), pr'_1 = (\{B\}, in, 1, +)$ and $pr'_2 = (\{B'\}, in, 1, +)$. The guard functions G_1, G_2 for B, B' must identify the correct tokens based on the $proc_{id}$, i.e., transitions B, B' may only consume the tokens having the correct $proc_{id}$. This information is encoded in the content attribute of the performative received via pr'_1, pr'_2. All tokens must be consumed by B and B' simultaneously.

3.2   Category II – Constrained Event Execution

The ISC patterns for this category are based on the same building blocks as those for Category I. However, there are two differences. First, simultaneous execution is not of importance and second, according to the real-world ISC examples, mostly ISC conditions correspond to thresholds, like, e.g., the amount in the before mentioned example for Category II. This leads to the situation that, as long as this threshold is not met, instances may be executed.

Constrained ISC Pattern (one process type)
Description: As long as the ISC threshold is not reached, all instances may execute the ISC transition. As soon as the ISC threshold has been reached, all affected instances must wait until the ISC threshold can be reset.
Formalization: Let $A \in T_{pre}, B \in T_{ISC}, pr = (\{A\}, out, +, 1)$ and $pr' = (\{B\}, in, 1, +)$. The guard function G for B must identify the correct tokens based on the $proc_{id}$, i.e., transition B may only consume the tokens having the correct $proc_{id}$. This information is encoded in the content attribute of the performative received via pr'.

Constrained ISC Pattern (multiple process types)
Description: As long as the ISC threshold is not reached, all instances may execute the ISC transitions. As soon as the ISC threshold is has been reached, all affected instances must wait until the ISC threshold can be reset.
Formalization: Let $A, A' \in T_{pre}, B, B,' \in T_{ISC}, pr_1 = (\{A\}, out, +, 1), pr_2 = (\{A'\}, out, +, 1), pr'_1 = (\{B\}, in, 1, +)$ and $pr'_2 = (\{B'\}, in, 1, +)$. The guard functions G_1, G_2 for B, B' must identify the correct tokens based on the $proc_{id}$, i.e., transitions B, B' may only consume the tokens having the correct $proc_{id}$. This information is encoded in the content attribute of the performative received via pr'_1, pr'_2.

3.3   Category III – Ordered Event Executions

ISC of this category span multiple process types. It holds that ISC transitions may only consume tokens if the preceding place contains the associated token and the preceding transition, that needs to be executed first and is present in a different process, has already been executed.

Ordering ISC Pattern
Description: As long as the instance containing the transition which precedes the ISC transition has not arrived at the synchronization point, the corresponding instance, i.e., the one with the same instance uid, located in a different process may not execute the ISC transition. As soon as the transition preceding the ISC transition has been executed the associated instance may execute the ISC transition.
Formalization: Let $B \in T_{pre}, C' \in T_{ISC}, pr_1 = (\{B\}, out, +, 1)$ and $pr'_2 = (\{C'\}, in, 1, +)$. The guard function G for C' must identify the correct tokens based on the $proc_{id}$. Transition C' can only consume the token having the correct $proc_{id}$. This information is encoded in the content attribute of the performative received via pr'_2.

3.4   Category IV – Non-concurrent Event Execution

For ISC of this category only one transition involved in the ISC is allowed to consume a token, all other transitions have to wait until it is finished. Consider, e.g., that two tasks B and B' may not be executed concurrently. In order to formalize this ISC pattern, an additional set $T_{post} \subseteq \bigcup_i T_i$ containing the transitions succeeding an ISC transitions must be introduced. This allows for checking whether one task has already finished since its succeeding transition was executed.

Non-concurrent ISC Pattern
Description: If an ISC transition has been started all other associated instances, i.e., those having the same instance uid, have to wait until it is completed. Afterwards, only one other associated instance may start its ISC transition and all remaining instances have to wait until it is finished. This continues until all instances have executed their ISC transitions.

Formalization: Let $A, A' \in T_{pre}, B, B' \in T_{ISC}, C, C' \in T_{post}$ and ports $pr_1 = (\{A\}, out, +, 1), pr_2 = (\{A'\}, out, +, 1), pr_1' = (\{B\}, in, 1, +), pr_2' = (\{B'\}, in, 1, +), \tilde{pr}_1 = (\{C\}, out, +, 1)$ and $\tilde{pr}_2 = (\{C'\}, out, +, 1)$. The guard functions G_1, G_2 for B, B' must identify the correct tokens based on the $proc_{id}$. Transitions B, B' can only consume the token having the correct $proc_{id}$. This information is encoded in the content attribute of the performative received via pr_1', pr_2'.

4 Evaluation of ISC Patterns

ISC patterns are evaluated through their application in processes in Sect. 4.1 and in existing approaches in Sect. 4.2, followed by a discussion in Sect. 4.3.

4.1 Application to Business Processes

Centrifuge Example. Figure 5 picks up the centrifuge example outlined in the introduction with corresponding ISC *Wait until centrifuge is filled*. In order to model the Simultaneous ISC pattern, a Proclet system is given by a timed colored WF-net and $ports = \{pr, pr'\}, pr = ((put\ in\ centrifuge), out, +, 1), pr' = ((centrifugation), in, 1, +)$ as well as one channel Ch.

Moreover, $(put\ in\ centrifuge) \in T_{pre}, (centrifugation) \in T_{ISC}, \Sigma = \{NUM, ID\}, var\ procid : ID, var\ slots : NUM$ and $\Sigma_{ISC} = \{NUM\} \subseteq \Sigma$ whereas ID is a timed color set.

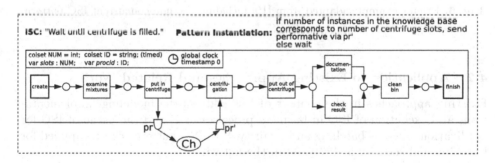

Fig. 5. Recap of laboratory process including the Simultaneous ISC pattern (one process type)

Printer Example. Figure 6 depicts three processes adapted from [19] whereas $\mathcal{P}1$ outlines the handling of flyer orders, $\mathcal{P}3$ the handling of poster orders and $\mathcal{P}2$ the corresponding billing process for both flyer and poster orders. In [19], six different ISC are outlined, but for illustration purposes, only one example is depicted in this paper while the remaining ISC examples are provided as supplementary material[2]. The ISC states *Flyers and posters as well as bills and posters cannot be printed concurrently on one printer since they require a different paper format* which can be modeled using the Non-concurrent ISC pattern. Each process is represented by a Proclet system $PS_i = (N_i, ports_i), i = 1, 2, 3$ based on a timed colored WF-net N_i, $ports_i = \{pr_i, pr'_i, \tilde{pr}_i\}$, with $pr_1 = ((send\ draft\ to\ customer), out, +, 1), pr'_1 = ((print\ flyer), in, 1, +),$ $\tilde{pr}_1 = ((deliver\ flyer), out, +, 1)$ and the remaining ports defined analogously, as well as one channel Ch. Moreover, $(send\ draft\ to\ customer), (write\ bill),$ $(design\ poster) \in T_{pre}, (print\ flyer), (print\ bill), (print\ poster) \in T_{ISC},$ $(deliver\ flyer), (deliver\ bill), (deliver\ poster) \in T_{post}, \Sigma_i = \{ID^2, RES\}$ and $\Sigma_{ISC} = \{ID^2, RES\}$ with corresponding variables as depicted in Fig. 6.

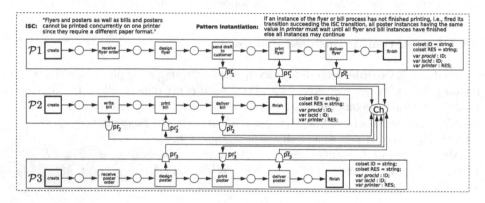

Fig. 6. Printer example adapted from [19] including the non-concurrent ISC pattern

4.2   Application to Existing Approaches and Related Work

Existing approaches in the context of ISC address the modeling, implementation, and execution of ISC in business processes [3,7] and the usage of ISC for applications such as batching and security. How ISC patterns can be applied for batching and security is discussed in the following.

Batching [10]. Batching can be either parallel, meaning that "instances for one activity are executed simultaneously and get terminated before the next activity is executed the same way" or sequential, i.e., "activities within a batch region are executed for one process instance (case) before the next one can be started." A batching region is determined by four parameters, the *i) groupingCharacteristic, ii) activationRule, iii) maxBatchSize* and *iv) executionOrder*. The identification of instances based on instance spanning attributes and related instances via the instance uid corresponds to i). The ISC, e.g., task `centrifugation` may only be started if the centrifuge is filled corresponds to ii) activationRule whereas

---

[2] http://gruppe.wst.univie.ac.at/projects/crisp/index.php?t=iscpatterns.

iii) the maxBatchSize is determined by, e.g., the number of centrifuge slots. The execution order in this case is parallel and the Simultaneous ISC pattern can be applied. For sequential processing, the Non-concurrent ISC Pattern can be applied. Since batching typically spans just one process type, the process must be duplicated in order to be able to apply the Non-concurrent ISC Pattern.

Security [11]. Security constraints such as access control and separation of duties within processes can be modeled using the Constrained ISC pattern, in one or multiple process type form. Consider, e.g., two tasks grant loan present in process $P1$ and check loan accommodations present in process $P2$. A user u having granted a loan with $uid = 123$ may not check the accommodation of the loan case with $uid = 123$. Based on token colors representing the user and the uid the execution of task check loan accommodations by user u can be prohibited for the case with $uid = 123$. Only a second user is allowed to execute task check loan accommodations for the instance with $uid = 123$.

4.3   Discussion

The presented ISC patterns can be considered *comprehensive* w.r.t. the existing ISC categorization [19] and collection of real-world ISC [3]. Still, new ISC examples might lead to additional ISC patterns. Besides, the current collection of ISC patterns does not cover ISC for handling exceptions which might be quite diverse since exceptions can be manifold. Existing workflow patterns for exception handling[3] seem to be a useful starting point for modeling ISC exception handling patterns. Moreover, processes and process instances might be subject to multiple ISC at once, i.e., ISC patterns must be *combinable* without interrupting and influencing each other. Regarding the *simplicity* of the formalization choice: Consider as an ISC example *five tokens need to be consumed simultaneously by transition B*. This could simply be modeled by having capacity 5 for the arc before task B and a timed WF-net without colors. So, for this simple ISC, Proclets and colors are actually not required. However, as mentioned before, ISC can have further conditions. Consider, e.g., *task B must be executed for five instances simultaneously by the same resource R1*. In this case, we need to check whether five instances have arrived before task B for R1, i.e., token colors are required in order to model and consequently check the resource. Additionally, we need a knowledge base that has stored all instances and corresponding data values and can be queried whether enough instances have arrived for resource R1. Hence, the expressiveness of Proclets based on timed colored WF-nets is mandatory.

5   Conclusion

This work presents 6 patterns for constraints spanning multiple process instances of one or multiple process types. These ISC patterns are based on a collection

---

[3] http://www.workflowpatterns.com/patterns/exception/.

of real-world ISC examples and an existing ISC categorization. Several requirements imposed by ISC, like support of instance correlation or the need for representing instance spanning attributes, led to selecting Proclets based on timed colored Workflow nets for ISC pattern formalization. ISC patterns are evaluated through an application to business processes as well as existing approaches such as batching and security. The discussion outlines several links to future work including the elicitation and formalization of ISC patterns for exception handling as well as investigating how ISC patterns can be combined without introducing, e.g., a blocking of the process execution. When implementing and executing ISC at runtime, aspects such as scalability become subject for investigation well.

References

1. van Der Aalst, W.M., Ter Hofstede, A.H., Kiepuszewski, B., Barros, A.P.: Distributed and parallel databases. Workflow Patterns **14**(1), 5–51 (2003)
2. Fahland, D., de Leoni, M., van Dongen, B., van der Aalst, W.: Checking behavioral conformance of artifacts. BPM Center Report BPM-11-08, BPMcenter.org (2011)
3. Fdhila, W., Gall, M., Rinderle-Ma, S., Mangler, J., Indiono, C.: Classification and formalization of instance-spanning constraints in process-driven applications. In: La Rosa, M., Loos, P., Pastor, O. (eds.) BPM 2016. LNCS, vol. 9850, pp. 348–364. Springer, Cham (2016). https://doi.org/10.1007/978-3-319-45348-4_20
4. Gall, M., Rinderle-Ma, S.: Visual modeling of instance-spanning constraints in process-aware information systems. In: Dubois, E., Pohl, K. (eds.) CAiSE 2017. LNCS, vol. 10253, pp. 597–611. Springer, Cham (2017). https://doi.org/10.1007/978-3-319-59536-8_37
5. Jensen, K., Kristensen, L.M.: Coloured Petri Nets. Springer, Heidelberg (2009). https://doi.org/10.1007/b95112
6. Ly, L.T., Maggi, F.M., Montali, M., Rinderle-Ma, S., van der Aalst, W.M.P.: Compliance monitoring in business processes: functionalities, application, and tool-support. Inf. Syst. **54**, 209–234 (2015)
7. Mangler, J., Rinderle-Ma, S.: Rule-based synchronization of process activities. In: Commerce and Enterprise Computing, pp. 121–128 (2011)
8. Mans, R., Russell, N.C., van der Aalst, W.M., Bakker, P.J., Moleman, A.J., Jaspers, M.W.: Proclets in healthcare. J. Biomed. Inform. **43**(4), 632–649 (2010)
9. Martin, N., Swennen, M., Depaire, B., Jans, M., Caris, A., Vanhoof, K.: Retrieving batch organisation of work insights from event logs. Decis. Support Syst. **100**, 119–128 (2017)
10. Pufahl, L., Meyer, A., Weske, M.: Batch regions: Process instance synchronization based on data. In: Enterprise Distributed Object Computing, pp. 150–159 (2014)
11. dos Santos, D.R., Ranise, S.: On run-time enforcement of authorization constraints in security-sensitive workflows. In: Cimatti, A., Sirjani, M. (eds.) SEFM 2017. LNCS, vol. 10469, pp. 203–218. Springer, Cham (2017). https://doi.org/10.1007/978-3-319-66197-1_13
12. Senderovich, A., Weidlich, M., Gal, A., Mandelbaum, A.: Queue mining for delay prediction in multi-class service processes. Inf. Syst. **53**, 278–295 (2015)
13. Van Der Aalst, W.: Process Mining: Discovery, Conformance and Enhancement of Business Processes, vol. 2. Springer, Heidelberg (2011). https://doi.org/10.1007/978-3-642-19345-3

14. Van Der Aalst, W.M., Barthelmess, P., Ellis, C.A., Wainer, J.: Proclets: a framework for lightweight interacting workflow processes. Int. J. Coop. Inf. Syst. **10**(04), 443–481 (2001)
15. Voglhofer, T., Rinderle-Ma, S.: Collection and elicitation of business process compliance patterns with focus on data aspects. Bus. Inf. Syst. Eng. **62**, 361–377 (2019)
16. Weber, B., Reichert, M., Rinderle-Ma, S.: Change patterns and change support features - enhancing flexibility in process-aware information systems. Data Knowl. Eng. **66**(3), 438–466 (2008)
17. Weske, M.: Business Process Management: Concepts, Languages, Architectures. Springer, Heidelberg (2007). https://doi.org/10.1007/978-3-540-73522-9 ⌐
18. Winter, K., Rinderle-Ma, S.: Discovering instance-spanning constraints from process execution logs based on classification techniques. In: Enterprise Distributed Object Computing Conference, pp. 79–88 (2017)
19. Winter, K., Stertz, F., Rinderle-Ma, S.: Discovering instance and process spanning constraints from process execution logs. Inf. Syst. **89**, 101484 (2020)

Contribution of Conceptual Modeling to Enhancing Historians' Intuition - Application to Prosopography

Jacky Akoka[1,2], Isabelle Comyn-Wattiau[3]([⊠]), Stéphane Lamassé[4], and Cédric du Mouza[1]

[1] CEDRIC-CNAM, Paris, France
jacky.akoka@lecnam.net, dumouza@cnam.fr
[2] Institut Mines Telecom-Business School, Evry, France
[3] ESSEC Business School, Cergy, France
wattiau@essec.edu
[4] LAMOP-Sorbonne University, Paris, France
stephane.lamasse@univ-paris1.fr

Abstract. Historians, and in particular researchers in prosopography, focus a lot of effort on extracting and coding information from historical sources to build databases. To deal with this situation, they rely in some cases on their intuition. One important issue is to provide these researchers with the information extracted from the sources in a sufficiently structured form to allow the databases to be queried and to verify, and possibly, to validate hypotheses. The research in this paper attempts to take up the challenge of helping historians capturing and assessing information throughout automatic processes. The issue emerges when too many sources of uncertain information are available. Based on the high-level information fusion approach, we propose a process that automatically supports historians' intuition in the domain of prosopography. The contribution is threefold: a conceptual data model, a process model, and a set of rules combining the reliability of sources and the credibility of information.

Keywords: Conceptual model · Process model · Uncertain information · Historian's intuition · Prosopography · Information fusion · Uncertain Knowledge Graph

1 Introduction

Historians, and in particular researchers in prosopography, generally study well documented small groups of elites and/or large groups of individuals, mostly anonymous and poorly documented. In both cases the reliability and the quality of the source material is crucial. Prosopography is a domain of research in the field of History related to the inquiry into the common characteristics of a group of historical actors by means of a collective study of their lives (Stone 1971). Prosopographical research has benefited from database technology, relying on relational databases to structure the data describing

G. Dobbie et al. (Eds.): ER 2020, LNCS 12400, pp. 164–173, 2020.
https://doi.org/10.1007/978-3-030-62522-1_12

these individuals. These databases allow researchers to conjecture and test hypotheses. Hypothesis testing is a process that involves performing several steps ranging from the processing of the information contained in different and multiple sources to the validation of the hypothesis. This is not a simple transformation process. It gives rise to several interpretations due to the use of natural language. The latter is ambiguous, information is incomplete and imprecise. The structured representation of this information must also encode the uncertainty that characterizes it.

Data fusion researchers have proposed a process model that facilitates the integration of data and knowledge from several sources (Esteban *et al.* 2005). There are many analogies between information fusion and the process implemented by historians and researchers in prosopography, which captures information from historical sources to reconcile it, aiming at verifying historical hypotheses on the basis of a given population. We propose to adapt the information fusion process to the development of prosopographical databases, automatically gathering the information contained in the historical sources and aspiring the data of the existing databases, if any.

Our contribution is threefold: i) a conceptual data model gathering and representing the basic concepts of prosopography, ii) a conceptual process model adapting and enriching the high-level information fusion process, and iii) a set of rules ensuring the combination of the credibility of information and the reliability of sources to provide the researchers with automatically consolidated information. The combination of these three artifacts makes it possible to consolidate and further develop the intuition of researchers in History, and in particular of those in prosopography.

2   Related Work

An important issue facing prosopographical researchers is how to make available the information extracted from different sources in a structured form to allow the databases to be queried and to verify, and possibly validate, hypotheses. Conceptual modeling helps to achieve this goal. Moreover, historians' ability to analyze this information by using their intuition may be limited by the fact that the information they capture originates from several sources and it can be inconsistent, ambiguous, and uncertain. Finally, it can be imprecise and incomplete. Providing the researchers in prosopography with an information fusion process will help them to develop a sharper intuition. The use of intuition is justified by the fact that History is very often seen as an interpretative discipline, allowing a plurality of opinions. In order to facilitate this interpretation, intuition is helpful, especially when expertise is not sufficient, when the problem and the data are unstructured, and finally when there is a lack of objective criteria (Barraclough 1966).

2.1   Conceptual Modeling for Prosopography

Although there are several conceptual models to represent prosopographical data, the most common conceptual model is that of the factoid. Prosopography of Anglo-Saxon England (PASE) is an example of a factoid model[1]. Other examples include the Roman

---

[1] http://www.pase.ac.uk/.

Republic project (Figueira and Vieira 2017) and Charlemagne's European conceptual model[2]. (Akoka *et al.* 2019) present a conceptual model that gathers and makes more generic the information contained in different prosopographical databases, namely the concepts of *People, Factoids, Places* and *Sources*. It also incorporates a representation of uncertainty.

Note that not all prosopographical databases use the factoid conceptual model. For example, Studium Parisiense[3] uses a logical model without reference to the factoids. CHARM[4] is a reference model for cultural heritage. Conceptual modeling of prosopographical projects also calls on ontologies. The Factoid Prosopography Ontology (FPO), ontology of the PASE project, is based on OWL/RDFS. The CIDOC-CRM ontology is not based on factoids but on temporal entities which generalize the concept of event (Doerr 2003). It represents information relating to cultural heritage. To our knowledge, these ontologies do not take into account vagueness of information. An approach for the quantification of uncertain information can be found in (Martin-Rodilla *et al.* 2019). As it can be seen, there is not a single conceptual data model that encompasses the different viewpoints of prosopographical researchers.

2.2 Information Fusion Process

Information fusion is "an automated process which involves combining data in the broadest sense to estimate or predict the state of some aspects of a problem space of interest" (Snidaro *et al.* 2016). Information fusion, used to improve the quality of the information being considered, can greatly improve the imperfection that characterizes information captured by historians including information inconsistencies. Moreover, historians may have to make choices, but they have to face information conflicts that can be solved using information fusion approaches (Luo and Kay 1988).

Many fusion approaches, models, and techniques have been proposed (Castanedo 2013). Data fusion approaches include probabilistic, evidential belief reasoning, and rough set-based fusion. Contributions in data fusion include (Alam *et al.* 2018; Snidaro *et al.* 2016; Pires *et al.* 2016; Yao *et al.* 2008; Menga *et al.* 2020; Blasch *et al.* 2012; Blasch *et al.* 2013). The objective of the first JDL Data Fusion model was to provide a process flow for sensor data fusion (Kessler *et al.* 1991).

In summary, and to the best of our knowledge, there is not a prosopographical conceptual process model adapting and enriching the high-level information fusion process. Building on the analogy between the information fusion process and the manual process of the historian confronting different sources of information, we propose a conceptual data model and a process model that can be completely automated.

3 The Conceptual Data Model

Information in one source can be supplemented, reinforced or contradicted by information in another source. When two pieces of information complement each other, in

---

[2] http://www.charlemagneseurope.ac.uk/.

[3] http://lamop-vs3.univ-paris1.fr/studium.

[4] http://www.charminfo.org.

most cases, the incompleteness can be reduced. When two pieces of information are confirmed, the uncertainty is reduced. When they contradict each other, they can be juxtaposed and then be subject to the expertise of the historian who will relies on rules, on the credibility she grants to the source or on her interpretation of the context in which the author has written. A challenge is therefore to design a model which captures all this information and their cohabitation.

3.1 The Basic Concepts of Our Approach

Our aim is to provide a unified model reconciling historians' viewpoints based mainly on four main concepts: *mention, factoid, fact,* and *hypothesis.*

Definition 1. *Mention: information found in a source.*

The mention is our finest grain information. It may be presented as affirmative (credibility $= 1$) or with a level of uncertainty ($0 <$ credibility < 1). It may also be defined with a given level of precision. An information fusion process for prosopographical research starts with source digitization, natural language processing (NLP) techniques encompassing the capture of mentions, followed by named entity recognition (NER) mechanisms to ensure the translation of mentions into factoids.

Definition 2. *Factoid: assertion based on one or several mentions with a certain level of agreement among historians.*

The factoid was coined in 1973 by (Mailer 1973) as a fact which has no existence before appearing in a magazine or newspaper. In the factoid model, it denotes an assertion made by the project team that a source 'S' at location 'L' states something ('F') about person 'P'. A mention is an atomic factoid, in the sense that it cannot be decomposed into simpler elements. Moreover, it is linked to a unique source. It is also marked by uncertainty and imprecision.

Definition 3. *Fact: assertion that is known or proved to be true.*

Oppositely to a factoid, an assertion is a fact when it receives a large consensus to be true. A fact may result from the reconciliation of several similar factoids. As a consequence, it may be less precise, representing to some extent the greatest common divisor of several factoids. A fact achieves a broad consensus between historians, forming an historical truth. Some mentions may automatically be considered as facts given the status of the source where they come from.

Definition 4. *Hypothesis: tentative statement about the relationship between two or more facts and/or factoids.*

Research in humanities aims at proving or disproving hypotheses. The latter may not only be defined on facts but frequently imply less agreed assertions, represented as factoids in our context.

3.2 The Conceptual Data Model

The conceptual model described in Fig. 1 is adapted from (Akoka *et al.* 2019) in order to meet several requirements: i) encompass and put together the different viewpoints of prosopographical researchers; ii) conform to the information fusion process; iii) automatically propagate the certainty of information throughout the main concepts (mention, factoid, fact, hypothesis) as explained below (Fig. 2). A factoid may be composed of simpler factoids. If two sources describe the same information, they constitute two mentions in our model. The researcher interprets the different factoids leading to facts. The latter may be simple or may aggregate simple facts. Both factoids and facts, represented by the generic entity Datum, may support hypotheses. Factoids as well as facts are related to the other main concepts of prosopography, i.e. Persons, Places, and Time that we don't represent here for space reasons.

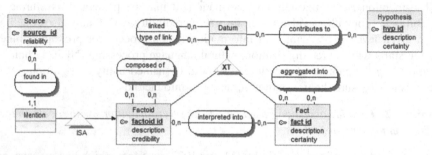

Fig. 1. The conceptual data model (an excerpt)

This conceptual data model provides researchers with a model whose aim is to integrate the different factoid visions and to reconcile the different prosopographical approaches. It also supports our process model, the aim of which is to automate the building process of the historian's intuition. The combination of this data model and the process model presented below will save prosopography researchers' time, allow better handling of the uncertainty, and the possibility of going back to the source databases to interpret the uncertainty.

3.3 The Conceptual Process Model

We describe the historical information fusion process by the means of a conceptual model (Fig. 2). To the best of our knowledge, it is the first time that the information fusion process model is adapted to digital humanities. The idea is to implement and make automatic the construction of the historian's intuition. Information capture (source preprocessing of information fusion) is based on NLP, ETL, and NER techniques and feeds the mentions of our conceptual data model. Credibility and reliability are also encoded. Making this step automatic releases the historian from this task so that she devotes herself to the generation of hypotheses. The certainty of the *mention* results from the combination (by a function to be defined) of the reliability of the source, combined with the credibility of the information as described in the source (for example, a very reliable source says: "it is very likely that..."). The main phases of our conceptual process model are described below.

1. Information Capture phase: basically, this phase consists in aspiring in *mentions*, information contained in the sources. We can assign a certainty combining the reliability of the source and the credibility of the information.

Fig. 2. Process model

2. Factoid Association phase (level 1 of data fusion, or object refinement) applies association techniques (spatio-temporal alignment, correlation, clustering, grouping, etc.) to bring together statements that are similar and thus consolidate their certainty in a *factoid* of the same grain but with a higher certainty or construct a more structured *factoid* grouping together the different similar *mentions*. The "factoid association" combines all similar *factoids* to generate new richer or safer *factoids*. It compares the *factoids* based on their similar dimensions like the people involved for example. Thus, it can also spot people with similar names (using metrics like edit distance) involved in similar *factoids*. For example, if a new source of information is received, we can trigger the "factoid association" using forward chaining to deduce all the *factoids* resulting from this new arrival of information. In backward chaining, starting from a factoid, it searches for the simpler factoids that compose it. Factoid association generates factoids from factoids. We could formalize the concepts of the greatest common divisor and the least common multiple or max and min in a lattice.

3. Fact Establishment phase (level 2 of data fusion or situation assessment) makes it possible to combine factoids to converge on a fact. It combines different statistical techniques (removal of false positives, definition of a certainty threshold, etc.) and makes it possible to deduce facts. Again, we can fire a forward chaining in a classic application of the whole process from the capture of new information to, in cascade, enrich the entire database. We can also, in backward chaining, verify a hypothesis and for this seek the presence of supporting facts and the presence of factoids sufficiently convergent to attest the fact. In addition, for all factoids reaching a certain degree of confidence, one can establish a fact. One can also directly integrate in facts *mentions* since the reliability of the source is very strong.

4. Hypothesis Test and Verification phase. It is analogous to the previous one. It relies on *factoids* and *facts* to confirm or refute a hypothesis.

5. Feedback propagation phase. To our knowledge, this phase is new in the information fusion process. When a *hypothesis* is confirmed (resp. infirmed), it makes it possible to back propagate in the various *factoids* and in the information relating to the sources, the enhanced (resp. diminished) reliability of these sources. It is also during this phase that we can imagine thus downgrading a *fact*.

4 Illustrative Example

Let us consider two different prosopographical data sources relating to historical figure Thomas Aquinas, considered as one of the main masters of scholastic philosophy and Catholic theology. Each source can be represented as an Uncertain Knowledge Graph (Fig. 3), logical representation of our conceptual data model. For space reason, we cannot describe the mapping between conceptual and logical levels. Uncertain Knowledge Graph (UKG) have been recently investigated (Chen *et al.* 2019). They represent knowledge as a set of relations R defined over a set of entities E. More precisely, it consists of a set of weighted triples UKG = {(t, s)}, with t = (e1, r, e2) a triple representing a relation fact where (e1, e2) $\in E^2$ and r $\in$ R, and s $\in$ [0, 1] represents the confidence score for this relation fact to be true.

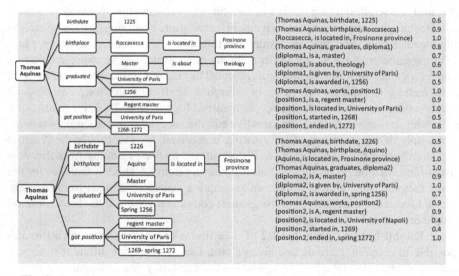

Fig. 3. Two prosopographical data sources represented as Uncertain Knowledge Graphs

A prosopographical data source can be considered as a collection of mentions. Basically a mention is a set of triples (subject, predicate, value) obtained using the n-ary relations transformation proposed by W3C[5]. Moreover, each triple is associated with a certainty score which represents the confidence we have for this relation to be true. As for UKG, we perform inference, for instance based on PSL logic (Chen *et al.* 2019). Since our objective is to integrate new prosopographical data, we must additionally define rules to combine information whose certainty can be reinforced or weakened. These rules are essentially expert rules. Thanks to these rules we can automate the process depicted in Fig. 2. We provide in the following some examples of these rules.

Similarity Detection: Before applying a composition rule for two triples (s1, p, v1) and (s2, p, v2) we check whether s1 and s2 refer to the same subject. So we assume the

---

[5] https://www.w3.org/TR/swbp-n-aryRelations/.

existence of a similarity function for each domain, denoted $\text{sim}\_D\colon D \times D \rightarrow \aleph$. This similarity is based on expert rules and largely differs from one domain to another.

Composition Rules: Let T be the set of domains organized as tree (or upper semi-lattice), thanks to a predicate: is located in, is a, etc. For a domain $D \in T$ and its associated predicate p, we denote $\text{LCM}_p\colon D \times D \rightarrow D$ the least common ancestor function for predicate. We also define the concept distance for a domain $D \in T$ $\text{dist}_p(v1, v2) = \min(\text{dist}_a(v1, \text{LCM}(v1, v2)), \text{dist}_a(v2, \text{LCM}(v1, v2)))$ where $\text{dist}_a(x, y)$ returns the difference between the level of y and x in the tree. So the closer one of the two values is to their LCM the smaller the concept distance is.

Rule 1 [Value-Consistent Predicate]: Assume a predicate p, and $\text{codomain}(p) \in T$, we have: $\{(s, p, v1), p1\} \wedge \{(s, p, v2), p2\} \wedge \text{dist}_p(v1, v2) \leq \tau$

$$\rightarrow \{(s, p, \text{LCM}(v1, v2)), \text{aggreg\_lcm}(p1, p2)\}$$

Aggreg_lcm is an aggregation function for the two probabilities. For consistent values it can be for instance max, avg, min, or $1 - (1 - p1) \times (1 - p2)$. τ is the distance threshold for the concept distance. Its objective is to avoid to deduce some information with an important loss of precision (for instance LCM(Paris, Versailles) = Parisian Region is accepted, but LCM(Paris, Roma) = Europe is not).

Rule 2 [Value-Inconsistent Predicate]: Assume a predicate p, and $\text{codomain}(p) \in T$. we have: $\{(s, p, v1), p1\} \wedge \{(s, p, v2), p2\} \wedge \text{dist}_p(v1, v2) \wedge p1 > p2 > \tau$

$$\rightarrow \{(s, p, v1), \text{aggreg\_inconsistent}(p1, p2)\}$$

Aggreg_inconsistent is an aggregation function for the two probabilities. For inconsistent values it can be for instance $\min(p1, p2)$, $p1 - p2$, or $p1 \times (1 - p2)$

Rule 3 [Fact Building]: Consider the set of all triples associated to a subject s, denoted Ω, and a threshold value π set for the system, that we call the fact threshold. We also denote with Ω^+ the subset of Ω composed by the triples with a certainty value greater than π. Then we decide that Ω^+ is a fact while Ω is a complex factoid.

In the example, if $\pi = 0.9$, 'Thomas Aquinas got a diploma and this diploma is a master' is a fact. Thomas Aquinas got a diploma and this diploma is a master in 1256 is a factoid. Assume we have a source S3: {(Thomas Aquinas, graduates, diploma3), 1.0} and {(diploma3, is A, doctorate), 0.4} and {(diploma3, is awarded in, 1256), 0.9}.
→: {(Thomas Aquinas, graduates, diploma2), 0.99} and {(diploma2, is A, master), 0.58} and {(diploma2, is awarded in, 1256), 0.98}. So now, the fact is Thomas Aquinas got a diploma and this diploma was received in 1256 and no more the previous one.

In the previous example, we tried to illustrate how our conceptual model may be derived into a logical knowledge graph and how our information fusion process may propagate the credibility of the mentions extracted from the sources to the facts but also infirm facts.

5   Validation of the Approach

(Prat *et al.* 2015) consider that a design science approach generally results in a set of artifacts constituting a system and proposes to validate the properties of this system. We use their framework to present the different validations we conducted. In italics, we mention the criteria that we were able to check.

The system composed of these two conceptual models is goal-directed. We mainly tried to assess the *goal attainment* criterion. The criterion *added value* is twofold. The combination of factoids assigned with credibility improves the state-of-the-art by providing the historians with an enriched set of information that would require too much time to be explored directly. Their confidence is based on the fact that they initially define the reliability of the sources, which is one component of the credibility computed on factoids. The second added value is due to the feedback propagation step which automatically updates the reliability of sources resulting from their confrontation.

In order to check the *utility* of the approach, we organized a focus group with historians. We explained the data model and the process model and questioned them on the ability of the approach to represent their reasoning. They were able to validate our objective: better define a process that can then be automated and considerably improve the state-of-the-art by embedding the codification of the credibility. They could also enrich our understanding by providing us with several publications where historians tried to explain their reasoning.

We also questioned the historians to check the *completeness* and the *minimality* of our conceptual data model. In our first version, the **mention** was an entity related to **factoid** but not a subtype of it. This idea was first considered as interesting. But they were unable to clearly distinguish between **mentions** and **factoids** whereas they were immediately convinced by the interest of representing both *factoids* and *facts*.

Regarding the conceptual process model, they think that it really represents their reasoning when analyzing directly information sources. In particular, depending on the category of sources (e.g. registers of universities), one can immediately translate the information contained in terms of *facts*. In other sources (e.g. testimonies), usually only *factoids* can be deduced and a credibility may be associated. In this sense, we can consider that we checked the *fidelity* of the process model *to the phenomenon it represents* (the construction of the historian's intuition).

This validation allowed us to check its *technical feasibility* using the mapping to knowledge graphs and testing some inference rules.

6   Conclusion and Future Research

The research question discussed in this paper is how to enhance historians' intuition. We answered the research question by developing an approach based on the combination of a conceptual data model and a conceptual process model. The conceptual data model captures the main concepts of prosopography while the process model implements and makes automatic the construction of the historian's intuition. This model is enriched with a feedback propagation step, useful when a hypothesis tested by historians is confirmed (resp. infirmed), allowing them to back propagate the results in the information relating to the historical sources. We also provided a set of rules combining the reliability of sources and the credibility of information manipulated by historians, in particular in prosopography. We illustrated the approach using two different data sources, represented as uncertain knowledge graphs. Finally, an argumentation is presented to validate our approach. Future research will include more experimentations and a comprehensive implementation, leading to the proposition of additional rules, and alternative methods for combining credibility depending on the context.

References

Akoka, J., Comyn-Wattiau, I., Lamassé, S., Du Mouza, C.: Modeling historical social networks databases. In: Proceedings of Hawaii International Conference on System Sciences (2019)

Alam, F., Mehmood, R., Katib, I., Albogami, N.N., Albeshri, A.: Data fusion and IoT for smart ubiquitous environments: a survey. IEEE Access **5**, 9533–9554 (2018)

Barraclough, G.: Gordon Wright, an introduction to contemporary history. (New York: Basic Books. 1964. Pp. vii, 272. $4.95.). Am. Hist. Rev. **71**(2), 510–511 (1966). https://doi.org/10.1086/ahr/71.2.510

Blasch, E., Steinberg, A., Das, S., Llinas, J., Chong, C.-Y., et al.: Revisiting the JDL model for information exploitation. In: International Conference on Information Fusion (2013)

Blasch, E.P.: High level information fusion (HLIF): survey of models, issues, and grand challenges. IEEE Aerosp. Electron. Syst. Mag. **27**, 4–20 (2012)

Castanedo, F.: A review of data fusion techniques. Sci. World J. **2013**, 1–19 (2013)

Chen, X., Chen, M., Shi, W., Sun, Y., Zaniolo, C.: Embedding uncertain knowledge graphs. In: AAAI, pp. 3363–3370 (2019)

Doerr, M.: The CIDOC conceptual reference module: an ontological approach to semantic interoperability of metadata. AI Mag. **24**(3), 75 (2003)

Esteban, J., Starr, A., Willetts, R., et al.: A review of data fusion models and architectures: towards engineering guidelines. Neural Comput. Appl. **14**, 273–281 (2005)

Figueira, L., Vieira, M.: Modelling a prosopography for the Roman republic. In: The Digital Prosopography of the Roman Republic Project, Digital Humanities Conference (2017)

Kessler, O., et al.: Functional description of the data fusion process, technical report for the office of naval technology data fusion development strategy. Naval Air Development Center (1991)

Luo, R.C., Kay, M.: Multisensor integration and fusion: issues and approaches. In: Proceedings of Sensor Fusion, SPIE, vol. 0931 (1988)

Mailer, N.: Marilyn: A Biography. Grosset & Dunlap, New York (1973)

Martin-Rodilla, P., Pereira-Fariña, M., Gonzalez-Perez, C.: Qualifying and quantifying uncertainty in digital humanities: a fuzzy-logic approach. In: Proceedings of the Seventh International Conference on Technological Ecosystems for Enhancing Multiculturality, pp. 788–794 (2019)

Menga, T., Jinga, X., Zheng, Y., Pedryczc, W.: A survey on machine learning for data fusion. Inf. Fusion **57**, 115–129 (2020)

Pires, I.M., Garcia, N.M., Pombo, N., Flórez-Revuelta, F.: From data acquisition to data fusion: a comprehensive review and a roadmap for the identification of activities of daily living using mobile devices. Sensors **16**(2), 184 (2016)

Prat, N., Comyn-Wattiau, I., Akoka, J.: A taxonomy of evaluation methods for information systems artifacts. J. Manag. Inf. Syst. **32**(3), 229–267 (2015)

Snidaro, L., García, J., Llinas, J., Blasch, E. (eds.): Context-enhanced information fusion. In: Advances in Computer Vision and Pattern Recognition, 2016 (2016)

Stone, L.: Prosopography. Daedalus **100**(1), 46–79 (1971)

Yao, J., Raghavan, V., Wu, Z.: Web information fusion: a review of the state of the art. Inf. Fusion **9**(4), 446–449 (2008)

A Code-Efficient Process Scripting Language

Maxim Vidgof[1]([⊠]) [iD], Philipp Waibel[1] [iD], Jan Mendling[1] [iD], Martin Schimak[2],
Alexander Seik[3], and Peter Queteschiner[3]

[1] Institute for Information Business, WU Wien, Vienna, Austria
{maxim.vidgof,philipp.waibel,jan.mendling}@wu.ac.at
[2] Plexiti, Vienna, Austria
martin.schimak@plexiti.com
[3] Phactum, Wickenburggasse 26/2, 1080 Vienna, Austria
{alexander.seik,peter.queteschiner}@phactum.at

Abstract. Business process management systems are an important piece of infrastructure for digital transformation initiatives. Rapid development of executable business processes is a key requirement in this context. Even though there are various process modeling languages available, none of them is designed with the ambition to be code efficient and expressive at the same time. In this paper, we investigated the research question how a process scripting language can be defined that addresses the four requirements of code efficiency, control flow expressiveness, data processing and event processing. To this end, we designed and implemented a process scripting language based on Kotlin. To analyze the language regarding the four requirements, we use the language in a case study of a real-world process of our industry partner.

Keywords: Process languages · Process modelling · Domain-specific languages · Kotlin

1 Introduction

Business process management systems (BPMS) play an increasingly important role for the digital transformation of many companies [10]. Since the inception in the 1980s as office automation [12] and then workflow management systems [11], BPMS technology has developed into a commodity that is available as open-source packages like Bonitasoft or Camunda [10] and as components in frameworks such as Uber's Cadence[1], Netflix Conductor[2] or Amazon Step Functions[3]. All these systems and frameworks have in common that business processes are specified using process modeling languages, either textual or visual ones.

---

[1] https://cadenceworkflow.io.
[2] https://netflix.github.io/conductor/.
[3] https://docs.aws.amazon.com/step-functions/latest/dg/welcome.html.

© Springer Nature Switzerland AG 2020
G. Dobbie et al. (Eds.): ER 2020, LNCS 12400, pp. 174–188, 2020.
https://doi.org/10.1007/978-3-030-62522-1_13

A plethora of process modeling languages has been proposed in the past with diverging strengths and weaknesses [27]. Many of the more important control flow patterns have been integrated into the Business Process Model and Notation (BPMN) as a lingua franca [1]. However, what is often neglected is the fact that BPMN is an underspecified language without proper support for data processing on the visual level. Other languages like Cadence are in essence programming languages for processes, but missing important abstractions. Indeed, it is a gap of current research that an executable process modeling language with proper data processing and powerful abstractions for development is missing.

In this paper, we address this research gap by presenting a process scripting language called Factscript that combines the strengths of different types of process modeling languages to overcome their weaknesses. More specifically, Factscript is designed as a code-efficient domain-specific language (DSL) that is meant to help developers for rapid implementation of business processes. We have implemented Factscript in Kotlin[4] with a deployment for Camunda BPMS. We demonstrate the language usage in a case study of a real-world process of our industry partner and analyze the language regarding requirements for a code-efficient process scripting language.

The rest of the paper is structured as follows. Section 2 discusses the background of our study with a focus on requirements for a code-efficient process scripting language. Section 3 describes the design of Factscript with reference to the design process for DSLs. Section 4 presents our case study and Sect. 5 concludes the paper.

2 Background

This section discusses different types of process modeling languages. First, we discuss visual languages, then code-based languages. We compare both in turn and identify requirements for a language that provides code efficiency while integrating control-flow expressiveness, data and event processing capabilities.

2.1 Visual Languages

Workflow management systems saw an increasing uptake in the 1990s. These systems mostly used proprietary process modeling languages [27, p. 93]. The Workflow Management Coalition was established in 1993 to achieve interoperability by defining standard interfaces. The standard for Interface 1 defined the exchange format for process models [27, p. 121]. By the turn of the millenium, the heterogeneity of languages became an increasing roadblock of practical adoption of workflow systems. An industry initiative led to the specification of the Business Process Execution Language for Web Services (BPEL4WS, later only WS-BPEL or just BPEL) sponsored by OASIS [13]. Research of the workflow pattern initiative consolidated various control flow concepts [2,23].

---

[4] https://kotlinlang.org/.

Neither BPEL nor the workflow patterns provide a visual language for process modeling, but both together define the key concepts that informed the definition of the Business Process Model and Notation (BPMN) [1]. BPMN supports the major control flow constructs that are identified by the workflow pattern initiative including sequence, parallel split and synchronization, choice and merge, multiple choice, and event-based choice [26]. The BPMN specification also defines a transformation to BPEL with a focus on control flow elements, message passing and data mapping [1]. The data mapping assumes that data properties are specified additionally to the visual elements of the BPMN model.

2.2 Code-Based Languages

In the early years of the 21st century, several code-based languages were proposed for supporting the orchestration of complex web services [27, p. 93]. Many of them where used as interchange formats and hardly for directly programming executable processes [17]. BPEL represents the convergence of process automation concepts building on web services at the time around 2007, and it has been so far the last code-based language for process execution that was standardized. Table 1 compares how BPEL supports the most important workflow patterns with BPMN and more recent languages.

Table 1. Control flow constructs in BPEL and BPMN

Workflow pattern	BPEL	BPMN	Netflix	Uber	AWS State Language
Sequence	Sequence	Sequence	Sequence	Sequence	Sequence
Parallel split	Flow	AND split	Parallel	-	FORK_JOIN
Synchronization		AND join			JOIN
Exclusive choice	If-Else	XOR split	Choice	If-Else	DECISION
Merge		XOR join			
Multiple choice	Flow	OR split	-	-	-
Merge		OR join			
Cycles (0:n Loop)	While	XOR join	-	While	Choice
Cycles (1:n Loop)	Repeat	XOR split	DO_WHILE	Do-While	Choice
Deferred choice	Pick	Event split	-	-	-

Today, BPEL is discontinued. Recently, new code-based languages for process execution have been developed for cloud computing [3,4] and microservice architectures [8,22]. Platforms like Netflix, Uber, and Amazon have developed their own frameworks, mostly open source, for implementing microservice-based architecture for their systems. Orchestrating these microservices is as much as a challenge as it was with web service architectures [9]. To address this need, the mentioned companies have developed highly scalable execution engines for processes and accompanying process model languages. These languages are mainly used by developers and are code-based with a JSON or Java syntax.

Prominent examples of such new code-based languages are Netflix Conductor, Uber Cadence, and Amazon AWS State Language. These three modeling languages support the orchestration of microservices, but with some differences. While Netflix Conductor and Amazon AWS State Language provide process modeling languages that are JSON-based, Uber Cadence is based on Java. Uber Cadence was designed to provide the developers with a syntax that developers are familiar with and that can be integrated directly into Java code. In contrast, Netflix and Amazon opted for a modeling language that is independent of the programming language and, thus, opt for JSON. For Amazon, the possibility to easily integrate AWS Cloud Services, e.g., AWS Lambda, was also important.

2.3   Requirements

The different process modeling languages exhibit strengths and weaknesses as summarized in Table 2. First, the novel languages of Netflix, Uber, and Amazon address the need for rapid development based on a compact syntax. Corresponding benefits of an efficient and natural problem specification have been emphasized by research on programming [21] and domain-specific languages [15,24]. An efficient syntax helps developers to achieve high programming productivity, for instance in terms of program length and total working time on a program [21]. Efficient syntax is a weakness of BPEL and BPMN. Second, the languages vary in their degree of workflow pattern support. While BPEL and BPMN are largely inspired by the workflow patterns, the new microservice languages have notable gaps in pattern support. Third, the languages differ in their data processing capabilities. While all code-based languages cover data processing, BPMN provides only an informal data specification at the visual level. Fourth, BPEL and BPMN are strong in event processing thanks to their ambition to support web service orchestration. The novel languages partially follow a closed system philosophy with limited event processing capabilities.

Table 2. Factscript Requirements and Existing Language Strengths and Weaknesses ("+" strength, "−" weakness)

Requirement	BPEL	BPMN	Netflix	Uber	AWS
R1 Efficient Syntax	−	−	+	+	+
R2 Control Flow	+	+	+/−	−	+/−
R3 Data Processing	+	−	+	+	+
R4 Event Processing	+	+	+/−	−	+/−

The aim of this research is to combine the strengths of the different languages. To this end, our research goal is to design a code-based process scripting language that addresses (R1) an efficient syntax, (R2) extensive control flow support, (R3) support of data processing, and (R4) support of event processing.

3 Conceptual Design of Factscript

This section discusses the design of Factscript according to the requirements identified in Sect. 2.3. For the development of Factscript, we followed the DSL development process presented by Mernik et al. [5,18,19]. It includes seven phases: *decision, analysis, design, implementation, testing, deployment,* and *maintenance.* Below, we focus on analysis, design and implementation.

3.1 Analysis Phase

In the analysis phase, we focus on three aspects that R2-R4 emphasize: *Expressiveness of control flow, expressiveness of data processing,* and *expressiveness of messaging and event handling.* For each of these aspects, domain experts were asked to select one representative language that we analyzed more deeply.

Expressiveness of Language Control Flow: The control flow of a process describes the different constructs that a language provides for defining the potential sequences of activities [14]. As BPMN supports the majority of control flow constructs [26] and is the de-facto standard in industry, we refer to this language regarding expressiveness of control flow. The major control flow constructs covered by BPMN are sequence, parallel split and synchronization, choice and merge (XOR), multiple choice and merge (OR), and event-based choice. In order to achieve the same level of control flow expressiveness for Factscript, we decided to include these constructs.

Expressiveness of Data Processing: Even though BPMN provides extensive control flow support, it does not offer proper support for data processing. We analyzed other languages with a focus on data processing. Many of them including BPEL, Uber Cadence, and AWS State Language use types for data variables. Achieving type safety similar to a programming language like Java or C# was therefore identified as important. Type safety has been shown to increase code quality [16]. Therefore, we decided to build on Kotlin as the basis for the data processing expressiveness. In this way, we are able to use the full range of data-related functionality of Kotlin for Factscript. Among others, these are the type safety and general data processing capabilities.

Expressiveness of Messaging and Event Handling: While BPMN offers a rich set of event handling and messaging elements on the visual level, its specification of these aspects is semi-formal. With the direct possibility to perform asynchronous and synchronous service calls and corresponding data handling, we opted for BPEL as a basis for this aspect. The BPEL core elements support the message interaction send, receive, and send/receive [25]. To achieve the same expressiveness for Factscript, we decided to provide constructs that permit the same message interactions. In combination with the message interaction, BPEL offers the possibility to wait and react to message events and timer events. This can also be done in combination with event-based gateways. The functionality to wait for specific messages or events in combination with a timeout option is often required. Therefore, we also decided to provide this in Factscript.

After analyzing the expressiveness of the languages BPMN, Kotlin, and BPEL, we formulated the levels of expressiveness that Factscript should have. Next, we describe the resulting syntax.

3.2 Design Phase

The central design aspect of a DSL is the set of its constructs and its syntax. Here, we specify the syntax of Factscript using EBNF. For better understanding, we split the syntax specification in three parts: *General Structure*, *Message and Event Handling* as well as *Control Flow*. The EBNF definition also includes some generic elements that we do not explain further, such as *booleanExpression*, *label*, etc. It also includes some elements specific to Kotlin language such as *messageType* and *factoryMethod*. We do not explain these elements either, but keep them in the listings to provide transparency to the reader.

General Structure. The general structure of the syntax and its elements are shown in Listing 1.1. The *flow* consists of an *api*, *execution* and the *report*. *Api* defines the starting event of a (sub-)process and may give *promise* of a returned message to expect. The *execution* element contains the body of a process with all its activities, events and other elements defined in sequential order. The *execution* element can contain any number of elements; it can also be empty. This is especially useful for defining APIs of processes deployed remotely. The *execute* statement provides the option to execute a single *command* or to start parallel execution of subflows. Finally, the *command* element represents the command instance to be executed.

Listing 1.1. EBNF Definition of General Structure Elements

```
1 flow = api, execution, report;
2 api = "on", ("command", messageType, [promise] ) | catchedEvent;
3 promise = "emit", "{", {("success" | "failure"), event}- "}";
4 execution = {execute | emit | await | issue | select | repeat};
5 execute = "execute", ( (command, {but}) | executeAll );
6 command = "command", "{", factoryMethod, "}";
```

Listing 1.2. Example of General Structure Elements

```
1 on command RetrievePayment::class emit {
2   success event PaymentRetrieved::class
3   failure event PaymentFailed::class
4 }
5 execute command {
6   ChargeCreditCard(reference = paymentId, charge = total)
7 }
8 emit event {
9   PaymentRetrieved(paymentId = paymentId, payment = total)
10 }
```

A simple example of a process is shown in Listing 1.2. First, the API of the process is defined including the message type of a starting event and the promised result (lines 1–4). Afterwards, a command is executed with some data attached to the remote call (lines 5–7). Finally, a message is sent (lines 8–10). Note that the *messageType* of the message corresponds to the *messageType* in the *promise*. It is also worth noting that "RetrievePayment::class" and "ChargeCreditCard(...)" are *messageType* and *factoryMethod*, respectively. The format of these elements, however, is specific to the programming language used to define the flow and thus not further discussed in this paper.

Message and Event Handling. Factscript supports message and event handling. All elements related to messages and events are defined in Listing 1.3. The elements *emit* and *await* are used to publish and subscribe to events, respectively. They correspond to throwing and catching message events in BPMN. *Issue* represents "Fire-and-Forget" semantics, which corresponds to a send task in BPMN. The *catchedEvent* represents a message or time event that is observed and deals with message correlation. *First* is a construct used to define an event-based gateway in Factscript, and *report* represents compulsory end event stating either *success* or *failure* of the process.

Listing 1.3. EBNF Definition of Message- and Event-related Elements

```
1 emit = "emit", ["success" | "failure" ], event;
2 event = "event", "{", factoryMethod, "}";
3 await = "await", (catchedEvent, {but}) | first;
4 catchedEvent = ("event",  messageType,  [having]) | time;
5 having = "having", { variable, "match", expression }-;
6 first = "first", "{", "on", catchedEvent, execution, { "}", "or", "{",  "on
       ", catchedEvent, execution, }- , "}";
7 time = "time", duration | limit;
8 duration = "duration", ["(", label, ")"], "{", isoPeriod, "}";
9 limit = "limit", ["(", label, ")"], "{", timeObject, "}";
10 issue = "issue", command;
11 report = "emit", ( "success" | "failure" ), event;
```

An example illustrating these constructs is shown in Listing 1.4. Note that this example is not a complete process definition but only a fragment. Here, the execution depends on which event is consumed *first* (line 1). In case a message of "PaymentApproval" class is received, some command will be executed (lines 2–3). If, however, the message is not received within 14 days, the path with the timer event is chosen (line 5) and "SendReminder" message activity is executed (line 6). Also note that the time in the *duration* is specified in ISO 8601 Date and Time Format[5], whereas a time *limit* would be specified as Kotlin time object.

Listing 1.4. Example of Event Handling

```
1 await first {
2   on event PaymentApproval::class
3   execute command ...
4 } or {
5   on time duration ("Two weeks") { "P14D" }
6   issue command { SendReminder(orderId) } ...
7 }
```

Control Flow. Those elements that define the control flow are presented in Listing 1.5. Exception handling is done with the *but* statement. *ExecuteAll* starts parallel execution of the contained subflows, whereas *select* allows to choose one

---

[5] https://www.w3.org/TR/xmlschema-2/#isoformats.

or multiple *paths* based on a *condition*. Whether one or more branches can be chosen, i.e., whether the choice is exclusive or inclusive depends on the use of "either" or "all" in the *select* statement. It is also possible to provide at most one *defaultPath* that is chosen in case none of the *conditions* holds. The *repeat* element is a simple statement to add a loop that executes *until* certain *condition* is met.

Listing 1.5. EBNF Definition of Control Flow Elements

```
 1 but = "but", "{", "on", (catchedEvent | catchedSuccess | catchedFailure),
     execution "}";
 2 catchedSuccess = "success", messageType;
 3 catchedFailure = "failure", messageType;
 4 executeAll = "all", "{", execution, { "}", "and", "{", execution }- , "}";
 5 select = "select", ("either" | "all"), path;
 6 path = "{", given, execution, "}", [or];
 7 given = "given", ["(", label, ")"], condition;
 8 condition = "condition", "{", booleanExpression, "}";
 9 or = "or", path | deafultPath;
10 defaultPath ="{", otherwise, execution, "}";
11 otherwise = "otherwise", ["(", label, ")"];
12 repeat = "repeat", "{", execution, until, "}";
13 until = "until", ["(", label, ")"], condition, "};
```

The example in Listing 1.6 shows an exclusive gateway (line 1). Here, two conditions are evaluated. The first option is "Yes" and it is selected if the variable *confirmed* is true (line 2). This is in essence a *booleanExpression* as mentioned in Listing 1.5. If the first *condition* does not hold, the second *path* is executed (lines 5–6). The second *path* is added via an *or* statement (line 4). Note that the *conditions* have to be mutually exclusive as *select either* is used.

Listing 1.6. Example of Control Flow Elements

```
1 select either {
2   given ("Yes") condition { confirmed }
3   ...
4 } or {
5   otherwise ("No")
6   emit failure event { CreditCardExpired(reference, charge)}
7 }
```

3.3   Implementation Phase

The implementation of Factscript is done using Kotlin as a programming language and can be downloaded from a GitHub repository[6]. The type-safety of Kotlin, together, with the support for creating DSLs[7] Kotlin is well suited for the Factscript implementation. Currently, it builds upon the Kotlin version 1.3.70 for its support by IDEs such as IntelliJ IDEA[8]. Camunda Workflow Engine[9] version 7.10.0 is currently used as the execution engine.

Figure 1 depicts the implementation architecture of Factscript. It has two top-level entities: *IntelliJ (1)* and *Camunda (7)*. The entity *IntelliJ (1)* includes

---

[6] https://github.com/factdriven (commit tag ER-2020-Demo).
[7] https://kotlinlang.org/docs/reference/type-safe-builders.html.
[8] https://www.jetbrains.com/idea/.
[9] https://camunda.com/products/bpmn-engine/.

the code of Factscript in Kotlin. This entity is responsible for providing the means to model the processes and also partly for executing it. The processes are modeled using the *Factscript Modeler (2)*, which uses the standard text editor of IntelliJ. The modeler uses the *Factscript Construct Definitions (3)* storage that holds the constructs that are implemented as Kotlin classes, interfaces, and annotations, which in turn use the *DslMarker* functionalities of Kotlin.

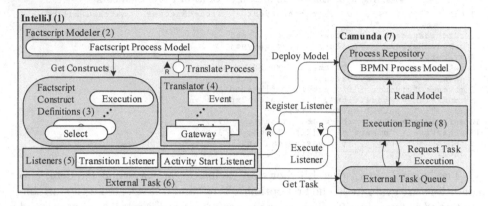

Fig. 1. Implementation architecture (the numbers are references to the descriptions)

After a process is modeled, the *Translator (4)* component translates the model into a BPMN process with additional Camunda specific extensions. In particular, our implementation uses the Camunda specific *Execution Listeners* and *External Task*. In the case of the *Execution Listeners*, our implementation listens to transitions and activity start events. These events are implemented as separate classes in the *Listeners (5)* component. Furthermore, each activity is executed as an external task. The external task implementation is the component *External Task (6)* at the bottom of the *IntelliJ (1)* top-level entity.

The process translated to BPMN is deployed in *Camunda (7)*, the second top-level entity. At this stage, Camunda creates a process instance in the *Execution Engine (8)*, which is then interacting with the implementations of the *Listener (5)* and the task in the *External Task (6)* components of the *IntelliJ (1)*.

4   Case Study

This section uses the implementation of Factscript in a case study of a real-world process of our industry partner. Based on this case, we analyze the language regarding the requirements defined in Sect. 2.3. The case study is about an order payment process that is part of an online ordering process.

4.1   Order Payment Case Study

The payment process is triggered by the *retrieve payment* command and performs the following steps: (1) First, the money is withdrawn from a prepaid customer account. (2) If there is not enough money in the account, the remaining money is charged from the customer's credit card. (3) If the credit card is expired, the customer has two weeks to update the credit card details. After the two weeks, the process ends with an exception, and the already withdrawn money is credited to the customer's account. (4) After charging the money from the credit card, the process checks if the total order cost is covered. If not, the credit card is charged again by returning to step (2). (5) After the payment is fully covered, the ordering process is informed by a *payment retrieved* event.

Listing 1.7 shows the payment process defined in Factscript. Listing 1.8 shows the required variable declarations. After defining these variables, they can be used by Factscript. Listing 1.9 shows the declaration of the *WithdrawAmount-FromCustomerAccount* type and the data processing method that listens to the *AmountWithdrawnFromCustomerAccount* message type. Due to page constraints, we omit the remaining type declarations in the listing. The complete example can be found on GitHub[10].

Listing 1.7. Case Study Process

```
1 on command RetrievePayment::class emit {
2   success event PaymentRetrieved::class
3   failure event PaymentFailed::class
4 }
5 execute command {
6   WithdrawAmountFromCustomerAccount(accountId, total)
7 } but {
8   on failure PaymentFailed::class
9   execute command {
10    CreditAmountToCustomerAccount(accountId, covered)
11  }
12 }
13 select ("Payment fully covered?") either {
14   given ("No") condition { covered < total }
15   repeat {
16     execute command {
17       ChargeCreditCard(orderId, total - covered)
18     } but {
19       on failure CreditCardExpired::class
20       await first {
21         on event CreditCardDetailsUpdated::class having "accountId" match {
                accountId }
22       } or {
23         on time duration ("Two weeks") { "P14D" }
24         emit failure event { PaymentFailed(orderId) }
25       }
26     }
27     until ("Payment fully covered?") condition { covered == total }
28   }
29 } or {
30   otherwise ("Yes")
31   emit success event { PaymentRetrieved(orderId) }
32 }
33 emit success event { PaymentRetrieved(orderId) }
```

---

[10] https://github.com/factdriven (commit tag ER-2020-Demo).

Listing 1.8. Case Study Variable Declarations

```
1 val orderId: String,      // Current order ID
2 val accountId: String,    // Customer account ID
3 var total: Float,         // Total amount the customer has to pay
4 var covered: Float = OF,  // Amount already paid
```

Listing 1.9. Case Study Type Declaration and Data Processing

```
1 data class WithdrawAmountFromCustomerAccount(val customer: String, val
      withdraw: Float)
2 fun apply(fact: AmountWithdrawnFromCustomerAccount) {
3   covered = covered + fact.withdrawn
4 }
```

Next, we discuss Listing 1.7. Lines 1–4 define that a new process instance is created when a *RetrievePayment* command is received. These lines also define the API of the process, i.e., a *PaymentRetrieved* event signalizes a successful payment, and a *PaymentFailed* event signalizes a failed payment.

Lines 5–12 withdraw the money from the customer's account. To withdraw the money, a separate service or another process is used that listens to *WithdrawAmountFromCustomerAccount* (this service is not shown in the listing). After the amount, or a part of it, has been withdrawn from the customers account, the separate service returns with an event of type *AmountWithdrawnFromCustomerAccount*. By receiving this event, the payment process instance saves the withdrawn amount in the *covered* variable. This happens in the separate apply function, shown in Listing 1.9, that is executed when a *AmountWithdrawnFromCustomerAccount* event is recognized. Lines 7–12 of Listing 1.7 define the action that is taken if the complete payment fails.

Line 14 checks if enough money could be withdrawn. If yes, the process is finished (line 31), and the *PaymentRetrieved* event is emitted. If not, lines 15–28 are executed. Line 17 charges the credit card with the missing amount, i.e., *total − covered*. Lines 19–25 define the steps that are taken when the credit card is expired. If it is expired, the process waits for a *CreditCardDetailsUpdated* event for two weeks. After that, the *PaymentFailed* event is issued. Lines 16–26 are repeated until the total amount is covered, i.e., *covered = total*, (line 27).

4.2 Requirements Analysis

In the following we use the provided case study and the definition of Factscript from Sect. 3.2, to analyse the requirements defined in Sect. 2.3:

(R1) Efficient Syntax: We evaluate the syntax in two steps. First, we evaluate the grammar based on metrics [6,20]. For this we use the tool presented in [20]. We use TERM (number of terminal symbols in the grammar), VAR (number of non-terminal symbols), HAL (describes the effort required to understand the grammar), and LRS (complexity of the grammar). These metrics allow us to judge simplicity, readability, and understandability of Factscript. Table 3 presents the resulting values of Factscript in comparison to the ones from Java 7 and Kotlin. We observe that in comparison to Java 7 and Kotlin, Factscript achieves lower values for all metrics. Especially, the lower values regarding HAL

and LRS suggest a lower complexity of the language, which suggests that it is easier to learn. Second, we evaluate the lines of code (LoC) required to describe the process in Listing 1.7 with the ones required in BPMN. To this end, we transform the process to BPMN. As can be seen in Listing 1.7, the definition needs 33 LoC and the variable and type declaration (Listing 1.8 and Listing 1.9) need additional 27 LoC, resulting in total 60 LoC. The corresponding BPMN (depicted in Fig. 2) needs in total 429 lines of XML code. While there are BPMN modelers available to create BPMN process models and automatically create the XML, this initial evaluation provides a first analysis of the compactness of Factscript. At this point it should also be mentioned that several other process description languages, e.g., Netflix Conductor or AWS Step Functions, lack a graphic modeler, which leads to the need to define the process textually.

Table 3. Factscript syntax complexity comparison

Metric	Java 7	Kotlin	Factscript
TERM	108	146	30
VAR	104	172	30
HAL	111.74	267.29	12.81
LRS	4717	145124	308

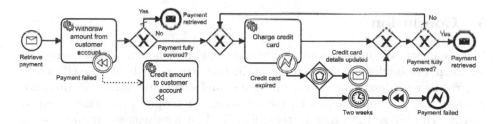

Fig. 2. Use case study process modeled in BPMN

(R2) Extensive Control Flow Support: As defined in Sect. 3.1 as baseline for the control flow aspects we use BPMN. As shown in Sect. 3.2 Factscript supports a vast amount of different constructs and all major BPMN constructs. By supporting the major BPMN constructs Factscript achieves the same level of expressiveness. In Listing 1.7 we further showed that with the help of Factscript constructs, i.e., XOR (line 13), loop (line 27), failure compensation (line 8), and the event-based choice (line 19), a real-world process can be implemented. For the comparison with BPMN we refer to Fig. 2.

(R3) Support of Data Processing: As can be seen in our case study Factscript supports data processing. In particular, each process can hold different variables

of different types, e.g., in the case study we used Float and String. These variables can then be accessed and manipulated during the execution of the process, as shown, e.g., in lines 14, 17, and 27 of Listing 1.7. This way, Factscript is type safe. While other process modeling languages also provide type safety for data variables, they often do not allow the direct manipulation of the variables, e.g., using mathematic operations like − or +, as it is supported by Factscript.

By using a modern IDE (in our case IntelliJ) as a development environment, the process designer is further supported by IDE functionalities like code completion and spell checking. These functionalities and the possibility to use an IDE that a developer is familiar with, further, help to decrease the error-proneness and improve the code quality [7]. These functionalities are often not given in the editors that are available for other process modeling languages.

(R4) Support of Event Processing: As can be seen in Listing 1.7 and in Sect. 3.2, Factscript provides different ways of event processing. On the one hand, it provides the means to send and receive events and commands. For instance, the process described in Listing 1.7 listens to a *ReceivePayment* command to start a process instance and emits an *PaymentRetrieved* event when the process instance is done. Similar to BPMN and BPEL, these events and commands can be defined at the start and end of a process, but also intermediate. On the other hand, Factscript provides support for additional events, e.g., time or error events. Moreover, Factscript supports event-based gateways that wait for a particular event and then follow the defined path (e.g., lines 20–25 of Listing 1.7). This way, Factscript achieves a similar event processing level as BPEL and BPMN.

5   Conclusion

In this paper, we investigated the research question how a process scripting language can be defined that addresses the four requirements of code efficiency, control flow expressiveness, data processing and event processing. To this end, we designed and implemented Factscript, a process scripting language based on Kotlin. To analyze the language regarding the four requirements and to discuss them, we presented a case study of a real-world process.

In future research, we aim to further extend Factscript in various directions. First, we plan to integrate the AWS Step Function process execution engine in addition to the Camunda BPMS. Second, we plan to evaluate the usability and readability of Factscript in a user study with developers.

Acknowledgement. The concept and design of Factscript as well as its implementation in Kotlin was done by Martin Schimak, plexiti GmbH.

This research is partially funded by FFG (ref. no. 876062).

References

1. Business Process Model and Notation (BPMN) version 2.0. Tech. rep. (2011)
2. van der Aalst, W.M.P., ter Hofstede, A.H., Kiepuszewski, B., Barros, A.P.: Distributed and parallel databases. Workflow Patterns **14**(1), 5–51 (2003)
3. Armbrust, M., et al.: A view of cloud computing. Commun. ACM **53**(4), 50–58 (2010)
4. Buyya, R., Yeo, C.S., Venugopal, S., Broberg, J., Brandic, I.: Cloud computing and emerging IT platforms: vision, hype, and reality for delivering computing as the 5th utility. Future Gener. Comp. Syst. (FGCS) **25**(6), 599–616 (2009)
5. Ceh, I., Crepinsek, M., Kosar, T., Mernik, M.: Ontology driven development of domain-specific languages. Comput. Sci. Inf. Syst. **8**(2), 317–342 (2011)
6. Crepinsek, M., Kosar, T., Mernik, M., Cervelle, J., Forax, R., Roussel, G.: On automata and language based grammar metrics. Comput. Sci. Inf. Syst. **7**(2), 309–329 (2010)
7. Dieste, O., et al.: Empirical evaluation of the effects of experience on code quality and programmer productivity: an exploratory study. In: International Conference on Software and System Process, ICSSP 2018, pp. 111–112. ACM (2018)
8. Dragoni, N., et al.: Microservices: yesterday, today, and tomorrow. Present and Ulterior Software Engineering, pp. 195–216. Springer, Cham (2017). https://doi.org/10.1007/978-3-319-67425-4_12
9. Dragoni, N., Lanese, I., Larsen, S.T., Mazzara, M., Mustafin, R., Safina, L.: Microservices: how to make your application scale. In: Petrenko, A.K., Voronkov, A. (eds.) PSI 2017. LNCS, vol. 10742, pp. 95–104. Springer, Cham (2018). https://doi.org/10.1007/978-3-319-74313-4_8
10. Dumas, M., La Rosa, M., Mendling, J., Reijers, H.A.: Process-aware information systems. Fundamentals of Business Process Management, pp. 341–369. Springer, Heidelberg (2018). https://doi.org/10.1007/978-3-662-56509-4_9
11. Georgakopoulos, D., Hornick, M., Sheth, A.: An overview of workflow management: from process modeling to workflow automation infrastructure. Distrib. Parallel Databases **3**(2), 119–153 (1995)
12. Hirschheim, R.A.: Office automation: a social and organizational perspective (1986)
13. Jordan, D., et al.: Web services business process execution language version 2.0. Tech. rep. (2007)
14. Kiepuszewski, B., ter Hofstede, A.H.M., van der Aalst, W.M.P.: Fundamentals of control flow in workflows. Acta Inf. **39**(3), 143–209 (2003)
15. Kosar, T., et al.: Comparing general-purpose and domain-specific languages: an empirical study. Comput. Sci. Inf. Syst. **7**(2), 247–264 (2010)
16. Mateus, B.G., Martinez, M.: An empirical study on quality of Android applications written in Kotlin language. Empir. Softw. Eng. **24**(6), 3356–3393 (2019)
17. Mendling, J., Nüttgens, M.: XML interchange formats for business process management. Inf. Syst. E-Bus. Manag. **4**(3), 217–220 (2006)
18. Mernik, M., Heering, J., Sloane, A.M.: When and how to develop domain-specific languages. ACM Comput. Surv. **37**(4), 316–344 (2005)
19. Mernik, M., Hrncic, D., Bryant, B.R., Javed, F.: Applications of grammatical inference in software engineering: domain specific language development. Sci. Appl. Lang. Methods **2**, 421–457 (2010)
20. Power, J.F., Malloy, B.A.: A metrics suite for grammar-based software. J. Softw. Maint. Res. Pract. **16**(6), 405–426 (2004)

21. Prechelt, L.: An empirical comparison of seven programming languages. Computer **33**(10), 23–29 (2000)
22. Richardson, C.: Microservices patterns: with examples in Java (2019)
23. Russell, N., van der Aalst, W.M.P., ter Hofstede, A.H.: Workflow Patterns: The Definitive Guide. MIT Press, Cambridge (2016)
24. Van Deursen, A., Klint, P., Visser, J.: Domain-specific languages: an annotated bibliography. ACM Sigplan Not. **35**(6), 26–36 (2000)
25. Weidlich, M., Decker, G., Großkopf, A., Weske, M.: BPEL to BPMN: the myth of a straight-forward mapping. In: Meersman, R., Tari, Z. (eds.) OTM 2008. LNCS, vol. 5331, pp. 265–282. Springer, Heidelberg (2008). https://doi.org/10.1007/978-3-540-88871-0_19
26. Wohed, P., van der Aalst, W.M.P., Dumas, M., ter Hofstede, A.H.M., Russell, N.: On the suitability of BPMN for business process modelling. In: Dustdar, S., Fiadeiro, J.L., Sheth, A.P. (eds.) BPM 2006. LNCS, vol. 4102, pp. 161–176. Springer, Heidelberg (2006). https://doi.org/10.1007/11841760_12
27. Zur Muehlen, M.: Workflow-Based Process Controlling: Foundation, Design, and Application of Workflow-Driven Process Information Systems. Logos Verlag, Berlin (2004)

Assessing the Compliance of Business Process Models with Regulatory Documents

Karolin Winter[1]([✉]), Han van der Aa[2], Stefanie Rinderle-Ma[1],
and Matthias Weidlich[3]

[1] Faculty of Computer Science, University of Vienna, Vienna, Austria
{karolin.winter,stefanie.rinderle-ma}@univie.ac.at
[2] Data and Web Science Group, University of Mannheim, Mannheim, Germany
han@informatik.uni-mannheim.de
[3] Department of Computer Science, Humboldt-Universität zu Berlin,
Berlin, Germany
matthias.weidlich@hu-berlin.de

Abstract. Implementing regulatory documents is a recurring, mostly manual and time-consuming task for companies. To establish and ensure regulatory compliance, constraints need to be extracted from the documents and integrated into process models capturing existing operational practices. Since regulatory documents and processes are subject to frequent change, the constant comparison between both is mandatory. Additionally, new regulations must be integrated and checked against existing process models. To address these challenges, we provide an approach that uses natural language processing to automatically support compliance assessment between regulatory documents and process model repositories. The outcome is a pairwise matching between parts of a regulatory document and process models from a repository. This matching can be used to either determine the coverage of regulations by a process model or to guide compliance assessment by ranking models based on their fitness and cost. The approach is implemented and applied in two real-world case studies: one from the energy domain and the other based on the General Data Protection Regulation.

Keywords: Compliance assessment · Regulatory documents · Business process models · Natural language processing

1 Introduction

Due to the potentially enormous fines for non-compliance with regulations such as the GDPR, establishing and monitoring regulatory compliance is a crucial task for companies. Although many companies have their business processes captured in process models using, e.g., Business Process Model and Notation (BPMN) [15], in practice, checking and ensuring their compliance with regulatory documents is still mostly conducted manually [11]. This might lead to

© Springer Nature Switzerland AG 2020
G. Dobbie et al. (Eds.): ER 2020, LNCS 12400, pp. 189–203, 2020.
https://doi.org/10.1007/978-3-030-62522-1_14

errors and high costs when implementing the regulations. Moreover, regulatory documents are constantly subject to change and new regulatory documents come into effect regularly [11].

In literature, several approaches for checking regulatory compliance based on process models exist [10]. However, existing compliance checking approaches abstract from the regulatory documents themselves and, instead, assume the existence of a set of extracted compliance constraints that are already captured using formalisms such as LTL or Event Calculus [10]. Although some approaches aim at extracting process descriptions [3] or compliance constraints [21] from regulatory documents, an approach to directly assess compliance between process models and regulatory documents during design time, is missing, despite providing the following advantages: i) it avoids misunderstanding, misinterpretation, and errors in the extraction and formalization of compliance constraints [11]; ii) it facilitates the monitoring of changes in the regulatory documents; iii) it enables the implementation of new regulatory documents; and iv) it supports sanity checks for process models with respect to regulatory compliance. This work aims to fill this gap by addressing the following research questions:

RQ1 How to identify which parts of a regulatory document relate to which process models in a repository?

RQ2 How to measure and assess compliance violations between a process model and regulatory constraints?

Addressing these research questions involves several challenges, like differences in granularity between documents and process models. As shown in previous work, regulatory documents are extensive and structured along topics, making it advisable to fragment the documents into paragraphs [21]. However, certain regulations might be implemented in various process models [16]. Hence, we aim to support complex many-to-many relations between parts of regulatory documents and process models. To assess compliance, we provide a matching of paragraph-model pairs using a fitness score ($\mapsto$ *RQ1*) and a cost score ($\mapsto$ *RQ2*). The *fitness score* determines the likelihood that a paragraph pertains to a particular process model, whereas the *cost score* quantifies the amount of detected process compliance violations. Our work particularly targets the detection of control-flow violations in terms of mandatory activities that are missing in a process, as well as activities that are performed in the wrong order. Furthermore, we detect resource-related violations in terms of activities that are not performed by the correct organizational entity.

Based thereon, we support two compliance assessment scenarios. When a matching between paragraphs and process models is pre-defined by a user, the cost score measures compliance, whereas the fitness score enables conclusions on the coverage of regulations by a model. In the absence of a given matching, the scores guide compliance assessment by ranking models that show high coverage, but low compliance, with respect to certain parts of a regulatory document.

The remainder of the paper is structured as follows. Section 2 illustrates the problem and highlights the main challenges addressed in this work. Section 3 describes our compliance assessment approach. Section 4 presents an evaluation based on two real-world case studies, followed by a discussion in Sect. 5. After a review of related work in Sect. 6, the paper concludes in Sect. 7.

P₁: A screen lock provides the possibility to conceal the information currently displayed on the screen. In order that access to an IT system is reliably prevented during a short absence of the IT user, it should only be possible to disable a screen lock after successful user authentication [**R₁**]. It should be possible for the user to activate the screen lock manually [**R₂**]. In addition, the screen lock should be automatically initiated after a predefined period of inactivity [**R₃**].

(a) Description of Screen-lock Regulation

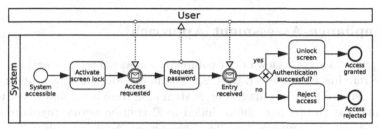

(b) Process model M_1: Screen-lock protection

Fig. 1. Running example of an IT security scenario, based on [16]

2 Problem Illustration and Challenges

This section presents an exemplary scenario to illustrate the challenges imposed by the problem of assessing the compliance between regulatory documents and business process models. To this end, we consider IT security regulations stemming from the *IT Baseline Catalogues* of the German Federal Bureau of Security in IT[1]. As a starting point, we consider a full regulatory document, consisting of multiple paragraphs, and a repository of process models. However, for illustrative purposes, we here present a single regulatory paragraph stemming from the English version of the document, as well as an accompanying process model.

The respective paragraph of the regulatory document, P_1, is presented in Fig. 1a and describes various rules associated with the protection of IT systems using screen locks[2]. Given such a paragraph, as part of a larger document, automated compliance assessment involves the following steps: (1) Extracting the compliance rules that paragraph P_1 imposes on processes, (2) identifying that the rules from P_1 relate to process model M_1, depicted in Fig. 1b, and (3) determining whether the rules from P_1 are properly implemented by M_1.

---

[1] www.bsi.bund.de/grundschutz.
[2] The identifiers (R1 to R3) have been inserted for clarity.

To perform these steps, a variety of challenges need to be addressed. For instance, step (1) requires an approach to differentiate between the sentences describing actual constraints and those providing additional clarification or context. To determine correspondences between a paragraph and a model in step (2), an automated approach needs to be able to deal with the inherently flexible nature of natural language, which allows the same constraints to be expressed in a broad range of manners, can lead to considerable differences in terminology between paragraph and model, as well as to differences in granularity [2]. Finally, step (3) requires the assessment of the exact constraint that a compliance rule imposes on a process and to consider how this constraint should be reflected in a corresponding process model.

3   Compliance Assessment Approach

Figure 2 presents an overview of our compliance assessment approach illustrated using the running example (cf. Sect. 2). The input consists of a process model repository $\mathcal{M}$ and a set of paragraphs $\mathcal{P}$ stemming from a regulatory document. We assume that the paragraphs included in $\mathcal{P}$ contain actual regulations, i.e., introductory sections and reference lists are omitted. As shown in Fig. 2, our approach first parses the process models in $\mathcal{M}$ and the paragraphs in $\mathcal{P}$. The former is straightforward, whereas the latter involves the identification and extraction of constraints imposed by the regulatory document, as well as, e.g., control flow aspects like strict orders between activities. The output is a pairwise matching of process models and paragraphs based on fitness and cost scores.

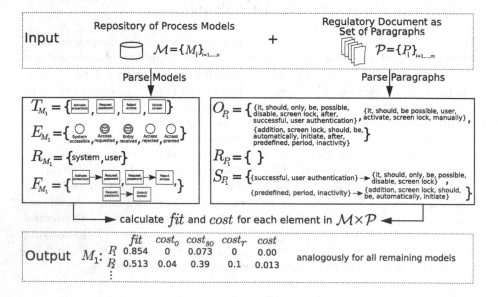

Fig. 2. Compliance assessment approach illustrated based on Fig. 1

The *fitness score* $fit(P, M)$ quantifies the likelihood that a paragraph $P \in \mathcal{P}$ pertains to a model $M \in \mathcal{M}$. The *cost score* $cost(P, M)$ quantifies the distance (i.e., cost), between the obligations expressed in paragraph P and the process implemented by model M. Our work targets both control-flow and resource-related compliance violations in terms of three violation types: (**V1**) an obligatory activity is not incorporated in the model, (**V2**) activities are executed in the wrong order and (**V3**) activities are not performed by the correct resource.

By combining $fit(P, M)$ with $cost(P, M)$, our approach is able to detect those paragraph-model pairs that have a strong semantic relation (i.e., P specifies rules that are relevant to model M), but are also likely subject to compliance issues.

3.1   Parsing Process Models

Process models can be created using a variety of modeling languages, such as Petri nets, EPCs, and the Business Process Model and Notation (BPMN). Since our work is independent of the specific notation used to define a process model, we define process models using a generic definition, given in Definition 1.

Definition 1. *A process model is a tuple M that consists of:*

- $N_M = T_M \cup E_M \cup G_M$ *is a finite set of nodes, with T_M a set of tasks, E_M a set of events, and G_M a set of gateways,*
- $F_M \subseteq N_M \times N_M$ *is the flow relation, s.t. (N_M, F_M) is a connected graph,*
- $t_M : G_M \rightarrow \{and, xor, or\}$ *is a function that maps each gateway to a type,*
- R_M *is a finite set of resources,*
- $u_M : R_M \nrightarrow T_M \cup E_M$ *is a partial function that maps resources to tasks and events.*

In the process model-parsing step, our approach parses all models in a repository (e.g., from JSON files) into a collection $\mathcal{M}$, where each model $M \in \mathcal{M}$ fits the provided definition. Whereas notations such as BPMN can be directly and fully mapped to this format, other notations may only result in a partially populated process model definition. For instance, a process model notation that lacks resources will result in an empty set R_M. This naturally prevents the detection of compliance violations involving resources (V3). Furthermore, we note that sub-processes can be flattened into one process model.

3.2   Parsing Regulatory Documents

In this step, our approach aims to extract constraints specified in paragraphs of a regulatory document together with those elements of constraints that enable the detection of compliance violations. In particular, for each paragraph $P \in \mathcal{P}$, the approach extracts a set O_P of obligatory activities that must be performed according to P, a strict order relation $S_P \subseteq O_P \times O_P$ that indicates pairs of activities that must be executed in a specific order, a set R_P of described resources, and a partial function $u_P : R_P \nrightarrow O_P$ that specifies which resources must execute which activities. These are extracted as follows.

Extracting Obligatory Activities O_P. The extraction of obligatory activities described in a paragraph P represents a two-step procedure. Our approach first distinguishes between sentences in P that describe actual process constraints, i.e., sentences that contain mentions of obligatory activities, and those that provide contextual information, e.g., *A screen lock provides the possibility to conceal the information currently displayed on screen.* To discern between these two types of sentences, we recognize that obligatory activities correspond to mentions of some action (typically a verb), associated with a closed-class of signal words, including *must, should, shall,* and *has to* (cf. [7]), whereas contextual sentences lack such obligations. We refer to the set of sentences with mentions of obligations, identified in this manner, as $P' \subseteq P$.

From the sentences in P', our approach then aims to extract individual activities. The extraction of activities using tailored techniques based on heuristics (cf. [8,17]) is known to be error prone for long, complex sentences [1]. Therefore, our approach rather splits each sentence in P' into one or more clauses, which can be achieved by employing existing NLP techniques, cf., spaCy [12]. Each clause is then added as an activity to O_P. For instance, for a complex sentence like: *The electrical supply must be interrupted, an entry in the logbook of the terminal is generated and the status is transmitted to the central system.*, our approach recognizes three clauses and, thus, three activities: [(1) *The electrical supply must be interrupted,* (2) *an entry in the logbook of the terminal is generated,* and (3) *the status is transmitted to the central system*].

Extracting Order Restrictions S_P. To extract order restrictions between the activities in O_P, we build on existing work on the extraction of process models from natural language text [8]. This extraction procedure identifies signal words, e.g., *then, after* or *afterwards,* to detect specific orders in which activities must be performed. For the running example, our approach recognizes two such order restrictions, both based on the marker *after,* resulting in S_P containing two restrictions: 1. *successful user authentication* → *it should only be possible to disable screen lock* and 2. *a predefined period of inactivity* → *screen lock should be automatically initiated.* Both examples indicate clear restrictions about which activity must be executed first (e.g., successful user authentication), before the next activity is allowed (e.g., disabling a screen lock).

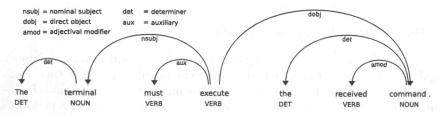

Fig. 3. Sentence with dependency tree and part-of-speech tags

Extracting Resource Responsibilities R_P. To identify the resources R_P associated with obligatory activities, we again employ NLP techniques such as dependency parsing and POS tagging. Figure 3 depicts a sentence with its corresponding dependency tree and POS tags obtained using spaCy [12]. In the displayed example, the resource corresponds to *the terminal*, identified as the nominal subject via the corresponding dependency label *nsubj*. However, given the flexibility of natural language, the same constraint could also have been expressed as, e.g., *The received command must be executed by the terminal.* This makes the resource the *agent* of the sentence. The corresponding element in R_P would then be given as {*terminal* → {*must, execute, received, command*}}.

3.3   Matching Paragraph-Model Pairs Based on Fitness and Cost

The compliance assessment between a process model repository and a regulatory document is based on the computation of fitness and cost scores between each paragraph-model pair in $\mathcal{P} \times \mathcal{M}$. The *fitness score* $fit(P, M)$ quantifies the likelihood that paragraph $P \in \mathcal{P}$ pertains to model $M \in \mathcal{M}$. The *cost score* $cost(P, M)$ quantifies the distance (i.e., cost), between the process constraints imposed by paragraph P and the actual process implemented by model M, computed as the total number of violations detected between P and M.

Fitness Score. The fitness score aims to quantify the likelihood that a paragraph P relates to a model M. For instance, we use fitness to recognize that paragraph P_1 from Fig. 1, which relates to screen lock protection, should be paired with model M_1, rather than, e.g., a process model related to password management. Our approach achieves this by first identifying correspondences between each obligatory activity in O_P and its most similar process model element (task or event) in $T_M \cup E_M$. We denote the similarity between some $o \in O_P$ and $t \in T_M \cup E_M$ using $sim(o, t) \in [0, 1]$. In our approach, we use existing *semantic similarity* measures for this quantification [12], which allows the approach to recognize when comparable process steps are described using synonymous terms. Based on these similarity values, we define a set $\mathcal{C}_{P,M} \subseteq O_P \times T_M \cup E_M$ containing the correspondences with the highest similarity scores for each $o \in O_P$. Thus, $(o, t) \in \mathcal{C}_{P,M}$ denotes that t is the process model element with the highest similarity to o. To omit unimplemented obligatory activities from consideration in the fitness computation, we introduce a threshold $\gamma \in [0, 1]$ that filters out correspondences with a low similarity score. We shall use $\mathcal{C}_{P,M,\gamma} = \{(o, t) \in \mathcal{C}_{P,M} \mid sim(o, t) > \gamma\}$ to denote the set of correspondences above this threshold. Based on this set, we define fitness as the average similarity values obtainable for the obligatory activities in O_P that are greater than γ, as given in Eq. 1.

$$fit(P, M, \gamma) = \frac{\sum_{(o,t) \in \mathcal{C}_{P,M,\gamma}} sim(o, t)}{|\mathcal{C}_{P,M,\gamma}|} \tag{1}$$

Consequently, $fit(P, M)$ receives a high value if there is a strong relation between the obligatory activities described in the paragraph P and the tasks and events contained in the process model M.

Cost Score. The cost score provides a quantitative assessment for compliance violations **V1–V3**. For a model $M \in \mathcal{M}$ and a paragraph $P \in \mathcal{P}$, the cost score $cost(P, M, \gamma, \delta) \in [0, 1]$ is defined as follows:

$$cost(P, M, \gamma, \delta) := w_o cost_o(P, M, \gamma) + w_{so} cost_{so}(P, M, \gamma) + w_r cost_r(P, M, \gamma, \delta) \quad (2)$$

where $w_o, w_{so}, w_r \in [0, 1]$ with $w_o + w_{so} + w_r = 1$ are weights that allow users to alter the relative importance of the violation types. Parameters γ and δ represent similarity thresholds that are explained below. Note that a high violation in one of the three cost scores can be weakened by the weights, e.g., if $cost_o = 1, cost_{so} = cost_r = 0$ and $w_o = w_{so} = w_r = \frac{1}{3}$ then the overall costs evaluate to $cost = \frac{1}{3}$. Another possibility is to take the maximum function instead of a weighted sum to compute the overall cost score. However, this can also be achieved by setting the weights accordingly, i.e., for the example, $w_o = 1, w_{so} = w_r = 0$.

Missed Obligatory Activities (V1). We define $cost_o(P, M)$ to quantify the amount of obligatory activities from P that are not implemented in model M. To recognize such cases, we define a threshold $\gamma \in [0, 1]$ that captures the minimal similarity value that is required for an obligatory activity o to be recognized as implemented in a model through task (or event) t, i.e., if $sim(o, t) < \gamma$ for $(o, t) \in \mathcal{C}_{P,M}$, the obligation imposed by activity o is considered violated in model M. The cost score between model and paragraph is then computed as follows:

$$cost_o(P, M, \gamma) := \frac{|\{(o, t) \in \mathcal{C}_{P,M} \mid sim(o, t) < \gamma\}|}{|O_P|} \quad (3)$$

Strict Order Violations (V2). Strict order violations occur when a regulatory document specifies that two activities should be executed in a specific order, whereas this order is not enforced in the model. To recognize such cases, we compare the strict order relation S_P extracted from a paragraph P to the flow relation F_M of the model. In particular, let $(o, o') \in S_P$ be a strict order constraint and let $(o, t), (o', t') \in \mathcal{C}_{P,M}$. Then, this strict order constraint is only satisfied if there is a path from t to t', i.e., $(t, t') \in F_M^+$, and not vice versa, i.e., $(t', t) \notin F_M^+$. However, the enforcement of such a constraint in the model shall only be assessed, if the model indeed includes sufficiently similar tasks (or events), as again determined by a parameter γ, for the obligatory activities o, o'. We therefore limit the relation S_P to these constraints as $S_{P,M,\gamma} = \{(o, o') \in S_P \mid \exists (o, t), (o', t') \in \mathcal{C}_{P,M} : sim(o, t) > \gamma \wedge sim(o', t') > \gamma\}$. Then, the cost score between model and paragraph is computed as follows:

$$cost_{so}(P, M, \gamma) := \frac{|\{(o, o') \in S_{P,M,\gamma} \mid \exists (o, t), (o', t') \in \mathcal{C}_{P,M} : (t, t') \in F_M^+ \wedge (t', t) \notin F_M^+\}|}{|S_{P,M,\gamma}|} \quad (4)$$

Resource Responsibility Violations (V3). Resource responsibility violations occur when the regulatory document specifies that an activity must be performed by a specific resource, whereas a different resource executes the corresponding process model task. Given an obligatory activity o and a process model task t, such that $(o, t) \in \mathcal{C}_{P,M}$, we compare the resource $r_P \in R_P$ assigned by u_P to o to the resource $r_M \in R_M$ assigned by u_M to t. Here, we consider that a resource responsibility is satisfied if r_P and r_M are sufficiently similar, i.e., if $sim(r_P, r_M) \geq \delta$. This way, we are able to recognize comparable resource descriptions, e.g., a *supervisor* to a *manager*. Let $R_{P,M,\gamma}$ be the resources in the document assigned to an activity for which there exists a γ-similar task in the process model, i.e., $R_{P,M,\gamma} = \{r \in r_P \mid \exists\, (o, t) \in \mathcal{C}_{P,M} : u_P(r) = o \wedge sim(o, t) > \gamma\}$. Furthermore, let $\phi(r, r', \gamma, \delta)$ be a predicate that holds true for resources $r \in R_{P,M,\gamma}$ and $r' \in R_M$ if their assigned documents and tasks are γ-similar, $(u_P(r), u_M(r')) \in \mathcal{C}_{P,M}$ and $sim(u_P(r), u_M(r')) > \gamma$, and the resources are δ-similar, $sim(r, r') > \delta$. Then, the cost score between model and paragraph is computed as follows:

$$cost_r(P, M, \gamma, \delta) := \frac{|\{r \in R_{P,M,\gamma} \mid \exists\, r' \in R_M : \phi(r, r', \gamma, \delta)\}|}{|R_{P,M,\gamma}|} \tag{5}$$

Compliance Assessment. The computed fitness and cost scores are applicable in two different scenarios that will be picked up in the evaluation.

The first application scenario presumes that the correct paragraph-model pairs are already known. Assessing a paragraph-model pair via the above scores then enables the following conclusions: The lower the costs, the better the compliance of a model to a paragraph. The fitness score, in turn, serves as a quality indicator of the process model. It indicates the coverage of the paragraph. Moreover, if an additional paragraph has a high fitness score, this paragraph is likely to contain compliance constraints that also refer to the model.

In a second application scenario, pre-defined paragraph-model pairs are not given. In this case, our approach acts as a sort of recommender system that displays a top-k list of paragraph-model correspondences. Here, k can, e.g., depend on the median of all fitness values, meaning that only paragraph-model pairs having a fitness score higher than the median are considered. The top-k pairs are then ranked based on their cost score, in order to highlight the pairs with the most compliance issues. Note that this result suggests a paragraph-model matching that shall serve as a basis for manual assessment by a domain expert.

4   Evaluation

The evaluation experiments comprise two real-world cases, intended to show the effectiveness of our compliance assessment approach. A prototype was implemented in Python3 taking as input a collection of .bpmn-files, e.g., exported from Signavio, and a collection of .txt-files, corresponding to paragraphs of a regulatory document. For the NLP tasks, e.g., parsing, analysis of grammatical relations, and similarity computation, we employ the spaCy library [12].

Section 4.1 reports on experiments conducted for Austrian's energy providers and demonstrates the first application scenario, i.e., the assessment of compliance between an already known paragraph-model matching. Section 4.2 presents a case study for the second scenario in the context of GDPR implementation, i.e., the detection of compliant paragraph-model pairs from scratch. While the former experiments are based on proprietary data, the GDPR data collection and the employed implementation are publicly available.[3] In both case studies, we assign equal values to the weights in the cost calculation ($w_o = w_{so} = w_r = 1/3$), set the resource threshold to $\delta = 0.8$, but vary γ. We conducted the experiments using an Intel Core i5-7200U @2.50 GHz processor (4 cores) and 8 GB RAM. Each experiment required at most 16 min, illustrating the feasibility of our approach from a computational perspective.

4.1 Smart Meters for Austrian Energy Providers

This case study demonstrates the first application scenario, i.e., compliance assessment for already known paragraph-model pairs.

Input. The input consists of a repository of 12 process models, which were established and verified by domain experts in the context of earlier work [6] and have one-to-one correspondences to 12 paragraphs of the related regulatory document for smart electricity meters.[4]

Evaluation Strategy. For each process model $M \in \mathcal{M}$, we establish a ranking $rank(M, \mathcal{P})$ in which all paragraphs in $\mathcal{P}$ are ranked according to their fitness score. Furthermore, we use $rank(M, P)$ to denote the ranking of paragraph P in $rank(M, \mathcal{P})$, with 1 being the highest rank and $\hat{P}_M \in \mathcal{P}$ to refer to the paragraph that actually corresponds to model M.

We quantify our approach's accuracy using common measures for recommender systems [18]: The *average precision* (AP) per model, as well as the *mean average precision* (MAP) for the whole model repository, defined as:

$$AP(M) = \frac{1}{rank(M, \hat{P}_M)}, \quad MAP(\mathcal{M}) = \frac{\sum_{M \in \mathcal{M}} AP(M)}{|\mathcal{M}|}$$

Since there is only a single relevant paragraph $\hat{P}_M$ per model, the AP value corresponds to the inverse of its rank. The mean value MAP is computed by averaging the AP values for all 12 models in $\mathcal{M}$. As such, it provides an overall quantification of how good the fitness score performs for this particular document collection. The cost score is evaluated in a qualitative manner.

Configurations. We employ two configurations for this use case that vary in the way that obligatory activities are extracted. One configuration employs the

---

[3] http://gruppe.wst.univie.ac.at/projects/RegMiner/index.php?t=prototypes.
[4] https://oesterreichsenergie.at/files/Downloads%20Netze/Oesterreich%20Use %20Cases%20Smart%20Metering_14122015_Version_1-1.pdf.

exact method defined in Sect. 3.2, yielding a set of obligatory activities O_P. The other configuration skips the filtering of sentences and, thus, transforms the clauses from all sentences into obligatory activities, yielding a set O'_P. This latter configuration is introduced given the procedural style present in this particular regulatory document, which uses fewer words to explicitly denote obligations.

Results. For the fitness score, the AP and MAP results are, respectively, depicted in Fig. 4 and Table 1. As displayed in Fig. 4, the O_P configuration achieves the best result for $\gamma = 0.8$.[5] In this case, 6 out of 12 models are matched to the correct paragraph (i.e., the paragraph is ranked in the first spot). However, for the remaining models, the average precision indicates that the correct paragraph was actually ranked low on the list.

The O'_P configuration performs better, in particular for $\gamma = 0.6$. In this case, for 9 out of 12 models the correct paragraphs are ranked in first place, while for the remaining models the correct paragraphs are ranked in second place. These results emphasize the potential of the fitness score, achieving a perfect correspondence for 75% and a top-2 ranking for all models. As shown in Table 1, this results in a mean average precision of $MAP = 0.875$. Fur-

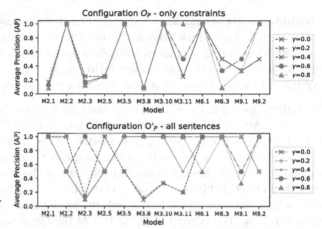

Fig. 4. Average precision per model for smart meters case study

thermore, the results reveal that the O'_P configuration performs better than O_P, due to the aforementioned descriptive nature of the regulatory document.

Table 1. Mean average precision for smart meters case study for O_P and O'_P

Configuration	$\gamma = 0.0$	$\gamma = 0.2$	$\gamma = 0.4$	$\gamma = 0.6$	$\gamma = 0.8$
O_P	0.528	0.528	0.528	0.579	0.581
O'_P	0.647	0.650	0.760	0.875	0.745

Regarding the cost score, the expected observations are confirmed, i.e., for higher γ values, the $cost_o$ increases while $cost_{so}$ and $cost_r$ decrease. Moreover,

---

[5] Due to limited space within the figures and since the values for AP and MAP are lower than for $\gamma = 0.8$ the results for $\gamma = 0.9$ are omitted.

the costs are mostly zero, correctly indicating that manually verified process models have few compliance violations.

4.2   General Data Protection Regulation – GDPR

The second case study corresponds to the second application scenario, i.e., the identification of compliant paragraph-model pairs.

Input. As input we take seven process models (taken from [4]), which capture how the main privacy constraints of the GDPR can be implemented within processes. Aside these seven process models, we consider GDPR Articles 5 to 50, since Articles 1 to 4 contain introductory statements, whereas Article 51 and onwards apply to supervisory authorities rather than organizations.

Evaluation Strategy. We exemplary describe the results for the model depicting a pattern for a *data breach*. In order to verify whether the approach works well, we identified in a manual analysis relevant articles. It turned out that Articles 33 and 34 contain most information on the situation of a data breach and Article 40 contains one constraint referring to that topic.

Results. As within the first case study, we tested several values for γ. For $\gamma = 0.0$, Article 29 has the highest fitness $(0.87508)^6$ and Article 16 has the lowest fitness score (0.73057). The median of the fitness score is at 0.79285 and except for three articles having a fitness greater than the median, the cost score evaluates to zero. Among these, Article 34 has the second highest fitness score, Article 33 the third highest fitness score while having both $cost = 0$. If we want to detect from scratch which paragraph-model pairs are most compliant, we would therefore have the correct ones on top of the list regarding fitness. For $\gamma = 0.4$ the same situation holds while for $\gamma = 0.6$ both articles are shifted down by one position, i.e., in third resp. fourth place and for Article 33 $cost_{so} = 1.0$. For $\gamma = 0.8$ both articles are further shifted down in the ranking and costs for Article 33 additionally increase while Article 34 has now $cost_o = 0.05$. In contrast to the first case study, the ideal γ is at 0.4 for this model-paragraph matching.

5   Discussion and Limitations

Within this section a reflection and discussion of results as well as limitations and suggestions how to resolve these are outlined.

The evaluation demonstrated the impact of parameter γ on the results. In particular, the higher γ, the fewer obligations are identified with corresponding obligatory activities, resulting in a lower MAP. However, MAP also decreases if too many smaller similarities are allowed. For the cost score, similar effects occur, i.e., a stricter threshold γ can lead to an increase of costs. In scenarios

---

[6] Article 29 has one of the highest fitness scores for almost each of the process models since this article just consists of one single constraint, i.e., the chance of having a high semantic similarity with one obligatory activity from a process model is high.

where a model-paragraph alignment is available, a suitable value for γ can be chosen by selecting the value that achieves the highest MAP. When such an alignment is not available, the parameter can be set based on the γ value that leads to the highest overall fitness score. For the case reported on in Sect. 4.1, this would result in $\gamma = 0.6$, which corresponds to the configuration with the second highest MAP value for the O_P configuration and to the highest MAP for the O'_P one. This thus suggests that the fitness score could be a useful proxy value for the parameter selection.

A limitation arises if resources have contrary names within the model and paragraph since semantic similarity would probably fail to identify them as similar. Adapting the threshold δ is one possibility but this would allow for undesired behaviour, i.e., resource cost could increase tremendously. Having a user defined mapping would be more feasible. By now, our approach focuses on mandatory tasks but there might be optional constraints within a paragraph, e.g., indicated by can. As future work we plan to adapt the cost score such that compliance violations caused by optional constraints are considered as well.

6   Related Work

Various approaches provide (semi-)automated support for business process compliance checking (see [11] for an overview). Our work targets so-called design-time compliance analysis, which aims at detecting compliance issues during development and implementation of a business process [13]. Most techniques in this regard require regulations to be first transformed into a formal representation, e.g., temporal logic [10], rather than operating on the regulatory document itself.

The extraction of process constraints from natural language text is typically conducted as part of a broader use case and is a core requirement for approaches that automatically extract process models from process-oriented texts [8,9,20]. Other approaches aim to elicit process constraints from rule-oriented texts, such as the extraction of requirements from documents [5,7,19] and declarative process constraints [1]. More broadly, constraint extraction from regulatory documents is related to requirements elicitation from text. According to the survey in [14], most of the existing approaches are manual or semi-automatic. Other related work compares textual process descriptions to process models [2,17]. However, those works assume that a textual process description relates to exactly one, already known process model, whereas the regulatory documents considered by our work can be subject to complex, many-to-many correspondences.

7   Conclusion

This work enables the automatic assessment of the compliance between process models and regulatory documents. For this, we presented a notion of fitness to identify which of the compliance constraints extracted from a regulatory document concern a certain model. In addition, we proposed a cost function to measure the distance between these constraints and the process as captured by the model, thereby highlighting potential violations. The effectiveness of our approach has been demonstrated in two case studies.

Our work supports companies to cope with frequent changes of regulations and of process models through automated support. As the first approach of its kinds, our work opens several avenues for future research. The approach can be expanded to incorporate additional types of compliance violations, such as those stemming from *prohibitive* rather than *obligatory* statements in regulatory documents, as well as those covering the data and time perspectives of processes. Furthermore, our proposed cost function can be employed to go beyond the detection of violations by helping to assess which process change operation may be employed to ensure compliant process execution.

References

1. van der Aa, H., Di Ciccio, C., Leopold, H., Reijers, H.A.: Extracting declarative process models from natural language. In: Giorgini, P., Weber, B. (eds.) CAiSE 2019. LNCS, vol. 11483, pp. 365–382. Springer, Cham (2019). https://doi.org/10. 1007/978-3-030-21290-2_23
2. Van der Aa, H., Leopold, H., Reijers, H.A.: Comparing textual descriptions to process models-the automatic detection of inconsistencies. Inf. Syst. **64**, 447–460 (2017)
3. Van der Aa, H., Leopold, H., Reijers, H.A.: Checking process compliance against natural language specifications using behavioral spaces. Inf. Syst. **78**, 83–95 (2018)
4. Agostinelli, S., Maggi, F.M., Marrella, A., Sapio, F.: Achieving GDPR compliance of BPMN process models. In: Cappiello, C., Ruiz, M. (eds.) Information Systems Engineering in Responsible Information Systems. CAiSE 2019. Lecture Notes in Business Information Processing, vol. 350. Springer, Cham (2019). https://doi.org/ 10.1007/978-3-030-21297-1_2
5. Bajwa, I.S., Lee, M.G., Bordbar, B.: SBVR business rules generation from natural language specification. In: AAAI Spring Symposium, pp. 2–8 (2011)
6. Böhmer, K., et al.: Application and testing of business processes in the energy domain. Big Data Management Systems in Business and Industrial Applications (2017)
7. Dragoni, M., Villata, S., Rizzi, W., Governatori, G.: Combining NLP approaches for rule extraction from legal documents. In: MIREL (2016)
8. Friedrich, F., Mendling, J., Puhlmann, F.: Process model generation from natural language text. In: Mouratidis, H., Rolland, C. (eds.) CAiSE 2011. LNCS, vol. 6741, pp. 482–496. Springer, Heidelberg (2011). https://doi.org/10.1007/978-3-642-21640-4_36
9. Ghose, A., Koliadis, G., Chueng, A.: Process discovery from model and text artefacts. In: Services, pp. 167–174 (2007)
10. Hashmi, M., Governatori, G.: Norms modeling constructs of business process compliance management frameworks: a conceptual evaluation. Artif. Intell. Law **26**(3), 251–305 (2017). https://doi.org/10.1007/s10506-017-9215-8
11. Hashmi, M., Governatori, G., Lam, H.-P., Wynn, M.T.: Are we done with business process compliance: state of the art and challenges ahead. Knowl. Inf. Syst. **57**(1), 79–133 (2018). https://doi.org/10.1007/s10115-017-1142-1
12. Honnibal, M., Montani, I.: spaCy 2: natural language understanding with Bloom embeddings, convolutional neural networks and incremental parsing (2017)

13. Kharbili, M.E., Medeiros, A.K.A.D., Stein, S., van der Aalst, W.M.: Business process compliance checking: current state and future challenges. In: MobIS (2008)
14. Meth, H., Brhel, M., Maedche, A.: The state of the art in automated requirements elicitation. Inf. Softw. Technol. **55**(10), 1695–1709 (2013)
15. Omg, O., Parida, R., Mahapatra, S.: Business process model and notation (BPMN) version 2.0. Object Manag. Group **1** (2011)
16. Rinderle-Ma, S., Kabicher-Fuchs, S.: An indexing technique for compliance checking and maintenance in large process and rule repositories. EMISAJ **11**, 1–24 (2016)
17. Sànchez-Ferreres, J., van der Aa, H., Carmona, J., Padró, L.: Aligning textual and model-based process descriptions. Data Knowl. Eng. **118**, 25–40 (2018)
18. Schröder, G., Thiele, M., Lehner, W.: Setting goals and choosing metrics for recommender system evaluations. In: UCERSTI2 (2011)
19. Selway, M., Grossmann, G., Mayer, W., Stumptner, M.: Formalising natural language specifications using a cognitive linguistic/configuration based approach. Inf. Syst. **54**, 191–208 (2015)
20. Sinha, A., Paradkar, A.: Use cases to process specifications in business process modeling notation. In: Web Services, pp. 473–480 (2010)
21. Winter, K., Rinderle-Ma, S.: Deriving and combining mixed graphs from regulatory documents based on constraint relations. In: Giorgini, P., Weber, B. (eds.) CAiSE 2019. LNCS, vol. 11483, pp. 430–445. Springer, Cham (2019). https://doi.org/10.1007/978-3-030-21290-2_27

Modeling Chatbots, Narratives and Natural Language

Model-Driven Chatbot Development

Sara Pérez-Soler(✉) ⓘ, Esther Guerra ⓘ, and Juan de Lara ⓘ

Universidad Autónoma de Madrid, Madrid, Spain
{Sara.PerezS,Esther.Guerra,Juan.deLara}@uam.es

Abstract. Chatbots are software services accessed via conversation in natural language. They are increasingly used to help in all kinds of procedures like booking flights, querying visa information or assigning tasks to developers. They can be embedded in webs and social networks, and be used from mobile devices without installing dedicated apps. While many frameworks and platforms have emerged for their development, identifying the most appropriate one for building a particular chatbot requires a high investment of time. Moreover, some of them are closed – resulting in customer lock-in – or require deep technical knowledge.

To tackle these issues, we propose a model-driven engineering approach to chatbot development. It comprises a neutral meta-model and a domain-specific language (DSL) for chatbot description; code generators and parsers for several chatbot platforms; and a platform recommender. Our approach supports forward and reverse engineering, and model-based analysis. We demonstrate its feasibility presenting a prototype tool and an evaluation based on migrating third party Dialogflow bots to Rasa.

Keywords: Chatbots · Model-driven engineering · DSLs · Migration

1 Introduction

Chatbots are software programs that interact with users via natural language (NL) conversation. Their use is booming because they can be used within webs and social networks – like Telegram, Twitter or Slack – without having to install dedicated apps [23]. Many companies are developing chatbots to offer 24/7 customer service while reducing costs, and their presence is percolating a wide range of areas such as education [26,29,30] or civic engagement [27].

The success of chatbots has led to the emergence of a plethora of technologies for their creation. Not only big software companies have made available chatbot creation tools, like Google's Dialogflow [9], IBM's Watson Assistant [28], Microsoft's bot framework [17] or Amazon's Lex [15], but many other proposals exist, like Rasa [21], FlowXO [10] and Pandorabots [18]. Among them, we find a variety of approaches. For example, Dialogflow and Watson offer low-code cloud development platforms that support the creation and deployment of bots, while Rasa is a framework that requires Python programming for bot development.

© Springer Nature Switzerland AG 2020
G. Dobbie et al. (Eds.): ER 2020, LNCS 12400, pp. 207–222, 2020.
https://doi.org/10.1007/978-3-030-62522-1_15

Overall, these chatbot creation tools are indisputably powerful (e.g., some provide NL processing, speech recognition, etc.). However, since there are so many options, choosing the most appropriate one to develop a chatbot with certain features is not easy. There may also be operational factors to consider in the decision, as for example, some options may imply vendor lock-in, and migrating chatbots between tools is not generally supported. Last but not least, some approaches have a steep learning curve and require expert knowledge.

To overcome these problems, we propose a model-driven engineering (MDE) approach [22] to chatbot development. This relies on a meta-model with core primitives for chatbot design, and a domain-specific language (DSL) to define bots independently of the implementation technology. Chatbots defined with the DSL can be analysed for "smells" of defects, and a ranked list of appropriate bot creation tools is recommended based on the chatbot definition and other requirements. Our DSL can be used for *forward engineering*, to produce the chatbot implementation from its specification; and for *reverse engineering*, to produce a model out of a chatbot implementation, which can then be analysed, refactored and migrated to other platforms. Currently, we provide code generators and parsers from/to Dialogflow and Rasa, but our architecture is extensible. We evaluate our approach migrating third-party Dialogflow chatbots to Rasa.

In the rest of the paper, Sect. 2 introduces chatbot design and motivates our work. Section 3 outlines our proposal. Section 4 describes the meta-model and the DSL. Section 5 details our platform recommender. Section 6 presents tool support. Section 7 reports an evaluation based on migration. Section 8 compares with related works, and Sect. 9 concludes and outlines future work.

2 Building a Chatbot: Background and Limitations

Chatbots (also called conversational agents) are software programs with a conversational user interface. They can be classified into *open-domain*, if they can converse on any topic with users, or *task-specific*, if they assist in a concrete task (e.g., bookings flights or shopping). Our work targets the latter kind of bots.

Figure 1 shows the typical working scheme of task-specific chatbots. They are designed around a set of *intents* that users may want to accomplish. Given a user utterance (e.g., *"I'd like to buy a flight ticket from Madrid to Vienna"*, label 1 in the figure), the chatbot tries to identify the corresponding intent (label 2). The approach for this depends on the particular chatbot creation tool. Some of them – like Pandorabots – permit defining patterns or regular expressions upon which the utterance is matched, while others – like Dialogflow, Lex

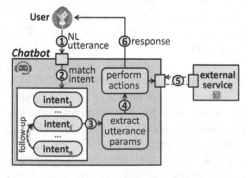

Fig. 1. Chatbot working scheme.

or Rasa – require declaring training phrases and apply NL processing (NLP) techniques. If the chatbot does not find any matching intent, some approaches allow having a default fallback intent. In addition, the conversation flow can be structured into expected sequences of intents (relation *follow-up* in the figure).

After matching an intent, the chatbot extracts the *parameters* of interest from the utterance (e.g., the origin and destination of the flight, label 3). Parameters may be typed by *entities*, which can be either predefined (e.g., date, number) or specific to a chatbot (e.g., flight class). If the utterance lacks some expected parameters (e.g., date of flight), the chatbot can be configured to ask for them.

As a last step, the chatbot can perform different actions depending on the intent, such as calling an external service (e.g., a booking information system, label 5) or replying to the user (label 6). The simplest response format is text, but some chatbot deployment platforms (e.g., Telegram, Twitter) also support images, URLs, videos or buttons.

There are numerous tools for creating chatbots that follow this scheme. These tools use different approaches, ranging from low-code form-based platforms (e.g., Dialogflow, Lex, Watson, FlowXO) to frameworks for programming languages (e.g., Rasa, Botkit [4]), libraries (e.g., Chatterbot [6]) and services (e.g., LUIS [16]). Such a variety makes it difficult to ascertain which tool is suitable to build a specific chatbot, as not every tool supports every possible feature (e.g., only a few provide NLP or multi-language support). Moreover, the conceptual model of the chatbot might be difficult to attain, as the chatbot definition frequently includes tool-specific accidental details. As a consequence, reasoning, understanding, validating and testing chatbots independently from the implementation technology becomes challenging. Finally, some platforms are proprietary which hinders chatbot migration and results in vendor lock-in.

In the following section, we present our proposal to overcome these problems.

3 Model-Driven Engineering of Chatbots

Figure 2 shows a scheme of our proposal. It provides a technology-agnostic DSL called CONGA (ChatbOt modelliNg lanGuAge) to design chatbots. This is built on the basis of a neutral, platform-independent meta-model resulting from an analysis of the existing approaches. The DSL permits modelling chatbots independently of any development platform, and validating quality criteria and well-formedness rules on the chatbot models. Section 4 introduces this DSL.

To facilitate the task of selecting a development tool for implementing a given chatbot model, we provide an extensible recommender that analyses the chatbot model as well as other requirements, to provide a ranked list of suitable tools. Section 5 explains the recommender system and its extensible architecture.

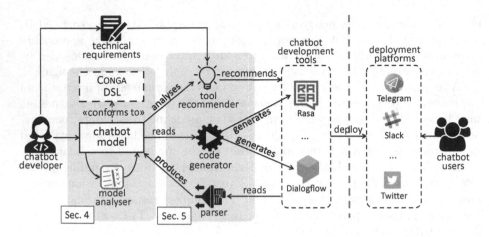

Fig. 2. Overview of our proposal.

In addition, the DSL is complemented with code generators that synthesize chatbot implementations from chatbot models for specific development tools (e.g., JSON configuration files in the case of Dialogflow, or Python programs and configuration files in the case of Rasa). The chatbots so generated can be deployed in different platforms (e.g., Telegram, Slack or Twitter) to make them available to users. Likewise, the DSL facilitates chatbot migration by the provision of parsers from several development platforms into the DSL. Our tool support for these scenarios is explained in Sect. 6, while its evaluation based on migration scenarios is presented in Sect. 7.

Overall, the advantages of our proposal are the following: it keeps the design of the chatbot independent of the specific development technology; it provides analyses applicable at the design level (i.e., prior to the implementation); it assists in the selection of an appropriate development tool; it enables both forward and backward engineering; and it reduces the risk of vendor lock-in.

4   CONGA: A DSL for Chatbot Design

Our DSL CONGA enables the design of chatbots conformant to the neutral meta-model of Fig. 3. This is a platform-independent meta-model which gathers recurrent concepts in chatbot development approaches. Table 1 summarizes the main concepts of the 15 approaches that we have revised to design our meta-model.

The main meta-model class is *Chatbot*, which has a *name* and a list of supported *languages* to allow the definition of multi-language chatbots. Chatbots can define *intents*, *entities*, *actions* and structure the dialogue via *flows*.

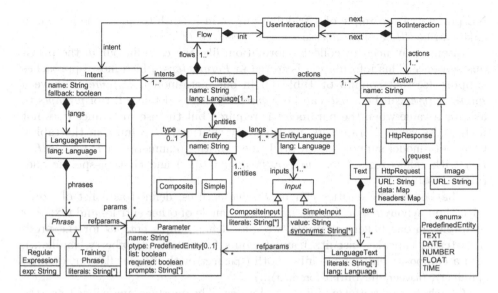

Fig. 3. Platform-independent chatbot design meta-model (simplified excerpt).

Table 1. Recurrent concepts of representative chatbot creation approaches.

Approach	Intent	NLP	Regular expr	Phrase params	Entities	Answ. text	Answ. image	Http Rq/Rs	Dialogue structure
Botkit [4]	no	no	yes	no	no	no	no	no	programm.
Bot framework [17]	yes	yes	yes	yes	yes	yes	yes	yes	tree
Chatfuel [5]	no	yes	no	no	no	yes	yes	yes	tree
Chatterbot [6]	no	yes	no	no	yes	no	no	no	context
Dialogflow [9]	yes	yes	no	yes	yes	yes	yes	yes	context
FlowXO [10]	yes	no	yes	no	yes	yes	yes	yes	tree
Landbot.io [14]	no	no	yes	no	no	yes	yes	yes	tree
Lex [15]	yes	yes	no	yes	yes	yes	yes	yes	session
LUIS [16]	yes	yes	yes	yes	yes	no	no	no	tree
Pandorabots [18]	yes	no	yes	yes	no	yes	yes	no	DSL
Rasa [21]	yes	yes	no	yes	yes	yes	yes	yes	tree
SmartLoop [24]	yes	yes	yes	yes	yes	yes	yes	no	context
Watson [28]	yes	yes	yes	yes	yes	yes	yes	yes	context
Xatkit [8]	yes	yes	yes	yes	yes	yes	yes	yes	context
Xenioo [31]	no	yes	yes	yes	yes	yes	yes	no	tree

Most analysed approaches (10 out of 15) rely on the notion of intent. In our meta-model, an *Intent* has a *name*, can be a *fallback* intent, and defines one set of regular expressions or NL training phrases per supported language. As Table 1 shows (3rd and 4th columns), all approaches support at least one of these two definition mechanisms, while 6 approaches can combine regular expressions with

NL phrases. An example of a training phrase in English to query the price of a cake can be *"How much does a chocolate cake cost?"*.

Intents may need to collect information, like the cake flavour in the previous sentence. This information is stored in *Parameters*, which most approaches support (see 5th column of Table 1). In our meta-model, *Parameters* have a *name*, a *type*, can be a *list*, can be *required*, and may define a list of *prompts* to ask for a value when the parameter is required but the user utterance does not include its value. Parameters are typed by entities (6th column in the table). Our meta-model supports both predefined entities (enumeration *PredefinedEntity* with values *text*, *date*, *number*, *float* and *time*) and chatbot-specific ones (class *Entity*).

Chatbot-specific entities can be *Simple* entities, defined as a list of words with their synonyms, or *Composite* entities, made of other entities and text. For example, in our bakery example, we may define simple entities for the products (cake, cupcake, biscuit...) and flavours (chocolate, strawberry, vanilla...), and a composite entity combining both (⟨product⟩ with ⟨flavour⟩ flavour, ⟨flavour⟩ ⟨product⟩, ⟨flavour⟩ flavoured ⟨product⟩...).

Chatbots can perform different *Actions*. The most common ones are the following (see 7th to 9th columns in Table 1): sending a *Text* response to the user, which requires specifying the actual text for each chatbot language; sending an *Image* which is identified by its *URL*; performing an *HttpRequest* to a given *URL*, optionally providing some *headers* and *data*; and sending to the user an *HttpResponse* for a previous *http* request.

Finally, a chatbot can define conversation *Flows*. As the last column of Table 1 shows, all approaches provide some way to structure the dialogue, and in particular, the meta-model has primitives to cover conversation trees and intent activation based on contexts and sessions. Pandorabots supports a richer mechanism based on a DSL – the Artificial Intelligence Markup Language (AIML)[1] – which our meta-model does not include due to its specificity. A flow is made of *UserInteractions* associated to an intent, and *BotInteractions* comprising one or more actions. A flow must start with a user interaction followed by a bot interaction, after which there may be other user interactions, and so on.

To facilitate the instantiation of this meta-model, we have designed a textual concrete syntax for it. Listing 1 illustrates its usage by showing an excerpt of the definition of a chatbot for a bakery to which users can consult prices and order different products like bread or cakes. The first line defines the chatbot name and the supported languages (English and Spanish). Lines 4–18 define an intent named *Price*, which declares a set of training phrases for each language of the chatbot. If a set of phrases does not specify a language (as is the case in line 5), then they are assumed to be in the first language declared by the chatbot (English in this example). The intent defines four parameters in lines 15–18. The training phrases can refer to them (e.g., [count_param] in line 6) and assign them

---
[1] http://www.aiml.foundation/.

a value in the context of the phrase (e.g., three in line 6). The parameters type can be a predefined entity, like *number*, or a user-defined one, like *flavour*.

Lines 21–29 show the definition of the simple entity *flavour*. This declares the admissible flavours for each language supported by the chatbot, together with their synonyms.

Lines 31–42 illustrate the definition of actions, specifically, a text response called *PriceResponse*. As in the training phrases, text responses can be in different languages, and use parameter values (e.g., [Price.bread_param] in line 34).

Finally, lines 44–49 define the conversation flow (i.e., sequences of user and chatbot interactions). The listing configures two flows, which always must start with a user interaction and the corresponding intent. Flows are defined once, independently of the language. The flow in line 45 takes place when the user utterance matches the *Price* intent, in which case, the chatbot performs the action *PriceResponse* defined in lines 32–42. The second flow (lines 46–49) corresponds to the intent *Buy*. In this case, the chatbot asks for the product type to buy, and the flow is split depending on the user answer (cake or bread). This branching can be recursively nested to enable a compact representation of alternative flows.

The DSL includes model validation rules of two kinds. The first ones are *integrity constraints* that ensure the well-formedness of chatbot models. For example, some of these rules forbid equally named elements (e.g., two *Actions* with the same name) and validate that each *Intent* has exactly one *LanguageIntent* for each language of the chatbot (attribute *Chatbot.lang*). The second kind of rules performs a static analysis of the chatbot definition to assess whether it adheres to *best practices* for chatbot design. Violating these rules may be a "smell" of a bad chatbot design. Currently, the DSL validates the following aspects: there is a fallback intent; text responses only use parameters of intents appearing in the conversation flow; there are no two intents with the same training phrase; all intents define either one regular expression or at least three training phrases; and training phrases do not start by a parameter typed by the predefined entity *text*, as this would match any user utterance which can be problematic.

```
1  chatbot Bakery language: en, es
2
3  intents:
4    Price:
5      inputs {
6        "How much are" (three)[count_param] (bread)[bread_param] "?",
7        "How much is a" (cake)[cake_param] "?",
8        "How much is a" (chocolate)[flavour_param](cake)[cake_param] "?"
9      }
10     inputs in es {
11       "¿Cuanto cuesta el" (pan)[bread_param] "?",
12       "¿Cuanto cuesta una" (tarta)[cake_param] "?",
13       "¿Cuanto cuesta un" (pastel)[cake_param] "de" (chocolate)[flavour_param] "?"
14     }
15     parameters:
16       bread_param, cake_param: entity product;
17       flavour_param: entity flavour;
18       count_param: entity number;
19
20 entities:
21   simple entity flavour:
22     inputs in en {
23       chocolate synonyms choco, cocoa, truffle;
24       ...
25     }
26     inputs in es {
27       chocolate synonyms choco, cacao, trufa;
28       ...
29     }
30
31 actions:
32   text response PriceResponse:
33     inputs {
34       "The" [Price.bread_param] "costs 1 euro per unit",
35       "The" [Price.flavour_param] [Price.cake_param] "costs 10 euro per unit",
36       "The" [Price.cake_param] "costs 10 euro per unit"
37     }
38     inputs in es {
39       "El" [Price.bread_param] "cuesta 1 euro por unidad",
40       "Las" [Price.cake_param] "de" [Price.flavour_param] "cuestan 10 euros por unidad",
41       "Las" [Price.cake_param] "cuestan 10 euros por unidad"
42     }
43
44 flows:
45   − user Price => chatbot PriceResponse;
46   − user Buy => chatbot Type {
47     => user Cake => chatbot Quantity => user num => chatbot BuyCakeHttp, buyCakeResponse;
48     => user Bread => chatbot Quantity => user num => chatbot BuyBreadHttp, buyBreadResponse;
49   }
```

Listing 1: Excerpt of chatbot model definition with the CONGA DSL.

5   Recommending a Chatbot Creation Tool

Due to the large amount of tools and approaches for chatbot creation (cf. Table 1), selecting the best option to build a particular chatbot becomes complex. To assist in this task, we provide a recommender that receives a chatbot model specified with CONGA and the answers to a questionnaire relative to other aspects of the chatbot (e.g., technical, organizational or managerial requirements), and from this information, it recommends an appropriate tool to implement the chatbot. The recommender builds on a model-based extensible architecture that enables the addition of new chatbot creation tools and the customization of the questions and model features the recommendation builds on.

Figure 4 shows the meta-model our *Recommender* relies on. To make a recommendation, it considers a list of chatbot *Requirements*, whose value can be retrieved either by means of a *Question* to the developer, or automatically via an *Analysis* of the chatbot model. Both kinds of requirements have a *name*, a *text*, a list of admissible *Options*, and can be *multi-response* or not. In addition, *Analysis* requirements define an *evaluator*, which is the (Java) class in charge of analysing the chatbot model. This latter class must extend the built-in abstract class *Evaluator* and implement its abstract method *evaluate*, which receives a chatbot model and returns the *Options* that this model fulfils. The recommendation consists of a list of *Tools*. For each tool, the recommender stores the requirement options that are *available*, *unavailable*, *unknown* or are ultimately *possible* (i.e., not natively supported but achievable using a workaround).

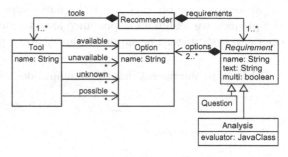

Fig. 4. Recommender meta-model.

The recommender currently considers the requirements in Table 2, and new ones can be added if needed. The table also shows the coverage of these requirements by two chatbot creation tools: Dialogflow and Rasa. Regarding analysis requirements, we check whether the chatbot model is multi-language (like in Listing 1), the targeted languages[2], and whether it uses predefined or chatbot-specific entities, calls to external services, parameters, training phrases or regular expressions. Rasa does not support multi-language bots, but a workaround is generating one bot per language, hence the value *possible* in the table.

Questions are chatbot requirements explicitly asked to the developer as they cannot be inferred from the chatbot model. The first seven questions in Table 2 deal with technical aspects. Specifically, we ask for the following issues: the social network the chatbot is to be deployed in (Dialogflow supports 16, and Rasa 8); the hosting server of the chatbot, since some platforms (e.g., Dialogflow) can host the chatbot themselves, but others (e.g., Rasa) require an external server; the level of support for version control, which is built-in in platforms like Dialogflow, while programming-based approaches like Rasa need to use an external version control system like *github*; the need to monitor the chatbot performance (e.g., Dialogflow provides some chatbot analytics); the persistence of utterances for their subsequent analysis; and the need to support speech recognition or sentiment analysis.

The last three questions in Table 2 tackle organizational and managerial aspects concerned with open-source and price model requirements, and the level of expertise of the development team. For example, the expertise for using Rasa is higher than for Dialogflow, since the former requires programming.

---

[2] For brevity, Table 2 shows the number of languages supported, not the list of them.

Since some requirements may be more important than others depending on the project, we assign an importance level to each requirement, which the developer can customize. The supported levels are: *irrelevant, relevant, double relevant*

Table 2. Requirements that the recommender currently takes into consideration.

Text	Multi-response	Options	Dialogflow	Rasa
Analyses				
Is the chatbot multi-language?	false	Yes	avail.	possib.
		No	avail.	avail.
Which are the chatbot languages?	True	-	21	all
Does the chatbot use new or predefined entities?	true	Predefined	avail.	avail.
		New entities	avail.	avail.
		None	avail.	avail.
Does the chatbot call to external services?	false	One	avail	avail.
		Multiple	possib.	avail
		None	avail.	avail.
Does the chatbot use phrase parameters?	false	Yes	avail.	avail.
		No	avail.	avail.
Does the chatbot need persistent or volatile parameter storage?	true	Persistent	avail.	avail.
		Volatile	avail.	avail.
		None	avail.	avail.
Does your chatbot need natural language processing or pattern matching?	true	NLP	avail.	avail.
		Pattern	unavail.	unavail.
Questions				
Which social networks do you want to deploy the chatbot in?	true	-	16	8
Do you want to deploy the chatbot on your own host?	false	Tool host	avail.	unavail.
		Own host	unavail.	avail.
Do you want to use a built-in version control system?	false	Yes	avail.	avail.
		No	avail.	avail.
Do you require native support for chatbot analytics?	false	Yes	avail.	unavail.
		No	avail.	avail.
Do you require native support for utterance persistence?	false	Yes	avail.	avail.
		No	avail.	avail.
Do you require the chatbot to support speech recognition?	false	Yes	avail.	unavail.
		No	avail.	avail.
Do you require the chatbot to support sentiment analysis?	false	Yes	avail.	unavail.
		No	avail.	avail.
Do you require to use an open-source tool?	false	Yes	unavail.	avail.
		No	avail.	avail.
Which price model do you plan to use?	true	Free	avail.	avail.
		Pay as you go	avail.	unavail.
		Quota	unavail.	unavail.
		Pay advanced feats	unavail.	avail.
What's the level of expertise of the development team?	false	Low	avail.	unavail.
		High	avail.	avail.

and *critical*. Irrelevant requirements are not considered for the recommendation, and critical ones are breaking factors (i.e., tools that do not comply with the requirement will not be recommended). For each tool, the recommender computes a score based on the supported requirements and their importance level. *Available* requirements add 1 to the score of a tool, *unavailable* ones add 0, *unknown* ones add 0.5, and *possible* ones add 0.75. In all cases, double relevant requirements score double. Then, the recommender orders the tools according to their score, and produces a report with the ranking of tools and how each requirement contributes to this ranking.

Incorporating a new chatbot creation tool (e.g., Watson) into our framework requires: (i) informing the tool options for every requirement in the recommender; (ii) providing a code generator from CONGA to the tool; (iii) optionally, providing a parser if reverse engineering is required. Our framework prevents the code generation for a tool whenever the chatbot requirements are *unavailable* in that tool. There may be some *possible* requirements though, meaning that their support is not native in the tool but they can be implemented. For instance, Rasa does not support multi-language chatbots, but this can be emulated by generating one chatbot per language. As another example, Dialogflow only supports one external service call per intent, and so, the generator only considers the first call and warns the developer.

6 Tool Support

We have built tool support for our approach. Fig. 5(a) shows the developed editor for the CONGA DSL, which uses the Eclipse Modeling Framework (EMF) [25] and Xtext. The editor provides syntax highlighting, autocompletion, and informs of errors and warnings found in the chatbot models.

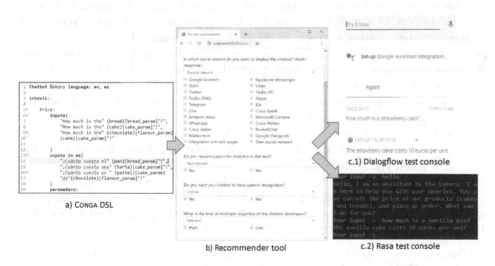

Fig. 5. Our tool in action for forward engineering. (a) CONGA editor. (b) Recommender. (c.1) Generated bot for Dialogflow. (c.2) Generated bot for Rasa.

Upon uploading a chatbot model to a web server, we can apply the recommender (Fig. 5(b)) and generate code for a specific chatbot creation tool. Currently, the recommender considers 14 up-to-date tools, and we provide generators and parsers from/to Dialogflow and Rasa. Anyhow, as previously explained, both aspects are extensible. Figures 5(c.1) and 5(c.2) show two generated chatbots for Dialogflow and Rasa in their respective development environments, from where the chatbots can be deployed into a social network.

7   Evaluation

This section reports on an evaluation of our approach on a migration scenario which involves both backward and forward engineering. The goal is to answer two research questions (RQs): **RQ1:** *Is* CONGA *expressive enough to capture the details of existing chatbots?* **RQ2:** *Can the migration process be fully automated?* For this purpose, we have migrated four Dialogflow agents developed by third parties (three from github, one built by Google) into Rasa. Table 3 summarizes the experiment results.

Table 3. Assessment metrics.

	Dialogflow					CONGA		Rasa			
	No. intents	No. ents.	Http req.	No. files	Lang	No. objects	No. lines	No. chatbots	No. Python lines	No. Markd. lines	No. yaml lines
Game	11	0	yes	30	en/fr	541	268	2	378	242	362
Room reservation	7	1	no	17	en	717	196	1	253	166	137
Coffee shop	21	8	no	60	en	931	393	1	657	394	269
Nutrition	4	7	no	23	en	833	610	1	802	81	99

Game[3] is a conversational agent for a numeric guessing game. It has 11 intents, no entities, one *http* request, and supports English and French. Its Dialogflow specification is made of 30 JSON files. From this specification, our parser creates a model with 541 objects and 268 lines of CONGA code. Since Rasa does not support multi-language chatbots, two Rasa chatbots are generated from the CONGA model, one for each language. These have 378 lines of Python code (to define parameters and actions), 242 lines of Markdown code (to define intents and flows) and 362 lines of YAML code (to configure the chatbot).

Room reservation[4] is a chatbot to book hotel rooms. It has 7 intents and one entity, and works in English. The migration produces a Rasa chatbot with 253 lines of Python code. Since the original Dialogflow chatbot has button actions, which are unsupported by CONGA, we had to add them manually in Rasa.

Coffee shop is a Dialogflow pre-built agent to order food to a coffee shop. Its specification is the most complex of the four chatbots, spanning 60 JSON files. These are parsed into a CONGA model with 931 objects.

---

[3] https://github.com/actions-on-google/dialogflow-number-genie-nodejs.

[4] https://github.com/dialogflow/dialogflow-java-client-v2/tree/master/samples/resources.

Nutrition[5] is a chatbot to query the nutritional value of meals. Although it is a small chatbot with 4 intents and 7 entities, it generates many lines of Python code because the entities have many entries.

Overall, we were able to migrate all Dialogflow chatbots but the button actions on the room reservation bot, which confirms the expressiveness of CONGA (RQ1). Except for that bot, migration was fully automatic (RQ2). These results are very promising, but more case studies are needed to strengthen the confidence in the capabilities of CONGA. Moreover, we manually checked that the produced Rasa chatbots preserved the original Dialogflow behaviour, but we plan to automate this check in future work (e.g., using tools like Botium[6]).

8 Related Work

The popularity of chatbots has promoted the appearance of many tools for their construction. In this section, we revise works built atop these tools to simplify some aspect of chatbot development.

Xatkit [8] (formerly known as Jarvis [7]) is a model-driven solution for developing chatbots. Similar to our approach, it proposes a meta-model and a textual DSL. However, differently from us, Xatkit has its own bot execution engine that builds on Dialogflow to identify the user intent using NLP, and does not generate code for existing chatbot development tools. Moreover, even though Xatkit is model-based, it does not address the recommendation of suitable chatbot platforms, nor reduces the risk of vendor lock-in by supporting chatbot migration.

In [3], Baudat et al. facilitate the definition of Watson chatbots by means of an OCaml library which produces the necessary JSON files, and the use of ReactiveML to orchestrate the dialog. While this approach is generative, it is limited to Watson and does not support reverse engineering.

There are some recent model-based proposals to automate the construction of chatbots for a specific task. For example, the framework in [1] permits creating chatbots for video game development; in [20], we generate Dialogflow chatbots to allow instantiating meta-models using a NL syntax; and in [19], we generate model query chatbots. Other works do not rely on models for automating chatbot creation, such as [13], where the authors enable a black-box reuse of components for creating chatbots for FAQ exploration. All these approaches are not general-purpose, but they produce chatbots for a specific task (creating video games, creating models, querying models, or exploring FAQs).

Conversely, in [2], the authors envision a reverse engineering process called *botification* to produce a conversational interface for existing web sites. The process parses a web page to produce a domain model, which serves to configure the allowed NL interactions. Botified webs improve the user experience for visually impaired users, and the development cost is low. We believe that our architecture could serve as a reference to implement this scenario.

---

[5] https://github.com/Viber/apiai-nutrition-sample.
[6] https://www.botium.ai/.

Another related line of research concerns crowd-powered conversational assistants [11,12]. While they are not auto-generated, as we do in this paper, they can auto-evolve by learning appropriate responses from previous ones.

Finally, some development tools are specific for voice-user interfaces. For example, tortu[7] supports the visual creation of conversation flows, but it does not allow code generation or bot migration. In a similar vein, VoiceFlow[8] offers a graphical DSL to create voice-based conversation flows that can be deployed on Google home or Alexa, but does not provide recommendation or migration facilities, and the deployment platforms are fixed.

Overall, our approach is novel as it provides a complete MDE solution comprising a unifying DSL for chatbot design, a recommender of up-to-date chatbot development tools according to given design and technical chatbot requirements, and supporting forward and backward engineering, including migration.

9   Conclusion and Future Work

Nowadays, we can find many tools for building chatbots. While these tools accelerate chatbot development, the chatbot design can become obscured under technical tool details. Moreover, selecting the most appropriate tool, or chatbot migration, require a high investment of time. To alleviate these problems, we have proposed an MDE approach to chatbot development that includes a textual DSL, a platform recommender, code generators and parsers. Our approach supports both forward and reverse chatbot engineering, and has been evaluated by migrating four Dialogflow chatbots developed by third parties to Rasa.

In the future, we plan to extend our framework with more chatbot creation tools, facilities for model-based testing, quick-fixes for violations of chatbot best-practices, and mechanisms to make CONGA extensible with platform-specific concepts, like buttons. We are currently migrating our editor of CONGA models to a web environment, and later we plan to perform a user study with developers to assess the advantages of our approach. Finally, we plan to create higher-level DSLs to define domain-specific chatbots (e.g., for education or commerce) which can be transformed into our framework for validation and code generation.

Acknowledgments. Work funded by the Spanish Ministry of Science (RTI2018-095255-B-I00) and the R&D programme of Madrid (P2018/TCS-4314).

---

[7] https://tortu.io/.
[8] https://www.voiceflow.com/.

References

1. Baena-Perez, R., Ruiz-Rube, I., Dodero, J.M., Bolivar, M.A.: A framework to create conversational agents for the development of video games by end-users. In: Dorronsoro, B., Ruiz, P., de la Torre, J.C., Urda, D., Talbi, E.-G. (eds.) OLA 2020. CCIS, vol. 1173, pp. 216–226. Springer, Cham (2020). https://doi.org/10.1007/978-3-030-41913-4_18

2. Baez, M., Daniel, F., Casati, F.: Conversational web interaction: proposal of a dialog-based natural language interaction paradigm for the web. In: Følstad, A., et al. (eds.) CONVERSATIONS 2019. LNCS, vol. 11970, pp. 94–110. Springer, Cham (2020). https://doi.org/10.1007/978-3-030-39540-7_7

3. Baudart, G., Hirzel, M., Mandel, L., Shinnar, A., Siméon, J.: Reactive chatbot programming. In: REBLS@SPLASH, pp. 21–30. ACM (2018)

4. Botkit. https://botkit.ai/. Accessed 2020

5. Chatfuel. https://chatfuel.com/. Accessed 2020

6. Chatterbot. https://chatterbot.readthedocs.io/. Accessed 2020

7. Daniel, G., Cabot, J., Deruelle, L., Derras, M.: Multi-platform chatbot modeling and deployment with the Jarvis framework. In: Giorgini, P., Weber, B. (eds.) CAiSE 2019. LNCS, vol. 11483, pp. 177–193. Springer, Cham (2019). https://doi.org/10.1007/978-3-030-21290-2_12

8. Daniel, G., Cabot, J., Deruelle, L., Derras, M.: Xatkit: a multimodal low-code chatbot development framework. IEEE Access **8**, 15332–15346 (2020)

9. Dialogflow. https://dialogflow.com/. Accessed 2020

10. FlowXO. https://flowxo.com/. Accessed 2020

11. Huang, T.K., Chang, J.C., Swaminathan, S., Bigham, J.P.: Evorus: a crowd-powered conversational assistant that automates itself over time. In: UIST, pp. 155–157. ACM (2017)

12. Jonell, P., Fallgren, P., Dogan, F.I., Lopes, J., Wennberg, U., Skantze, G.: Crowd-sourcing a self-evolving dialog graph. In: CUI, pp. 14:1–14:8. ACM (2019)

13. de Lacerda, A.R.T., Aguiar, C.S.R.: FLOSS FAQ chatbot project reuse. how to allow nonexperts to develop a chatbot. In: OpenSym. ACM (2019)

14. Landbot.io. https://landbot.io/. Accessed 2020

15. Lex. https://aws.amazon.com/en/lex/. Accessed 2020

16. LUIS. https://www.luis.ai/. Accessed 2020

17. Microsoft Bot Framework. https://dev.botframework.com/. Accessed 2020

18. Pandorabots. https://home.pandorabots.com/. Accessed 2020

19. Pérez-Soler, S., Daniel, G., Cabot, J., Guerra, E., de Lara, J.: Towards automating the synthesis of chatbots for conversational model query. In: Nurcan, S., Reinhartz-Berger, I., Soffer, P., Zdravkovic, J. (eds.) Enterprise, Business-Process and Information Systems Modeling. BPMDS 2020, EMMSAD 2020. Lecture Notes in Business Information Processing, vol. 387. Springer, Cham. https://doi.org/10.1007/978-3-030-49418-6_17

20. Pérez-Soler, S., González-Jiménez, M., Guerra, E., de Lara, J.: Towards conversational syntax for domain-specific languages using chatbots. J. Object Technol. **18**(2), 5 (2019)

21. Rasa. https://rasa.com/. Accessed 2020

22. Schmidt, D.C.: Guest editor's introduction: model-driven engineering. Computer **39**(2), 25–31 (2006)

23. Shevat, A.: Designing Bots: Creating Conversational Experiences. O'Reilly, Sebastopol (2017)

24. SmartLoop. https://smartloop.ai/. Accessed 2020
25. Steinberg, D., Budinsky, F., Merks, E., Paternostro, M.: EMF: Eclipse Modeling Framework, 2nd edn. Pearson Education, London (2008)
26. Tegos, S., Demetriadis, S.N.: Conversational agents improve peer learning through building on prior knowledge. Educ. Technol. Soc. **20**(1), 99–111 (2017)
27. Väänänen, K., Hiltunen, A., Varsaluoma, J., Pietilä, I.: CivicBots – chatbots for supporting youth in societal participation. In: Følstad, A., et al. (eds.) CONVERSATIONS 2019. LNCS, vol. 11970, pp. 143–157. Springer, Cham (2020). https://doi.org/10.1007/978-3-030-39540-7_10
28. Watson. https://www.ibm.com/cloud/watson-assistant/. Accessed 2020
29. Winkler, R., Hobert, S., Salovaara, A., Söllner, M., Leimeister, J.M.: Sara, the lecturer: improving learning in online education with a scaffolding-based conversational agent. In: CHI, pp. 1–14. ACM (2020)
30. Meyer von Wolff, R., Nörtemann, J., Hobert, S., Schumann, M.: Chatbots for the information acquisition at universities – a student's view on the application area. CONVERSATIONS 2019. LNCS, vol. 11970, pp. 231–244. Springer, Cham (2020). https://doi.org/10.1007/978-3-030-39540-7_16
31. Xenioo. https://www.xenioo.com/en/. Accessed 2020

Supporting Collaborative Modeling via Natural Language Processing

Fatma Başak Aydemir[1]([⊠]) and Fabiano Dalpiaz[2]

[1] Boğaziçi University, Istanbul, Turkey
`basak.aydemir@boun.edu.tr`
[2] Utrecht University, Utrecht, The Netherlands
`f.dalpiaz@uu.nl`

Abstract. Engineering large-scale systems requires the collaboration among experts who use different modeling languages and create multiple models. Due to their independent creation and evolution, these models may exhibit discrepancies in terms of the domain concepts they represent. To help re-align the models without an explicit synchronization, we propose a technique that provides the modelers with suggested concepts that they may be interested in adding to their own models. The approach is modeling-language agnostic since it processes only the text in the models, such as the labels of elements and relationships. In this paper, we focus on determining the similarity of compound nouns, which are frequently used in conceptual models. We propose two algorithms, that make use of word embeddings and domain models, respectively. We report an early validation that assesses the effectiveness of our similarity algorithms against state-of-the-art machine learning algorithms with respect to human judgment.

Keywords: Collaborative modeling · Conceptual modeling · Natural language processing · Semantic similarity

1 Introduction

The systems we build are growing in size and complexity [25]; many examples are before our eyes such as intelligent transportation systems, healthcare infrastructures, and smart grids. Due to the complex interactions between systems and their subsystems [30], we need to analyze cross-cutting system concerns such as performance, security, safety, privacy, and fairness, through approaches like aspect-oriented design [7].

Specific expertise is necessary to study these different aspects, thereby demanding collaboration among multiple experts. Since physically bringing these experts to the same location is quite costly and even not possible due to unforeseen situations such as a pandemic, the collaboration among these individuals increasingly relies on mediated, asynchronous interaction over the Internet thanks to the rise of digital transformation.

© Springer Nature Switzerland AG 2020
G. Dobbie et al. (Eds.): ER 2020, LNCS 12400, pp. 223–238, 2020.
https://doi.org/10.1007/978-3-030-62522-1_16

One of the challenges in this setting is to create consistent models. Modeling techniques can ensure consistency via, e.g., aspect weaving [14,34], when a common meta-model exists. As an alternative, recent work [24] has proposed near real-time modeling frameworks for enabling collaboration on the same model and for resolving conflicts.

We take a complementary standpoint. Instead of integrating the models into a consistent supermodel, we propose algorithms for achieving *model alignment*; two models are aligned when they capture similar if not the same domain concepts and relations. If the models are aligned, it means that the experts have analyzed the same part of the domain, and can therefore conduct trade-off analyses between the various aspects.

We assist model alignment by *suggesting concepts* that the modelers may want to include in their models. We suggest concepts that are missing in a model but are captured in other models in the same project. To identify candidate concepts, we automatically search for element and relationship labels with identical or similar noun phrases.

Identifying matching or missing concepts is not trivial. On one hand, our experience in system specification [23] has shown that modelers (and designers in general) often use *compound nouns* to describe a domain, e.g., 'company car', 'car engine', 'car rental'. On the other hand, interpreting the meaning of compound nouns is renown to be difficult [20,22]. As a consequence, finding synonym compound words is all but simple.

Our work takes a lightweight approach to matching terms, in which we do not assume the definition of a shared meta-model [24], the existence of a domain ontology [11], or knowledge about the semantics of the model elements [21].

In this paper, we make three specific contributions toward the alignment of multiple models without requiring knowledge of or aligning the meta-models:

1. We propose the Concept Suggester service that relies on natural language processing (NLP) heuristics to propose additional concepts to the modelers; see Sect. 2. This paper extends the vision of the service sketched in previous work [2].
2. We devise two algorithms, that use different approaches, for computing the similarity of two-word compound nouns (Sect. 3).
3. We report on an experiment that assesses the performance of our heuristics against off-the-shelf machine learning algorithms (Sect. 4).

After discussing related work in Sect. 5, we conclude and present future work in Sect. 6.

2   The Concept Suggester Service

The *Concept Suggester* service supports the asynchronous collaboration among two or more modelers by analyzing the changes they make in their own models, and by recommending ("suggesting") which domain concepts they may be interested to include in their models by analyzing the domain concepts that are represented in other models.

2.1   Motivation and System Overview

The concept suggester service was conceived in the context of the PACAS research project[1] regarding the decision making processes in the air traffic management domain. In this setting, multiple organizations (such as governments, airports, and airlines) investigate possible solutions from different perspectives through models that are built using various modeling languages. Currently, experts from various organizations, working in different time-zones and locations, build their models during face-to-face workshops. Besides costs and carbon footprint, this type of workshops become impossible in time of a pandemic. Note that this situation applies to other kinds of information systems in which different experts collaborate to model the system from different perspectives.

This setting poses some challenges. How to ensure that the individual models, created independently, analyze the same domain by representing the same domain concepts (*C1*)? Also, in case of competing collaboration (e.g., airline companies), the modelers may want to not disclose sensitive information while allowing alignment (*C2*). Finally, how to ensure the use of unified terminology (*C3*)? This challenge stems from the different backgrounds of experts, which may result in different labels for the same concepts.

Our service focuses on overcoming these challenges. Regarding *C1*, it keeps track of the concepts modelled in each model, without looking into the actual meaning of the models. When domain concepts are identified that miss in other models, those concepts are suggested to increase model completeness. *C2* is addressed by not sharing with other modelers the actual content of the models and the relationships between concepts. Regarding *C3*, a domain ontology is consulted when making suggestions to encourage including standard terms rather than the jargon of the individual modelers. Note that, by not requiring a shared meta-model, the experts are free to use their modeling languages.

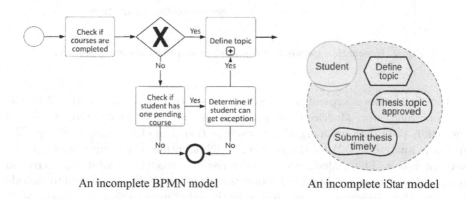

An incomplete BPMN model   An incomplete iStar model

Fig. 1. Early models for a thesis management system

---

[1] https://www.sesarju.eu/projects/pacas.

Illustration. Figure 1 presents two incomplete models drawn in the early phases of the design of a thesis management system for a higher education institution. Our service recognizes the concepts modelled during each modeling session, and keeps track of the modelled concepts for each model. It also tracks the missing concepts for each model, and suggest them to the modeler. In this illustrative example the **course** concept appears in the BPMN model (Fig. 1a), but the iStar goal model (Fig. 1b) lacks it. Then, our service suggests this concept to the modeler to support the modeling process.

The Concept Suggester was originally built for the PACAS project to support the collaboration among air traffic management experts working on security, safety, performance, etc. Through its integration in the PACAS collaborative modeling platform[2], we obtained feedback from domain experts that led to the version described here.

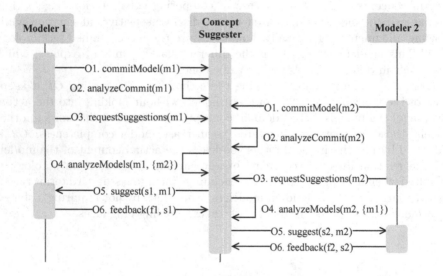

Fig. 2. Interaction between two modelers and the Concept Suggester.

Figure 2 shows a typical interaction between two modelers, mediated by the Concept Suggester. Modeler 1 commits a model m1 that she created. A *commit* operation (O1) denotes a significant change that a modeler aims to share. The model is analyzed (O2) by the service, which identifies the noun phrases in the element labels. Then, Modeler 2 commits her own model m2, which was created independently from m1. Modeler 1 requests suggestions (O3) of concepts to include in her model: the service, after analyzing the other model m2, looks for concepts in m2 that do not appear in m1, which are suggested (O5) to Modeler 1. This actor provides feedback (O6) on the usefulness of the suggested concepts. A similar cycle takes place between Modeler 2 and the service.

---

[2] https://pacas.disi.unitn.it/pacas.

2.2   NLP Heuristics for Term-Concept Matching

Operations O2 and O4 use NLP algorithms that process the element labels in a committed model (O2), and that identify domain concepts that the committed model does not include but that are included in other models of the project (O4). Below, *terms* are the noun phrases in model elements, while *concepts* are the elements in a domain model. The BPMN diagram of Fig. 3 shows the NLP that takes place between O1 and O4.

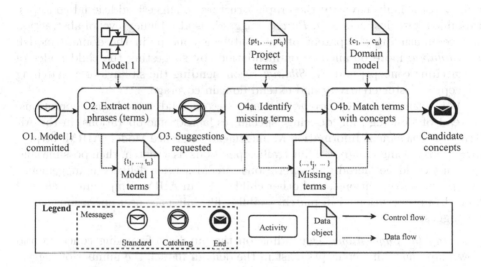

Fig. 3. From model commit to candidate concepts to suggest.

The process starts when Model 1 is committed (O1). Noun phrases are extracted from the committed model (O2), resulting in the set of terms from that model. Then, when the modeler requests suggestions for concepts to include in her model, the extracted terms are compared against project terms from other models (O4a), with the goal of identifying project terms that do not appear in the processed model. Then (O4b), these missing terms are matched against the domain model, filtering out those terms that are not domain-specific, and resulting in the candidate concepts to recommend.

Matching Heuristics. Many algorithms exist to determine whether two terms or concepts do match, ranging from exact lexical match to more advanced metrics like semantic similarity. Some examples: *i. Exact string match*: two terms/concepts match only if they are the same string; *ii. Substring match*: one term/concept is a substring or a superstring of another; *iii. Similarity*: the semantic similarity between the terms/concepts is above a certain threshold, e.g., computed by counting the shared *is-a* relationships in an ontology [17]; *iv. Relatedness*: like similarity, but based on the number of relationships—of any type, *is-a* or otherwise—that two concepts share in an ontology [17].

Exact string match provides the most restricted set of suggestions since it does not leave room for concept exploration. It is therefore particularly useful towards the end of the overall modeling process to ensure model alignment. The other heuristics provide suggestions in a broader spectrum, and may be useful earlier in the modeling process, for they suggest divergence, triggering creativity and increasing the scope of the model.

Suggesting Concepts. When missing concepts are found by O4, and we possess a domain model that has a graph structure (e.g., a taxonomy or an ontology), O5 can optionally navigate the graph structure to suggest additional concepts. Possible strategies include: *i. Parent:* suggestions at a higher level of abstraction by recommending the parent of the matching concept in the domain model; *ii. Children:* more detailed recommendations by suggesting the child nodes of a matching concept; and *iii. Sibling*: recommending the siblings of a matching concept to foster creativity and extend domain coverage.

For example, using *parent*, we may recommend 'aerodrome operations' instead of 'de-icing', for 'de-icing' specializes 'aerodrome operations' in the Air Traffic Management Information Management Reference Model (AIRM, http:// airm.aero). Using *children*, if 'air traffic operations' is a match, then possible suggestions could be 'aerodrome operations', 'ATM service delivery management', 'airspace user operations', and other child nodes in AIRM. Employing *sibling*, if 'aerodrome operations' is a match, a sibling like 'airspace user operations' could be suggested.

Filtering the Suggestions. Depending on the number of missing concepts and how many matching concepts exist in the domain model, the number of suggestions might grow rapidly. Our experience with domain experts in PACAS led us to devising some strategies: *i. Fixed number:* a maximum number of suggested concepts is set (our domain experts suggested five to ten suggestions at a time); *ii. User feedback:* when a modeler expresses a suggestion is irrelevant (O6), the service blacklists that concept and related ones; *iii. Frequency:* the most recurring concepts that are present in other models are suggested; *iv. Limiting the matches per missing term:* this filter selects a limited number of matches per missing term, so to support divergence.

3   Similarity for Compound Nouns

In our initial implementation [2], we adopted nouns as units of computation, for which off-the-shelf NLP libraries exist that can measure similarity. When we observed that many labels use compound words, we switched to noun compounds as the unit of computation, and realized that the NLP literature is much weaker on compounds similarity [20,22]. As such, we developed two heuristics for supporting this task.

The first heuristic (Sect. 3.1) combines semantic similarity measures that rely on word2Vec and WordNet and that use general-purpose corpora. The second heuristic (Sect. 3.2), instead, uses a domain glossary as a type of domain model. Both heuristics return a similarity score in the [0, 1] interval.

3.1 Using Word Embeddings and WordNet

This heuristic measures the similarity between a pair of two-word compounds through a combination of *i.* their lexical similarity with *ii.* the semantic similarity between the words that compose the compounds, determined using word embeddings and WordNet. We use word embeddings because of their good results for short text similarity [18].

Algorithm 1: Similarity of two words.

---

1 **Function** tws
   | **Data:** wordA, wordB
2 | similarity ← word2VecSim(wordA, wordB)
3 | **if** similarity $> \sigma$ **then**
4 | | **if** (synsets(wordA) ∩ synsets(wordB)) $\neq \emptyset$ **then**
5 | | | **return** 1
6 | **return** similarity

Algorithm 1 calculates the similarity of two words. Line 2 invokes the word2Vec similarity algorithm that relies on word embeddings; word2Vec is implemented in state-of-the-art NLP toolkits like spaCy and NLTK. If the obtained similarity is greater than a given threshold σ, line 4 checks if they are synonyms by intersecting their synonym sets in WordNet. If the intersection is not empty, the algorithm returns 1: full similarity, i.e., synonymy. In all other cases, it returns the similarity value from word2Vec.

Algorithm 2: Similarity of two-word compounds.

---

1 **Function** getCompoundSimilarity
   | **Data:** cwordA =[w1, w2], cwordB =[w3, w4]
2 | **return** $\gamma \cdot$ tws(w1, w3) $+ \delta \cdot$ tws(w2, w4) $+ \epsilon \cdot$ (tws(w1, w4) $+$ tws(w2, w3))

Algorithm 1 is invoked by Algorithm 2 and determines the similarity of a pair of two-word compounds. This second algorithm measures the similarity of each word with the other words in the other compound by calling Algorithm 1 for each combination, and combines the results into the overall similarity score using a weighted sum. The values of the similarity threshold σ (Algorithm 1), and the weights for the similarity of first words, second words, and cross words γ, δ, and ϵ (Algorithm 2) are assigned as 0.6, 0.3, 0.4, and 0.15, respectively, for they correlate best with an evaluation by human experts [6] ($r = 0.621$: moderate to strong correlation). Future research is needed to further validate these weights.

3.2   Using domain model matching

The `getSimilarityViaDM` algorithm computes the similarity between two n-word compounds with the help of a domain model. The idea is to denote similarity between two compounds only when both are similar to a given concept in the domain model. Differently from the heuristic in Sect. 3.1, this algorithm is domain specific.

Algorithm 3 formalizes this intuition. Given two compound words and a domain model, the similarity score is first set to zero (line 2). Then, a cycle iterates through all concepts in the domain model (lines 3–10), and calculates the similarity between the two words with respect to the domain concept at hand. Lines 4 and 5 calculate the match score between each word and the domain concept (details below). If both match scores are greater than zero (line 7), the similarity between the two words w.r.t. the given concept is computed as the average of the match scores (line 8). If the score is greater than the maximum similarity score between the two compounds computed w.r.t. previously processed domain concepts (line 9), the maximum similarity score is updated (line 10).

Algorithm 3: Similarity score between compound words via a domain model.

1 **Function** getSimilarityViaDM
    Data: wordA, wordB, domainModel
2   simScore ← 0
3   **foreach** dc ∈ domainModel **do**
4   matchScoreA ← getMatchScore(wordA, dc)
5   matchScoreB ← getMatchScore(wordB, dc)
6   abScore ← 0
7   **if** matchScoreA > 0 ∧ matchScoreB > 0 **then**
8   abScore ← $\dfrac{\text{matchScoreA} + \text{matchScoreB}}{2}$
9   **if** abScore > simScore **then**
10   simScore ← abScore

11   **return** simScore

The function `getMatchScore` calculates the match score between a compound word w and a concept dc in the domain model. It assigns a full match score (1.0) when w and dc are the same string, and a slightly lower score (0.75) when w is a substring of dc (e.g., w = 'air traffic' and dc = 'air traffic controller'). Following a similar rationale, it considers the case of a substring of w that excludes the first word: we assign score 0.5 when that corresponds to the domain concept (w = 'congested air traffic' dc = 'air traffic'), and 0.4 when the shortened version of w is a substring of dc. Finally, it assigns even lower scores (0.3 and 0.2) by considering the substring of w that removes the last word; e.g., a score of 0.3 would be assigned with w = 'air traffic control' and dc = 'traffic control'. The scores for the two substring variants differ because the former case (removing the first word of a compound) corresponds to following bottom-up a specialization relationship, the principle used by similarity metrics based on WordNet.

4   Evaluation

We evaluate the effectiveness of our measures for the similarity of compounds with respect to human judgment; our research question is the following:

RQ Given the similarity measures obtained by the techniques of Sect. 3, which one aligns best with human judgment?

4.1   Experimental Setup

We identified four categories to measure the similarity of two-word compound pairs: *Cross*–the first word of a compound is the same as the second word of the other compound in the pair; *First*–the compounds share the same first word; *Second*–the compounds share their second word; *None*–the compounds do not share any word. Next, we randomly picked five instances of these categories from the set of concepts that we have extracted from the website of the Master of Business Intelligence (MBI) program of Utrecht University (archived as *Exp. MBIThesisWebSite* in [3]). The left part of Fig. 4 shows these pairs of compounds and their corresponding categories.

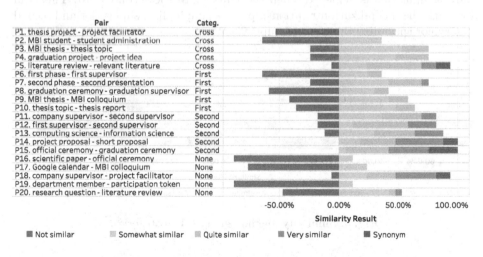

Fig. 4. Similarity tagging of the 20 pairs of compounds.

The second author created a domain model. This was done by first executing a Python script (*Exp. ParseNounChunks* in [3]) that extracts noun chunks from the MBI website. Then, the output was analyzed manually to retain only domain-specific terms and to identify synonyms among those terms. This manual processing required 1 h of work, and the output is *Exp. DomainModel* in [3].

Via an online survey (*Exp. Survey* in [3]), we asked humans to assess the similarity between these pairs via a 5-point Likert type scale consisting of the values *not similar*, *somewhat similar*, *quite similar*, *very similar*, and *synonym*. We measured the compounds' similarity using four methods: *i.* word embeddings with WordNet (Sect. 3.1), *ii.* domain model matching (Sect. 3.2), *iii.* spaCy's similarity algorithm that relies on word embeddings [31], and *iv.* an implementation of semantic similarity[3] that trains Google BERT on the STS benchmark [5].

Participants. We sent the survey to the students and academic staff of the MBI program as they are familiar with the domain; we received 17 responses. The participants spent an average of 6 min and 55 s to fill the survey. Besides evaluating the similarity of pairs using the scale described above, the participants could also indicate the most challenging pairs and provide feedback.

4.2   Results: Gold Standard

The right part of Fig. 4 and Fig. 5 show the results of the similarity tagging for each of the compounds and grouped by category (cross, first, second, none), respectively. We converted the 5-point Likert scale to a $[0, 1]$ similarity score with 0.25 increments, and assigned the mean of the scores assigned by the taggers as the gold standard score. All the responses are in *Exp. RawData* in [3]. Although our little sample size requires caution in our interpretation, it seems that the highest similarity is achieved when the pairs share the second word. This is in line with the specialization relationship: for example, first supervisor and second supervisor specialize the concept supervisor.

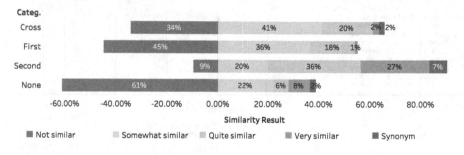

Fig. 5. Similarity tagging, grouped by categories.

8 taggers found the couple company supervisor - project facilitator (P18) among the most difficult pairs to evaluate, followed by four couples highlighted by 6 taggers each: graduation project - project idea (P4), literature review - relevant literature (P5), and project proposal - short proposal (P14). The participants'

---

[3] https://github.com/AndriyMulyar/semantic-text-similarity.

opinions show how difficult it is to evaluate compounds by focusing on similarity, rather than focusing on relatedness (operationalized via co-occurrence by most NLP toolkits).

4.3   Results: Algorithms

Figure 6 compares the similarity values by the different heuristics and the gold standard, splitting the results per category. The outputs of the algorithms are in *Exp. OutputOfAlgorithms* in [3]. The figure highlights important differences when comparing the heuristics against the four categories: (1) *spaCy* consistently assigns the highest score out of the tested heuristics; (2) the *domain model* heuristic generally assigns the lowest score; (3) for the category *Cross*, the algorithms consistently score higher than the *gold standard*; and (4) in the category *Second*, which is linked to the is-a relationship, BERT seems to correlate very well with the gold standard. Furthermore, while SpaCy gives the highest scores to the compounds that share the second word, the domain model heuristic consistently assigns the lowest scores, thereby requiring some tuning. As a side note, four of the most difficult pairs to compare (P18, P5, P12, P14) are also among the most similar pairs in the gold standard.

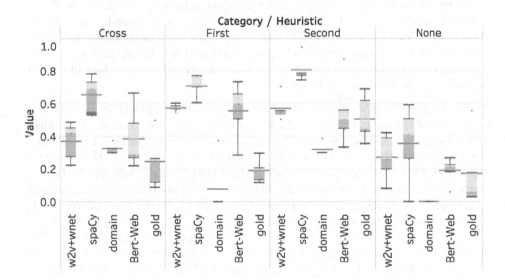

Fig. 6. Box-plot that compares the different heuristics and the gold standard, grouped by category. The green, horizontal lines denote the average value for a given algorithm and a specific category. (Color figure online)

Standard Correlation Analysis. We apply the 2-tailed Spearman correlation ρ, the standard method utilized by the semantic similarity community [5]. This is adequate even in our small sample: we assessed that the gold standard is normally

Table 1. Samples correlations (Spearman's ρ and significance p) and Euclidean distance d between the treatments and the gold standard, $n = 20$. Legend: * denotes significance at $p < 0.05$ and ** at $p < 0.01$.

Sample 1	Sample 2	ρ	Sig. p	d	Sample 1	Sample 2	ρ	Sig. p	d
w + W	GS	0.495*	0.026	1.101	w + W	B-W	0.833**	0.000	0.643
spaCy	GS	0.731**	0.000	1.804	w + W	DM	0.086	0.720	1.496
B-W	GS	0.473*	0.035	1.203	spaCy	DM	.449*	0.047	2.194
DM	GS	0.347	0.134	**0.984**	B-W	DM	0.256	0.276	1.472
w + W	spaCy	0.788**	0.000	0.935	B-W	spaCy	0.747**	0.000	1.196

distributed using the Shapiro-Wilk test ($W = 0.927$, $p = 0.134$), then we visually inspected the relationship between each pair of treatments (e.g., spaCy vs. gold, domain model vs. gold) and we identified a non-linear, monotonic relationship. The results of Table 1, columns ρ and Sig. p, provide an initial answer: spaCy has a *strong* positive correlation with the gold standard (GS) ($0.6 < \rho < 0.79$, significance $p < 0.01$), both word2Vec + WordNet (w + W) and BERT-Web (B-W) have a *moderate* positive correlation ($0.4 < \rho < 0.59$, significance at $p < 0.05$), while we found *no* significant correlation between the domain model (DM) heuristic and the gold standard. When analyzing between-algorithms correlations, we found (i) a *strong* positive correlation between word2Vec + WordNet and spaCy ($p < 0.01$), and (ii) a *very strong* positive correlation between word2Vec + WordNet and BERT-Web. The first correlation can be explained since Algorithm 1 invokes spaCy's implementation of word2Vec. The second correlation, instead, shows alignment between our algorithm and the state-of-the-art in NLP, i.e., BERT-based solutions.

Use-Case Specific Correlation Analysis. Spearman's ρ identifies correlations regardless of the actual value in the algorithms' range: for example, if an algorithm assigns consistency 0.8 to all samples, and another assigns 0.2 to all samples, the correlation will be perfect. In our use case, however, this makes a difference, for we are interested in algorithms that identify concepts to be recommended to modelers (see Sect. 2). Therefore, we apply the Euclidean distance metric as a better measure of how close the values for each couple of words are, compared to the gold standard. In this case, spaCy turns out to be the worst ($d = 1.804$): this is confirmed by visually inspecting the box-plots in Fig. 6. The algorithm that best resembles human tagging is the domain model approach ($d = 0.984$), followed by our other heuristic based on word2Vec and WordNet, and then BERT-Web. These results seem to indicate that the development of specific heuristics for compounds lead to closer results to the gold standard than off-the-shelf similarity techniques, although modern approaches like BERT offer relatively good performance.

5   Related Work

Viewpoints. The need of analyzing the perspectives of multiple stakeholders in a project is well known in requirements engineering [26]. Fischer *et al.* [13] define a *viewpoint* as a language that reflects certain aspects of a *meta-model*, while a *view* presents a model according to a viewpoint. Several tools support viewpoints and views, e.g., Sirius [33] which builds on the Eclipse stack, or MetaEdit+ [12]. Such works are the modeling infrastructure on top of which the Concept Suggester can be plugged.

Model Alignment. Sànchez-Ferreres *et al.* [27] align textual and graphical representations of the same processes using NLP, machine learning, and integer linear programming. Similarly, van der Aa *et al.* [1] detect inconsistencies between the text and model of the same process. Delfmann *et al.* [10] adopts an NLP powered approach and naming conventions. Our approach focuses on multi-model alignment and does not impose any restrictions on model labels.

Matching. Ontology matching deals with matching multiple ontologies [29]. Schema matching identifies semantically related objects in databases [15] whereas process matching aims to detect common activities or similar processes [4]. Our research problem is different, for detecting structural similarity and matching the underlying schema of models are out of our scope. We provide a lightweight solution to support collaboration by providing suggestions from a domain model.

Real-Time Collaboration. Some infrastructures support a near real-time, web-enabled, collaboration among modelers. Nicolaescu *et al.* [24] use a shared meta-model to generate visual model editors for a given viewpoint, they enable modelers to create views for a viewpoint and propose algorithms for managing shared editing conflicts. Debreceni *et al.* [9] focus on asynchronous collaboration, one can lock model chunks based on properties to be preserved. While these works focus on collaboration on the same model, we support modelers in the same project who do not share the same model.

Model Labels. Kögel *et al.* [19] propose initial ideas on recommending modelers which elements may have to be changed when the same modeler alters a namesake or referenced element in another model. Grammel *et al.* [16] generate trace links between models by checking their similarity. They propose three similarity measures that rely on the number of namesake attributes, the number of shared parent and children nodes, and that follow the instance-of relationships. While we share similar ideas, we focus on the collaboration among multiple modelers and assume no meta-model knowledge.

Similarity. Calculating the similarity of compounds significantly less explored than the similarity of single words. One family of techniques combines the lexical similarity between the first and second words of the compounds [8,28]. Our Algorithm 2 combines the lexical similarity of not only the first and second words but all combinations of word pairs of the compounds. An alternative family of techniques consider two pairs of compounds similar if they are mentioned in similar contexts [32] within a large corpus [32]; instead, Algorithm 3 consults a domain model which has fewer words than a corpus.

6   Discussion and Conclusions

We have presented an approach that helps modelers in a collaborative modeling project to align their models without requiring a shared meta-model or mandating the use of identical labels. This adds flexibility to a project where multiple modeling languages are used since it removes to adjust the shared meta-model. Our approach also limits the data sharing, only the modeled concepts are shared with the service, not how concepts are connected to each other. Also, there is no direct model sharing with the other modelers. This supports competitive collaboration situations. We have implemented our approach as a web service and integrated it to the PACAS collaborative modeling platform.

We detailed two heuristics that determine the similarity of compound nouns, which are frequently used in conceptual models.

Conclusions. Our experiment shows that, when measuring the similarity of compound words, spaCy's implementation of word2Vec correlates the highest with the gold standard followed by our techniques based on word embeddings and domain models. Although preliminary, this could be a valuable finding for the information systems community, for a machine learning algorithm based on term co-occurrence in a general-purpose corpus showed better results than heuristics that make use of domain models. Our algorithms are a preliminary attempt to support the analysis and comparison of model labels that contain compound words; this research topic is under-explored.

Threats to Validity. Conclusion. Low statistical power is the major threat for our experiment: we experimented with only 5 pairs of compounds per category. *Internal.* Maturation may have occurred, as the survey respondents form their understanding of how to assess similarity as they answer the questions. To mitigate this effect, we presented the pairs in a random order. *Construct.* Mono-operation bias exists due to the choice of one specific case. Also, we intentionally decided not to give a definition of similarity, for that may introduce a bias in favor of some heuristics. *External.* While we asked the respondents to assess the similarity, the notion of similar depends on the chosen similarity metric (e.g., looking for synonyms, finding related concepts).

Future Work. We are currently designing an experiment where the subjects are given suggestions while they model. Additional research is necessary to assess if spaCy's off-the-shelf implementation outperforms our algorithms, or this is rather due to the choice of inadequate weights (e.g., σ, γ, δ in Sect. 3.1) for our algorithms.

References

1. van der Aa, H., Leopold, H., Reijers, H.A.: Comparing textual descriptions to process models - the automatic detection of inconsistencies. Inf. Syst. **64**, 447–460 (2017)
2. Aydemir, F.B., Dalpiaz, F.: Towards aligning multi-concern models via NLP. In: Proceedings of the MoDRE-RE (2017)
3. Aydemir, F.B., Dalpiaz, F.: Online appendix: supporting collaborative modelling via NLP. Figshare. https://figshare.com/s/e4a13da8404bcb74e0a0
4. Beheshti, S.-M.-R., et al.: Process matching techniques. In: Beheshti, S.-M.-R., et al. (eds.) Process Analytics, pp. 61–90. Springer, Cham (2016). https://doi.org/10.1007/978-3-319-25037-3_3
5. Cer, D.M., Diab, M.T., Agirre, E., Lopez-Gazpio, I., Specia, L.: SemEval-2017 task 1: semantic textual similarity - multilingual and cross-lingual focused evaluation. CoRR abs/1708.00055 (2017). http://arxiv.org/abs/1708.00055
6. Claasen, R.: SimCom: measuring similarity of compound terms (2017), B.Sc. Thesis. https://github.com/RELabUU/concept-suggestor
7. Clarke, S., Baniassad, E.: Aspect-Oriented Analysis and Design. Addison-Wesley, Boston (2005)
8. Curran, J.R.: From distributional to semantic similarity (2004)
9. Debreceni, C., Bergmann, G., Ráth, I., Varró, D.: Property-based locking in collaborative modeling. In: Proceedings of MODELS, pp. 199–209 (2017)
10. Delfmann, P., Herwig, S., Lis, L.: Unified enterprise knowledge representation with conceptual models-capturing corporate language in naming conventions. In: ICIS, p. 45 (2009)
11. Euzenat, J., Shvaiko, P.: Ontology Matching, vol. 18. Springer, Heidelberg (2007). https://doi.org/10.1007/978-3-540-49612-0
12. Fill, H.G., Karagiannis, D.: On the conceptualisation of modelling methods using the ADOxx meta modelling platform. Enterp. Model. Inf. Syst. Archit. **8**(1), 4–25 (2015)
13. Fischer, K., Panfilenko, D., Krumeich, J., Born, M., Desfray, P.: Viewpoint-based modeling-towards defining the viewpoint concept and implications for supporting modeling tools. In: Proceedings of EMISA, pp. 123–136 (2012)
14. France, R., Ray, I., Georg, G., Ghosh, S.: Aspect-oriented approach to early design modelling. IEE Proc.-Softw. **151**(4), 173–185 (2004)
15. Gal, A.: Uncertain schema matching. Synth. Lect. Data Manag. **3**(1), 1–97 (2011)
16. Grammel, B., Kastenholz, S., Voigt, K.: Model matching for trace link generation in model-driven software development. In: Proceedings of MODELS, pp. 609–625 (2012)
17. Harispe, S., Ranwez, S., Janaqi, S., Montmain, J.: Semantic similarity from natural language and ontology analysis. Synth. Lect. Hum. Lang. Technol. **8**(1), 1–254 (2015)
18. Kenter, T., De Rijke, M.: Short text similarity with word embeddings. In: Proceedings of CIKM, pp. 1411–1420 (2015)
19. Kögel, S., Groner, R., Tichy, M.: Automatic change recommendation of models and meta models based on change histories. In: Proceedings of ME@MODELS, pp. 14–19 (2016)
20. Lapata, M.: The disambiguation of nominalizations. Comput. Linguist. **28**(3), 357–388 (2002)

21. Leopold, H., van der Aa, H., Offenberg, J., Reijers, H.A.: Using hidden Markov models for the accurate linguistic analysis of process model activity labels. Inf. Syst. **83**, 30–39 (2019)
22. Levi, J.N.: The Syntax and Semantics of Complex Nominals. Academic Press, Cambridge (1978)
23. Lucassen, G., Robeer, M., Dalpiaz, F., van der Werf, J.M.E.M., Brinkkemper, S.: Extracting conceptual models from user stories with visual narrator. Requir. Eng. **22**(3), 339–358 (2017). https://doi.org/10.1007/s00766-017-0270-1
24. Nicolaescu, P., Rosenstengel, M., Derntl, M., Klamma, R., Jarke, M.: Near real-time collaborative modeling for view-based web information systems engineering. Inf. Syst. **74**, 23–39 (2018)
25. Northrop, L., et al.: Ultra-large-scale systems: the software challenge of the future. Technical report, Software Engineering Institute, Carnegie Mellon University (2006)
26. Nuseibeh, B., Kramer, J., Finkelsteiin, A.: Viewpoints: meaningful relationships are difficult! In: Proceedings of ICSE, pp. 676–681 (2003)
27. Sànchez-Ferreres, J., Carmona, J., Padró, L.: Aligning textual and graphical descriptions of processes through ILP techniques. In: Dubois, E., Pohl, K. (eds.) CAiSE 2017. LNCS, vol. 10253, pp. 413–427. Springer, Cham (2017). https://doi.org/10.1007/978-3-319-59536-8_26
28. Séaghdha, D.O., Copestake, A.: Using lexical and relational similarity to classify semantic relations. In: Proceedings of the 12th Conference of the European Chapter of the Association for Computational Linguistics, pp. 621–629 (2009)
29. Shvaiko, P., Euzenat, J.: Ontology matching: state of the art and future challenges. IEEE Trans. Knowl. Data Eng. **25**(1), 158–176 (2011)
30. Sommerville, I., et al.: Large-scale complex IT systems. Commun. ACM **55**(7), 71 (2012)
31. Trask, A., Michalak, P., Liu, J.: sense2vec - a fast and accurate method for word sense disambiguation in neural word embeddings. CoRR abs/1511.06388 (2015)
32. Turney, P.D.: Similarity of semantic relations. Comput. Linguist. **32**(3), 379–416 (2006)
33. Viyović, V., Maksimović, M., Perisić, B.: Sirius: a rapid development of DSM graphical editor. In: Proceedings of INES, pp. 233–238 (2014)
34. Whittle, J., Jayaraman, P., Elkhodary, A., Moreira, A., Araújo, J.: MATA: a unified approach for composing UML aspect models based on graph transformation. In: Transactions on Aspect-Oriented Software Development VI, pp. 191–237 (2009)

Automatic Generation of Chatbots
for Conversational Web Browsing

Pietro Chittò[1], Marcos Baez[2]([✉]), Florian Daniel[1], and Boualem Benatallah[3]

[1] Politecnico di Milano, Via Ponzio 34/5, 20133 Milan, Italy
`pietro.chitto@mail.polimi.it, florian.daniel@polimi.it`
[2] Université Claude Bernard Lyon 1, Lyon, France
`{marcos-antonio.baez-gonzalez,boualem.benatallah}@univ-lyon1.fr`
[3] University of News South Wales, Sydney, Australia
`boualem@cse.unsw.edu.au`

Abstract. In this paper, we describe the foundations for generating a chatbot out of a website equipped with simple, bot-specific HTML annotations. The approach is part of what we call *conversational web browsing*, i.e., a dialog-based, natural language interaction with websites. The goal is to enable users to use content and functionality accessible through rendered UIs by "talking to websites" instead of by operating the graphical UI using keyboard and mouse. The chatbot mediates between the user and the website, operates its graphical UI on behalf of the user, and informs the user about the state of interaction. We describe the conceptual vocabulary and annotation format, the supporting conversational middleware and techniques, and the implementation of a demo able to deliver conversational web browsing experiences through Amazon Alexa.

Keywords: Non-visual browsing · Conversational browsing · Chatbots

1 Introduction

Conversational agents are emerging as an exciting new platform for accessing online services that promise a more natural and accessible interaction paradigm. They have shown great potential for regular users in hands-free and eyes-free scenarios but also for making services more accessible to people with disabilities and visual impairments [11], as well as groups, such as older adults, often challenged by service design choices [9]. This new generation of agents is however not able to natively access the Web, requiring web developers and content creators to implement specific "skills" to offer their content and services on Amazon Alexa, Google Asssitant and other platforms. This requirement represents a huge barrier for developers and creators who might not have the skills or resources to invest, and a missed opportunity for making the Web accessible to everyone.

Integrating conversational capabilities into software enabled services is an emerging research topic [3], as pushed by recent works by Castaldo et al. [5] on inferring bots directly from database schemas, Yaghoub-Zadeh-Fard et al. [13] on

© Springer Nature Switzerland AG 2020
G. Dobbie et al. (Eds.): ER 2020, LNCS 12400, pp. 239–249, 2020.
https://doi.org/10.1007/978-3-030-62522-1_17

deriving bots from APIs, and by Ripa et al. [12] on generating informational bots out of website content. While these works are facilitating chatbot integration at different levels of the Web architecture, they do not address the challenges of generating chatbots from both *content* and *functionality* available in websites.

In this paper, we take a software engineering approach and study how to enable conversational browsing of websites equipped with purposefully designed annotations. This represents the first step towards our vision [2] of enabling users to access the content and services accessible through rendered UIs by "talking to websites" instead of by operating the graphical UI using keyboard and mouse. We start with an annotation-driven approach as the focus is to lay the foundation for conversational browsing and to identify all necessary conversational features and technical solutions, which can then lead to the development of support tools and automatic approaches. In doing so, we make the following contributions:

- conceptual vocabulary for augmenting websites with conversational capabilities, able to describe domain knowledge (content and functionality) while abstracting interaction knowledge (enacting low level interactions with sites);
- an approach, architecture and techniques for generating a chatbot out of a website equipped with simple, bot-specific HTML annotations;
- prototype implementation and technical feasibility of the proposed automatic chatbot generation approach.

In the following we describe a concrete target scenario, the overall approach, and the prototype implementation.

2   Scenario and Requirements

We describe our target scenario by illustrating the interactions of a user browsing a typical research project website using a smart speaker such as Amazon Echo (Fig. 1). After the user requests access to the research project website, a conversational agent tailored to the website content, functionality and domain knowledge is automatically generated to mediate the interactions between the user and the target website. During these interactions, i) the user is informed of the available features, ii) can browse the website in dialog-based natural language interactions with the agent, and iii) the agent identifies and performs the appropriate web browsing actions on the target website on behalf of the user.

Before diving into the requirements posed by the envisioned scenario, we need to introduce some concepts related to chatbot development, in what refers to *task-oriented* chatbots. Modern task-oriented chatbots are built on a frame-based architecture, which relies on a domain ontology (composed of frame, slots and values) that specify the type of user intentions the system can recognize and respond to [8]. *Intents* refer to the task requested by the user and the *actions* to the specific operations performed by the chatbot to serve the intent. Identifying user intents given a *request* in natural language (e.g., "Tell me about Florian Daniel") requires a natural language processing component *trained* with a dataset of examples (e.g., researcher_info: ["Tell me about @researcher", "Who

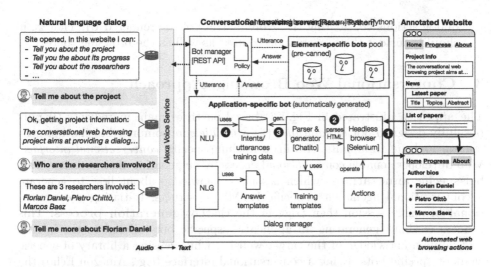

Fig. 1. Conversational browsing scenario: the user talks to a bot not the website.

is @researcher?", ...]) to correctly classify the request and infer the slots and values (e.g., intent: researcher_info, researcher : "Florian Daniel"). Then the *dialog management* component, based on intent, the input provided and the conversation context, decides on the appropriate *action* (e.g., parse associated DOM element). A *response* is generated using a natural language generation component that elaborates the results and presents them in a format that fits the conversation medium (refer to [8] for more on chatbot design and architecture).

Having introduced the scenario and main concepts, we refine some key requirements to enabling conversational browsing as identified earlier [2]:

R1 **Orientation:** The bot must be able to summarize the content and/or functionalities offered by the website, to guide users through site offers at any point and to provide for basic access structures (e.g., "In this site you can...").

R2 **Inferring intents and parameters:** The bot must be able to understand the user's intent and enact suitable actions in response. Intents may be *application-agnostic* (e.g., fill a form field) or *application-specific* (e.g., post a new paper). The latter requires the bot to infer the intents from the website.

R3 **Training and vocabulary:** The bot should be able to speak and understand the language of the target website, so as to identify intents and elaborate proper responses. This requires deriving domain knowledge directly from the website, training the bot to identify application-specific intents.

R4 **Browsing actions enactment:** As the bot mediates between the user and the website, enacting an action in response to an identified intent requires a strategy for translating high-level user requests into automated low level interactions with the website.

R5 **Dialog control from rendered UIs:** As the user browse the website conversationally, the chatbot should track the state of the dialog and choose dialog actions considering the evolving state of the rendered UI. That is, it should consider the conversation context as well as the browsing context.

3   Conversational Web Browsing: Approach

The approach illustrated in Fig. 1 is based on three main ingredients (i) purposefully designed bot *annotations*, (ii) a *middleware* comprised of chatbot generation and run-time units, and iii) a medium-specific *conversational interface*. Web developers enable conversational access by augmenting their websites with bot-specific **annotations**, which associate knowledge about how to generate a conversational agent with specific HTML constructs. Initiating a conversational browsing session then triggers the chatbot **generation process**. This process is about generating an application-specific bot tailored to the intents and domain knowledge of the target website, while reusing a library of generic element-specific bots. Using a conversational interface (e.g., Amazon Echo) the user can start a dialog with the website. At **run-time**, the middleware processes the user requests in natural language, selects the relevant bot and executes the appropriate actions on the rendered GUI of the website.

Supporting conversational browsing is non trivial and requires weighing several options. The most important decisions that resulted in our solution are:

- **Domain vs. interaction knowledge:** Using a website generally requires the user to master two types of knowledge, *domain knowledge* (to understand content and functionalities) and *interaction knowledge* (to use and operate the site). This distinction is powerful to separate concerns in conversational browsing. Domain knowledge, e.g., about the research project and scientific publications, must be provided by the developer, as this varies from site to site. Interaction knowledge, e.g., how to fill a form or read text paragraph by paragraph, can be pre-canned and reused across multiple sites. We thus distinguish between an *application-specific* bot and a set of *element-specific* bots [R1,R2]. The former masters the domain, the latter enable the user to interact with specific content elements like lists, text, tables, forms, etc.
- **Modularization:** Incidentally, the distinction between application- and element-specific bots represents an excellent opportunity for modularization and reuse. Application-specific bots must be generated for each site anew [R3]; element-specific bots can be implemented and *trained once and reused multiple times*. They can be implemented for specific HTML elements, such as a form, or they can be implemented for a very specific version thereof, e.g., a login form. However, the presence of application- and element-specific bots introduces the need for a suitable bot selection logic.
- **Bot selection:** As a user may provide as input any possible utterance at any instant of time, referring to either application-specific or element-specific intents, it is not possible to pre-define conversational paths through a website. Instead, some form of random access must be supported. We introduce for this purpose a so-called bot manager, which takes as input the utterance

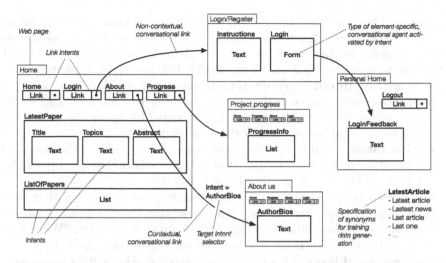

Fig. 2. Informal graphical model of a project website explaining the core concepts of application-specific, conversational browsing. Labels in italics define the used graphical notation. Gray-shaded intents are copied from the Home page.

and forwards it to the bots registered in the system [R5]. Depending on the context (e.g., the last used bot) and the confidence provided by each invoked bot, it then decides which bot is most likely to provide the correct answer [R1,R2]. Thanks to the bot manager, the ensemble of application-specific and element-specific bots presents itself as one single bot to the user.

4   Annotating Websites with Conversational Knowledge

The goal of the work presented in this paper is to prevent asking developers to provide full-fledged chatbots for their websites in order to support conversational browsing. The challenge is asking them to provide as little information as possible – the annotation – such that, together with the content and functionality that are already in the site (its GUI), it is possible to automatically generate a chatbot.

Conceptual Model. Let's start with introducing the key concepts that enable conversational browsing. Figure 2 uses an intuitive, graphical notation to contextualize them in a model of a simple website about a research project, e.g., our project on conversational browsing. The site consists of a set of pages, of which the model ignores the actual content; the design of such content has traditionally been approached by modeling languages like WebML [6] or IFML [4]. Instead, the model hypothesizes a conceptual vocabulary that could extend the pages, subsuming the presence of suitable content[1]. We identified these concepts through a literature and systems review and prototyping efforts:

---

[1] Note that here we do not want to introduce an own, new modeling notation for conversational browsing; Fig. 2 serves an intuitive, illustrative purpose only.

- **Intents:** These are the core ingredients of conversational browsing. Intents annotate HTML constructs and thereby qualify their contents as relevant for the enactment of the intents' actions [R2]. More importantly, intents enable the user to access content and functionality. We distinguish three types:
  - **Selection intents** identify HTML constructs the developer wants to make accessible through the chatbot. In order to guide user inside complex pages, selection intents can be structured hierarchically, which tells the bot to read out options at different levels of detail.
  - **Link intents** enable the user to navigate among pages of the site. Each navigation may reset the context of the conversation and prompt the bot to inform the user of the new intents available.
  - **Built-in intents** are the intents that the framework comes with in order to support basic interactions, such as orienting the user inside a page by proactively telling him/her which options are available (e.g., "What is the page about?")[R1]. Built-in intents do not require any annotation.
- **Conversational links:** These are the counterpart of hyperlinks in conversational browsing and tell link intents their target [R4]. Similar to conventional links, we distinguish two types of conversational links:
  - **Non-contextual** conversational links are links that can be navigated with the help from the bot and result in the loading and rendering of a new page, causing the bot to start a new browsing context. That is, each page accessed through a non-contextual link causes the bot to inform the user about the content of the page [R1]. For example, Login follows a non-contextual link to a new page (with a different menu of options), triggering the bot to inform of the available options (Instructions, Login).
  - **Contextual** conversational links are links that are directed not only toward a new page but also toward a specific target intent. If a user thus accesses a page through a contextual link, the bot will immediately start performing the action associated with the target intent [R5], e.g., About (contextual link) will trigger AboutBios (reading the associated text).
- **Bot types:** If a selection intent identifies the HTML construct to act upon, i.e., if it cannot be further split into sub-intents (e.g., LatestPaper → Title), the type of element-specific bot able to perform the expected action can be specified (Title: Text). As explained earlier, the number of element-specific bots is theoretically unlimited, but we identify the need for a minimum set of element-specific bots able to manage the following content elements [R2]:
  - **Text**, i.e., text organized into headings, sub-headings and paragraphs. Element-specific actions are reading out loud the full text, reading the titles only, jumping back and forth among paragraphs, etc.
  - **List**, i.e., an ordered or unordered lists of items. Element-specific actions are telling the number of items, reading them out, navigating them, etc.
  - **Table**, i.e., content organized in rows and columns. Element-specific actions are reading by cells, navigating by rows, reading by column, etc.
  - **Form**, i.e., input fields grouped together and accompanied by a submission button. Element-specific actions are telling which inputs are required, filling individual fields, confirming inputs, submitting, etc.

bot-intent: associates a page-wide unique *intent identifier* to the HTML construct holding it.

bot-desc: provides a *text explanation* that the bot can use to inform the user about the meaning of the intent.

bot-keys: specifies a comma-separated list of *synonyms* as alternative names of the intent.

bot-type: specifies the type of *element-specific bot* to use to process the HTML construct's internal HTML markup (e.g., Text Reader).

Fig. 3. Simplified code excerpt of the <body> of the Home page in Fig. 2 with annotations for conversational browsing. Application-specific annotations enable navigation and content access; element-specific ones instruct the Text Reader.

- **Domain vocabulary:** It is necessary to equip all intents in the website with their domain-specific vocabulary. This can be achieved by accompanying intents with *labels* and *synonyms* that can be used to generate combinations of phrases and to train the application-specific bot [R3]. For instance, the intent LatestPaper with the words "latest paper, recent paper" or similar.
- **Intent description:** Intent descriptions are simple textual explanations that the bot can use to tell the user which intents a given page supports. For instance, the LatestPaper intent could be described using the words "tell you about the last paper published by the project" [R1].

Given a website, is important to note how the sensible selection of which HTML construct to annotate and how to connect them with conversational links allows the developer to construct pre-defined **dialog flows** guiding the user through the content and functionalities published by a website [R5].

Annotation Format. *Annotating* a website now means associating conversational knowledge (knowledge about how to generate a conversational agent) with specific HTML constructs in a page. The *cues* for the generation of the agent come in the form of HTML attributes and developer-provided values. Informed by the conceptual model, the concrete attributes for the generation of **application-specific** bots are highlighted in Fig. 3. The figure provides a practical example of the use of these attributes, and the use of one **element-specific** attribute: **bot-attribute**, which identifies element-specific *content types* that the respective element-specific bot can understand. While some annotations may seem redundant (e.g., can be derived from HTML tags), developers not always follow the semantics of HTML tags. For instance, one of the most used tags today is the <div> tag, which lacks semantics. Explicit annotations can also allow developers indicate what elements to expose to the chatbot.

As research progresses, we intend to maintain an up-to-date version of the annotation format on **GitHub** and to improve it with the help from the community. Please refer to https://github.com/floriandanielit/conversationalweb.

5   Generating Application-Specific Conversational Agent

The generation process can be divided into two phases: (i) the generation of the *application-specific training data* and the training of the NLU (natural language understanding), and (ii) the generation of a suitable *conversational context model* to enable the bot manager to manage the dialog. The generation of the application-specific training data follows the steps highlighted in Fig. 1 using circled numbers: the headless browser loads the current page of the website and builds its DOM ❶, the parser and generator extracts intent identifiers and the list of intent synonyms ❷ and generates a dataset of utterances for training ❸; the NLU uses the dataset to learn intents and application-specific vocabulary ❹.

The **conversational context model** is generated by the parser and generator once the NLU is successfully trained. It consists in a tree representation[2] of the intents contained in the current page: $CT = \langle N, C \rangle$, where N is the set of nodes, where each node represents one application-specific intent in the page, and $C = N \times N$ represents the set of non-cyclic, directed child relationships of the tree. Each node $n \in N, n = \langle intent, type, desc, keys, elem, link \rangle$ contains the identifier, type, description and keywords of the respective intent, the HTML element it is associated with, and the possible conversational link in case the intent is a link intent. The root node $r \in N$ represents the information intent associated with the <body> element of the current page. Intermediate nodes represent access intents with sub-intents; leaf nodes (nodes without children) represent intents to be processed using a given *type* of element-specific bot.

The bot manager now uses the so constructed context model to decide which bot to choose to advance the conversation with the user. The proposed policy works as follows: as the user provides input, the bot manager checks if the last used bot (the *current* bot) is able to understand the input, i.e., if it is able to identify an intent with a confidence that exceeds a given threshold τ. If yes, the respective answer is forwarded to the user, otherwise it forwards the input to all direct children of the current bot, and recursively to the sub-children if none is successful. If any of them is able to identify an intent with sufficient confidence, that bot becomes the new current bot and its answer is forwarded to the user. If the current bot corresponds to a leaf node and is not able to understand the user input, it escalates the input to upper levels until there is a higher level bot able to understand the input or the escalation reaches the root node. If none is able understand the input, the user is asked to reformulate his/her request.

---

[2] The tree is a result of the hierarchical organization enabled by selection intents, e.g., LatestPaper→Title(Text Reader).

6 System Implementation and Technical Validation

The conversational browsing infrastructure outlined in Fig. 1 has been implemented making use of ready technologies: *Alexa Voice Service* for voice to text conversion, *Rasa NLU* (https://rasa.com/) for natural language understanding, *Selenium* (https://selenium.dev/) as headless browser integrated with *Mozilla Firefox*, and *Chatito* (https://github.com/rodrigopivi/Chatito) for the generation of training data. Custom integration and chatbot code was written in *Python*. For the tests with Alexa, the infrastructure was deployed on Heroku.

While the training phase of the chatbot could be done once of the entire site, in our current prototype we opted for a page-by-page training, in order to support dynamically generated pages. As the focus of the prototype was technical feasibility, it is not yet optimized for performance. However, tests on a local machine (Omen by HP 15-DH0, Intel Core i7, 16 GB of RAM, SSD hard-drive, Win10 64bit) show that page loading and rendering, training data generation and bot training requires up to few seconds, an acceptable performance for some scenarios. Fetching pages from the Web adds an additional overhead. The construction of the context model is negligible in terms of execution time.

The element-specific bots of the prototype are custom Rasa bots with predefined intents, actions and NLU models. Demo videos illustrating the components of the approach can be found at https://bit.ly/2OckzZW.

7 Related Work

The problem of **non visual web browsing** has produced two main approaches: *markup-based* approaches such as VoiceXML [10] and *voice-enabled screen readers* integrated into web browsers [1]. VoiceXML [10] is a W3C markup language for voice applications typically accessed using a phone. Applications are stand alone and could complement websites, but there is no native integration of the two. Voice-based screen readers (e.g., [1]) aim at lowering the complexity of managing shortcuts in navigating with screen readers, enabling users to utter browsing commands in natural language ("press the cart button"). While valuable, these approaches were developed to support desktop web browsing: they require users to be aware of the layout of the pages and perform low-level, step-by-step interactions, or to create macros to automate tasks.

As for **chatbot development**, general platforms and tools support the development of stand-alone chatbots (e.g., DialogFlow, Instabot.io). Another approach is that of deriving chatbots directly from database schemas, API definitions and web content. Prominent works in this regard are the ones by Castaldo et al. [5] exploring the idea of conversational data exploration, by inferring a chatbot directly from annotated database schema; Yaghoub-Zadeh-Fard et al. [13] generating a conversational interface directly from API specifications (e.g., OpenAPI). Website content has also been used for chatbot generation. Popular in e-commerce and CRM, approaches such as SuperAgent [7] can generate conversational FAQ based on the content to visitors directly on the website. Ripa et al. [12] focus on making informational queries over content intensive websites accessible via voice-based interfaces (e.g., smart speakers), relying on augmentations provided by end-users. While all these works illustrate the diversity of approaches, they require either (bot) programming knowledge (and effort), are constrained by an application domain, or are limited to Q&A.

8   Conclusion and Outlook

This paper contributes with abstractions, techniques and conceptual vocabulary for superimposing conversational bots over websites. These contributions along with the software infrastructure enable the (semi)automatic generation of chatbots directly from websites, and can be leveraged by authoring tools to enable developers, even without chatbot skills, to obtain chatbots effectively and efficiently. The solution presented is a proof-of-concept implementation not optimized for large applications, and thus presents points for improvement that are the focus of our ongoing work. As a next step, we will out user studies with different types of target users (end users and developers) and derive guidelines for conversational browsing. We are also already studying how to use machine learning and AI along with existing Web technical specifications (e.g., HTML5) to replace some explicit annotations by automatic recognition.

References

1. Ashok, V., Borodin, Y., Puzis, Y., Ramakrishnan, I.: Capti-speak: a speech-enabled web screen reader. In: W4A, p. 22. ACM (2015)
2. Baez, M., Daniel, F., Casati, F.: Conversational web interaction: proposal of a dialog-based natural language interaction paradigm for the web. In: Følstad, A., et al. (eds.) CONVERSATIONS 2019. LNCS, vol. 11970, pp. 94–110. Springer, Cham (2020). https://doi.org/10.1007/978-3-030-39540-7_7
3. Baez, M., Daniel, F., Casati, F., Benatallah, B.: Chatbot integration in fewpatterns. IEEE Internet Computing (2020)
4. Brambilla, M., Fraternali, P., et al.: The interaction flow modeling language (IFML), version 1.0. Technical report, OMG, http://www.ifml.org (2014)
5. Castaldo, N., Daniel, F., Matera, M., Zaccaria, V.: Conversational data exploration. In: Bakaev, M., Frasincar, F., Ko, I.-Y. (eds.) ICWE 2019. LNCS, vol. 11496, pp. 490–497. Springer, Cham (2019). https://doi.org/10.1007/978-3-030-19274-7_34
6. Ceri, S., Fraternali, P., Bongio, A., Brambilla, M., Comai, S., Matera, M.:Designing Data-Intensive Web Applications. Morgan Kaufmann (2002)
7. Cui, L., Huang, S., Wei, F., Tan, C., Duan, C., Zhou, M.: Superagent: a customer service chatbot for e-commerce websites. ACL **2017**, 97–102 (2017)
8. Jurafsky, D., Martin, J.H.: Dialog systems and chatbots. Speech Lang. Process. **3** (2017). https://web.stanford.edu/~jurafsky/slp3/24.pdf
9. Kowalski, J., et al.: Older adults and voice interaction: a pilot study with google home. In: CHI 2019 Extended Abstracts, pp. 1–6 (2019)
10. Oshry, M., Auburn, R., Baggia, P., Bodell, M., Burke, D., Burnett, D., et al.: Voice extensible markup language (voicexml) 2.1. w3c recommendation (2007)

11. Pradhan, A., Mehta, K., Findlater, L.: Accessibility came by accident use of voice-controlled intelligent personal assistants by people with disabilities. CHI **2018**, 1–13 (2018)

12. Ripa, G., Torre, M., Firmenich, S., Rossi, G.: End-user development of voice user interfaces based on web content. In: Malizia, A., Valtolina, S., Morch, A., Serrano, A., Stratton, A. (eds.) IS-EUD 2019. LNCS, vol. 11553, pp. 34–50. Springer, Cham (2019). https://doi.org/10.1007/978-3-030-24781-2_3

13. Yaghoub-Zadeh-Fard, M.A., Zamanirad, S., Benatallah, B., Casati, F.: Rest2bot: Bridging the gap between bot platforms and rest apis. Companion Proc. Web Conf. **2020**, 245–248 (2020)

Modeling Narrative Structures in Logical Overlays on Top of Knowledge Repositories

Hermann Kroll[(✉)] ⓘ, Denis Nagel ⓘ, and Wolf-Tilo Balke ⓘ

Institute for Information Systems, TU Braunschweig, Braunschweig, Germany
{kroll,nagel,balke}@ifis.cs.tu-bs.de

Abstract. An important part of the scientific discourse is the exchange of knowledge in the form of stringent, well-arranged, and interconnected arguments. These 'scientific storylines' allow to put central entities, observations, experiments, etc. into perspective and thus ease the understanding of underlying mechanisms, dependencies, or theories. Moreover, taking a bird's eye view allows to discern recurring *narrative patterns* that have proven helpful for validating, comparing, and fusing information across individual publications and even between disciplines. However, current knowledge repositories still struggle with representing such information in a structured way. This is because narratives do not only contain factual bits of information, but also parts like temporal developments, causal dependencies, etc. In this paper, we present an innovative conceptual model using a *logical overlay structure* to bridge the gaps between individual types of knowledge repositories. We also explain how *narrative bindings* validate modeled narratives in the sense of provenance. In brief, narrative overlays plus adequate bindings allow to effectively fuse knowledge and improve retrieval and discovery tasks by structurally aligning underlying repositories only driven by some narrative. Finally, we practically demonstrate the usefulness of our model by applying it to a scientific narrative in the PubMed bio-medical collection.

Keywords: Narratives · Logical overlays · Knowledge graphs

1 Introduction

A lot of today's world – theories, insights, and decisions – has become 'data-driven'. Making sense of vast amounts of data is usually realized using structured knowledge repositories, e. g. relational databases, knowledge graphs, digital libraries, or data set registries [1,12]. Yet, the theories, insights, etc. are usually not *part of* such repositories, but have to be managed outside. In this paper, we propose a conceptual model that integrates derived knowledge in the general form of narratives on top of knowledge repositories. The basic idea can be compared to peer-to-peer networks: built on top of a *physical* IP-based routing

G. Dobbie et al. (Eds.): ER 2020, LNCS 12400, pp. 250–260, 2020.
https://doi.org/10.1007/978-3-030-62522-1_18

infrastructure, direct connections in a *logical overlay* allow for creating advantageous network topologies that can subsequently be used for improved routing, content sharing, etc. In the same way, we argue for a logical overlay as an abstraction layer on top of knowledge repositories that, in turn, allows us to capture narratives, bind them to knowledge repositories, and assess essential characteristics such as their individual validity or plausibility.

Unlike fictional narratives that tend to involve many protagonists and hence are notoriously hard to represent [2], narratives used in practical information systems are usually more limited and quite concise. Such narratives usually relate recurring explanation patterns or chains of arguments that are investigated, modeled, and schematically represented for subsequent sharing, discussion, and reuse by researchers in a variety of scientific domains [10]. Prime examples include chemical reactions and metabolic pathways in bio-medicine.

Throughout this paper, we will use a pharmaceutical use case with an often occurring narrative pattern of a simple drug-drug interaction as a running example (Fig. 1). In brief, assume that an *active ingredient* is *metabolized* in the body by some *gene system*, but exactly this system is *inhibited* by some other *drug* administered at the same time. Then the active ingredient is *accumulated* in the body, which in turn may *cause* severe adverse effects in the form of *diseases*.

Looking at this simple pharmaceutical example narrative describing a typical kind of adverse drug-drug interaction, we already get a first idea of the concepts, which we will conceptualize in the following sections. There are *entities* like active ingredients, gene systems, or drugs, there are *relationships* between them, such as being metabolized by something or inhibiting something, there are *events*, such as the accumulation of some active ingredient in the body, and there are *causal or temporal structures* such as the failed metabolization causing an accumulation of some active ingredient or the adverse effect diseases being a consequence of this accumulation.

It also becomes clear why -although technically it would be possible-on a practical level existing knowledge bases usually do not capture all of the information in narratives: Narratives may relate causal mechanisms or developments over time, which may refer to special cases only and may not be generally applicable. In this way, unlike the factual information collected in knowledge graphs, narratives usually do not feature truth values [13]. Entities and events related by a narrative may happen only in individual cases (in the sense of anecdotes), may be more or less probable (or possible), and only in the best case may be generally valid [7]. Moreover, the use of narratives may heavily determine their structures, e. g. more schematic for rigid scientific argumentation vs. quite free for storytelling. Therefore a new kind of representation is needed, enriched with strong links to factual knowledge or actual contexts. Our contributions are:

- We design a conceptual model for narratives and propose narratives to represent scientific argumentation in a structured way (Sect. 2).
- We introduce narrative bindings to verify (or at least plausibilise) each narrative by grounding its parts to individual knowledge repositories (Sect. 2).

– As a first real-world use case, we demonstrate that our model in extension with narrative queries is applicable for *scientific narratives* in the PubMed bio-medical collection (Sect. 3).

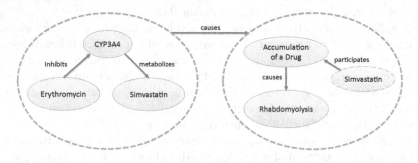

Fig. 1. Adverse drug-drug interaction as a sample pharmaceutical Narrative

2   Modeling Scientific Narratives

In this section, we propose a model for narratives working along a typical pharmaceutical narrative (Fig. 1) as a sample use case.

2.1   Narratives in Science

A narrative structure forms the backbone of virtually every scientific publication. And while scientific narratives tend to be much more limited and restricted than general narratives in fictional stories, their basic structure is similar. This includes protagonists driving the story, and events impacting their behavior. In this paper, we consider real-world objects and concepts, i. e. **entities** as the story's main protagonists. Considering the example above, the drugs *simvastatin* and *erythromycin*, the disease *rhabdomyolysis* and the gene system *CYP3A4* are the entities of interest. We denote the set of all entities by $\mathcal{E}$. In the scope of an individual narrative, entities might interact with each other, which can be expressed in the form of subject-predicate-object *relationships*, e. g. *CYP3A4 metabolizes simvastatin*. Here, we refer to the well-known Resource Description Framework (RDF) for modeling factual knowledge [9]. Each relation is identified via a *predicate label* like *inhibits* or *metabolizes*. Besides entities, a narrative may speak about simple *literals* in the place of objects, i. e. strings or numerical values. For example, the treatment of patients with simvastatin is naturally associated with a specific dosage, e. g. simvastatin may be applied in a dose of 20 mg per day. We denote the set of all literals by $\mathcal{L}$. Relationships between different entities or entities and literals can be understood as factual information. Prime examples are properties, e. g. *CYP3A4 metabolizes simvastatin*, as well as structural and ontological information about entities, i. e. the type or class of an entity. We call these relationships between entities and literals in a narrative **factual knowledge** denoted by $\mathcal{R}_F$. The set of possible predicate labels used for such factual knowledge is denoted by Σ_F. Hence, $\mathcal{R}_F \subseteq \mathcal{E} \times \Sigma_F \times (\mathcal{E} \cup \mathcal{L})$.

Besides entities and literals, narratives usually feature **events**. In our running example, the *accumulation of a drug* in the body of some patient is such an event, which might be observed and reported during a study. It describes the observation that the level of a drug in the patient's body increases. Hence, events can be understood in the sense of some labeled observation, which happens as the story progresses, i. e. an event is an observed state or a change of a state. Events may also feature a temporal dimension, i. e. an event occurs, having a starting point and sometimes an endpoint in time. We denote the set of all events by Γ.

In most scientific narratives, events are arranged in some order to describe the story's progress, e. g. the *accumulation of a drug* leads to a severe adverse effect inducing the disease *rhabdomyolysis*. There is much research invested in analyzing the characteristics of relationships between events [2,3,8]. There are several kinds of such relationships: Temporal relationships describe the temporal order of events, i. e. *a drug has to be administered* first, before *side effects may occur*. Causal relationships describe that an event causes some other event, e. g. *heart failure* leads to a *patient's death*. While temporal and causal relationships almost exclusively exist between events, entities can also be related to events. Usually, this either indicates that the entity participates in or is affected by some event. Whereas factual knowledge is more about properties and ontological information of entities, relations between events describe an argumentation's progress. Hence, we compose the progress of a narrative by a set of **narrative relationships** denoted by $\mathcal{R}_N$. In brief, narrative relations feature special, non-factual labels and can be placed between events or between events and entities, but not between entities. We denote the set of all narrative relation labels by Σ_{NR}. Hence, the set of narrative relationships $\mathcal{R}_N \subseteq (\Gamma \times \Sigma_{NR} \times (\mathcal{E} \cup \Gamma)) \cup (\mathcal{E} \times \Sigma_{NR} \times \Gamma)$.

Both narrative relations between entities and events, as well as factual knowledge between entities and literals, form the essential backbone of a narrative. A narrative might be composed inductively, e. g. the metabolism and inhibition behavior of CYP3A4, simvastatin, and erythromycin, which *as a whole* leads to the drug's accumulation. This behavior is also reflected by Hauser et al. [5], who characterize recursive elements as a key element in human language: a story can be composed using arbitrary sub-stories.

Definition 1. *A narrative is defined inductively:*

1. *A directed edge-labeled graph (V, E) is a narrative with $V \subseteq \mathcal{E} \cup \mathcal{L} \cup \Gamma$ being nodes and $E \subseteq \mathcal{R}_F \cup \mathcal{R}_N$ being edges.*
2. *If n_1, n_2 are narratives and $p \in \Sigma_{NR}$, then (n_1, p, n_2) is also a narrative.*

That means a narrative can be understood as edge-labeled directed graphs with events, entities, and literals as nodes and labeled edges between them.

Modeling the real world usage of narratives, we also allow them to show a recursive structure. In our running example, the metabolization of simvastatin by CYP3A4 and its inhibition by erythromycin is a three-node narrative, which takes part as a new node in a second narrative on a higher level. Narratives can thus act as nodes in specific narrative relations, e. g. administering both drugs, shown on the left side of Fig. 1, *causes* an *accumulation*, resulting in an adverse effect, shown on the right side of Fig. 1. Please note that we intuitively visualize recursive narratives as directed edge-labeled graphs where nodes may encapsulate narratives: such nodes are depicted by dashed circles, which enclose a complete graph structure of another narrative. This means that the content of encapsulating nodes is again a directed graph, with entities, literals, and events being the nodes and the relations being the edges.

2.2   Narrative Bindings

With narratives formally defined, we now introduce narrative bindings connecting the narrative itself as a logical overlay to underlying knowledge repositories. Binding a narrative n to a knowledge repository kr means *grounding* n with data from kr as evidence. We understand the notion of knowledge repositories in a broad sense, i. e. any structured or unstructured form of data storage, such as knowledge graphs, relational databases, document collections, or data set registries.

Definition 2. *Let n be a narrative, e be an edge of the narrative n and kr be a knowledge repository, a narrative binding nb binds the edge e against the knowledge repository kr with $nb = (e, kr)$. We say that e is bound by nb.*

Due to the recursive structure of narratives, there exist two types of edges: edges between events, entities and literals and edges between enclosed narratives. Returning to our running example, narrative bindings might easily ground the factual knowledge in the narrative, i. e. (*erythromycin, inhibits, CYP3A4*) and (*CYP3A4, metabolizes, simvastatin*), to a knowledge graph capturing important

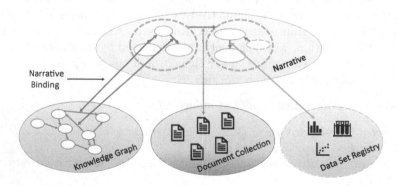

Fig. 2. Narratives as logical overlays on top of knowledge repositories

properties of genes and drugs. It is important to note that each subgraph of a narrative can be bound to a different knowledge repository. If all parts of a narrative can be bound, we consider the narrative to be *grounded*. Formally,

Definition 3. *Let n be a narrative and NB be a set of narrative bindings, we call n grounded by NB, if all edges of n are bound by at least some nb $\in$ NB.*

With narratives, we introduce a novel model to express any form of scientific discussion in a structured fashion, of course without making any claims to its validity. However, using bindings to ground a narrative against underlying knowledge repositories, at least provides some evidence for the narrative in the sense of *plausibility*. Regarding a specific knowledge repository, computing bindings in real-world applications relies on available methods for information retrieval, natural language processing and querying capabilities. Still, it is essential to note that a successful binding does not imply any *guarantees* on a narrative's validity, which is obviously heavily impacted by the quality of the respective repositories, but also by the somewhat difficult to assess the validity of information fusion over different sources [7].

3   Narrative Queries

We have modeled narratives to represent scientific argumentations in a structured way that is usable for information systems. However, how can we use scientific narratives in real-world applications? We introduce narrative queries with variables to support sense-making processes, i.e. generating new hypotheses [12]. We denote the set of all variable symbols by $\mathcal{V}$ and write each symbol by a leading question mark. A **narrative query** nq is some narrative n, where each entity, event or literal might be replaced by a variable symbol of $\mathcal{V}$. Hence, each narrative is also a (variable-free) narrative query.

Considering our running example, we might formulate a narrative query by replacing any node by some variable $?X$. By substituting variables we can then fill nodes by arbitrary entities, literals or events. In the following, we use the SPARQL notation[1]. The set of variables used in a narrative query nq is denoted by $vars(nq) = \{?v_1, \ldots, ?v_n\}$. A **substitution** μ from $\mathcal{V}$ to $\mathcal{E} \cup \mathcal{L} \cup \Gamma$ is a partial function: $\mu : \mathcal{V} \rightarrow \mathcal{E} \cup \mathcal{L} \cup \Gamma$. We define the subset of $\mathcal{V}$, where μ is defined, as the domain of μ, shortly $dom(\mu)$. The substitution of the variables in a narrative query nq by μ yields a narrative n, if all variables of the query are in $dom(\mu)$. We use $\mu(nq) = n$ as a shortcut for this substitution.

An **answer** to a narrative query nq is a pair $(\mu(nq), NB)$ with a substitution $\mu(nq)$ and a set of narrative bindings NB, such that the following holds: 1. $vars(nq) \subseteq dom(\mu)$, 2. $\mu(nq) = n$, and 3. n is grounded by NB. As a consequence, answering a narrative query nq requires two steps: 1. obtaining all substitutions $\{\mu_1, \ldots, \mu_n\}$ and 2. obtaining narrative bindings grounding $\mu_i(nq)$ for each $\mu_i \in$

---

[1] https://www.w3.org/TR/rdf-sparql-query/.

$\{\mu_1, ..., \mu_n\}$. If a narrative query does not include variables, its answer is the empty substitution and a set of narrative bindings grounding the respective narrative.

Obviously, testing arbitrary substitutions for their narrative bindings is an expensive task. But, by first computing possible narrative bindings for the fixed parts of a narrative query, the set of feasible substitutions can be severely restricted. Moreover, finding such narrative bindings in structured knowledge repositories allows for the usage of efficient query languages such as SPARQL.

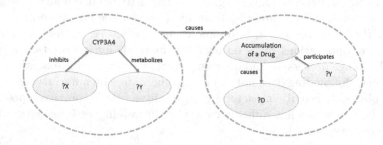

Fig. 3. A pharmaceutical narrative query

3.1 Answering a Narrative Query with SemMedDB and PubMed

As a small showcase, we pose a narrative query in the biomedical domain. We compute all narrative bindings against two knowledge repositories, namely SemMedDB and PubMed. SemMedDB[2] is a knowledge graph comprising nearly 19 million medical facts in version 2019. PubMed[3] is the world's most extensive biomedical library with around 30 million publications and is publicly available as the PubMed Medline 2020. Let us design a pharmaceutical narrative query nq based on our running example, see Fig. 3. It asks for two drugs $?X$ and $?Y$, which both interact with the gene system $CYP3A4$. This interaction leads to an adverse effect $?D$ triggered by the accumulation of drug $?Y$ in the body. A possible answer to the query nq are the substitution μ with $\mu(?X) = erythromycin$, $\mu(?Y) = simvastatin$ and $\mu(?D) = rhabdomyolysis$ and the respective narrative bindings NB against SemMedDB and PubMed. In fact, $\mu(nq)$ is exactly our running example narrative.

But, how can we compute all answers to nq? Since $?X$ and $?Y$ are part of purely factual knowledge inside the narrative query, we can formulate a suitable SPARQL statement to query SemMedDB for possible substitutions of $?X$ and $?Y$ automatically. In contrast, as $?D$ does not participate in a factual, but in a narrative relationship, we can derive valid substitutions for $?D$ by searching for publications in PubMed, which talk about $\mu_i(?X)$, $\mu_i(?Y)$ and $CYP3A4$ for

---

[2] https://skr3.nlm.nih.gov/SemMedDB/.
[3] https://pubmed.ncbi.nlm.nih.gov.

each substitution $\mu_i \in \{\mu_1, \ldots, \mu_n\}$. If diseases are mentioned within such a publication, they serve as possible substitution μ_i for $?D$. As an example, if a publication talks about *simvastatin, erythromycin, CYP3A4* and *rhabdomyolysis*, we derive the corresponding μ with $\mu(?X) = erythromycin$, $\mu(?Y) = simvastatin$ and $\mu(?D) = rhabdomyolysis$. Using SemMedDB2019 and the PubMed Medline 2020 we computed 1264 possible substitutions. These substitutions $\{\mu_1, \ldots, \mu_n\}$ can derive the narratives $\{n_1, \ldots, n_n\}$ by $\mu_i(nq) = n_i$ with $\mu_i \in \{\mu_1, \ldots, \mu_n\}$. Due to the nature of how we have computed the substitutions, each narrative in $\{n_1, \ldots, n_n\}$ is already grounded by bindings against SemMedDB and PubMed. This small experiment demonstrates that answering a narrative query can automatically derive a large set of grounded narratives.

4   Discussion

In sum, we introduce a novel narrative overlay model to represent scientific argumentations in a formal way. In contrast to integrating all knowledge repositories into a single one, which is obviously an prohibitive task, narratives are designed as logical overlays on top of different types of knowledge repositories. We introduce narrative bindings to bind a narrative against some knowledge repository, i. e. the narrative can be grounded by data of this knowledge repository. Grounding means to find evidence for the narrative in the sense of *plausibility*. Finding suitable narrative bindings to ground a narrative is still an open research task. We showed that (for easy cases) bindings might simply be computed using established query languages like SPARQL. However, query processing is not always that easy, e. g. entity and relation alignments must be computed automatically or at least semi-automatically. In the future, transforming the process of manually defining bindings to automatically computing them is worth investigating.

Designing narratives is a task for domain experts who are familiar with domain-specific argumentations. A domain expert can ground her narrative by suitable bindings, which give hints and, more or less, evidence about the correctness and validity of her narrative. In a first use case, incorporating narrative queries, we demonstrate how such a process is done in the biomedical scientific domain. Moreover, a narrative query that includes variables enables a domain expert to automatically design a template. This template can be used later to derive suitable narratives by computing narrative bindings against already established knowledge repositories. As an application, our example narrative query might be used to discover new knowledge, e. g. the interaction between *simvastatin* and *erythromycin* is inferred, iff the corresponding narrative is grounded. Hence, narrative queries support workflows for knowledge discovery by obtaining substitutions for variables and grounding them. Suppose a narrative cannot be grounded, but parts of it can be. In that case, a researcher can decide whether the not grounded parts are worth of investigation for future work.

Moreover, domain experts design narrative queries with hints for the computation of bindings once, and several researchers benefit from these templates later. A young researcher might efficiently utilize a narrative query to generate a new hypothesis or to find suitable provenance information by having a look at the obtained narrative bindings. Especially in domains where researchers are not familiar with query languages, pre-designed narrative queries in conjunction with hints for the computation of bindings assist their process by automatically querying different knowledge graphs. Although the design of our pharmaceutical narrative query might take some time, the query is used to explain thousands of drug-drug interactions with adverse effects. The showcase demonstrates that our narrative query is ready-to-use in the pharmaceutical domain for querying and obtaining bindings against SemMedDB and PubMed automatically. Narratives as logical overlays together with narrative queries enable domain experts to collect knowledge from several different kinds of knowledge repositories. In this way, domain experts can boost their applications' quality without the need for a complex integration of existing repositories.

5   Related Work

Extending the reach of knowledge graphs has been an extensive field of study for many years. In knowledge graphs reification [6], as applied in the singleton notation [11], and different strategies to capture provenance information [14] have been proposed. These extensions aim to capture contextual or situational knowledge that is usually not expressed due to the restrictive data structure of RDF using binary relations. These approaches usually require high manual expenditures, which contradicts the general idea of RDF to facilitate large scale knowledge repositories in an easy way. And even in these cases, storing complete narrative structures is usually not pursued.

Detecting stories in natural language texts is a topic that has sparked much interest. Chambers et al. discussed the idea of modeling texts by extracting temporally ordered sequences of events [2]. Li et al. discussed the generation of stories by using crowd-sourced plot graphs [8]. These stories are then analyzed to find their commonalities and to determine relevant events, as well as orders of event sequences. These works describe a story as a sequence of events. In contrast, we focus on modeling a complete scientific argumentation within a single model. The general characteristics of argumentation structures have been thoroughly analyzed by Toulmin et al. [13]. Argumentation mining aims to find suitable arguments to a topic automatically, i.e. extracting positive and negative arguments (pro and contra) [4,10]. Especially in the scientific domain, where work is usually published in the form of a solid argumentation, a deeper understanding of such an argumentation and its structure is essentially needed.

6   Conclusion

Capturing argumentations in the form of narratives in a structured way has sparked much interest. While capturing arbitrary narratives raises many problems, we focus on scientific narratives, which are usually more limited and quite concise. In this paper, we conceptualize scientific argumentations in a novel narrative model, combining factual knowledge and narrative patterns within its scope. Utilizing a single knowledge repository to form a proper scientific narrative is not sufficient. Argumentations typically operate on different types of knowledge, e. g. on factual knowledge or situational knowledge, like observed results of an experiment. Grounding narratives by narrative bindings gives evidence about the narrative's validity and correctness - in the sense of plausibility. By understanding narratives as logical overlays that can be bound against different kinds of knowledge repositories, we bypass the extensive integration of different knowledge repositories. Hence, we argue to keep the sources separated and to build logical overlays on top of them. In a biomedical showcase, we utilize a narrative on top of two large-scale knowledge repositories demonstrating the applicability of narratives. Indeed, narrative structures are commonly used in a wide range of scientific argumentations, e. g. chemical pathways, new theories in physics, the behavior of systems and algorithms in computer science, sociological observations and many more. Narratives are designed as logical overlays to enable information systems to represent and ground scientific argumentations against several knowledge repositories within a single model. In the future, we will investigate applications utilizing scientific narratives to boost the quality of research tasks like hypothesis generation.

References

1. Auer, S., Kovtun, V., Prinz, M., Kasprzik, A., Stocker, M., Vidal, M.E.: Towards a knowledge graph for science. In: Proceedings of the 8th International Conference on Web Intelligence, Mining and Semantics, pp. 1 6, WIMS 2018, ACM (2018). https://doi.org/10.1145/3227609.3227689
2. Chambers, N., Jurafsky, D.: Unsupervised learning of narrative event chains. In: Proceedings of ACL-08: HLT, pp. 789–797 (2008)
3. Chang, D.-S., Choi, K.-S.: Causal relation extraction using cue phrase and lexical pair probabilities. In: Su, K.-Y., Tsujii, J., Lee, J.-H., Kwong, O.Y. (eds.) IJCNLP 2004. LNCS (LNAI), vol. 3248, pp. 61–70. Springer, Heidelberg (2005). https://doi.org/10.1007/978-3-540-30211-7_7
4. Habernal, I., Gurevych, I.: Argumentation mining in user-generated web discourse. Comput. Linguist. **43**, 125–179 (2017). https://doi.org/10.1162/COLI_a_00276
5. Hauser, M.D., Chomsky, N., Fitch, W.T.: The faculty of language: what is it, who has it, and how did it evolve? Science **298**, 1569–1579 (2002). https://doi.org/10.1126/science.298.5598.1569
6. Hernández, D., Hogan, A., Krötzsch, M.: Reifying RDF: what works well with wikidata? In: Proceedings of the 11th International Workshop on Scalable Semantic Web Knowledge Base Systems, CEUR Workshop Proceedings, vol. 1457, pp. 32–47. CEUR-WS.org (2015)
7. Kroll, H., Kalo, J.-C., Nagel, D., Mennicke, S., Balke, W.-T.: Context-compatible information fusion for scientific knowledge graphs. In: Hall, M., Merčun, T., Risse, T., Duchateau, F. (eds.) TPDL 2020. LNCS, vol. 12246, pp. 33–47. Springer, Cham (2020). https://doi.org/10.1007/978-3-030-54956-5_3

8. Li, B., Lee-Urban, S., Johnston, G., Riedl, M.: Story generation with crowdsourced plot graphs. In: 27th AAAI Conference on Artificial Intelligence (2013). https://doi.org/10.5555/2891460.2891543

9. Manola, F., Miller, E., McBride, B., et al.: Rdf primer. W3C recommendation **10**(1–107), p. 6 (2004)

10. Mochales, R., Moens, M.F.: Argumentation mining. Artif. Intell. Law **19**, 1–22 (2011). https://doi.org/10.1007/s10506-010-9104-x

11. Nguyen, V., Bodenreider, O., Sheth, A.: Don't like RDF reification?: making statements about statements using singleton property. In: Proceedings of the 23rd International Conference on World Wide Web, pp. 759–770, WWW 2014, ACM (2014). https://doi.org/10.1145/2566486.2567973

12. Spangler, S., Wilkins, A.D., Bachman, B.J., Nagarajan, M., Dayaram, T., Haas, P., et al.: Automated hypothesis generation based on mining scientific literature. In: Proceedings of the 20th ACM SIGKDD International Conference on Knowledge Discovery and Data Mining, pp. 1877–1886. KDD 2014, ACM (2014). https://doi.org/10.1145/2623330.2623667

13. Toulmin, S.E.: The Uses of Argument. Cambridge University Press, Cambridge (1958)

14. Wylot, M., Cudré-Mauroux, P., Hauswirth, M., Groth, P.: Storing, tracking, and querying provenance in linked data. IEEE Trans. Knowl. Data Eng. **29**, 1751–1764 (2017). https://doi.org/10.1109/TKDE.2017.2690299

Towards a Conceptual Model for Data Narratives

Faten El Outa[1], Matteo Francia[3], Patrick Marcel[1]([envelope]),
Veronika Peralta[1], and Panos Vassiliadis[2]

[1] University of Tours, Blois, France
{faten.outa,patrick.marcel,veronika.peralta}@univ-tours.fr
[2] University of Ioannina, Ioannina, Greece
pvassil@cs.uoi.gr
[3] University of Bologna, Cesena, Italy
m.francia@unibo.it

Abstract. Data narration is the activity of producing stories supported by facts extracted from data analysis, possibly using interactive visualizations. In spite of the increasing interest in data narration in several communities (e.g. journalism, business, e-government), there is no consensual definition of data narrative, let alone a conceptual or logical model of it. In this paper, we propose a conceptual model of data narrative for exploratory data analysis. It is based on four layers that reflect the transition from raw data to the visual rendering of the data story: factual, intentional, structural and presentational. This model aims to support the entire lifecycle of building a data narrative, starting from an intentional goal: fetch and explore data, bring out highlights, derive important messages, structure the plot of the data narrative, and render it in a visual manner. Our contributions include a description of the model and its instantiation for several real examples showing that it covers data narration needs.

Keywords: Data narrative · Visual narrative · Data storytelling · Data exploration

1 Introduction

Narrating a story is considered as one of the oldest activities in the world, and a pillar of information communication as a mean of education. Often mistaken with storytelling, which describes the social and cultural activity of sharing stories [13], narration is the use of techniques to convey a story to an audience [12]. Recently, data narration, i.e., narrating with data visualizations [7], received increasing interest in several communities (e.g. journalism, business, e-government). It is defined as the activity of producing narratives supported by facts extracted from data analysis, using interactive visualizations [2]. More concretely, such data narratives can be viewed as ordered sequences of steps,

© Springer Nature Switzerland AG 2020
G. Dobbie et al. (Eds.): ER 2020, LNCS 12400, pp. 261–270, 2020.
https://doi.org/10.1007/978-3-030-62522-1_19

each of which can contain words, images, visualizations, audio, video, or any combination thereof, and which are based on data [8].

Apart from these general considerations, and to the best of our knowledge, there is no consensual definition of data narrative, let alone a conceptual or logical model of it. While data narrative essentially attracted attention from the visualization community [2,8], we believe that (i) a more global approach to it is needed from domains including visualization, data management, data exploration and machine learning, and (ii) conceptual modeling of the domain should drive further researches, to help the understanding, standardization, reuse and sharing of data narratives. Such a clear foundation of the aspects and design choices in the domain of data narration provided to system builders and algorithm designers will allow to facilitate rapid exploration with automation, to support iterative and collaborative workflows, etc. [14].

The main contribution of this paper is a conceptualization of the domain of data narrative. We propose a novel conceptual model that provides a structured, principled definition of the key concepts of the domain, along with their relationships, and clarifies their role and usage. This model aims to guide an author to build a data narrative from scratch: fetch and explore data, abstract important messages based on an intentional goal, structure the contents of the data story, and render it in a visual manner. Note that automatic decisions for producing a narrative (e.g., automatically deciding the visualization technique given a specific message) or methodological aspects (e.g., guidelines for using the model) are out of the scope of our work.

The paper is organized as follows: Sect. 2 describes background concepts, presents related work and introduces our definition of data narrative. The proposed model is presented in Sect. 3. Finally, Sect. 4 concludes and presents future research directions.

2   From Narrative to Data Narrative

While various models of narratives have been proposed (see [6] for a survey), none of them qualifies for data narrative. However, some aspects of classical narration theory, as described e.g., by Chatman [4], should be reviewed to understand the fundamental structure of narration. This is the topic of Subsect. 2.1. In addition, to understand what is particular to the process of communicating the result of a data analysis through visual artifacts, we review recent works on visual narration from the data visualization community. Without offering a precise model nor a consensual definition of data narration, these works shed a light on important aspects of it. This is the topic of Subsect. 2.2. Finally, reviewing these aspects helps us to clarify the terminology and to propose a definition of data narrative that will structure the proposed model.

2.1   Narratives

Narrative theoreticians agree that there are at least two levels in any narration: some events happen (what is told) and these events are presented and transmitted to an audience in a certain way (how is it told). In the most widely used structuralist terminology, the answer to the "what" question is called a **story** and the answer to the "how" question is called a **discourse** [1]. Chatman [4] distinguishes narration's elements based on the what and how questions, defining narrative as a couple of story (content of the narrative) and discourse (expression of it). The story has a form, that is the set of possible objects, events, etc., and a substance, which is a **composition** of story elements (i.e., events, settings, behaviors, characters) as pre-processed by the author's cultural code. A discourse has a form of expression, which is a translation of the story content to a **structured combination** of the story elements. In other words, this means that, out of the entire story as it actually happened, when constructing a discourse, the author picks an interesting subset to present. The discourse also has a substance that includes the set of all **media** used to show structured elements, like text, pictures, tables or charts. In summary, the story can be seen as the logical form of the narrative, while the discourse is its presentable manifestation, obtained through author's editions: prunes unimportant parts out, magnifies some others deemed interesting, rearranges the order of presentation to make it more interesting, etc.

2.2   Visual Data Narration

While using many terms (e.g., narrative visualization, visual storytelling, data driven storytelling), the data visualization community has recently brought much attention to visual data narration [2]. Kosara and McKinley [8] intuitively define a data story as an ordered sequence of steps, each of which primarily consists of visualization, which can include text and images but essentially are based on data. The authors note that journalists work with a model of story construction where the order of events is consistent and clear, for the story to be comprehensible. Journalists **collect information, which gives them the key facts**, and then they tie those facts together into a story. The authors note that the goals, tasks and tools used during the research phase differ from those in the writing phase , and that **only some of the material from the research phase end up in the final story**, most of the source material only serving as raw background information. Segel and Heer [10] insist that the notion of a chain of causally related events is central to the definition. One typical difference between traditional storytelling and data narration, highlighted in [10], concerns the potential for interactivity in the latter. In an effort to understand what makes a good sequence of visualizations, Hullman et al. [7] estimate the cognitive cost of transiting from one visualization to another. More recently, Chen et al. [5] distinguishes (a) visual analytics, which requires to see all aspects of complex data, explore their interrelationships, and is supported by multiple coordinated views and sophisticated interaction techniques, from (b) storytelling, which is meant to convey only interesting and/or important information extracted through the analysis, presented in a simple and easily understandable way. The two processes differ in their purposes, target users, kind of information dealt with, and methods of presenting the information and interacting with it. To support telling stories of visual analytics findings, there should be an intermediate step between analysis and storytelling, in which **the analyst assembles and organizes information pieces to be communicated.**

2.3   Our Definition of Data Narrative

Inspired by Chatman [4] and Chen et al. [5], we propose the following definition for data narrative: *A data narrative is a structured composition of messages that (a) convey findings over the data, and, (b) are typically delivered via visual means in order to facilitate their reception by an intended audience.*

We borrow Chatman's terminology and extend his structure of narrative considering that data narrative must describe how the content of the story (Chatman's events and existents) is derived from data. This is done by distinguishing 4 layers in our model of data narrative: the first two layers represent the *story* and the last two represent the *discourse*. In the story, a *factual* layer represents the story form while an *intentional* layer represents the story substance. In the discourse, a *structural* layer represents the discourse form and a *presentational* layer represents the discourse substance. Specifically, and originally compared to classical models of narration, the factual layer includes an entity for *findings* based on facts and models collected from data, and the intentional layer includes entities for *messages* derived from findings, where the narrative *characters* (e.g., important business objects) demonstrate interesting measurements. The factual layer can be thought of as the "objective" one, describing the work around data exploration and model construction, while the intentional layer reflects the "subjective" editorial work of pre-processing findings to turn them into messages. Note that our model of data narrative is agnostic of a specific data model; all the specific details on how data and facts are produced to serve the information goal and support the extraction of findings are encapsulated in a *collector* entity. The structural layer includes entities modeling the arrangement of the messages into a structured combination of presentable discourse elements, and the presentational layer includes entities for the assignment of a presentable set of media to each of the narrative's discourse structure.

3   The Model

This section presents the conceptual model for data narrative depicted in Fig. 2, using UML class diagram notation, but omitting class properties for readability purposes. Subsection 3.1 presents an intuitive introduction to model components with a motivating example, while Subsect. 3.2 describes the model, organized in 4 layers.

In what follows, we use the terms *author* or *analyst* for the designer of the data narrative. The author is not necessarily a business analyst, she can be a data journalist, or a plain data enthusiast, aiming to produce a report of findings. We also assume an *audience* for the produced outcome, which includes the people that will see, read or hear the story. Both author and audience can represent several persons, or be confounded into one person.

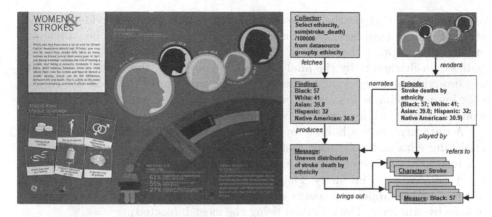

Fig. 1. Example of data narrative, available at https://www.good.is/infographics/facts-about-women-and-strokes (left); and a partial object diagram for a particular message (right).

3.1 Motivating Example

This subsection illustrates the components of our model (signaled in italics) using a simple visual data narrative about women and strokes, published by GOOD[1]. For illustration purpose, we describe a plausible process for defining analytical questions and collecting data, which is not precised by the author.

The final result, a *visual narrative* is depicted in Fig. 1 (left side), taking the form of an infographic. The *plot* warns women about stroke risks by combining diverse information about risks, symptoms and incidents. The plot structures the discourse by arranging messages in coherent pieces of discourse: *acts* narrating a major piece of information and a major part of the narration with a significant communication, and *episodes*, subparts of lesser importance on their own, narrating specific messages. In this example, there is a unique act and six episodes. This act is rendered with a *dashboard* displaying complementary visual information. Six *dashboard components* render the six episodes. For instance, the top right corner of Fig. 1 displays stroke deaths by ethnicity. Visual artifacts (in this case, circle sizes) are used for carrying the message (here, putting in evidence that black women are the most impacted by stroke deaths).

We summarize the *messages* in the example, from top-left to bottom-right: (m_1) the overall situation of women's stroke in the USA, (m_2) the uneven distribution of stroke death by ethnicity, (m_3) the risks unique to women, (m_4) the rates of women stroke deaths and incidents, (m_5) the poor ability of patients to identify symptoms, and (m_6) the impact of ethnicity in stroke incidents.

Typically, a data narrative starts with an *analysis goal* and a set of *analytical questions*, reflecting the author's intention. Here, the author's analysis goal is to narrate facts about women and strokes in the USA. An example of analytical question is: Which characteristics of women (age, ethnicity, weight, etc.) have

---

[1] https://www.good.is/infographics/facts-about-women-and-strokes.

an impact on stroke deaths? Message m_2 answers this question, evidencing that ethnicity is a critical factor. It brings out ethnicity as a *character*, i.e., a relevant entity or concept of the story, in addition to women and stroke, both already pointed as characters by the analysis goal. Analogously, the ratios by ethnicity are brought out as relevant *measures*, i.e., relevant figures in the story. We can note here that characters may appear in several episodes, esp. the main cast (e.g. women, stroke), while others are only supporting in an episode (e.g. symptoms).

A data *exploration* is built by the author, who called several *collectors* for analysing data and collecting *findings* in order to answer analytical questions. For example, a collector queried a dataset of female patients in the USA, asking for stroke deaths by ethnicity. The ratios of stroke deaths by ethnicity constitute a finding that supports message m_2, stating the uneven distribution of stroke deaths by ethnicity (black women being the most impacted).

Figure 1 (right side) illustrates a partial object diagram concerning message m_2, from the collection of findings to the rendering of an episode.

3.2 Model Description

The model we propose for data narrative is depicted in Fig. 2. As introduced in Sect. 2, the organization in 4 layers, adapted from Chatman [4], reflects the transition from raw facts to the visuals communicated to the audience of the data narrative. On their way to the reader, the facts traverse:

1. **Factual layer**. The factual layer models the *exploration* of facts (i.e., the underlying data), via a set of *collectors* that allow for manipulating facts with varied tools. *Findings* emerged from explored facts are candidates for participating in the story.
2. **Intentional layer**. The intentional layer models the substance of the story, identifying the *messages*, *characters* and *measures* the author intends to communicate and tracing how they are obtained through *analytical questions*, according to an *analysis goal*.
3. **Structural layer**. The structural layer models the structure of the data narrative, organizing its *plot* in terms of *acts* and *episodes*.
4. **Presentational layer**. The presentational layer models the rendering of the data narrative, i.e., a *visual narrative*, that is communicated to the reader through visual artifacts (*dashboards* and *dashboard components*).

To understand the organization of the model, one should note that the concept of *message* is the model's corner stone, which is clearly evidenced by the way we have related message to the other concepts. Essentially, a specific message is rooted in the facts analyzed, conveying essential findings in the data that answer a, and may raise new, analytical question(s). This specific message is then the discourse structural building block: episodes narrate specific messages, and acts, built as sets of episodes, narrate a broader message. A message is also indirectly connected to the presentational layer: a global message is visually conveyed by one dashboard, each of the dashboard components illustrating one specific message. We now detail each layer by describing its entities and their relationships.

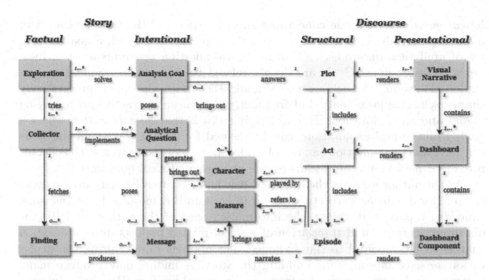

Fig. 2. The data narrative model, organized in layers

Factual Layer. Data narratives need data. Data represent the facts that support a story. The factual layer concerns the processes of looking for data in a set of data sources, analyzing them, and obtaining added value and findings. Data are collected via a set of *collectors*, that can be queries in a query language or interface supported by the data sources, extraction tools (e.g. wrappers or loaders), or more generally, all kind of programs able to interact and retrieve data from sources. They may just retrieve data from sources or include functionalities for filtering, checking, building models and reasoning with data. For example, a collector may cluster data, compute correlations, detect outliers or emphasize contradictory data in order to produce insights. For the sake of generality, we do not assume a particular structuring of data (e.g., databases or unstructured files) nor a particular way of collecting findings (e.g., via queries, data analytics or other algorithms), but use collector as an abstraction of data access and manipulation. *Findings* are, among the facts retrieved by collectors, those that are more striking, surprising or relevant and worth narrating in the story. Findings are more than just data returned by collectors, they result from the analysis of facts. A collector may *fetch* one or several findings, or conversely, it may evidence no narrating-worthy finding. The set of actions conducted to collect findings is called a data *exploration*. It aims at keeping trace of the set of collectors tried for addressing an information need. Each collector is part of an exploration while an exploration typically *tries* many collectors.

Intentional Layer. The intentional layer models the devising of the substance of the story based upon the author's analysis goal. An *analysis goal* represents the main objective of a story, i.e., the intended information that should be explained, detailed and transmitted to the reader. A goal is carved up into a set of *ana-*

lytical questions, each one concerning specific aspects of the goal, and a set of *messages* are raised in order to answer these questions. Indeed, a goal *poses* a set of analytical questions, and an analytical question *generates* a set of messages, possibly none. Goals are deeply related to explorations. Sometimes, an exploration is built for solving a clear goal, other times, the goal is progressively shaped while exploring data, but frequently, there is an interactive process tying a goal and an exploration. The underlying idea is that an exploration *solves* a goal, while several explorations can be devised for solving a goal. In the same way, an analytical question can be solved by one or more collectors, each collector providing *implementation* means to one or more analytical questions.

As the author explores the data and new findings are collected, progressively the author distills and structures them in her mind. A message is, at the same time, (a) a partial answer to the information need of the author, and (b) the distilling, merging, and translation of a set of related findings into information that is to be conveyed to the audience. The findings raised during the exploration *produce* messages for building the story. A finding may produce many messages and a message results from one or several findings. Possibly, new analytical questions can be *posed* based on the message found, inviting for more exploration. To further structure messages, we introduce two important components of them, *characters* and *measures*, that capture important data values that characterize a message and their fact-based quantification. Both characters and measures belong to the universe understandable by the audience. Messages *bring out* characters (e.g., a set of products causing a drop in sales) and the related measures (e.g. amount of sales for those products). In addition, some characters are previously known and *brought out* directly by the analysis goal (e.g., sales in France). Noticeably, messages serve as a baseline for structuring the story: an episode *narrates* a message. In this way, the intentional layer acts as a bridge between the exploration of facts (factual layer) and the structuring of the story (structural layer). In particular, a message, based on a finding, is the base for building an episode.

Structural Layer. This layer concerns the form of expression of the data narrative. While previous layers deal with the contents of the narrative, this layer focuses on its discourse. It is important to stress, that there is a design part served here. The idea is that after deciding to address a goal via analytical questions and exploring data, the analysis has resulted in a set of messages to be conveyed to the audience. As reported in Sect. 2, the literature suggests that, before presenting the messages, there is a synthesis of a story as a coherent composition, where messages must be conveyed to the audience in an organized way [4,5,8]. Plots, acts and episodes model the parts of the synthesis of the narrative's content into this composition. A *plot* is the arrangement of messages in a way easily understandable by the audience. To achieve this, the author must put in order a part of the audience-intended report with the messages that conveys an interesting piece of information. Following the terminology of traditional narration, we introduce an *act* as a constituent part of the plot, which is the mean to convey a specific piece of information. Practically, this means that an act corresponds to a major piece of information and a major part of the plot. Each act is composed of several subparts of lesser importance on their own, which we call episodes. An *episode* is the granular piece of the narrative that conveys a message. A plot *includes* one or several acts and an act *includes* one or several episodes. A plot *answers* a goal and an episode *narrates* a message, the episode text being the shaping of the message. Accordingly, characters and measures brought out by the message appear in the episode text, possibly starring or being highlighted according to author's narration style. One or many characters can *play* in one or many episodes. Analogously, one or many measures can *be referred* in one or many episodes.

Presentational Layer. This layer focuses on how the structured story is presented to the audience. Acts and episodes are represented and organized in order to be understandable by the audience. Visualization aspects are the focus of this layer. A *visual narrative renders* a plot. It can be a slideshow, a notebook, a blog, or any other visual art allowing for the visual representation of a story. A visual narrative *contains* a set of *dashboards*, each one *rendering* an act. We use the term dashboard since it is general enough to accommodate varied types of visualizations (e.g. a Business Intelligence dashboard, an infographics, a section in a python notebook, a section in a blog or web page). In the same way, a dashboard contains a set of *dashboard components*, each one *rendering* an episode. Dashboard components include text, images, charts, maps, animations, etc. We remark that a story can be rendered in several ways or formats (e.g., an infographics and a video). In the same way, acts and episodes can be rendered by several dashboards and dashboard components.

4   Conclusion

This paper introduced a conceptual model for data narrative, by extending a classical model of narration [4] to reflect the transition from raw data to the visual rendering of information derived from data analysis. Our model translates fundamental concepts of narration to their respective counterparts when it comes to data narrations and involves the collection of data, the extraction of key findings and the corresponding messages to the audience, the structuring of a presentation of these findings and the ultimate presentation via visual -or other-means via a set of dashboards. To showcase the model, we implemented a proof of concept web application helping an author structuring a data narrative while interactively exploring a database. The code is available on Github[2].

Among the possible refinements of the model, we identified the following as the most desirable: adding a support for transitions between episodes/acts, supporting different semantic structuring (e.g. linear, causality [8], Martini glass

---

[2] https://github.com/OLAP3/pocdatastorytelling.

[10]), adding support for plausibilization and coherence of messages and arguments, distinguishing main cast from supporting cast among the narrative characters and adding a layer for interactivity [9] balancing between author- and reader-driven stories. We also aim at improving the web application through tests with data journalists. On the longer run, we plan to tightly integrate the model with our past works on data explorations [3,11].

References

1. Akleman, E., Franchi, S., Kaleci, D., Mandell, L., Yamauchi, T., Akleman, D.: A theoretical framework to represent narrative structures for visual storytelling. In: Bridges, pp. 129–136 (2015)
2. Carpendale, S., Diakopoulos, N., Riche, N.H., Hurter, C.: Data-driven storytelling (dagstuhl seminar 16061). Dagstuhl Rep. **6**(2), 1–27 (2016)
3. Chanson, A., et al.: The traveling analyst problem. In: DOLAP (2020)
4. Chatman, S.: Story and Discourse: Narrative Structure in Fiction and Film. Cornell University Press, Ithaca (1980)
5. Chen, S., et al.: Supporting story synthesis: Bridging the gap between visual analytics and storytelling. TVCG pp. 1–1 (2018)
6. Elson, D.K.: Modeling narrative discourse. Ph.D. thesis, Columbia Univ. (2012)
7. Hullman, J., Drucker, S.M., Riche, N.H., Lee, B., Fisher, D., Adar, E.: A deeper understanding of sequence in narrative visualization. IEEE TVCG **19**(12), 2406–2415 (2013)
8. Kosara, R., Mackinlay, J.: Storytelling: the next step for visualization. IEEE Comput. **46**, 44–52 (2013)
9. Sarikaya, A., Correll, M., Bartram, L., Tory, M., Fisher, D.: What do we talk about when we talk about dashboards? IEEE TVCG **25**(1), 682–692 (2019)
10. Segel, E., Heer, J.: Narrative visualization: telling stories with data. IEEE TVCG **16**(6), 1139–1148 (2010)
11. Vassiliadis, P., Marcel, P., Rizzi, S.: Beyond roll-up's and drill-down's: an intentional analytics model to reinvent OLAP. Inf. Syst. **85**, 68–91 (2019)
12. Wikipedia: Narration. https://en.wikipedia.org/wiki/Narration
13. Wikipedia: Storytelling. https://en.wikipedia.org/wiki/Storytelling
14. Wongsuphasawat, K., Liu, Y., Heer, J.: Goals, process, and challenges of exploratory data analysis: an interview study. CoRR abs/1911.00568 (2019)

Subcontracting, Assignment, and Substitution for Legal Contracts in Symboleo

Alireza Parvizimosaed[1]([✉])(iD), Sepehr Sharifi[1]([✉])(iD), Daniel Amyot[1]([✉])(iD),
Luigi Logrippo[1,2]([✉])(iD), and John Mylopoulos[1]([✉])(iD)

[1] School of EECS, University of Ottawa, Ottawa, Canada
{aparv007,sshar190,damyot,logrippo,jmylopou}@uottawa.ca
[2] Université du Québec en Outaouais, Gatineau, Canada

Abstract. *Legal contracts* specify obligations and powers among legal subjects, involve assets, and are subject to quality constraints. *Smart contracts* are software systems that monitor the execution of contracts to ensure compliance. As a starting point for developing software engineering concepts, tools, and techniques for smart contracts, we have proposed Symboleo, a formal specification language for contracts. The complexity of real-life contracts (e.g., in the construction and transportation industries) requires specification languages to support execution-time operations for contracts, such as subcontracting, assignment, delegation, and substitution. This paper formalizes such concepts by proposing for them a syntax and axiomatic semantics within Symboleo. This formalization makes use of primitive operations that support the transfer or sharing of right, responsibility, and performance among contracting and subcontracting parties. A prototype compliance checking tool for Symboleo has also been created to support monitoring compliance for contracts that include subcontracting aspects. A realistic freight contract specified in Symboleo is provided as an illustrative example for our proposal, and is used for a preliminary evaluation with positive results.

Keywords: Contracts · Formal specification languages · Legal subcontracts · Smart contracts · Subcontracting

1 Introduction and Motivation

Legal contracts specify *obligations* and *powers* among contractual *roles*. They involve assets, and define constraints enforcing specific modalities. In a world of digital transformations, many aspects of contracts are being automated. In particular, *smart contracts* are software systems that monitor the execution of legal

---

Partially funded by an NSERC Strategic Partnership Grant titled "Middleware Framework and Programming Infrastructure for IoT Services" and by SSHRC's Partnership Grant "Autonomy Through Cyberjustice Technologies".

G. Dobbie et al. (Eds.): ER 2020, LNCS 12400, pp. 271–285, 2020.
https://doi.org/10.1007/978-3-030-62522-1_20

contracts by contracting parties to ensure compliance. Smart contracts have received much attention in the literature and news recently because of their potential application in multiple areas, including Finance, Commerce, Government, and Agriculture. We are interested in developing concepts, tools, and techniques for building monitorable smart contracts. As a starting point for this endeavour, we have proposed *Symboleo*[1], a formal specification language for legal contracts [14].

Real-life contracts (e.g., in the construction and transportation industries) are complex artifacts, based on rich ontologies and expressive specification languages. They can change during execution time in the sense that obligations and powers may be cancelled by a party that has the power to do so. Assignments to parties may be changed as well through subcontracting, assignment, delegation, novation, and substitution. Intermediate contractors may further subcontract to third parties, leading to a chain of delegations of performance and responsibilities (i.e., who does what and who is responsible for what). For example, large construction projects engage multiple subcontractors in a hierarchy of contracts in order to reduce construction cost and save time [15].

The contributions of this work include (a) a set of execution-time operations that allow the sharing or change of rights, performance responsibilities, and liabilities among contracting parties; (b) syntax and axiomatic semantics for these operations; (c) the definition of the legal notions of subcontracting, assignment, and substitution in terms of the primitive operations; (d) a compliance checking tool that includes reasoning with subcontracts, substitutions, and assignments; (e) a preliminary evaluation of our proposal using a realistic freight contract with subcontracting.

The rest of the paper is structured as follows. Section 2 gives a quick overview of Symboleo, while Sect. 3 introduces primitive execution-time operations along with their syntax and semantics, which support the transfer or sharing of performance or responsibility. Section 4 discusses how the legal concepts of subcontracting, assignment, and substitution can be expressed in terms of the proposed primitive operations. In Sect. 5, we adopt a realistic freight contract from the literature, specify it in Symboleo and show how to deal with subcontracting, assignment and others with our proposal. Section 6 highlights how such contract specifications can be analyzed with a compliance checker tool. Section 7 discusses related work, while Sect. 8 concludes.

2   Overview of Symboleo

Contracts can be understood as prescriptions of allowable legal process executions. They specify obligations and powers that determine *who* is responsible to *whom* for *what* and *when*. The *how* is left to the responsible party to determine. In this respect, contracts can be seen as outcome-oriented processes, in the sense that they specify what should be the outcome of a contract execution, without

---

[1] From the Greek word $\Sigma \upsilon \mu \beta o \lambda \alpha \iota o$, meaning contract and pronounced '*simvoleo*'.

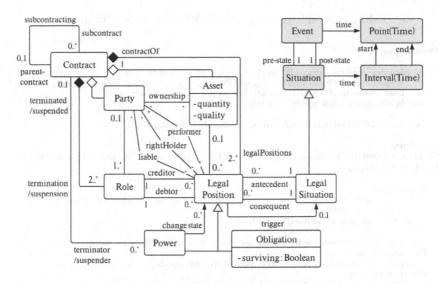

Fig. 1. Symboleo's contract ontology

specifying all the activities that have to be performed. Contracts are very different from business processes in that powers can change the status of obligations, e.g., by cancelling obligations or imposing new ones during contract execution. The concepts of our contract ontology are briefly reviewed in the following. Other definitions can be found in [14].

As shown in Symboleo's ontology (Fig. 1), a legal contract (or just **contract** henceforth) is defined as a collection of **obligations** and **powers** between two or more **roles**. A **contract** is concerned with at least one **asset** (contractual consideration) from each contractual **role**. For a contract execution, **roles** are assigned to **parties** (persons or legal entities) that take part in the contract execution.

A **legal position** is either an **obligation** or a **power** that defines a legal relationship between a **debtor** and a **creditor**, has a (possibly null) **legal situation** as activation condition (**antecedent**), and obliges the **debtor** to bring about another **legal situation** (**consequent**). **Legal positions** can be instantiated via propositional **triggers** representing a legal situation. **Obligations** are legal duties of a **debtor** towards a **creditor** to bring about a **consequent**, while **powers** define the right of a **creditor** to create, change, suspend, or cancel **legal positions**. **Antecedents**, **consequents**, and **triggers** are propositions constraining the occurrence of instantaneous **events** and **situations** holding over a time **interval**. The full ontology of Symboleo, which extends the UFO-L foundational legal ontology [6] (e.g., see shaded concepts in Fig. 1), is described in more detail in [14].

The aim of the Symboleo language is to enable contract creators to specify *parameterized* contract templates that can be instantiated with different parameter values. Symboleo's formal semantics also enables checking contracts for safety and liveness properties, which respectively verify that bad things do not happen (e.g., payment loopholes or privacy violations) and that good things eventually happen (e.g., assets will be delivered and will be paid for) during the execution of a contract instance.

Table 1. Sample sale-of-goods (SOG) contract specification

Domain salesD

/* Includes concepts that are specializations of the contract ontology concepts such as Buyer/Seller, Goods and Delivered/Paid, which are specializations of Role, Asset and Event, respectively. Additional attributes may also be specified. */
Goods **isA** Asset **with** goodsID: Integer;
...
Delivered **isA** Event **with** delAddress: String, delDueDate: Date;

endDomain
Contract salesC(seller: Seller, buyer: Buyer, ID: Integer, amnt: Integer, curr: Currency, delAdd, delDd: String)

   Declarations
   /* Here, the values of the parameters are passed on to the variables that were defined in the domain model. */
   goods : Goods **with** goodsID := ID;
   ...
   delivered : Delivered **with** delAddress := delAdd, delDueDate := delDd;
   Preconditions
   isOwner(seller, goods) AND NOT isOwner(buyer, goods);
   Postconditions
   isOwner(buyer, goods) AND NOT isOwner(seller, goods);
   Obligations
   O_1 : O(Seller, Buyer, true, **happensBefore**(delivered, delivered.delDueD));
   O_2 : O(Buyer, Seller, true, **happensBefore**(paid, paid.payDueD));
   Powers
   P_1 : **violates**(O_2, _) → P(Seller, Buyer, true, **terminates**(salesC));
   SurvivingObl
   /* Some obligations will remain active even after the contract has terminated successfully, namely confidentiality obligations. */
   Constraints
   not(isEqual(buyer, seller));

endContract

We illustrate the workings of Symboleo using a sale-of-goods example. Suppose there is a contract between a buyer and a seller, consisting of three template clauses, namely two obligations and one power (*right*) guarded by a trigger:

O1. The Seller shall deliver the Goods <*goodsID*> to the Buyer at address <*delAdd*> before the delivery due date <*delDd*>.
O2. The Buyer shall pay the amount of <*amnt*> in currency <*curr*> to the Seller before the payment due date <*payDd*>.
P1. In case of violation of the payment obligation (O2), the Seller has the right to terminate the contract.

A contract specification has a *domain* section and a *contract body* section (Table 1). Domain-dependent concepts and axioms are defined in the domain section as specializations of Symboleo's ontology (Fig. 1). The contract body starts with the contract's *signature*, which contains parameters and their types. Parameter values are used to instantiate a contract. Aside from the specification of obligations, powers, and *surviving obligations* (that persist after the successful termination of a contract, e.g., a non-disclosure clause), pre/post-conditions and constraints on the contract execution are also specified in the contract body.

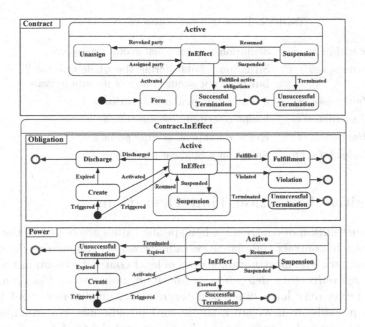

Fig. 2. UML statecharts for obligations, powers, and contracts [14]

The first two clauses of this contract are obligations (O_1 and O_2 respectively), while the third is a power (P_1). As seen in the example, legal positions have as signatures [trigger→] $O(debtor, creditor, antecedent, consequent)$ for obligations and [trigger→] $P(creditor, debtor, antecedent, consequent)$ for powers.

The lifecycle of a contract/obligation/power instance is captured by UML statecharts defined in Fig. 2 [14]. State transitions are events that are recorded on ledgers (preferably with assured integrity as in blockchains) that enable the monitoring function of smart contracts. A contract is initially in its Form state and transitions to the InEffect state when it is signed and its effective date is reached. Since O_1 and O_2 do not have a trigger (true by default), they transition to the Create state when the contract transitions to the InEffect state. However, P_1 will be instantiated whenever its trigger becomes true, i.e., the event $violated(O_2)$ happens or O_2 transitions to the Violation state. After becoming InEffect (i.e., the antecedent becomes true), the creditor of P_1 has the power to bring about the consequent (exertion of power), i.e., transitioning the contract to the Unsuccessful Termination state, which results in all other active obligations and powers transitioning to their Unsuccessful Termination state. After exertion, the power itself transitions to its Successful Termination state.

The statecharts act as the baseline for Symboleo's semantics. In [14], the semantics of transitions are given in terms of axioms that use the predicates listed in Table 2, inspired by the Event Calculus [13].

Table 2. Primitive predicates of Symboleo

e within s	Situation s holds when event e happens
occurs(s, T)	Situation s holds during the whole interval T, but does not occur in any of its subintervals
Initiates(e, s)	Event e brings about situation s
Terminates(e, s)	Event e terminates situation s
Happens(e, t)	Event e happens at time point t
HoldsAt(s, t)	Situation s holds at time point t

3   Primitive Execution-Time Operations

During the execution of contracts, when specific values are bound to the parameter variables of contract templates, certain *operations* can change the contract state at runtime. The most notable types of legal contract execution-time operations are *subcontracting, delegation, substitution, novation* and *assignment.*

These terms may have different interpretations in different legal jurisdictions, and possibly even within a single legal jurisdiction. For example, while *assignment* is defined as transferring the claims and rights of an assignor to an assignee in the Common Law system, some courts in the USA will also treat it as transferring a contract as a whole, depending on the intentions inferred from the assignment clause [9].

Despite various intention-dependent definitions, the actions underlying these operations can be categorised as sharing or transferring rights, responsibilities, or performance of parties. In this paper, we have extended the original Symboleo ontology [14] with such relationships, defined between Party and Legal Position in Fig. 1. Note that "liable" here is a synonym of "responsible". From a syntactic viewpoint:

- **rightHolder(x, p):** for an obligation/power instance x, party p is *rightHolder.*

- **liable(x, p):** for an obligation/power instance x, party p is *liable.*

- **performer(x, p):** for an obligation/power instance x, party p is *performer.*

These terms are used in **Axioms** 1, 2, 3 and 4 of the augmented axiomatic semantics of Symboleo, based on the predicates of Table 2. For all obligation instances o, power instances *pow.* and party instances p, there exists a time point t for which the following hold:

$$happens(activated(o), t) \; \wedge \; holdsAt(bind(o.debtor, p), t)$$
$$\rightarrow initiates(activated(o), liable(o, p)) \wedge initiates(activated(o), performer(o, p)) \tag{1}$$

$$happens(activated(o), t) \; \wedge \; holdsAt(bind(o.creditor, p), t)$$
$$\rightarrow initiates(happens(activated(o), rightHolder(o, p)) \tag{2}$$

Table 3. Primitive execution-time operations

$shareR(x, p)$	Party p becomes a rightHolder for obligation/power instance x
$shareL(x, p)$	Party p becomes liable for obligation/power instance x
$shareP(x, p)$	Party p becomes a performer for obligation/power instance x
$transferR(x, p_{old}, p_{new})$	Party p_{new} becomes a rightHolder for obligation/power instance x and p_{old} is no longer a rightHolder for x
$transferL(x, p_{old}, p_{new})$	Party p_{new} becomes liable for obligation/power instance x and p_{old} will no longer be liable for x
$transferP(x, p_{old}, p_{new})$	Party p_{new} becomes a performer for obligation/power instance x and p_{old} is no longer a rightHolder performer for x

$$
\begin{aligned}
happens(activated(pow), t) \ \wedge \ & holdsAt(bind(pow.creditor, p), t) \\
\rightarrow \ initiates(activated(pow), & rightHolder(pow, p)) \\
\wedge \ initiates(activated(pow), & performer(pow, p))
\end{aligned} \tag{3}
$$

$$
\begin{aligned}
happens(activated(pow), t) \ \wedge \ & holdsAt(bind(pow.debtor, p), t) \\
\rightarrow \ initiates(activated(pow), & liable(pow, p))
\end{aligned} \tag{4}
$$

In other words, after the time an obligation instance o is activated, the party bound to the debtor role of o is the *performer* of o and is *liable* for o (**Axiom 1**), and the party bound to the creditor role of o is the *rightHolder* of o (**Axiom 2**).

After the time a power instance *pow* is activated, the party bound to the creditor role of *pow* is the *rightHolder* and the *performer* of *pow* (**Axiom 3**), and the party bound to the debtor role of pow is *liable* for *pow* (**Axiom 4**).

Based on the above axioms, we define a set of primitive contract execution-time operations (Table 3) to express what can happen during the execution of a contract instance. An execution-time operation is initiated/terminated by an event with a corresponding name (e.g., *shareR* is initiated/terminated using event *shared R*). The semantics of the primitive sharing and transfer operations defined in Table 3 are exemplified with *shareR* and *transferR* (a party can share or transfer her rights under a contract to another party). The semantics of the other four primitive operations are defined with similar axioms not presented here due to space limitations.

Axiom 5: Given active obligation/power instance x, party p, and the fact that $sharedR(x, p)$ is the event that initiates the sharing of x with p, at some time t the following holds:

$$
\begin{aligned}
happens(sharedR(x, p), t) \ \wedge \ holdsAt(active(x), t) \ \rightarrow \\
initiates(sharedR(x, p), rightHolder(x, p))
\end{aligned} \tag{5}
$$

Axiom 6: Given active obligation/power instance x, party instances p_{new} and p_{old}, and the fact that $transferredR(x, p_{old}, p_{new})$ is the event that initiates the transfer of rights, then the following holds:

$$happens(transferredR(x, p_{old}, p_{new}), t) \wedge holdsAt(active(x), t) \wedge$$
$$holdsAt(rightHolder(x, p_{old}), t) \rightarrow$$
$$initiates(transferredR(x, p_{old}, p_{new}), rightHolder(x, p_{new})) \wedge \tag{6}$$
$$terminates(transferredR(x, p_{old}, p_{new}), rightHolder(x, p_{old}))$$

These new primitive operation can now be used to implement various interpretations (e.g., from different jurisdictions) of contract execution-time operations. The next section defines three operations for general international law.

4   Assignment, Substitution, and Subcontracting

Although execution-time operations can have different meanings according to the practices in different jurisdictions or the intentions of the contractual parties, we focus here on the definitions of *assignment (of rights)*, *substitution (of contractual parties)*, and *subcontracting* due to their more stable and consistent definitions in different contexts and their frequent application in everyday practice.

We formally specify syntax (parametric shorthand) and semantics (axioms) for these operations in Symboleo, to enable contract performance monitoring. Shorthands are situations in Symboleo and are captured as Prolog predicates in our tool. In the following axioms, O and P respectively represent the sets of all obligation instances and all power instances in the contract. Also, the dot (.) operator is used in some axioms to navigate our ontology, à la OCL.

Assignment (of rights): $assignR(\{x_1, ..., x_n\}, p_{old}, p_{new})$
Semantics: A party can assign the rights that she is entitled to under a contract to a third-party [9]. Its axiom builds upon $transferR$ (Axiom 6).
Axiom 7: For any set of obligation/power instances $x = \{x_1, ..., x_n\}$ that party p_{old} is the rightHolder of, if p_{old} assigns her rights for x to another party p_{new}, then the rights for x are transferred from p_{old} to p_{new}. Here, $assignedR(x, p)$ is the event that initiates the assignment, leading to many primitive transfers.

$$\forall x \in \mathcal{P}(O \cup P), \forall x_i \in x : happens(assignedR(x, p_{old}, p_{new}), t) \wedge$$
$$holdsAt(rightHolder(x_i, p_{old}), t) \rightarrow happens(transferredR(x_i, p_{old}, p_{new}), t) \tag{7}$$

Contractual Party Substitution: $substituteC(c, r, p_{old}, p_{new})$
Semantics: A party p_{old} who has a role r in contract c can substitute herself with another party p_{new} and transfer all of the rights, responsibilities, and performance of all the active obligations/powers x to p_{new}, given the consent of all original parties and of p_{new} [9].

Axiom 8: Given the consent of p_{old}, p_{new}, and other parties of the contract c to $substituteC(c, r, p_{old}, p_{new})$, and given contract c, obligation/power x, and role r, and the fact that $substitutedC(c, r, p_{old}, p_{new})$ is the event that occurs and initiates the substitution, then there exists a time t for which this holds:

$$\forall x \in c.legalPosition : happens(consented(substitutedC(c, r, p_{old}, p_{new})), t)$$
$$\wedge\ happens(substitutedC(c, r, p_{old}, p_{new}), t)\ \wedge\ holdsAt(active(c), t)$$
$$\wedge\ holdsAt(bind(c.r, p_{old}), t)\ \rightarrow$$
$$initiates(substitutedC(c, r, p_{old}, p_{new}), bind(c.r, p_{new}))$$
$$\wedge\ terminates(substitutedC(c, r, p_{old}, p_{new}), bind(c.r, p_{old})) \tag{8}$$
$$\wedge\ happens(transferredR(c.x, p_{old}, p_{new}), t)$$
$$\wedge\ happens(transferredL(c.x, p_{old}, p_{new}), t)$$
$$\wedge\ happens(transferredP(c.x, p_{old}, p_{new}), t)$$

Subcontracting: $subcontract(\{o_1, ..., o_m\}$ **to** $\{\{c_1, pa_1\}, ..., \{c_n, pa_n\}\}$ **with** $\{constr_1, ..., constr_n\})$. Subcontracting involves sharing performance of a set of contractual obligations with one or more other parties through subcontracts $c_1, ..., c_n$. Since single contractual counter-party is a simple and popular case of subcontracting, this paper focuses on this case and leaves the generic forms (i.e., multiple multilateral subcontracts) to future work.

Semantics: As Axiom 9 indicates, subcontracting is a legal way of granting new parties this privilege. Subcontractors fulfill the subcontracted obligations once they successfully terminate the corresponding well-designed subcontracts, which trigger events that bring about the consequents of the delegated obligations.

For instance, a seller may hire a carrier to transport goods from a warehouse to port A, another one to ship the goods from port A to port B, and a third one to transport the goods from port B to the final destination. In this case, successful termination of three subcontracts fulfills the corresponding obligations of the original contract. However, *violation*, *suspension*, and *unsuccessful termination* of subcontracts do not alter the state of the original contract's obligations since the contractor, as a liable party and primary performer, can run an alternative plan (e.g., subcontractor replacement) and consequently fulfill its original obligations. Contractors may stipulate some constraints to supervise further subcontracts, e.g., to acquire a main contractor's consent to shift its burden to a third party.

Axiom 9: For any set of obligation instances o in O that is *subcontracted* out under a set of contracts in C to a set of parties in PA subject to a set of domain assumptions expressed as additional propositional constraints $(\{constr_1, ..., constr_n\})$, then the performance of all subcontracted obligations is shared with all of the (sub)contractual counter-parties.

$$\forall o \in \mathcal{P}(O), \forall cp \in \mathcal{P}(C \times PA) :$$
$$happens(subcontracted(o, cp, \{constr_1, ..., constr_n\}), t)\ \wedge \tag{9}$$
$$constr_1 \wedge ... \wedge constr_n\ \rightarrow \forall o_i \in o, \forall (c, pa) \in cp : happens(sharedP(o_i, pa), t)$$

5   Case Study: Multiple Freights as Subcontracts

The sale-of-goods contract from Sect. 2 has a delivery clause, and there are many examples of businesses subcontracting such obligations to third parties under a separate contract whose post-condition implies the satisfaction of the subcontracted obligation's consequent. One of the results (post-conditions) of a *Freight contract*'s successful completion (e.g., Tables 4 and 5) is that the goods (meat here) have been delivered by the *Shipper* to the desired delivery address (*delAdd*). Likewise, for proper chaining, a precondition allows execution of a freight contract only if the goods have been delivered to the required lading location (*pkAdd*).

Subcontracting of an obligation is the act of delegating the satisfaction of a consequent (*contractual performance*) of that obligation to another party under a new contract [9]. The subcontract, also a contract, can be created at runtime via a power that *implicitly* exists in the contract (as stated in formula 10). Right holders of such powers are restricted to subcontract obligations for which they are liable and all partners consent. The power to assign claims and subcontracts are present for both parties unless explicitly disallowed in the *constraints* part of the contract specification.

$$
\begin{aligned}
pow_x : P\,(&creditor, debtor, rightHolder(pow_x) = Liable(o_1) = ... = Liable(o_m) \wedge \\
&(\forall c \in \{c_1, ..., c_n\}, \exists r \in c.Role, bind(r, rightHolder(pow_x))) \wedge \\
&(\forall p \in PA, \forall o \in \{o_1, .., o_m\} : p = Liable(o) \rightarrow \\
&\quad happens(consented(p, subcontracted(o, \{(c_1, p_1), ..., (c_n, p_n)\}), \_))), \\
&happens(subcontracted(\{o_1, ..., o_m\}, \{(c_1, p_1), ..., (c_n, p_n)\}), \_))
\end{aligned}
\tag{10}
$$

The contract in Table 4 is a freight agreement between a shipper of goods (meat) and a carrier who provides shipping services. Table 5 contains a (non-instantiated) specification that will act as a template for the subcontract(s) of the delivery obligation of the sample contract introduced in Sect. 2.

Assume the seller's warehouse of the sales-of-goods (SOG) example from Table 1 is located in Buenos Aires (Argentina) and the buyer's warehouse is located in Ottawa (Canada). The seller might decide not to fulfill the delivery obligation by himself, but rather would subcontract it to three different carriers: one to $carrier_{BA}$, for freight from the seller's warehouse to the port of Buenos Aires; one to $carrier_{Hal}$, for freight from Buenos Aires to Halifax; and one to $carrier_{Ott}$ for freight from Halifax to the buyer's warehouse in Ottawa. Notice that the pre/post-conditions of the freight contract specification ensure that all three freight contracts are executed sequentially. For example, the freight contract from Halifax to Ottawa is not executed before the goods are delivered to Halifax as a result of the successful execution of the contract with $carrier_{Hal}$.

6   Analysis

Contracts can be very complex artifacts that hide unwelcome consequences for some of their parties. To mitigate this risk, we developed an analysis tool[2] that

---

[2] The tool is available at https://sites.google.com/uottawa.ca/csmlab.

Table 4. Freight contract template example

Agreement is entered into effect between *<party1>* as Shipper, and *<party2>* as Carrier.
O1 The Carrier agrees to transport the goods as stated in tender sheet (*<qnt>* of *<qlty>* quality meat, in proper refrigerated conditions, from *<pkAdd>*, to *<delAdd>* on *<delDueDate>*).
O2 The Shipper should pay *<amt>* ("amount") in *<curr>* ("currency") to the Carrier for its services within 3 days after delivery of goods.
O3 The Shipper is additionally subjected to *<intRate>*% interest rate on the amount due if payment is breached.

Table 5. Freight contract specification in Symboleo

Domain freightD

Shipper **isA** Role **with** pickupAddress: String;
Carrier **isA** Role **with** office: String;
Meat **isA** PerishableGood **isA** Asset **with** quantity: Integer, quality: MeatQuality;
Paid **isA** Event **with** amount: Integer, currency: Currency, from: Role, to: Role, payDueDate: Date;
Delivered **isA** Event **with** item : Meat, delAddress: String, delDueDate: Date;
MeatQuality **isA** Enumeration('PRIME', 'AAA', 'AA', 'A');
terminates{delivered, paid};

endDomain

Contract freightC(shipper: Shipper, carrier: Carrier, effDate: Date, qnt: Integer, qlty: MeatQuality, amt: Integer, curr: Currency, delAdd: String, delDd: Date, pkAdd: String, intRate: Integer)

    Declarations
        goods : Meat **with** quantity := qnt, quality := qlty;
        paid : Paid **with** amount := amt, currency := curr, from := shipper, to := carrier,
            dueD:=payDueDate;
        paidLate : Paid **with** amount := amt*(1 + intRate/100), currency := curr, from :=
            shipper, to := carrier;
        delivered . Delivered **with** item := goods, delAddress := delAdd, delDueDate := delDd;
        atLocation : Situation **with** what : Asset, where : String; // *External situ. monitoring*
    Preconditions
        atLocation(goods, pkAdd)
    Postconditions
        atLocation(goods, delAdd)
    Obligations
        O_1 : O(carrier, shipper, true, happensBefore(delivered, delivered.delDueDate));
        O_2 : **happens**(delivered, t) → O(shipper, carrier, true, happensBefore(paid, t + 3 days));
        O_3 : **violates**(O_2) → O(shipper, carrier, true, **happens**(paidLate, _));
    Powers // *None*
    SurvivingObls // *None*
    Constraints
        not(isEqual(shipper, carrier));

endContract

takes as input a set of scenarios (each consisting of a sequence of events), along with the expected final states of the contract for each scenario, and actually runs each scenario to validate that it does end in the expected final state. The tool was implemented by using an existing reactive event calculus tool (jREC [10]), written in Java and Prolog, which was extended to support the Symboleo semantics and performs abductive reasoning on given scenarios. We designed six

Table 6. Test cases

Test case	Freight	SOG
1. Buyer pays off order but Carrier delivers the meat under inappropriate conditions resulting in spoiled meat	V1	V1, Fu2
2. Carrier's transport is unable to ship loaded meat, and instead the shipper (i.e., Seller) delivers it himself to the Buyer under proper conditions before due date, and gets paid	V1	Fu1, Fu2
3. Buyer refuses payment and neither Carrier nor Shipper delivers the meat till 10 days after due date	V1	V1, V2, A3
4. Carrier delivers meat while Shipper awaits more than 10 days for Buyer's payment	V2, A3	Fu1, V2, A3
5. Buyer refuses to pay off the agreed amount before due date and then the Seller terminates the contract and does not allow unloading the good at due location	V1	V2, ST3, UT_{SOG}
6. Buyer pays original Seller after assigning payment rights to a third party	-	V2, A3

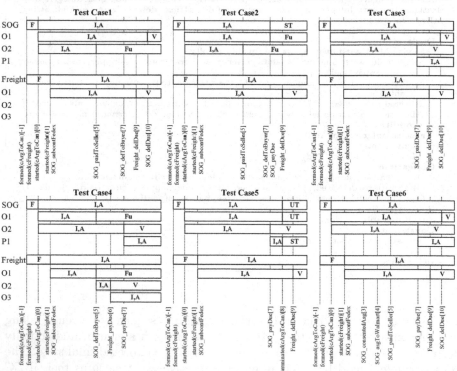

Fig. 3. Test results showing the states of contracts/clauses over events[time]

scenarios and corresponding test cases (Table 6) combining the SOG and Freight contracts. All tests involve meat sales between a seller in Argentina and a buyer in Ottawa, with freight subcontracting to a carrier. These test cases cover many possible states of obligations, powers, and contracts, especially boundary cases.

In Table 6 and Fig. 3, V = Violation, F = Form, Fu = Fulfillment, I = InEffect, A = Active, UT = Unsuccessful Termination, and ST = Successful Termination of a contractual clause (i.e., states from Fig. 2). For example, the first test case violates the first obligation(V1) of Freight and (V1) of SOG, but fulfills SOG's second obligation (Fu2). In Fig. 3, the vertical axis shows the states of the contracts and their clauses (O1, O2, O3, P1), and the horizontal axis characterizes events over time (with time units between brackets). The delivery obligation is subcontracted to the Fedex carrier (SOG_subcontFedex) through a freight contract. However, in Test Case 6, after consent, Fedex assigns its payment rights to Walmart. As the freight contract proceeds independently, the delivery obligation of the freight contract stays active after the termination of SOG until its due date arrives and violates the obligation at time 9. Our tool monitors runtime responsibility, right, and performance relationships of parties. The results indicate that the execution of these tests complies with expected results, which partially validates Symboleo's axioms and our new subcontracting and substitution operations.

7   Related Work

Multi-agent systems investigate runtime commitment operations, namely delegation and assignment. Kafalı and Torroni [7] propose eight forms of social commitment delegations by discharging and instantiating commitments. Implicit and explicit delegations partially express semantics of obligation delegation and substitution operations respectively. Implicit operation generates a commitment between a party and a third party while keeping the original commitment. Explicit operations cancel the original commitment and then create the new commitment. They also introduce causal delegation chains and delegation trees to perform reasoning on sequences of delegated commitments [8]. Similar to explicit operations, Chesani et al. [3] and Dalpiaz et al. [5] formalize commitment delegation and assignment by means of debtor and creditor replacement axioms, respectively. This delegation transfers responsibility. In contrast, the approaches of Chopra and Singh [4] and Yolum and Sing [16] hold the responsibility of the original debtor. These operations, compared to Symboleo's, shift liability and performance altogether and deal only with social norms. Delegation semantics are incomplete since the fulfillment/violation influence of an implicit delegation on the original commitment is not defined.

Legal liability, right, and delegation concepts have been studied through temporal logics. Sartor [12] develops notions of obligative and permissive rights, which express the right of debtors and creditors, respectively, regarding Hohfeldian concepts. These legal positions are manipulated at runtime by means of potestative right and legal power normative operations. Norman and Reed [11] adopt tense logic axiomatization to specify the semantics of responsibility and performance transmission and sharing during obligation delegation. In a similar fashion, these legal notions are formally expressed by a CTL*-based logic [1]. These languages typically specify primary legal norms such as right holder and responsibility delegation, whereas Symboleo considers runtime operations at the level of substitution, assignment, and subcontracting via primary operations.

8 Conclusions and Future Work

This paper advances the state-of-the-art by extending Symboleo with execution-time operations supporting dynamic assignment of rights, consensual substitution of a contractual party, and subcontracting of obligations. Primitive operations for the sharing and transfer of right, responsibility, and performance of legal positions enable the support of higher-level operations in specific jurisdictions. Axiomatic semantics were defined and prototyped in a compliance checker, which enabled some initial validation for various scenarios involving a sale-of-good contract and a freight sub-contract. These contributions open the door to powerful and necessary functionalities for monitoring legal contracts.

For future work, we intend to further generalize our language and axioms to support multiple multilateral subcontracts, and to improve Symboleo's syntax to make it more usable by legal experts. We will also make our compliance checker more general and robust. Moreover, we propose to convert Symboleo specifications to nuXmv [2], to model check properties for contracts.

Acknowledgment. The authors thank E. Jonchères, V. Callipel, D. Restrepo Amariles, P. Bacquero, F. Gélinas, G. Sileno, T. van Engers, and T. van Binsbergen (lawyers and professors from the Autonomy Through Cyberjustice Technologies project) for their feedback on Symboleo and guidance on subcontracting, as well as A. Roudak for his feedback on our compliance checker.

References

1. Aldewereld, H., Dignum, V., Vasconcelos, W.W.: Group norms for multi-agent organisations. ACM Trans. Auton. Adapt. Syst. (TAAS) **11**(2), 1–31 (2016)
2. Cavada, R., et al.: The NUXMV symbolic model checker. In: Biere, A., Bloem, R. (eds.) CAV 2014. LNCS, vol. 8559, pp. 334–342. Springer, Cham (2014). https://doi.org/10.1007/978-3-319-08867-9_22
3. Chesani, F., Mello, P., Montali, M., Torroni, P.: Representing and monitoring social commitments using the event calculus. Auton. Agents Multi-Agent Syst. **27**(1), 85–130 (2013)
4. Chopra, A.K., Singh, M.P.: Multiagent commitment alignment. In: Proceedings of The 8th International Conference on Autonomous Agents and Multiagent Systems, vol 2, pp. 937–944. FAAMAS (2009)
5. Dalpiaz, F., Cardoso, E., Canobbio, G., Giorgini, P., Mylopoulos, J.: Social specifications of business processes with Azzurra. In: 9th International Conference on Research Challenges in Information Science (RCIS), pp. 7–18. IEEE CS (2015)

6. Guizzardi, G., Wagner, G., Almeida, J.P.A., Guizzardi, R.S.: Towards ontologi- cal foundations for conceptual modeling: the unified foundational ontology (UFO) story. Appl. Ontology **10**(3–4), 259–271 (2015)
7. Kafalı, Ö., Torroni, P.: Social commitment delegation and monitoring. In: Leite, J., Torroni, P., Ågotnes, T., Boella, G., van der Torre, L. (eds.) CLIMA 2011. LNCS (LNAI), vol. 6814, pp. 171–189. Springer, Heidelberg (2011). https://doi.org/10. 1007/978-3-642-22359-4_13
8. Kafalı, Ö., Torroni, P.: Comodo: collaborative monitoring of commitment delega- tions. Expert Syst. Appl. **105**, 144–158 (2018)
9. Kirby, J.: Assignments and transfers of contractual duties: integrating theory and practice. Victoria U. Wellington L. Rev. **31**, 317 (2000)
10. Montali, M.: jREC (2016). https://www.inf.unibz.it/~montali/tools.html
11. Norman, T.J., Reed, C.: A logic of delegation. Artif. Intell. **174**(1), 51–71 (2010)
12. Sartor, G.: Fundamental legal concepts: a formal and teleological characterisation. Artif. Intell. Law **14**(1–2), 101–142 (2006). https://doi.org/10.1007/s10506-006- 9009-x
13. Shanahan, M.: The event calculus explained. In: Wooldridge, M.J., Veloso, M. (eds.) Artificial Intelligence Today. LNCS (LNAI), vol. 1600, pp. 409–430. Springer, Heidelberg (1999). https://doi.org/10.1007/3-540-48317-9_17
14. Sharifi, S., Parvizimosaed, A., Amyot, D., Logrippo, L., Mylopoulos, J.: Symboleo: A specification language for smart contracts. In: 28th IEEE International Require- ments Engineering Conference (RE 2020), IEEE CS, pp. 384–389 (2020)
15. Tam, V.W., Shen, L., Kong, J.S.: Impacts of multi-layer chain subcontracting on project management performance. Int. J. Proj. Manag. **29**(1), 108–116 (2011)
16. Yolum, P., Singh, M.P.: Reasoning about commitments in the event calculus: an approach for specifying and executing protocols. Ann. Math. Artif. Intell. **42**(1–3), 227–253 (2004)

Ontology and Conceptual Modeling

Towards a Reference Ontology for Digital Platforms

Thomas Derave[1]([X]) (iD), Tiago Prince Sales[2]([X]) (iD), Frederik Gailly[1]([X]) (iD),
and Geert Poels[1]([X]) (iD)

[1] Department of Business Informatics and Operations Management, Ghent University,
Tweekerkenstraat 2, 9000 Ghent, Belgium
{thomas.derave,frederik.gailly,geert.poels}@UGent.be
[2] Faculty of Computer Science, Free University of Bozen-Bolzano, Bolzano, Italy
tiago.princesales@unibz.it

Abstract. Digital platforms can be categorized into different types including
'multi-sided platform', 'digital marketplace', 'crowdfunding platform', 'sharing
economy platform' and 'on-demand platform'. As there is a lack of knowledge
regarding the requirements and design of these digital platform types, we developed a method to design a digital platform reference ontology based on a taxonomy. The taxonomy provides an overview of digital platform properties, with
the property values expressing the possible variations between digital platforms
depending on their type. For each property value, we can create a digital platform
reference ontology module using the five-step approach proposed by Ruy et al.
[1] based on the patterns of the Unified Foundational Ontology (UFO). UFO is a
high-level ontology that provides us with basic concepts for objects, events, social
elements and their types, relations and properties. These digital platform reference
ontology modules can be combined as building blocks to compose our reference
ontology for expressing the functionality for digital platforms of all types. We
believe this reference ontology can be a step towards a better understanding of
digital platform functionality, better communication between stakeholders and
eventually may facilitate future research and development of digital platforms.

Keywords: Digital platform · Multi-sided platform · UFO · Ontology ·
Taxonomy

1 Introduction

The platform economy refers to activities in business, culture and social interaction that
are performed on or are intermediated by digital platforms [2]. Well-known examples of
such platforms are Airbnb, eBay, Etsy, Ticketswap, Tinder, Lime and Uber. Characteristic
of the platform economy is that these activities were previously provided differently by
firms [3, 4]. Information technology is the most important original enabling force of
the platform economy. Therefore, the platform economy is not only a new economic
phenomenon, but also a success of advances in information technology [5].

© Springer Nature Switzerland AG 2020
G. Dobbie et al. (Eds.): ER 2020, LNCS 12400, pp. 289–302, 2020.
https://doi.org/10.1007/978-3-030-62522-1_21

Existing digital platforms categorized in types like digital marketplace, on-demand platform and multi-sided platform, have a lot in common, but also have substantial differences in functionality. However, there is little research on the platform economy from the perspective of information technology, as most studies looked into business models and economic/societal impact [5]. Consequently, there is a lack of knowledge regarding the requirements and design of the different types of digital platforms. Therefore, it is not known whether software products for developing platforms, like the open-source Sharetribe Go [6] for creating sharing economy platforms, support all the functionality expected for a certain type of platform.

This paper contributes to filling the lack of knowledge of digital platform functionality by proposing a method using the patterns of the Unified Foundational Ontology (UFO) [7] to create a reference ontology. Following our method, the reference ontology will be based on a taxonomy that was already developed as a first part of this research project. The taxonomy gives an overview of digital platform properties, with the property values expressing the possible variations between digital platforms depending on their type. For each property value, we plan to create a digital platform reference ontology module. The entirety of these modules composes the reference ontology, which thus describes the general functionality of any digital platform and the more specific functionality of each digital platform type in relation to its property values as defined in the taxonomy. By organizing the ontology into modules, it is possible to select and combine modules to create a unique ontology for each digital platform type. Additionally, when new platform types arise, additional ontology modules can be added to the reference ontology. As a result, our reference ontology can accommodate the evolution of the sharing economy and combine existing and emerging platform variations to model new types.

We believe this reference ontology can be a step towards a better understanding of digital platform functionality. Apart from supporting communication between stakeholders in platform development, it can support ontology-driven development of platforms. Summarizing, the reference ontology is envisioned as a common language for expressing digital platform functionality that can be used to facilitate future research and development of digital platforms.

This paper is structured as follows; In Sect. 2 we provide background on the digital platform taxonomy created in previous research. In Sect. 3 we explain our methodology for creating the reference ontology. In Sect. 4 we present two modules of our ontology, as the other modules are work in progress. After, we discuss the validation of our ontology using an ontology expert. In Sect. 5 we discuss limitations and future research and in Sect. 6 we give the conclusion.

2   Background: Digital Platform Taxonomy

The digital platform taxonomy was created during previous research following the method of Nickerson et al. [8]. As background to the reference ontology design presented in this paper, we present a simplified version of the taxonomy development and resulting taxonomy schema.

First, a working definition of a digital platform was defined. Due to the dispersal of digital platform research across a number of fields, there is a miscellany of perspectives concerning a digital platform. To reach our objective, the working definition of a digital platform needs to be independent of its type. As we wish to cover a wide range of digital platform types, we relate the platform economy to the broader concept of service economy, and therefore combine the knowledge of [2, 9–11] in defining a digital platform as 'a service offering by the digital platform management to the users that may be bound to an agreement. The primary service offered are interactions between users and these interactions are enabled by a software system'. This definition is very broad, as the intended interactions can consist solely of information transfer (e.g. WhatsApp, Tinder) but can also include offerings of products (e.g. eBay), services (e.g. Airbnb) or investments (e.g. Kickstarter).

Second, we searched for secondary studies (literature reviews) on digital platforms to identify digital platform types and their definitions. Our literature search ended up with six literature reviews [3, 12–16]. Out of these literature reviews and the primary sources they refer to (and which we also studied), nine digital platform types where identified: Multi-Sided (MS) platform [17]; transaction platform [18]; investment platform [11]; crowdfunding platform [19]; digital marketplace [20]; Peer-to-Peer (P2P) sharing and collaborative consumption platform [21]; sharing economy platform [22]; on-demand platform [23]; and second-hand P2P platform [18]. Third, we compared the definitions of these nine types to each other to identify the digital platform properties whose values distinguish between these types. And during the last step, we conceptualized and validated the properties and property values using a sample of existing platforms[1]. The resulting taxonomy schema is shown in Table 1.

Table 1. Digital platform taxonomy schema

Property	Values				
Market sides	One-sided			Multi-Sided	
Affiliation	Registration	Subscription	Main Content Creation	Transaction	Investment
Centralization	Decentralized			Centralized	
Participation	B2C		B2B	P2P	C2C
Offering orientation	Product		Result		User
Immediate access	True			False	
Under-utilized	True			False	

---

[1] The full sample of existing digital platforms we used in our validation can be found on http://model-a-platform.com/sample-of-existing-digital-platforms/.

Market sides [17] is the number of different groups of platform users. Affiliation [16] refers to different ways that users (per group) can be connected to the platform. Centralization [12, 24] is the way the users can connect to each other. This can be via a decentralized search by the users of one side, or via a centralized, automated matching by the platform software. Participation and offering orientation are only applicable if the platform has multiple sides. Participation [20, 25] indicates if the market that is intermediated by the platform is Business-to-Business (B2B), Business-to-Consumer (B2C), Consumer-to-Consumer (C2C) or Peer-to-Peer (P2P); the latter case holds when platform participants are considered as 'equals', where C2C is a specialisation of P2P when users of at least two sides are only allowed to be private persons. The offering orientation [26] differentiates between product selling, result-oriented services or user-oriented offerings including leasing, renting, sharing and pooling of a product. Finally, immediate access and under-utilized capacity are only relevant for user-oriented offerings. A digital platform offers immediate access [27, 28] if the offering can be provided at the moment of ordering. Under-utilized [22] indicates excess capacity of the offered product.

3 Methodology

Our research methodology for building and evaluating the envisioned reference ontology for digital platforms is shown in Fig. 1 and explained below.

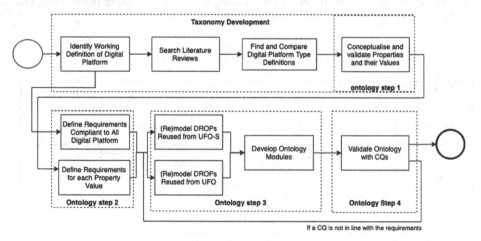

Fig. 1. Methodology

The taxonomy schema of Sect. 2 gives a structured overview of the properties and property values of digital platforms. Each unique combination of property values provides an intentional definition of a digital platform type, some of which might have an empty extension as no instances have been developed yet. Based on these intentional definitions, we develop the digital platform reference ontology. Our ontology development process uses the patterns of the UFO, a high-level ontology that provides us with basic concepts for objects, events, social elements and their types, relations and properties [7]. To create the reference ontology, we use the five-step approach proposed by Ruy et al [1].

1. The first step is to modularize the digital platform domain. These modules are already provided by our taxonomy schema, as we create an ontology module for each property value. This means that the reference ontology can model any digital platform type that is defined by the taxonomy by combining the relevant ontology modules.
2. A second step is to define requirements for each module. These are the requirements that a digital platform has to fulfil to be defined as an instance of a certain digital platform type. First, we define the requirements related to the general functionality of any digital platform. For this, we reuse the literature-based working definition that we used for the taxonomy development in Sect. 2. After, requirements for the different property values are defined.
3. In a third step we develop the ontology. First, the requirements are modelled using Domain-Related Ontology Patterns (DROPs). A DROP represents a recurrent modelling fragment in a certain domain. Conform the approach of [1], we searched for core ontologies we can reuse. A digital platform can be seen as a service offering to its users, and depending on the type the users are able to offer services (apart from other types of product) through the digital platform. For part of the requirements we therefore reuse UFO-S [29], a core ontology that provides a clear account of service-related concepts, to extract DROPs. The other requirements are then modelled using DROPs directly reused from the foundational UFO ontology. All DROPs are developed by analogy [30], i.e. reproducing and completing the structure with the specific knowledge, using OntoUML [31], a UFO-based conceptual modelling language that is capable of representing objects, events and social entities. After, we combine the DROPs into ontology modules; a general reference ontology module compliant with all digital platforms and a separate ontology module for each property value. In this paper we only present the one-sided and multi-sided ontology modules.
4. The fourth step is the validation. We use the method of [32] to define Competency Questions (CQs) as a set of queries that the ontology must be capable of answering in order to be considered competent for conceptualizing the domain it was intended for [33]. These CQs are asked to ontology experts to check if our ontology modules reflect what was expected of them. As long as the responses to the CQs are not in line with the requirements, the DROPs need to be remodelled to make sure our ontology captures the knowledge as needed.

4   Digital Platform Ontology

In a first sub-section, we present the general reference ontology module. This module is part of any ontology application that is created for a digital platform, independent of its type. In the second sub-section, we present two modules that describe the functionality related to the market sides property of our taxonomic schema: the 'one-sided' and 'multi-sided' platform ontology module. The value of this property depends on whether one or more than one distinctive group of platform users is served by the platform[2]. In the third sub-section, we discuss the ontology validation process and illustrate it for the ontology modules presented in the first and second sub-sections.

4.1   General Reference Ontology Module

Our working definition of a digital platform for the taxonomy development (see Sect. 2) was the following: 'A digital platform is a service offering by the digital platform management to the users that may be bound to an agreement. The primary service offered are interactions between users and these interactions are enabled by a software system'. Based on this working definition, we define the following requirements compliant to all digital platforms:

1.   A digital platform is a service offering;
2.   This service offering is offered by digital platform management towards a certain target platform user community consisting of target platform users;
3.   This service offering is bound to an agreement between the platform user and the platform management.
4.   This service offering is enabled by software;
5.   Platform users may participate in platform-supported interaction between each other.

Based on these requirements we create the general ontology module, which is independent of platform type. Figure 2 shows this module, modelled in OntoUML, with a color coding referring to the sub-ontologies of UFO: UFO-A, an ontology of objects (in red); UFO-B, an ontology of events (in yellow); and UFO-C, an ontology of social constructs (in green and blue). A 'type' entity (in purple) is used for categorizing entities [34] of different sub-ontologies.

Figure 2 also shows how we modelled each requirement by means of a DROP. For the sake of clarity, the numbering of these DROPs is the same as the requirements. Requirements 1 to 3 are modelled with DROPs reused from the service domain ontology UFO-S. In UFO-S, a service offer is an event creating a social construct, or in this case a relatorKind as it has the ability to connect two entities. This relatorKind called 'service offering', connects a service provider and a target customer community and this service offering can eventually result in the establishment of another relatorKind called 'service agreement' [29]. These UFO-S patterns are than reused to model DROP 1 to 3.

---

[2] Other ontology modules are still work in progress and published at http://model-a-platform.com/digital-platform-ontology/.

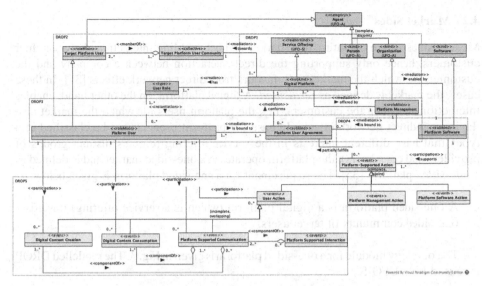

Fig. 2. General module of the digital platform reference ontology (Color figure online)

Requirements 4 and 5 are more specific for digital platforms and could not be modelled by reusing DROPs extracted from UFO-S. However, we could model these requirements by reusing DROPs directly from the foundational ontology UFO.

The general module of the digital platform reference ontology can be read as follows. A digital platform is a service offering as defined in UFO-S (DROP1). The digital platform is offered by the organization managing the platform (a.k.a. platform management) towards a target platform user community. This community is a collection of target platform users and can be persons or organizations (DROP2). From the moment a target platform user is bound to an agreement (in this case a platform user agreement) with the platform management, he becomes a platform user (DROP3). The digital platform is enabled by the platform software (DROP4), that supports different kinds of platform supported actions. These platform supported actions are divided into user actions (i.e., platform actions performed by users), platform management actions (i.e., platform actions performed by platform management) and platform actions (i.e., autonomous platform actions). The most basic user actions are digital content creation (e.g., sending a message) and digital content consumption (e.g., receiving a message). When both creation and consumption take place, we talk about a communication action. To fulfil the fifth requirement of a digital platform, the platform software must allow platform user interaction (DROP5), which requires mutual communication between users (e.g., sending, receiving, replying, receiving).

4.2 Market Sides

Most businesses are operating in a market without enabling interactions between their customers, hence only supporting the direct interaction between a company and the customer, for which the market only favours from direct network effects [35]. In these cases, the market is defined as *zero-sided*. A digital platform, on the other hand, enables interactions between the customers, i.e., the platform users for which the market also flaviours indirect network effects. In case the platform users cannot be classified into types that have different interests in the service offering (e.g., as distinct groups of providers and consumers), the platform operates in a one-sided market and is defined as a *one-sided* platform [35]. The requirement for a one-sided platform is given below:

6. A one-sided platform is a digital platform (which is a service offering) towards a one-sided community of target users.

The ontology module for a one-sided platform is given in Fig. 3. The modelled DROP is reused from UFO-S.

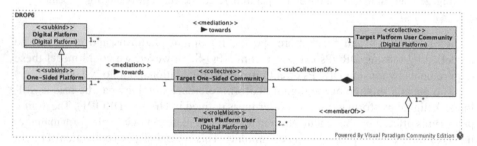

Fig. 3. One-sided platform ontology module

Unfortunately, for *Multi-Sided (MS) markets* there is no a clear and widely accepted definition [16]. The term was first used by noble price winners Rochet and Tirole [36] and defined as a market including at least two distinct but interdependent sides to have direct and clearly identified interactions with each other. Economically speaking, for a market to be MS it requires an increase in value to users on one side of the market with the number of participating users on another side [37]. This is known as 'cross-side network effects', sometimes referred to as 'indirect network effects'. The management of MS platforms (these are platforms operating in a MS market) typically face the chicken-and-egg problem [38], having difficulties to find users of one side without having users of the other side. It is gradually becoming acknowledged that such platforms pose specific challenges to market regulation and innovation policy as this strategy has strong indirect network effects that can lead to dominant market power and monopolies [39]. As this paper focusses on the digital platform functionalities to aid in future platform software design, we leave the economical and regulatory requirements stated by [36, 37] and others out of scope and focuss on the enabling of interactions between users of different sides.

As stated by [17], users of each side need to be affiliated with the market. By 'affiliation', it is meant that users make a platform-specific investment to be able to interact to each other directly [16]. But how to define these platform-specific investments? Is someone searching an apartment in Airbnb before registration a user? Is an artist whose music is offered on Spotify without his formal acceptance a user? We narrow the affiliation definition of [16] as we did for our taxonomy and define a user as an agent that is registered, subscribed, has created main content, has entered in a transaction or has entered in an investment using the MS platform software.

Based on the literature, the requirements for a MS platform are constructed and given below:

7. A MS platform is a digital platform (which is a service offering) towards multiple sides.
8. Users of both sides are affiliated with the platform after a user affiliation action. This affiliation is a platform user agreement and can be by registration, subscription, main content creation, making a transaction or making an investment.
9. The software enabling the MS platform offering allows for interactions between the users of at least two sides

The ontology module for a MS platform is given in Fig. 4. DROP 7 is reused from UFO-S. DROPs 8 and 9 are reused from UFO.

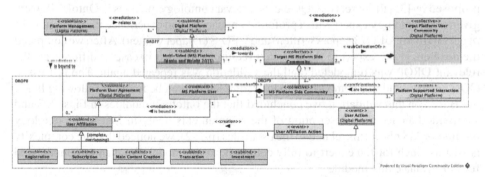

Fig. 4. Multi-sided platform ontology module (part 1)

A digital platform can have different user roles that allow users to conduct certain actions. For most one-sided digital platforms, all users have equal participation rights (e.g. WhatsApp), but a MS platform has at least two roles (e.g. homeowners and renters on Airbnb). The user role can change by performing an affiliation action and the users of a different role are allowed to perform actions that for other roles are prohibited (e.g. create new accommodation offering for homeowners, book accommodation for customers). The requirements for the user roles of a MS platform are given below:

10. A MS platform ensures at least two user roles.
11. User instances of different roles are allowed to perform different user actions.

12. A user can change its user role by performing a user affiliation action.

The ontology module for the user roles is given in Fig. 5. All DROPs are reused from UFO.

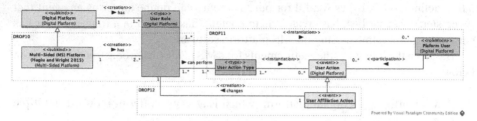

Fig. 5. Multi-sided platform ontology module (part 2: user roles)

4.3 Ontology Validation with CQs

To validate the ontology, we define sets of CQ's for each ontology module. The CQs are formulated as queries and come forth out of the requirements as CQs play the role of a type of requirement specification against which the ontology can be evaluated [40]. As proposed by [32] these sets of CQs and the relevant ontology modules in OntoUML were given to an ontology expert with a profound knowledge and experience in ontologies (11 papers written), UFO (3 papers written) and UFO-S (1 paper written). After, we compared the answers of the expert to the intended requirements, and in case of differences, the relevant DROP was remodeled, and the validation was repeated again. The full list of CQs, answers and our comparison to the requirements can be found at following link[3].

Based on this validation, we concluded that the ontology modules in Figs. 2, 3 and 4 provided an accurate description of the requirements. Only in Fig. 5, the ontology module of MS platforms related to the user roles (part 2), we noticed that the complexity is still too high for the expert to fully comprehend the model. We plan to remodel and further evaluate this module.

5 Discussion

This paper is only a first step towards the reference ontology and proposes the method with three modules; The general digital platform module, the one-sided module and the multi-sided module. In the future we plan to further develop the digital platform reference ontology with a module for each property value of our taxonomy. These other ontology modules are still work in progress and published at following link[4].

During this development, the ontology can be validated and further improved in three ways. First, we plan to expand the number of UFO and UFO-S experts used in

---

[3] http://model-a-platform.com/validation-of-the-digital-platform-reference-ontology/.

[4] http://model-a-platform.com/digital-platform-ontology/.

Sect. 4.3, as the validation of only one expert is not sufficient. Second, we plan to apply our ontology to the existing digital platforms used in the development of our taxonomy. This way we make sure that our ontology includes the functionalities of a broad range of platforms. As an example, we apply our current ontology model to the meal delivery platform Uber Eats [5] in Fig. 6 (appendix). For a third validation, we plan to use the simulation method of [41] to identify anti-patterns. Otherwise, these anti-patterns capture error prone modelling decisions that can result in the creation of models that allow for unintended model instances (representing undesired state of affairs).

6 Conclusion

To increase the knowledge regarding the requirements and design of digital platforms and their types, we proposed our method to develop a digital platform reference ontology based on a taxonomy and presented three ontology modules. These types, including 'multi-sided platform', 'digital marketplace', 'crowdfunding platform', 'sharing economy platform' and 'on-demand platform' are partly similar, but also differ in many aspects including the functionality they offer to their users. Our ontology can help comprehend the complexity and functionality requirements of existing digital platform depending on their type.

The ability to see through the fog in the digital platform domain is important, as the complexity within this domain is ever increasing. For example in the transportation sector, Uber is planning to combine car, train, plane, bike and scooter (rental) services into one transaction to get the customers to their destination in the cheapest, convenient and fastest way possible. These combinations of platform types with different types of providers are also called mega-platforms [42], hybrid platforms [24] or integrated platforms [11] and have the ability to further shake up and interrupt out-dated markets.

So what can be the implications of our research? First of all it helps both researchers and practitioners in their communication and decision making, as the ontology can be used as a common language all stakeholders can understand. Second, it is possible for them to improve and enlarge this ontology and make it compatible with other research fields. At this point, the ontology mainly focusses on the functionality requirements. But since our method makes use of ontology modules, it is fairly easy to enlarge this ontology and create modules that include terminology, entities, relationships and social constructs of interrelated domains to aid in the regulation, business model creation and social responsibility fields of digital platforms. Third, ontology modeling can play an essential role in areas such as database design, information systems and software development [7]. It can help the decision-making of developers and entrepreneurs and support ontology-driven development of new platforms.

We acknowledge that there are some limitations to our research. First, the ontology is not yet validated using our sample of 48 existing platforms of different types and functionality. And even then, the sample only represents a small portion of the current digital platform domain. Second, our ontology only represents the current state of the digital platform domain, but developments will require modifications to the ontology.

---

[5] www.ubereats.com.

Despite these limitations we believe that an ontology can be a vital tool to accelerate the development of new digital platforms and hopefully push the sector into a more alternative and socially responsible direction.

Appendix

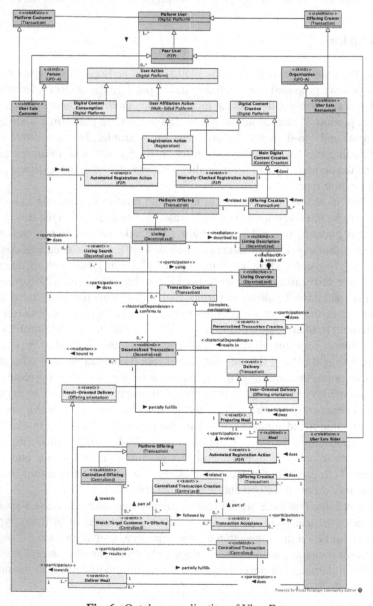

Fig. 6. Ontology application of Uber Eats

References

1. Ruy, F.B., Guizzardi, G., Falbo, R.A., Reginato, C.C., Santos, V.A.: From reference ontologies to ontology patterns and back. Data Knowl. Eng. **109**, 41–69 (2017)
2. Kenney, M., Zysman, J.: The rise of the platform economy. Issues Sci. Technol. **32**, 61–69 (2016)
3. Görög, G.: The Definitions of sharing economy: a systematic literature review. Management **13**, 175–189 (2018)
4. Puschmann, T., Alt, R.: Sharing economy. Bus. Inf Syst. Eng. **58**, 93–99 (2016)
5. Yin, C., Wang, X., Rong, W., Wang, T., David, B.: A system framework for sharing economy. In: Proceedings 2018 IEEE 22nd International Conference Computer Supported Cooperative Work in Design, CSCWD 2018, pp. 779–784 (2018)
6. Sharetribe: Sharetribe Go (2019). https://github.com/sharetribe/sharetribe
7. Guizzardi, G.: Ontological Foundations for Structural Conceptual Models (2005)
8. Nickerson, R.C., Varshney, U., Muntermann, J.: A method for taxonomy development and its application in information systems. Eur. J. Inf. Syst. **22**, 336–359 (2013)
9. Wu, L.: Understanding collaborative consumption business model: case of car sharing systems. DEStech Trans. Mater. Sci. Eng. 403–409 (2017)
10. Apte, U.M., Davis, M.M.: Sharing economy services: business model generation. Calif. Manage. Rev. **61**, 104–131 (2019)
11. Evans, P.C., Gawer, A.: The rise of the platform enterprise a global survey. Cent. Glob. Enterp. 1–30 (2016)
12. Sutherland, W., Jarrahi, M.H.: The sharing economy and digital platforms: a review and research agenda. Int. J. Inf. Manage. **43**, 328–341 (2018)
13. Nguyen, S., Llosa, S.: On the difficulty to define the sharing economy and collaborative consumption – literature review and proposing a different approach with the introduction of "collaborative services." Journée la Relat. à la Marque dans un Monde Connect. 19–25 (2018)
14. Codagnone, C., Biagi, F., Abadie, F.: The passions and the interests: unpacking the "Sharing Economy." (2016)
15. Ranjbari, M., Morales-Alonso, G., Carrasco-Gallego, R.: Conceptualizing the sharing economy through presenting a comprehensive framework. Sustainability **10**(7), 2336 (2018)
16. Sanchez-Cartas, J.M., Leon, G.: Multi-sided platforms and markets: a literature review. SSRN Electron. J. 1–62 (2019)
17. Hagiu, A., Wright, J.: Multi-sided platforms. Int. J. Ind. Organ. **43**, 1–32 (2015)
18. Acquier, A., Daudigeos, T., Pinkse, J.: Promises and paradoxes of the sharing economy: an organizing framework. Technol. Forecast. Soc. Change **125**, 1–10 (2017)
19. Haas, P., Blohm, I., Leimeister, J.M.: An empirical taxonomy of crowdfunding intermediaries. In: 35th International Conference Information Systems Building a Better World Through Information Systems, ICIS 2014, pp. 1–18 (2014)
20. Täuscher, K., Laudien, S.M.: Understanding platform business models: a mixed methods study of marketplaces. Eur. Manag. J. **36**, 319–329 (2018)
21. Chasin, F., von Hoffen, M., Cramer, M., Matzner, M.: Peer-to-Peer Sharing and Collaborative Consumption Platforms: a Taxonomy and a Reproducible Analysis. Springer, Heidelberg (2018)
22. Frenken, K., Schor, J.: Putting the sharing economy into perspective. Environ. Innov. Soc. Transitions. **23**, 3–10 (2017)
23. Mamonova, Y.: Sharing Economy vs. On-Demand Economy: The Major Differences (2018)
24. Acquier, A., Carbone, V., Massé, D.: How to create value (s) in the sharing economy: business models. Scalability Sustain. **9**, 5–25 (2019)

25. Ehikioya, S.A.: A formal model of peer-to-peer digital product marketplace. Int. J. Networked Distrib. Comput. **6**, 143–154 (2018)
26. Ritter, M., Schanz, H.: The sharing economy: a comprehensive business model framework. J. Clean. Prod. **213**, 320–331 (2019)
27. Andersson, M., Hjalmarsson, A., Avital, M.: Peer-to-peer service sharing platforms: driving share and share alike on a mass-scale. In: Proceedings of 34th International Conference Information Systems, vol. 4, pp. 2964–2978 (2013)
28. Gobble, M.A.M.: Defining the sharing economy. Res. Technol. Manag. **60**, 59–61 (2017)
29. Nardi, J.C., et al.: A commitment-based reference ontology for services. Inf. Syst. **54**, 263–288 (2015)
30. Falbo, R.A., Guizzardi, G., Gangemi, A., Presutti, V.: Ontology patterns: clarifying concepts and terminology. CEUR Workshop Proc. **1188**, 14–26 (2013)
31. Guizzardi, Giancarlo., Fonseca, Claudenir M., Benevides, Alessandro Botti., Almeida, João Paulo A., Porello, Daniele, Sales, Tiago Prince: Endurant types in ontology-driven conceptual modeling: towards OntoUML 2.0. In: Trujillo, Juan C., Davis, Karen C., Du, Xiaoyong, Li, Zhanhuai, Ling, Tok Wang, Li, Guoliang, Lee, Mong Li (eds.) ER 2018. LNCS, vol. 11157, pp. 136–150. Springer, Cham (2018). https://doi.org/10.1007/978-3-030-00847-5_12
32. Bezerra, C., Freitas, F., Santana, F.: Evaluating ontologies with competency questions. In: Proceedings of 2013 IEEE/WIC/ACM International Joint Conferences on Web Intelligence Intelligent Agent Technologies – Work, WI-IATW 2013, vol. 3, pp. 284–285 (2013)
33. Gharib, M., Mylopoulos, J.: COPri - A Core Ontology for Privacy Requirements Engineering (2018)
34. Carvalho, V., Giancarlo, G., …: Extending the Foundations of Ontology-based Conceptual Modeling with a Multi-Level Theory. In: International Conference on Conceptual Modeling (2015)
35. Filistrucchi, L., Geradin, D., Van Damme, E., Affeldt, P.: Market definition in two-sided markets: theory and practice. J. Compet. Law Econ. **10**, 293–339 (2014)
36. Rochet, J., Tirole, J.: Platform competition in two-sided markets, pp. 5–6 (2001)
37. Hagiu, A.: Strategic decisions for multisided platforms. Polym. Eng. Sci. **58**, 928–942 (2018)
38. Evans, D.S.: The Antitrust economics of two-sided markets. SSRN Electron. J. **20**, (2005)
39. Katharina, H.: Innovation comes from platforms rather than from individual applications. https://ec.europa.eu/digital-single-market/en/news/innovation-comes-platforms-rather-individual-applications
40. Asunción, G.-P., Mariano, F.-L., Oscar, C.: Ontological Engineering (2003)
41. Guizzardi, Giancarlo, Sales, Tiago Prince: Detection, simulation and elimination of semantic anti-patterns in ontology-driven conceptual models. In: Yu, Eric, Dobbie, Gillian, Jarke, Matthias, Purao, Sandeep (eds.) ER 2014. LNCS, vol. 8824, pp. 363–376. Springer, Cham (2014). https://doi.org/10.1007/978-3-319-12206-9_30
42. Radonjic-Simic, M., Richter, S., Pfistere, D.: Reference Model and Architecture for the Post-Platform Economy (2019)

An Ontological Analysis of the Notion of Treatment

Paul Johannesson(✉) and Erik Perjons

Department of Computer and Systems Sciences, Stockholm, Sweden
{pajo,perjons}@dsv.su.se
http://dsv.su.se

Abstract. Treatments are entities of central importance in many practices and applications, including both medical and technical ones. Treatments exhibit a number of intricate characteristics that give rise to practical as well as theoretical modelling challenges. One issue is that treatments can be viewed as endurants as well as events, the latter ones being temporally extended and having both a completed life history and a planned life for their future. There is also a normative relationship between a treatment viewed as an endurant and its life history. Other issues include various abstraction levels of treatments and their divisions into subtreatments. We address these issues by proposing an ontologically grounded modelling pattern of treatments based on an ontological analysis of the event notion in UFO. We also use this analysis to suggest visualizations of treatments.

Keywords: Treatments · Ontology · UFO · Modelling pattern

1 Introduction

Treatments are ubiquitous in many domains and practices, where they are used to improve, maintain, restore or cure some object that is malfunctioning. In health practices, treatments aim to remedy existing or potential health problems, typically following a diagnosis. Medical treatments can be divided into three broad categories: curative treatments that aim to cure a patient of an illness, palliative treatments that aim to relieve symptoms from an illness, and preventive treatments that aim to prevent the onset of an illness. Treatments also occur in engineering and technical contexts, where they are used to improve or repair equipment as well as materials, for example in surface engineering.

The conceptual modelling of treatments gives rise to a number of issues and challenges, practical as well as theoretical ones. One of these issues is that treatments can have both a partially completed life history and a future life to be unfolded, which requires the modelling of future, or expected, events. Another issue is how to represent the normative relationships between a treatment viewed as an agreement (an endurant) and a treatment viewed as a life history (an event). The life history itself as well as its constituent events can, completely or

© Springer Nature Switzerland AG 2020
G. Dobbie et al. (Eds.): ER 2020, LNCS 12400, pp. 303–314, 2020.
https://doi.org/10.1007/978-3-030-62522-1_22

partially, fulfil the agreement. For example, a treatment agreement can include a number of planned events, and the agreement is fulfilled only if these events actually occur. Still another issue concerns the fact that treatments can be expressed with different levels of specificity, which affects the conditions for determining how, and to what extent, they are fulfilled. Finally, another issue is how to divide treatments into parts or subtreatments. The goal of this paper is to propose a modelling pattern for treatments that addresses the above issues and to outline how it can be used for visualizing treatments. As a basis for the pattern, we have carried out an ontological analysis of treatments based on the Unified Foundational Ontology (UFO) [5].

The rest of the paper is structured as follows. Section 2 provides a brief overview of UFO and discusses the modelling of events. Section 3 introduces the ontological analysis of treatments and the modelling pattern for treatments. Section 4 discusses how the pattern can provide a basis for the visualizations of treatments. Finally, Sect. 5 provides conclusions and a discussion of open issues and future work.

2   Theoretical Basis

Our analysis will be based on the Unified Foundational Ontology (UFO), which is a top-level ontology that unifies a number of foundational ontologies and provides foundations for conceptual modelling based on philosophically well-founded principles, [5].

UFO makes a key distinction between individuals and universals [9]. *Individuals* in UFO are entities that possess a unique identity, while *universals* are abstract patterns of features that can be realized in one or several individuals. Individuals can be divided into endurants and events, see Fig. 1. An *endurant* is an individual that is wholly present whenever it is present, e.g. a mountain or a car. An *event*, on the other hand, is made up of temporal parts, which are not all present whenever the event is present. For example, when a business process or an election campaign is present, only one of its temporal parts is present. Note that an event is not viewed as instantaneous but as extended over time.

Endurants can be specialized into substantials and moments. *Substantials* are existentially-independent endurants, e.g., a tree or a person. In contrast, *moments* are individuals that inhere in other individuals, meaning that they are existentially-dependent on their bearers, e.g., the smile of a person or the marriage between two spouses. Moments can be either intrinsic moments or relators. *Intrinsic moments* are moments that are dependent on a single endurant, e.g., the colour of a car, while *relators* are dependent on two or more endurants, e.g., a marriage.

Qualities are intrinsic moments that can be measured, while *modes* are intrinsic moments that cannot be directly measured, such as desires, beliefs, intentions, conceptions, and symptoms. A *disposition* is an intrinsic moment that can be manifested in certain situations through the occurrence of some event. For example, the fragility of a vase can be manifested through its breaking in a situation

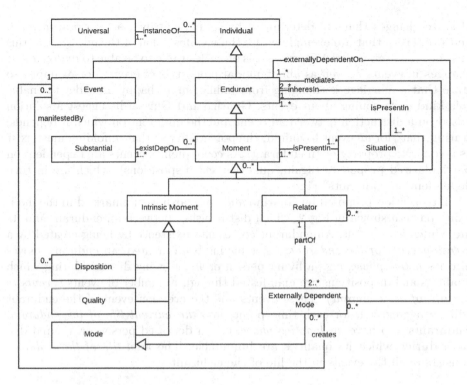

Fig. 1. A fragment of UFO for individuals

where it is hit by a hammer. However, a disposition may never be manifested, e.g., a fragile vase may never break.

Relators come into existence when a relationship between two or more endurants is established. For example, a marriage between two persons comes into existence as a consequence of a wedding. This event will give rise to a number of externally dependent modes, i.e., modes that are dependent on the marriage, including emotions, commitments and claims between the two persons. The marriage relator aggregates all these externally dependent modes.

UFO clearly distinguishes between endurants and events, but as pointed out by Guarino and Guizzardi in [4], this distinction is not unproblematic, and they challenge it by asking a number of questions about endurant-like characteristics of events. They start by noting that endurants can bear both essential and accidental properties; that they can qualitatively change in certain aspects while remaining the same; and that they can be the subject of counterfactual reasoning. And they ask whether the same can be said about events: "Can events genuinely change their properties while remaining the same? Can an event be the bearer of modal properties? In particular, can an event exhibit properties contingently? Can an event be different from what it is?" [4]. According to classical axiomatized ontologies of events [11], all of these questions are answered in the negative. An event is here defined by the sum of its parts, and it can be seen as a succession of state changes that are determined by its participants, a temporal interval, and properties that are exemplified by the manifestation of the event. Still, this answer may seem unsatisfactory, as it is often desirable to be able to reason about changes in events as well as about modal properties of events, for example, to state that a marriage is changing from indifferent to happy. In order to enable this kind of reasoning about events, Guarino and Guizzardi suggest a solution based on a distinction between an event and the endurant on which it depends, stating that "for an event to unfold, the potentiality of that unfolding must exist as a concrete property of an endurant. As consequence, events are dependent on particularized properties (again, qualities and dispositions), which are in turn dependent on endurants" [4].

The solution proposed by Guarino and Guizzardi is summarized in the modelling pattern shown in Fig. 2, which distinguishes between an endurant and its life, which is an event. An endurant comes into existence by being created by a *creation event of the endurant*. After having been created, an endurant moves into its *active phase*, e.g., a living person or an on-going disease, during which qualities and dispositions are manifested through a number of events (*events in the life of the endurant*). These events and the creation event of the endurant will be aggregated, for each time point, into *the current life of the endurant*. Endurants also have an *inactive phase*, e.g., a deceased person or a cured disease, during which its qualities are immutable. The *final life of the endurant* consists of all the events in the life of the endurant.

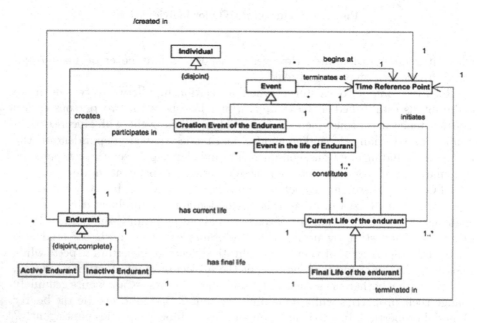

Fig. 2. A modelling pattern for representing events, from [4]

3   A Modelling Pattern for Representing Treatments

The modelling pattern for representing events, see Fig. 2, will be used as a basis for analysing the notion of treatment, meaning that a number of classes will be introduced to express its various aspects. The analysis is documented in the form of a modelling pattern, as shown in Fig. 3.

First, there will be a class *Treatment Regimen* classifying endurants that are agreements for treatments, including commitments for performing specific actions as well as overall goals that these actions are expected to produce. Such goals are about improving, maintaining, restoring or curing the object of the treatment. For example, a treatment regimen can specify that a certain medication should be taken twice a day for two weeks, resulting in an infection being cured. There will also be a class for events for creating treatment regimens, called *Regimen Creation*, corresponding to the class *Creation Event of the Endurant* in Fig. 2.

As for any endurant, a treatment regimen has a life, which is an event. For any time point, the life of a treatment can be divided into two parts, the administered treatment and the planned treatment, modelled by the classes *Administered Treatment* and *Planned Treatment* in Fig. 3. Here, the administered treatment includes all the treatment events that have occurred up to a certain time point, corresponding to *Current Life of the Endurant* in Fig. 2. The planned treatment, on the other hand, consists of all the *expected treatment events* to occur during the remainder of the treatment.

The notion of a planned treatment raises (at least) two ontological challenges. First, at a specific time point, there may certainly exist many possible future lives of a treatment, and it may be questioned whether it is fruitful to single out one of these and designate it as the planned treatment. One argument for doing so is to include those events prescribed by the treatment that would occur if nothing extraordinary takes place, i.e., if only the expected treatment events occur. For example, the planned treatment of a medication treatment regimen would include those drug intakes that should occur if the patient's condition develops in the anticipated way. Thus, a planned treatment is similar to a "happy path" in software testing and engineering, which is a scenario that features no exceptional or error conditions [6]. A second issue concerns the ontological status of an expected event. In the traditional ontological view, events are seen as static entities "frozen in time" that can only be referred to in the past [4]. But as pointed out by Sales in the context of value analysis, there can also be a "need to refer to envisioned events, whose expected temporal properties are not completely fixed (so that they may change in time before the event occurs), but still are considered as first-class citizens in our domain of discourse" [10]. Being able to talk explicitly about planned treatments, i.e., about the future of a treatment, seems to be most desirable. Therefore, we accept the notion of expected, or envisioned, events, though we recognize the need for further ontological clarification.

There is a normative, or fulfilment, relationship between a treatment regimen as an endurant and its life, in the sense that the events of the latter should

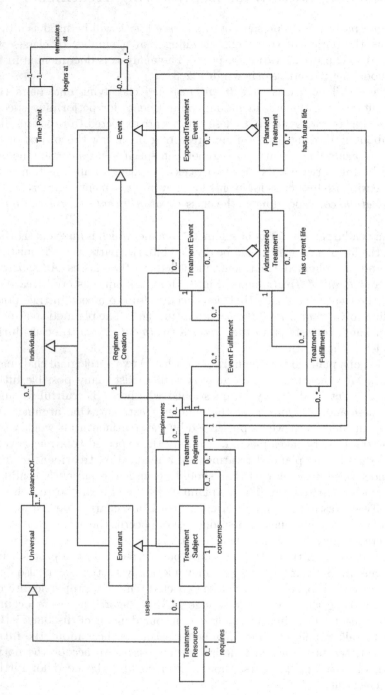

Fig. 3. A modelling pattern for representing treatments

be carried out in accordance with the prescriptions specified by the treatment regimen. This relationship can be modelled through an association *fulfils* between *Treatment Regimen* and *Treatment Event,* specifying that one treatment event has completely fulfilled a treatment regimen. However, sometimes a treatment event only partially fulfils the prescriptions of a treatment regimen, for example, an infusion may have to be aborted prematurely, implying that a drug has only been partially administered. There may also be other kinds of deviations, such as one medication being replaced by a similar one. Thus, there is a need for an additional relator, *Event Fulfilment,* that relates a treatment event to a treatment regimen, specifying how, and to what extent, the former has fulfilled the latter. Further, not only individual treatment events can be seen as fulfilling a treatment regimen but also an entire administered treatment, in the sense that its effects are in accordance with the goals and expectations of the treatment regimen. Therefore, we also introduce a relator *Treatment Fulfilment* between *Adminstered Treatment* and *Treatment Regimen.*

Treatment regimens can be formulated on different levels of specificity. For example, a treatment regimen on a low level of specificity may state only that some drug should be administered twice a day, while a corresponding regimen on a higher level also may include the exact time points of administration. On a still higher level of specificity, a regimen may indicate the professional role required for the drug administration, for example an ICU nurse. A treatment event may then fulfil a treatment regimen on one level of specificity, while it simultaneously does not fulfil a corresponding treatment regimen on a higher level. In order to model specificity levels, we introduce an association *implements* for the class *Treatment Regimen,* as shown in Fig. 3. One treatment regimen implements another treatment regimen if any treatment event fulfilling the first regimen also fulfils the second one.

A treatment regimen concerns a treatment subject, an endurant, for example, an engine, a patient, or a group of patients. Furthermore, it can refer to other resources, treatment resources, that are to be used in the treatment. For treatment regimens on a low level of specificity, treatment resources may be referred to as universals, while on a higher level, they may instead be referred to as individuals. For example, on a low level of specificity, only the type of a spare part may be indicated, while on a higher level, a particular physical object is given. However, in some cases, universals may be used also on high levels of specificity, for example, medical pills are seldom specified as endurants. In such cases, even an administered treatment may refer to universals.

4   Visualizations of Treatments

Treatments can be visualized by focusing on their temporal dimension and graphically representing their included treatment events. In the following, we will outline a visual notation for treatments, administered as well as planned ones, that follows the principle of "no syntax without semantics" [2], which in this context means that there should be no graphical element without a corresponding modelling construct.

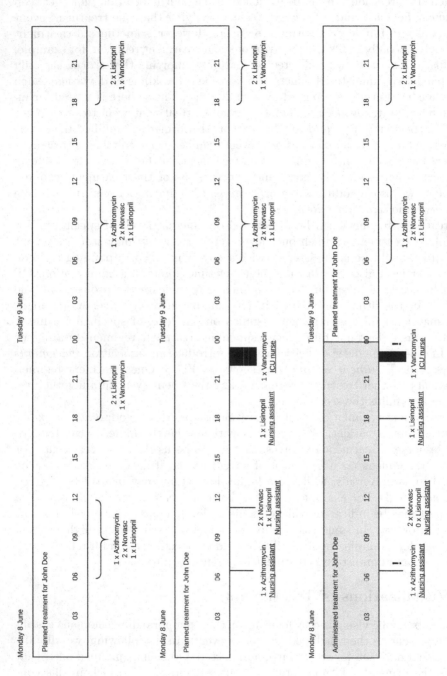

Fig. 4. Visualizing administered and planned treatments

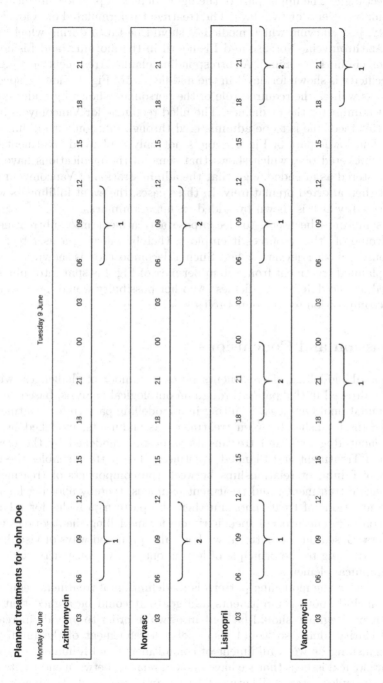

Fig. 5. Visualizing subtreatments

A planned treatment can be visualized, as shown in Fig. 4, as a horizontally extended rectangle. The upper part of the figure depicts a planned (medication) treatment for a patient for two days. The treatment is formulated on a low level of specificity, just showing which medicines should be taken during which time intervals (Azithromycin, Norvasc and Lisinopril in the morning, and Lisinopril and Vancomycin in the evening). A corresponding planned treatment on a higher level of specificity is shown for day 1 in the middle part of Fig. 4, showing specific time points as well as the required role of the personnel (shown by underscored labels) that administer the medicines. The filled rectangle for Vancomycin indicates that this medicine is to be administered through infusion with a duration of 90 min. The lower part of Fig. 4 depicts not only a planned treatment but also an administered one, which shows that some of the medications have not been administered as intended, e.g., that the administration of Vancomycin was started but then aborted prematurely. In these cases, the event fulfilments were not as expected, which is shown by added exclamation marks.

It can sometimes be useful to decompose a treatment into subtreatments based on (some of) the resources it employs, thereby allowing a user to focus on the resources most relevant for her. Such a decomposition is shown in Fig. 5, where the planned treatment from the upper part of Fig. 4 is split into subtreatments based on the different medicines. Another possibility would have been to base the decomposition on personnel roles.

5   Discussion and Conclusions

The conceptual modelling of treatments poses a number of challenges, which have been addressed in this paper through an ontological analysis, based on the Unified Foundational Ontology, resulting in a modelling pattern for treatments. The pattern distinguishes between treatments as endurants, modelled by the class Treatment Regimen, and treatments as events, modelled by the classes Administered Treatment and Planned Treatment. The pattern enables the representation of fulfilment relationships between the components of treatments, as well as entire treatments, and treatment regimens, thereby allowing for representing evaluations of treatments. Further, the pattern provides for relating treatments on different levels of specificity and for modelling the resources used in treatments. Based on the pattern, we have also proposed ways of visualizing treatments, adhering to the principle of letting ontological constructs guide the choice of graphical elements.

One issue with the modelling pattern is its definition of treatment regimens, which now include both commitments and goals. It could be argued that the class Treatment Regimen should be split into two in order to provide increased conceptual clarity; doing so would also enable a refinement of the fulfil relators, distinguishing between fulfilment of commitments and fulfilment of goals. Another ontological issue is that we have allowed relators between endurants and events, for example, between Treatment Event and Treatment Regimen, which is not according to UFO.

To the best of our knowledge, the modelling of treatments has not received systematic attention in the conceptual modelling literature, though there exists some relevant work in the health care research area, e.g., [1] and [8]. However, treatments are in several respects similar to plans, though they have their specific characteristics, such as the need for continuous evaluation, the multiple levels of specificity, and the varying degrees of plan fulfilment. Still, there are many similarities between treatment regimens and plans, in particular that they both include agreements that prescribe a course of action. Thus, a topic of further research is to investigate how the proposed analysis and modelling pattern can be generalised to cater for plans, and compare the results to existing approaches to modelling plans, for example, the notion of schedule in [7]. Another research direction is instead to focus on the particular characteristics of treatments, e.g., the different kinds of deviations that may occur in the fulfillment of treatment regimens. The fulfilment of agreements and commitments has been discussed in the modelling literature, e.g., in [3], but without paying much attention to the various ways in which fulfilments may only partially succeed. Yet another research direction is to investigate the ontological status of expected events that are not fixed as ordinary events but may be subject of change. Finally, it would be worthwhile to extend the scope of analysis and not consider treatments in isolation but as integral parts of larger practices, which would also include monitoring, evaluation and modifications of treatment regimens, thereby investigating how context influences treatments.

Acknowledgements. The authors wish to thank Susanne Bergman, Annika Karlsson, Pernilla Karlsson, Emil Sanders and Monica Winge for discussions on conceptualizations in health care.

References

1. Burt, J., Rick, J., Blakeman, T., Protheroe, J., Roland, M., Bower, P.: Care plans and care planning in long-term conditions: a conceptual model. Prim. Health Care Res. Dev. **15**(4), 342–354 (2014)
2. Crane, T.: The language of thought: no syntax without semantics. Mind Lang. **5**(3), 187–213 (1990)
3. Geerts, G.L., McCarthy, W.E.: The ontological foundation of REA enterprise information systems. In: Annual Meeting of the American Accounting Association, Philadelphia, PA. vol. 362, pp. 127–150. (2000) msu.edu
4. Guarino, N., Guizzardi, G.: Relationships and events: towards a general theory of reification and truthmaking. In: Adorni, G., Cagnoni, S., Gori, M., Maratea, M. (eds.) AI*IA 2016 Advances in Artificial Intelligence, pp. 237–249. Springer, Cham (2016). https://doi.org/10.1007/978-3-319-49130-1_18
5. Guizzardi, G.: Ontological foundations for structural conceptual models, PhD thesis. University of Twente (2005)
6. Hasling, B., Goetz, H., Beetz, K.: Model based testing of system requirements using UML use case models. In: 2008 1st International Conference on Software Testing, Verification, and Validation, pp. 367–376 (April 2008)
7. Hruby, P.: Model-Driven Design Using Business Patterns. Springer, Berlin (2010)

8. Khoo, C.S.G., Na, J.C., Wang, V.W., Chan, S.: Developing an ontology for encoding disease treatment information in medical abstracts. DESIDOC J. Libr. Inf. Technol. **31**(2), 103–115 (2011)

9. Nardi, J.C., et al.: A commitment-based reference ontology for services. Inf. Syst. **54**, 263–288 (2015)

10. Sales, T.P.: Ontological Foundations for Strategic Business Modeling: The Case of Value, Risk and Competition. Ph.D. thesis, University of Trento (April 2019)

11. Simons, P.: The formalization of Husserl's theory of wholes and parts. In: Simons, P. (ed.) Philosophy and Logic in Central Europe from Bolzano to Tarski: Selected Essays, pp. 71–116. Springer, Dordrecht (1992). https://doi.org/10.1007/978-94-015-8094-6_4

Transformation of Ontology-Based Conceptual Models into Relational Schemas

Gustavo L. Guidoni[1,2], João Paulo A. Almeida[1(✉)], and Giancarlo Guizzardi[1,3]

[1] Ontology and Conceptual Modeling Research Group (NEMO),
Federal University of Espírito Santo, Vitória, Brazil
jpalmeida@ieee.org
[2] Federal Institute of Espírito Santo, Colatina, Brazil
gustavo.guidoni@ifes.edu.br
[3] Free University of Bozen-Bolzano, Bolzano, Italy
gguizzardi@unibz.it

Abstract. Despite the existence of several strategies for transforming structural conceptual models into relational schemas, there are a number of features of ontology-based conceptual models that have not been taken into account in the existing literature. Most approaches fail to support conceptual models that: (i) include overlapping or incomplete generalizations; (ii) support dynamic classification; (iii) have multiple inheritance; and (iv) have orthogonal hierarchies. This is because many of the approaches discussed in the literature are based on the object-relational mapping and, as a consequence, assume primitives underlying object-oriented programming languages (instead of conceptual modeling languages). This paper addresses this gap, focusing on the realization of taxonomic hierarchies of ontology-based conceptual models. We explore some ontological meta-properties that characterize classes in these models (sortality and rigidity) to guide the transformation and avoid some problems in existing approaches.

Keywords: Object-relational mapping · Transformation · Impedance mismatch · Ontology primitives

1 Introduction

Conceptual models play an important role in the design of relational databases, and are often used to guide the definition of relational schemas. Several systematic model transformation approaches to this end have been explored in the academic literature and incorporated in production-ready tools [23]. In these approaches, elements and patterns of a resulting relational schema have their origin traced back to corresponding elements and patterns of a source conceptual model. By using a model transformation approach, design decisions are incorporated into transformation specifications; automated model transformation then shields designers from manual (error-prone) realization steps.

© Springer Nature Switzerland AG 2020
G. Dobbie et al. (Eds.): ER 2020, LNCS 12400, pp. 315–330, 2020.
https://doi.org/10.1007/978-3-030-62522-1_23

A significant challenge of a model transformation approach is to preserve the semantics of a source model. This is because, often, source and target models are based on different paradigms, employ different concepts, which results in a variety of technical problems. A manifest example of this is the so-called "Object-Relational Impedance Mismatch" [15], which results from a "semantic gap" with object-oriented constructs not bearing a direct correspondence with constructs in relational schemas.

The existing transformation approaches that target relational schemas vary in a number of ways, including: (i) the primitives with which the source conceptual model is defined (e.g., as given by the source modeling language and its underlying abstractions), (ii) the realization strategies employed to bridge the semantic gap, (iii) the non-functional properties of the resulting database systems (such as time performance, ease of use, maintainability), and (iv) level of automation.

Consider, for example, approaches to transform an object-oriented inheritance hierarchy into relational schemas (such as those discussed by [2,16]). Concerning the adopted primitives (i), their vast majority assume objects are classified statically (i.e., objects cannot change classes at runtime); some of them assume single inheritance only. Concerning the realization strategies employed (ii), approaches adopt variations of *one table per class, one table per leaf class* and *one table per hierarchy*. Strategy choices are either fixed in a particular approach or discussed with general heuristics. For example, when discussing these approaches, Ambler [2] argues that if priority is given to the support for polymorphism, then the best strategy is *one table per class*, at the cost of performance. Keller [16] indicates the use of *one table per hierarchy* strategy if the transformation purpose is performance and maintainability.

Despite the existence of several strategies for transforming object-oriented models into relational schemas, there are a number of features of ontology-based conceptual models that have not been taken into account in the existing literature. Most approaches do not cater for source conceptual models that: (i) include overlapping or incomplete generalizations; (ii) support dynamic classification; (iii) have multiple inheritance; and (iv) have orthogonal hierarchies. This is because many of the approaches discussed in the literature are based on the object-relational mapping and, as a consequence, assume primitives underlying object-oriented programming languages (instead of conceptual modeling languages). This paper addresses this gap, focusing on the realization of taxonomic hierarchies of ontology-based conceptual models, which do not adhere to the constraints of inheritance hierarchies in programming languages. Further, by exploring ontological distinctions for types—specifically the formal metaproperties of *sortality* and *rigidity*—we are able to devise a novel transformation strategy and avoid some problems in existing approaches.

This paper is further structured as follows. Section 2 presents the primitives we assume in a source conceptual model. It also introduces a running example. Section 3 identifies predominant strategies in the literature to transform class hierarchies into relational schemas; it identifies limitations that motivate us to investigate a novel approach. Section 4 presents the ontology-based approach, which is applied to the running example. Section 5 discusses how the proposed approach is positioned with respect to the dominant strategies and other related work. Section 6 presents concluding remarks.

2 Primitives of the Source Conceptual Model

We assume that the basic elements of a taxonomy in a structural conceptual model are *classes* and their relations of *specialization* (also called "is-a", *subclassing*, or *inheritance* relations). Classes are used to capture common properties of entities they classify, and, in a taxonomic hierarchy, more general classes are specialized into more specific (sub-)classes, which "inherit" attributes and associations of their superclasses (for brevity, we call here both the attributes and associations of a class its "features"). We assume conceptual modelling approaches share these ground notions, nevertheless, there are variations including additional supporting mechanisms, their semantics and their possible range of use, as discussed in the remainder of this section.

Multiple Inheritance. A first source of variation concerns the possibility of a subclass to specialize more than one superclass. In a taxonomic hierarchy with multiple inheritance, a class can be a subclass of different classes [6]. A subclass in such a hierarchy inherits the properties of all its superclasses. Multiple inheritance has been avoided in some programming languages as it leads to some implementation difficulties. In conceptual modeling, however, multiple inheritance is hardly dispensable, as it enables opportunities for modularity and reusability [7].

Overlapping Classification. Another variation concerns whether an object can simultaneously instantiate multiple classes which are not related by specialization. For example, a person may instantiate both the BrazilianCitizen and the ItalianCitizen subclasses of Person. In UML, this can be explicitly supported with the so-called *overlapping generalization sets*, in which a set of non-disjoint classes specialize the same superclass. Additionally, this kind of scenario can be supported with different–orthogonal–hierarchies that specialize a common superclass based on different criteria. For example, persons may be classified according to their age and according to citizenship status. In this setting, a Brazilian adult would instantiate both the BrazilianCitizen and the Adult subclasses of Person (each from a different generalization set).

Non-Exhaustive Classification. A related variation concerns whether specializing subclasses "cover" the specialized superclass, i.e., whether they jointly exhaust all the classification possibilities for the superclass. In UML, this can be explicitly supported with the so-called *complete* generalization sets, which are opposed to *incomplete* generalization sets. In the case of an incomplete generalization set, it is possible for an instance of the superclass not to instantiate any of the subclasses in the set. For example, it is possible for a person to be stateless (in the sense of not being considered a national by any State), and hence a nationality generalization set could be marked as "incomplete" even in the case all known nationalities are explicitly modeled.

Dynamic Classification. Another variation we consider concerns whether instances can change the set of classes they instantiate throughout their existence. For example, a `Person` may be reclassified from `Child` to `Adult` with the passing of time. This is not possible if static classification is assumed. Many modeling languages support only static classification given their roots in object-oriented programming languages that likewise only support static classification; in these languages, the class that an object instantiates is defined at object instantiation time, and remains fixed throughout that object's life cycle. Nevertheless, in conceptual modeling, dynamic classification has been considered an important feature and studied by several authors [1,9,21,22,25]. Dynamic classification enlarges the realm of classes to include those which apply contingently or temporarily to their instances. Examples include the ontological notions of *phases* (such as `Child` and `Adult`), and *roles* (such as `BrazilianCitizen`, `ItalianCitizen`, `Employee` and `Customer`).

Abstract and Concrete Classes. Finally, we assume that the conceptual modeling technique may distinguish between abstract and concrete classes. Abstract classes have no "direct" instances, i.e., all of their instances are also instances of specializing subclasses. Concrete classes in their turn are not bound by this constraint (and thus can have "direct" instances).

Running Example. Figure 1 shows a UML model exploring all of the aspects of a source conceptual model we address in this paper, and is used further as a running example. It includes: (i) an overlapping and incomplete generalization set, in which `Persons` are specialized according to—none or more than one—enumerated countries of citizenship; (ii) a generalization set orthogonal to the first one, in which `Persons` are classified dynamically according to life phase; (iii) multiple inheritance, with each `PersonalCustomer` being both a `Customer` and an `Adult Person`, as well as each `CorporateCustomer` being both a `Customer` and an `Organization`); (iv) orthogonal classification hierarchies (with `Organization` being classified as a `CorporateCustomer` when it establishes a relation with another `Organization` and also possibly being classified as a `PrimarySchool` in which children may be enrolled or as a `Hospital`); (v) an abstract class `NamedEntity`, which is specialized into `Person` and `Organization` and an abstract class `Customer`, which is specialized into concrete classes `PersonalCustomer` and `CorporateCustomer`.

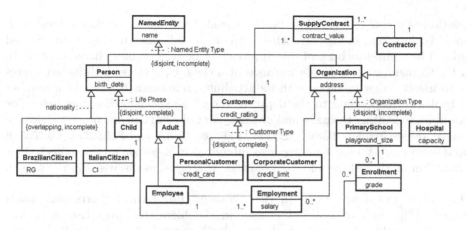

Fig. 1. Running example

3 Current Realization Strategies

The relational model does not directly support the concept of inheritance, and, hence, realization strategies are required to preserve the semantics of a source conceptual model in a target relational schema. Such strategies are described by several authors [3,8,16,18,23] under various names. In this section, we review the most salient strategies in the literature. We discuss their applicability in relation to the source conceptual modeling primitives under discussion.

One Table Per Class. This strategy is also called "Class table" [8], "Vertical inheritance" [23] or "One class one table" [16]: In this strategy, each class gives rise to a separate table, with columns corresponding to the class's features. In this strategy, specialization between classes in the conceptual model gives rise to a foreign key in the table that corresponds to the subclass (henceforth "subclass tables" for simplicity). This foreign key references the primary key of the table corresponding to the superclass (henceforth "superclass table" for simplicity). For example, when applying this strategy under the hierarchy formed by the classes `Customer`, `PersonalCustomer` and `CorporateCustomer` in Figure 1, all classes are transformed into tables. Foreign keys in the `PERSONAL_CUSTOMER` and `CORPORATE_CUSTOMER` tables refer to the primary key of the `CUSTOMER` table. The relational schema directly reflects the organization of classes in the conceptual model, and no restriction on the primitives of the model are imposed. Multiple inheritance can be supported by using a composite foreign key in subclass tables (`PERSONAL_CUSTOMER` in fact has a composite key referencing the primary keys of the `ADULT` and `CUSTOMER` tables). Constraints on a generalization set (overlapping and non-exhaustive classification) are reflected in integrity constraints concerning the cardinality of entries in the subclass tables for a particular row in each superclass table. Dynamic classification is implemented by deletion of a row in a subclass table (cascaded to further subclass tables) and, possibly, insertion in another. Abstract classes and concrete classes are treated alike. The main drawback of this approach is its performance characteristics. In order to manipulate a single instance of a class, e.g., to read all its attributes or to insert a new instance with its attributes, one needs to traverse a number of tables corresponding to the depth of the whole specialization hierarchy. For example, consulting the name and credit_card of a Person one needs to traverse four(!) tables, namely NAMED_ENTITY, PERSON, ADULT and PERSONAL_CUSTOMER (and even more tables if we are also interested in a person's nationality). This limitation motivates the adoption of other strategies, as discussed in the sequel.

One Table Per Leaf Class. In this strategy, also termed "horizontal inheritance" [23], each of the leaf classes in the hierarchy gives rise to a corresponding table. Features of all (non-leaf) superclasses of a leaf class are realized as columns in the leaf class table. No foreign keys emulating inheritance are employed in this approach. The strategy can be understood as reiterated application of an operation of "flattening" of superclasses. For example, when applying this strategy under the hierarchy formed by the classes Customer, PersonalCustomer and CorporateCustomer in Fig. 1, the credit_rating attribute of the Customer correspond to columns in both the PERSONAL_CUSTOMER and CORPORATE_CUSTOMER tables (which also has columns for attributes of its other superclasses: birth_date and address respectivelty). Any references to a superclass (e.g., the references realized as foreign keys of a SUPPLY-CONTRACT) now refer to an entry in either of the subclass tables (in this case PERSONAL_CUSTOMER or CORPORATE_CUSTOMER). Referential integrity tends to be problematic if the number of leaf classes is large. For example, if there are two references from a superclass to another class in the model and ten leaf classes, there will be the need to maintain referential integrity for twenty references. Special attention is required when the conceptual model has multiple inheritance, because of possible name collision (easily addressed with name conventions). (If multiple inheritance is disallowed, the strategy becomes equivalent to *one table per inheritance path*.) This strategy addresses the performance issue discussed for the *one table per class*, at the cost of polymorphic queries. Consider, for example, a query for all customers to ascertain average credit_rating. In the *one table per class* strategy such a query involves only one table. In this strategy, however, the query requires the union of PERSONAL_CUSTOMER and CORPORATE_CUSTOMER). The higher the class in the specialization hierarchy, the higher the number of classes involved in a polymorphic query. Regardless of the performance characteristics, there is a more serious concern when it comes to supporting overlapping generalization sets and orthogonal hierarchies. In the presence of overlapping classification, there is an issue with the identification of an instance of the superclass. Consider the "flattening" of Person in our example. In case a person has double Brazilian and Italian citizenship, there would be a row in the BRAZILIAN_CITIZEN table and another row in the ITALIAN_CITIZEN table denoting the same person, but without a correlating identifier. This problem is also present for orthogonal hierarchies of an abstract superclass. (There would be, e.g., a row in the ADULT table corresponding to a row in the BRAZILIAN_CITIZEN table.) Further, there is a problem with the preservation of identity in dynamic classification (when objects change classes, a row is deleted from one table and added to another, all attributes that are inherited from superclasses must be copied to the new row). Differently from *one table per class*, there is no stable identifier.

One Table Per Hierarchy. This strategy, also called "Single-table" [8] or "One inheritance tree one table" [16], can be understood as the opposite of *one table per leaf class*, applying a "lifting" operation to subclasses instead of the "flattening" of superclasses. Consider, e.g., the hierarchy formed by Customer, PersonalCustomer and CorporateCustomer. Customer is the top-level class in this hierarchy, and will thus give rise to a corresponding CUSTOMER table. Attributes of each subclass become columns in the superclass table, with mandatory attributes corresponding to optional columns. This strategy usually requires the creation of an additional column to distinguish which subclass is (or which subclasses are) instantiated by the entity represented in the row (a so-called "discriminator" column). The "lifting"operation is reiterated until the top-level class of each hierarchy is reached. In principle, the performance problems discussed for the other strategies do not appear in this approach. However, as discussed in [23], standard database integrity mechanisms cannot prevent certain inconsistencies. In our example, the ENROLLMENT table would have foreign keys to the top-level class NAMED_ENTITY, since Person and Primary School would be "lifted" to the corresponding top-level class. Thus, the discriminator would have to be checked to make sure that only children are enrolled in primary schools, because the database would admit any named entity enrolled in another named entity, e.g., hospitals enrolled in hospitals. In addition, the greater the number of leaf classes in a hierarchy, the greater the number of optional columns that remain unattributed in every row. This approach is problematic in the face of multiple inheritance. If multiple inheritance is admitted, then there may be top-level classes that are not disjoint (e.g., Customer and NamedEntity). This means that there will be rows in more than one table denoting the same individual, a problem which also appeared in *one table per leaf class*, albeit for different reasons. Dynamic classification at the top of the hierarchy (such as the case of Customer) also poses a challenge, not unlike the one faced by *one table per leaf class*.

4   Ontological Semantics to the Rescue

In the previous section, we have observed that there are a number of deficiencies of existing conceptual model transformation approaches, with (i) poor performance in various data manipulation operations, (ii) failure to explore beneficial database mechanisms, and/or (iii) lack of support for various conceptual modeling primitives including orthogonal classification hierarchies, overlapping non-exhaustive generalization sets as well as dynamic classification and multiple inheritance.

In contrast with all the aforementioned approaches, our proposal in this paper explores the *ontological semantics* [12] of the elements represented in a conceptual model. By identifying formal ontological meta-properties of the classes in a model, including *sortality* and *rigidity*, we are able to guide the transformation. We use here the ontological distinction underlying the Unified Foundational Ontology (UFO) [12], which have their roots in OntoClean [11]. Here we discuss only the ontological distinctions that are needed in this paper. For further reference and formalization, see [12,14].

Take a subject domain focused on objects (as opposed to events or occurrences). Central to this domain we will have a number of object *kinds*, i.e., the genuine fundamental types of objects that exist in this domain. The term "kind" is meant here in a strong technical sense, i.e., by a kind, we mean a type capturing essential properties of the things it classifies. In other words, the objects classified by that kind could not possibly exist without being of that specific kind. In Fig. 1, we have represented two object kinds, namely, `Person` and `Organization`. These are the fundamental kinds of entities that are deemed to exist in the domain. Kinds tessellate the possible space of objects in that domain, i.e., all objects belong necessarily to exactly one kind.

Static subdivisions (or subtypes) of a kind are naturally termed *subkinds*. In our example, the kind `Organization` is specialized in the subkinds `Primary School` and `Hospital`. Object kinds and subkinds represent essential properties of objects, i.e., properties that these objects instantiate in all possible situations. They are examples of what are termed *rigid* or static types. There are, however, also types that represent contingent or accidental properties of objects (termed *anti-rigid* types). These include *phases* and *roles*. Phases represent properties that are intrinsic to entities; roles, in contrast, represent properties that entities have in a relational context, i.e., contingent relational properties. In our example, we have a *phase partition* including `Child` and `Adult` (as phases in the life of a `Person`). Several other types in the example are *roles*: `Employee`, `Contractor`, `BrazilianCitizen` and `ItalianCitizen` (the last two in the context of a relation with a national state, not represented in the model, for simplicity).

Kinds, subkinds, phases, and roles are all object *sortals*. In the philosophical literature, a sortal is a type that provides a uniform principle of identity, persistence, and individuation for its instances. A sortal is either a kind (e.g., `Person`) or a specialization of a kind (e.g., `Child`, `Employee`, `Hospital`), i.e., it is either a type representing the essence of what things are or a sub-classification of entities that "have that same type of essence". There are also types that apply to entities of multiple kinds, these are called *non-sortals*. An example of non-sortal is `Customer` (which can be played by both people and organizations). We call these role-like types that classify entities of multiple kinds *role mixins*. Another example of non-sortal is `NamedEntity`. However, it is a rigid non-sortal, classifying objects of various kinds statically.

In addition to objects, there are also *existentially dependent* endurants, i.e., endurants that depend on other endurants for their existence. Here, we highlight the so-called *relators*, which reify a relationship *mediating* endurants. In our example, an instance of `Employment` can only exist as long as a particular instance of `Person` (playing the `Employee` role) and a particular instance of `Organization` (playing the corresponding `Employer` role, omitted here) exist. The meta-properties we have discussed for object types also apply to relator types. In our example, `Employment`, `Enrollment` and `SupplyContract` are relator kinds.[1]. Relators are composed of another type of dependent endurant termed a *qua-entity* (or *role instance*) [12]. Each qua-entity composing a relator inheres in one of the relatum of that relator while being relationally dependent on the other relata.

Figure 2 revisits Fig. 1, now including class stereotypes according to the ontological distinctions discussed above, which are part of UFO-based OntoUML profile [12]. According to the rules that apply to OntoUML (formally characterized in [14]):

- non-sortals (such as «category» and «roleMixin»), when present in a model, are always superclasses (and never subclasses) of sortals (such as «kind», «subkind», «role», «phase», «relatorKind»);
- non-sortals are abstract and are only instantiated through their sortal subclasses;
- sortals that are not kinds («subkind», «role», «phase» or «role») specialize *exactly one* kind (or «relatorKind»), from which they inherit their principle

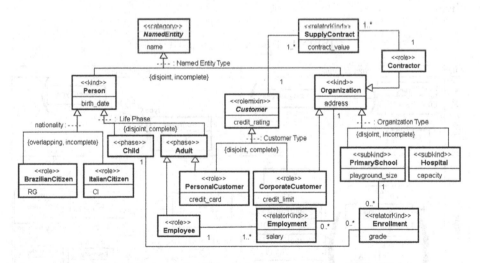

Fig. 2. Running example with OntoUML stereotypes added.

---

[1] It is not in the scope of this paper to discuss strategies for the representation of *n*-to-*n* relationships. With the reification of these relationships into relators, the challenge is already addressed at the conceptual model level, with many other benefits [10].

of identity. So, there is no multiple inheritance of kinds, since all kinds are mutually disjoint;

– rigid types («kind», «subkind», «category», «relatorKind») never specialize anti-rigid types («role», «roleMixin» or «phase»).

We can now use the ontological distinctions to articulate a transformation strategy. In a nutshell, this strategy results in a schema composed of tables corresponding to the *kinds* of entities in the domain. Because of this, it is termed *one table per kind.*

The first two steps of our approach are based on the operations of *flattening* and *lifting*, which are guided by the aforementioned ontological distinctions. Non-sortals are flattened towards sortals (step 1). Sortals are lifted until their kinds are reached (step 2). These operations basically correspond to the graph transformation *model abstraction rules* proposed in [13]. In particular, the former to the *non-sortal abstraction rule* (R_2), and the latter to a combination of the *sortal abstraction rule* (R_3) and the *subkind and phase partition abstraction rule* (R_4). Flattening is performed from all top-level non-sortals. In our running example, the `name` attribute `NamedEntity` is flattened to `PERSON` and `ORGANIZATION`. The same applies to `credit_rating` in `Customer`. When all non-sortals have been flattened, lifting is performed recursively from the leaves of the inheritance tree, propagating mandatory attributes as optional, until kinds are reached[2]. Table 1 shows the two operations as graph transformations. The classes flattened or lifted are shown in grey. For lifting, there are two cases. When a generalization set is involved (a), a discriminator enumeration is introduced, with labels corresponding to each $SubType_j$ in the set. Otherwise (b), a Boolean attribute suffices.

Table 1. Transformation patterns.

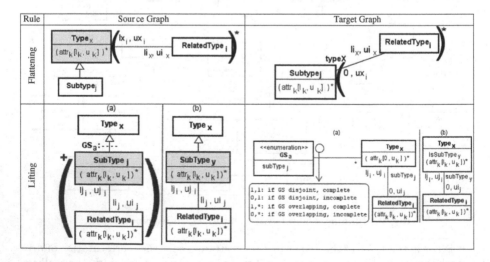

---

[2] For the implementation repository see https://github.com/nemo-ufes/ontouml2db.

After these operations have been carried out, as a final step of our approach (step 3), tables are produced for each of the classes in the refactored model. The tables corresponding to dependent entities must have foreign keys to the entities on which they depend. This is the case for tables corresponding to relator kinds, and also for the discriminating tables in the case of overlapping generalization sets. In the latter case, each row in a discriminator table represents a qua-entity connecting role players with the corresponding (reified) role class. As previously discussed, qua-entities and relators are existentially dependent entities.

Figure 3 presents the schema that results from the application of these transformation steps in the conceptual model in Fig. 2. We obtain the five tables corresponding to object kinds: PERSON, ORGANIZATION, and three corresponding to relator kinds: EMPLOYMENT, ENROLLMENT and SUPPLY_CONTRACT. An additional table for the discriminator that results from the overlapping generalization set nationality is introduced (PERSON-NATIONALITY, representing a qua-entity connecting a person to a particular nationality type). Finally, for all the tables representing dependent entities types, we introduce the corresponding dependency keys.

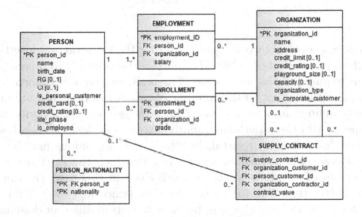

Fig. 3. Resulting relational schema in running example *one table per kind*.

5   Discussion and Comparison to Alternative Approaches

Table 2 summarizes the comparison between the proposed *one table per kind* strategy and the three dominant strategies in the literature, where: n is the total number of classes in the source conceptual model, h is the maximum height of the hierarchy (i.e., maximum path size from a top-level class to a leaf class), n_l is the number of leaf classes in the hierarchy, n_t the number of top-level classes, and n_k is the number of kinds. Note that the number of kinds (n_k) is equal to or lower than the number of leaf classes (i.e., $n_k \leq n_l \leq n$), and that they are equal ($n_k = n_l$) only in case there are no subkinds, roles and phases. Thus, the number of tables to required to represent entities in the domain in the proposed *one table per kind* strategy is equal to or lower than that required by *one table per class* and *one table per leaf class*. The comparison with *one table per hierarchy* requires us to consider the number of top-level classes (n_t). The two approaches result in the same number of tables when there are no non-sortals ($n_k = n_t$).

Table 2. Comparison between realization strategies.

Realization strategy	N° of tables representing entities	N° of joins to retrieve an entity	N° of tables affected in insert operation	N° of tables in union to read one attribute (polymorphic query)	Multiple inheritance	Orthogonal hierarchies	Dynamic classification performance
One table per class	n	h	$h+1$	1	Yes	Yes	Poor
One table per leaf class	n_l	1	1	n_l	Yes	No	Poor
One table per hierarchy	n_t	1	1	1	No	Yes	Good
One table per kind	n_k	1	1	n_k (1, if defined in sortal)	Yes	Yes	Good

The table also presents worst-case figures for the retrieval and insertion of an entity (with all its attributes). *One table per class* fares poorly in this comparison, with h joins required in the worst case. The performance of polimorphic queries is considered, with respect to the number of tables involved in a union to read one attribute defined in a superclass. *One table per leaf class* performs poorly in this respect. All others perform equally, except *one table per kind* when the attribute is defined in a non-sortal, in which case, n_k unions may be required in the worst case (when the non-sortal class in which the attribute is defined classifies entities of all kinds in the model). Even in this case, the approach is equal to or better than *one table per leaf class* (since $n_k \leq n_l$). Table 3 shows the values for these variables for a number of models in different domains (those also employed in [13]), revealing that height of the hierarchy ranges from two to six, and the number of kinds in a model is typically one fourth or one fifth of the total number of classes. The average number of leaf classes (n_l) is 39, contrasted with 15 for kinds.

Table 3. Variable occurrences by OntoUML model.

Variables	OntoUML models										
	Cloud vulnerability	ECG	G.805	MPOG	Normative acts	OpenBio	OpenFlow	Open provenance	PAS 77	Software requirements	Average
n	30	49	123	15	59	231	20	33	66	17	64
h	3	2	6	4	3	5	2	2	3	2	3
n_l	12	18	70	7	43	163	8	12	41	11	39
n_t	5	4	14	3	5	9	4	8	5	2	6
n_k	12	18	18	5	10	37	6	17	19	7	15

Problems with multiple inheritance in *one table per hierarchy* do not appear in *one table per kind* because there is no multiple inheritance of kinds. Multiple inheritance of non-kind sortals (subkinds, phases and roles) does not pose a problem, as discriminators identify the instantiated classes. Multiple inheritance of non-sortals creates no problems because they are flattened into kinds. Problems with orthogonal hierarchies and overlapping generalization sets in *one table per leaf class* also do not arise as a consequence of the transformation strategy. Kinds tables are where the entities primary keys are placed, and hence there is no problem with the same entity being represented in several tables. Flattening of non-sortals poses no problem in this scenario. In the lifting of non-kind sortals, orthogonal hierarchies and overlapping generalization sets are, not unlike multiple inheritance, reflected in discriminators in the kind table. Dynamic classification is supported naturally as reclassification is simply change in discriminators. This is not the case with *one table per class* and *one table per leaf class*, which require deletion and insertion, posing a problem for referential integrity.

In addition to the dominant strategies we have discussed, there are approaches which use the distinction between abstract and concrete classes, with impact on performance characteristics. For example, *one table per concrete class* is a variant of *one table per class* in which abstract classes are flattened out. Since flattening of abstract classes reduces the height of the hierarchy, this strategy has the potential of improve the performance of retrieving and inserting an entity. Nevertheless, that performance is still much dependent on the size of the concrete class hierarchy. Further, dynamic classification performance remains a challenge in this approach. By identifying the ontological meta-properties of classes in the source conceptual model, we are able to better navigate performance tradeoffs, beyond what can be achieved with the abstract–concrete distinction. For example, strategies such as *one table per rigid sortal* become possible, approximating *one table per concrete class* in terms of performance but circumventing its difficulty with dynamic classification. This approach is favored by Rybola and Pergl [20], who focus on the transformation of sortals. In his Ph.D. thesis, Rybola [19] proposes the transformation of non-sortals with a pattern that introduces a table for each class. In this sense, his approach approximates *one table per class*, but produces even more tables due to the patterns employed to address the relation between the non-sortal and sortal hierarchies. This exacerbates the performance issues when accessing or inserting an object. The techniques proposed in that work can be adapted to our strategy. In particular, quite sophisticated integrity rules and validation triggers were proposed to preserve the semantics of the original constructs from the source OntoUML model.

Over the years, a number of authors have compared the various object-relational mapping strategies in terms of system infrastructure (performance and storage) and relational schema design (understanding and maintainability). Among these, Keller [16] points out the infrastructure and design "forces" that govern the development of a relational schema, as well as some characteristics used in the application design, such as polymorphism. The author also exposes the consequences of using the strategies, which also is done by Fowler [8] when identifying the strengths and weaknesses of each strategy. Ambler [2] performs a brief comparison between the strategies and is concerned with the practical differences between the relational and the object-oriented paradigms. Philippi [18] establishes the consequences of mapping strategies in relation to the infrastructure and design aspects of the relational schema when the inheritance hierarchy is associated with other classes of the model along with association cardinality. In turn, Torres [23] does not perform a systematic comparison between the strategies, but identifies their adoption in the various object-relational mapping tools. A common characteristic of all these efforts is their focus on the primitives of object-oriented programming languages as opposed to conceptual modeling primitives.

Some authors [4, 18] have identified three types of approaches to bridge the gap between an object model and a relational schema: (i) the "forward engineering" approach (also called object-relational mapping), in which the relational schema is generated from the class model that must be persisted (often together with the necessary code to propagate object persistence to the database); (ii) the "reverse engineering" approach (also called relational-object mapping), in which classes are produced from the existing relational structure; and (iii) the "meet-in-the-middle" approach, in which conceptual model and relational schema are designed, implemented and evolved separately, requiring some middleware to perform the correspondence between the objects and the database. Our approach is clearly positioned in the "forward engineering" camp.

6   Conclusions

The study of ontological foundations in conceptual modeling has produced a number of advances over the last decades. This paper extends some of these advances to relational schema design. We have shown that considering the ontological status of classes in a conceptual model makes it possible to conceive of novel transformation strategies that cannot be articulated with ontologically neutral conceptual modeling primitives. We have shown that the *one table per kind* strategy has performance characteristics that differ from the dominant approaches in the literature. Further, it supports multiple inheritance, orthogonal and overlapping hierarchies and dynamic classification.

We hypothesize that *one table per kind* can improve schema comprehension, as well as query writing and readability. This is because of the role that kinds play in cognition. There is a significant body of evidence in cognitive psychology [17, 26, 27], that object *kinds* are the most salient category of types in human cognition, being responsible for our most basic operations of object individuation and identity. Further, there is empirical evidence that the ontological distinctions employed here (those underlying OntoUML) contribute to improving the quality of conceptual models without requiring an additional effort to produce them [24]. In future work, we intend to assess whether the benefits trickle down to the system-level when coupled with the transformation strategy proposed here. We also intend to evaluate the impact of the various strategies on maintainability, in particular when considering the evolution of the relational schema (e.g., with the introduction/removal of classes, attributes, associations and the required data migration). Usability, maintainability and database performance analysis requires careful consideration of application-specific demands. Thus, considering application sensitivity is a clear issue for further work and application characteristics (e.g., demands on polymorphic queries) could guide the selection of a strategy.

Finally, recent developments have shown that there is a fruitful interplay between ontology-based techniques and database realization. For example, Ontology-Based Data Access (OBDA) approaches such as Ontop [5], have shown that is possible to expose relational data in terms of a computational ontology. This is done in a meet-in-the-middle fashion by relying on the manual specification of a mapping from a computational ontology to an existing relational schema. We understand that synthesizing ODBA mappings with our approach is feasible, and would allow transparent ontology-based access to the produced relational schemas.

Acknowledgments. This research is partly funded by the Brazilian Research Funding Agencies CNPq (grants 312123/2017-5 and 407235/2017-5) and CAPES (23038.028816/2016-41).

References

1. Albano, A., Bergamini, R., Ghelli, G., Orsini, R.: An object data model with roles. In: Proceedings of 19th International Conference on Very Large Data Bases, pp. 39–51. Morgan Kaufmann (1993)
2. Ambler, S.W.: Mapping objects to relational databases, White Paper, AmbySoft Inc (1997)
3. Ambler, S.W.: Agile Database Techniques: Effective Strategies for the Agile Software Developer. Wiley, New York (2003)
4. Cabibbo, L.: Objects meet relations: on the transparent management of persistent objects. In: Persson, A., Stirna, J. (eds.) CAiSE 2004. LNCS, vol. 3084, pp. 429–445. Springer, Heidelberg (2004). https://doi.org/10.1007/978-3-540-25975-6_31
5. Calvanese, D., et al.: Ontop: answering SPARQL queries over relational databases. Semant. Web **8**(3), 471–487 (2017)
6. Cardelli, L.: A semantics of multiple inheritance. In: Kahn, G., MacQueen, D.B., Plotkin, G. (eds.) SDT 1984. LNCS, vol. 173, pp. 51–67. Springer, Heidelberg (1984). https://doi.org/10.1007/3-540-13346-1_2
7. Carré, B., Geib, J.: The point of view notion for multiple inheritance. In: Yonezawa, A. (ed.) Proceedings OOPSLA/ECOOP 1990, pp. 312–321. ACM (1990)
8. Fowler, M.: Patterns of Enterprise Application Architecture. Addison-Wesley Longman Publishing, Boston (2002)
9. Gottlob, G., Schrefl, M., Röck, B.: Extending object-oriented systems with roles. ACM Trans. Inf. Syst. **14**(3), 268–296 (1996)
10. Guarino, N., Guizzardi, G.: We need to discuss the *relationship*: revisiting relationships as modeling constructs. In: Zdravkovic, J., Kirikova, M., Johannesson, P. (eds.) CAiSE 2015. LNCS, vol. 9097, pp. 279–294. Springer, Cham (2015). https://doi.org/10.1007/978-3-319-19069-3_18

11. Guarino, N., Welty, C.A.: An overview of ontoclean. In: Handbook on Ontologies, pp. 201–220. Springer (2009)
12. Guizzardi, G.: Ontological foundations for structural conceptual models. Ph.D. thesis, University of Twente (10 2005)
13. Guizzardi, G., Figueiredo, G., Hedblom, M.M., Poels, G.: Ontology-based model abstraction. In: Proceedings of RCIS 2019, pp. 1–13. IEEE (2019)
14. Guizzardi, G., Fonseca, C.M., Benevides, A.B., Almeida, J.P.A., Porello, D., Sales, T.P.: Endurant types in ontology-driven conceptual modeling: towards OntoUML 2.0. In: Trujillo, J.C. (ed.) ER 2018. LNCS, vol. 11157, pp. 136–150. Springer, Cham (2018). https://doi.org/10.1007/978-3-030-00847-5_12
15. Ireland, C., Bowers, D., Newton, M., Waugh, K.: A classification of object-relational impedance mismatch. In: Proceedings of 1st DBKDA, pp. 36–43, March 2009
16. Ireland, C., Bowers, D., Newton, M., Waugh, K.: A classification of object-relational impedance mismatch. In: Proceedings of 1st DBKDA, pp. 36–43, March 2009
17. Macnamara, J.T., Macnamara, J., Reyes, G.E.: The Logical Foundations of Cognition. No. 4 in Vancouver Studies in Cognitive Science, Oxford University Press on Demand, New York (1994)
18. Philippi, S.: Model driven generation and testing of object-relational mappings. J. Syst. Softw. **77**, 193–207 (2005)
19. Rybola, Z.: Towards OntoUML for Software Engineering: Transformation of OntoUML into Relational Databases. PhD thesis, Czech Technical University in Prague (2017)
20. Rybola, Z., Pergl, R.: Towards OntoUML for software engineering: Transformation of kinds and subkinds into relational databases. Comput. Sci. Inf. Syst. **14**(3), 913–937 (2017)
21. Steimann, F.: On the representation of roles in object-oriented and conceptual modelling. Data Knowl. Eng. **35**(1), 83–106 (2000)
22. Steimann, F.: The role data model revisited. Appl. Ontology **2**(2), 89–103 (2007)
23. Torres, A., et al.: Twenty years of object-relational mapping: a survey on patterns, solutions, and their implications on application design. Inf. Softw. Technol. **82**, 1–18 (2017)
24. Verdonck, M., Gailly, F., Pergl, R., Guizzardi, G., Martins, B., Pastor, O.: Comparing traditional conceptual modeling with ontology-driven conceptual modeling: an empirical study. Inf. Syst. **81**, 92–103 (2019)
25. Wieringa, R.J., de Jonge, W., Spruit, P.: Using dynamic classes and role classes to model object migration. TAPOS **1**(1), 61–83 (1995)
26. Xu, F.: From lot's wife to a pillar of salt: evidence that physical object is a sortal concept. Mind Lang. **12**(3–4), 365–392 (1997)
27. Xu, F., Carey, S.: Infants metaphysics: the case of numerical identity. Cogn. Psychol. **30**(2), 111–153 (1996)

Towards an Ontology Network on Human-Computer Interaction

Simone Dornelas Costa[1,2(✉)], Monalessa Perini Barcellos[2],
Ricardo de Almeida Falbo[2],
and Murillo Vasconcelos Henriques Bittencourt Castro[2]

[1] Computer Department, Federal University of Espírito Santo (UFES), Alegre, Brazil
`simone.costa@ufes.br`
[2] Ontology and Conceptual Modeling Research Group (NEMO), Computer Science Department, Federal University of Espírito Santo (UFES), Vitória, Brazil
`{monalessa,falbo}@inf.ufes.br, murillo.castro@aluno.ufes.br`

Abstract. Engineering interactive computer systems is a challenging task that involves concerns related to the human-computer interaction (HCI), such as usability and user experience. HCI is a wide domain, where ontologies are useful instruments for supporting knowledge-related problems. However, HCI ontologies have been built and used in isolation. Ideally, in wide domains, ontologies should not be stand-alone artifacts. They should relate to each other, forming a network of interlinked semantic resources, i.e. an ontology network. Therefore, in this paper we introduce HCI-ON, a Human-Computer Interaction Ontology Network composed of ontologies that we have developed and others found in the literature. HCI-ON organizes and integrates knowledge, serving as a basis to several applications. We also discuss mechanisms to evolve HCI-ON and present some envisioned applications.

Keywords: Human-Computer Interaction · Ontology · Ontology network

1 Introduction

Developing Interactive Computer Systems (ICS) is a challenging task, which involves a diverse body of knowledge and multidisciplinary teams, joining people from different backgrounds with their own technical language, terms and knowledge [4,5]. To an ICS reach high usability levels, it is necessary to take HCI aspects into account. HCI is a wide domain and as the area matures, new terms are proposed and new meanings are assigned to existing terms. This makes it difficult to establish a common conceptualization about HCI, leading to semantic interoperability problems, such as ambiguity and imprecision when interpreting shared information. Ontologies can be useful to capture and organize knowledge to deal with these problems. They have been applied in the HCI context to

G. Dobbie et al. (Eds.): ER 2020, LNCS 12400, pp. 331–341, 2020.
https://doi.org/10.1007/978-3-030-62522-1_24

knowledge representation [7,20], to aid in interaction design [2,27,34] and evaluation [24], interface adaptation [3,16,25], semantic annotation [13,21], among others.

We investigated the state of the art of ontologies on HCI through a systematic literature review and we found 22 ontologies. However, there are several HCI aspects not covered by them. Since HCI is a complex domain, it is not possible to build a large monolithic ontology to cover the entire domain. Contrariwise, HCI ontologies should be built incrementally in an integrated way, forming a network. An ontology network (ON) is a collection of ontologies related together by means of dependency and alignment relationships [33]. ONs enable to establish a comprehensive conceptualization that provides a common understanding about the domain and can be used as a reference to solve problems related to the conceptualization as a whole or to extracts of it. Hence, integrating several ontologies into an ON provides a framework that can be explored to potentialize and increase the set of solutions in its universe of discourse.

In this paper we argue that HCI ontologies should be organized as an ON, to provide comprehensive knowledge about the domain and support knowledge evolution. We introduce the Human-Computer Interaction Ontology Network (HCI-ON), an ON composed of ontologies that we have developed and others we found in the literature. Since HCI-ON is very extensive, our focus here is to provide a general view of its three-layered architecture and discuss its evolution mechanisms. Section 2 briefly presents the background for the paper. Section 3 presents HCI-ON architecture and the HCI Design Ontology. Section 4 discusses how to evolve HCI-ON by adding new and existing ontologies to it. Finally, Sect. 5 presents some envisioned applications and our final considerations.

2   Background

HCI involves multidisciplinary knowledge and people from different communities. The lack of a common conceptualization shared by the communities interested in HCI can lead to communication, knowledge transferring and semantic interoperability problems.

Ontologies have been acknowledged as quite appropriate to solve semantic conflicts, for reducing conceptual ambiguities and inconsistencies, for making knowledge structures clearer and can be used for establishing a common conceptualization of a domain of interest. According to [28], ontologies can be organized in a three-layered architecture: (i) *foundational ontologies* model the very basic and general concepts and relations that make up the world (e.g., objects, events); (ii) *core ontologies* refine (i) by adding detailed concepts and relations in a specific area (e.g., service, process); and, (iii) *domain ontologies* describe a particular domain in reality (e.g., the anatomy of the human body) by specializing concepts from (i) or (ii).

For a complex domain, representing its knowledge as a single ontology results in a large and monolithic ontology that is hard to manipulate, use, and maintain [33]. On the other hand, representing each sub-domain in isolation is a costly task that leads to a very fragmented solution that is again hard to handle [26]. In such cases, building an *ontology network* (ON) is an adequate solution [33]. In an ON, ontologies are connected to each other through relationships, such as *dependency* and *alignment*. The former occurs when, in order to define its own model, an ontology refers to concepts and relations defined in another ontology (i.e., an ontology reuses concepts from another). The latter is a way to put different models in correspondence by establishing equivalency mappings between entities from different ontologies (i.e., the same as, a generalization of, a specialization of) [33].

To investigate existing ontologies in HCI, we have performed a systematic literature review (SLR) [15] and found 22 ontologies: [1–3, 6, 7, 9, 11, 13, 16–21, 24, 25, 27, 29, 31, 32, 34, 35]. These ontologies cover different, but related HCI aspects. Some of them focus on UI (User Interface) design and evaluation, representing aspects related to both the user and the system, but without describing the HCI phenomenon itself [2, 11, 16, 17, 32, 34]. Others address only one of the parts involved in the HCI phenomenon: user [21, 27] or system [1, 6, 13, 18, 29]. Four ontologies describe the HCI phenomena: [7, 31, 35] and [20]. However, [7] and [20] are specific to some kinds of interaction, namely: haptic [20] or by means of gestures [7]. [3] covers different aspects involving adaptation. [9] is specific to context of use. Three works [16, 17, 25] focus on people with disabilities. [19] addresses the characterization of user feedback and [24] focuses on usability guidelines and related elements. Further information about the 22 ontologies and its concepts is available at http://bit.ly/SLR_OntoInHCI.

Although a variety of HCI aspects are addressed by these ontologies, there are aspects not covered by any of them (e.g., HCI evaluation and design processes, prototype, among others). Moreover, none of them reused or even discuss how to reuse or integrate ontologies. In fact, HCI ontologies have been developed to solve specific problems in specific contexts, without a concern with integration. This approach has proven to be inadequate to integrate, use and share knowledge [26]. To speed up the development and use of HCI ontologies, we advocate that they should be built incrementally, reusing existing ontologies, and forming a network. This motivated us to work on HCI-ON.

3   HCI-ON: A Human-Computer Interaction Ontology Network

Figure 1 presents HCI-ON (current version). Since HCI is related to Software Engineering, HCI-ON is integrated to SEON (Software Engineering Ontology Network) [26]. In the figure, each circle (network node) represents a core or a domain ontology. Obfuscated circles represent ontologies under development. Arrows represent dependency relationships, indicating that concepts from the target ontology are reused by the source ontology (in red from HCI-ON to SEON). Circle size varies according to the number of concepts of the ontology.

To truly enjoy the benefits of keeping the ontologies in a network, we need to take advantage of the existing resources available in the ON for gradually improving and extending it. It is crucial to establish a sustainable architecture that supports growing the ON by adding new ontologies to it or integrating existing ontologies into it. In this sense, in HCI-ON, we adopted a three-layered architecture (Fig. 1). At the *foundational layer*, we adopted UFO (Unified Foundational Ontology) [12], which is also used in SEON. By doing that, we keep the same foundation on both ONs concepts, making easier to connect them. At the *core layer*, we developed the Human-Computer Interaction Ontology (HCIO) [8]. Its purpose is to clarify the main notions and establish an explicit common and shared conceptualization about the HCI phenomenon. HCIO describes what an interactive system is, which types of actions users perform when interacting with an interactive system and, finally, what a human-computer interaction is. It is at the heart of HCI-ON. Finally, at the *domain layer*, there are domain-specific ontologies, namely: HCI Design Ontology (HCIDO); HCI Evaluation Ontology (HCIEO); UI Types and Elements Ontology (UIT&EO); HCI Modality Ontology (HCIMO); Context of Use Ontology (CUO); Cognitive HCI Ontology (CHCIO); and Semiotic HCI Ontology (SHCIO). HCIDO and HCIEO address aspects related to, respectively, HCI design and evaluation, such as the process, produced artifacts and stakeholders, among others. HCIMO treats, in a general way, HCI styles/paradigms (modalities of interaction). It connects to UIT&EO to indicate Input and Output (I/O) devices and types of interface used in these approaches. UIT&EO addresses interface types and their elements, associating them with the possible types of I/O equipment to be used in each element. CUO describes the elements that characterize a context of use, describing physical and social environments in which the interaction occurs. CHCIO and SHCIO also describe the HCI phenomenon. The former does that by adopting the Seven Stages of Action perspective proposed by [22], while the latter adopts the meta-communication perspective proposed by [30].

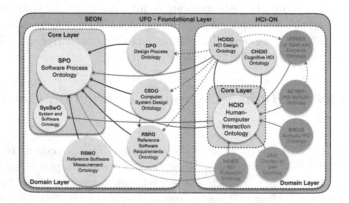

Fig. 1. HCI-ON architecture.

The decision on which domain ontologies we should develop was made in order to cover relevant aspects of the HCI domain, providing knowledge to talk about the whole life cycle of an HCI project (from design, UI, modalities of interaction, evaluation to context of use). Moreover, they allow describing the HCI phenomenon under cognitive and semiotic perspectives. The ontologies in the domain layer support the HCI-ON growth, since each of them can be extended to address more specific sub-domains or related domains. Next, we present a fragment of the HCI Design Ontology (HCIDO).

3.1 HCI Design Ontology

The HCI Design Ontology (HCIDO) addresses aspects such as which types of HCI objects can be designed, the involved artifacts and agents that deal with them. HCIDO was developed by specializing concepts mainly from HCIO (HCI-ON) and CSDO (SEON). CSDO deals with the design of computer systems. We built CSDO based mainly on the conceptual model proposed by Ralph and Wand [23], who define design (in general) as "a specification of an object, manifested by an agent, intended to accomplish goals, in a particular environment, using a set of primitive components, satisfying a set of requirements, subject to constraints". To develop HCIDO, we reused CSDO by specializing its concepts and connecting them with specializations of HCIO concepts. By doing that, we address HCI design by connecting design aspects to HCI objects.

Figure 2 presents an overview of an HCIDO fragment and its dependencies with ontologies from SEON and HCI-ON. The black single-dashed horizontal lines separate concepts from different ontologies, and the red double-dashed lines separate the layers. The top-most is the foundational layer, where concepts from UFO are placed. Following a top-down direction, there are three ontologies at the core layer: SPO and SysSwO (SEON); and HCIO (HCI-ON). They provide details about the agents and objects involved in SE and HCI and relationships between them. At the bottom, there is the domain layer, where HCIDO is located, directly connected to CSDO (SEON), UIT&EO and HCIO. Different colors are used to indicate concepts from different ontologies. Next, we describe HCIDO concepts. In the text, concepts are written in **bold** and examples (i.e., instances) in *italics*.

From HCIO, there are three concepts that characterize possible objects of interest in HCI Design, all of them are **Software Items**, i.e., pieces of software produced in software processes [10]. The first, **User Interface Program**, represents software items that aim at producing a certain result through execution on a computer, dealing with **User Interface**, which is composed of **Input Equipment** and **Output Equipment** (not shown in Fig. 2). The second, **Interactive Software System**, is a software item constituted by at least one **User Interface Program** and, being a Software System, it intends to determine the behavior of the computer towards the external environment [10]. The third, **Interactive Computer System**, is a computer system that has **User Interface**. It is a combination of hardware and software used to process, transform, store, display or transmit information or data by receiving input, and communicating output to users [14]. For example, *Microsoft Visual Studio (MVS)* is an instance of **Interactive Software System**. Among the many programs that

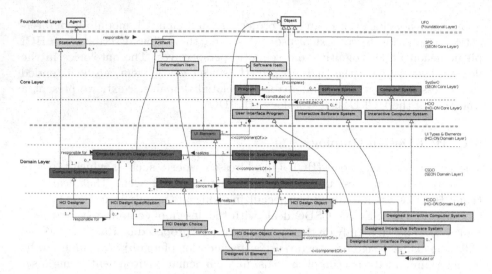

Fig. 2. HCIDO and related ontologies.

constitute it, the ones that deal with its graphical interface are instances of **User Interface Program**. The *MVS* loaded and running on a computer, together with input and output equipment to interact with the user, comprises an instance of **Interactive Computer System**.

We consider that, in the context of HCI, **User Interface Programs**, **Interactive Software Systems** (including their **User Interfaces**) and **Interactive Computer Systems** (involving software and hardware components) are the kind of objects that can be designed. Therefore, in HCIDO, we define **HCI Design Object** as the designed objects in the HCI phenomenon, being either a **Designed User Interface Program**, a **Designed Interactive Software System** or a **Designed Interactive Computer System**. What adds the "designed" characteristic to these objects is the existence of an **Artifact** with a detailed description of them in terms of their design (e.g., a prototype or a document describing their components and connections among them). This artifact is an **HCI Design Specification**, which consists of a collection of several **Information Items**, named **HCI Design Choices**, each one concerning how a specific **HCI Design Object Component** should be. **HCI Design Object Components** are smaller parts that, connected, form an **HCI Design Object**, which thus realizes the **HCI Design Specification** where its components are described. **Designed UI Elements** are **UI Elements** (e.g. windows, buttons, toolbars) from UIT&EO that compose a **Designed User Interface Program**. Finally, the **HCI Designer** is the agent (a person or a group) responsible for creating and maintaining the **HCI Design Specification**.

Taking the *MVS* example, in an HCI design scenario, it is a **Designed Interactive Software System**. The team or person in charge of designing it (i.e., the **HCI Designer**) sketched a prototype (**HCI Design Specification**) showing how *MVS* graphical user interface should be. This prototype encoded several **HCI Design Choices**, like the description of how a toolbar (a **Designed UI Element**) should look and be positioned on the screen. This toolbar is implemented as an **HCI Design Object Component** in the *MVS* graphical user interface program (**Designed User Interface Program**), which is a constituent of the **Designed Interactive Software System** (*MVS*). What makes the *MVS* an **HCI Design Object** is the fact that it has a design specification describing its characteristics (i.e., an **HCI Design Specification**) and once it was created satisfying that specification, it realizes that.

Although not shown in Fig. 2, HCIDO also addresses concepts related to the mental aspects involved in HCI design. For example, both the design object and its specification exist in the mind of the designer before being materialized as the objects and artifacts showed in Fig. 2. Moreover, as it can be seen in Fig. 1, HCIDO connects to RSRO. This relation allows to align the HCI Design Specification to the functional (e.g., functionalities that the software should provide) and non-functional (e.g., usability requirements to be satisfied) requirements that must be met by the software item. It makes explicit that the HCI Design Specification must describe HCI Design Choices able to meet the software item requirements, connecting the HCI Design process to the Requirements Engineering process.

4   Evolving HCI-ON

An ON is constantly evolving. Each ontology added to ON contributes for it as a whole. When a new ontology is added, it reuses elements from the networked ontologies. These, in turn, may be adapted to keep consistency and share the same semantics along the whole network.

To evolve HCI-ON, one can (i) develop new ontologies from scratch and add them to the network; or (ii) add existing ontologies to the network. In (i), the ontologies must be developed grounded in UFO, to share the same foundation of all networked ontologies, and they must be added to the network through dependency relationships. We have developed the HCI-ON ontologies shown in Fig. 1 by following this procedure. In (ii), one can use dependency or alignment relationships. In the first case, it is necessary to re-engineer the existing ontology in the light of UFO, so that the ontology will share the same HCI-ON basic conceptualization and, thus, it will be possible to integrate it into the network properly. When two or more existing ontologies addressing the same subject represent together the conceptualization of a new ontology to be added to HCI-ON (i.e., they are complementary), they must be merged and re-engineered in the light of UFO. After re-engineering, the ontology can be added to HCI-ON through dependency relationships. For example, we can merge and re-engineer the ontologies [21] and [27] to produce a Persona Ontology; [3,16,17,21] and [25] to produce a User Capacity and Accessibility Ontology and add them to HCI-ON.

Existing ontologies can also be added to the ON as they are, through alignment relationships (i.e., indicating equivalence between concepts of different ontologies). For example, the terms People [31], Person [21] and Person [27] have the same meaning than HCIO's Person concept. Aligning existing ontologies to HCI-ON makes the ON conceptualization more comprehensive. Moreover, it allows the plugged ontologies not to be changed (not affecting applications in which they are used) and, even so, extend their conceptualizations. Figure 3 shows the ontologies we found in our SLR plugged into HCI-ON. Since they were not re-engineered, they are not grounded in UFO.

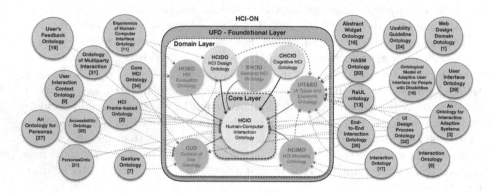

Fig. 3. Evolving HCI-ON.

5   Final Considerations

In this paper, we advocate that HCI ontologies should be built forming a network that organizes and structures knowledge. This motivated us to create HCI-ON, which aims to provide a comprehensive conceptualization about HCI.

We envisioned some applications to HCI-ON. First, it can be useful to solve knowledge and semantics-related problems. For example, it can be used for communication purposes, to support knowledge management (KM) systems, aiding in knowledge representation (e.g., semantic annotation), integration, search, and retrieval. HCI-ON conceptual model can also be used as a basis to design KM systems integrating several HCI sub-domains. HCI-ON can also be used to annotate HCI-related documents (e.g., text document, spreadsheets, images), allowing easily to retrieve and integrate information from these documents. It can make it possible, for example, to keep traceability between software requirements, HCI design components that meet the requirements and results of the evaluation of HCI components against those requirements. HCI-ON can also aid in systems integration. In integration scenarios spanning different HCI sub-domains, the benefits of using HCI-ON stand out. Instead of spending effort to integrate several ontologies, one can just extract the HCI-ON portion to be used. Another application concerns semantic interoperability among standards. Considering that different standards often presents a diverse vocabulary leading to semantic conflicts, HCI-ON can serve as the reference conceptualization to harmonize them, so that they share the same conceptualization and can be properly used in a combined way.

We have experienced the benefits of ONs by using SEON in applications as the ones we cited before. However, when talking about ICS, HCI conceptualization is also necessary. Therefore, we intend to use HCI-ON in these applications and explore it to provide solutions integrating HCI aspects to SE practices, by connecting HCI designers and software engineers. In this sense, currently, we are working on a knowledge-based solution to HCI design and evaluation.

References

1. Bakaev, M., Gaedke, M.: Application of evolutionary algorithms in interaction design: from requirements and ontology to optimized web interface. In: NW Russia Young Researchers in Electrical and Electronic Engineering Conference, pp. 129–134 (2016)
2. Bakaev, M., Avdeenko, T.: User interface design guidelines arrangement in a recommender system with frame ontology. In: Yu, H., Yu, G., Hsu, W., Moon, Y.-S., Unland, R., Yoo, J. (eds.) DASFAA 2012. LNCS, vol. 7240, pp. 311–322. Springer, Heidelberg (2012). https://doi.org/10.1007/978-3-642-29023-7_31
3. Bezold, M., Minker, W.: A framework for adapting interactive systems to user behavior. J. Ambient Intell. Smart Env. **2**(4), 369–387 (2010)
4. Carroll, J.M.: Human computer interaction (HCI). In: Soegaard, M., Dam, R.F. (eds.) The Ency of HCI, chap. 2, 2nd edn. The Interaction Design Foundation, pp. 21–61 (2014)
5. Castro, M.V.H.B., Costa, S.D., Barcellos, M.P., Falbo, R.D.A.: Knowledge management in human-computer interaction design: a mapping study. In: Proceedings of the XXIII Iberoamerican Conference on Software Engineering, CIbSE 2020, Curitiba, November 0–13 (2020)
6. Celino, I., Corcoglioniti, F.: Towards the formalization of interaction semantics. In: Proceedings of the International Conference on Semantic Systems, pp. 10:1–10:8 (2010)
7. Chera, C., Tsai, W., Vatavu, R.: Gesture ontology for informing service-oriented architecture. In: International Symposium on Intelligent Control, pp. 1184–1189. IEEE (2012)
8. Costa, S.D., Barcellos, M.P., Falbo, R.D.A., Conte, T., Oliveira, K.M.D.: A core ontology on the human-computer interaction phenomenon (2020, under review)
9. Devaurs, D., Rath, A., Lindstaedt, S.: Exploiting the user interaction context for automatic task detection. Appl. Artif. Intell. **26**, 58–80 (2012)
10. Duarte, B.B., de Castro Leal, A.L., Falbo, R.d.A., Guizzardi, G., Guizzardi, R.S.S., Souza, V.E.S.: Ontological foundations for software requirements with a focus on requirements at runtime. Appl. Ontology **13**(2), 73–105 (2018)
11. Elyusufi, Y., Seghiouer, H., Alimam, M.A.: Building profiles based on ontology for recommendation custom interfaces. In: International Conference on Multimedia Computing and Systems, pp. 558–562 (2014)
12. Guizzardi, G.: Ontological foundations for structural conceptual models. Ph.D. thesis, University of Twente (2005)
13. Haller, A., Groza, T., Rosenberg, F.: Interacting with linked data via semantically annotated widgets. In: Pan, J.Z., Chen, H., Kim, H.-G., Li, J., Wu, Z., Horrocks, I., Mizoguchi, R., Wu, Z. (eds.) JIST 2011. LNCS, vol. 7185, pp. 300–317. Springer, Heidelberg (2012). https://doi.org/10.1007/978-3-642-29923-0_20

14. ISO 9241–210: ISO 9241–210:2019(en) - ergonomics of human-system interaction - part 210: Human-Centred design for interactive systems (2019)
15. Kitchenham, B.A., Charters, S.: Guidelines for performing systematic literature reviews in software engineering. Technical Report Kele University and University of Durham (2007)
16. Kultsova, M., Potseluico, A., Zhukova, I., Skorikov, A., Romanenko, R.: A two-phase method of user interface adaptation for people with special needs. In: Kravets, A., Shcherbakov, M., Kultsova, M., Groumpos, P. (eds.) CIT&DS 2017. CCIS, vol. 754, pp. 805–821. Springer, Cham (2017). https://doi.org/10.1007/978-3-319-65551-2_58
17. Lebib, F.Z., Mellah, H., Mohand-Oussaid, L.: Ontological interaction modeling and semantic rule-based reasoning for user interface adaptation. In: Proceedings of the International Conference on Web Information Systems and Tech, INSTICC, pp. 347–354. SciTePress (2016)
18. Martín, A., Rossi, G., Cechich, A., Gordillo, S.: Engineering accessible web applications an. aspect-oriented approach. World Wide Web **13**(4), 419–440 (2010)
19. Mezhoudi, N., Vanderdonckt, J.: A user's feedback ontology for context-aware interaction. In: World Symp on Web Applications and Networking, pp. 1–7. IEEE (2015)
20. Myrgioti, E., Bassiliades, N., Miliou, A.: Bridging the HASM: an owl ontology for modeling the information pathways in haptic interfaces software. Expert Syst. Appl. **40**(4), 1358–1371 (2013)
21. Negru, S., Buraga, S.: A knowledge-based approach to the user-centered design process. In: Fred, A., Dietz, J.L.G., Liu, K., Filipe, J. (eds.) IC3K 2012. CCIS, vol. 415, pp. 165–178. Springer, Heidelberg (2013). https://doi.org/10.1007/978-3-642-54105-6_11
22. Norman, D.A.: The Design of Everyday Things: Revised and Expanded Edition, 2nd edn. Basic Books, New York (2013)
23. Ralph, P., Wand, Y.: A proposal for a formal definition of the design concept. In: Lyytinen, K., Loucopoulos, P., Mylopoulos, J., Robinson, B. (eds.) Design Requirements Engineering: A Ten-Year Perspective. LNBIP, vol. 14, pp. 103–136. Springer, Heidelberg (2009). https://doi.org/10.1007/978-3-540-92966-6_6
24. Robal, T., Marenkov, J., Kalja, A.: Ontology design for automatic evaluation of web user interface usability. In: Portland International Conference on Management of Engineering and Technology, pp. 1–8. IEEE (2017)
25. Romero Mariño, B., Rodríguez Fórtiz, M.J., Hurtado, M., Haddad, H.M.: Accessibility and activity-centered design for ICT users: romero ACCESIBILITIC ontology. IEEE Access **6**, 60655–60665 (2018)
26. Ruy, F.B., Falbo, R.D.A., Barcellos, M.P., Costa, S.D., Guizzardi, G.: SEON: a software engineering ontology network. In: Blomqvist, E., Ciancarini, P., Poggi, F., Vitali, F. (eds.) EKAW 2016. LNCS (LNAI), vol. 10024, pp. 527–542. Springer, Cham (2016). https://doi.org/10.1007/978-3-319-49004-5_34
27. Salma, G., Marouane, E.L.: Operating an application for modeling persona by using ontologies. J. Theor. Appl. Info. Tech. **88**(1), 57–64 (2016)
28. Scherp, A., Saathoff, C., Franz, T., Staab, S.: Designing core ontologies. Appl. Ontology **6**(3), 177–221 (2011)
29. Shahzad, S., Granitzer, M., Helic, D.: Ontological model driven GUI development: user interface ontology approach. In: International Conference on Computer Sciences and Convergence Information Technology, pp. 214–218. IEEE (2011)
30. Souza, C.S.D.: The Semiotic Engineering of Human-Computer Interaction. The MIT Press, Cambridge (2005)

31. Storrs, G.: A conceptualisation of multiparty interaction. Interact. Comput. **6**(2), 173–189 (1994)
32. Suàrez, P.R., Jùnior, B.L., De Barros, M.A.: Applying knowledge management in UI design process. In: Proceedings of Conference on Task Models and Diagrams, pp. 113–120. ACM (2004)
33. Suárez-Figueroa, M.C., Gómez-Pérez, A., Motta, E., Gangemi, A.: Ontology Engineering in a Networked World. Springer, Heidelberg (2012). https://doi.org/10.1007/978-3-642-24794-1
34. Tourwé, T., Tsipokova, E., González-Deleito, N., Hristoskova, A.: Ontology-driven elicitation of multimodal user interface design recommendations. In: Belgian/Netherlands Artificial Intelligence Conference, p. 8 (2011)
35. Zamzami, E.M., Budiardjo, E.K., Suhartanto, H.: Requirements recovery using ontology model for capturing end-to-end interaction of proven application software. Int. J. Softw. Eng. Appl. **7**(6), 425–434 (2013)

Ontology-Based Modeling and Analysis of Trustworthiness Requirements: Preliminary Results

Glenda Amaral[1]([✉])(iD), Renata Guizzardi[2](iD), Giancarlo Guizzardi[1](iD), and John Mylopoulos[3](iD)

[1] CORE/KRDB, Free University of Bozen-Bolzano, Bolzano, Italy
{gmouraamaral,giancarlo.guizzardi}@unibz.it
[2] NEMO/UFES, Espírito Santo (UFES), Vitoria, Brazil
rguizzardi@inf.ufes.br
[3] University of Ottawa, Ottawa, Canada
jm@cs.toronto.edu

Abstract. The advent of Artificial Intelligence (AI) technologies has made it possible to build systems that diagnose a patient, decide on a loan application, drive a car, or kill an adversary in combat. Such systems signal a new era where software-intensive systems perform tasks that were performed in the past only by humans because they require judgement that only humans possess. However, such systems need to be trusted by their users, in the same way that a lawyer, medical doctor, driver or soldier is trusted in performing the tasks she is trained for. This creates the need for a new class of requirements, *Trustworthiness Requirements*, that we have to study in order to develop techniques for their elicitation, analysis and operationalization. In this paper, we propose a foundation to develop such techniques. Our work is based on an *Ontology of Trust* that answers questions about the nature of trust and the factors that influence it. Based on the answers, we characterize the class of trustworthiness requirements. Among other things, this characterization supports the requirements engineer in defining thurstworthiness requirements, identifying the risks presented by the system-to-be, and understanding the signals the system must emit to gain and maintain trust.

Keywords: Trustworthiness requirements · AI systems · OntoUML

1 Introduction

Trust is an essential ingredient of everyday life. We relate to people, organizations and things because we trust them to deliver on a certain goal, task or asset. Trust is especially important in the case of safety-critical services that can directly affect human lives, such as medical diagnosis, autonomous driving, military technology, terrorism detection, and other situations that pose risks to

G. Dobbie et al. (Eds.): ER 2020, LNCS 12400, pp. 342–352, 2020.
https://doi.org/10.1007/978-3-030-62522-1_25

human life and health. And although we tend to be tolerant if a "translation service produces grammatically incorrect sentences or if a cell phone camera misses to recognize a person" [12], tolerating the possibility of a single wrong decision in "critical decision-making systems such as security, healthcare, or finance, where human lives or significant assets are at stake" [12], is not acceptable. As systems are being developed, with or without AI technologies, that do make critical decisions, it is essential that their users trust them in the same way they trust their doctors, drivers and police. In the context of AI systems this was a key conclusion of the High-Level Expert Group on Artificial Intelligence (AI HLEG), which elaborated a set of ethics guidelines for trustworthy AI, as part of the European Strategy on Artificial Intelligence [9]. A similar conclusion was drawn in the "Explainable AI" initiative launched by the United States Defense Advanced Research Projects Agency (DARPA) [8], with the objective of making deep learning systems more trustworthy and controllable. These considerations call for studying a new class of requirements, namely, *Trustworthiness Requirements*, so that we can understand their nature and develop proper analysis techniques.

But what exactly is trust? And what makes a system trustworthy? In this work, we answer these questions in terms of a recently proposed Reference Ontology for Trust (ROT) [1]. Then, we combine ROT with the Non-Functional Requirements Ontology (NFRO) [7], which has the basic concepts to allow the definition of functional and non-functional requirements. This combination allows us to define the class of trustworthiness requirements and their relation to concepts such as trust, capability, vulnerability and risk, among others.

Here, we characterize trustworthiness requirements as a special class of *quality requirements* (in the sense of [7]) where the desired states-of-affairs are stakeholder mental states that include an *attitude* of trust towards the system-to-be. This trust is based on the system's track record in delivering its intended services (driving, diagnosing, decision-making, etc.), the availability of valid information on that track record (no falsehoods or half-truths), as well as transparency on the delivery of the system's services.

The remainder of this paper is structured as follows. Section 2 discusses the ontological foundations in which our analysis is grounded. Section 3 introduces trustworthiness requirements and related concepts. Section 4 presents our proposal, a *Reference Ontology of Trustworthiness Requirements*. We conclude in Sect. 5 with some final considerations.

2   Research Baseline

In this paper, we provide an ontological analysis of trustworthiness requirements and trustworthiness-related risks, grounded in the Unified Foundational Ontology (UFO) [4]. In our analysis we shall rely on the trust-related concepts defined in the Reference Ontology of Trust proposed in [1] and on the ontological interpretation of non-functional requirements presented in [7].

The Reference Ontology of Trust (ROT). Based on UFO, Amaral et al. [1] present a Reference Ontology of Trust (ROT) which formally characterizes the concept of trust, as well as clarifies the relation between trust and risk, and represents how risk emerges from trust relations.

ROT makes the following ontological commitments on the nature of trust:

- Trust is always about a trustor's intention. An agent trusts another only relative to a goal, for the achievement of which she counts upon the trustee.

- Trust is a complex mental state of a trustor regarding a trustee. This complex mental state is composed of: (i) a trustor's intention, whose propositional content is a goal of the trustor; (ii) the belief that the trustee has the capability to perform the desired action; and (iii) the belief that the trustee's vulnerabilities will not prevent her from performing the desired action.

- The trustor is necessarily an "intentional entity". Briefly put, the trustor is a cognitive agent, an agent endowed with goals and beliefs.

- The trustee is not necessarily a cognitive system. The trustee is an entity capable of having an impact on a goal of the trustor.

- Trust is context dependent. The trustor may trust in the trustee in a certain context but may not trust her for the same action in a different context.

- Trust always implies risk. By trusting, the trustor accepts to become vulnerable to the trustee in terms of potential failure of the expected action and result, as the trustee may not perform the expected action or the action may not have the desired result.

Figure 1 depicts a ROT excerpt, which captures most of the aforementioned ontological notions. As in the original ROT ontology, this model is represented in OntoUML [5]

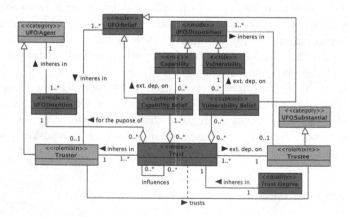

Fig. 1. A fragment of ROT depicting the mental aspects of trust

In ROT, TRUST is modeled as a complex mode (a dependent entity) composed of a TRUSTOR INTENTION, whose propositional content is a goal of the TRUSTOR, and a set of BELIEFS that inhere in the TRUSTOR and are externally dependent on the *dispositions* [2,6] that inhere in the TRUSTEE. These beliefs include: (i) the BELIEF that the TRUSTEE has the CAPABILITY to perform the desired action (CAPABILITY BELIEF); and (ii) the belief that the TRUSTEE'S VULNERABILITIES will not prevent her from performing the desired action (VULNERABILITY BELIEF). The TRUSTEE'S VULNERABILITIES and CAPABILITIES are dispositions that inhere in the TRUSTEE, which are manifested in particular situations, through the occurrence of events [6].

ROT relies on the Common Ontology of Value and Risk (COVER) proposed by Sales et al. [15] to represent the relation between trust and risk. A central notion for characterizing risk in COVER is a chain of events that impacts on an agent's goals, which the authors name Risk Experience. Risk Experiences focus on unwanted events that have the potential of causing losses and are composed by threat and loss events. A THREAT EVENT is the one with the potential of causing a loss, which might be intentional or unintentional. A THREAT EVENT might be the manifestation of a VULNERABILITY (a special type of disposition whose manifestation constitutes a loss or can potentially cause a loss from the perspective of a stakeholder). The second mandatory component of a Risk Experience is a LOSS EVENT, which necessarily impacts intentions in a negative way [15]. When actions related to a trust relation are performed, they may satisfy the goals of the trustor or, in the worst case, they may not have the desired result. In this case, the resulting situation stands for a THREAT SITUATION that may trigger a THREAT EVENT, which may cause a loss. The LOSS EVENT is a RISK EVENT that impacts intentions in a negative way.

The Ontology of Non-functional Requirements (NFRO). In [7], the authors propose a UFO-based ontological interpretation of non-functional requirements. In NFRO, requirement is defined as a goal. Requirements are specialized into NFRs (also named quality goals) and functional requirements (FRs). FRs refer to a function (a capability, capacity) that has the potential to manifest certain behavior in particular situations, while NFRs refer to qualities taking quality values in particular quality regions. For example, a software system is considered to have good usability if the value associated to its "usability" requirement maps to a region "good" in the "usability" quality space. Figure 2 depicts a selected subset of the NFRO that are relevant for our discussions on trustworthiness requirements. For an in-depth discussion and formal characterization of qualities, quality types, quality regions, and quality spaces, refer to [4].

3   Trustworthiness Requirements

Requirements are prescriptions of intended states-of-affairs that the system-to-be should bring about. Traditionally, these states-of-affairs were system-related, such as functions the system should deliver, or qualities it should possess with respect to performance, reliability, usability etc. Social requirements and physical requirements have been introduced in the literature more recently with the advent of socio-technical and cyber-physical systems [11,13]. For example, "schedule meeting" is a social requirement because the desired state-of-affairs

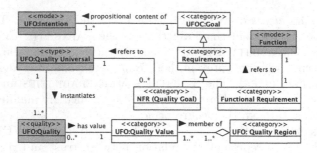

Fig. 2. A fragment of the ontology of non-functional requirements

is one that includes a new meeting, where meeting is a social artifact (a bundle of rights, commitments, powers, etc. binding a number of participants). On the other hand, "distance from nearby physical objects ≥ 50 cm" is a physical requirements for an autonomous vehicle. Personal requirements constitute a forth category of requirements where the desired states-of-affairs involve attitudinal (mental) properties of (some of) the system's stakeholders. For example, "$\geq 70\%$ of departments members are using the meeting scheduling system" is a personal requirement (more specifically, an acceptance requirement) in that the system-to-be has to bring members of the department to a state of mind where they are willing to use the system. Trustworthiness requirements are personal requirements as well in that their desired states-of-affairs are ones where some of the stakeholders trust the system.

But how can an agent earn the trust of the recipients of its services? Firstly, the agent can make available to its users its credentials (degrees, accreditations, certificates, awards) that suggest that "it knows its craft", "it is doing a good job", and the like. The agent can also make available information on its track record, such as reviews from service recipients and statistics on its experience. Moreover, all information that is used must be true (no half-truths and no lies). Politicians are able to convince a certain segment of their electorate to trust them; however, if done through the use of half-truths and lies in the process, this can make them trusted but unworthy of trust, or untrustworthy.

Trustworthiness means more than trust in other ways as well. A trustworthy agent must be delivering its service in a professional and effective manner. For example, a medical doctor agent may be trusted by most of its patients because of its accreditations and its affiliation with a healthcare organization, but it is not trustworthy unless it also delivers reliable healthcare services to its patients. Reliability here includes availability, the good doctor is available when you need it, but also effectiveness in its diagnoses and treatments of its patients. A medical doctor you rarely succeed to make an appointment with isn't trustworthy, nor is one whose diagnoses are often contradicted by expert colleagues.

Another element of trustworthiness is transparency in the delivery of an agent's services. Transparency is influenced by many factors [10]. In the context of an agent delivering a service, transparency includes offering information on what the agent is doing, as well as rationale for its decisions (aka explainability).

On the basis of these considerations, a trustworthiness requirement can be AND-refined into a *reliability requirement*, a *truthful information communication requirement* and a *transparency requirement* for the service being delivered.

Trustworthiness requirements are quality requirements [7]. This means that they constrain the level of presence of a quality in its subject. For example "being red" is a property that constrains the colour quality of its subject to be in the red region of a color quality space (a chromatic map known as the color spindle). Likewise "being trustworthy" is a constraint for agents or services to fall in the trustworthiness region of a space that also includes an untrustworthiness region.

Of course, trustworthiness isn't only a black-and-white quality requirement. It also includes weaker versions that can be defined by refinement operators [7]:

- Probabilistic refinements: These consider what percentage of the uses of the system's services were deemed trustworthy by the recipients of these services. For example, for a diagnostic system, a trustworthiness requirement could be "$\geq 80\%$ of uses were found trustworthy";
- Fuzziness refinements: Here, we weaken the notion of trustworthiness by making it fuzzy to include things that are "almost trustworthy", "fairly trustworthy", "definitely not untrustworthy".
- Subjectivity refinements: These are requirements of the form "$\geq N\%$ of users asked consider the system trustworthy". Note that unlike probabilistic refinements, subjectivity refinements focus on users, not uses.

These refinement operators can also be applied to the sub-goals of a trustworthiness requirement, to yield a full space of requirements concerning the trustworthiness quality.

4 Ontology-Based Modeling and Analysis Of Trustworthiness Requirements

Understanding the elements of stakeholder trustworthiness towards the system to be is important because they reveal the qualities and properties the system should have in order to be considered trustworthy and effectively promote well-placed trust. Note that as trust is contextually dependent (the trust degree of a trustor in a trustee may vary from a context to another) the implementation of trustworthiness requirements depends on the specific application. For example, a user trusts a system in collecting her location data but not when she is in sensitive places, such as when she is being treated at a hospital, since such information may lead to disclose a health issue.

Another advantage of making the components of trust explicit is that this knowledge can be used as input to the definition of trust-warranting signals that ensure trustworthy behavior. In other words, once the system's capabilities and vulnerabilities related to the trust of the stakeholder are known, it is possible to reason about the signals that the system should emit to indicate that it is capable of successfully realizing the capabilities and prevent the manifestation of the vulnerabilities. For example, information about how privacy and security measures are implemented could be provided as signals of the trustworthiness of a system. Other relevant examples of trust-warranting signals are data certificates and data provenance information, both relevant for systems dealing with large amounts of data, to avoid bias and unfair results.

Finally, the identification of trust components is equally important to the assessment of risks related to the capabilities and vulnerabilities, which are the focus of stakeholders' beliefs. As previously discussed, *capabilities* are dispositions that inhere in an agent and, as such, are manifested in particular situations, through the occurrence of events [6]. As defined in the Common Ontology of Value and Risk (COVER) [15], a *threat event* is a type of *risk event* that may be the manifestation of a capability of the system, in case it fails to realize this specific capability in order to bring about an outcome desired by the stakeholder. According to COVER, the threat event may lead to a *loss event*, which negatively influences the stakeholder's intention. For example, suppose that a network malfunction prevents a medical system to access the server containing patient data and, as a result of that, it cannot deliver its capability of providing a diagnosis. In this case, the network malfunction is a threat event, which leads to a lack of diagnosis loss event.

Similarly, *vulnerabilities* are also a special type of disposition, whose manifestation causes or can potentially cause a loss, under the perspective of a stakeholder. Therefore, a threat event may be the manifestation of a vulnerability and eventually trigger a loss event. To illustrate this point, let us imagine that our medical system has a security vulnerability and is thus hacked, leading to the leak of patient data. In this case, the hacking threat event, resulting from the manifestation of the system's security vulnerability, triggered the patient privacy loss event.

We represent the concepts related to TRUSTWORTHINESS REQUIREMENTS in the OntoUML model depicted in Fig. 3, and the emergence of risks in this scenario in Fig. 4.

As shown in Fig. 3, we modeled REQUIREMENT as a GOAL, which is the propositional content of an INTENTION of a STAKEHOLDER. QUALITY REQUIREMENT is a type of REQUIREMENT, and TRUSTWORTHY REQUIREMENT is a type of QUALITY REQUIREMENT. STAKEHOLDERS are represented as AGENTS that play the role of trustor, while the SYSTEM is an existentially independent object that plays the role of trustee. The SYSTEM intends to satisfy the TRUSTWORTHINESS REQUIREMENTs.

As pointed out in Sect. 3, the analysis of the trustworthiness requirement involve its decomposition in three other quality requirements, namely, *reliability requirement, truthful information communication requirement* and *transparency requirement*. Thus, we include in the model of Fig. 3, a composition relation between TRUSTWORTHINESS REQUIREMENT and QUALITY REQUIREMENT. Additionally, this model supports the representation of the mentioned sub-requirements as instances of the QUALITY REQUIREMENT concept. All QUALITY

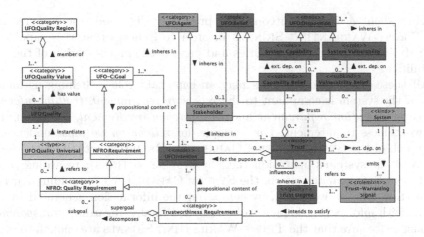

Fig. 3. Modeling trustworthiness requirements in OntoUML

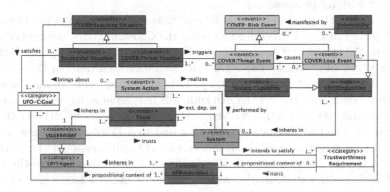

Fig. 4. Modeling the emergence of trustworthiness-related risks

REQUIREMENTS are such that they restrict the value of the qualities at hand to a particular set of values of the corresponding QUALITY REGION. TRUST-WORTHY REQUIREMENT restrict the values of qualities referring to reliability, transparency and information truthfulness to particular set of values accordingly.

As for TRUST, we represent it as a complex mode composed of a STAKE-HOLDER's INTENTION, whose propositional content is a GOAL of the STAKE-HOLDER, and a set of BELIEFS that inhere in the STAKEHOLDER and are externally dependent on the dispositions [2,6] that inhere in the SYSTEM. These beliefs include: (i) the BELIEF that the SYSTEM has the CAPABILITY to perform the desired action (CAPABILITY BELIEF); and (ii) the BELIEF that the SYSTEM's VULNERABILITIES will not prevent it from exhibiting the desired behavior (VULNERABILITY BELIEF). The SYSTEM's VULNERABILITIES and CAPABILITIES are dispositions that inhere in the SYSTEM, which are manifested in particular situations, through the occurrence of events [6]. We adopt the interpretation of capability proposed by Azevedo et al. [2], who defined capability as the power to bring about a desired outcome. As previously discussed, the SYSTEM can emit TRUST-WARRANTING SIGNALS in order to indicate that it is capable of successfully realizing the capabilities and prevent the manifestation of the vulnerabilities.

All these ontological concepts play an important role in helping us understand if the system is compliant to the *reliability requirement, truthful information communication requirement* and *transparency requirement*, composing the trustworthiness requirement. For example, for *reliability*, we must understand how much of the STAKEHOLDER'S CAPABILITY BELIEF is actually met by the results of the system's operation (i.e., by SYSTEM ACTIONS); regarding *truthful information communication*, the SYSTEM CAPABILITY of providing truthful information may be validated, by comparing the information generated by the system with information known to be real; and finally, regarding *transparency*, we must make sure that the TRUST-WARRANTING SIGNALS are enough to make the STAKEHOLDER satisfied w.r.t how often and how well the system explains its decision-making process.

We represent the emergence of trustworthiness-related risks in the OntoUML model depicted in Fig. 4. In order to realize the CAPABILITIES, the SYSTEM performs some ACTIONS that bring about a RESULTING SITUATION. The RESULTING SITUATION may satisfy the STAKEHOLDER'S GOALS (and in this case it is considered a SUCCESSFUL SITUATION) or, in the worst case, it may not have the desired result and the STAKEHOLDER will not be able to achieve her goal. In this case, the RESULTING SITUATION stands for a THREAT SITUATION that may trigger a THREAT EVENT, which may lead to a LOSS EVENT that impacts intentions in a negative way, as it hurts the STAKEHOLDER'S INTENTIONS of reaching a GOAL. Analogously, System's Vulnerabilities may enable the occurrence of Risk Events that, in the worst case, may cause a LOSS EVENT which will hurt the STAKEHOLDER'S INTENTIONS of reaching her GOAL.

5   Final Remarks

In this paper, we presented an ontological analysis characterizing the concept of trustworthiness requirements of software systems, as well as the emergence of risks when using such system.

The elicitation of trust requirements has been broadly studied and different approaches have been proposed in the literature to support the capture and implementation of trust requirements in the context of software systems [3,9,11,14]. Despite the wide number of efforts to properly analyse trustworthiness requirements and trust-related issues, little has been said about what constitutes the stakeholders' trust in the system, what it depends upon and how trustworthiness-related risks can be identified. Differently from other approaches, our proposal analyses the components of the trust complex mental state of the trustor in order to identify what the system should have for stakeholders to trust it. These elements are fundamental for a better understanding and proper elucidation of trustworthy requirements. Moreover, they are key for the identification of trustworthiness-related risks that may arise when the requirements are not fulfilled accordingly.

As future work, we plan to further validate our ontology by doing real case studies and having experts evaluate the results. We also plan to define ontological patterns, based on this ontology, to support the modeling and analysis of trustworthiness requirements, aiming at facilitating the development of trustworthy systems. Finally, we plan to propose a systematic process for identifying trustworthiness requirements, grounded on these patterns and on the ontological account of trustworthiness requirements presented here.

Acknowledgment. CAPES (PhD grant# 88881.173022/2018-01) and OCEAN project (UNIBZ).

References

1. Amaral, G., Sales, T.P., Guizzardi, G., Porello, D.: Towards a reference ontology of trust. In: Panetto, H., Debruyne, C., Hepp, M., Lewis, D., Ardagna, C.A., Meersman, R. (eds.) OTM 2019. LNCS, vol. 11877, pp. 3–21. Springer, Cham (2019). https://doi.org/10.1007/978-3-030-33246-4_1
2. Azevedo, C.L.B., et al.: Modeling resources and capabilities in enterprise architecture: A well-founded ontology-based proposal for ArchiMate. Inf. Syst. **54**, 235–262 (2015)
3. Giorgini, P., Massacci, F., Mylopoulos, J., Zannone, N.: Modeling social and individual trust in requirements engineering methodologies. In: Herrmann, P., Issarny, V., Shiu, S. (eds.) iTrust 2005. LNCS, vol. 3477, pp. 161–176. Springer, Heidelberg (2005). https://doi.org/10.1007/11429760_12
4. Guizzardi, G.: Ontological foundations for structural conceptual models. Telematica Instituut/CTIT (2005)
5. Guizzardi, G., Wagner, G., Almeida, J.P.A., Guizzardi, R.S.S.: Towards ontological foundations for conceptual modeling: the unified foundational ontology (UFO) story. Appl. Ontology **10**(3–4), 259–271 (2015)
6. Guizzardi, G., Wagner, G., de Almeida Falbo, R., Guizzardi, R.S.S., Almeida, J.P.A.: Towards ontological foundations for the conceptual modeling of events. In: Ng, W., Storey, V.C., Trujillo, J.C. (eds.) ER 2013. LNCS, vol. 8217, pp. 327–341. Springer, Heidelberg (2013). https://doi.org/10.1007/978-3-642-41924-9_27
7. Guizzardi, R., et al.: An ontological interpretation of non-functional requirements. Proc. FOIS. **14**, 344–357 (2014)
8. Gunning, D., Aha, D.W.: Darpa's explainable artificial intelligence program. AI Mag. **40**(2), 44–58 (2019)
9. Hleg, A.I.: Ethics Guidelines for Trustworthy AI. B-1049 Brussels (2019)
10. Leite, L., Cappelli, C.: Software transparency. Bus. Inf. Syst. Eng. **2**(3), 127–139 (2010)
11. Mohammadi, G.: Trustworthy Cyber-Physical Systems. Springer, Wiesbaden (2019)
12. Nassar, M., Salah, K., ur Rehman, M.H., Svetinovic, D.: Blockchain for explainable and trustworthy artificial intelligence. Wiley Interdis. Rev. Data Min. Knowl. Discovery **10**(1), e1340 (2020)
13. Paja, E., Chopra, A.K., Giorgini, P.: Trust-based specification of sociotechnical systems. Data Knowl. Eng. **87**, 339–353 (2013)

14. Rosemann, M.: Trust-aware process design. In: Hildebrandt, T., van Dongen, B.F., Röglinger, M., Mendling, J. (eds.) BPM 2019. LNCS, vol. 11675, pp. 305–321. Springer, Cham (2019). https://doi.org/10.1007/978-3-030-26619-6_20
15. Sales, T.P., Baião, F., Guizzardi, G., Almeida, J.P.A., Guarino, N., Mylopoulos, J.: The common ontology of value and risk. In: Trujillo, J.C. (ed.) ER 2018. LNCS, vol. 11157, pp. 121–135. Springer, Cham (2018). https://doi.org/10.1007/978-3-030-00847-5_11

Upper-Level Types of Occurrent Based on the Principle of Ontological Conservation

Fabrício Henrique Rodrigues$^{(\boxtimes)}$ ⓘ, Joel Luís Carbonera ⓘ, and Mara Abel

Informatics Institute, Federal University of Rio Grande do Sul, Porto Alegre, Brazil
{fabricio.rodrigues,joel.carbonera,marabel}@inf.ufrgs.br

Abstract. Ontologies are usually focused on describing the things that exist in time (i.e., continuants, objects), but the things that happen (i.e., occurrents, processes, events) also play an important role in representing the world. This paper explores the view of occurrents as transitions between situations to propose a framework for the ontological analysis of occurrents. We analyzed this view in light of the notion of material constitution to characterize the subtypes of occurrent according to the differences between the situation that precedes and the one that follows from the happening of the occurrent. With that, we propose the principle of ontological conservation as well as four types of occurrents.

Keywords: Ontologies · Occurrents · Events · Material constitution · Ontological conservation

1 Introduction

In Computer Science, ontologies are *explicit specifications of conceptualizations* [9] that formally describe the meaning of the terms of a given universe of discourse. An ontology may include concepts to represent both things that exist, i.e., *continuants*[1],– as well as things that happen – i.e., *occurrents*[2]. In spite of the somewhat widespread view that continuants are ontologically prior to occurrents (i.e., continuants are all that exist and events represent just the distribution of matter and objects in space and time) [7], it seems that great part of our reality is fundamentally dependent on occurrents (e.g., from chemical reactions to business transactions).

In practical terms, a good model of occurrents can support several ontology-based reasoning activities, such as pre- and post-condition inference, discovery of temporal relations, inference of missing or implicit events, and identification

---

[1] Also known as endurants and usually referred to as objects. In this work we use the terms continuant and endurant, employing object, substantial to refer only to independent continuants.

[2] Also known as perdurants and usually referred to as events or processes. In this work we use any of the four terms interchangeably.

© Springer Nature Switzerland AG 2020
G. Dobbie et al. (Eds.): ER 2020, LNCS 12400, pp. 353–363, 2020.
https://doi.org/10.1007/978-3-030-62522-1_26

of incompatible descriptions of a same event [4]. This support can help in a variety of tasks, which include discrete event simulation [12], representation of narratives [19], causal and temporal reasoning [17], as well as the interpretation of the occurrence of events given their products [5].

There are several definitions for the notion of occurrent. A widespread basic definition presents occurrent as things that *happen in time*, that may accumulate temporal parts and that involve continuants as participants [18]. Another important point of view considers occurrents as *transitions* between situations or states [3,13]. It complements the definition of occurrent as something that happens in time by providing further insights on its ontological nature, allowing to answer the question of what is happening (i.e., a new situation is superseding a previous one). Moreover, it has some appeal from a computational point of view, since it provides a way to identify occurrents by means of the analysis of static data representing temporal snapshots of the world (which is, arguably, the most common way we store information, e.g., recording the states of things instead of their transitions). In spite of that, existing taxonomies usually do not take into account this view of occurrents.

Thus, in this work we propose a framework for the ontological analysis of occurrents as transition between situations. To do so, we recall the notion of *material constitution* to propose the *principle of ontological conservation*. Then we use these notions to analyze the concept of occurrent focusing on the possible differences between the situations it connects. From that, we identify three types of properties and four types of occurrents derived from them.

In the remaining of the paper, Sect. 2 presents our main assumptions; Sect. 2.3 presents the principle of ontological conservation; Sect. 3 brings our view on occurrents; Sect. 4 presents the types of properties and occurrents identified in this work; Sect. 5 discusses related works and discuss the contributions of our approach; finally, Sect. 6 brings our concluding remarks.

2   Assumptions

This section presents the assumptions underlying our proposed framework.

2.1   Material Constitution

Constitution is the relation between something and what it is made of [8]. In this work, we adopt the so-called *Constitution View* [2] restricted to the case of material objects (as in [8]). In this view, the relation of constitution is distinct from that of composition (i.e., if x constitutes y, then x is not a part of y). Furthermore, for [2], the fundamental idea of constitution is that when an individual of a given *primary kind* is in certain *favorable circumstances*, a new individual of another primary kind comes into existence. Such individuals are *distinct* but *spatially coincident* as long as the constitution relation holds. The primary kinds of a constituted individual and of its constituent are in different ontological levels, being, respectively, higher- and lower-level types in relation to each other.

The primary kind of an individual determines what it most fundamentally is. It is when a primary kind is instantiated that a new individual comes into existence. In addition, each primary kind specifies the persistence conditions for its individuals (i.e., the conditions for an individual to remain in existence). Favorable circumstances represent the necessary and sufficient conditions for establishing a relation of constitution between two entities. They are contingent conditions such that if we submit an individual of a primary kind A to them, it makes the case that a distinct individual of another primary kind B comes into existence without the A individual ceasing to exist.

Constitution and Existence. Given this definition of constitution, we could consider that every independent continuant falls into one of two possible categories. It may be a *constituted object*, which is constituted by another independent continuant of a lower-level primary kind. Alternatively, it may be a portion of *basic ontological substrate* (whatever the nature of such substrate may be[3]), i.e., an individual of a primary kind on an eventual basic ontological level whose instances are not constituted by anything else. Thus, besides the case of basic ontological substrate, coming into existence is a matter of coming to be constituted by an individual of a lower-level type that is in favorable circumstances for this. Likewise, remaining in existence involves keeping some constituent in these circumstances, and ceasing to exist is a matter of ceasing such favorable circumstances.

2.2   Situations

In this work, we regard a situation as a particular configuration of a part of reality that is understood as a whole [1, 13, 14], which defines a particular state of affairs [12], and that satisfies certain conditions of unity imposed by relations and categories associated with the situation [14]. Thus, situations are continuants disjoint from substantials and moments [6]. Each situation is determined by the mereological sum of instantaneous snapshots of certain substantials[4], moments (intrinsic and/or relational) inhering in such substantials and/or formal relations among them [6] at a given time point [12, 14]. With that, situations are instantaneous and bound to specific time points [13, 14], so that two situations in different time instants are necessarily different, even if they are qualitatively indistinguishable (i.e., referring to the same continuants which bear the same properties and take part in the same relations, e.g., the situation of a person standing still now and the same person standing still five minutes ago are two different situations) [13].

---

[3] For example, in [2] it is suggested that aggregates of subatomic particles would be the ultimate constituents of ordinary material objects.

[4] A snapshot of a substantial is a set of attributions about such substantial [12].

2.3 Ontological Conservation

In Physics, the notion of *law of conservation* refers to principles that state that certain physical quantities do not change over time within an isolated physical system [16]. An example of such principles is the Law of Conservation of Mass[5], which states that, in a closed system, the total mass involved in a chemical reaction (taking into account all its reactants and products) remains the same throughout the reaction, so that no mass is created nor destroyed.

An analogous principle can be formulated for the realm of ontology. As previously stated, substantials are either constituted objects or portions of basic ontological substrate. Assuming that such basic ontological substrate cannot be created or destroyed, we propose what we call the *Principle of Ontological Conservation*, i.e., given a closed system, the amount of basic ontological substrate remains the same along the time. In other words, the situations that supersede each other within a system must comprise the same amount of basic substrate. With that, any object that may come into existence within the system would be a rearrangement of the basic ontological substrate circumscribed by the system (usually in an indirect way, by the rearrangement of constituted objects that already exist in a way that establishes the favorable circumstances for the constitution of the new object). Likewise, whenever an object ceases to exist, the substrate that constituted it (directly or indirectly) continues to exist within the system (usually as constituted objects of another primary kind). In this context, the principle of ontological conservation can be used as a guide for delimitation and modeling of occurrents.

3   A View on Occurrents

In this work, we regard occurrents as transitions between situations, consisting in changes and/or "unchanges" in the properties of the objects that are present in such situations (i.e., the participants of the occurrent). Therefore, an occurrent is characterized by the differences and similarities between the situations it connects. We also assume that those situations must be in some way related to each other to form a valid occurrent (in order to rule out spurious occurrents, e.g., the one linking the situation of Usain Bolt preparing for a 100 m run to the situation of Elton John playing the last chord of a song). However, what would be this relation between situations that justifies the transition between them?

With an occurrent being the changes and/or unchanges in its participant objects, we could intuitively say that the linked situations refer to the same set of objects (eliminating, e.g., the occurrent involving Usain Bolt and Elton John). However, this restriction would exclude any occurrent of *creation* since what characterizes it is the presence in the ending situation of an object that is not

---

[5] In fact, this is just an approximate law of conservation since mass can be converted into other forms of mass-energy [16]. However, we use it as an illustration of the concept for its simplicity.

present in the initial situation. A similar restriction would apply to occurrents of *destruction*.

To account for this problem, we can found a criterion on the principle of ontological conservation. By this principle, the amount of *basic ontological substrate* remains the same along the time in a closed system. Thus, just as the total mass involved in a chemical reaction is conserved throughout its occurrence, the amount of basic ontological substrate involved in an occurrent would remain the same during its occurrence. With that, the situations linked by an occurrent would relate to each other by having the same amount of substrate underlying the objects in each situation. Then, an occurrent would be a transition between situations that comprise the *same maximal amount of basic ontological substrate*.

According to this definition, the creation of a statue from a portion of clay would be a valid occurrent: it links two situations comprising the same portion of clay, which initially is simply a lump of the material and ends up in favorable circumstances to constitute a statue. By comprising the same portion of clay, both situations comprise the same amount of basic ontological substrate that underlies this clay.

On the other hand, the occurrent of a sidewalk getting wet, defined as linking an initial situation comprising a dry sidewalk and an ending situation gathering a sidewalk covered by water, would not be valid. In this case, both initial and ending situations comprise the same sidewalk, but the portion of water in the latter is not present in the former. Also, the initial situation does not comprise anything that constituted such water, or that was constituted by it. Therefore, the ending situation includes an additional amount of basic ontological substrate (i.e., the one that ultimately constitutes the portion of water). Due to this extra amount of substrate created within the considered system, such occurrent violates the principle ontological conservation. For this occurrent to be valid, the initial situation must include the portion of water (or what would later constitute it). It would be the case, for example, if the occurrent is defined as the movement of a portion of water onto the sidewalk, linking a situation in which the water and the sidewalk are not in contact and an ending situation in which they are touching each other.

4   Types of Occurrent

This section presents some intuitions that underlie our classification and that help to identify different types of properties as well as the possible types of occurrent according to the type of property affected by the occurrence.

4.1   Underlying Intuitions

Let's consider the concept of *statue*, understood as the physical piece of art constituted by some portion of solid material representing a given *figure*. Here *statue* is regarded as a primary kind, therefore providing an identity criterion for its instances, which, let's suppose, includes the reference link between the statue and the represented figure. Besides this reference, it also has many other properties (e.g., size, specific contours), some of them composing the favorable conditions to its existence (e.g., being in solid-state).

Considering that, imagine that we have a statue of a man, constituted by a lump of some malleable metal. First of all, there may be the case in which the statue remains as it is: the statue is in a given situation in time t_0 and in a similar situation in time t_1 - the only difference being the time point to which the situation is bounded. (Case $C1$)

If we slightly bend the material that constitutes the nose of the statue, we will change properties of the statue (e.g., its specific contours). However, it will certainly be the same statue (e.g., Michelangelo's David would still be the same even if Michelangelo had carved its nose a little further). Nothing comes into nor goes out of existence; it is just a simple change in the given statue. (Case $C2$)

Nevertheless, sometimes it may be the case that a new statue is brought into or sent out of existence, and it may happen in two fashions. First, let us imagine that we have the same man-shaped metal statue and keep changing and remodeling it until it acquires the shape of a dog. At this point, we can say that the initial man-shaped statue no longer exists. Besides, we can also say that a dog-shaped statue was brought into existence. It is as the original statue was transformed into the new dog-shaped statue. (Case $C3$)

In an alternative case, we may initially have some portion of malleable metal and, after bending different parts of this portion of metal, we end up with the desired shape of a man. At this point, a man-shaped statue comes into existence. We can keep making small changes in its shape while it still remains as the same statue, keeping its identity. However, if we melt the whole portion of metal that constitutes the statue, we will no longer be able to recognize the man shape that characterized the original statue, so that we can say that such a statue ceased to exist. More than that, there would no longer exist any statue at all, since we no longer have a solid object (a necessary condition for a statue). Finally, if we solidify the portion of metal and mold it to the shape of a dog, we will create a new statue again. In this case, we would have the creation of a statue, followed by its destruction, followed by the creation of another statue. (Case $C4$)

In both cases $C3$ and $C4$, we have similar initial and ending situations and we apparently refer to equivalent situation transitions. However, there are important differences between them. In $C3$ there is a *transformation* from one statue to another one. Then the *coming into existence* of a statue *necessarily* follows from a *going out of existence* of the other statues, with both occurrences *essentially* tied to each other. On the other hand, in $C4$, we simply have a chain of *destruction* of a statue and *creation* of another one which just *contingently* follow one another (e.g., it might be the case that, after the destruction, the following creation never happens or the creation might happen without the prior destruction).

In the statue transformation ($C3$), there is no temporal interval between one statue ceasing to exist and another one coming into existence so that there is no change in the count of statues in the world due to this occurrent. In contrast, in $C4$, there is an interval between the destruction of one statue and the creation of the other, during which there is one less statue in the world. In other words, in the transformation case ($C3$), the portion of metal constitutes some statue (though not the same one) during the whole interval. Contrariwise, in the alternative case ($C4$), the portion of metal is changed in such a way that the favorable circumstances that support the existence of a statue are not present during some interval. Thus, it ceases to be a statue altogether.

4.2   Three Categories of Properties

In the given intuitions, all the exemplified occurrents refer to what happens with the properties of the involved objects. In fact, given the notion of occurrent as a transition between situations that comprise the same maximal amount of basic ontological substrate, even what is created or destroyed is the result of a change in the properties of something of a lower-level type that was already present.

Nevertheless, we intuitively recognize the difference between certain types of occurrent, especially between those in which objects are created or destroyed and those in which they just suffer simple changes or remain as they are. Thus, if every occurrent is just a matter of changing (or not changing) some property(ies) of the involved objects, the difference between such types of occurrent must be based on the types of the affected properties.

Such types of properties seem to be related to the role of the property in relation to the existential status of the object - i.e., simply characterizing it, allowing its (re)identification, or providing the necessary conditions for the existence of something of a given type (e.g., *being solid*, for a statue). Therefore, we classify properties of objects according to the type of effect that their modification may bring about. This property modification is understood in a broad sense, comprising changes in the value of a quality (e.g., change of color), acquiring/losing a property (e.g., a portion of iron that, after a magnetization process, acquires the disposition of attracting other objects made of iron), and other general property changes (e.g., acquiring/losing parts). With that, we identified 3 types of properties, as described in what follows.

Ordinary properties: Properties that are neither related to the identity of the object, nor related to the favorable circumstances for its existence. They are properties that, if modified, the characteristics of the object are changed, but it does not cause any object to come into existence or to go out of existence.

Identity-related properties: Properties that, if modified, cause a change in the identity of the object (i.e., the object is changed in a way that it can no longer be recognized as the same individual as the one existing prior to the change in the property, even though being an individual of the same type).

Favorable properties: Properties that, if modified, establish the favorable circumstances for an individual to come into existence or cease the favorable circumstances that support the existence of some individual.

It is important to note that the status of a property is dependent on particular types of object. That is, for example, the general shape is an identity-related property for a statue, but not for a portion of clay.

4.3 Four Types of Occurrents

Based on the presented types of property, we propose the following classification.

States: States are occurrents in which the linked situations only differ in their *temporal positions*. No other property of its objects are modified. Thus, this type of occurrent can be seen as the maintenance of a configuration of a part of the world. This corresponds to the case $C1$ in Sect. 4.1.

Simple Changes: Simple changes are occurrents that only modifies *ordinary properties* of the objects. Thus, the exact same individual objects arranged in the initial situation are present in the ending situation, though presenting some different properties. This corresponds to the case $C2$ in Sect. 4.1.

Transformations: Transformations are occurrents in which *identity-related* properties are modified and the individual(s) that bear the modified identity-related properties have their identity changed. With that, both initial and ending situations will comprise individuals of the same type, but numerically distinct from each other, so that the individual in the ending situation is such that it has come from the individual in the initial situation (i.e., they share the same basic ontological substrate, but have some identity-relate property for their type modified). Moreover, the number of instances of the considered type does not change in any temporal interval during the transformation. Finally, the "going out of existence" of the transform and individual and the coming into existence of the transformed individual are *simultaneous* and *essentially* tied together. This corresponds to the case $C3$ in Sect. 4.1.

Existential occurrents: Existential occurrents are those in which *favorable properties* are modified, affecting the favorable circumstances for the existence of some participants. Is specialized in two different types: *creation* and *destruction*. In a creation, the modification in favorable properties results in the establishment of favorable circumstances for the appearance of a new individual of a given type. In a destruction, the modification in favorable properties results in the "removal" of the favorable conditions that were supporting the existence of an individual of a given type, causing it to cease to exist. This corresponds to the case $C4$ in Sect. 4.1.

5 Related Work

Current ontologies employ a variety of classification criteria to build their taxonomies for occurrents [18], some of them considering the transition character of occurrents. The types proposed in this work have some parallel in [15] and in [12]. Nevertheless, differently from our approach, the types presented in these ontologies focus on the involved objects, with no reference to the substrate that constitutes them. Without that, they provide no means to rule out spurious occurrents, such that of an object appearing out of nothing or disappearing leaving no trace.

This work also introduces a criterion of individuation given by the principle of ontological conservation which seems to advance previous proposals. In [10], an occurrent is everything that happens to a selected set of focal individual qualities during a temporal interval. This criteria works very well for *States* or *Simple Changes* (they are just a matter of keeping/altering properties of some participants). However, problems seem to arise in *Transformations* and *Existential Occurrents*, since they involve participants that exist in one of the ends of the occurrent but not in the other and thus there is no focal quality to track throughout the whole occurrent. In our framework, coming into or going out existence is a matter of alterations of favorable properties of a conserved ontological substrate, making it possible to individuate such occurrents focusing on favorable properties of the involved ontological substrate.

6   Concluding Remarks

In this work, we presented a framework for the ontological analysis of occurrents based on the notion of occurrent as a transition between situations. We articulate the idea of constitution and its implications for the existence of objects to propose the principle of ontological conservation. With that, we identified three main types of property of objects and four types of occurrent related to what can happen regarding these properties.

The proposed framework provides a guide to the modeling of occurrents, offering criteria to assess the correctness of models of occurrents and to fix modeling problems that may arise. Among other features, the very definition of occurrent proposed here (i.e., a transition between situations that comprise the same maximal amount of basic ontological substrate) provides a powerful individuation criterion for occurrents. With that, it is possible to rule out spurious occurrents that link situations comprising unrelated objects and reveal hidden participants not considered in the modeling. Thus, applying this framework in the development of ontologies may contribute to approximate the set of valid models of an ontology to the truly *intended ones*.

This work was restricted to the case of occurrents involving objects. However, we implicitly assume the existence of similar types occurrents (e.g., creation, destruction, change) regarding properties (as mentioned in [11]). The investigation of such types is left as future work.

Acknowledgments. This study was financed in part by the Coordenação de Aperfeiçoamento de Pessoal de Nível Superior - Brasil (CAPES) - Finance Code 001 and Conselho Nacional de Desenvolvimento Científico e Tecnológico (CNPq).

References

1. Almeida, J.P.A., Costa, P.D., Guizzardi, G.: Towards an ontology of scenes and situations. In: 2018 IEEE Conference on Cognitive and Computational Aspects of Situation Management (CogSIMA), pp. 29–35. IEEE (2018)
2. Baker, L.R.: The Metaphysics of Everyday Life. Cambridge University Press, Cambridge (2007)

3. Bennett, B., Galton, A.P.: A unifying semantics for time and events. Artif. Intell. **153**(1–2), 13–48 (2004)

4. Borgo, S., Bozzato, L., Aprosio, A.P., Rospocher, M., Serafini, L.: On coreferring text-extracted event descriptions with the aid of ontological reasoning. arXiv preprint arXiv:1612.00227 (2016)

5. Carbonera, J.L., Abel, M., Scherer, C.M.: Visual interpretation of events in petroleum exploration: an approach supported by well-founded ontologies. Expert Syst. Appl. **42**, 2749–2763 (2015)

6. Costa, P.D., Guizzardi, G., Almeida, J.P.A., Pires, L.F., Van Sinderen, M.: Situations in conceptual modeling of context. In: 2006 10th IEEE International Enterprise Distributed Object Computing Conference Workshops (EDOCW 2006), p. 6. IEEE (2006)

7. Galton, A., Mizoguchi, R.: The water falls but the waterfall does not fall: new perspectives on objects, processes and events. Appl. Ontol. **4**(2), 71–107 (2009)

8. Fonseca Garcia, L., Carbonera, J.L., Rodrigues, F.H., Roca Antunes, C., Abel, M.: What rocks are made of: towards an ontological pattern for material constitution in the geological domain. In: Laender, A.H.F., Pernici, B., Lim, E.-P., de Oliveira, J.P.M. (eds.) ER 2019. LNCS, vol. 11788, pp. 275–286. Springer, Cham (2019). https://doi.org/10.1007/978-3-030-33223-5_23

9. Gruber, T.R., et al.: A translation approach to portable ontology specifications. Knowl. Acquis. **5**(2), 199–221 (1993)

10. Guarino, N., Guizzardi, G.: Relationships and events: towards a general theory of reification and truthmaking. In: Adorni, G., Cagnoni, S., Gori, M., Maratea, M. (eds.) AI*IA 2016. LNCS (LNAI), vol. 10037, pp. 237–249. Springer, Cham (2016). https://doi.org/10.1007/978-3-319-49130-1_18

11. Guizzardi, G., Guarino, N., Almeida, J.P.A.: Ontological considerations about the representation of events and endurants in business models. In: La Rosa, M., Loos, P., Pastor, O. (eds.) BPM 2016. LNCS, vol. 9850, pp. 20–36. Springer, Cham (2016). https://doi.org/10.1007/978-3-319-45348-4_2

12. Guizzardi, G., Wagner, G.: Towards an ontological foundation of discrete event simulation. In: Proceedings of the 2010 Winter Simulation Conference, pp. 652 664. IEEE (2010)

13. Guizzardi, G., Wagner, G., de Almeida Falbo, R., Guizzardi, R.S.S., Almeida, J.P.A.: Towards ontological foundations for the conceptual modeling of events. In: Ng, W., Storey, V.C., Trujillo, J.C. (eds.) ER 2013. LNCS, vol. 8217, pp. 327–341. Springer, Heidelberg (2013). https://doi.org/10.1007/978-3-642-41924-9_27

14. Herre, H.: General formal ontology (GFO): a foundational ontology for conceptual modelling. In: Poli, R., Healy, M., Kameas, A. (eds.) Theory and Applications of Ontology: Computer Applications. Springer, Dordrecht (2010). https://doi.org/10.1007/978-90-481-8847-5_14

15. Kaneiwa, K., Iwazume, M., Fukuda, K.: An upper ontology for event classifications and relations. In: Orgun, M.A., Thornton, J. (eds.) AI 2007. LNCS (LNAI), vol. 4830, pp. 394–403. Springer, Heidelberg (2007). https://doi.org/10.1007/978-3-540-76928-6_41

16. Conservation Law: Encyclopaedia britannica. britannica.com/science/conservation-law

17. Mele, F., Sorgente, A.: The temporal representation and reasoning of complex events. In: CILC, pp. 385–399 (2011)

18. Rodrigues, F.H., Abel, M.: What to consider about events: a survey on the ontology of occurrents. Appl. Ontol. **14**(4), 343–378 (2019)
19. Tao, C., Wei, W.Q., Solbrig, H.R., Savova, G., Chute, C.G.: Cntro: a semantic web ontology for temporal relation inferencing in clinical narratives. In: AMIA Annual Symposium Proceedings, vol. 2010, p. 787. American Medical Informatics Association (2010)

A Core Ontology for Economic Exchanges

Daniele Porello[1] (ID), Giancarlo Guizzardi[2] (ID), Tiago Prince Sales[2] (ID),
and Glenda Amaral[2(✉)] (ID)

[1] ISTC-CNR Laboratory for Applied Ontology, Trento, Italy
daniele.porello@cnr.it
[2] Conceptual and Cognitive Modeling Research Group (CORE),
Free University of Bozen-Bolzano, Bolzano, Italy
{giancarlo.guizzardi,tiago.princesales,gmouraamaral}@unibz.it

Abstract. In recent years, there has been an increasing interest in the development of well-founded conceptual models for Service Management, Accounting Information Systems and Financial Reporting. Economic exchanges are a central notion in these areas and they occupy a prominent position in frameworks such as the Resource-Event Action (REA) ISO Standard, service core ontologies (e.g., UFO-S) as well as financial standards (e.g. OMG's Financial Industry Business Ontology - FIBO). We present a core ontology for economic exchanges inspired by a recent view on this phenomenon. According to this view, economic exchanges are based on an agreement on the actions that the agents are committed to perform. This view enables a unified treatment of economic exchanges, regardless the object of the transaction. We ground our core ontology on the Unified Foundational Ontology (UFO), discussing its formal and conceptual aspects, instantiating it as a reusable OntoUML model, and confronting it with the REA standard and the UFO-S service ontology.

Keywords: Economic exchanges · Preferences · Enterprise modeling · Business ontology · Unified Foundational Ontology

1 Introduction

The nature of economic exchanges has been thoroughly debated in philosophy, economics, and social sciences, since at least the Eighteenth century, when the epistemological status of the main concepts of the economic theory was intensively discussed in search of a solid foundation, cf. [10]. Two important issues regarding the nature of economic exchanges —which are quite pressing for a fruitful ontological understanding of economic interactions— are the nature of the things being exchanged and the matter of the agreement between the transacting agents. Do we transact goods, services, objects, actions, events, or promises? Are we motivated to transact because of converging or inverse interests?

To approach these delicate points, we shall rely on the *Action Theory of Economic Exchanges* (ATE) [12], a recent perspective from the area of philosophy of economics. The motivation for this choice is three-fold. Firstly, it allows for a

G. Dobbie et al. (Eds.): ER 2020, LNCS 12400, pp. 364–374, 2020.
https://doi.org/10.1007/978-3-030-62522-1_27

quite general view of economic exchanges concerning heterogeneous items (e.g. both goods and services). Secondly, the ATE explains why and under which conditions an economic exchange takes place. Finally, the ATE models economic exchanges from the perspective of both agents involved in a transaction, the so-called "helicopter view", cf. [11]. For the above-mentioned reasons, we claim that ATE is more apt to guide a foundational analysis of economic exchanges than, for instance, the ISO standard for Accounting Information Systems REA (Resource-Event-Action) [13]. In particular, REA focuses mainly on exchanges of resource items. It does not explain why a transaction happens and it takes the partial perspective of a single actor of the exchange. As we shall see, the REA modeling style can indeed be retrieved within the ATE, which is in fact a richer perspective.

In the subsequent sections, we shall develop an ontological account of economic transactions according to the ATE. The goal of this paper is to use the ATE as a guide to lay down the main aspects of a core ontology of economic interactions. To make our investigation precise and applicable to designing well-founded Information Systems, we shall place our analysis within the Unified Foundational Ontology (UFO) [7–9]. One of the reasons for using UFO is its rich treatment of relations [4], a compelling feature, as we shall see, for modeling concepts in economics. Moreover, UFO is associated to a well-founded UML profile (OntoUML) [7], which has been extensively used for developing an onto-logically sound methodology for conceptual modeling. So to put the ATE to work in modeling applications, we present a reusable OntoUML model of economic exchanges.

To demonstrate the expressiveness and generality of our core ontology, we use it to analyze and ground both REA and UFO-S. The latter is a core ontology of services, which has been shown to be able to harmonize different views of service, ranging from marketing-oriented views (e.g., Service Dominant Logic) to a capability-oriented views in service science, to technology-oriented views (as in Archimate) [14]. Moreover, it was successfully employed to analyze a number of prominent mainstreams service modeling languages (e.g., SoaML, USDL, Archimate) [15]. Finally, it influenced the efforts towards defining a federal government ontology of services for the national infrastructure of open data in Brazil[1]. As we show here, both REA and UFO-S can be seen as a special case of our core ontology.

A closely related work to the one presented here is [2], which also approaches economic exchanges in UFO. Another related work is [20], which starts the development of an ontology of commercial exchanges in the foundational ontology BFO. In comparison to the latter, by leveraging on UFO's theory of relations, our work is able to capture the nature of economic offering and agreements as *full-fledged endurants* [5] and, as such, as entities capable of genuine changes in time (as opposed to modeling only the events and descriptions related to this phenomenon). This benefit is also present in [2] (and for the same reason). Our main difference with respect to that approach is our explicit connection to the

---

[1] See http://wiki.gtinda.ibge.gov.br/Ontologia-Servicos-Publicos.ashx.

notion of *economic preference* and its explicit grounding on a modern philosophy theory of economic exchange (ATE).

The paper is organized as follows. Section 2 presents the ATE and a brief view on the UFO and OntoUML. Section 3 presents the main contribution of this paper, i.e., a well-founded ontology of ATE in light of UFO. Section 4 concludes by showing the application of this ontology to analyze and ground REA and UFO-S.

2   Background: ATE and UFO

2.1   The Action Theory of Economic Exchanges (ATE)

The core assumption made by the Action Theory of Exchanges (ATE) [12] is that, in any economic transaction, the "object" of the transaction is a pair of *actions* to be performed by the relevant agents involved in it. The main assumptions of the ATE are summarised below:

Definition 1. *Agents a and b are transacting about actions ϕ and ψ iff*

1. Preferences and beliefs:
   1.1 *a prefers that a does ϕ and b does ψ, to a does not ϕ and b does not ψ.*
   1.2 *b prefers that a does ϕ and b does ψ, to a does not ϕ and b does not ψ.*
   1.3 *a believes that promising to b to do ϕ on condition that b does ψ is a way to make b to do ψ.*
   2 Offer and acceptance:
   2.1 *Because of 1.1. and 1.3, a promises to b that a will do ϕ, if b does ψ*
   2.2 *Because of 1.2, b accepts the offer.*
   3 Provisions:
   3.1 *Because of 2.2, b does ψ. Therefore, a is obliged to do ϕ.*
   3.2 *Because of 2.1 and 3.1, a does ϕ.*

Three points are worth noticing. Firstly, by viewing the object of transactions as actions, the ATE is capable of accounting for economic transactions about goods as well as services. In the case of services, the agreement is about the respective actions to be performed by the relevant parties. E.g. a customer and a delivery company agree on the pair of actions ϕ: "*a* pays the agreed amount to company *b*" and ψ: "The company *b* delivers the requested service to *a*". In the case of goods, the preferred pair of actions can be expressed in terms of the transfer of ownership, the action of transferring the ownership of an item: e.g. ϕ: "*a* transfer the ownership of her laptop to *b*" and ψ: "*b* pays the agreed amount to *a*".

Secondly, the assumption about the *convergence* of the agents' preferences to the same pair of actions is an important bit here, as it is capable of explaining why two agents are in fact transacting with each other (and not with other parties). The actions to which the agents commit explicitly mention the relevant agents of the actions, which are in fact the very agents involved in the transaction: when an actual transaction between a and b happens, a is intending to transact precisely with b, and not to an other agent.

Thirdly, the ATE is a quite rich reconstruction of the steps happening in an economic exchange. If the preconditions in point 1 of Definition 1 are met, an economic transaction starts with an offering, cf. point 2.1, which is based on the preference of one agent for a certain course of action and on the belief that, by promising something to another agent, this course of action can take place. Moreover, an economic offering generates obligations, i.e. commitments. In point 2.1, a promises to (commits to) do ϕ, if b does ψ (a conditional commitment). In point 3.1, since b has accepted the offer, b is committed to do ψ, then once B has done ψ, a is obliged to do ϕ (an unconditional commitment). Thus the ATE's mechanism for explaining why economic transactions happen works by turning a conditional commitment into an unconditional commitment, under the suited conditions. For this reasons, ATE also provides an explanation of why and under which circumstances an economic exchange happens. As we shall see, the unfolding of commitments in ATE is quite similar to what happens to service offerings in UFO-S, cf. [14].

2.2   The Unified Foundational Ontology (UFO)

UFO is an axiomatic theory combining results from formal ontology in philosophy, linguistics, cognitive science and philosophical logics [8]. Over the years, UFO has been systematically designed as a foundation for addressing basic concepts in conceptual modeling. In order to ground our models on UFO, we employ OntoUML, a UFO-based ontology-driven conceptual modeling language [7]. OntoUML is a version of UML class diagrams constructed to reflect the categories and axiomatization of UFO. UFO and OntoUML have been successfully employed in academic, industrial and governmental settings to create conceptual models in a variety of different application domains [8].

UFO separates individuals in endurants (aka objects) and perdurants (aka events). Individuals instantiate types. Types are also separated into relational (or n-ary) types (RELATION) and unary types, in particular, ENDURANT TYPE that classify endurants. For a complete review on UFO, one should refer to [4,7,9].

We focus here on endurant types. They comprise SUBSTANTIAL TYPE, e.g. types whose instances are ordinary objects (e.g. a flower, a person), and MOMENT TYPE, that is, types whose instances are aspects of objects (e.g. the colour of a rose, the courage of a person). MOMENT TYPE is further classified into INTRINSIC MOMENT TYPE and EXTRINSIC MOMENT TYPE. The former includes types whose instances are aspects of objects that do not depend on other entities (e.g. the courage of a person). The latter includes types whose instances are *relational* aspects, i.e. they inhere in an entity but existentially depend on something external to that entity. Examples of relational aspects include the love of a mother for her child and the mutual commitments of a conjugal relationship. EXTRINSIC MOMENT TYPE is in turn divided into two subclasses: EXTRINSIC MODE TYPE (or single-sided relators, [4]) and RELATOR TYPE. The former refers to types whose instances inhere in a single endurant, but are externally dependent on other endurants. So, the love of a mother for her child is a mode that inheres in the mother and externally depends on the child. By contrast, a relator requires a mutual pattern of dependence between the relational qualities that inhere in (at least) two distinct entities. For instance, the conjugal commitments in a marriage constitute a relator as the (mereological) sum of the commitments of the two partners, each commitment being externally dependent on the other partner. A further condition on externally dependent modes and on relators is that each of them is founded on a unique event, e.g. the conjugal relator is founded on the marriage event. For a formalisation of this notions, we refer to [4].

Anticipating our view of economic transactions, economic offering shall be represented as relators: they are the sum of the commitments and of the obligations of the parties involved in the transaction.

Orthogonal to the specialization of ENDURANT TYPES w.r.t. the nature of their instances, UFO also specialize them regarding their relation to the ontological notions of *essence*, *rigidity*, and *relational dependence* [7]. ENDURANT TYPES can be either SORTALS or NON-SORTALS. SORTALS are either KINDS or specializations of a KIND. A KIND is a central notion here as it defines what endurants in this domain are *essentially*, i.e., in all possible situations (the set of all our possible instances is a tessellation of rigid, i.e., static KINDS). An antirigid (i.e., dynamic, contingent) SORTAL specializing a KIND is a ROLE. *Roles* are also relationally dependent, i.e., individuals (contingently) play ROLES in the scope of a relation. NON-SORTALS are types that classify individuals of multiple KINDS. A rigid (static) NON-SORTAL is termed a CATEGORY; a role-like anti-rigid NON-SORTAL that can be played by individuals of multiple KINDS is termed a ROLE MIXIN.

3 The Action Theory of Economic Exchanges in UFO

The core ingredients for representing the ATE in UFO are: *agents, preferences, actions, beliefs and commitments, economic offerings, and economic exchanges.* The focus here is on economic offerings and transactions.

AGENT is a rigid non-sortal type, i.e., a type that essentially classifies individuals of different *kinds*, i.e., individuals that have different ontological natures [7]. The class AGENT may include individual or collective agents (e.g. organisations, companies, etc.), with their specific ontological differences [3,16].

Since agents (i.e. entities with *intentionality*) are necessarily agents (in the modal sense), we stereotype the type AGENT as an OntoUML *Category*. Agents can play the "role" of VALUE BEHOLDER in a value ascription relation, the relation by which an agent assigns a value to an entity. We represent the type VALUE BEHOLDER as a *role mixin* because: (i) it classifies entities only contingently, (ii) one is a value beholder due to a relational condition; (iii) it is a *Non-Sortal*, i.e., it can classify entities of multiple kinds.

A VALUE ASCRIPTION is a *mode* [7,19]. As we discussed, a mode is an existentially dependent entity that, as such, can only exist by inhering in some other individual. In particular, a value is a *externally dependent mode*, i.e., a mode that inheres in an individual but which is also externally dependent on a different entity. So, a value ascription is a sort of mental state inhering in the value beholder that is also externally dependent on a number of entities in VALUE ENTITY. A value ascription mode takes a value in at least one (but possibly several) VALUE MAGNITUDE SPACES, via the *quality* of VALUE (a quality of the value ascription). These spaces have, in OntoUML, the semantics of abstract conceptual spaces, delimiting the possible values a property can be projected into, cf. [7] (e.g. we can account for cardinal or ordinal measures of value).

Finally, a PREFERENCE, cf. [17], of an agent between two entities is relational mode (between the agent and the two entities) but a complex one (i.e., a complex mental state). A (binary) preference concerning two entities is a mode inhering a value beholder that is essentially composed of exactly *two* existing value ascriptions (it is the mereological sum of them), inhering in that very same value beholder: *i*) the value of the first entity given the second entity and *ii*) the value of the second entity given the first entity.[2]

The (ternary) relation *prefers* (a relational type in UFO, cf. [4]) in "*i* prefers *x* over *y*" connects the rolemixin VALUE BEHOLDER *i* with two other rolemixins PREFERRED ENTITY *x* and DEPRECATED ENTITY *y*.

To apply this view of preferences to ATE (step 1.1 and 1.2 of Definition 1), we need to understand ontologically what are the entities about which the agents have preferences. In ATE, preferences are definitely about *pairs of actions* (cf. point 1.1.) Actions are particular types of events in UFO, so preferences are *prima facie* about events that are composed of two actions.[3]

This point is however quite delicate, for the reasons highlighted in [18].

The solution adopted here is to view preferences as being about *types* of actions. This solution enables flexibility in describing the object of the preference. Firstly, agents may have preferences over actions that may not actually occur or even over negative actions: instead of introducing a category of possible or negative actions, we can do by introducing the right type of actions, which may not be instantiated in the actual world. Secondly, types enable a flexible degree of determination of the actions at issue: we do not need to assume that agents can fully determinate the events they are preferring. Summing up, an OntoUML module for preferences is depicted in Fig. 1, where PREFERRED ENTITY and DEPRECATED ENTITY are thus to be intended as types of types of events.

3.1 Economic Offering and Economic Transactions

We can finally approach the modeling of economic transactions. We start from the offering event, cf. OFFERING. This event is the foundation (cf. creation in OntoUML) of a relator ECONOMIC OFFERING which is composed of the (mereological) sum of (the externally dependent modes given by) the conditional commitment of the offerer and of the offeree. OFFERER and OFFEREE are again roles

---

[2] The preference depends on the context of comparison between the entities, cf. [19,20].

[3] By assuming a mereology of events, cf. [1], the event "A doing ϕ and B doing ψ" is defined as the mereological sum of the two events "A doing ϕ" and "B doing ψ".

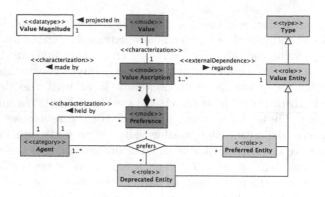

Fig. 1. OntoUML model of preference relations.

mixins here. The important aspects is that, at this point, the commitments and claims are *conditional*, which corresponds to stage 2.1 of Definition 1. According to our discussion in Section 4.1 about the entities that are related by preferences in ATE, the conditional commitments are about types of actions, cf. commits to in OntoUML. The OFFERED CONTRIBUTION TYPE and the COUNTERPART CONTRIBUTION TYPE are in fact types of types of events. The offering is based on the preferences of the offerer, according to stage 2.1 of Definition 1. Notice that here is where we changed Massin and Tieffenbach's model from ATE by viewing preferences as defined on *types* of actions. Accordingly, an instance of the class ECONOMIC EXCHANGE TYPE is a type of event constructed by means of two types of events: the OFFERED CONTRIBUTION TYPE and the COUNTERPART CONTRIBUTION TYPE. We are modeling the constructed type by means of the relation requires. The idea is that a type in ECONOMIC EXCHANGE TYPE classifies events that have two components: a component classified by a type in OFFERED CONTRIBUTION TYPE and a component in COUNTERPART CONTRIBUTION TYPE.[4]

The relation participate to events of type models the fact that the offerer participates in all the events of the offered contribution type and the offeree participates in all the events of the counterpart contribution type. This point accounts for the fact that the convergent preferences of the two agents have to mention the relevant agents involved in the transaction.[5] Figure 2 represents the OntoUML modeling of economic offerings.

To shorten the exposition, here we model the situation where the offer proposed by the offerer is immediately accepted, and no negotiation takes places between the parties, see Fig. 3. If the offer is accepted by the offeree, then the event of the offering founds a new relator of ECONOMIC AGREEMENT between

---

[4] We leave a proper treatment of the requires relation for a dedicated work.

[5] For reasons of space, we omit a number of aspects of ATE. E.g. the economic offer is also based on beliefs, cf. point 1.2 and 1.3. We can easily integrate beliefs as in [14].

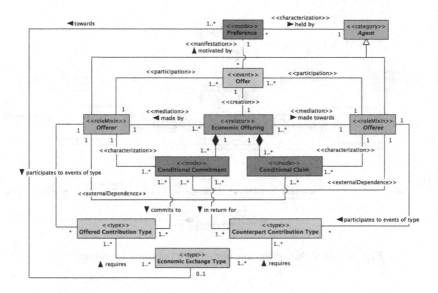

Fig. 2. OntoUML diagram depicting economic offerings.

the two agents. This step provides the ontological counterpart of stage 2.2. of
Definition 1. The new relator complies with the previously created economic
offering relator. This new relator has parts the new (now) *unconditional* commitments of the agents to fulfill the promised courses of actions (of the required
type). This step realises the final outcome of Definition 1, namely the actualisa-
tion of steps 2.1 and 2.2 based on the provisions 3.1 and 3.2. The actual event
of ECONOMIC EXCHANGE is required then to have as parts the event (action) of
fulfilment of the offerer commitments as well as the event (action) of the fulfilment of the requested counterparts. Those events are of the right type, i.e. the
OFFERED CONTRIBUTION and the COUNTERPART CONTRIBUTION match the
type in OFFERED CONTRIBUTION TYPE and COUNTERPART CONTRIBUTION
TYPE (respectively), cf. the relation instantiation.

4   ATE at Work: Generalising REA and UFO-S

We conclude by discussing the relationship between our account of the ATE,
UFO-S, and REA. We start showing how REA can be retrieved by isolating a
part of our OntoUML model of ATE.

In REA, economic transactions are intended as events, i.e. "occurrences in
time wherein ownership of an economic resource is transferred from one person to
another person" [13]. This aspect is captured by the realisation of the economic
transaction in ATE, i.e. when the commitments are fulfilled, they trigger the
relevant events, cf. Fig. 3. Moreover, although REA seems to view resources
(e.g. endurants) as objects of the transaction, what is brought about in economic
exchanges is the transferring of ownership of an item, which is in fact an event,

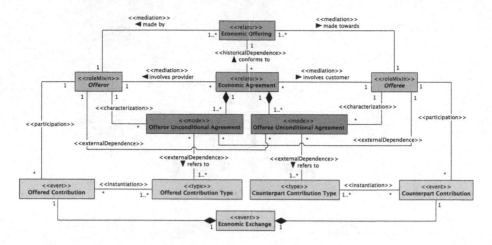

Fig. 3. OntoUML diagram depicting economic exchanges.

see [6]. This is indeed a specific type of action, which can be straightforwardly accounted by ATE. E.g., suppose that agent a is selling a bike to agent b. We can specify the relevant types of actions involved as follows: a and b both prefer the type of actions "a transfer the ownership of the bike to b and b pays the agreed price" to the type of actions "a does not transfer the ownership of the bike to b and b does not pay the agreed amount". In the analysis of REA in [11], the economic agreement is captured by means of the duality relations, (e.g. transfer duality, [11], p. 16). In [11], duality relations are modeled as relators, as we do here. This enables a direct comparison with our framework: duality relators are simply a specific type of our ECONOMIC AGREEMENT, restricted to specific types of actions, e.g. transfer of ownership. Hence, REA modeling is a submodel of our OntoUML version of ATE. Therefore, our modeling provides, on the one hand, a generalisation of REA to transactions involving any type of services and, on the other hand, an explanation of why the transaction occurs: it is based, as we have seen, on the convergent preferences of the agents and on the commitment generated by the offering steps.

We confront now our OntoUML model of ATE with UFO-S. As we anticipated, the mechanism of turning conditional commitment into unconditional commitments is at the core of UFO-S. There, commitments are generated by the service offering, cf. [14], as in ATE are generated by the economic offering. In this perspective, ATE provides a simple generalisation of UFO-S from service offering to any kind of economic offering. Service offering are reinterpreted, in our view, as offering about types of actions, which serves to accommodate the ontological worries about committing to possible or negative events. Moreover, ATE nicely complements the model of UFO-S by providing an explanation of why the offering is proposed in the first place and of why it can be accepted by the counterpart. The beginning of the offering is grounded in ATE on the assumptions concerning the converging preferences. So ATE complements UFO-

S by providing an explanation of why the service offering is proposed and under which conditions it is accepted. In practice, we can integrate the model of UFO-S of the relator of service agreement (cf. [14], p. 181) with our model of Fig. 2.

References

1. Almeida, J.P.A., Falbo, R.A., Guizzardi, G.: Events as entities in ontology-driven conceptual modeling. In: Laender, A.H.F., Pernici, B., Lim, E.-P., de Oliveira, J.P.M. (eds.) ER 2019. LNCS, vol. 11788, pp. 469–483. Springer, Cham (2019). https://doi.org/10.1007/978-3-030-33223-5_39
2. Blums, I., Weigand, H.: A financial reporting ontology for market, exchange, and enterprise shared information systems. In: Gordijn, J., Guédria, W., Proper, H.A. (eds.) PoEM 2019. LNBIP, vol. 369, pp. 83–99. Springer, Cham (2019). https://doi.org/10.1007/978-3-030-35151-9_6
3. Ferrario, R., Masolo, C., Porello, D.: Organisations and variable embodiments. In: Proceedings of the 10th FOIS, pp. 127–140. IOS Press (2018)
4. Fonseca, C.M., Porello, D., Guizzardi, G., Almeida, J.P.A., Guarino, N.: Relations in ontology-driven conceptual modeling. In: Laender, A.H.F., Pernici, B., Lim, E.-P., de Oliveira, J.P.M. (eds.) ER 2019. LNCS, vol. 11788, pp. 28–42. Springer, Cham (2019). https://doi.org/10.1007/978-3-030-33223-5_4
5. Guarino, N., Guizzardi, G.: "We need to discuss the *relationship*": revisiting relationships as modeling constructs. In: Zdravkovic, J., Kirikova, M., Johannesson, P. (eds.) CAiSE 2015. LNCS, vol. 9097, pp. 279–294. Springer, Cham (2015). https://doi.org/10.1007/978-3-319-19069-3_18
6. Guarino, N., Guizzardi, G., Sales, T.P.: On the ontological nature of REA core relations. In: Value Modeling and Business Ontologies (VMBO), pp. 89–98 (2018)
7. Guizzardi, G.: Ontological Foundations for Structural Conceptual Models. Telematica Instituut/CTIT (2005)
8. Guizzardi, G., et al.: Towards ontological foundations for conceptual modeling: the Unified Foundational Ontology (UFO) story. Appl. Ontol. **10**(3–4), 259–271 (2015)
9. Guizzardi, G., Fonseca, C.M., Benevides, A.B., Almeida, J.P.A., Porello, D., Sales, T.P.: Endurant types in ontology-driven conceptual modeling: towards OntoUML 2.0. In: Trujillo, J., et al. (eds.) ER 2018. LNCS, vol. 11157, pp. 136–150. Springer, Cham (2018). https://doi.org/10.1007/978-3-030-00847-5_12
10. Hodgson, G.M.: Markets. In: Durlauf, S.N., Blume, L.E. (eds.) The New Palgrave: Dictionary of Economics. LNCS, pp. 3918–3925. Palgrave Macmillan UK, London (2008). https://doi.org/10.1007/978-1-349-58802-2_1035
11. Laurier, W., Kiehn, J., Polovina, S.: REA 2: a unified formalisation of the Resource-Event-Agent ontology. Appl. Ontol. **13**(3), 201–224 (2018)
12. Massin, O., Tieffenbach, E.: The metaphysics of economic exchanges. J. Soc. Ontol. **3**(2), 167–205 (2016)
13. McCarthy, W.: ISO 15944–4 - REA Ontology. ISO, June 2007
14. Nardi, J., et al.: A commitment-based reference ontology for services. Inf. Syst. **54**, 263–288 (2015)
15. Nardi, J., et al.: An ontology-based diagnosis of mainstream service modeling languages. In: Proceedings of the IEEE 23rd EDOC, pp. 112–121. IEEE (2019)
16. Porello, D., Bottazzi, E., Ferrario, R.: The ontology of group agency. In: Proceedings of the 8th FOIS, Rio de Janeiro, pp. 183–196. IOS Press (2014)

17. Porello, D., Guizzardi, G.: Towards an ontological modelling of preference relations. In: Ghidini, C., Magnini, B., Passerini, A., Traverso, P. (eds.) AI*IA 2018. LNCS (LNAI), vol. 11298, pp. 152–165. Springer, Cham (2018). https://doi.org/10.1007/978-3-030-03840-3_12
18. Porello, D., et al.: An ontological account of the action theory of economic exchanges. In: Proceedings of the 14th VMBO, vol. 2574, pp. 157–169. CEUR-WS.org (2020)
19. Sales, T.P., Guarino, N., Guizzardi, G., Mylopoulos, J.: An ontological analysis of value propositions. In: Proceedings of IEEE 21st EDOC, pp. 184–193. IEEE (2017)
20. Vajda, J., Merrell, E., Smith, B.: Toward an ontology of commercial exchange. In: Proceedings of the 5th JOWO, vol. 2518. CEUR-WS.org (2019)

Applications of Conceptual Modeling

Towards a Model-Driven Architecture for Interactive Digital Twin Cockpits

Manuela Dalibor(✉)⬭, Judith Michael⬭, Bernhard Rumpe⬭, Simon Varga⬭,
and Andreas Wortmann⬭

Software Engineering, RWTH Aachen University, Aachen, Germany
dalibor@se-rwth.de,
https://www.se-rwth.de/

Abstract. Digital twins promise tremendous potential to reduce time
and cost in the smart manufacturing of Industry 4.0. Engineering and
monitoring interactive digital twins currently demands integrating different piecemeal technologies that effectively hinders their application and
deployment. Current research on digital twins focuses on specific implementations or abstract models on how digital twins could be conceived.
We propose model-driven software engineering to realize interactive digital twins and user-specific cockpits to interact with the digital twin
by generating the infrastructure from common data structure models.
To this end, we present a model-driven architecture for digital twins,
its integration with an interactive cockpit, and a systematic method of
realizing both. Through this, modeling, deploying, and monitoring interactive digital twins becomes more feasible and fosters their successful
application in smart manufacturing.

Keywords: Digital Twins · Information systems · Model-driven
software engineering · Smart manufacturing

1 Introduction

Motivation and Challenges. Digital Twins (DTs) of Cyber-Physical Production
Systems (CPPSs), including their hardware and software components, promise
tremendous potential to reduce time and cost in smart manufacturing [18].
Clearly, DTs need means for information representation [4], interactive control
of CPPSs [19] and optimization functionalities [23], *e.g.,* for adapting machine
configurations to yield higher part quality. Suitable visualizations must provide
CPPS information in a human-processable form and enable controlling the DT.
We call these services *digital twin cockpit* hereafter.

Funded by the Deutsche Forschungsgemeinschaft (DFG, German Research Foundation)
under Germany's Excellence Strategy - EXC 2023 Internet of Production - 390621612.
We thank the Institute for Plastics Processing in Industry and Craft at RWTH Aachen
University and the ARBURG GmbH + Co KG for the provided machine equipment.

G. Dobbie et al. (Eds.): ER 2020, LNCS 12400, pp. 377–387, 2020.
https://doi.org/10.1007/978-3-030-62522-1_28

Research Question. How can we facilitate rapid engineering of interactive digital twin cockpits through integrating architecture and data modeling?

Our Approach. We propose a method to engineer interactive digital twin cockpits systematically by generating their infrastructure based on *common data models* created with Domain-Specific Languages (DSLs). We employ an architecture modeling language to specify the internal structure of the DT, the interface between the DT and the physical system, and the interface between the DT and the DT cockpit. This facilitates the engineering of a DT cockpit and ensures consistent integration with the DT.

Outline. In the following, Sect. 2 presents preliminaries. Section 3 illustrates challenges of the problem domain by example of injection molding. Section 4 explains our approach and its reference architecture. Section 5 describes how to create a digital twin cockpit for injection molding. Section 6 discusses our approach and related work. Section 7 concludes.

2 Preliminaries

A significant reason for the challenges of modern software systems engineering lies in the conceptual gap [10] between the problem domains and the solution domain software engineering. Overcoming this gap with handcrafted solutions requires immense effort and gives rise to so-called accidental complexities [10], *i.e.,* problems of the solution domain, which are not conceptually relevant in the problem domain. *Model-Driven Software Engineering (MDSE)* [21] is an umbrella term for software development methodologies that employ models as primary development artifacts to reduce the conceptual gap and with it accidental complexities.

Digital Twins in Smart Manufacturing. DTs are often described as a digital duplicate of a physical entity [9], enabling its management and control [8] or supporting design and production decisions, and thus speeding up the development process. DTs rely on information about the current system state to provide, *e.g.,* predictive maintenance or design support [14]. Since modern CPPSs are equipped with various sensors and produce large amounts of data, it is crucial to reduce the data into an amount the DT can process. Thus we introduce the Digital Shadow (DS). *A digital shadow is a set of models and data traces, that in addition to the data also includes context describing metadata for its intended purpose.* Hence, a DS contains precisely the data that the DT requires to perform its task and can, *e.g.,* be enriched with information about the data's origin or accuracy. Based on a survey among the participants of the German cluster of excellence "Internet of Production"[1], which comprises 25 departments and 200 researchers we conceived the following definition for a DT: *A digital twin of a system consists of a set of models of the system, a set of digital shadows and their aggregation and abstraction collected from a system, and a set of services*

---

[1] Internet of Production: https://www.iop.rwth-aachen.de.

that allow using the data and models purposefully with respect to the original system. Thus DTs might comprise, for instance, engineering models (*e.g.,* geometries, physical behavior, energy consumption, *etc.*), software models (structure, behavior, deployment, *etc.*), and services (such as cockpits visualizing data and providing services, optimization of CPPS use *etc.*).

MontiArc. [7] is an architecture description language. Its elements comprise component types that exchange messages through their interface of typed, directed ports. Components are connected via unidirectional connectors and support hierarchical decomposition through which a system's functionality can be decomposed hierarchically. A component encapsulates a subset of the system's functionality, and either is composed or atomic. Composed components consist of other components and their behavior emerges from these subcomponents and their interaction. Due to defined interfaces MontiArc facilitates exchangeability of components to adapt a system's behavior. Atomic components perform computations via embedded behavior models or handcrafted behavior implementations. Leveraging results from software language engineering, its language and code generation capabilities can be extended flexibly [6].

MontiGem. [1] generates web-based Enterprise Information System (EIS), *e.g.,* for finance cockpits or IoT dashboards using Class Diagrams (CDs), Object Constraint Language (OCL), tagging and GUI-DSL models, describing Graphical User Interfaces (GUIs), as input. The provided domain models directly influence the generated data structure, the database schema, the GUI layout, and view models. Integrating these DSLs, a variety of aspects of the resulting application can be modeled. Using these input models, MontiGem produces code for a pre-existing application framework that is used to build and execute the EIS. To ensure consistency-by-construction between front- and backend, models are used as a common source for information. Using CDs, we generate data classes and the database schema, the communication infrastructure using the command pattern and default website GUIs and views [11]. Additional GUI models can be used to detail and customize the layout of the generated pages. From an OCL model that constrains the data structure, the generator derives validators for data objects that conform to this structure. We use a Tagging DSL to enrich models with information for enabling different generator configurations or adding implementation-specific adaptations. The MontiGem generator framework creates a EIS that enables creating, viewing, editing, or deleting data sets [11].

3   Modeling Challenges in Injection Molding

Injection molding [15] is a plastic processing technique in which a plastic granule is heated and injected under pressure into an injection mold. Injection molding is one of the leading production techniques for plastic parts and can be considered as a representative of a classic mass production process. Figure 1 illustrates the typical components of an injection molding machine.

The machine operator can configure the operation point via the user interface. A plastic granule is inserted into the machine through a hopper. Within

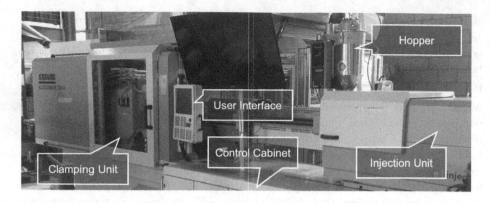

Fig. 1. The ARBURG Allrounder 520 injection molding machine from the example.

the injection unit, the plastic granule is heated and molten into the desired consistency. The screw transfers the plastic to the nozzle. Next, the injection unit injects the molten plastic into the mold while applying high pressure. The clamping unit keeps the mold closed during injection so that the applied pressure is countered and the mold halves do not open up. After a cooling time, the machine ejects the workpiece from the mold.

Various device components with multiple influencing variables and process parameters are directly involved in the successful realization of an injection molded part. During the injection molding process, temperature and pressure sensors measure the process parameters. These already indicate the quality of the produced workpiece, and an experienced operator can derive how to adapt the configuration to meet required quality criteria. Injection molding machines are *sensitive to stress and contextual changes* as, *e.g.,* in the environmental temperature. Thus, the same configuration does not always yield workpieces of equal quality.

Visualizing process and context information for users to make changes in the configuration traceable and automating countermeasures (*e.g.,* increasing the pressure) before further defective products are finished can significantly decrease production time and reduce material consumption. To support such operations, a DT cockpit should:

C1 Provide real-time information about machine states and operating context,
C2 Provide role-specific views and aggregated data showing information at different levels of detail,
C3 Remain consistent with the DT if the DT is adapted to and deployed on new CPPS,
C4 Allow for interaction with the DT and to call specific operations on the DT and the CPPS.

4 Modeling Digital Twin Cockpits

Developing a controlling cockpit for DTs is paramount to facilitate the trust of machine operators and customers in the DT's activities. Since the DT consists of many components, we aim at reusing models that describe its structure or behavior and derive the cockpit's code. By generating the cockpit, it remains adaptable and can evolve if the underlying domain model or the DT evolves (*challenge C3*). Figure 2 shows the architecture of our system. The architecture structures into five layers: (1) Cyber-Physical Layer, (2) Data Layer, (3) Connection Layer, (4) Application Layer, and (5) Visualization Layer.

The main components are (A) the CPPS, the actual machine and its control interface, (B) the Digital Twin monitoring and influencing the machine, (C) the Data Lake with data from different information sources the DT relies on and the DT cockpit visualizes and (D) the DT Cockpit, providing aggregated information and visualizations of the system's state and enabling interaction with the DT.

The **Cyber-Physical Layer** describes the production system, which is monitored and controlled by the DT. The CPPS component provides an interface that enables reading sensor values. Further, it can receive commands via this interface and return feedback after processing these. Runtime data that the sensors within the CPPS collect is stored in the data lake. Our DT realization requires ports for sending commands, receiving feedback and collecting machine-specific data, as depicted in Fig. 2. We specify the CPPS and its ports in MontiArc since the language provides typed and directed ports. Thus, we can ensure that other components access the CPPS's ports only in the intended ways and that exchanged data conforms to a specified type.

The Data Lake within the **Data Layer** is an extensive data storage that can span multiple databases containing data from the CPPS and its operating context. The Data Lake also encapsulates the MontiGem database that includes all processed data and additional information, *e.g.,* user profiles or settings. These data structures are described with CDs that serve as input from which MontiGem generates the data structure, the infrastructure for storing the data of the DT cockpit as well as data update functionalities or observation methods to recognize data updates. The Data Lake provides an interface to query data for the DT and the DT cockpit. To represent the CPPS's state, the DT aggregates, processes, and transforms this data to DSs which the DT cockpit visualizes.

The components in the **Connection Layer** communicate with the physical layer and provide data for the application layer. The DataProcessor component creates and shares knowledge about the system's state by producing *digital shadows* based on data contained in the data lake. It queries data from specific databases within the data lake and further processes and transforms these data to create DSs. The DT cockpit visualizes these DSs that provide, *e.g.,* real-time information about the CPPS's state (meeting *challenge C1*). The Executor within the DT obtains a solution describing what the CPPS is supposed to do and transforming descriptions into commands sent to the CPPS. The CPPS returns

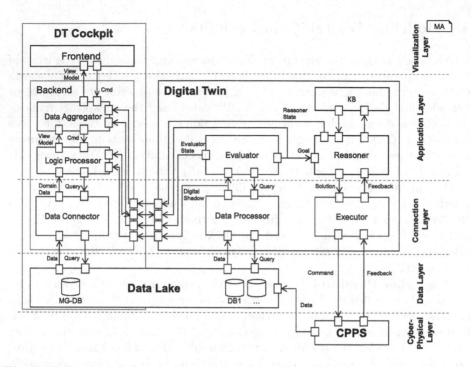

Fig. 2. The integrated digital twin and digital twin cockpit architecture in MontiArc.

feedback evaluated by the Executor. Depending on the evaluation results, the Executor sends further commands that contribute to fulfilling the solution.

The components of this layer depend on the descriptions of exchanged data. Thus, the structure of this data must be defined. We use CDs to derive the structure of exchanged objects automatically. This enables generating storage and query functionality for the specified data objects and generating the communication interfaces between the DT and DT cockpit. They stay compatible if a model changes, as both rely on the same structure description.

The **Application Layer** contains the main functionality of the DT including its ability to detect unintended behavior of the CPPS and deciding on reactions to these. The purpose of the Evaluator is to monitor the system behavior and detect possible malfunctions. It queries information about the system or its context from the data processor and receives DSs in return. If the Evaluator detects unintended behavior, it creates a goal and sends it to the Reasoner. The Reasoner uses knowledge about the CPPS, similar systems, and the system's operating context to decide how to realize this goal. If several possible solutions exist, it determines the best solution, *e.g.,* depending on costs, energy consumption, or time efficiency. The Evaluator's behavior is modeled with a domain-specific event language [5], which describes events based on DSs that encapsulate data from different points in time. The Reasoner's behavior is specified as a statechart, reacts to inputs, changes, its state, and triggers actions.

In the DT cockpit, the `LogicProcessor` handles relevant data and states of the DT. This data is queried and further processed by the `DataAggregator` sending commands to the `LogicProcessor`, which evaluates these. The resulting data can then be send to the frontend to visualize the system's data and states. Commands are used to write data back in the system or to set specific goals for the DT. Currently, only the infrastructure is generated. The behavior of those components needs to be described by handwritten code.

The **Visualization Layer** includes all graphical components of the DT cockpit used to visualize DS and configure the DT and the CPPS. The visualizations of the DT cockpit frontend are generated from MontiGem GUI models. The data accessible at runtime is part of the GUI models and conforms to its representation in the CDs. Thus, the visualization is in sync with data provided by the components of the DT. Different views on the same data objects are available to show different levels of detail. This allows to use the application in different parts of an organization: Visualizations with detailed technical information provide in-depth insight into the current system. Other, more high-level views, display an abstract status, *e.g.,* for management purposes, or data analysis. By generating the frontend based on specifications in the GUI models, we provide role-specific views of the data provided by the production system (meeting *challenge C2*).

The user can supervise the DT and its behavior by interaction through the GUI (meeting *challenge C4*). The GUI displays all information provided by the data processor, *e.g.,* the state of the production system, static information, such as available users or connected devices. Additionally, dynamic information can provide an accurate status of the running system, *e.g.,* a currently running process step of different parts of the system. The user of the digital twin cockpit directly influences the DT behavior via the GUI, *e.g.,* specify the next goal.

We combine information from a variety of models to create the DT cockpit and reuse the CDs describing the DT data structure for generating the cockpit. This has two important advantages: (1) CDs have to be written only once, (2) the communication between data processor and application backend is trivial. This common data basis provides consistency-by-construction and has an immediate impact on the generated code, as the DT cockpit always fits the DT. Moreover, using MDSE methods, the DT cockpit can adapt to changing requirements flexibly.

5   Application to Injection Molding

To show the practical application of our approach, we have realized a DT and DT cockpit for injection molding (*cf.* Sect. 3). We display the DSs of the injection molding process to illustrate the machine state.

Our dashboard (Fig. 3) for the operator role *visualizes the data* in the injection molding process. The operator can see the currently observed machine as well as pressure and temperature data. In the top right is a real-time display of the current status of the process. To interact with the machine, there is a button below which triggers a full machine stop. Other views include raw data from the data lake such as logs for the last process events, structure and architecture models as well as data for each pressure and temperature sensor. For each machine in the production process, the status and statistical information about their produced parts are visualized. In conclusion, the presented DT connects to the CPPS and creates DSs representing the CPPS's state. The DT cockpit integrates with the DT and visualizes the DSs that the DT provides. Since both, the DT and the DT cockpit base on the same domain model, and the concrete implementation is derived from this model, changes within this model are consistently reflected in both systems. If, *e.g.*, a new sensor is added to the CPPS, only one change in the data model is required to realize an adaptation in the DT and to add a new graphical element representing the sensor in the DT cockpit.

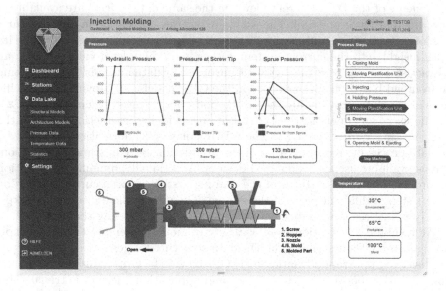

Fig. 3. Screenshot of the dashboard for the injection molding process.

6   Discussion and Related Work

Our method to systematically engineer a DT and its interactive monitoring cockpit leverages CDs for data structure modeling, the MontiArc architecture description language to define the integrated system's software architecture, and MontiGem to model aggregation and presentation of manufacturing data. As they rely on the same language workbench, integrating these approaches is effortless. Besides learning these, operating manufacturing equipment demands for translating their models into executable programming language artifacts. While in the past generators were required for a multitude of languages, this is mitigated by the rise of OPC-UA, ROS-Industrial and other manufacturing middlewares. We have *evaluated* our reference architecture in injection molding and ultra-short pulse laser cutting. While the results indicate that the seamless development of digital twins and their cockpits can reduce wastrel and, hence, optimize the use of resources, we still need to evaluate our reference architecture and the DSLs in a greater variety of contexts.

Related research in DTs often investigates their application in IoT or production use cases [3,16,22]. For instance, [3] describes an architecture with similar layers as our approach and follows a micro-service encapsulation suited for IoT. [22] uses digital twins for monitoring and optimization of hollow glass production lines. [16] sketches an architecture and visualization for digital twins and describes possible views for an oil separation process use case. In [12], a monitoring and assistance system for Human-Machine Interaction is described. Our approach differs from those mentioned in the *use of models to describe the architecture and behavior of the system*. Besides that, we *completely generate* the DT and DT cockpit in contrast to other generative approaches for EIS, which focus either on models to describe the structure and behavior of an application [13] or interface modeling and interface generation [17,20]. Our approach generates a fully runnable EIS [11]. MontiGem uses multiple different input DSLs and supports an easy to use extension mechanism to provide adaptability and allow for agility and continuous regeneration [1,2].

7 Conclusion

We presented an approach to engineer interactive DTs systematically together with their cockpit. Our approach relies on modeling and generating the infrastructure of DT and cockpit based on shared data structures. Models of our DT architecture operate on these data structures. GUI models aggregate, abstract, and represent their contents to the user in connected DT cockpits. This facilitates creating, deploying, and monitoring interactive DTs that can provide real-time information about machine states and the operating context, feature role-specific views with aggregated data and adapt to changes in the underlying models. This fosters their successful application in smart manufacturing to optimize processes and making better use of production equipment.

References

1. Adam, K., Michael, J., Netz, L., Rumpe, B., Varga, S.: Enterprise information systems in academia and practice: lessons learned from a MBSE project. In: 40 Years EMISA (EMISA 2019). LNI, vol. P-304, pp. 59–66. GI e.V. (2020)
2. Adam, K., et al.: Model-based generation of enterprise information systems. In: Enterprise Modeling and Information Systems Architectures (EMISA 2018), vol. 2097, pp. 75–79. CEUR-WS.org (2018)
3. Alam, K.M., El Saddik, A.: C2ps: a digital twin architecture reference model for the cloud-based cyber-physical systems. IEEE Access **5**, 2050–2062 (2017)

4. Bakliwal, K., Dhada, M.H., Palau, A.S., Parlikad, A.K., Lad, B.K.: A multi agent system architecture to implement collaborative learning for social industrial assets. IFAC-PapersOnLine **51**(11), 1237–1242 (2018)

5. Bibow, P., et al.: Model-driven development of a digital twin for injection molding. In: Dustdar, S., Yu, E., Salinesi, C., Rieu, D., Pant, V. (eds.) CAiSE 2020. LNCS, vol. 12127, pp. 85–100. Springer, Cham (2020). https://doi.org/10.1007/978-3-030-49435-3_6

6. Butting, A., Haber, A., Hermerschmidt, L., Kautz, O., Rumpe, B., Wortmann, A.: Systematic language extension mechanisms for the MontiArc architecture description language. In: Anjorin, A., Espinoza, H. (eds.) ECMFA 2017. LNCS, vol. 10376, pp. 53–70. Springer, Cham (2017). https://doi.org/10.1007/978-3-319-61482-3_4

7. Butting, A., Kautz, O., Rumpe, B., Wortmann, A.: Architectural programming with MontiArcAutomaton. In: International Conference on Software Engineering Advances (ICSEA), pp. 213–218. IARIA XPS Press (2017)

8. Dietz, M., Putz, B., Pernul, G.: A distributed ledger approach to digital twin secure data sharing. In: Foley, S.N. (ed.) DBSec 2019. LNCS, vol. 11559, pp. 281–300. Springer, Cham (2019). https://doi.org/10.1007/978-3-030-22479-0_15

9. Duansen, S., Chen, L., Ding, J.: A hierarchical digital twin model framework for dynamic cyber-physical system design, pp. 123–129 (February 2019)

10. France, R., Rumpe, B.: Model-driven development of complex software: a research roadmap. In: Future of Software Engineering (FOSE 2007), pp. 37–54 (2007)

11. Gerasimov, A., Michael, J., Netz, L., Rumpe, B., Varga, S.: Continuous transition from model-driven prototype to full-size real-world enterprise information systems. In: 25th Americas Conference on Information Systems (AMCIS 2020), pp. 1–10. AIS Electronic Library (AISeL), Association for Information Systems (2020)

12. Josifovska, K., Yigitbas, E., Engels, G.: A digital twin-based multi-modal UI adaptation framework for assistance systems in Industry 4.0. In: Kurosu, M. (ed.) HCII 2019. LNCS, vol. 11568, pp. 398–409. Springer, Cham (2019). https://doi.org/10.1007/978-3-030-22636-7_30

13. Peñil, P., Posadas, H., Nicolás, A., Villar, E.: Automatic synthesis from UML/MARTE models using channel semantics. In: International Workshop on Model Based Architecting and Construction of Embedded System, ACES-MB 2012, pp. 49–54. ACM (2012)

14. Rauch, L., Pietrzyk, M.: Digital twins as a modern approach to design of industrial processes. J. Mach. Eng. **19**, 86–97 (2019)

15. Rosato, D.V., Rosato, M.G.: Injection Molding Handbook. Springer, Heidelberg (2012). https://doi.org/10.1007/978-1-4615-4597-2

16. Schroeder, G., et al.: Visualising the digital twin using web services and augmented reality. In: International Conference on Industrial Informatics (INDIN), pp. 522–527. IEEE (2016)

17. Stocq, J., Vanderdonckt, J.: A domain model-driven approach for producing user interfaces to multi-platform information systems. In: Proceedings of the Working Conference on Advanced Visual Interfaces, AVI 2004, pp. 395–398. ACM (2004)

18. Tao, F., Zhang, H., Liu, A., Nee, A.Y.C.: Digital twin in industry: state-of-the-art. IEEE Trans. Ind. Inform. **15**(4), 2405–2415 (2019)

19. Tao, F., Zhang, M.: Digital twin shop-floor: a new shop-floor paradigm towards smart manufacturing. IEEE Access **5**, 20418–20427 (2017)

20. Valverde, F., Valderas, P., Fons, J., Pastor, O.: A MDA-based environment for web applications development: from conceptual models to code (March 2019)

21. Völter, M., Stahl, T., Bettin, J., Haase, A., Helsen, S., Czarnecki, K.: Model-Driven Software Development: Technology, Engineering, Management. Wiley, Hoboken (2013)
22. Zhang, H., Liu, Q., Chen, X., Zhang, D., Leng, J.: A digital twin-based approach for designing and multi-objective optimization of hollow glass production line. IEEE Access **5**, 26901–26911 (2017)
23. Zhang, H., Zhang, G., Yan, Q.: Digital twin-driven cyber-physical production system towards smart shop-floor. J. Ambient Intell. Humaniz. Computi. **10**, 1–15 (2018)

Empowering Virus Sequence Research Through Conceptual Modeling

Anna Bernasconi$^{(\boxtimes)}$ ⓘD, Arif Canakoglu ⓘD, Pietro Pinoli ⓘD, and Stefano Ceri ⓘD

Dipartimento di Elettronica, Informazione e Bioingegneria, Politecnico di Milano,
Via Ponzio 34/5, 20133 Milano, Italy
{anna.bernasconi,arif.canakoglu,pietro.pinoli,stefano.ceri}@polimi.it

Abstract. The pandemic outbreak of the coronavirus disease has attracted attention towards the genetic mechanisms of viruses. We hereby present the Viral Conceptual Model (VCM), centered on the virus sequence and described from four perspectives: biological (virus type and hosts/sample), analytical (annotations, nucleotide and amino acid variants), organizational (sequencing project) and technical (experimental technology).

VCM is inspired by GCM, our previously developed Genomic Conceptual Model, but it introduces many novel concepts, as viral sequences significantly differ from human genomes. When applied to SARS-CoV-2 virus, complex conceptual queries upon VCM are able to replicate the search results of recent articles, hence demonstrating huge potential in supporting virology research.

Our effort is part of a broad vision: availability of conceptual models for both human genomics and viruses will provide important opportunities for research, especially if interconnected by the same human being, playing the role of virus host as well as provider of genomic and phenotype information.

Keywords: Conceptual model · Open data · SARS-CoV-2 · Viral genomics · Biological research

1 Introduction

Despite the advances in drug and vaccine research, diseases caused by viral infection pose serious threats to public health, both as emerging epidemics (e.g., Zika virus, Middle East Respiratory Syndrome Coronavirus, Measles virus, or Ebola virus) and as globally well-established epidemics (such as Human Immunodeficiency Virus, Dengue virus, Hepatitis C virus). The pandemic outbreak of the coronavirus disease COVID-19, caused by the "Severe acute respiratory syndrome coronavirus 2" virus species SARS-CoV-2 (according to the GenBank [42] acronym[1]), has brought unprecedented attention towards the genetic mechanisms of coronaviruses.

---

[1] SARS-CoV-2 is generally identified by the NCBI taxonomy [18] ID 2697049.

G. Dobbie et al. (Eds.): ER 2020, LNCS 12400, pp. 388–402, 2020.
https://doi.org/10.1007/978-3-030-62522-1_29

Thus, understanding viruses from a conceptual modeling perspective is very important. The sequence of the virus is the central information, along with its annotated parts (known genes, coding and untranslated regions...) and the nucleotide/amino acids variants, computed with respect to the reference sequence chosen for the species. Each sequence is characterized by a *strain name*, which belongs to a specific virus species. Viruses have complex taxonomies (as discussed in [27]): a species belongs to a genus, to a sub-family, and finally to a family (e.g., Coronaviridae). Other important aspects include the host organisms and isolation sources from which viral materials are extracted, the sequencing project, the scientific and medical publications related to the discovery of sequences; virus strains may be searched and compared intra- and cross-species. Luckily, all these data are made available publicly by various resources, from which they can be downloaded and re-distributed.

Our recent work is focused on data-driven genomic computing, providing contributions in the area of modeling, integration, search and query answering. We had previously proposed a conceptual model focused on human genomics [8], which was based on a central entity ITEM, representing files of genomic regions. The simple schema evolved into a knowledge graph [5], including ontological representation of many relevant attributes (e.g., diseases, cell lines, tissue types...). The approach was validated through the implementation of the integration pipeline META-BASE [6], which feeds an integrated database, searchable through the GenoSurf interface [10]. On the basis of this experience, we are already developing the ViruSurf interface[2] [11] for inspecting the content of a database for virus sequences, constructed by using VCM as reference conceptual schema. Based on these considerations, in this paper we contribute as follows:

- We propose a new **Viral Conceptual Model (VCM)**, a general conceptual model for describing viral sequences, organized along specific dimensions that highlight a conceptual schema similar to GCM [8];
- We provide a list of **interesting queries** replicating newly released literature on infectious diseases; these can be easily answered by using VCM as reference conceptual schema.

The manuscript is organized as follows: Sect. 2 overviews current technologies available for virus sequence data management. Section 3 proposes our VCM, describing the central entity SEQUENCE and the dimensions that characterize it. We show examples of applications in Sect. 4 and review related works in Sect. 5. Section 6 discloses our vision for future developments.

2   Current Scenario

The landscape of relevant resources and initiatives dedicated to data collection, retrieval and analysis of virus sequences is shown in Fig. 1. We partitioned the space of contributors by considering: institutions that host data sequences, primary sequence deposition databases, tools provided for directly querying and

---

[2] GenoSurf: http://gmql.eu/genosurf/; ViruSurf: http://gmql.eu/virusurf/.

searching them, and then organizations and tools hosting secondary data analysis interfaces that also connect to viral sequence databases. White rectangles represent resources identified using their logo. Relations between them are of three kinds: institutions *host* deposition databases, retrieval tools *query* deposition databases, secondary databases/interfaces *include data from* deposition databases, typically adding other features.

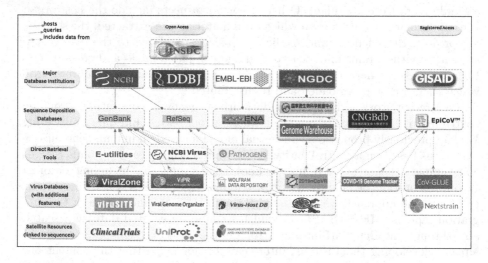

Fig. 1. Current relevant resources and initiatives dedicated to data collection, retrieval and analysis of virus sequences, divided by open and registered access.

The three main organizations providing open-source viral sequences are NCBI (US), DDBJ (Japan), and EMBL-EBI (Europe); they operate within the broader contexts provided by the International Nucleotide Sequence Database Collaboration[3]. NCBI hosts the two, so far, most relevant open viral sequence databases: RefSeq [34] provides a stable reference for genome annotation and gene identification/characterization; GenBank [42] contains an annotated collection of publicly available DNA/RNA sequences. It is continuously updated thanks to the abundant sharing of multiple laboratories and data contributors around the world (note that SARS-CoV-2 nucleotide sequences have increased from about 300 around the end of March 2020, to 13,314 as of August 1st, 2020). EMBL-EBI hosts the European Nucleotide Archive [1], which accepts submissions of nucleotide sequencing information, including raw sequencing data, sequence assembly information and functional annotations.

Several tools are available for querying and searching these databases; E-utilities [41], NCBI Virus [24], and Pathogens[4] are tools and portals directly provided by the INSDC institutions for supporting the access to their viral

---

[3] http://www.insdc.org/.

[4] https://www.ebi.ac.uk/ena/pathogens/.

resources, however lacking the possibility of querying based on annotations and variants. A number of databases and data analysis tools refer to these viral sequences databases: ViralZone [25] by the SIB Swiss Institute of Bioinformatics, which provides access to SARS-CoV-2 proteome data as well as cross-links to complementary resources; the Virus Pathogen Database and Analysis Resource (ViPR, [37]), an integrated repository of data and analysis tools for multiple virus families, supported by the Bioinformatics Resource Centers program; viruSITE [47], an integrated database for viral genomics; the Viral Genome Organizer[5], implemented by the Canadian Viral Bioinformatics Research Centre, focusing on search for sub-sequences within genomes.

Another cluster of resources[6] is connected to the Chinese National Genomics Data Center (at the Beijing Institute of Genomics) and the China National GeneBank; these include the National Microbiology Data Center and the Genome Warehouse, as well as other virus database retrieval tools. Note that not all such resources have a related webpage in English, therefore can be difficult to use.

While the INSDC consortium provides full open access to sequences, the GISAID Initiative [44] was created in 2008 with the explicit purpose of offering an alternative to traditional public-domain data archives, as many scientists hesitated to share influenza data due to their legitimate concern about not being properly acknowledged, among others. GISAID hosts EpiFlu^{TM}, a large sequence database, which started its mission for influenza data and is now expanding with EpiCoV^{TM} having a particular focus on the SARS-CoV-2 pandemic (75,509 sequences for SARS-CoV-2 on August 1st, 2020). Some interesting portals have become interfaces to GISAID data with particular focuses: NextStrain [23] overviews emergent viral outbreaks based on the visualization of sequence data integrated with geographic information, serology, and host species; CoV-GLUE [45], contains a database of replacements, insertions and deletions observed in sequences sampled from the pandemic.

Many other accessory resources link to viral sequence data, including: drug databases, particularly interesting as they provide information about clinical studies (see ClinicalTrials[7]), protein sequences databases (e.g., UniProtKB/Swiss-Prot [39]), and cell lines databases (e.g., Cellosaurus [3]).

3   Conceptual Modeling for Viral Genomics

We previously proposed the Genomic Conceptual Model (GCM, [8]), an Entity-Relationship diagram that recognizes a common organization for a limited set of concepts supported by most genomic data sources, although with different names and formats. The model is centered on the ITEM entity, representing an elementary experimental file of genomic regions and their attributes. Four views depart from the central entity, recalling a classic star-schema organization that

---

[5] https://4virology.net/virology-ca-tools/vgo/.

[6] NGDC: https://bigd.big.ac.cn/; CNGB: https://db.cngb.org/.

[7] http://clinicaltrials.gov/.

is typical of data warehouses [9]; they respectively describe: i) the *biological* elements involved in the experiment: the sequenced sample and its preparation, the donor or patient; ii) the *technology* used in the experiment, including a specific assay (i.e., technique); iii) the *management* aspects: the projects/organizations involved in the preparation and production; iv) the *extraction* parameters used for internal selection and organization of items.

GCM is employed as a driver of integration pipelines for genomic datasets, fueling user search-interfaces (such as GenoSurf [10]). Lessons learnt from that experience include the benefits of having: a central *fact* entity that helps structuring the search; a number of surrounding *dimensions* capturing organization, biological and experimental conditions to describe the facts; a direct representation of a data structure suitable for conceptually organizing genomic elements and their describing information. a data layout that is easy to learn for first-time users and that helps the answering of practical questions (demonstrated in [4]).

We hereby propose the Viral Conceptual Model (VCM), which is influenced by our past experience with human genomes, with the comparable goal of providing a simple means of integration between heterogeneous sources. However, there are significant differences between the two conceptual models. The human DNA sequence is long (3 billions of base pairs) and has been understood in terms of *reference genomes* (named h19 and GRCh38) to which all other information is referred, including genetic and epigenetic signals. Instead, viruses are many, their sequences are short (order of thousands of base pairs) and each virus has its own reference sequence; moreover, virus sequences are associated to a host sample of another species.

With a bird's eye view, the VCM conceptual model is centered on the SEQUENCE entity that describes individual virus sequences; sequences are analyzed from the *biological* perspective (HOSTSAMPLE and VIRUS), the *technological* perspective (EXPERIMENTTYPE), and the *organizational* perspective (SEQUENCINGPROJECT). Three other entities, NUCLEOTIDEVARIANT, ANNOTATION, and AMINOACIDVARIANT represent an *analytical* perspective of the sequence, allowing to analyze its characteristics, its sub-parts, and the differences with respect to reference sequences for the specific virus species. We next illustrate the central entity and the four perspectives.

Central Entity. A viral SEQUENCE can regard DNA or RNA; in either cases, databases of sequencing data write the sequence as a DNA *NucleotideSequence*: possible characters include guanine (G), adenine (A), cytosine (C), and thymine (T)[8], but also eleven "ambiguity" characters associated with all the possible combinations of the four DNA bases [38]. The sequence has a specific *Strand* (positive or negative), *Length* (ranging from hundreds to millions, depending on the virus), and a percentage of read G and C bases (*GC%*). As quality of sequences is very relevant to virologists, we also include the percentage of ambiguous bases (i.e., *N%*) to give a more complete information on reliability of the sequencing process. Each sequence is uniquely identified by an *AccessionID*, which is retrieved directly from the source database (GenBank's are usually formed by

---

[8] In RNA sequencing databases uracil (U) is replaced with thymine (T).

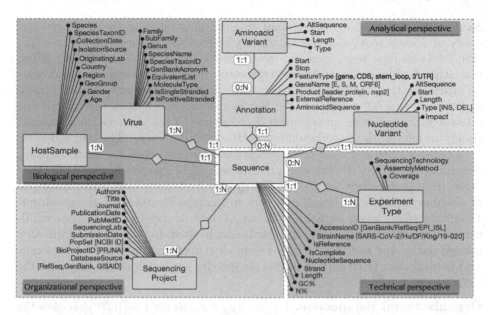

Fig. 2. The Viral Conceptual Model: the central fact SEQUENCE is described by four different perspectives (biological, technical, organizational and analytical).

two capital letters, followed by six digits, GISAID by the string "EPI_ISL_" and six digits). Sequences can be complete or partial (as encoded by the Boolean flag *IsComplete*) and they can be a reference sequence (stored in RefSeq) or a regular one (encoded by *IsReference*). Sequences have a corresponding *StrainName* (or isolate) assigned by the sequencing laboratory, somehow hard-coding relevant information (e.g., hCoV-19/Nepal/61/2020 or 2019-nCoV_PH_nCOV_20_026).

Technological Perspective. The sequence derives from one experiment or assay, described in the EXPERIMENTTYPE entity (cardinality is 1:N from the dimension towards the fact). It is performed on biological material analyzed with a given *SequencingTechnology* platform (e.g., Illumina Miseq) and an *AssemblyMethod*, collecting algorithms that have been applied to obtain the final sequence, for example: BWA-MEM, to align sequence reads against a large reference genome; BCFtools, to manipulate variant calls; Megahit, to assemble NGS reads. Another technical measure is captured by *Coverage* (e.g., 100× or 77000×).

Biological Perspective. Each sequence belongs to a specific VIRUS, which is described by a complex taxonomy. The most precise definition is the *Species-Name* (e.g., Severe acute respiratory syndrome coronavirus 2), corresponding to a *SpeciesTaxonID* (e.g., 2697049, according to the NCBI Taxonomy [18]), related to a simpler *GenBankAcronym* (e.g., SARS-CoV-2) and to many comparable forms, contained in the *EquivalentList* (e.g., 2019-nCoV, COVID-19, SARS-CoV2, SARS2, Wuhan coronavirus, Wuhan seafood market pneumonia virus, ...). The species belongs to a *Genus* (e.g., Betacoronavirus), part of a

SubFamily (e.g., Orthocoronavirinae), finally falling under the most general category of *Family* (e.g., Coronaviridae). Each virus species corresponds to a specific *MoleculeType* (e.g., genomic RNA, viral cRNA, unassigned DNA), which has either double- or single-stranded structure; in the second case the strand may be either positive or negative. These possibilities are encoded within the *IsSingleStranded* and *IsPositiveStranded* Boolean variables. An assay is performed on a tissue extracted from an organism that has hosted the virus for an amount of time; this information is collected in the HOSTSAMPLE entity. The host is defined by a *Species*, corresponding to a *SpeciesTaxonID* (e.g., 9606 for Homo Sapiens, according to the NCBI Taxonomy). The sample is extracted on a *CollectionDate*, from an *IsolationSource* that is a specific host tissue (e.g., nasopharyngeal or oropharyngeal swab, lung), in a certain location identified by the quadruple *OriginatingLab* (when available), *Region*, *Country*, and *GeoGroup* (i.e., continent) – for such attributes ISO standards may be used. In some cases information related to the *Age* and *Gender* of the individual donating the HOSTSAMPLE may also be available. Both entities of this perspective are in 1:N cardinality with the SEQUENCE.

Organizational Perspective. The entity SEQUENCINGPROJECT describes the management aspects of the production of the sequence. Each sequence is connected to a number of studies, usually represented by a research publication (with *Authors*, *Title*, *Journal*, *PublicationDate* and eventually a *PubMedID* referring to the most important biomedical literature portal[9]). When a study is not available, just the *SequencingLab* and *SubmissionDate* are provided. In rare occasions, a project is associated with a *PopSet* number, which identifies a collection of related sequences derived from population studies (submitted to GenBank), or with a *BioProjectID* (an identifier to the BioProject external database[10]). We also include the name of *DatabaseSource*, denoting the organization that primarily stores the sequence. In this perspective all cardinalities are 1:N as sequences can be part of multiple projects; conversely, sequencing projects contain various sequences.

Analytical Perspective. This perspective allows to store information that is useful during the secondary analysis of genomic sequences. The NUCLEOTIDE-VARIANT entity contains sub-parts of the main SEQUENCE that differ from the reference sequence of the same virus species. They can be identified just by using the *AltSequence* (i.e., the nucleotides used in the analyzed sequence at position *Start* for an arbitrary *Length*, typically just equal to 1) and a specific *Type*, which can correspond to insertion (INS), deletion (DEL), substitution (SUB) or others. The content of the attributes of this entity is not retrieved from existing databases; instead it is computed in-house by our procedures. Indeed, we use the well-known dynamic programming algorithm of Needleman-Wunsch [32], that computes the optimal alignment between two sequences. From a technical point of view, we compute the pair-wise alignment of every sequence to the reference

---

[9] https://www.ncbi.nlm.nih.gov/pubmed/.
[10] https://www.ncbi.nlm.nih.gov/bioproject/.

sequence of RefSeq (e.g., NC_045512 for SARS-CoV-2); from such alignment we then extract all insertions, deletions, and substitutions that transform (i.e., edit) the reference sequence into the considered sequence. Finally, we include the *Impact* information, an annotation of the variant computed using SnpEff tool [12], which calculates the effect that the variant produces on known genes; a variant may, for example, be irrelevant, silent, produce small changes in the transcript or be deleterious for the transcript.

ANNOTATIONs include a number of sub-sequences, each representing a segment (defined by *Start* and *Stop* coordinates) of the original sequence, with a particular *FeatureType* (e.g., gene, peptide, coding DNA region, or untranslated region, molecule patterns such as stem loops and so on), the recognized *Gene-Name* to which it belongs (e.g., gene "E", gene "S" or open reading frame genes such as "ORF1ab"), the *Product* it concurs to produce (e.g., leader protein, nsp2 protein, RNA-dependent RNA polymerase, membrane glycoprotein, envelope protein...), and eventually arelated *ExternalReference* when the protein is present in a separate database such as UniProtKB. Additionally, for each ANNOTATION we also store the corresponding *AminoacidSequence*(encoded according to the notation of the International Union of Pure and Applied Chemistry[11]). Example codes are A (Alanine), D (Aspartic Acid), F (Phenylalanine).

The AMINOACIDVARIANT entity contains sub-parts of the *AminoacidSequence* stored in the specific ANNOTATION, which differ from the reference amino acids of the same virus species. These variants are calculated similarly to the NUCLEOTIDEVARIANTs (a comparable approach is used within CoV-GLUE. Also here we include the *AltSequence*, the *Start* position, the *Length*, and a specific *Type* (SUB, INS, DEL...).

4   Answering Complex Biological Queries

In addition to very general questions that can be easily asked through our conceptual model (e.g., retrieve all viruses with given characteristics), in the following we propose a list of interesting application studies that could be backed by the use of our conceptual model. In particular, they refer to the SARS-CoV-2 virus, as it is receiving most of the attention of the scientific community. Figure 3 represents the reference sequence of SARS-CoV-2[12], highlighting the major structural sub-sequences that are relevant for the encoding of proteins and other functions. It has 56 region ANNOTATIONS, of which Fig. 3 represents only the 11 genes (ORF1ab, S, ORF3a, E, M, ORF6, ORF7a, ORF7b, ORF8, N, ORF10) plus the RNA-dependent RNA polymerase enzyme, with approximate indication of the corresponding coordinates. We next describe biological queries supported by VCM, from the easy to complex ones, typically suggested by existing studies.

---

[11] https://en.wikipedia.org/wiki/Nucleic_acid_notation#IUPAC_notation.

[12] It represents the positive-sense, single-stranded RNA virus (from 0 to the 29903th base) of NC_045512 RefSeq staff-curated complete sequence (*StrainName* "Wuhan-Hu-1"), collected in China from a "Homo Sapiens" HOSTSAMPLE in December 2019.

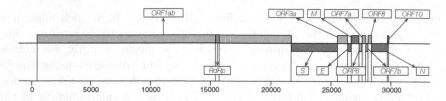

Fig. 3. Location of major structural protein-encoding genes (as red boxes: S = Spike glycoprotein, E = Envelope protein, M = Membrane glycoprotein, N = Nucleocapsid phospoprotein), accessory protein ORFs = Open Reading Frames (as blue boxes), and RNA-dependent RNA polymerase (RdRp) on the sequence of the SARS-CoV-2. (Color figure online)

Q1. The most common variants found in SARS-CoV-2 sequences can be selected for US patients; the query can be performed on entire sequences or only on specific genes.

Q2. COVID-19 European patients affected by a SARS-CoV-2 virus can be selected when they have a specific one-base variant on the first gene (ORF1ab), indicated by using the triple <start, reference_allele, alternative_allele>. Patients can be distributed according to their country of origin. This conceptual query is illustrated in Fig. 4, where selected attribute values are specified in red, in place of attribute names in the ER model; values in NUCLEOTIDEVARIANT show one possible example. *Country* is in blue as samples will be distributed according to such field.

Q3. According to [14], E and RdRp genes are highly mutated and thus crucial in diagnosing COVID-19 disease; first-line screening tools of 2019-nCoV should perform an E gene assay, followed by confirmatory testing with the RdRp gene assay. Conceptual queries are concerned with retrieving all sequences with mutations within genes E or RdRp and relating them to given hosts, e.g. humans affected in China.

Q4. Tang *et al.* [49] claim that there are two clearly definable "major types" (S and L) of SARS-CoV-2 in this outbreak, that can be differentiated by transmission rates. Intriguingly, the S and L types can be clearly distinguished by just two tightly linked SNPs (Single Nucleotide Polymorphisms, i.e., a specific kind of variant) at positions 8,782 (within the ORF1ab gene from C to T) and 28,144 (within ORF8 from T to C). Then, queries can correlate these SNPs to other variants or the outbreak of COVID-19 in specific countries (e.g., [21]).

Q5. To inform SARS-CoV-2 vaccine design efforts, it may be needed to track antigenic diversity. Typically, pathogen genetic diversity is categorized into distinct *clades* (i.e., a monophyletic group on a phylogenetic tree). These clades may refer to 'subtypes', 'genotypes', or 'groups', depending on the taxonomic level under investigation. In [21], specific sequence variants are used to define clades/haplogroups (e.g., the *A group* is characterized by the 20,229 and 13,064 nucleotides, originally C mutated to T, by the 18,483 nucleotide T mutated to C,

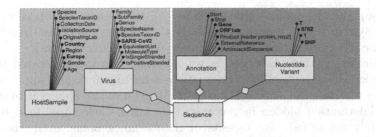

Fig. 4. Visual representation of query **Q2**.

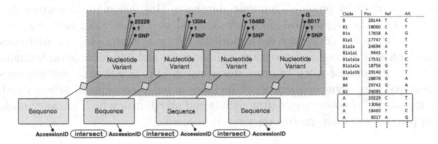

Clade	Pos	Ref	Alt
B	28144	T	C
B1	18060	C	T
B1a	17858	A	G
B1a1	17747	C	T
B1a1a	24694	A	T
B1a1a1	9445	T	C
B1a1a1a	17531	T	C
B1a1a1a	18756	G	T
B1a1a1b	29140	G	T
B4	28878	G	A
B4	29742	G	A
B2	29095	C	T
A	20229	C	T
A	13064	C	T
A	18483	T	C
A	8017	A	G
⋮	⋮	⋮	⋮

Fig. 5. Illustration of the selection predicate for the *A clade* [21], used in query **Q5**.

and by the 8,017, from A to G). VCM supports all the information required to replicate the definition of SARS-CoV-2 clades requested in the study. Figure 5 illustrates the conjunctive selection of sequences with all four variants corresponding to the *A clade group* defined in [21].

Q6. Morais Junior et al. [26] propose a subdivision of the global SARS-CoV-2 population into sixteen subtypes, defined using "widely shared polymorphisms" identified in nonstructural (nsp3, nsp4, nsp6, 27 nsp12, nsp13 and nsp14) cistrons, structural (spike and nucleocapsid), and accessory (ORF8) genes. VCM supports all the information required to replicate the definition of all such subtypes.

5   Related Work

The genomics community has always made great use of specialized ontologies (see the collective OBO Foundry [46], including the Gene Ontology [13]). In addition, the use of conceptual modeling to describe genomics databases dates back to the late nineties, including a functional model for DNA databases named "associative information structure" [33], a model representing genomic sequences [31], and a set of data models for describing transcription/translation processes [36]. Later, a stream of works developed conceptual modeling-based data warehouses, including: the GEDAW UML Conceptual schema [22] (for a gene-centric data warehouse), the Genomics Unified Schema [2], the Genome Information Management System [15] (a genome-centric data warehouse), and the GeneMapper Warehouse [17] (integrating expression data from genomic sources).

More recently, there has been a solid stream of works dedicated to data quality-oriented conceptual modeling: [19] presents an ontological approach, [40] introduces the Human Genome Conceptual Model and [35] applies it to uncover relevant information hidden in genomics data lakes. Conceptual modeling has been mainly concerned with aspects of the *human* genome, even when more general approaches were adopted; in [8] we presented GCM, describing metadata associated with genomic experimental datasets available for model organisms.

In the variety of types of genomic databases [16], aside the resources dedicated to humans [7], several ones are devoted to viruses [43]; however, very few works relate to conceptual data modeling. Among them, [48] considers host information and normalized geographical location, and [29] focuses on influenza A viruses. The closest work to ours, described in [45], is a flexible software system for querying virus sequences; it includes a basic conceptual schema[13]. In comparison, VCM covers more dimensions and attributes, which are very useful for supporting research queries on virus sequences.

6   Discussion and Future Developments

This paper responds to an urgent need: understanding the conceptual properties of SARS-CoV-2 so as to facilitate research studies. The model applies to any type of virus and can be used as a basis for the development of search systems. In the past, we first presented the conceptual model for human genomics [8], then we developed the Web-based search system GenoSurf [10]. Inspired by our previous experience, we practically employed the VCM by directly translating it into a logical schema and then into a solid relational database implementation that supports the ViruSurf [11] search interface (http://gmql.eu/virusurf) in the back end. We started by focusing on the sequences of SARS-CoV-2; we include them from five sources, i.e., GenBank, RefSeq, COG-UK, GISAID, and NMDC. After SARS-CoV-2, we are progressively adding sequences of other virus species that could provide relevant comparative information for dealing with the COVID-19 pandemic, e.g., for vaccine and drug development.

While the need for data is pressing, there is also a need of conceptually well-organized information. In our broad vision, the availability of conceptual models for both human genomics and viruses will provide important opportunities for research, amplified to the maximum when human and viral sequences will be interconnected by the same human being, playing the role of host of a given virus sequence as well as provider of genomic and phenotype information.

In this direction, we are participating to the COVID-19 Host Genetics Initiative[14], aiming at *bringing together the human genetics community to generate,*

---

[13] http://glue-tools.cvr.gla.ac.uk/images/projectModel.png.
[14] https://www.covid19hg.org/.

share and analyze data to learn the genetic determinants of COVID-19 sus-ceptibility, severity and outcomes. We are coordinating the production of a data dictionary for the phenotype definition, which is now being used as a reference by participating institutions, hosted by EGA [20], the European Genome-phenome Archive of EMBL-EBI[15]. When both phenotype and viral sequences datasets will be accessible, other more powerful studies will be possible. Some early findings have been already published connecting virus sequences with phenotypes, so far with very small datasets (e.g., [28] with only 5 patients, [30] with 9 patients, and [49] with 103 sequenced SARS-CoV-2 genomes). As reaffirmed by these works, there is need for additional comprehensive studies linking the viral sequences of SARS-CoV-2 to the phenotype of patients affected by COVID-19; such studies will be produced in the near future as result of ongoing clinical protocols.

In the future we will continue our modeling and integration efforts for virus genetics in the context of humans, by interacting with the community of scholars who study viruses. We may add more discovery-oriented entities to the model, that could be of use in a future scenario, e.g., a new pandemic offspring. We will expand our schema in several directions: 1) we will add both validated and predicted epitopes (i.e., antigen parts to which antibodies attach) with their sequence, lineage, host, evidence, reference or algorithm, type of response; 2) we will link entities to specific external/ontological knowledge, which is being dis-covered nowadays, e.g., each variant to COVID-19 morbidities and each epitope to the specific strain and geographic population it refers to; 3) we will also link sequences to complete tree-structured taxonomies of viruses and host organisms.

In this way, we will be able to cover a wider spectrum of domain specific queries. A user researching on diagnosis could ask, for example, what sequence patterns are unique to the whole or sub-part of the database (i.e., do not appear in viruses within the database). Whereas, a user working on vaccine development could be interested in what are the epitopes that cover the whole database or a partition of it, for MHC types prevalent in different infected humans. Possibly, other dimensions will be necessary, such as drug resistance information and drug resistance-associated mutations.

Acknowledgements. This research is funded by the ERC Advanced Grant 693174 GeCo (Data-Driven Genomic Computing), 2016–2021. The authors would like to thank Ilaria Capua, Luca Ferretti, Alice Fusaro, Susanna Lamers, Francesca Mari, Carla Mavian, Alessandra Renieri, Stephen Tsui, and Limsoon Wong for their precious con-tributions during the phase of requirements elicitation and for their inspiration towards future developments of this research.

References

1. Amid, C., et al.: The European nucleotide archive in 2019. Nucleic Acids Res. **48**(D1), D70–D76 (2020)

---

[15] We coordinated about 50 active participants and released the "Freeze 1" version of the data dictionary on April 16, 2020 (http://gmql.eu/phenotype/).

2. Babenko, V., et al.: GUS the genomics unified schema a platform for genomics databases. http://www.gusdb.org/. Accessed 1 Aug 2020
3. Bairoch, A.: The cellosaurus, a cell-line knowledge resource. J. Biomol. Tech. JBT **29**(2), 25 (2018)
4. Bernasconi, A., et al.: Exploiting conceptual modeling for searching genomic metadata: a quantitative and qualitative empirical study. In: Guizzardi, G., et al. (eds.) Advances in Conceptual Modeling, pp. 83–94. Springer, Cham (2019). https://doi.org/10.1007/978-3-030-34146-6_8
5. Bernasconi, A., et al.: From a conceptual model to a knowledge graph for genomic datasets. In: Laender, A.H.F., et al. (eds.) Conceptual Modeling, pp. 352–360. Springer, Cham (2019). https://doi.org/10.1007/978-3-030-33223-5_29
6. Bernasconi, A., et al.: META-BASE: a novel architecture for large-scale genomic metadata integration. IEEE/ACM Trans. Comput. Biol. Bioinform. (2020)
7. Bernasconi, A., et al.: The road towards data integration in human genomics: players, steps and interactions. Briefings Bioinform. **4**, 80 (2020)
8. Bernasconi, A., et al.: Conceptual modeling for genomics: building an integrated repository of open data. In: Mayr, H.C., et al. (eds.) Conceptual Modeling, pp. 325–339. Springer, Cham (2017). https://doi.org/10.1007/978-3-319-69904-2_26
9. Bonifati, A., et al.: Designing data marts for data warehouses. ACM Transactions on Software Engineering and Methodology **10**(4), 452–483 (2001)
10. Canakoglu, A., et al.: GenoSurf: metadata driven semantic search system for integrated genomic datasets. Database **2019**, 132 (2019)
11. Canakoglu, A., et al.: ViruSurf: an integrated database to investigate viral sequences. Nucleic Acids Research, gkaa846 (2020). https://doi.org/10.1093/nar/gkaa846
12. Cingolani, P., et al.: A program for annotating and predicting the effects of single nucleotide polymorphisms, SnpEff: SNPs in the genome of Drosophila melanogaster strain w1118; iso-2; iso-3. Fly **6**(2), 80–92 (2012)
13. Consortium, G.O.: The gene ontology resource: 20 years and still going strong. Nucleic Acids Res. **47**(D1), D330–D338 (2019)
14. Corman, V.M., et al.: Detection of 2019 novel coronavirus (2019-nCoV) by real-time RT-PCR. Eurosurveillance **25**(3), 200045 (2020)
15. Cornell, M., et al.: GIMS: an integrated data storage and analysis environment for genomic and functional data. Yeast **20**(15), 1291–1306 (2003)
16. De Francesco, E., et al.: A summary of genomic databases: overview and discussion. In: Biomedical Data and Applications, pp. 37–54. Springer, Heidelberg (2009). https://doi.org/10.1007/978-3-642-02193-0_3
17. Do, H.H., et al.: Flexible integration of molecular-biological annotation data: the genmapper approach. In: Bertino, E., Christodoulakis, S., Plexousakis, D., Christophides, V., Koubarakis, M., Böhm, K., Ferrari, E. (eds.) EDBT 2004. LNCS, vol. 2992, pp. 811–822. Springer, Heidelberg (2004). https://doi.org/10.1007/978-3-540-24741-8_47
18. Federhen, S.: The NCBI taxonomy database. Nucleic Acids Res. **40**(D1), D136–D143 (2012)
19. Ferrandis, A.M.M., et al.: Applying the principles of an ontology-based approach to a conceptual schema of human genome. In: Ng, W., Storey, V.C., Trujillo, J.C. (eds.) ER 2013. LNCS, vol. 8217, pp. 471–478. Springer, Heidelberg (2013). https://doi.org/10.1007/978-3-642-41924-9_40
20. Flicek, P., et al.: The European Genotype Archive: Background and implementation [white paper] (2007). https://www.ebi.ac.uk/ega/sites/ebi.ac.uk.ega/files/documents/ega_whitepaper.pdf

21. Gudbjartsson, D.F., et al.: Spread of SARS-CoV-2 in the Icelandic population. New Engl. J. Med. **382**, 2302–2315 (2020)
22. Guérin, E., et al.: Integrating and warehousing liver gene expression data and related biomedical resources in GEDAW. In: Ludäscher, B., Raschid, L. (eds.) DILS 2005. LNCS, vol. 3615, pp. 158–174. Springer, Heidelberg (2005). https://doi.org/10.1007/11530084_14
23. Hadfield, J., et al.: Nextstrain: real-time tracking of pathogen evolution. Bioinformatics **34**(23), 4121–4123 (2018)
24. Hatcher, E.L., et al.: Virus variation resource-improved response to emergent viral outbreaks. Nucleic Acids Res. **45**(D1), D482–D490 (2017)
25. Hulo, C., et al.: ViralZone: a knowledge resource to understand virus diversity. Nucleic Acids Res. **39**, D576–D582 (2011)
26. Junior, I.J.M., et al.: The global population of SARS-CoV-2 is composed of six major subtypes. bioRxiv (2020)
27. Koonin, E.V., et al.: Global organization and proposed megataxonomy of the virus world. Microbiol. Mol. Biol. Rev. **84**(2), 156 (2020)
28. Lescure, F.X., et al.: Clinical and virological data of the first cases of COVID-19 in Europe: a case series. The Lancet Infect. Dis. **20**, 6 (2020)
29. Lu, G., et al.: Influenza A virus informatics: genotype-centered database and genotype annotation. In: Second International Multi-Symposiums on Computer and Computational Sciences (IMSCCS 2007), pp. 76–83. IEEE (2007)
30. Lu, R., et al.: Genomic characterisation and epidemiology of 2019 novel coronavirus: implications for virus origins and receptor binding. The Lancet **395**(10224), 565–574 (2020)
31. Médigue, C., et al.: Imagene: an integrated computer environment for sequence annotation and analysis. Bioinformatics (Oxford, England) **15**(1), 2–15 (1999)
32. Needleman, S.B., et al.: A general method applicable to the search for similarities in the amino acid sequence of two proteins. J. Mol. Biol. **48**(3), 443–453 (1970)
33. Okayama, T., et al.: Formal design and implementation of an improved DDBJ DNA database with a new schema and object-oriented library. Bioinformatics (Oxford, England) **14**(6), 472–478 (1998)
34. O'Leary, N.A., et al.: Reference sequence (RefSeq) database at NCBI: current status, taxonomic expansion, and functional annotation. Nucleic Acids Res. **44**(D1), D733–D745 (2015)
35. Palacio, A.L., et al.: A method to identify relevant genome data: conceptual modeling for the medicine of precision. In: Trujillo, J.C., et al. (eds.) ER 2018. LNCS, vol. 11157, pp. 597–609. Springer, Cham (2018). https://doi.org/10.1007/978-3-030-00847-5_44
36. Paton, N.W., et al.: Conceptual modelling of genomic information. Bioinformatics **16**(6), 548–557 (2000)
37. Pickett, B.E., et al.: ViPR: an open bioinformatics database and analysis resource for virology research. Nucleic Acids Res. **40**(D1), D593–D598 (2012)
38. Nomenclature Committee of the International Union of Biochemistry (NC-IUB): Nomenclature for incompletely specified bases in nucleic acid sequences: Recommendations 1984. Proceedings of the National Academy of Sciences of the United States of America **83**(1), 4–8 (1986)
39. UniProt Consortium: UniProt: a worldwide hub of protein knowledge. Nucleic Acids Res. **47**(D1), D506–D515 (2019)

40. Reyes Román, J.F., Pastor, Ó., Casamayor, J.C., Valverde, F.: Applying conceptual modeling to better understand the human genome. In: Comyn-Wattiau, I., Tanaka, K., Song, I.-Y., Yamamoto, S., Saeki, M. (eds.) ER 2016. LNCS, vol. 9974, pp. 404–412. Springer, Cham (2016). https://doi.org/10.1007/978-3-319-46397-1_31

41. Sayers, E.: The E-utilities in-depth: parameters, syntax and more. Entrez Programming Utilities Help [Internet] (2009). https://www.ncbi.nlm.nih.gov/books/NBK25499/

42. Sayers, E.W., et al.: GenBank. Nucleic Acids Res. **47**(D1), D94–D99 (2019)

43. Sharma, D., et al.: Unraveling the web of viroinformatics: computational tools and databases in virus research. J. Virol. **89**(3), 1489–1501 (2015)

44. Shu, Y., et al.: GISAID: Global initiative on sharing all influenza data-from vision to reality. Eurosurveill. **22**(13), 30494 (2017)

45. Singer, J., et al.: CoV-Glue: a web application for tracking SARS-CoV-2 genomic variation (2020). Preprints 2020, 2020060225

46. Smith, B., et al.: The obo foundry: coordinated evolution of ontologies to support biomedical data integration. Nat. Biotechnol. **25**(11), 1251–1255 (2007)

47. Stano, M., et al.: viruSITE-integrated database for viral genomics. Database **2016**, e00152 (2016)

48. Tahsin, T., et al.: Named entity linking of geospatial and host metadata in genbank for advancing biomedical research. Database **2017**, 93 (2017)

49. Tang, X., et al.: On the origin and continuing evolution of SARS-CoV-2. Nat. Sci. Rev. (2020)

Modeling Interactive Smart Spaces

Mattia Gianotti⬥, Fabiano Riccardi⬥, Giulia Cosentino(✉)⬥,
Franca Garzotto⬥, and Maristella Matera⬥

Department of Electronics, Information and Bioengineering, Politecnico di Milano,
Milano, Italy
{mattia.gianotti,fabiano.riccardi,giulia.cosentino,
franca.garzotto,maristella.matera}@polimi.it

Abstract. The Internet of Things (IoT) enables the creation of *Interactive Smart Spaces* (ISSs) where different types of digital devices are integrated in the ambient or embedded in physical objects, and can sense human actions to control equipment, modify environmental parameters, or create multi-sensory effects. These IoT-enhanced interactive systems can support human activities in different contexts, e.g., education, entertainment, home assistance, rehabilitation, to name a few. This paper explores a *human-centered* perspective in the design of ISSs, which takes into account some salient characteristics of these systems and introduces new conceptual modeling issues going beyond representing hardware, software, and connectivity features of IoT devices. *Interaction* in particular emerges as a crucial modeling dimension, needed to capture the interplay occurring not only among multiple connected IoT devices but also among the users and the materials or the spaces embedding such devices. The paper presents a novel conceptual model for Interactive Smart Spaces and exemplifies the identified abstractions through a case study, modelling a complex ISS for children' play and learning that has been installed at two local schools and two therapeutic centers in our country.

Keywords: Interactive Smart Spaces · Interactive IoT · Smart objects · Interaction modeling

1 Introduction

In early '90s, Mark Weiser envisioned that pervasive devices and services would have become parts of our daily life [27]. Internet of Things (IoT) technologies have largely accelerated this trend. Initial IoT solutions focused on the creation of arrays of distributed connected sensors (Wireless Sensor Networks) to support automation systems relieving users from repetitive tasks (e.g., plants monitor or automatic controls). In this class of IoT systems, the interaction between

Supported by the Italian Ministry of University and Research (MIUR) under grant PRIN 2017 "EMPATHY".

the system and the user was of secondary priority. Nevertheless, thanks to the ever-increasing opportunity to integrate IoT into everyday objects and physical spaces, many environments we live in are augmented today through an interleaving between the cyber and the physical worlds [6]. Novel interactive systems are emerging that empower people in different activities and contexts of everyday life [9,10,14,24]. A more human-centered perspective has progressively emerged, in which the interactive capability of IoT-enhanced physical objects and spaces (hereinafter *smart objects* and *smart spaces*) becomes more and more central, raising new requirements and challenges for conceptual modelling. In this scenario, the scope of conceptual modeling would go beyond representing features related to hardware, software, connectivity, and communication among multiple devices, and should also address the *interactions* between the users and the materials or spaces embedding such devices. New conceptual modeling primitives are therefore needed to: i) represent the IoT-enabled interaction capabilities of smart objects and smart spaces, and their interactive behaviour, abstracting from the underlying technology; ii) describe how these features are orchestrated in order to offer an optimal *smart interactive experience* to the user [1]. Such primitives would help designers focus on the salient human-centered aspects of IoT-enhanced systems, paving the ground towards the definition of new methods and tools for interaction design in the IoT arena, as well as new technological architectures for this class of systems.

This paper presents an attempt to address this modelling challenge. After an overview of the relevant state of the art reported in Sect. 2, in Sect. 3 we discuss the relevant features that characterize Interactive Smart Spaces (ISSs) and classify them in order to contextualize our ISS model. Following the "separation of concerns" principle, we distinguish between two main design dimensions for ISSs, which results into two sub-models - *Structural Model* and *Interactive Behavior Model*, presented in Sect. 4. To exemplify our primitives and highlight their expressive power, Sect. 5 describes (fragments of) the conceptual model of a sophisticated multi-sensory ISS called "Magic Room". In Sect. 6 we depict the future directions of our research, and highlight the potential of an interaction-centered modeling approach for End-User Development research in the arena of interactive IoT systems.

2   Related Work

In the last decades researchers had proposed different modelling approaches for IoT systems related to Smart Spaces. Four major topics emerge: privacy and security of data transmission [2,25,26], orchestration of device behaviour [4,12,21,23], data gathering and propagation [8,19], and design of single devices and smart objects [5,12]. The role of the user is neglected or simply considered as a pure source of data, and existing approaches take into account only marginally (or not at all) the need of modeling human interaction in Interactive Smart Spaces. Haller et al. [18] present a distribution map for the computation and the interaction between what they call "augmented entities" and users through devices, resources and services without a distinction between human and non-human actors. Zeng et al. [28] describe the behaviour of a IoT-enhanced system through a two-levels Petri net. The top-level net describes the social flow between the different humans, and the physical flow between humans and objects; the lower level describes the flow of data between the digital twins of humans and the objects. Still, the model does not cover the interactive capabilities of smart physical objects. Gračanin et al. [17] present a two-tier architecture framework to encompass the interaction between the users and the system, but its expressiveness is limited to interactions that are directed by the user to the system through a client-based approach. In order to simulate and verify planned agents' distributed tasks, Zhao et al. [29] propose a methodology based on BIM-Sim 3D to simulate the human activities, their analysis and the configuration of the space. This method, however, may fail to capture the intrinsic unpredictability of users and describe the complex variability of activities. Markopoulos et al. [22] discuss how the Unified Modeling Language (UML) can be used as a reference representation language for interaction design; still, the authors do not provide any insight on how the UML primitives discussed can be applied to IoT-enhanced interactive systems.

3   Characterizing Interactive Smart Spaces

An *Interactive Smart Space* (ISS) is an ecosystem of smart resources, based on a variety of IoT devices [3], from basic sensors and actuators to digitally enhanced physical objects (*smart objects* [20]) and software services, featuring mutual cross-interactions and interactions with humans to support the accomplishment of user goals at multiple levels of complexity. ISSs call for a human-centered vision of IoT, where the involvement of human actors is central: it is the interactive dimension that distinguishes - at the highest degree - ISSs from other categories of "smart spaces" where the IoT technology is embedded in the physical environment and its physical components. Beside the high level of interactivity, another feature that characterizes many ISSs is the richness of digital media content and multisensory stimuli the user can experience in these environments. In a user-centered perspective, we can therefore characterize ISSs along two main dimensions:

- *Interaction Intensity*: interaction-intensive ISSs enable (and motivate) users to interact frequently and actively with the physical space and its components, using multiple modes of interacting with them, from touch and manipulation to gestures, movements, or voice, leading to a continuous exchange of actions and stimuli between the system and the user.
- *Content Intensity*: content-intensive ISSs provide a vast amount of digital media contents that are generated automatically, or by effect of interaction, offering engaging experiences enriched by multiple stimuli and, when contents are integrated in the fabric of the physical space, a feeling of immersiveness.

Different degrees of interaction intensity and content intensity lead to a wide spectrum of ISS types, ranging from Automated Interactive Smart Spaces (having low interaction intensity and low content intensity) to Multi-sensory Smart Spaces (having high interaction intensity and high content intensity).

An *Automated Interactive Smart Space* is a digitally-enriched physical space where the orchestration of IoT devices and the integrated software services are largely finalized to automating some tasks or ambient functionality. In many cases these ISSs focus on monitoring some variables characterizing the environment (e.g., temperature, luminosity, user presence or proximity) to enact actions that change the state of the physical environment by means of some physical devices installed in it (e.g., "switching on" the heating or the lights or "opening" the window blinds). In this class of systems, the interaction by human agents exists but it is often "implicit" or limited. For example, the user "implicitly" interacts with the room by entering it (which triggers the activation of the lighting). Explicit user actions are restricted to simple instructional tasks, such as controlling some devices or home appliances using a touch interface, manipulating a physical affordance, or issuing vocal commands to a conversational agents such as Alexa.

Multi-sensory smart spaces are characterized by providing multiple modes for the user to interact with devices, digital contents embedded in the physical spaces, and smart objects [11], and by the capability to generate a wide amount of digital media contents and sensory effects that stimulate all senses. Multi-sensory smart spaces offer opportunities for a countless variety of interaction-intensive and content-intensive user experiences that make this type of ISSs appropriate for many domains such as education, training, tourism, entertainment, or rehabilitation. The conceptual model discussed in this paper provides primitives to describe ISSs in the whole range of possible types.

4   Modeling Interactive Smart Spaces

The main abstractions of our conceptual approach are depicted in the meta-model shown in Fig. 1. Abstractions are organized in two main sub-models: the *Structural Model* and the *Interactive Behaviour Model*. The *Structural Model* supports the representation of the human and technological "actors", their interaction capability, i.e., which actions they can perform and perceive ("sense") and which perceivable effects they can generate ("actuate"), as well as the digital contents that are involved in the user experience. The *Interactive Behavior Model* supports the representation of the interactive behaviour of all actors and how cross-interactions are orchestrated for the users to perform tasks and activities at different levels of complexity.

4.1   Structural Model

The Structural Model is built around the notion of *Actors* (both *Human* and *Technological*), that are the building blocks of any ISS as their properties and

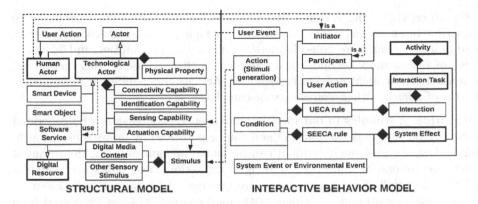

Fig. 1. Metamodel. Larger borders denote key elements.

their cross-interactions enact the ISS interactive experience. *Stimuli* and *Digital Resources* then support the execution of the interactive experience.

Human Actor. Human Actors (i.e., the users), are described by their interaction capability, i.e., the *User Actions* (*Actions* for short) they are expected to perform while interacting with Technological Actors. Considering the user as an actor perceiving stimuli and acting on the surrounding space distinguishes an ISS from other cyber-physical systems that mainly consists of networks of physical and computational components.

Technological Actor. Technological Actors are characterized by a mix of digital and physical features. They make use of IoT equipment that enables one or more of the following capabilities: *sensing* (detecting signals generated by other Actors), *actuation* (generating data, content, or human-perceivable stimuli of any nature), *connectivity* (exchanging signals with other Technological Actors or systems), and *identification* (being identifiable in a unique way by other systems, e.g., by means of RFID tags). Technological Actors can also be characterized by *physical properties*, e.g., the material they are built of, the shape, or the physical affordance, if these "product design" features are relevant for the interactive experience. We envision two types of Technological Actors: smart devices and smart objects. *Smart devices* are self-standing (often off-the-shelf) equipment. Examples of smart devices with sensing capability only are luminosity sensors. Examples of smart devices with actuation capability only are smart lights, sound players, digital displays, or projectors. A tablet that the user brings around, "senses" the user's current position, and reacts by displaying related content, has both sensing and actuation capability. *Smart objects* are everyday life objects (e.g., a toy or a piece of furniture) or purposely-crafted physical items which are augmented with capabilities of sensing, actuation, connectivity, or identification. Compared with smart devices, modeling physical properties is more relevant for this class of Actors, as the interaction with them is typically tangible and involves some form of manipulation consistently with the object's affordance. Given the variety of technologies associated to ISSs, it is useful to describe Technological Actors at two levels. At a *high level*, Technological Actors are represented as mere "placeholders" of interaction capabilities, and "containers" of one or more technological components that expose sensing, actuation, connectivity, or identification capabilities. Actuation capability is described in terms of *stimuli*, either elementary or complex.

Stimulus. A stimulus in our model is any phenomenon that can be generated by a digital device as "actuation" and can be perceived by user's senses: touch, sight, hearing, and smell. Stimuli can be mono- or multi-sensory, depending if they involve one or more senses. Images, animations, and lights are examples of visual stimuli. Sound and music are example of hearing stimuli. Example of multisensory stimuli are videos with aural content, bubbles generated by a bubble machine (which can be touched and seen) and the vibration of a smart toy (which might involve touch and sight).

Digital Resource. Digital Resources are digital-only, immaterial components that, depending on the type of ISS, contribute at different degrees to the user experience or are needed for computational purposes. Digital resources are of two types: i) *Digital media content*: in ISSs, many experiences are content-intensive (see Sect. 3) and content consumption is a large part of the user experience; mono- or multi-media content is generated by Technological Actors to give feedback during interaction, to create immersivity effects in the environment, to promote engagement, or to prompt the user during specific activities; ii) *software services*: these are software components exposing data and operations needed for computational purposes, and appear in the conceptual representation of the ISSs as placeholders to encapsulate technical features enabling interaction.

4.2 Interactive Behaviour Model

The Interactive Behavior Model provides the primitives to represent how the user experience unfolds along the time and how users interact with Technological Actors to reach their goals during the experience. It comprises two sub-models, at two levels of abstraction: the *Activity Interaction Model* and the *Expanded Activity Interaction Model*. Both models borrow some concepts and notations from the choreographic process model of BPMN [7]. BPMN is a well-known modeling language; it supports the specification of business processes and of collaborations among different stakeholders by means of a notation similar to UML Activity Diagrams. We re-interpret BPMN through the lens of human-ISS interaction, and extend/adapt some BPMN primitives to account for the specific modeling requirements of the human activities in ISSs, which are characterized by the "collaboration" between Human and Technological Actors.

Activity Interaction Model. This sub-model supports the high-level representation of the logic of the human activities in the ISS, and provides three abstractions: *Activity, Interaction Task*, and *System Effect*.

An *Activity* is a human "process" taking place within the ISS. It is represented by conventional flow diagrams composed by *Interaction Tasks*, *System Effects*, and control structures.

Interaction Tasks are the tasks performed by the user to reach the goal of the process. An Interaction Task encapsulates the *Interactions*, i.e., the user's actions with Technological Actors, needed to complete the task. At a high level, the representation of an Interaction Task declares what the users are expected to achieve (e.g., "select an item") but not how they achieve it, and with whom, omitting the specification of the specific Interactions and the associated Technological Actors. These latter aspects are represented in the Expanded Activity Interaction Model.

A *System Effect* is a set of perceivable, possible combined, stimuli generated automatically in response to *System Events* or *Environmental Events*, i.e., events that are outside of direct users' control. Such stimuli might have various goals, for example: to provide feedback when an Interaction Task is completed; to prompt the user to perform an Interaction Task; to increase engagement and serendipity at some point of time during the experience in the ISS; to adapt the physical space to weather condition. At high level, stimuli specifications are omitted in the representation. A System Effect declares what it is expected to achieve but not how, the latter being described in the Expanded Activity Interaction Model.

Expanded Activity Interaction Model. The Expanded Activity Interaction Model refines activity specifications by exposing the key features of Interaction Tasks and System Effects, zooming into the details of the specific User Actions performed within each Interaction Task and their direct effects (stimuli), and about the perceivable phenomena that take places place in the environment automatically during the Activity.

Each Interaction Task is described as a flow of *Interactions*. An Interaction is described by: 1) the Human Actor(s) performing the Interaction, hereinafter referred to as *Initiator(s)*; 2) the *User Action* performed by the Initiator(s) according to the available interaction capability (as described in the Structural Model); 3) the Actors - either Human or Technological - participating in the Interaction, hereinafter referred to as *Participants*; 4) a set of *UECA Rules*, which relate User Actions to their direct effects, i.e., stimuli. UECA rules account for the intrinsically event-driven logic of human-technology interaction, and their specification is guided by the sensing and actuation capabilities of the participant Technological Actors (described in the Structural Model). UECA rules have an ECA (Event-Condition-Action) rule format where the Event is a "User Event" associated to the detection of the "User Action" by the Participant Technological Actor(s); the "Condition" predicates on the User Event; the "Action" describes the stimuli actuated by the Participant Technological Actor(s) if the Condition is satisfied.

Depending on the available technology, different Interactions can be included within the same Interaction Task to specify multiple ways to accomplish the task, using different interaction paradigms (e.g., based on movements, gestures, object manipulation, or voice). In this way, the model enables to represent multimodal interaction, which is one of the most relevant peculiarities of ISSs, particularly to support different user profiles and account for different user skills.

In the Expanded Behavioral Model, a System Effect is described by: *Participants* - Technological Actors holding the actuation capability needed to generate the required stimuli; a set of *SEECA* rules, i.e., ECA rules that define the System or Environmental Events that, under given conditions, trigger such stimuli (Fig. 2).

5   Case Study: Magic Room

We exemplify the concepts introduced in the previous sections by modeling the salient interaction features of the *Magic Room*. This is a sophisticated multisensory smart space for children's play, learning, and rehabilitation that we developed in the context of a national project and installed at two local schools and two therapeutic centers in Italy [13–16]. Children's experiences in the Magic Room have various goals: *i)* promoting well-being and relaxation; *ii)* providing controlled stimulation for the vestibular, proprioceptive and tactile sensory systems to improve "sensory integration" capability; *iii)* developing children's cognitive skills through learning-by-doing and embodied learning approaches. The design process of the Magic Room was participatory and iterative, and unfolded for a period of approximately four months, involving ten primary school teachers, three special educators, five therapists (psychologists, experts in neuro-developmental disorders), and our technical team (two interaction designers and three computer engineers). Our model was used as a common language to communicate and externalize ideas during brainstorming, to share and discuss design proposals and alternatives at different levels of abstraction and refinement, and to integrate the contributions from all members of the heterogeneous project team. We organized three initial workshops devoted to: i) present to educators and therapists the technology we integrate; ii) explain the key concepts of our model and rephrase the description of technology in terms of the main Technological Actors and their interactive capabilities; iii) identify children's profiles and needs, and elicit caregivers' goals. Then educators and therapists focused on the definition of children's activities, working autonomously and in

Fig. 2. Children playing in the magic room; in the centre: interaction with the smart sphere

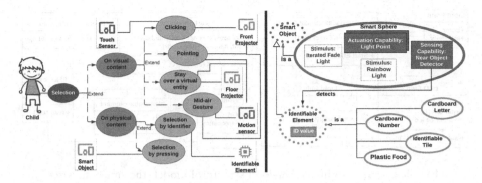

Fig. 3. Excerpts from the structural model of the magic room: the specification of a user action, *selection*, by the human actor *Child* (left). The high-level specification of the technological actor *smart sphere* (right).

team, and progressively reporting the results to the technical team for discussion. Caregivers mainly used the Interactive Behavioral Model, in an informal way, drafting boxes (for Interaction Tasks and System Effects) and arrows (to indicate the temporal order among them) in a blackboard, identifying Initiators and Participants, and writing inside the boxes the textual descriptions of what they would like the users to do during each Interaction Task, and the generated stimuli. In parallel, they also identified some physical materials and objects useful for the various activities, and the interactive capability that would expect from them, paving the ground for the definitions of the Structural Model, finally mapping these Technological Actors to Activities as Participants in the various Interaction Tasks. The technical team elaborated these drafts and translated them into more precise specifications, using the full gamut of primitives of our model. Designers and engineers specified the Structural Model at high level and low level respectively. Engineers were also responsible of the full specifications of the Behavioral Model (refining the graphs for Interaction Task flows, System Effects, and associated rules). When needed, we reshaped some design solutions suggested by domain experts in light of the constraints of the technology, and returned back to them to discuss and validate the updated proposals. For lack of space, in the rest of the section we present only few examples of the conceptual model of the Magic Room, extracted from the specification of one activity - *Battleship*, a smart space version of classic battle-ship board game.

5.1 Structural Model

Actors and Digital Resources: High Level Model. The Human Actors in the Magic Room are *Child* and *Caregiver*. The Technological Actors are: front and floor projectors, Kinect body-motion sensor, RFID cards and readers attachable to various materials, portable and ambient smart lights, sound players, aroma and soap bubbles emitters, a tablet offering an app for caregiver to control the execution flow of Activities and Interaction Tasks. There are also several Smart

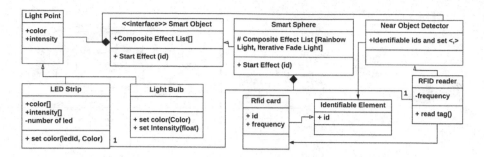

Fig. 4. Excerpts from the low-level structural model: the smart sphere.

Objects: Smart Toys (embedding motion and pressure sensors and light or sound actuators), Paper- or plastic-based Identifiable Objects (RFID tagged items), and a Smart Sphere (described in Fig. 3 - right side). A *Smart Sphere* embeds a sensor (a *Near Object Detector*) able to generate an object identifier when it detects the proximity of an *Identifiable Element*). The Smart Sphere also includes a number of light actuators ("Light Points"). These can generate composite light effects such as *Rainbow Light* and *Iterated Fade Light*, represented on the right side of Fig. 3.

The Magic Room also features a large number of Digital Media Content such as videos, animations, images, sounds, and music.

Children interact with projections and smart objects, while Caregivers operate on the tablet.

Technological Actors: Low-Level Model. The UML class diagram in Fig. 4 represents the Smart Sphere at a lower level, in terms of its attributes and functions. The *Smart Sphere* is a *Smart Object* that exposes two composite light stimuli (Rainbow and Fade) and a method to generate them. Its *Light Points* use *LED strips*, with associated attributes and methods controlling light effects. The Smart Sphere also uses a *Near Object Detector* to sense the proximity of RFID tags embedded in *Identifiable Elements* (*RFID card*) and to read its unique ID.

User Actions. Figure 3 illustrates an excerpt of Structural Model concerning the User Action *Selection* associated to the Human Actor "Child". The User Action is specified first by describing what can be selected, either *visual* or *physical content*, and then how the selection is performed through some Technological Actors. For example, the Child can "select" a *visual content* by executing a *mid-air gesture* (sensed by the motion sensor) in front of Digital Media Contents projected by the *Wall Projector*. The Child could *stay over a virtual entity* projected on the floor by the *Floor Projector*; s/he can also *select by pressing*, when interacting with *physical content* represented by a *Smart Object*; or s/he can *select by identifier*, using an *Identifiable Element*, i.e., a Smart Object that has identification features (embedding RFID cards) and can be detected by proximity by a Smart Objects that have RFID sensing capability (e.g., the Smart Sphere).

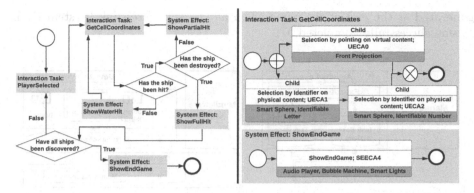

Fig. 5. Activity interaction model of battleship (left) and the expanded activity interaction model for the interaction task enabling the cell coordinates' selection (right).

5.2   Interactive Behaviour Model

Interactive Activity Model. Fig. 5 exemplifies the behavioral specification for the Activity "Battleship". The flow diagram (left side of Fig. 5) includes the *Interaction Task "GetCellCoordinates"* to select a cell in the battleship grid, and a number of *System Effects* that generate visual and auditory feedback to outline partial or full hit, water hit, or end of game.

The fragment of the *Expanded Activity Interaction Model* shown on the right side of Fig. 5 presents the details of the Interaction Task "GetCellCoordinates". The diagram provides two alternative modalities to accomplish this Interaction Task (mid air gestures and tangible interaction), each one associated to different *Interactions*: The user can either "point on" a virtual content (a cell of the Battle grid projected on the front screen), or can place - on top of the Smart Sphere - two Identifiable Cards for the cell coordinates, one with a number and one with a letter. Each box associated to an Interaction shows the Human Actor (Initiator) who executes the action(s) (upper area of the box) and the Participant Technological Actors (Smart Sphere and Identifiable Objects) involved in the Interaction (bottom area of the box). The middle area of the Interaction box includes the User Action (for example "Selection by Identifier on Physical content") and the UECA rules, for example "UECA 1", the specification of which (omitted in figure for lack of space) is: *<USER EVENT:Sensed (ID); CONDITION:Type(ID)= "Letter"; ACTION: Activate("Smart_Sphere", "rainbow_light")>*. The rule means that if the Identifiable Object selected by the user and sensed by the Smart Sphere (Participant) is a letter (i.e., the first coordinate of the cell selection), then the Smart Sphere generates a multi-color, rainbow-like light stimulus.

At low level, a *System Effect* (see bottom of Fig. 5 - right side) is represented by a box having empty top area (being the stimuli generated by System or Environmental Events without intentional human intervention) and SEECA rules, e.g., rule SEECA4, which defines the stimuli (music, lights, soap bubbles) generated at the end of the game when all the ships are sunk (System Event "game successfully completed").

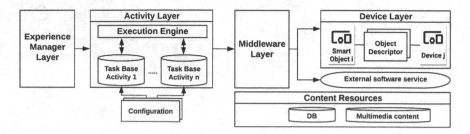

Fig. 6. Magic room architecture

5.3   From Models to Software Architectures

The abstractions presented in the previous sections guided the definition of a multi-layer architecture for the Magic Room (Fig. 6) characterized by modularity, flexibility, and extensibility. The Activity specifications in the Interactive Behavioural Model and the Technology Actor specifications in the Structural Model guide the definition of a JSON-based configuration file that the *Execution Engine* interprets as low-level rules governing the interactive capabilities of Technological Actors. During the execution of an Activity, the Execution Engine manages the transition between interactive tasks, and triggers the execution of the rules governing interactions, while the *Experience Manager* controls the flow of different activities. The Execution Engine leverages on the *Content Resources* component and on the Middleware, demanding to these modules the low-level execution of the activated rules. The *Middleware* manages the low-level functionality of each Technological Actor, as expressed in the Low-Level Structural Model, abstracting from the technology heterogeneity of the IoT products by means of adequate wrappers. The Middleware also supports the runtime discovery and instantiation of the different devices, depending on the interaction capabilities required by the Interaction Tasks in execution. To enhance a plug and play approach, devices expose their structural content and specific functions by means of *Object Descriptors*.

6   Conclusions

This paper has discussed some modeling requirements that characterize Interactive Smart Spaces (ISSs), pinpointing the importance of considering the human as the principal actor in this class of systems, and addressing the interaction capabilities as fundamental for empowering users in this spaces and enabling the accomplishment of complex tasks. Limited research in the IoT arena has taken this perspective so far. In addition, we have presented a novel conceptual model that enables designers of ISSs to focus on the salient human-centered aspects of IoT-enhanced user activities, and to organize the design along multiple dimensions and levels of abstractions. The proposed model deserves additional refinements, but also in its current form it has demonstrated its expressive power and its capability of supporting the design and conceptual specification of a very complex, content-intensive and interaction-intensive smart space, discussed as case study in the paper. Our model and our overall approach can pave the ground towards innovative methods for conceptual design in the IoT arena, and may also lead to the definition of more modular and standardized technological architectures for future highly interactive IoT systems.

An interaction-centered modeling approach is also the first step towards the definition of novel solutions to support the appropriation process of interactive IoT technology by end users; adequate abstractions like the ones presented in this paper can provide a base of concepts upon which to create the building blocks for End-User Development methods and tools [10]. This issue is particularly important in contexts - like education and rehabilitation - where Interactive Smart Spaces could have a significant potential but there is a strong need of personalization of the user experiences. Since it is not possible to predict at design time all the possible relevant configurations of activities as built-in components of an ISS, users would benefit from the possibility of eventually defining their interactive experiences or configuration parameters by themselves [1], without any knowledge about the underlying implementation. This view raises new research challenges, addressing the way the interaction capabilities of ISS should be modelled through metaphors and design patterns that make sense to the users, and would enable them to customize or even create from scratch their own interactive smart experiences, starting from flexible activity skeletons and a repertoire of interactive capabilities that they can manage and organize.

References

1. Ardito, C., Buono, P., Desolda, G., Matera, M.: From smart objects to smart experiences: an end-user development approach. IJHCS **114**, 51–68 (2018)
2. Arruda, M.F., Bulcão-Neto, R.F.: Toward a lightweight ontology for privacy protection in IoT. In: Proceedings of SAC 2019, pp. 880–888. ACM (2019)
3. Atzori, L., Iera, A., Morabito, G.: The internet of things: a survey. Comput. Netw. **54**(15), 2787–2805 (2010)
4. Bassi, A., et al.: Enabling Things to Talk. Springer, Cham (2013)
5. Bermudez-Edo, M., Elsaleh, T., Barnaghi, P., Taylor, K.: IoT-lite: a lightweight semantic model for the internet of things and its use with dynamic semantics. Pers. Ubiquit. Comput. **21**(3), 475–487 (2017)
6. Conti, M., et al.: Looking ahead in pervasive computing: challenges and opportunities in the era of cyber-physical convergence. Pervasive Mob. Comput. **8**(1), 2–21 (2012)
7. Cortes-Cornax, M., Dupuy-Chessa, S., Rieu, D., Dumas, M.: Evaluating choreographies in BPMN 2.0 using an extended quality framework. In: Dijkman, R., Hofstetter, J., Koehler, J. (eds.) BPMN 2011. LNBIP, vol. 95, pp. 103–117. Springer, Heidelberg (2011). https://doi.org/10.1007/978-3-642-25160-3_8

8. Costa, B., Pires, P.F., Delicato, F.C.: Modeling SOA-based IoT applications with SoaML4IoT. In: 2019 IEEE 5th World Forum on Internet of Things (WF-IoT), pp. 496–501. IEEE (2019)

9. Delprino, F., Piva, C., Tommasi, G., Gelsomini, M., Izzo, N., Matera, M.: Abbot: a smart toy motivating children to become outdoor explorers. In: Proceedings of AVI 2018, pp. 1–9 (2018)

10. Desolda, G., Ardito, C., Matera, M.: Empowering end users to customize their smart environments: model, composition paradigms, and domain-specific tools. ACM Trans. Comput. Hum. Inter. (TOCHI) **24**(2), 1–52 (2017)

11. Foglia, L., Wilson, R.A.: Embodied cognition. WIREs Cogn. Sci. **4**(3), 319–325 (2013)

12. Fortino, G., Russo, W., Savaglio, C., Shen, W., Zhou, M.: Agent-oriented cooperative smart objects: from IoT system design to implementation. IEEE Trans. Syst. Man, Cybern. Syst. **48**(11), 1939–1956 (2018)

13. Garzotto, F., Beccaluva, E., Gianotti, M., Riccardi, F.: Interactive multisensory environments for primary school children. In: Proceedings of CHI 2020, CHI 2020, p. 1–12. Association for Computing Machinery, New York (2020)

14. Garzotto, F., Gelsomini, M.: Magic room: a smart space for children with neurodevelopmental disorder. IEEE Pervasive Comput. **17**(1), 38–48 (2018)

15. Gelsomini, M., Leonardi, G., Garzotto, F.: Embodied learning in immersive smart spaces. In: Proceedings of CHI 2020, pp. 1–14 (2020)

16. Gelsomini, M., et al.: Magika, a multisensory environment for play, education and inclusion. In: Extended Abstracts of the 2019 CHI Conference on Human Factors in Computing Systems, pp. 1–6 (2019)

17. Gračanin, D., Handosa, M., Elmongui, H.G., Matković, K.: An approach to user interactions with IoT-enabled spaces. In: Proceedings of ConTEL 17, pp. 139–146. IEEE (2017)

18. Haller, S., Serbanati, A., Bauer, M., Carrez, F.: A domain model for the internet of things. In: 2013 Proceedings of Green Computing and Communications and Internet of Things and Cyber, Physical and Social Computing, 2013, pp. 411–417, August 2013

19. Jahed, K., Dingel, J.: Enabling model-driven software development tools for the internet of things. In: Proceedings of MiSE 2019, pp. 93–99. IEEE Press (2019)

20. Kortuem, G., Kawsar, F.: Market-based user innovation in the internet of things. In: 2010 Internet of Things (IOT), pp. 1–8. IEEE (2010)

21. Maheswaran, M., Wen, J., Gowing, A.: Design of a context aware object model for smart spaces, things, and people. In: Proceedings of IEEE ICC 2015, pp. 710–715, June 2015

22. Markopoulos, P., Marijnissen, P.: UML as a representation for interaction designs. Proc. OZCHI **2000**, 240–249 (2000)

23. Ning, D., Wang, Y., Guo, J.: A data oriented analysis and design method for smart complex software systems of IoT. In: Proceedings of ISSI 2018, pp. 1–6, September 2018

24. Petrelli, D., Lechner, M.: The meSch project-material encounters with digital cultural heritage: reusing existing digital resources in the creation of novel forms of visitor's experiences. In: Proceedings CIDOC 2014 (2014)

25. Sahinel, D., Akpolat, C., Görür, O.C., Sivrikaya, F.: Integration of human actors in IoT and CPS landscape. In: Proceedings of WF-IoT, pp. 485–490, April 2019

26. Skarmeta, A., Hernández-Ramos, J.L., Bernabe, J.B.: A required security and privacy framework for smart objects. In: 2015 ITU Kaleidoscope: Trust in the Information Society (K-2015), pp. 1–7, December 2015

27. Weiser, M.: The computer for the 21st century. Sc. Am. **265**(3), 94–105 (1991)
28. Zeng, J., Yang, L.T., Ma, J.: A system-level modeling and design for cyber-physical-social systems. ACM Trans. Embed. Comput. Syst. **15**(2), 35:1–35:26 (2016)
29. Zhao, Y., Pour, F.F., Golestan, S., Stroulia, E.: BIMSim3d: multi-agent human activity simulation in indoor spaces. In: Proceedings of the International Workshop on Software Engineering for Smart Cyber-Physical Systems, pp. 18–24. IEEE Press (2019)

The Conceptual Schema of Ethereum

Antoni Olivé[✉] [iD]

Department of Service and Information System Engineering, Universitat Politècnica
de Catalunya – Barcelona Tech, Barcelona, Catalonia, Spain
`antoni.olive@upc.edu`

Abstract. There is an abundant literature on Ethereum, but as far as we know
what is missing is its explicit conceptual schema. We present here the conceptual
schema of Ethereum in UML. The schema should be useful to those that want
to understand Ethereum and to those that develop the schema of Ethereum-based
DApps. We present a few population constraints, and show that they suffice for
the specification at the conceptual level of what is understood by immutability of a
blockchain. We also show that the well-known reification construct and an initial
constraint suffice to specify at the conceptual level that the Ethereum blockchain
stores the full state history.

Keywords: Conceptual modeling · Conceptual schema · Blockchain ·
Ethereum · Immutability

1 Introduction

This paper reports the main results of a project aiming at developing the conceptual
schema of Ethereum, a popular open-source platform for blockchain-based decentralized
applications [1]. The project had two main goals: (1) to know the conceptual schema of
that system, and (2) to check the degree to which the constructs that have been developed
in the conceptual modeling field allow the complete specification of a complex system
like Ethereum. Of particular concern was how to specify immutability at the conceptual
level.

The rationale of the first goal was that so far most of the Ethereum literature is
written from either a technical or an economic perspective [2]. Application developers, researchers and students in general that need to learn the foundations of Ethereum
have easily available a large number of books, papers and web documents (such as, for
example, [3–5]), but they usually include (and, sometimes, focus on) many complex
implementation details that make their understanding difficult [6].

From a conceptual modeling point of view, it is easy to see that what is missing in
the above literature is the explicit conceptual schema. Ethereum, like all blockchains,
is basically a particular kind of distributed database [7, 8] and, as such, it *necessarily*
has a conceptual schema. The important role of the explicit definition of that schema
not only in the development of database and of information systems, but also in their
understanding, has been recognized since long ago [9–11].

G. Dobbie et al. (Eds.): ER 2020, LNCS 12400, pp. 418–428, 2020.
https://doi.org/10.1007/978-3-030-62522-1_31

The rationale of the second goal was that blockchains in general, and Ethereum in particular, have some features whose conceptualization is not obvious. We wanted to check whether the constructs provided by conceptual modeling languages are sufficient to deal with those features. One of them, which is present in all blockchains, is *immutability* [12]: what kind of integrity constraints are needed to specify immutability? The other feature, which is specific to Ethereum, is that, besides the transactions, it maintains the *full state history* of the state of the instances of *Account*, which is the main entity type represented in the blockchain. The question is then: do we need a temporal conceptual model [13–15] to specify the full state history?

We describe here the main result of our project: the conceptual schema of Ethereum in UML. We deal only with the main elements of the structural schema; the behavioral one, at the conceptual level, is simpler. We have found that standard UML, extended with a few known temporal constraints, suffices for defining that schema, including the blockchain immutability and its full state history.

The structure of the paper is as follows. Section 2 introduces the temporal constraints that will be needed. Section 3 presents the conceptual schema of Ethereum. Section 4 reviews related work. Section 5 briefly summarizes the paper and suggests further work.

2 Population and Initial Constraints

In this section, we define the temporal constraints that will be used in this paper[1]. These constraints have been previously presented in the literature using several terms and formalisms [16–19]. We use here the terminology of the temporal constraints defined in [20] and indicate how to use the constraints as stereotypes in UML.

We assume that entities and relationships are instances of their types at particular time points (or states). By *lifespan* we mean the set of times during which the system operates. We represent by $E(e, t)$ the fact that e is an instance of entity type E at t. We denote by $R(p_1: E_1, \dots, p_n: E_n)$ the schema of a relationship type named R with entity type participants $E_1, \dots, E_n$, playing roles $p_1, \dots, p_n$, respectively. Attributes will be considered as ordinary binary relationship types. We represent by $R(e_1, \dots, e_n, t)$ the fact that entities $e_1, \dots, e_n$ participate in a relationship instance of R at t.

2.1 Entity Type Population Constraints

The *population* of an entity type E is the set of its instances at some time (or state). An entity type is *constant* when its population is always the same. An entity type E is *permanent* when once an entity e becomes an instance of E, e continues to be an instance until the end of the lifespan. It can be seen that a constant entity type is also permanent. On the other hand, if E is a covering generalization of a set of permanent entity types, then E is also permanent.

In UML, the above constraints can be defined as stereotyped constraints to which we give the short names of k (for constant) and p (for permanent).

---

[1] See [23] for the first-order logic formalization of the constraints and examples.

2.2   Relationship Type Population Constraints

The *population* of a relationship type R is the set of its instances (relationships) that exist at some time (or state). We say that a relationship type $R(p_1: E_1, \ldots, p_n: E_n)$ is *constant* with respect to a participant p_i if the instances of R in which an instance e_i of E_i participates are the same during the temporal interval in which e_i exists. Similarly, R is *permanent* with respect to participant p_i if the instances of R in which an instance e_i of E_i participates never cease to exist while e_i is an instance of E_i.

A relationship type R is *constant* if it is constant with respect to all its participants. Similarly, R is *permanent* if it is permanent with respect to all its participants. It can be seen that a constant relationship type is also permanent.

In UML, the above constraints can be defined as stereotyped constraints to which we give the same short names as before: k (for constant) and p (for permanent).

2.3   Creation-Time Constraint

A creation-time constraint ϕ of an entity type E is a constraint that its instances must satisfy only at the time when they become an instance of E [21]. Formally:

$$\forall e, t((E(e, t) \land \neg \exists t'(t' < t \land E(e, t')) \rightarrow \phi(e, t))$$

3   Ethereum

Figure 1 is a broad view of the main concepts of the conceptual schema of Ethereum in UML. In the figures, greyed rectangles denote entity types whose complete definition is shown in other figures. The *Blockchain* consists of a set of *Block*s, which in turn consist of a set of *Transaction*s. The state of the system consists of a set of *Account*s and their properties. Transactions change that state. For each block, the system stores the state of the accounts (*AccountState*) at the moment when the transactions included in the block have been processed and the block has been added to the blockchain. In what follows we describe in detail those concepts.

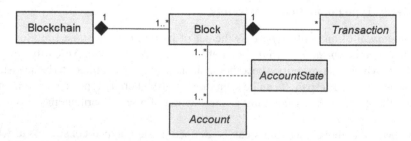

Fig. 1. Main concepts of the conceptual schema of Ethereum

3.1 Accounts

There are two kinds of accounts: Externally Owned Account (abbreviated as *EOAccount*) and *ContractAccount*, see Fig. 2. Both are permanent. Their generalization is the abstract entity type *Account*, which is also permanent.

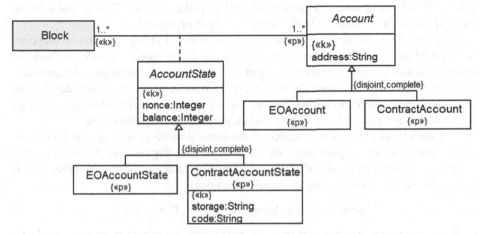

Fig. 2. Accounts and their states in Ethereum

Accounts are identified by means of their *address*, which is a constant attribute. An externally owned account is created and controlled by a user. Its address is determined from the user public key, which in turn is determined from the user private key. The sets of private/public keys of the users are stored in their wallets (not shown in the Figure).

A contract account is controlled by the code it contains, and its address is assigned by the system when the account is created. A contract account can be created by a user or by the code of another contract account.

Besides their address, both kinds of accounts have two attributes, called *nonce* and *balance*. For externally owned accounts, attribute *nonce* indicates the number of transactions sent from them, while for contract accounts it indicates the number of contract-creations made by them. Attribute *balance* indicates the amount of *ether*, the cryptocurrency of Ethereum, owned by the account. The balance is represented in *wei*, the smallest subunit of ether.

Attributes *code* and *storage* apply only to contract accounts. Attribute *code* contains the code that is executed when called by a transaction or by another contract account. The code is written in the EVM code language, and it is executed by the Ethereum Virtual Machine. Normally, the code of an account cannot change, but there is the possibility of executing a *destruct* operation with the effect that the code and the storage are removed from the account. Note that if *code* could not be destructed, then we could define it as a constant attribute of *ContractAccount*.

Contract accounts have also an attribute called *storage*, which is used by the contract code. A contract can neither read nor write to any storage apart from its own.

In Ethereum, there are two kinds of states: world state and account state. An *account state* is the set of values of the attributes of an account at a given moment. A *world state* is the set of all accounts existing at a given moment and their account state at that moment.

For each block, Ethereum stores the world state at the moment when the transactions included in a block have been processed and the block has been added to the blockchain. Therefore, the world state of a given block includes all accounts and their state existing after all transactions included in the block have been processed.

The world and the account states have been modeled in Fig. 2 by the association between *Block* and *Account*, and its reification, the entity type *AccountState*. Both the association and *AccountState* are permanent. In the association, the role *block* is constant, meaning that the set of accounts to which a block is associated with is fully determined when the block is added to the system, and cannot be changed. The role *account* in that association is permanent because new instances can be added at any time.

For each block, there is an instance of the association *block-account* (and therefore of *AccountState*) for each account that exists at the time the block is created. This can be easily expressed by means of a creation-time constraint (see Sect. 2.3). In logic, if R is the association *block-account*, the constraint would be:

$$\phi(b, t) \equiv \forall a(Account(a, t) \rightarrow R(b, a, t))$$

Note that given that *Account* is permanent, once an account is created, it will be associated with the block within which it was created and with all future blocks.

An instance of *AccountState* is an account state of the corresponding account. There are two permanent subtypes of *AccountState*, *EOAccountState* and *ContractAccountState*, similarly to the two subtypes of *Account*. The account attributes have been defined in these entity types, and all of them are constant.

The current values of the account attributes could have been defined as derived attributes of *Account* and of *ContractAcccount*. These attributes would not be constant. However, for simplicity, this has not been done in Fig. 2. The derivation rules would indicate that their value is that of the *AccountState* or *ContractAccountState* instances corresponding to the same account in the last block.

The set of instances of *AccountState* of a block is the world state corresponding to that block. Given the population constraints of *AccountState*, *Account*, *Block* (we will see that is also permanent) and those of the association *block-account* it follows that Ethereum stores the full history of its states.

With respect to immutability, the schema fragment of Fig. 2 indicates that the instances of *Account* and *AccountState* cannot be deleted and their attributes cannot be modified. Moreover, the instances of the association *block-account* of a block cannot be changed. However, and this is a subtle and necessary point, it is possible to add instances of that association to accounts.

3.2 Transactions

There are two kinds of transactions: *MessageCall* and *ContractCreation*, see Fig. 3. Both are permanent. Their generalization, the abstract entity type *Transaction*, is also permanent. All attributes of transactions are constant.

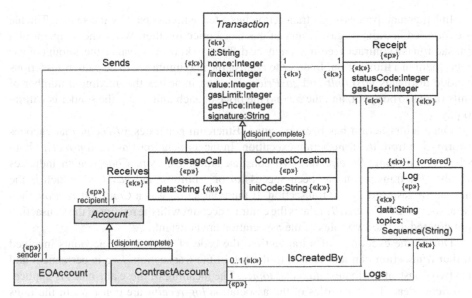

Fig. 3. Transactions in Ethereum

Transactions can be identified in three ways. The first is by means of attribute *id*, which is automatically computed when the transaction is created. The second is the tuple (*sender*, *nonce*). Transactions are originated by externally owned accounts, which send them to the network for processing. The association *Sends* indicates the *sender* of a transaction. The association is permanent, with role *sender* permanent (an account can send several transactions) and role *transaction* constant (the sender is determined when the transaction is created and cannot be changed later). Transactions sent by an externally owned account are numbered consecutively (*nonce*) starting at zero. The third way of transaction identification involves attribute *index*, which will be explained in the next section.

A message call is a transaction sent to a recipient. The association *Receives* indicates the *recipient*. The association is permanent with role *messageCall* constant and role *recipient* permanent. If the recipient is an externally owned account, the ether indicated in the attribute *value* is transferred from the sender to the recipient. If the recipient is a contract account, then its *code* is executed using the transaction attribute *data* as input. In this case, the transaction *value* may or may not be transferred to the recipient account.

A contract creation is a transaction that creates a new contract account. The *code* of the new account is obtained from the *initCode* attribute and it can be executed in future message calls. The transaction *value* is the starting balance of the new account (may be zero).

In order to ensure that a transaction has been originated by the sender, the transaction includes a *signature* attribute. The signature is obtained from the private key of the sender and the transaction attributes. Given a transaction, anyone can check that only the owner of the sender account could have sent it.

In Ethereum, processing a transaction has a fee, which is paid by the sender. The fee is expressed in units of gas. A unit of gas has a price in ether. When the recipient of a transaction is a contract account, it may be difficult to know in advance the amount of gas to be spent in a transaction. In order to control the maximum fee to be paid, transactions include attributes *gasLimit* and *gasPrice*. The first indicates the maximum number of units of gas to be spent, and the second the price of each unit of gas the sender is willing to pay.

Once a transaction has been executed, Ethereum generates a *Receipt* that encodes information from the transaction execution. In the association *transaction-receipt* both roles are constant. *Receipt* has two constant attributes: *statusCode,* which indicates whether the transaction has been successful or a failure, and *gasUsed,* which is the amount of gas used by the transaction. If the transaction was a *ContractCreation*, then the association *IsCreatedBy* relates the contract account with the receipt of the transaction that created it. The two roles of the association are constant.

During the execution of a transaction, the code of the contract accounts involved in that transaction can add entries to the log of the transaction. *Log* is permanent and has two constant attributes: *data* and *topics.* The meaning of these attributes is application dependent. The two roles of the association *log-receipt* are constant. In the *Logs* association, *contractAccount* is permanent while *log* is constant.

With respect to immutability, the schema fragment of Fig. 3 states that the instances of *Transaction*, and its subtypes, *Receipt* and *Log* cannot be deleted and their attributes cannot be modified. Three associations (*transaction-receipt*, *log-receipt* and *IsCreatedBy*) are constant, meaning that their instances cannot be deleted and no new instances can be added to the existing participants in those associations. The other three associations (*Sends*, *Receives*, *Logs*) are permanent, which implies that their instances cannot be deleted, but it is possible to add new instances to entities with a permanent role.

3.3 Blocks

In Ethereum, the blockchain consists of an ordered sequence of blocks. Figure 4 shows the entity types *Blockchain* and *Block* and the composition association between them. *Blockchain* is constant, and its population consists of a single instance, while *Block* is permanent and its population consists of many instances. The role *blockchain* is permanent because new blocks are added to the composition, while the role *block* is constant because a block is associated to the blockchain when it is created and cannot be changed.

All attributes of *Block* are constant. The first two are identifiers of blocks. Attribute *id* is a hash computed by the system from the block's contents, which includes several attributes irrelevant to our conceptual modelling purposes. Attribute *number* is derived. The corresponding derivation rule defines its value as the index of the block in the composition. The first block has a number of zero.

As has been indicated, the role *block* in the blockchain composition is constant. However, in this case the role *block* is *ordered*, which means that the blocks of the blockchain are ordered (a sequence in this case). This raises a subtle point: what precludes the change of the order of the blocks in the sequence? We could define a new population constraint for this purpose but in this case it is not necessary. It suffices to define attribute

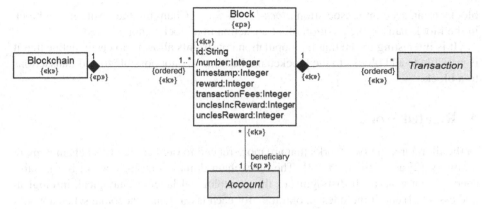

Fig. 4. Blocks in Ethereum

number as constant, which implies that the position of a block in the sequence cannot change.

Attribute *timestamp* indicates the time when the block was added to the blockchain. An obvious constraint is that it must be greater than that of the previous block in the sequence.

Blocks are prepared and added to the blockchain by *miners*, which are specialized network nodes. The miner of a block is compensated (in ether) for the work done. The compensation is sent to an account designated by the miner, given by the association *block beneficiary* in Fig. 4. The compensation includes a reward (attribute *reward*) and the fees of all transactions included in the block (attribute *transactionFees*). In some cases, a block may include up to two special stale blocks, called uncle blocks, which do not include transactions. If it is so, then the *beneficiary* receives an additional reward (attribute *unclesIncReward*), and the uncles receive the reward given by attribute *unclesReward*. For simplicity, Fig. 4 shows neither the uncle blocks nor their beneficiaries.

A block, in turn, consists of an ordered sequence of transactions. Figure 4 shows the composition association between *Block* and *Transaction*. Note that both roles in that association are constant: the instances of the composition are determined when a block and a transaction are created and cannot be changed. A block and its transactions are recorded in the blockchain at the same time.

In addition to the two ways indicated in the previous section, an instance of *Transaction* can be identified by the block of which it is a part and the *index* attribute (Fig. 3). This is a derived attribute whose value is the position of the transaction in the block. The attribute is constant, which – among other things – means that the position on a transaction in the block cannot be changed.

With respect to immutability, the schema fragment of Fig. 4 indicates that the single instance of *Blockchain* exists since the beginning of the system's lifespan and, as well as the instances of *Block*, it cannot be deleted. The attributes of both types cannot be changed. One association (*block-transaction*) is constant. The other two are permanent. It is possible to add blocks to the blockchain (association *blockchain-block*) and to add blocks to an account (association *block-beneficiary*). Changing the position of a block in the blockchain or the position of a transaction in a block is not allowed.

It is interesting to see that the population constraints allow us to easily define that it is possible to add blocks to the blockchain, but that it is not possible to add transactions to a block.

4 Related Work

In the literature, the two works that are more related to ours are the blockchain domain ontology [2] and EthOn [6, 22]. The blockchain domain ontology is not blockchain-specific, but general. It distinguishes three ontological layers (datalogical, infological and essential) and it includes an ontology for each layer. Our conceptual schema would basically be placed in their infological layer. The ontology corresponding to this level, the infological ontology, consists of six entity types, five associations, and one attribute. The conceptual schema that we have presented here is much more detailed because it is blockchain-specific.

EthOn is an ontology in RDF Schema and OWL that formalizes most of the concepts used in the Ethereum platform as described in the "yellow paper" [1]. The scope of EthOn is different from that of our conceptual schema. EthOn includes in an integrated ontology both the concepts related to the data stored in the platform and the concepts related to the implementation. In the classical terminology used in conceptual modelling [9], it can be said that EthOn describes in an integrated view both the conceptual and the internal schema of Ethereum. On the other hand, EthOn does not specify the population constraints of its concepts needed to specify their immutability, and it does not formalize the full state history.

5 Conclusions

We have presented the conceptual schema of Ethereum in UML. As far as we know, this is the first time that the schema is presented in the literature. We hope the schema will be useful to those that want to understand Ethereum and to those that develop the schema of Ethereum-based DApps [23].

We have presented and formalized a few population constraints, and we have shown that they suffice for the specification at the conceptual level of what is understood by immutability of a blockchain. Finally, we have shown that the well-known reification construct and an initial constraint suffice to specify at the conceptual level that the Ethereum blockchain stores the full state history.

This work can be extended in several directions. We point out two of them here. First, it would be useful to complete the structural schema that we have presented with a few remaining details, and to develop the behavioral one. Second, a work similar to the one presented here could be done with other blockchain platforms.

Acknowledgments. The author is greatly indebted to Joan Antoni Pastor and Jordi Estapé for their comments to earlier drafts of this paper.

References

1. Wood, G.: Ethereum: a secure decentralised generalised transaction ledger (2020). https://eth ereum.github.io/yellowpaper/paper.pdf
2. de Kruijff, J., Weigand, H.: Understanding the blockchain using enterprise ontology. In: Dubois, E., Pohl, K. (eds.) CAiSE 2017. LNCS, vol. 10253, pp. 29–43. Springer, Cham (2017). https://doi.org/10.1007/978-3-319-59536-8_3
3. Antonopoulos, A.M., Wood, G.: Mastering Ethereum: Building Smart Contracts and DApps. O'Reilly Media, Newton (2018)
4. Dameron, M.: Beigepaper: an Ethereum technical specification (2019). https://github.com/ chronaeon/beigepaper/blob/master/beigepaper.pdf
5. Kasireddy, P.: How does Ethereum work, anyway? (2017). https://medium.com/@preethika sireddy/how-does-ethereum-work-anyway-22d1df506369
6. Pfeffer, J.: EthOn—Introducing semantic Ethereum. Organized Ethereum knowledge (2017). https://media.consensys.net/ethon-introducing-semantic-ethereum-15f1f0696986
7. Dinh, T.T.A., Liu, R., Zhang, M., Chen, G., Ooi, B.C., Wang, J.: Untangling blockchain: a data processing view of blockchain systems. IEEE TKDE 30(7), 1366–1385 (2018)
8. Kim, H.M., Laskowski, M.: Toward an ontology-driven blockchain design for supply-chain provenance. Int. Syst. Account. Finance Manag. 25(1), 18–27 (2018)
9. ANSI: ANSI/X3/SPARC study group on data base management systems. Interim report. FDT, Bull. ACM SIGMOD 7(2) (1975)
10. Mylopoulos, J.: Conceptual Modelling and Telos. In: Loucopoulos, P., Zicari, R. (eds.) Conceptual Modelling, Databases and CASE, pp. 49–68. Wiley, Hoboken (1992)
11. Delcambre, L.M.L., Liddle, S.W., Pastor, O., Storey, V.C.: A reference framework for conceptual modeling. In: Trujillo, J., et al. (eds.) ER 2018. LNCS, vol. 11157, pp. 27–42. Springer, Cham (2018). https://doi.org/10.1007/978-3-030-00847-5_4
12. Hofmann, F., Wurster, S., Ron, E., Böhmecke-Schwafert, M.: The immutability concept of blockchains and benefits of early standardization. In: 2017 ITU Kaleidoscope: Challenges for a Data-Driven Society (ITU K), Nanjing, pp. 1–8 (2017)
13. Gregersen, H., Jensen, C.S.: Temporal entity-relationship models-a survey. IEEE TKDE 11(3), 464–497 (1999)
14. Combi, C., Degani, S., Jensen, C.S.: Capturing temporal constraints in temporal ER models. In: Li, Q., Spaccapietra, S., Yu, E., Olivé, A. (eds.) ER 2008. LNCS, vol. 5231, pp. 397–411. Springer, Heidelberg (2008). https://doi.org/10.1007/978-3-540-87877-3_29
15. Artale, A., Franconi, E.: Foundations of temporal conceptual data models. In: Borgida, A.T., Chaudhri, V.K., Giorgini, P., Yu, E.S. (eds.) Conceptual Modeling: Foundations and Applications. LNCS, vol. 5600, pp. 10–35. Springer, Heidelberg (2009). https://doi.org/10.1007/978-3-642-02463-4_2
16. Costal, D., Olivé, A., Sancho, M.-R.: Temporal features of class populations and attributes in conceptual models. In: Embley, D.W., Goldstein, R.C. (eds.) ER 1997. LNCS, vol. 1331, pp. 57–70. Springer, Heidelberg (1997). https://doi.org/10.1007/3-540-63699-4_6
17. Cabot, J., Olivé, A., Teniente, E.: Representing temporal information in UML. In: Stevens, P., Whittle, J., Booch, G. (eds.) UML 2003. LNCS, vol. 2863, pp. 44–59. Springer, Heidelberg (2003). https://doi.org/10.1007/978-3-540-45221-8_5
18. Artale, A., Parent, C., Spaccapietra, S.: Evolving objects in temporal information systems. Ann. Math. Artif. Intell. 50(1–2), 5–38 (2007). https://doi.org/10.1007/s10472-007-9068-z
19. McBrien, P.: Temporal constraints in non-temporal data modelling languages. In: Li, Q., Spaccapietra, S., Yu, E., Olivé, A. (eds.) ER 2008. LNCS, vol. 5231, pp. 412–425. Springer, Heidelberg (2008). https://doi.org/10.1007/978-3-540-87877-3_30

20. Olivé, A.: Conceptual Modeling of Information Systems. Springer, Heidelberg (2007). https://doi.org/10.1007/978-3-540-39390-0
21. Olivé, A.: A method for the definition of integrity constraints in object-oriented conceptual modeling languages. Data Knowl. Eng. **59**(3), 559–575 (2006)
22. Pfeffer, J.: EthOn: An Ethereum Ontology. https://consensys.github.io/EthOn/EthOn_spec.html. Accessed March 2020
23. Olivé, A.: The conceptual schema of Ethereum and of the ERC–20 token standard. http://hdl.handle.net/2117/328036 (2020)

Towards Privacy Policy Conceptual Modeling

Katsiaryna Krasnashchok(✉) , Majd Mustapha , Anas Al Bassit ,
and Sabri Skhiri

EURA NOVA, 1435 Mont-Saint-Guibert, Belgium
{katherine.krasnoschok,majd.mustapha,anas.albassit,
sabri.skhiri}@euranova.eu

Abstract. After GDPR enforcement in May 2018, the problem of implementing privacy by design and staying compliant with regulations has
been more prominent than ever for businesses of all sizes, which is evident from frequent cases against companies and significant fines paid due
to non-compliance. Consequently, numerous research works have been
emerging in this area. Yet, to this moment, no publicly available model
can offer a comprehensive representation of privacy policies written in
natural language, that is machine readable, interoperable and suitable
for automatic compliance checking. Meanwhile, regarding the use of personal data, privacy policies stay one of the main means of communication
between a Controller and a Data Subject. In this paper, we propose a
conceptual model for fine-grained representation of privacy policies. We
reuse and adapt existing Semantic Web resources in the spirit of interoperability. We represent our model as an ODRL profile and enrich it with
vocabularies for describing personal data processing in great detail, making it suitable for further usage in downstream applications, to support
adoption and implementation of privacy by design.

Keywords: Privacy · ODRL · GDPR · Semantic Web

1 Introduction

Compliance with data protection regulations, in particular, GDPR, often leads to
difficulties in the implementation of business applications. Although the GDPR
officially came into force in May 2018, very few companies are now fully in
compliance. In their 2019 report[1], the International Association of Privacy Professionals showed that out of 370 companies studied, fewer than half report
being GDPR-compliant. Moreover, among EU companies, 43% admit they are
only "moderately compliant", while naming GDPR compliance as top priority. In addition, Big Data introduces new challenges for companies, in terms

---

[1] https://iapp.org/resources/article/iapp-ey-annual-governance-report-2019/.

Supported and funded by the Walloon region, Belgium.

© Springer Nature Switzerland AG 2020
G. Dobbie et al. (Eds.): ER 2020, LNCS 12400, pp. 429–438, 2020.
https://doi.org/10.1007/978-3-030-62522-1_32

of management of data ingestion in real time, and access management for the datasets obtained with different contracts (web policies, data processing agreements, etc.). Pending a commonly accepted implementation of privacy by design, many companies opt for paper and manual procedures.

Meanwhile, contracts and policies written in natural language enclose the regulations of personal data processing from different perspectives – Data Subject, Data Controller, Data Processor. These documents mainly consist of deontic statements – permissions, prohibitions and obligations, which can be translated manually into business rules by domain experts. The goal of this paper is to facilitate automation of this process by proposing a conceptual model for privacy policies and data processing agreements (DPAs). The intention is to model the "operational" parts of the documents, i.e. the deontic rules that can support automated compliance checking and be transformed into access control rules over data. To this end, we focus on the rules from the perspective of a Controller or a Processor that cover the processing (collection, transfer, etc.) of personal data.

This work is developed within the ASGARD project and its RUNE track, whose objective is the automation of privacy by design. The main contribution is the proposed conceptual model – SAVE (Semantic dAta priVacy modEl), tailored to privacy policies and DPAs. SAVE combines deontic concepts with diverse taxonomy of data processing terms, by utilizing the principles of ontology reuse, avoiding reinventing the concepts and facilitating semantic interoperability. Further down the road, the conceptual model, as a part of the final privacy-by-design system, will be used to (i) check the compliance of data processing requests against policies; (ii) generate access control rules over datasets; (iii) represent written documents through NLP means; (iv) generate templates for NL policies from the model instances.

The paper is structured as follows: in Sect. 2 we discuss the state of the art in privacy models. Section 3 describes SAVE and the process of its synthesis. Next, we outline the usage of SAVE and its general aspects in Sect. 4. Finally, Sect. 5 concludes our paper, lays out work in progress and future plans.

2   Related Work

Although numerous works have been emerging in the area of privacy modeling, to this moment, no universally accepted model for privacy policies and contracts exists that is adopted by the industry. Multiple solutions have been proposed by exploring different aspects of privacy by design, and have been released as annotated datasets [20], UML models [2,4,18], and Semantic Web resources [1,5–14,19]. In this Section we compare existing privacy policy and/or GDPR-related models, based on the set of criteria relevant in our context. Table 1 contains the results of the analysis. The values are +, − or +/− for partial match of the criterion, unless stated otherwise. The following paragraphs detail our criteria and drawn conclusions.

GDPR Awareness. We operate in the context of lawful personal data processing, defined by the GDPR. Therefore, we assess to which extent each model acknowledges GDPR and if it contains relevant concepts, e.g., legal basis. Partial match indicates the models considering pre-GDPR [4,8] directives. Our analysis shows that not all latest privacy related research is GDPR-aware: some models are legislation-agnostic [3], even if they mention the regulation [9].

Privacy Policy (PP) Concepts. Here we include terms occurring in privacy policies related to personal data processing, such as personal data types, processing actions, purposes, participants, etc. The level of granularity is essential, as some models only contain the top-level concepts [2–5,8,10–13] or miss some categories [9,20], and are not capable of describing the rich set of rules expressed by the policies. Such works are marked as a partial match.

Deontic Concepts. Privacy policies and DPAs contain permissions, prohibitions, and obligations, regulating the processing of personal data. Deontic concepts are, therefore, necessary for representing them. Generally, though, privacy models focus mostly on permissions [7] or obligations [4,11]. Based on our analysis, models offering deontic concepts come from the Semantic Web field [1,10,19].

Interoperability/Reusability. It is crucial for the adoption of privacy by design that the conceptual models are agreed upon, reusable and represented in an interoperable format. Partial match concerns models in well structured and flexible formats (e.g., UML [2,4], UML/OCL [18]), or even in multiple formats [3], but still less (semantically) interoperable than Semantic Web solutions. Models that are not available publicly [1,9,10] are also marked as partial match.

Annotated Data. Since we plan to use our model for semi-automatic translation of privacy policies and DPAs, we started our search with available corpora. It appears that annotated data is not a priority for privacy systems, as they assume that the policies are expressed in their proposed model/language. In fact, OPP-115 [20] is practically the only commonly used annotated privacy policy corpus.

Specification Maturity Level. Here we mainly talk about Semantic Web models. The most mature ones, become, for example, a W3C Recommendation, like ODRL. Nevertheless, we admit that this process is lengthy, and lately published resources can stay in the state of a draft for some time, and that should not prevent the researchers from adopting them. The rest of the works we marked as not-applicable, including unavailable Semantic Web resources [1,6,9,10].

Reasoning/Compliance Checking. In this criterion we highlight the models that allow for or implement compliance checking [5,10]. Our comparison shows that most of the models are descriptive, and while some provide partial query or questionnaire based reasoning [1,9,12] or define compliance conceptually [4,8], they still require a lot of additional effort for automated compliance checking.

3   Model

In the process of creating SAVE, we followed the guidelines of the NeOn methodology [16]. In particular, "reusing and merging ontological resources" scenario was used in the initial model design, and future work on SAVE will go according to "reusing, merging and re-engineering ontological resources" scenario, as we improve our model to fit the objectives of the downstream applications. The methodology prescribes a set of activities to be performed in order to arrive at the final "ontology network". For our scenario, they are ontology search, assessment, comparison, selection, aligning and merging [16]. The first three steps were performed along with the study of the state of the art (see Table 1). The remaining three activities are described in this Section.

Table 1. Related work comparison

Models/ Criteria	GDPR Aware	PP Concepts	Deontic Concepts	Inter-operability/ Reusability	Annotated Data	Specification Maturity Level	Reasoning/ Compliance Checking
ODRL [19]	−	−	+	+	−	W3C Rec	−
Korba and Kenny [8]	+/−	+/−	+/−	+/−	−	N/A	+/−
Coen-Porisini et al. [4]	+/−	+/−	+/−	+/−	−	N/A	+/−
Caramujo and da Silva [2]	−	+/−	−	+/−	−	N/A	−
OPP-115 [20]	−	+/−	−	−	+	N/A	−
Tom et al. [17]	+	+/−	−	+/−	−	N/A	+/−
GDPRtEXT [11] GDPRov [12]	+	+/−	+/−	+	−	Draft	+/−
ODP Pandit et al. [13]	+	+/−	−	+	−	Draft	−
PrivOnto [9]	−	+/−	−	+/−	+	N/A	+/−
PrOnto [10]	+	+/−	+	+/−	−	N/A	+
Agarwal et al. [1]	+	−	+	+/−	−	N/A	+/−
RSL-IL4Privacy [3]	−	+/−	+	+/−	−	N/A	+
Torre et al. [18]	+	+	+/−	+/−	−	N/A	−
Joshi and Banerjee [6]	+	+	+/−	+	−	N/A	+
ORCP (ODRL) [5]	+	+/−	+	+	−	**Draft**	+
DPV [14]	+	+	−	+	−	**Draft**	−
SPECIAL [7]	+	+	+/−	+	−	Draft	+

3.1   Model Selection

In creating our conceptual model, we targeted existing solutions that can be reused, merged and re-purposed for expressing privacy policies and DPAs, and potentially allow for compliance checking in downstream applications. The comparative analysis has brought us to the following two models.

ORCP. Upon inspection of the state of the art, we concluded that ODRL [19] model suits our needs the best[2], and recently proposed ORCP profile [5] has already taken a step forward to GDPR-aware policies. Full description of the profile can be found in ORCP documentation[3], here we only recall relevant changes introduced to ODRL by ORCP:

- New `Rule` subclasses: `Obligation` and `Dispensation`. Additionally, rules can be nested, e.g., a `Prohibition` related to a `Permission`.
- New `Purpose` class with `purpose` property, connecting a `Rule` to its purpose.
- `LegalBasis` class and `legalBasis` property, in the domain of `Rule`. The class is further specialized with possible legal basis values.
- ODRL's `Party` class was enriched with subclasses encoding GDPR-related roles, e.g., `Controller` and `Processor`, with respective properties.
- ODRL's `Asset` class was replaced with `Resource` class.

ORCP was designed for modeling GDPR articles relevant for compliance checking of business requests. While this use case is correlated with our context, modeling privacy policies and DPAs requires specialization of the concepts that goes beyond general statements of the GDPR. For instance, privacy policies often mention precise personal data types, e.g., "email address", when describing their rules, as opposed to the general `PersonalData` class introduced in ORCP.

DPV. To specialize ODRL/ORCP we chose Data Privacy Vocabulary (DPV)[4] [14], released by Data Privacy Vocabularies and Controls Community Group[5]. DPV contains dedicated vocabularies, describing privacy and data concepts appearing in privacy policies. Each of these vocabularies is a taxonomy covering a broad range of classes, that were synthesized from different sources and approved by the group members. `PersonalDataHandling` class representing a particular operation on personal data is connected to the top-level classes, including:

- `PersonalDataCategory` – the data types mentioned in policies.
- `Purpose` – purposes of personal data processing.
- `Processing` – actions performed on data.
- `LegalBasis` – legal bases for processing. DPVCG released a separate vocabulary with GDPR classification of legal bases[6], which SAVE also adopted.

---

[2] PrOnto [10] has been the main candidate from the start for its reasoning capabilities, however, the ontology is not publicly available and cannot be reused.
[3] https://ai.wu.ac.at/policies/orcp/regulatory-model.html.
[4] https://www.w3.org/ns/dpv.
[5] https://www.w3.org/community/dpvcg/.
[6] https://www.w3.org/ns/dpv-gdpr.

- **DataController**, **DataSubject**, and **Recipient** – roles involved in personal data processing.
- **TechnicalOrganisationalMeasure** – measures that need to be implemented for lawful handling of personal data.

3.2   Alignment

After the resource selection stage is completed, we proceed with ontology alignment. Considering that in SAVE we wish to keep core functional components of ODRL model, namely policies and deontic rules, we identified "anchor points" – concepts in ORCP that can be mapped to the corresponding concepts in DPV. Next, the relationships between the mapped concepts were defined. We use `owl:equivalentClass` to connect classes that express the same concept, and `rdfs:subClassOf` to define an "is-a" relationship. For properties, we redefine the domain or range, or express an "is-a" connection with `rdfs:subPropertyOf`. The resulting alignments are depicted in Table 2. For the most anchor concepts in ORCP (rows 1–4), the "attachment" of DPV concepts brought a great deal of detail in the form of consolidated class hierarchies of terms. In case of legal bases (rows 5–10), which in DPV are defined by the GDPR articles, and are more free-form in ORCP, we identified separately the DPV legal bases that describe exactly or specialize the ORCP ones, and the remaining articles are handled implicitly by the alignment between the parent concepts (row 4). Participants of the data processing (rows 11–13), which belong to different top-level classes in DPV, were mapped to `orcp:Party` in order to be connected to `orcp:Rule`. DPV's `TechnicalOrganisationalMeasure` does not seem to have a matching concept in ORCP, therefore we attach it to the `orcp:Rule` concept through `dpv:hasTechnicalOrganisationalMeasure` property (row 14). Technical and organizational measures are often mentioned in obligations and constraints, and therefore their inclusion adds more expressiveness to our model. Finally, the property for a Data Subject party was added to SAVE from DPV (row 15).

3.3   Merging

In the next phase, we use the alignments above to merge the ontologies: each two equivalent classes are merged into one, the specializations (`rdfs:supClassOf`, `rdfs:subPropertyOf`) stay unchanged. The resulting conceptual model is encoded as an ODRL profile, with the specification document[7], as well as the ontology[8], publicly available. From merging two selected models, SAVE inherited the advantages of both and gained the power to represent privacy policies and DPAs in a fine-grained and functional manner, while supporting semantic interoperability. An extensive use-case demonstrating the instances of the model extracted from a privacy policy is available online[9], with more examples from a DPA presented in the specification.

---

[7] http://rune.research.euranova.eu/.

[8] http://rune.research.euranova.eu/save.ttl.

[9] http://rune.research.euranova.eu/demo/Policy.html.

4   Discussion

The aim of developing SAVE is to facilitate the automation of GDPR compliance through policies and access control regarding personal data. So far we have presented the model, which describes to the maximum level of detail the conditions of personal data handling. In this Section we discuss the quality of the model, remaining steps to its validation and outline the plans for its usage.

The rules we produce with SAVE will allow us to obtain concrete access control rules for data at different levels of granularity (e.g., a table or a column). And in order to be able to use the model fully, the rules from one document need to be combined into an ODRL `Policy`. Clearly, possible ambiguities in the policies' language can lead to incorrect representations, causing conflicts between rules, that can be further complicated by the hierarchical relationships between concepts in DPV. In simple cases, the native ODRL mechanism of conflict resolution can be applied. And for conflicts that cannot be solved by a single ODRL strategy, new conflict resolution methods need to be devised by the downstream applications. We are currently starting the implementation of SAVE evaluator, where conflict resolution will be one of the primary features, possibly including post-processing by domain experts for final decisions.

When it comes to reasoning and compliance checking of business requests, we are in the process of developing a tool for validating business requests against policies represented in SAVE. The tool is based on SHACL[10], which has recently become a W3C standard, and started attracting attention as an inference rule

Table 2. Ontology alignments established by SAVE

	DPV/DPV-GDPR concept	Relation	ORCP/ORDL concept
1	PersonalDataCategory	owl:equivalentClass	PersonalData
2	Processing	owl:equivalentClass	Action
3	Purpose	owl:equivalentClass	Purpose
4	LegalBasis	owl:equivalentClass	LegalBasis
5	A6-1-a-explicit-consent A6-1-a-non-explicit-consent A9-2-a	rdfs:subClassOf	Consent
6	A6-1-b	owl:equivalentClass	Contract
7	A6-1-c	owl:equivalentClass	LegalObligation
8	A6-1-d A9-2-c	rdfs:subClassOf	VitalInterest
9	A6-1-f	owl:equivalentClass	LegitimateInterest
10	A6-1-e A9-2-g A9-2-i A9-2-j	rdfs:subClassOf	PublicInterest
11	DataController	owl:equivalentClass	Controller
12	DataProcessor	owl:equivalentClass	Processor
13	DataSubject ThirdParty	rdfs:subClassOf	Party
14	hasTechnicalOrganisationalMeasure	rdfs:domain	Policy or Rule
15	hasDataSubject	rdfs:subPropertyOf	function

---

[10] https://www.w3.org/TR/shacl/.

engine. Using SHACL's advanced features will provide us with means for multi-level compliance checking, constraint validation, as well as conflict detection and resolution. At later stages, the regulations extracted by [5] from GDPR can be viewed as a top level of policies, and the compliance can be verified in the chain of GDPR policies/written policies/business requests.

Another promising usage of SAVE is automatic generation of written document templates from model instances. Natural language privacy policies will not disappear in the near future, so standardizing their generation from verified and already compliant policy instances will make them more interpretable and clear.

5   Conclusion and Future Work

In this paper we have presented SAVE – Semantic dAta priVacy modEl, that is GDPR-aware, fine-grained and reusable, with potential for semantic inter-operability and automated compliance checking. The model has been built on the principles of ontology reuse and merging [16], thus inheriting the expressive power and functionality of each of its components, and gaining a set of features that is unique and valuable. The proposed model has the potential to represent a wide range of privacy-related agreements, which can be seen from the use-case and examples available online.

SAVE has been created with the final goal of making privacy policies and DPAs functional: starting from semi-automatic parsing of written documents, obtaining their semantic representation, and finally, applying reasoning for inferring access control rules over datasets. Each of these subtasks represents an ongoing track in the ASGARD project. With such diverse functionalities, as a part of a family of interconnected applications, we expect to improve our model and make it industry-ready, in order to support the adoption of privacy by design.

Currently we are working on further validation and evaluation of SAVE. We plan to continue following NeOn guidelines [15] and organize evaluation process in terms of domain coverage, modeling quality and application suitability. Through collaboration with universities in Belgium, we will use assessment by humans as frame of reference, for legal domain is a special area where any automation has to be done under close supervision of domain experts. We will ask the judges to assess our model and the use-case instances in terms of syntactic correctness, accuracy and trust [15]. We expect constant feedback about the model to ensure that we stay on the course of compliance.

On the way to automated parsing of privacy policies, we are working on establishing the mapping between OPP-115 [20] attributes and SAVE concepts, in order to jump-start the extraction of model instances from written policies. With this mapping, and the annotation of missing concepts, we will be able to translate documents into our machine-readable conceptual model, that can be further checked, corrected and approved by domain experts (e.g., DPO of a company). We realize that, inevitably, fully automated translation of legal documents into machine-readable form is prone to inaccuracies, therefore, we work towards a human-in-the-loop system, that can be functional from the start and simultaneously learn from experts in the active learning environment.

Other current and future work directions, all aimed towards the final privacy-by-design system, include (i) designing and implementing conflict resolution strategies for policy construction; (ii) formalizing the rules generated by SAVE in order to perform "access control" inference over them; (iii) expanding the model to include deontic rules concerning Data Subjects' rights and actions, as well as consent handling concepts, which SAVE inherited from DPV, but has not fully incorporated into the model yet; and (iv) automatic generation of NL privacy policies and DPAs from SAVE instances.

References

1. Agarwal, S., Steyskal, S., Antunovic, F., Kirrane, S.: Legislative compliance assessment: framework, model and GDPR instantiation. In: Medina, M., Mitrakas, A., Rannenberg, K., Schweighofer, E., Tsouroulas, N. (eds.) APF 2018. LNCS, vol. 11079, pp. 131–149. Springer, Cham (2018). https://doi.org/10.1007/978-3-030-02547-2_8

2. Caramujo, J., da Silva, A.M.R.: Analyzing privacy policies based on a privacy-aware profile: the Facebook and LinkedIn case studies. In: 2015 IEEE 17th Conference on Business Informatics. IEEE, July 2015. https://doi.org/10.1109/cbi.2015.44

3. Caramujo, J., Rodrigues da Silva, A., Monfared, S., Ribeiro, A., Calado, P., Breaux, T.: RSL-IL4Privacy: a domain-specific language for the rigorous specification of privacy policies. Requir. Eng. 24(1), 1–26 (2018). https://doi.org/10.1007/s00766-018-0305-2

4. Coen-Porisini, A., Colombo, P., Sicari, S.: Privacy aware systems. In: Software Engineering for Secure Systems, pp. 232–259. IGI Global (2011). https://doi.org/10.4018/978-1-61520-837-1.ch009

5. De Vos, M., Kirrane, S., Padget, J., Satoh, K.: ODRL policy modelling and compliance checking. In: Fodor, P., Montali, M., Calvanese, D., Roman, D. (eds.) RuleML+RR 2019. LNCS, vol. 11784, pp. 36–51. Springer, Cham (2019). https://doi.org/10.1007/978-3-030-31095-0_3

6. Joshi, K.P., Banerjee, A.: Automating privacy compliance using policy integrated blockchain. Cryptography 3(1), 7 (2019). https://doi.org/10.3390/cryptography3010007

7. Kirrane, S., Fernández, J.D., Bonatti, P.A., Milosevic, U., Polleres, A., Wenning, R.: The SPECIAL-K personal data processing transparency and compliance platform. CoRR abs/2001.09461 (2020). https://arxiv.org/abs/2001.09461

8. Korba, L., Kenny, S.: Towards meeting the privacy challenge: adapting DRM. In: Feigenbaum, J. (ed.) DRM 2002. LNCS, vol. 2696, pp. 118–136. Springer, Heidelberg (2003). https://doi.org/10.1007/978-3-540-44993-5_8

9. Oltramari, A., et al.: PrivOnto: a semantic framework for the analysis of privacy policies. Semant. Web 9(2), 185–203 (2018). https://doi.org/10.3233/sw-170283

10. Palmirani, M., Martoni, M., Rossi, A., Bartolini, C., Robaldo, L.: PrOnto: privacy ontology for legal reasoning. In: Kő, A., Francesconi, E. (eds.) EGOVIS 2018. LNCS, vol. 11032, pp. 139–152. Springer, Cham (2018). https://doi.org/10.1007/978-3-319-98349-3_11

11. Pandit, H.J., Fatema, K., O'Sullivan, D., Lewis, D.: GDPRtEXT - GDPR as a linked data resource. In: Gangemi, A., et al. (eds.) ESWC 2018. LNCS, vol. 10843, pp. 481–495. Springer, Cham (2018). https://doi.org/10.1007/978-3-319-93417-4_31

12. Pandit, H.J., Lewis, D.: Modelling provenance for GDPR compliance using linked open data vocabularies. In: Proceedings of the 5th Workshop on Society, Privacy and the Semantic Web - Policy and Technology (PrivOn2017) Co-located with 16th International Semantic Web Conference, ISWC 2017, Vienna, Austria, 22 October 2017. CEUR Workshop Proceedings, vol. 1951. CEUR-WS.org (2017). http://ceur-ws.org/Vol-1951/PrivOn2017_paper_6.pdf

13. Pandit, H.J., O'Sullivan, D., Lewis, D.: An ontology design pattern for describing personal data in privacy policies. In: Proceedings of the 9th Workshop on Ontology Design and Patterns (WOP 2018) Co-located with 17th International Semantic Web Conference, ISWC 2018, Monterey, USA, 9th October 2018. CEUR Workshop Proceedings, vol. 2195, pp. 29–39. CEUR-WS.org (2018). http://ceur-ws.org/Vol-2195/pattern_paper_3.pdf

14. Pandit, H.J., et al.: Creating a vocabulary for data privacy. In: Panetto, H., Debruyne, C., Hepp, M., Lewis, D., Ardagna, C.A., Meersman, R. (eds.) OTM 2019. LNCS, vol. 11877, pp. 714–730. Springer, Cham (2019). https://doi.org/10.1007/978-3-030-33246-4_44

15. Sabou, M., Fernandez, M.: Ontology (network) evaluation. In: Suárez-Figueroa, M.C., Gómez-Pérez, A., Motta, E., Gangemi, A. (eds.) Ontology Engineering in a Networked World, pp. 193–212. Springer, Heidelberg (2012). https://doi.org/10.1007/978-3-642-24794-1_9

16. Suárez-Figueroa, M.C., Gómez-Pérez, A., Fernández-López, M.: The NeOn methodology for ontology engineering. In: Suárez-Figueroa, M.C., Gómez-Pérez, A., Motta, E., Gangemi, A. (eds.) Ontology Engineering in a Networked World, pp. 9–34. Springer, Heidelberg (2012). https://doi.org/10.1007/978-3-642-24794-1_2

17. Tom, J., Sing, E., Matulevičius, R.: Conceptual representation of the GDPR: model and application directions. In: Zdravkovic, J., Grabis, J., Nurcan, S., Stirna, J. (eds.) BIR 2018. LNBIP, vol. 330, pp. 18–28. Springer, Cham (2018). https://doi.org/10.1007/978-3-319-99951-7_2

18. Torre, D., Soltana, G., Sabetzadeh, M., Briand, L.C., Auffinger, Y., Goes, P.: Using models to enable compliance checking against the GDPR: an experience report. In: 2019 ACM/IEEE 22nd International Conference on Model Driven Engineering Languages and Systems (MODELS). IEEE, September 2019. https://doi.org/10.1109/models.2019.00-20

19. W3C ODRL Community Group: ODRL information model 2.2 (2018). https://www.w3.org/TR/odrl-model/

20. Wilson, S., et al.: The creation and analysis of a website privacy policy corpus. In: Proceedings of the 54th Annual Meeting of the Association for Computational Linguistics (Volume 1: Long Papers). Association for Computational Linguistics (2016). https://doi.org/10.18653/v1/p16-1126

Schema Design, Evolution, NoSQL

An Empirical Study on the Design and Evolution of NoSQL Database Schemas

Stefanie Scherzinger[1]($\boxtimes$) and Sebastian Sidortschuck[2]

[1] Universität Passau, Passau, Germany
stefanie.scherzinger@uni-passau.de
[2] SPARETECH.io, Stuttgart, Germany
sebastian.sidortschuck@sparetech.io

Abstract. We study how software engineers design and evolve their domain model when building applications against NoSQL data stores. Specifically, we target Java projects that use object-NoSQL mappers to interface with schema-free NoSQL data stores. This is a popular software stack. Given the source code of ten real-world database applications, we extract the NoSQL database schema thus implied in the application code. We can confirm that schemas are generally denormalized, as is recommended practice in data modeling for NoSQL data stores. Further, we analyze the entire project history, and with it, the evolution history of the NoSQL database schema. We show that NoSQL schemas evolve in all analyzed projects, and observe a comparatively high frequency in schema changes. In doing so, we conduct the so far largest empirical study on NoSQL schema design and evolution.

Keywords: Schema evolution · NoSQL Databases · Empirical study

1 Introduction

Schema-flexible NoSQL data stores are popular backends for database applications. In particular, data stores like MongoDB allow for flexible changes to the domain model during agile application development.

Even though such data stores do not enforce a global schema, the application code generally assumes that persisted entities adhere to a certain (if loose) database schema. Given that schema-flexibility is one of the major selling points of NoSQL data stores, this raises the question how this implied *NoSQL database schema* evolves in real-world projects.

In this paper, we study the dynamics of NoSQL database schema evolution. Our study is in the tradition of well-received studies on relational schema evolution, e.g. [6,12,14,17,19,25], which have allowed invaluable insights for researchers working in this field: Knowing the frequency with which the schema evolves, and which changes are actually common, is the absolute prerequisite for crafting solutions that can have practical impact. After all, schema evolution is

© Springer Nature Switzerland AG 2020
G. Dobbie et al. (Eds.): ER 2020, LNCS 12400, pp. 441–455, 2020.
https://doi.org/10.1007/978-3-030-62522-1_33

still considered one of the grand challenges in data management research [20], despite decades of research in this area. To our knowledge, ours is the most ambitious and encompassing study in the domain of NoSQL data stores so far, comprising ten open source applications.

So far, little is known about NoSQL schema evolution that is based on systematic, empirical study (versus anecdotal evidence): Earlier studies have had a different focus (such as specific features of object-NoSQL mapper libraries [15]), or perform data flow analysis in the application code of a single application to detect schema changes (c.f. [13]).

In this paper, we focus on the software stack shown in Fig. 1a, namely Java applications that use an object-NoSQL mapper to store data in either Google Cloud Datastore[1] or MongoDB[2], both popular and mature data stores.

Contributions. In particular, our paper makes the following contributions:

- We analyze the ten projects with the largest NoSQL database schemas among over 1.2K candidate projects on GitHub, and perform static code analysis over their commit history.
- We formulate three central research questions, namely (RQ1) whether the NoSQL database schema is *denormalized* (the recommended practice throughout the literature for NoSQL practitioners), (RQ2) which *growth in complexity* we can observe in NoSQL database schemas over the project development time, and (RQ3) *how* the schema evolves, identifying the common changes.
- We discuss our findings w.r.t. related studies on relational schema evolution, in particular the study by Qiu et al. [14]. We observe that the frequency of schema changes is comparatively high. We are further able to show evidence of evolutionary changes to the NoSQL database schema in all analyzed projects. In particular, property type changes seem to play a smaller role in NoSQL schema evolution when compared to relational schema evolution.

Structure. We introduce the preliminaries in Sect. 2. In Sect. 3, we describe our methodology, and state our research questions. In Sect. 4, we present the results of our study, which we then discuss in Sect. 5. We point out threats to the validity of our results in Sect. 6, and give an overview over related work in Sect. 7. We conclude with an outlook on future work.

2   Preliminaries

Physical Entities. We consider two popular NoSQL data stores: Google Cloud Datastore (called Datastore hereafter) is commercial and hosted on the Google Cloud Platform, MongoDB is open source. Both data stores are schema-free

---

[1] https://cloud.google.com/datastore/, available since 2009.
[2] https://www.mongodb.com/, available since 2019.

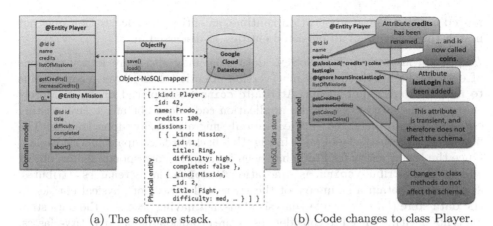

(a) The software stack.   (b) Code changes to class Player.

Fig. 1. (a) The object-NoSQL mapper separates the domain model from the NoSQL data store (adapted from [7]). (b) Not all code changes are actually schema-relevant.

(however, MongoDB offers *optional* schema validation). Both manage document-like data, which we refer to as the (physical) *entities*. On an abstract level, an entity is a collection of key-value pairs, or *properties*. Entities may be nested and properties may be multi-valued. We sketch a Datastore entity representing a player and his or her missions in a role playing game in Fig. 1a, in (simplified) JSON notation, to abstract away from system-proprietary storage formats.

Domain Models. In principle, each entity in a schema-free data store may have its very own, unique structure. However, in database applications, it is safe to assume that the software engineers have agreed on some *domain model*, as sketched in Fig. 1a. In our setting, the domain model is captured by Java class declarations, yet in the figure, we use the more compact UML notation. (For now, we ignore the @-labeled annotations.) Class Player declares attributes for an identifier, a name, an amount of credits, and a list of missions. Each mission also has an identifier, a title, a level of difficulty, and tracks its completion.

Object-NoSQL Mappers. Object mappers are state-of-the-art in building database applications [7]. Like object-relational mappers, the object-NoSQL mappers Objectify[3] and Morphia[4] map Java objects to entities. Objectify is tied to Datastore, and Morphia to MongoDB. With object-NoSQL mappers, developers merely specify their domain model as Java classes that are annotated with the keyword @Entity. Each *entity-class* has a unique key (annotated with @Id). The object mapper provides methods for saving and loading: In Fig. 1a, the class name and the identifying attribute are mapped to the designated properties _kind and _id. Objectify maps a player's list of missions to an array of

---

[3] https://github.com/objectify/objectify.
[4] https://github.com/MorphiaOrg/morphia.

nested entities. Yet at application runtime, an entity-class declaration may not match the structure of all persisted entities, as discussed next.

Lazy Data Migration. The NoSQL data store may also store legacy versions of entities. Figure 1b shows a new version of entity-class Player, changed due to new software requirements. Attribute `coins` has replaced `credits`. Merely changing the entity-class in the application code does not affect any existing entities. Instead, persisted entities are only migrated lazily, upon loading: The new version of entity-class Player in Fig. 1b is backwards-compatible with Fig. 1a. Once the legacy entity for Frodo has been loaded, the corresponding Java object will have an attribute `coins`, as annotation `@AlsoLoad` lazily renames attributes.

Thus, to obtain a summary of the structural variety of physical entities in the data store (based on code analysis alone, not having access to the data store contents itself), we need to consider the entire evolution history of entity-classes.

NoSQL Database Schema Evolution. We base our notion of the *NoSQL database schema* (or shorter, *NoSQL schema*) on the domain model. This idea of treating entity-classes as schema declarations is re-current in literature, c.f. [5,16]. Note that not all Java attributes are relevant for the NoSQL database schema: Attributes that are transient, e.g., carrying Objectify annotation `@Ignore`, are not schema-relevant: The value of `hoursSinceLastLogin` in Fig. 1b is not persisted (it may be derived from `lastLogin`). Also, class methods are not schema-relevant. Thus, code changes that only affect transient attributes or class methods are part of software evolution, but not of schema evolution. Therefore, they are not considered *schema changes* in this work.

Denormalized Entity-Classes. The recommendation in working with Datastore and MongoDB is to denormalize the schema.[5] This can be done by either nesting entities, or by using multi-valued properties, such as the array of `Missions` in Fig. 4. There are various motivations for denormalization, one being that traditionally, the query languages do not provide a join operator (such is still the case in Google Cloud Datastore, and this also used to be the case for MongoDB), so join results are materialized in the data store. Other reasons are limited (or no) support of referential integrity constraints, as well as limited support of transactional updates.

In the following, we say an entity-class is denormalized if it does not declare flat, relational-style tuples in first normal form, i.e., with atomic attribute values only. So unless all schema-relevant attributes have Java primitive types (such as `Integer`, `String`, `Boolean`, ...), we say the entity-class is denormalized. As we discuss in Sect. 3.3, this is a conservative yet practical approach. As an example, the entity-class declaration for players, sketched in Fig. 1, is considered denormalized, due to the multi-valued attribute `listOfMissions`.

---

[5] E.g., "6 Rules of Thumb for MongoDB Schema Design" at https://www.mongodb. com/blog/post/6-rules-of-thumb-for-mongodb-schema-design-part-2, June 2015.

3   Methodology

3.1   Context

We used BigQuery[6] to identify relevant open source repositories on GitHub, as of September 4th, 2018. We consider a repository (which we synonymously refer to as a project) relevant if it contains Java import statements for Objectify or Morphia. We cloned over 1.2K candidate repositories and excluded any repositories that (1) have fewer than 20 commits (to exclude tinker projects), (2) are the Morphia or Objectify source code (or forks thereof), (3) or are flagged as forks from repositories already covered, with no schema-relevant code changes after the fork. We analyze the project history using `git log`[7], and parse and aggregate the log output using Python scripts.

Among all projects analyzed, we determined the maximum number of entity-classes throughout the project history, and settled on the top-5 projects for Objectify and Morphia. Table 1 lists these projects with their life cycles up to the latest commit at the time of our analysis. (The name of the third Morphia-based project is abbreviated from "NoSQLDataEngineering"). We also state the total number of commits at the time (**#C**). We state the minimum and maximum number of entity-classes in the project history (**#ECs**), as well as the number of entity-classes added and removed over time (**#ECs+/−**). We further state the number of lines of code between the first and last analyzed commit (**LoC**, measured with `cloc`[8] and reported in thousands).

Table 1. Characteristics of the studied NoSQL database applications.

	Project	Life Cycle	#C	#ECs	#ECs+/−	LoC (K)
Objectify	Cryptonomica/cryptonomica	04/16–09/18	185	0–29	+30/−1	0–526
	FraunhoferCESE/madcap	12/14–03/18	853	0–82	+94/−51	0–17
	google/nomulus	03/16–09/18	2,025	51–55	+112/−61	138–224
	nareshPokhriyal86/testing	01/15–02/15	25	0–79	+79/−0	0–449
	Nekorp/Tikal-Technology	04/15–11/15	59	0–43	+44/−1	0–49
Morphia	altiplanogao/tallyframework	06/15–06/16	167	0–24	+59/−44	0–5
	bujilvxing/QinShihuang	10/16–12/16	154	0–36	+38/−2	0–21
	catedrasaes-umu/NoSQLD.E.	11/16–09/18	711	0–28	+125/−103	0–280
	GBPeters/PubInt	10/16–02/18	69	0–27	+37/−10	0–5
	MKLab-ITI/simmo	07/14–02/17	142	0–51	+78/−29	0–5

---

[6] Google BigQuery is a commercial cloud service. This data warehousing tool allows for querying the GitHub open data collection, mostly non-forked projects with an open source license: https://cloud.google.com/bigquery/.

[7] The exact command pattern for reproducability: `git log --before=2018-09-04T00:00:00 --cherry-pick --date-order --pretty=format: ''%H;%aI;%cI;%P''`.

[8] https://github.com/AlDanial/cloc (Version 1.74).

3.2   Research Questions

RQ1: Are NoSQL schemas denormalized? We perform static code analysis on entity-class declarations.

RQ2: What is the growth in complexity of the NoSQL schema? We capture schema complexity based on metrics recognized in literature.

RQ3: How does the NoSQL schema evolve? We classify evolutionary changes to the NoSQL schema.

3.3   Analysis Process

Locating Entity-Classes. We replay the commit histories and use the Java parser QDox[9] to parse class declarations. We identify entity-classes by the object mapper annotation @Entity, which may also be inherited.

Denormalization. To determine whether an entity-class is denormalized, we parse its Java declaration. We analyze the types of the schema-relevant attributes. Unless all have primitive types (such as Integer, String, or Boolean), we assume that the entity-class is denormalized. In most cases, we correctly recognize denormalization: (1) if the entity-class declaration contains container classes (e.g., a Java Collection), and therefore an attribute is multi-valued. (2) Equally, the entity-class may contain nested entity-classes, giving it a hierarchical structure.

However, there are also cases where this approach is a conservative simplification, and we might falsely categorize an entity-class as denormalized: an attribute type may be declared in a third-party library, which is inaccessible to us (see also our discussion in Sect. 6). Also, an attribute type may be a custom type that the developers declared. To realize that a custom type is just a wrapper for a basic Java type, we would have to run more involved code analysis. Note that underlying this problem are the *inherent* limitations of static code analysis. *Identifying Schema Changes.* We identify commits with schema-relevant changes by comparing succeeding versions of the application source code: We register when (1) a new entity-class is added or an entity-class is removed, (2) a schema-relevant attribute is added or removed, and (3) changes to schema-relevant attributes, such as to their type, default initialization, or even object mapper annotations. We only focus on changes which we can recognize programmatically. Recognizing renaming or splitting an entity-class, or renaming an attribute, are instances of schema matching and mapping [2], and cannot be fully automated.

4   Results of the Study

4.1   RQ1: Are NoSQL Schemas Denormalized?

We analyze the entity-class declarations in their most current version w.r.t. denormalization. The results are visualized in Fig. 2. For each analyzed project,

---

[9] https://github.com/paul-hammant/qdox (Version 2.0-M9).

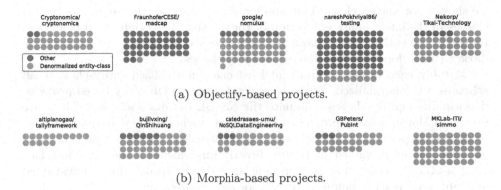

(a) Objectify-based projects.

(b) Morphia-based projects.

Fig. 2. Visualization of denormalized NoSQL database schemas. (Color figure online)

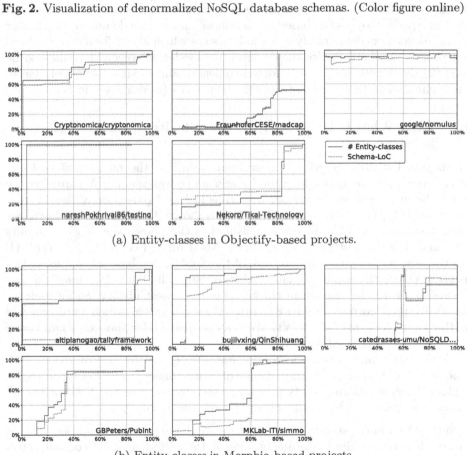

(a) Entity-classes in Objectify-based projects.

(b) Entity-classes in Morphia-based projects.

Fig. 3. Evolution trend. Horizontal axes: Project progress, in percentage of commits analyzed. Vertical axes: Complexity of the schema w.r.t. the maximum for two metrics. (Visualization modeled after [14]).

we show a dot matrix chart. The number of dots matches the number of entity-classes in the latest analyzed version of the schema. The brighter (orange) dots represent the entity-class declarations which we recognize as denormalized. The darker (blue) dots represent the other entity-classes.

Notably, each project contains at least one denormalized entity-class, so all schemas are denormalized. With the exception of two Objectify-based projects, denormalized entity-classes dominate the NoSQL database schemas. There are even two Morphia-based projects where all entity-classes are denormalized.

Closer inspection of the denormalized entity-classes reveals that 20% have at least one multi-valued attribute directly implementing the Java interface Collections. While this is a rough analysis, it seems that multi-valued attributes are not the dominant driver for denormalization.

Results. We find that each project has denormalized entity-classes. However, without qualitative studies based on developer surveys, we do not know whether (1) the developers deliberately chose a data store which allows for a denormalized schema, as this better suits their conceptual model. However, it could also be that (2) developers are actually forced to denormalize their data model, due to the technological limitations of NoSQL data stores (as discussed in Sect. 2).

4.2 RQ2: What is the Growth in Complexity of the NoSQL Schema?

In empirical studies on relational schema evolution, the number of tables is considered a simple approximation for schema complexity [9]. Accordingly, we track the number of entity-classes over time in Fig. 3 (based on a visualization idea from [14]). For each project, one chart is shown. On the horizontal axis, we track the progress of the project, measured as the percentage of git commits analyzed. For the madcap project, this is based on 853 commits (c.f. Table 1). On the vertical axis, we track the size of the NoSQL database schema using two metrics. One is the number of entity-classes (blue solid line). This metric is also normalized w.r.t. its maximum throughout the project history. So for madcap, the 100% peak corresponds to 82 entity-classes, some of which were removed in the later phase of the project. We refer to Table 1 for the exact number of entity-classes added and removed.

The second line denotes a "proxy metric" [9] for the size of the NoSQL schema, where we count the lines of code of entity-classes (including superclasses, excluding comments and empty lines), and thereby compute the *Schema-LoC*.[10] There is shrinkage, yet overall, schema complexity increases.

Results. 1) As in the study by Qiu et al. on relational software evolution [14], we can confirm that while the projects differ in their life-spans and commit activ-

---

[10] In our context, this proxy-metric is preferable to counting (schema-relevant) attributes: In static code analysis, abstract container classes and polymorphism make it impossible to know the types of nested attributes at compile time. With Schema-LoC, we are able to abstract from this issue, and entity-classes with more schema-relevant attributes have more lines of code accordingly.

ity, in nearly all projects, the NoSQL schema grows over time. However, there are phases of refactoring, causing dips. **2)** Apparently, Schema-LoC lends itself nicely as a proxy-metric, and we obtain high correlation coefficients when comparing to the number of entity-classes. As Schema-LoC depends on the number of attributes in an entity-class, we can retrace an effect reported in [14], namely that entity-classes and their attributes (corresponding to tables and columns) have largely analogous dynamics. **3)** In general, the schema grows more than it shrinks. This is in line with studies on relational schema evolution. **4)** One observation in [14] was that the schema stabilizes early: There, for 7 out of 10 projects, 60% of the maximum number of tables is reached in the first 20% of the commits. Interestingly, in our study, the number of entity-classes reaches the 60% in only 4 projects. **5)** In [14], less than 2% of all commits contain valid schema changes (across all ten projects analyzed there). In our study, the share of commits with schema-relevant changes is between 2.8% and over 30%, with 4 projects reaching over 20%. Clearly, we observe higher schema churn rates.

4.3   RQ3: How Does the NoSQL Schema Evolve?

In Fig. 4, we capture the distribution of schema changes according to the kind of change, broken down by project. From left to right, we visualize entity-classes added and removed, and further, schema-relevant attributes added, removed, or changed otherwise. Note that when a new entity-class is added, we do *not* count this as adding its attributes at the same time.

Notably, the distributions are project specific. We discuss two projects that stand out. In the fourth Objectify-based project, adding an entity-class makes up for nearly all changes. Considering the project characteristics in Table 1 reveals that this project is an outlier in several regards: With only 25 commits, it has barely made the bar for being considered in our analysis (see Sect. 3.1). At the same time, this project holds the second largest number of entity-classes in any project considered in this analysis. With a life cycle of two months, this project was in a very early stage of development at the time of this analysis. Possibly, the developers kick start their data model by declaring entity-classes in bulk.

In contrast, the second Morphia-based project stands out as the project with the least share of entity-class additions. Since the `git` commit messages are in Chinese (which the authors of this paper do not master), we find it difficult to retrace the developers' motivation. What is noticeable in Fig. 3b is that while the number of entity-classes increases in less than 10 distinct steps, the proxy metric Schema-LoC changes in more fine-granular steps. Thus, the entity-classes undergo more frequent changes. This matches the distribution plotted, as then the share of entity-class creations is smaller by comparison.

In Fig. 4b, we break down the schema-relevant attribute changes listed in Fig. 4a: **(a)** For some projects, types change. **(b)** For others, the initialization changes. A drill-down reveals that (as may be expected) adding an initial value is the most frequent change, followed by changing the initialization value. **(c)** In other cases, mapper annotations that affect the schema are added or removed. The most frequent annotations added are `@PersistField` and `@Reference`. The

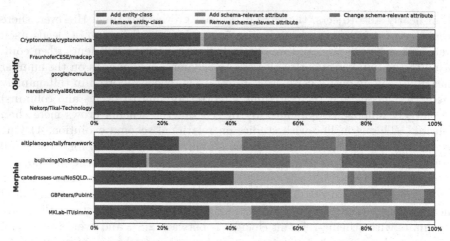

(a) Relative distribution of schema changes, by project.

	Project	Type	Initialization	Annotations
Objectify	Cryptonomica/cryptonomica	2	0	3
	FraunhoferCESE/madcap	9	0	6
	google/nomulus	11	2	58
	nareshPokhriyal86/testing	0	0	0
	Nekorp/Tikal-Technology	0	0	3
Morphia	altiplanogao/tallyframework	7	3	54
	bujilvxing/QinShihuang	32	33	15
	catedrasaes-umu/NoSQLDataEngineering	43	0	13
	GBPeters/PubInt	0	2	2
	MKLab-ITI/simmo	7	5	18

(b) Drill-down into further changes to schema-relevant attributes.

Fig. 4. Distinguishing different schema changes: (a) Relative shares of schema changes by project. (b) Drill-down into changes to schema-relevant attributes (absolute values).

first is from a third-party framework. Since it is schema-relevant, we report it. The second supports referential constraints. Sporadically, third-party annotations are added to declare additional constraints, such as @Min.

Results. **1)** We can confirm the observations from related work on relational schema evolution that schema changes are generally not distributed uniformly [14,24]. **2)** As already observed for RQ2, the trend is that entity-classes are added more frequently than they are removed. We see a similar pattern for schema-relevant attributes, in line with studies on relational schema evolution. Overall, in 9 out of 10 projects, additions collectively account for more than 50% of the changes. In 5 projects, they even account for over 70% of the changes. **3)** While additions are generally more frequent, there are also projects where removals of entity-classes occur to a non-significant degree. Related work [22] on relational schema evolution has shown that there are what the authors call *survivor tables*, which are short-lived. The observation that entity-class removals are very project-specific has also been made in [14]. **4)** Among all annotation changes, only 15 concern referential constraints (annotation @Reference). The authors of two related studies on relational schema evolution, both [14] and [21], have observed that changes concerning referential integrity constraints are also rare in relational schema evolution. With NoSQL data stores, this is to be expected, as referential integrity constraints are not enforced to the same extent. **5)** While Qiu et al. [14] found changes in attribute types to be the number one change for half of the projects analyzed. We do not observe this effect here.

5 Discussion

We can reproduce the main results from related work on relational schema evolution: There is strong evidence of NoSQL schema evolution, and additions are dominant schema changes. However, we do not see the schema stabilizing in the early phases of all projects, which may partly be due to shorter project life spans: The ten projects studied in [14] are PHP applications backed by relational databases, and have longer life cycles (two with ten years), more commits (starting at nearly 5K), and more lines of code. This is to be expected with a more mature software stack. Still, we do suspect that NoSQL developers evolve their schema more continuously. One indicator supporting this hypothesis is that a larger share of the commits contains code changes that affect the schema.

What stands out is that in relational schema evolution, type changes have been found to be among the most frequent schema changes [14,25], and we do not see this effect in NoSQL schema evolution. One conjecture is that in the SQL data definition language (and its many dialects), there is a richer set of types. For instance, character data may be stored as char(n) varchar(n), nvarchar(n), or clob (a listing which is not necessarily exhaustive). In contrast, in Google Cloud Datastore, there are merely the Java types String and Text. Thus, it is plausible that we observe fewer type changes in NoSQL schemas.

The fact that denormalization is common shows that solutions for managing relational schema evolution, involving flat tuples, will not transfer immediately. Rather, when devising frameworks, we may want to turn to related work on frameworks for handling schema evolution in XML (e.g. [8,11]) or object-oriented databases (e.g. [26]) for inspiration on what has shown to be feasible.

6 Threats to Validity

Construct Validity. **(1)** With applications using older versions of Objectify and Morphia, we cannot rely on the @Entity-annotation to identify entity-classes, and further consider the @Id annotation. To be confident that this does not lead to false positives, we performed manual checks. **(2)** In static analysis, we encounter a limitation with attribute types from third-party libraries, and tracking down these libraries is out of scope. Thus, there are attributes that are not fully captured by Schema-LoC. Yet as this is a proxy-metric to start with, we consider this threat acceptable. Further, third-party libraries cause entity-classes to be recognized as denormalized. Having sampled and inspected the entity-class declarations, we are confident that – given the inherent limitations of static code analysis – the risk of false positives is acceptable. (**3**) We treat each single commit as a new version of the schema. There are software development teams that operate by continuous deployment, so tested code is immediately and autonomously deployed to the production environment. There, in theory, each commit containing a schema change also comprises a new schema version. Yet rather often, a release to production comprises more than one commit. Unfortunately, we are not able to tell in static code analysis which commits were released when. There are development teams that tag release commits, but this is not consistent practice across all studied projects. Therefore, we must go by the simplifying assumption that each schema-relevant commit also constitutes a new schema version. (**4**) Our analysis focused on the repositories with the largest schemas, which introduces a certain bias, as it may very well be that smaller schemas show different schema volatility.

External Validity. We next discuss threats in generalizing our results to other software stacks. (**1**) It would be desirable to search additional repositories, and extend to further NoSQL data stores, object mapper libraries, and programming languages. (**2**) Extending our analysis to projects that do not use object-mappers requires a different kind of static code analysis, and was implemented in a related study that involved a single MongoDB project [13]. At the same time, object mappers are state-of-the art in modern application development, and by now, Objectify and Morphia are actually part of official Datastore and MongoDB tutorials (even though they started as independent projects). Thus, we are confident that we analyze a relevant stack. (**3**) There is the fundamental question whether studies on open source projects generalize to commercial projects.

7   Related Work

Database schema evolution is a timeless research area, with various proposals how to systematically manage schema changes. Providing tool support, however, is not the scope of this paper. In the following discussion of related work, we therefore focus on empirical studies on schema evolution in open source projects.

The availability of public code repositories has enabled empirical studies on relational schema evolution [6,12,14,17–19,22,23,25]. Among their key findings, these studies show that the schema evolves. They confirm that adding tables or columns are frequent changes. In these settings, the schema is specified declaratively (usually in SQL). Accordingly, the term *schema modification operations* (SMOs) [6] does not transfer well to our stack: Rather than declarative DDL statements, we need to parse raw Java code: While the authors of [25] also parse application code, they do so to extract declarative SQL statements embedded in code. While the authors in [4] also analyze object mapper class declarations, they target applications backed by a relational database. However, their primary focus is not on analyzing the schema captured by the mapper code, but rather on code changes to improve application performance and security.

So far, there are only few empirical studies on schema evolution in NoSQL data stores. Our work builds on an earlier analysis [15] on the adoption of mapper annotations for lazy schema evolution, which is a different focus. The authors in [13] present an approach for identifying a schema evolution history in MongoDB-based Java applications. Different from us, the authors do not assume that an object-NoSQL mapper is used to access the data store. Rather, they analyze direct calls to the MongoDB API. The schema derived is similar to our notion of the NoSQL schema, since it captures the perspective of the application code. The authors analyze a single open source project, whereas our study has a broader basis, considering ten projects. Different from our intent, their goal is a comprehensive visualization of the schema evolution history.

There is a growing body of work on schema extraction [1,5,10] from large collections of JSON data. While schema extraction is a bottom-up approach, starting from the data, we proceed top-down, analyzing the application code.

8 Conclusion and Outlook

In the history of data management research, empirical studies on schema evolution have always played a crucial role: They provide factual, rather than anecdotal, evidence. For decades, the source code of database applications was difficult to obtain for researchers, yet with the availability of source code repositories such as GitHub, source code analysis has actually turned into an established research area [3]. In this paper, we tie into this tradition and present the first study on NoSQL schema evolution involving ten real-world open source projects. We are able to reproduce many of the insights of related studies on relational schema evolution, but we are also able to point out differences.

Despite our successful findings, interesting questions remain unanswered. We remark on three, starting with (1) the generalizability of our observations to other projects, requiring us to investigate repositories with comparable software stacks (e.g., using the Python MongoDB-mapper library Mongoose). (2) Originally, we set out to compile detailed statistics on the structure of denormalized entity-classes, such as their nesting depth. However, we found that Java code written by experienced developers (e.g., as is the case with Google nomulus) is highly polymorphic, which is problematic in static code analysis. Alternative holistic analysis techniques, such as data flow analysis of the entire application code, as done in [13], might reveal further insights into NoSQL schema evolution. (3) We see evidence that the schema evolves, but we do not know the factors that influence NoSQL schema evolution. This calls for follow-up work, where we take the git commit messages into account, which often convey the reason for a schema change. What is also needed are qualitative studies, surveying developers who routinely deal with NoSQL schema evolution.

Acknowledgements. This project was funded by *Deutsche Forschungsgemeinschaft* (DFG, German Research Foundation) grant #385808805. We thank Wolfgang Mauerer, Uta Störl and Gabriela Tapken for feedback, and Sven Apel for pointing out QDox.

References

1. Baazizi, M.-A., Colazzo, D., Ghelli, G., Sartiani, C.: Parametric schema inference for massive JSON datasets. The VLDB J. **28**(4), 497–521 (2019). https://doi.org/10.1007/s00778-018-0532-7
2. Bellahsene, Z., Bonifati, A., Rahm, E.: Schema Matching and Mapping, 1st edn. Springer, Heidelberg, Incorporated (2011)
3. Bird, C., Menzies, T., Zimmermann, T.: The Art and Science of Analyzing Software Data, 1st edn. Morgan Kaufmann Publishers Inc., San Francisco (2015)
4. Chen, T.H., et al.: An empirical study on the practice of maintaining object-relational mapping code in java systems. In: Proceedings MSR 2016 (2016)
5. Chillón, A.H., Ruiz, D.S., Molina, J.G., Morales, S.F.: A model-driven approach to generate schemas for object-document mappers. In: IEEE Access, vol. 7 (2019)
6. Curino, C.A., Tanca, L., Moon, H.J., Zaniolo, C.: Schema evolution in Wikipedia: toward a web information system benchmark. In: Proceedings ICEIS 2008 (2008)
7. Fowler, M.: Patterns of Enterprise Application Architecture. Addison-Wesley Longman Publishing Co. Inc., Boston (2002)
8. Guerrini, G., Mesiti, M., Sorrenti, M.A.: XML schema evolution: incremental validation and efficient document adaptation. In: Proceedings XSym 2007 (2007)
9. Jain, S., Moritz, D., Howe, B.: High variety cloud databases. In: Proceedings ICDE Workshops 2016 (2016)
10. Klettke, M., Störl, U., Scherzinger, S.: Schema extraction and structural outlier detection for JSON-based NoSQL data stores. In: Proceedings BTW 2015 (2015)
11. Klímek, J., Malý, J., Necaský, M., Holubová, I.: eXolutio: methodology for design and evolution of XML schemas using conceptual modeling. Informatica, Lith. Acad. Sci. **26**(3), 453–472 (2015)
12. Lin, D.Y., Neamtiu, I.: Collateral evolution of applications and databases. In: Proceedings IWPSE-Evol 2009 (2009)
13. Meurice, L., Cleve, A.: Supporting schema evolution in schema-less NoSQL data stores. In: Proceedings SANER 2017 (2017)
14. Qiu, D., Li, B., Su, Z.: An empirical analysis of the co-evolution of schema and code in database applications. In: Proceedings ESEC/FSE 2013 (2013)
15. Ringlstetter, A., Scherzinger, S., Bissyandé, T.F.: Data model evolution using object-NoSQL mappers: folklore or State-of-the-art? In: Proceedings BIGDSE 2016 (2016)
16. Scherzinger, S., Cerqueus, T., Cunha de Almeida, E.: ControVol: a framework for controlled schema evolution in NoSQL application development. In: Proceedings ICDE 2015 (2015)
17. Sjøberg, D.: Quantifying schema evolution. Inf. Software Technol. **35**(1), 35–44 (1993)
18. Skoulis, I., Vassiliadis, P., Zarras, A.V.: Open-source databases: within, outside, or beyond lehman's laws of software evolution? In: Proceedings CAiSE 2014 (2014)
19. Skoulis, I., Vassiliadis, P., Zarras, A.V.: Growing up with stability. Inf. Syst. **53**, 363–385 (2015)
20. Stonebraker, M.: My top ten fears about the DBMS field. In: Proceedings ICDE 2018 (2018)

21. Vassiliadis, P., Kolozoff, M.-R., Zerva, M., Zarras, A.V.: Schema evolution and foreign keys: a study on usage, heartbeat of change and relationship of foreign keys to table activity. Computing **101**(10), 1431–1456 (2019). https://doi.org/10.1007/s00607-019-00702-x

22. Vassiliadis, P., Zarras, A.V.: Survival in schema evolution: putting the lives of survivor and dead tables in counterpoint. In: Dubois, E., Pohl, K. (eds.) CAiSE 2017. LNCS, vol. 10253, pp. 333–347. Springer, Cham (2017). https://doi.org/10.1007/978-3-319-59536-8_21

23. Vassiliadis, P., Zarras, A.V., Skoulis, I.: How is life for a table in an evolving relational schema? birth, death and everything in between. In: Proceedings ER 2015 (2015)

24. Vassiliadis, P., Zarras, A.V., Skoulis, I.: Gravitating to rigidity: patterns of schema evolution - and its absence - in the lives of tables. Inf. Syst. **63**, 24–46 (2017)

25. Wu, S., Neamtiu, I.: Schema evolution analysis for embedded databases. In: Proceedings ICDEW 2011 (2011)

26. Xue, L.: A survey of schema evolution in object-oriented databases. In: Proceedings of the TOOLS 1999 (1999)

A Study on the Effect of a Table's Involvement in Foreign Keys to its Schema Evolution

Konstantinos Dimolikas, Apostolos V. Zarras, and Panos Vassiliadis[(✉)] [iD]

Department of Computer Science and Engineering, University of Ioannina,
Ioannina, Greece
{kdimolikas,zarras,pvassil}@cs.uoi.gr

Abstract. In this paper, we study the evolution of tables in a schema with respect to *the structure of the foreign keys to which tables are related*. We organize a hierarchy of topological complexity for the structure of foreign keys, based on a modeling of schemata as graphs, where tables are classified in increasing order of complexity as: *isolated* (not involved in foreign keys), *source* (with outgoing foreign keys only), *lookup* (with incoming foreign keys only) and *internal* (with both kinds). Our study reveals that this hierarchy reflects also the update behavior of tables: topologically simple tables are more likely to have a life with few or zero schema updates, whereas, topologically complex tables are more likely to undergo high numbers of updates. Early versions of the database attract the large majority of births of complex tables, as opposed to the simple ones, demonstrating a pattern of reducing the introduction of complex, heavily updated constructs in the schema as time progresses.

Keywords: Schema evolution · Foreign keys · Software evolution

1 Introduction

How is the structure of the foreign keys to which a table is related affecting its behavior during schema evolution? In this paper, we study the evolution of tables in a schema, from the perspective of their *topology* of foreign keys. We study the histories of 6 relational schemata and we extract births and deaths of the tables, as well as the intra-table updates (attribute additions, deletions, data type and primary key updates) they went through from the subsequent versions of their schema definition files. We also extract their foreign key relations, too. We exploit the graph modeling of [9] to model tables as nodes and foreign keys as directed edges, and thus treat a schema version as a graph. A *Diachronic Graph* is the union of all the graphs of the different versions and the main tool we will employ to relate the graph-based characteristics and the activity of tables.

 Our first contribution lies in the introduction of a concise taxonomy of graph topological patterns, classifying tables into (a) *isolated* (zero total degree), (b) *source* (zero fan-in), (c) *lookup* (zero fan-out), and, (d) *internal* tables (with

© Springer Nature Switzerland AG 2020
G. Dobbie et al. (Eds.): ER 2020, LNCS 12400, pp. 456–470, 2020.
https://doi.org/10.1007/978-3-030-62522-1_34

both fan-in and fan-out degrees). All the degrees are measured over the afore-mentioned Diachronic Graph. *Our object of study has been the relationship of the topological profile of tables with their evolutionary activity.* We have discovered that there is indeed a relationship and the hierarchy of topological complexity actually relates to the behavior of tables. Specifically, our findings indicate that:

1. The topologically complex, *internal tables demonstrate high intra-table schema update activity* and, at the same time, they are almost in their entirety born in the initiating version of the database - in other words, *subsequent versions do not come with births of such topologically complex, internal tables.*
2. At the other end of the complexity spectrum *isolated tables undergo very little or zero change* and, despite the fact that a fair percentage of them is present in the original version of the database, isolated tables *are the most likely to be added in subsequent versions of the history.*
3. In-between the spectrum of isolated and internal tables, *source tables appear to be more similar to isolated, resisting change and being more likely to appear later in the life of a database, and lookup tables being more similar to the internal ones.*

The above have (unexpectedly) revealed that *evolutionary behavior is dependent upon a hierarchy of topological complexity: more topologically complex tables appear to be fewer, active and born only early, with the opposite behavior to topologically simple tables.* Our final contribution is that we discuss our explanation of this observation, which we attribute to the *gravitation to rigidity* phenomenon (i.e., the progressive aversion of developers to modify the schema), along with its implications.

Outline. In Sect. 2 we survey related work. In Sect. 3, we delineate the graph modeling used to represent schemata, the data sets and their preprocessing. In Sect. 4 we relate the topological categories of the individual tables to their activity and in Sect. 5 we conclude with a discussion of our results.

2 Related Work

Related work in the area of studying schema evolution has been initiated mainly in the turning of the millennium, due to the existence of Free Open Source Software (FOSS) projects that contained databases for their operation. Till then, it was very hard for the research community to have the necessary data to study -let alone publish the findings-in the area of schema evolution. A single case is found in [5] . During the last decade, several works appeared that mainly studied the growth of schemata [1–4,13]: we know by now that schemata grow slowly over time, and, in fact with decreasing rate [4], and alterations of change (mostly table insertions and updates) with long periods of calmness [6,7]. The study of individual tables has been performed in [10–12] revealing several survival and growth patterns.

To the best of our knowledge, the first work that studied how foreign keys evolve in the context of schema evolution of relational databases is [8] and its long version, [9]. The study was mainly done from the macroscopic, schema-level point of view and revealed that the evolution of foreign keys depends a lot on the idiosyncrasy of the database itself. In some cases, foreign keys are treated as an integral part of the system, evolving along with their tables, whereas in some other cases, only a small subset of the tables is involved in foreign keys, while birth and death of foreign keys is mostly out of synch with the respective table events. The extremity of this treatment is demonstrated in two data sets where the foreign keys where completely removed from the schema. Another serious problem observed was that within the 20 data sets collected, the mere existence of foreign keys was evident in only 7 of them. In [9], the way that the total degree of the graph modeling affects survival is discussed too: high degree tables are survivors (with removed tables being mostly low or zero degree) and active. The current paper differentiates itself from the related work as it complements the macroscopic observations of [9] on how the *entire schema* evolves, with observations *at the level of individual tables*, and characterizes the evolution of individual tables *with respect to their graph characteristics, and in particular, classes of their graph topology.*

3   Background and Experimental Setup

In this section, we discuss our underlying graph model for schemata with foreign keys, our data sets and tool, the classification of tables in topological categories, and the handling of the problem of tables with more than one label in their history.

3.1   Modeling as a Graph and the Diachronic Graph

We follow the modeling of [9], which we also quote here for completeness. We treat a relational schema as a set of relations, along with their foreign key constraints. A relation is characterized by a name, a set of attributes and a primary key. A foreign key constraint is a 1:1 mapping between a set of attributes S in a relation, R_S, called the source of the foreign key, and a set of attributes T in a relation R_T, called the target of the foreign key. At the extensional level, the semantics of the foreign key denote a subset relation between the instances of the source and the instances of the target attributes. We model a database schema as a directed graph $G(V; E)$, with relations as nodes and foreign keys as directed edges, originating from their source and targeted to their target. *The Diachronic Graph* of the history of a schema is the union of all the nodes and edges that ever appeared in the history of the schema.

3.2   Data Sets and Their Preprocessing

We base our study to the 6 data sets of [8,9] (Fig. 1). Our set includes CMS's, resource management toolkits and scientific databases. Two of the datasets,

SlashCode and Zabbix, demonstrate the explicit removals of foreign keys from the schema, with the former also introducing foreign keys late in the schema history. We have decided to work only with the periods where foreign keys were present in the schema (versions 74 to 260 for Slaschcode and 1 to 150 for Zabbix), since no table could possibly have any topological properties outside these periods. All the metrics reported have been obtained via our Parmenidian Truth tool that models, visualizes and quantifies the evolution of schemata with foreign keys. Both due to the identical nature of the data sets and their processing, and the lack of space, we refer the reader to [8,9] for a discussion of the *threats to validity* for the scope (Free Open Source Software), external, and measurement validity. *Both our tool and our data are publicly available for the research community at our Github repository* https://github.com/DAINTINESS-Group.

Datasets	Versions	Tables @start	Tables @end	Tables @DG	Tables Growth	FKs @start	FKs @end	FKs @DG	FKs Growth
Atlas	85	56	73	88	30,4%	61	63	88	3,3%
BioSQL	47	21	28	45	33,3%	17	43	79	152,9%
Castor	194	62	74	91	19,4%	6	10	13	66,7%
Egee	17	6	10	12	66,7%	3	4	6	33,3%
Slashcode	399	42	87	126	107,1%	0	0	47	0,0%
Zabbix	160	15	48	58	220,0%	10	2	38	-80,0%

Fig. 1. Statistics for the datasets used in our study [8,9]

3.3   The Topological Categories of Tables

In this subsection, we present the topological categories of tables based on their references to and from other tables. Figure 2 depicts the distribution of tables over the combination of their in- and out-degrees at the Diachronic Graph for the 6 datasets. In the sequel, we introduce the different *topological categories*, or *labels*, which are determined on the basis of the topology of the Diachronic Graph (Fig. 3).

Figure 2 shows the strong presence of *isolated* tables, i.e., tables with no inciting edges and zero total degree, in 4 of the 6 datasets. Moreover, in 2 of these datasets, namely Castor and SlashCode, zero degree tables constitute an overwhelming majority.

Leaving isolated tables aside, the next most populous category consists of *source* tables with no incoming references and at least one outgoing foreign key. This category of tables includes populations varying from 19% to 62%.

The third category includes tables with only incoming references, so we refer to them with the label *lookup*. In the 6 datasets, there is a small group of tables that lie in this category, not exceeding the value of 36%, and in 5 out of the 6 data sets they are less than 20% of the tables. However, due to their "reusable" nature, they typically achieve degrees much higher than the source tables.

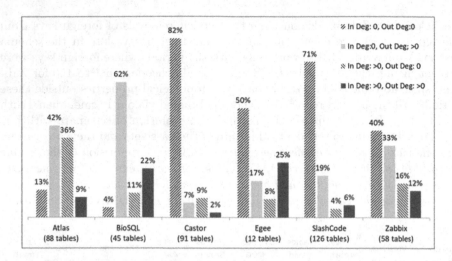

Fig. 2. Breakdown of tables wrt In- and Out-Degrees at the Diachronic Graph

The last category contains tables that have both in- and out-degrees. We refer to this category as *internal* tables. By definition, internal tables come with the most complicated topological structure. Although Fig. 2 shows that this category is not very large, it comes with interesting properties, as we will demonstrate in the sequel.

Name	Figure	Description
ISOLATED		Tables without FK's
SOURCE	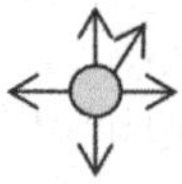	Tables having only outgoing FK's
LOOKUP	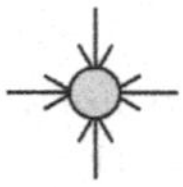	Tables having only incoming FK's
INTERNAL	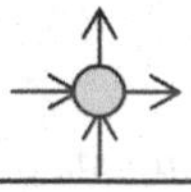	Tables with at least 1 incoming and at least 1 outgoing FK

Fig. 3. Table Categories Based on the Topology of the Diachronic Graph

3.4   Table Labeling for Multi-label Nodes

Having introduced the topological categories, the next issue to resolve was the labeling of the tables. *Given just a single graph as input, the labeling of the tables is straightforward with a single pass over the nodes, as the categories are disjoint and independent of a node's neighborhood.*

The problem arises when the entire history of a schema is concerned. In this case, the input to the problem is a sequence of graphs. Then, it is possible that there are tables that change label throughout their history and as a result we end up with the following categories of tables with respect to their labels:

- *Single label* tables, which have a unique topological label throughout their entire lives.
- *Multi-label* tables, which have more than one label during their existence in the dataset.

		#Tables with...	
Datasets	**Total #tables**	single label	>1 label
Atlas	88	76	12
BioSQL	45	39	6
Castor	91	84	7
Egee	12	9	3
SlashCode	126	97	29
Zabbix	58	30	28

Fig. 4. Distribution of Tables over the Single and Multi-labels Categories

Figure 4 presents the distribution of tables between the ones with a single label and those with more than one label. Apart from Zabbix, in the rest of the datasets, the large majority of tables have a single label in their lives.

A problem that arises is that we would like to relate the labels of the tables to their activity profile and a multi-labeling scheme would not facilitate a statistical study along these lines. So fundamentally, we want to address the problem: *can we assign a single topological label to a table in a way that does not invalidate our statistical analysis and characterizes a table as accurately as possible?* To address this problem, we have manually inspected the tables with change-of-category and decided to assign a single label to each of them, since their number is so small that would not entail any major loss of information. We have distilled the phenomena of label changes for a table in 6 categories.

1. Changes that include an ephemeral transition to a different category and the return to the former category.
2. Changes from the *isolated* category to a different category.
3. Changes soon after the table's "birth".

4. Changes leading to labels assigned for a short period in terms of the number of versions.
5. Changes caused by changing self-references to the table.
6. All other changes.

The resolution of multiple labels into a representative, single label has been straightforward. See Fig. 5 on the categories and the rules for their resolution.

4   Research Findings

In this Section, we relate the topological category of a table to its behavioral characteristics in order to assess whether the former is correlated to the latter.

4.1   Birth

In this subsection we investigate if the birth versions of the tables are related to their topological categories. We are particularly interested in the relationship between the probability that a table is born in the originating version of the schema history and the topological category it belongs to, as, based on previous findings, a large percentage of the schema was created at the very early stages of the schema's history. In this context, we can formulate the relevant research question as follows:

Research Question: how is the topological category of a table related to the probability of being born in the originating version of the schema history?

Figure 6 depicts the potential the tables of each topological category have to exist in the first version of their schema's history. As we want to perform

Rule	Description of Changes	Specific Criteria	Rule Decision
R0	No category change	$label_i = label_{i-1}$	The respective category
R1	Ephemeral category changes (DO-UNDO) in successive versions	$label_{i-1} = label_{i+1} \neq label_i$	Remove ephemeral $label_i$ and keep the remaining category $label_{i+1}$
R2	Changing from ISOLATED to another category	$label_{i-1} \neq label_i$, $label_{i-1} = ISO$	Remove ISO and keep the post-change label $label_i$
R3	Changing category in less than 10 versions after the First Known Version (FKV)	$label_{i-1} \neq label_i$, $i<10$	Remove the first labels and keep the post-change label $label_i$
R4	Changing to a category for a short period of less than 10 versions	$label_i = ... = label_{i+k}$, $k<10$, $label_{i-1} \neq \{label_i, ..., label_{i+k-1}\}$	Remove the period's labels & keep the pre-change label, $label_{i-1}$
R5	Changing category due to the presence of self-references	*An FK is added from the table to itself* $\Rightarrow$ $label_i = INTERNAL$	Remove $label_i$ & keep the pre-change label, $label_{i-1}$
R6	Changes not abiding by any of the previous rules	-	Return the Most Frequent Label in the table's history

Fig. 5. Rules for Tables' Categories Determination

Probability To Be Born @V0 Per Topological Category (Percentages Over #Tables Of Each Topological Category)

	Isolated		Source		Lookup		Internal		ALL TABLES	
	#Tables	Born @v0	#Tables	Born @v0	#Tables	Born @v0	#Tables	Born @v0	#Tables	Born @v0
Atlas	11	9%	38	61%	32	78%	7	100%	88	64%
BioSQL	2	100%	29	38%	8	50%	6	67%	45	47%
Castor	75	64%	6	83%	9	89%	1	100%	91	68%
SlashCode	35	43%	22	73%	7	86%	4	100%	68	60%
Zabbix	22	9%	20	30%	11	45%	3	67%	56	27%

Fig. 6. Probability to be "born" in the First Version per Topological Category (*blue italics*: lower than average, red bold: higher than average, both by at least 10%)

statistical analyses, Egee is omitted due to its very small size. The patterns that we encounter with reference to the probability of tables being "born" in the earliest version of their schema can be summarized as follows:

- The tables of the *internal* category are 100% certain to be "born" in the originating version in three out of the five datasets. In BioSQL and Zabbix, although the overall population of the *internal* tables is not present in the first version, the probability for an internal table to be born at v0 is 67% for both data sets. Overall, there is no doubt that internal tables are almost entirely early born and *it is really highly unlikely to see internal tables being born later in the life of a schema.*
- *Lookup* tables have higher probabilities to be "born" in the first version compared to the respective average probability, and in fact, their majority is present at the first version of the schema for 4 out of 5 data sets.
- Coming to *source* tables, the probability for a *source* table to be introduced in the first version of its dataset's history is, approximately, in accordance with the average probability and, in all datasets, it is lower than the respective potential of the *lookup* tables. In 2 out of 5 data sets, this probability is lower than the average probability of being born at v0. This signifies that it is easier for DBA's to add new source tables to the database during the evolution of the schema than it is to add lookup and internal ones.
- The tables of the *isolated* category have the lowest potential for being "born" in the originating version of their datasets, in four of the five datasets. Equivalently, we can claim that it is easier to add tables of this category over the course of a database's schema evolution than introducing tables of any other category.

The common features among the datasets related to the probability for a table to be "born" in the originating version if it belongs to a certain topological category are supported to some extent by the statistical evidence that assess the independence of the birth version from the topological categories. Specifically, we performed the Chi-square and Fisher statistical tests by utilizing a contingency table consisted of four rows representing the topological categories and

Breakdown of Tables over their Activity Class
(Percentages over Total #Tables)

	Total #Tables	Activity Class			Activity Class (%)		
		RIGID	QUIET	ACTIVE	RIGID	QUIET	ACTIVE
Atlas	88	18	43	27	*20%*	**49%**	31%
BioSQL	45	16	13	16	**36%**	*29%*	36%
Castor	91	57	31	3	**63%**	34%	*3%*
SlashCode	68	15	38	15	*22%*	**56%**	*22%*
Zabbix	56	23	30	3	41%	**54%**	*5%*

Fig. 7. Distribution of Tables per Activity Class (for each data set, the largest value is in red bold and the *smallest* in *blue italics*

two columns corresponding to tables born in the first version and those that are not. The p-values that do not exceed the limit of 5% are 4.74E-02 for Atlas, 1.36E-02 for SlashCode and 3.22E-02 for Zabbix.

To sum up, we observe that internal and lookup tables are more likely to be born in the originating version of their dataset's history, which, expressed in a different way, means that it is quite unlikely that they are "born" after this version. In contrast, source tables follow the trend of the general population and isolated tables are the ones with higher chances to be born in versions succeeding the originating one.

4.2 Activity

The next issue that we are interested in is that of the update profile of the tables with respect to their topological categories. To ease the process of analyzing the update behavior of the tables with respect to their topological categories we utilize the activity classes defined in [11], which are summarized as follows:

– *Rigid* tables experience no updates throughout their entire life in the dataset.
– *Quiet* tables are tables with the total number of updates not exceeding the value of 5 and the Average Transitional Update (ATU) to be less than 0.1.
– *Active* tables are tables which undergo more than 5 updates and have an ATU higher than 0.1.

The *Average Transitional Update* (ATU) of a table is defined as the fraction of the sum of updates the table undergoes throughout its life over its duration [11]. The updates include attribute addition, deletion, change of data type and change of primary key.

Research Question: is there a relationship between the topological category of a table and its update activity?

Figure 7 presents the distribution of the tables over the aforementioned activity classes. Tables tend to be mostly rigid and quiet. Next, we examine the impact of the topological categories of the update activity of the tables. The upper part of Fig. 8 depicts the probability for a table of a certain topological category to develop a certain update activity during its existence in its dataset. We outline the most interesting information derived from this figure in the following list:

- *Isolated* tables experience no or few updates with a probability that is higher than 82%. Overall: *isolated tables are mostly rigid and very ralely active!*
- The likelihood for a *source* table to undergo no or few changes throughout its life is at least 82% in all datasets, apart from BioSQL. *Source tables follow quite closely the overall pattern of the dataset, and they tend to be mostly quiet or rigid, and rarely active.*
- Activity shifts "rightwise" in Fig. 8, when it comes to *lookup* tables. Again, lookup tables are mostly quiet, but now, the odds are more in favor of being active, compared to the average behavior and compared to the probability of being rigid. In 3 out of 5 data sets, active lookup tables surpass 35%. *Overall, lookup tables are more prone to changes both with respect to categories of less topological complexity and with respect to the average behavior (which is expected, since the categories of low topological complexity are the most numerous ones).*
- *Internal* tables are mostly active! With the exception of Castor, having just one internal table, in all other cases, the majority of active internal tables is absolute. In other words, *the internal tables are expected to be mostly active, with a probability higher than in any other activity category!*

The bottom part of Fig. 8 presents the probability for a table with a certain activity profile to belong to a specific topological category. In a nutshell, we can identify the subsequent commonalities among the datasets:

- *Rigid tables are mostly isolated, or source, in the case where isolated tables do not really exist in the dataset.* The probability for a rigid table to be lookup is much lower compared to average and almost zero to be internal in 4 of the 5 data sets.
- It is fairly straightforward to observe that *the distribution of the quiet tables over the topological categories is in agreement with the aggregate one in all datasets.* In three of the five datasets, *quiet* tables are likely to belong to the *source* category, with the exceptions of Castor and SlashCode, in which *quiet* tables tend to be *isolated.*
- *Active tables are mostly inclined towards higher topological complexity.* In all data sets, (even in BioSQL where the distribution follows the average distribution of the entire data set very closely), the chances for an active table to belong to a topologically complex category are much higher than average. It is as if an attracting force is pulling active tables to the rightmost columns of higher topological complexity.

The statistical evidence provided by Chi-square and Fisher tests is fairly strong. We utilized a contingency table of four rows, each for a topological category, and three columns for the different activity classes. The p-values derived

PROBABILITY FOR A TABLE OF A TOPOLOGICAL CATEGORY TO DEVELOP A CERTAIN UPDATE ACTIVITY (PERCENTAGES OVER TOTAL #TABLES OF EACH TOPOLOGICAL CATEGORY)

| | TOPOLOGICAL CATEGORY | | | | | | | | | | | | | | | | | | | | |
| | ISOLATED | | | | SOURCE | | | | LOOKUP | | | | INTERNAL | | | | Aggregate per Activity Class | | | |
	Total #Tables	RIGID	QUIET	ACTIVE	Total #Tables	RIGID	QUIET	ACTIVE	Total #Tables	RIGID	QUIET	ACTIVE	Total #Tables	RIGID	QUIET	ACTIVE	Total #Tables	RIGID	QUIET	ACTIVE
Atlas	11	27%	55%	18%	38	29%	58%	13%	32	13%	47%	41%	7	0%	0%	100%	88	20%	49%	31%
BioSQL	2	100%	0%	0%	29	34%	31%	34%	8	25%	38%	38%	6	33%	17%	50%	45	36%	29%	36%
Castor	75	67%	32%	1%	6	67%	17%	17%	9	33%	56%	11%	1	0%	100%	0%	91	63%	34%	3%
SlashCode	35	34%	54%	11%	22	14%	68%	18%	7	0%	43%	57%	4	0%	25%	75%	68	22%	56%	22%
Zabbix	22	55%	41%	5%	20	35%	65%	0%	11	27%	73%	0%	3	33%	0%	67%	56	41%	54%	5%

PROBABILITY FOR A TABLE OF AN ACTIVITY CLASS TO BELONG TO A CERTAIN TOPOLOGICAL CATEGORY (PERCENTAGES OVER TOTAL #TABLES OF EACH ACTIVITY CLASS)

| | ACTIVITY CLASS | | | | | | | | | | | | | | | | | | | | |
| | RIGID | | | | | QUIET | | | | | ACTIVE | | | | | Aggregate per Topological Category | | | | |
	Total #Tables	ISOLATED	SOURCE	LOOKUP	INTERNAL	Total #Tables	ISOLATED	SOURCE	LOOKUP	INTERNAL	Total #Tables	ISOLATED	SOURCE	LOOKUP	INTERNAL	Total #Tables	ISOLATED	SOURCE	LOOKUP	INTERNAL
Atlas	18	17%	61%	22%	0%	43	14%	51%	35%	0%	27	7%	19%	48%	26%	88	13%	43%	36%	8%
BioSQL	16	13%	63%	13%	13%	13	0%	69%	23%	8%	16	0%	63%	19%	19%	45	4%	64%	18%	13%
Castor	57	88%	7%	5%	0%	31	77%	3%	16%	3%	3	33%	33%	33%	0%	91	82%	7%	10%	1%
SlashCode	15	80%	20%	0%	0%	38	50%	39%	8%	3%	15	27%	27%	27%	20%	68	51%	32%	10%	6%
Zabbix	23	52%	30%	13%	4%	30	30%	43%	27%	0%	3	33%	0%	0%	67%	56	39%	36%	20%	5%

Fig. 8. Probability for a Table of a Topological Category to Develop Specific Update Activity and vice versa.

from these tests are below the critical value of 5% in four of the five datasets (except Biosql), ranging from 9.6E-05 (Zabbix) to 3.89E-02 (Castor). *The statistical results confirm that tables with different topological categories are subjects to different amounts of updates. Altogether, we established that the topological category of a table is related to its update activity. Isolated and source tables are inclined towards zero or few updates in their lifetime, lookup tables with few or many changes and internal tables with an inclination to active lives with many updates.*

Why do Active Tables Change? The answer is that *they grow in schema size, i.e., in number of attributes.* We studied *schema resize* to see how attribute additions and deletions affect tables. In terms of their number of attributes, 2%–6% of tables shrink, 25%–47% of tables increase, and 50%–69% remain stable. Compared to the average probability of resize, we observe two different patterns that are consistent in all datasets: (a) *isolated* and *source* tables follow the average probability for size reduction, have higher probability for size steadiness and lower for size expansion, and, (b) *lookup* and *internal* tables have a potential for size reduction lower than the average with few exceptions, a probability for size steadiness below the average and a higher likelihood for size expansion.

5   An Unexpected Finding and Lessons Learned

The purpose of this research was to uncover patterns in the evolutionary behavior of tables with respect to their relationship with foreign keys, in order to derive useful knowledge on how developers evolve tables. In the process, we encountered patterns that were rather unexpected, although explainable in retrospect.

A Topological Hierarchy and Its Evolutionary Behavior. After observing that different topological categories differ in their evolution, we came at an unexpected finding: there is *a hierarchy of topologically increasing complexity* reflected on how tables are evolved by developers of FOSS projects.

$$Top.\ Complexity\ Hierarchy:\ Isolated \rightarrow Source \longrightarrow Lookup \rightarrow Internal \quad (1)$$

We have discovered that the complexity spectrum that results from this hierarchy relates to the behavior of tables. On the high end of the complexity spectrum, the internal tables demonstrate quite a different life than the isolated tables at the other end of it. *Complex internal tables* demonstrate high activity –which means the undergo attribute additions, deletions and type updates– whereas *isolated* tables undergo very little if zero change. Remember that we are studying data sets with hundreds of commits spanning into several years of monitoring. At the very same time, internal tables are almost totally born at the earliest version of the database history: *in other words, there are no internal, topologically complex, and, probably active, tables born after the initiation of the database.* The phenomenon is quite opposite for isolated tables: despite the fact that a fair percentage of them is present in the original version of the database, isolated tables are the most likely to be added in subsequent versions of the history. *As time passes, it appears as if people are disinclined to add more complex structures to their database!* In-between the spectrum of isolated and internal tables, *source* tables appear to be more similar to the isolated ones, resisting change and being more likely to appear later in the life of a database, and *lookup* tables being more similar to the internal ones. Last but not least, let us mention that *isolated and source tables are the most populous categories whereas lookup and internal tables are progressively smaller in numbers.*

In a nutshell, this study reveals *the existence of a complexity spectrum ranging from (a) a populous, rigid, easily born, topologically simple end, all the way to (b) a less populous, active (due to attribute additions), early born (and not later), topologically complex end.*

Why is this Happening? As also noted in the past [8,12], the main force that seems to govern schema evolution, at least in the Free Open Source Software (FOSS) setting that we study, is *gravitation to rigidity*, due to the difficulty of altering the schema of a database when surrounding code is built upon it. The same seems to be observed here too: *(a) inactive, topologically simple tables are much more populous and easy to create than complex and active ones; (b) very few tables change topological category (Fig. 4), with most changes in the ephemeral or short-lasting categories of label-changes; (c) different topological categories seem to have different evolutionary behaviors* – specifically, most of the activity of the high-end of the complexity spectrum is due to the addition of attributes to the existing structures, quite differently from the lower end of the spectrum, where administrators are more inclined towards building new tables.

We conjecture that an explanation for this difference in behavior is the *avoid-to-break-the-code* principle: adding new information via new tables, which can later be removed if not useful, does not result in the necessity to update the surrounding code that queries and updates the existing tables. This leads to *maintenance-by-addition* and simplifies the life of developers, at the expense, of course, of increasing the size of the schema and fragmenting the information into many tables. So, developers augment the database with simple topologies, and if complex topologies need expansion, this is done via attribute injection. A second reason that we conjecture affects the evolutionary profile of tables, is the deployment of projects. Remember we are studying FOSS projects, built to be selected by other organizations. Once a FOSS project has been adopted and deployed by an organization, future upgrades might result in the change of the schema too. Upgrading the schema in the presence of existing data is a painful experience, and simple structures and maintenance-by-addition reduce this pain.

Guidelines based on Our Findings. Apart from advancing our knowledge with solid evidence, our empirical study on how schema evolution relates to foreign keys in FOSS projects addresses several audiences, as it provides both (a) maintenance clues to curators and evaluators of FOSS projects, and, (b) insights on the adaptability of the relational model to the research community.

Curators. Project curators can expect that the tendency of the schema in the future will be to expand in terms of (a) topologically simple structures and (b) injection of attributes to early-born, complex topological structures. Enforcing maintenance-by-addition will allow lower impact to the surrounding code. In the FOSS universe, where development is not as strictly controlled as in closed projects, it is necessary to reserve cycles and time for schema cleanup and application refactoring to avoid the unregulated management of the schema.

FOSS Evaluators. When selecting a software projects for adoption, an evaluator may use our toolset to analyze the schema history of the schema, in order to see how actively maintained it is, and via what kind of changes. An evaluator will need to also assess the threats posed by the absence of (a) foreign keys and (b) maintenance actions from the side of the curators.

Researchers. We believe that the main recipients for this line of work are the members of the research community, much more than the other categories. The reason is that the nature of the situation boils down to the fundamentals of the relational model and how relational databases can be coupled to surrounding applications. We, as the research community, need to come up with more flexible ways of building applications on top of databases and/or tools that accurately highlight the points of maintenance in the surrounding code, in the event of schema evolution.

References

1. Cleve, A., Gobert, M., Meurice, L., Maes, J., Weber, J.H.: Understanding database schema evolution: a case study. Sci. Comput. Program. **97**, 113–121 (2015)
2. Curino, C., Moon, H.J., Tanca, L., Zaniolo, C.: Schema evolution in wikipedia: toward a web information system benchmark. In: Proceedings of ICEIS 2008 (2008)
3. Lin, D.Y., Neamtiu, I.: Collateral evolution of applications and databases. In: Proceedings of the Joint International and Annual ERCIM Workshops on Principles of Software Evolution (IWPSE) and Software Evolution (Evol) Workshops, pp. 31–40. IWPSE-Evol 2009 (2009)
4. Qiu, D., Li, B., Su, Z.: An empirical analysis of the co-evolution of schema and code in database applications. In: Proceedings of the 2013 9th Joint Meeting on Foundations of Software Engineering, pp. 125–135. ESEC/FSE 2013 (2013)
5. Sjøberg, D.: Quantifying schema evolution. Inf. Software Technol. **35**(1), 35–44 (1993)
6. Skoulis, I., Vassiliadis, P., Zarras, A.: Open-source databases: within, outside, or beyond Lehman's laws of software evolution? In: 26th International Conference on Advanced Information Systems Engineering (CAiSE 2014), Thessaloniki, Greece, 16–20 June 2014 (2014)
7. Skoulis, I., Vassiliadis, P., Zarras, A.V.: Growing up with stability: how open-source relational databases evolve. Inf. Syst. **53**, 363–385 (2015)
8. Vassiliadis, P., Kolozoff, M.-R., Zerva, M., Zarras, A.V.: Schema evolution and foreign keys: birth, eviction, change and absence. In: Mayr, H.C., Guizzardi, G., Ma, H., Pastor, O. (eds.) ER 2017. LNCS, vol. 10650, pp. 106–119. Springer, Cham (2017). https://doi.org/10.1007/978-3-319-69904-2_9
9. Vassiliadis, P., Kolozoff, M.-R., Zerva, M., Zarras, A.V.: Schema evolution and foreign keys: a study on usage, heartbeat of change and relationship of foreign keys to table activity. Computing **101**(10), 1431–1456 (2019). https://doi.org/10.1007/s00607-019-00702-x

10. Vassiliadis, P., Zarras, A.V.: Schema evolution survival guide for tables: avoid rigid childhood and you're en route to a quiet life. J. Data Semantics **6**(4), 221–241 (2017)
11. Vassiliadis, P., Zarras, A.V., Skoulis, I.: How is life for a table in an evolving relational schema? birth, death and everything in between. In: Johannesson, P., Lee, M.L., Liddle, S.W., Opdahl, A.L., López, Ó.P. (eds.) ER 2015. LNCS, vol. 9381, pp. 453–466. Springer, Cham (2015). https://doi.org/10.1007/978-3-319-25264-3_34
12. Vassiliadis, P., Zarras, A.V., Skoulis, I.: Gravitating to rigidity: patterns of schema evolution - and its absence - in the lives of tables. Inf. Syst. **63**, 24–46 (2017)
13. Wu, S., Neamtiu, I.: Schema evolution analysis for embedded databases. In: Proceedings of the 2011 IEEE 27th International Conference on Data Engineering Workshops, pp. 151–156. ICDEW 2011 (2011)

A Workload-Driven Document Database Schema Recommender (DBSR)

Vincent Reniers(✉) ⓘ, Dimitri Van Landuyt ⓘ, Ansar Rafique ⓘ,
and Wouter Joosen ⓘ

imec-DistriNet, KU Leuven, Celestijnenlaan 200A, 3000 Leuven, Belgium
{vincent.reniers,dimitri.vanlanduyt,ansar.rafique,
wouter.joosen}@cs.kuleuven.be

Abstract. Database schema design requires careful consideration of the application's data model, workload, and target database technology to optimize for performance and data size. Traditional normalization schemes used in relational databases minimize data redundancy, whereas NoSQL document-oriented databases favor redundancy and optimize for horizontal scalability and performance.

Systematic NoSQL schema design involves multiple dimensions, and a database designer is in practice required to carefully consider (i) which data elements to copy and co-locate, (ii) which data elements to normalize, and (iii) how to encode data, while taking into account factors such as the workload and data model.

In this paper, we present a workload-driven document database schema recommender (DBSR), which takes a systematic, search-based approach in exploring the complex schema design space. The recommender takes as main inputs the application's data model and its read workload, and outputs (i) the suggested document schema (featuring secondary indexing), (ii) query plan recommendations, and (iii) a document utility matrix that encodes insights on their respective costs and relative utility. We evaluate recommended schema in MongoDB using YCSB, and show significant benefits to read query performance.

Keywords: NoSQL database design · Document database schema recommender · NoSQL database cost models

1 Introduction

In the Big Data era, the systematic collection of enormous data volumes has become the norm in various industry sectors, such as Healthcare, E-commerce and Telecom. Heterogeneous data emerges from many sources and in large volumes, from users, sensors, to logging mechanisms. These have to be stored and processed appropriately in database systems that can scale horizontally.

The un- or semi-structured nature of these data elements, coupled with their large influx, poses challenges to traditional relational database systems which

© Springer Nature Switzerland AG 2020
G. Dobbie et al. (Eds.): ER 2020, LNCS 12400, pp. 471–484, 2020.
https://doi.org/10.1007/978-3-030-62522-1_35

adhere to a strict and rigid schema, and are limited in elastic and horizontal scalability. In order to handle such heterogeneous data, a new class of database systems has emerged, commonly referred to as NoSQL [3,12,21]. These provide support for specialized data models and features such as schema flexibility, leading to improvements in horizontal and elastic scalability. These benefits are achieved by relaxing the ACID properties of relational databases, in favor of eventual consistency [21], and secondly, by simplifying standard SQL operations [12].

General schema design guidelines for document-oriented NoSQL databases [10,14], such as MongoDB [2] and Couchbase [1], recommend data denormalization by embedding data elements (or copies thereof) into a single record (i.e. a document) to allow them to be served in a single look-up request. As table records are horizontally partitioned (sharded) across multiple nodes, a look-up may involve a costly JOIN operation traversing several physical nodes, which in turn significantly increases latency and overall strain on the database. Furthermore, some NoSQL databases do not support JOIN operations and favor denormalization, for example in MongoDB when using sharded collections, and instead these queries have to be implemented client-side. The main disadvantage of denormalization is that data redundancy will increase, and maintaining consistency across multiple copies will involve multiple write and update operations.

In general, the different options to denormalize NoSQL database schemas vary widely [3,11,14], and each single schema design decision will in effect represent a trade-off between aspects of data locality, storage usage, consistency, performance, and scalability. Making appropriate trade-off decisions requires in-depth knowledge of the application data model and its workload [19], the capabilities of the target database, and thus requires extensive expert knowledge. In practice, the database designer (or application developer) is fraught with finding a balance between normalization and de-normalization. In essence, this is a multi-dimensional optimization problem in which the combinatorial explosions of schema design possibilities hinders the ability to systematically enumerate this design space and search-based approaches are required [8].

In recent years, schema recommenders –mainly for columnar data stores– have emerged in related work (e.g., NoSE [18] or Bermbach et al. [5]) that implement such a search-based approach. These recommender systems take an (i) application's data model, and (ii) query workload, and suggest an appropriate NoSQL schema. However, to our knowledge, a systematic approach has not been presented for flexible NoSQL document-oriented databases.

In this paper, we propose DBSR, a document-based schema recommender that generates candidate schemas and employs a search-based approach to identify the most suitable candidates (evaluated in terms of query plan efficiency and projected cost). To evaluate DBSR, we have extended the Yahoo! Cloud Serving Benchmark (YCSB) [9] with dedicated workloads that integrate DBSR query plans. Our evaluation efforts show that significant benefits can be achieved in read query performance, but that this comes at an additional storage cost.

The remainder of the paper is structured as follows, Sect. 2 motivates the paper and explains the used terminology. Section 3 introduces DBSR in terms of its algorithms and data structures. Section 4 elaborates on the pruning algorithms for query plans and documents. Section 5 evaluates DBSR, with emphasis on the pruning algorithms, and the generated recommendations. Finally, Sect. 6 discusses related work, whereas Sect. 7 concludes the paper.

2 Motivating Example and Terminology

The motivating example for this paper is presented in Fig. 1. This example is based on an online auction system, and adopted from the RUBiS benchmark [6]. Starting from the ER model, a graph can be created with tables as nodes, and relationships as edges. At each point in the graph, a document can be constructed using the node as the top-level document, with options to either embed or reference the relationships to other nodes. The resulting document D can be defined as a directed acyclic graph (DAG).

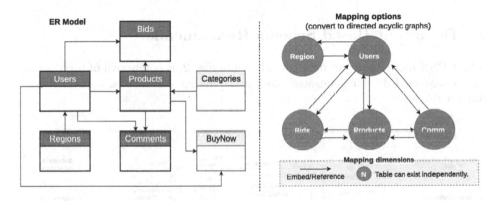

Fig. 1. RUBiS conceptual data model and mapping options.

It is a main rule of thumb in NoSQL design guidelines to group data that are frequently accessed together [1,2]. When a client visits a **Product** page, typically this person will be interested in the ongoing **Bids** for this **Product**, as well as in **Comments** made by previous buyers. Document collections optimized for the workload JOIN sequences $Seq_{P \rightarrow B}$ and $Seq_{P \rightarrow C}$ service this information with a single look-up without traversing documents D_B containing a **Bid** or document D_C containing a **Comment** separately, since these documents may be horizontally partitioned across several physical nodes. The optimized documents D for each sequence are $D_{P|B}$ and $D_{P|C}$, of which $P|B$ and $P|C$ represent an embedded relationship, resulting in a single **Product** record that respectively embeds its **Bids** or **Comments**. The workload read sequence $Seq_{P \rightarrow B}$ its original query plan $QP_{P \rightarrow B}$ is then replaced by a single look-up plan $QP_{P|B}$. Further optimization creates document $D_{P|\{B,C\}}$ which embeds in a `Product` record both `Bids` and `Comments`. This example its document tree consists of a maximum height (H) of 2, and at each child a width (W) of maximum 2 embedded relationships. An additional relationship X embedded in this document can be clarified using brackets, for example by replacing B with $\{B|X\}$, increasing overall height to 3.

Although each query can potentially be optimized in this manner, this would quickly lead to significant increases in data redundancy, since each relationship copies the referenced data and embeds it locally.

Problem Statement. This example illustrates the complexity of the solution space, even for a simplified example. Designing a schema demands in-depth knowledge of the workload and its data model, and the capabilities of the target database, and involves making trade-offs between query performance, data redundancy, data consistency, etc.

Approach. In this paper, we adopt a search-based approach to generate candidate schemas and automatically rank them in terms of relative query plan efficiency and projected cost. Next, we explain how our schema recommender (DBSR) supports this process.

3 Document-Based Schema Recommender

The DBSR framework[1] architecture shown in Fig. 2, is comprised of input models, a workload-driven generator, cost and ranking algorithms, a pruner, and output models.

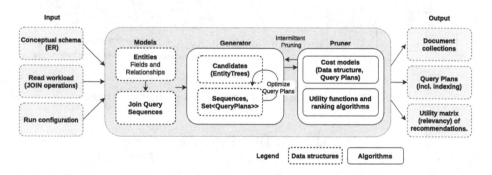

Fig. 2. DBSR: Architectural overview.

The generator takes as main inputs (i) the application's data model, (ii) a read workload of `JOIN` queries, and (iii) additional configuration parameters. The framework eventually outputs: (i) a document schema with secondary indexing, (ii) suggested query plans over these document collections, and (iii) a document utility matrix showing the relative efficiency in answering workload queries.

---

[1] DBSR framework repository: https://github.com/vreniers/DBSR.

3.1   Workload-Driven Schema Generation

As discussed in [20], two alternative approaches can be adopted to generate document data structures from an input workload: either a top-down, or bottom-up approach. We apply a bottom-up approach, which is globally more efficient, and starts from single-level document data structures for each table, rather than entirely denormalized documents (i.e. materialized views). Initial query plans are created from the workload that JOIN these single-level documents in multiple steps. Each query plan is optimized by merging used data structures into a larger document, and thereby eliminating a JOIN step that may traverse physical nodes.

Iterative Optimization of Query Plans. Figure 3 depicts the iterative loop of the generator. When a query plan is selected for optimization, the generator merges documents to eliminate a join step, thereby creating new larger documents, and a shortened query plan. All other query plans, that are notified of the novel data structure, can create new query plans based on the original plan and the new document. These plans are also added onto the stack for optimization.

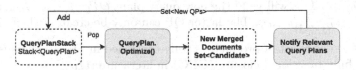

Fig. 3. Iterative loop optimizes query plans, which generates new documents and plans.

Stop Conditions. The generator will eventually stop when either (a) the query plan optimization stack becomes empty as no new data structures are generated and thus no novel query plans are added onto the stack, or (b) the maximum number of iterations (as stated in the run configuration) is reached.

3.2   Initial Query Plans and Data Structures

The iterative process starts from a set of initial data structures and query plans. We describe how these are created by example. Suppose that we have a sequence $Seq_{U \to P}$ that consists of a read query on the Users table, followed by the join operation on the Products table. The generator will first create a document candidate for each read query in this sequence, and this candidate data structure contains only the fields that are effectively used. We thus get the data structures D_{U_1} and D_{P_1}, which may be a subset of the original user table T_U and product table T_P. The generator then formulates for each sequence the possible query plans to answer the sequence, using these root data structures. This will yield in this case a single query plan $QP_{U_1 \to P_1}$.

Typically, the workload consists of more than one read sequence, and multiple initial data structures are created per sequence. Therefore, we could for example end up with 3 variants of the Users table $D_{U_1}, D_{U_2}, D_{U_3}$. In this case, D_{U_1} could be the entire normalized Users table, whereas D_{U_2}, D_{U_3} represent subsets with different columns.

After generating all initial data structures, all possible query plans are generated for all the sequences. The read sequence that utilizes D_{U_3} can create at least two query plans, in which one case D_{U_3} is used, and in the other case the superset D_{U_1}. Since this can quickly lead to an exceedingly large set of query plans and candidate data structures, the user can force the generator to only make combinations of entire tables, and not subsets of columns from each table.

3.3   Query Plan Creation

Each time query plan optimization results in document structures, the generator will check whether these document structures D are novel. When for example $D_{U_1|P_1}$ is a novel data structure, each query plan that uses D_{U_1} or D_{P_1} is notified of its existence. Each query plan will then check if it can replace each used document D by the new data structure.

Replacement Rules. Suppose the query plan $QP_{U_1 \to P_1 \to C_1}$ is notified of the existence of $D_{U_1|P_1}$. This will yield the new query plans $QP_{U_1|P_1 \to P_1 \to C_1}$ and potentially also $QP_{U_1 \to U_1|P_1 \to C_1}$. The latter QP can only be created when either:

Rule 1: The entire set of products is fully contained in $D_{U_1|P_1}$. This is referred to as a fully functional closure (**FFC**) in literature [17].

Rule 2: The result required to reach P_1, namely U_1, was queried in the previous step of the join query, and we are traversing the same relationship.

Query Plan Inner-compaction. These replacements based on the original query plan can typically be compacted. Suppose the query plan $QP_{U_1|P_1 \to P_1 \to C_1}$. In this example, we have already obtained the necessary Product information in the first step, and thus this query plan becomes $QP_{U_1|P_1 \to C_1}$. We list the different cases in which such compactions are allowed below:

Case 1: $A|B \to B$ The subsequent data has already been queried.
Case 2: $A \to A|B$ The previous data can also be queried in the next query.
Case 3: $B \to A|B|C$ If B is a FFC in $A|B|C$, then B can be eliminated.

The query plan can compact itself in multiple iterations until nothing changes.

Secondary Indexing. Suppose we have the Sequence $Seq_{P \to C}$ that is answered using the query plan $QP_{U_1|P_1 \to C_1}$ which joins Product information with buyer's Comments. Since the Product information is at the $2nd$-level in the nested document $D_{U_1|P_1}$, the query will require secondary indexing on the nested field Users.Products.id to select the relevant records. Query plans automatically keep track whether they require secondary indexes, which is in turn reflected in their cost. In the schema recommendation, the best query plans will be listed, and when these plans use secondary indexing, it will have to be implemented, which brings an additional cost.

3.4 Document Merge Operation

The merging of data structures is the key underpinning functionality that drives the document generation process. We explain the process by example: suppose we optimize the root query plan $QP_{U \to P \to C}$, then it will attempt to merge together $D_U + D_P$ and $D_P + D_C$. When this is allowed, new document structures $D_{U|P}$ and $D_{P|C}$ are created, which embed relational data into the parent document.

Merge Rules. The merge between two documents D_1 and D_2 happens at the initiative of a query plan, and is only allowed when the following rules uphold:

Rule 1: $D_1 \not\subset D_2$. The first document is not a subset of the second.
Rule 2: $D_1.$canMerge(D_2). Documents are complex trees of embedding, and their compatibility needs to be checked. The canMerge function checks: (i) if D_2 answers a subset of the sequences of D_1, and if either (ii.a) there is an overlap between D_1 and D_2, or (ii.b) D_1 can be connected to the top or bottom of D_2 its tree.
Rule 3: Let $T =$merge(D_1, D_2), then $Dim(T) \leq MaxDim$. The new document's maximum height and width (at each node) must be below the configured thresholds. This prevents the creation of exceedingly large documents.
Rule 4: Let $T =$merge(D_1, D_2), then T.isValidCyclic(). If T has repeating Entities, then these must correspond with at least one Sequence that makes use of this repetition.
Rule 5: Let $T =$merge(D_1, D_2), then $D_1 \subset T$ and $D_2 \subset T$.

Merge Between Document Trees. When D_1 can be merged with D_2, they are merged at the basis of their entire intersection (the largest overlap) that can be found in the largest tree. If the intersection is empty, the two documents are merged at the first leaf node that can form a connection between the top node of the other tree, or vice versa. This is illustrated in Fig. 4.

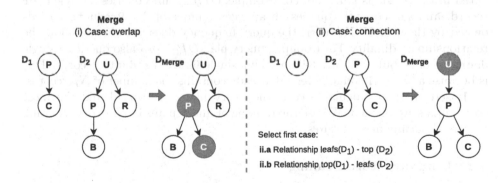

Fig. 4. Document merges at largest overlap or a relationship between two nodes.

The next section explains the mechanism of pruning documents and query plans at the basis of cost models and utility functions.

4 Pruning Algorithms

The set of query plans as generated in the previous steps will be established through many iterations and thus can grow exceedingly large. Since database recommendation is considered to be a NP-hard problem, Sect. 4.1 describes the mechanism for query plan pruning to force convergence or termination. Once all query plan optimization activities have terminated, we are left with numerous document data structures from which have to select the most suitable. Section 4.2 explains the pruning algorithms employed for this.

4.1 Query Plan Pruning and Compaction

At a configurable threshold of query plans (e.g. ≥ 30.000), we can apply two alternative mechanisms to reduce the query plan set: (i) query plan outer-compaction, or (ii) query plan pruning.

Query Plan Outer-compaction. In the overall set, a smaller query plan, for example $QP_{U_1|P_1}$, may be a subset of larger plans such as $QP_{U_1|P_1 \rightarrow P_1}$. Therefore, all query plans that are in bucket k, and thus have k join steps, are passed to the query plans in bucket $k+1$, which check whether or not they are redundant.

Query Plan Pruning and Cost Models. The second, and main mechanism, maintains an intermediate ranking of all the query plans per Sequence based on their efficiency. The efficiency of a query plan is calculated at the basis of their cost to execute, which takes into account per individual query: (i) the records selected, and (ii) the result size retrieved, which both may be impacted by (iii) the use of secondary indexing.

Query Frequency. An important cost factor is the frequency of records selected at a join step, and thus at an individual query. This typically follows the cardinality of the relationship between the first query at this step, and the last query executed in the previous join step. For example, $QP_{U \rightarrow P}$ first queries a single User record, and subsequently queries an average number of N_P Products records owned by the user U. However, the query frequency does not always follow the relationship cardinality. For example, query plan $QP_{U \rightarrow U|P}$ also queries a single Users records, but it is only followed by a single Users|Products records. This is because a Users|Products record already contains the number of N_P records.

Based on their calculable cost, the query plans are sorted and the most costly plans are pruned. We use the ranking of query plans to subsequently rank traversed document structures.

4.2 Data Structure Pruning

In the resulting recommendation set, only the N best document structures are chosen along with advice on the ideal query plans to answer the given workload.

The effectiveness of a document D can be defined by the number of total query plans it appears in and their respective query ranks. However, this indicator would simply be skewed by the quantity of plans in which the document appears, rather than their quality. Consequentially, we need a metric to determine a query plan's utility, before we can determine the utility of a document.

Query Plan Utility Function. A fitness function for a query plan takes as input its relative rank (with higher being better) between other query plans of the intended read **Sequence**, and the total rank. The linear fitness function skews the document utility by the quantity of query plans it appears in. The non-linear fitness function distributes more utility to higher-tier query plans (e.g. steps $k = 1$). We have implemented both a linear, and a non-linear fitness function.

$$linearFitness(qp, totalSeqRank) = \frac{2 * qp.Rank}{totalSeqRank} \tag{1}$$

$$nonLinearFitness(qp, totSeqRank) = \frac{linearFitness(qp, totSeqRank)}{qp.queryLength^2} \tag{2}$$

Document Ranking. The fitness of a document for a specific query **Sequence**, is the weighted sum of its relative fitness from its query plans that are subscribed to the document. Each value is also weighted by the query's frequency in the workload to stress its importance. Based on the overall fitness outcomes of each document, they can be ranked from least to most effective.

5   Evaluation

We evaluate the DBSR framework in the specific case of the online auction data model and workload found in the RUBiS benchmark [6]. Our evaluation approach is two-fold: (i) we analyse the impact of the configuration parameters on the document generation and pruning process, and (ii) we perform an experimental performance evaluation to assess the quality of recommended schemas and its query plans in a MongoDB cluster, compared to a normalized approach.

5.1   Document Generation and Pruning

The parameters that influence the resulting schema and its dimensions the most are: (a) the maximum document tree's height H, and (b) the maximum width W which is the maximum number of relationships embedded per single node in the tree, and potentially (c) the degree of pruning.

Table 1 shows the candidate documents in the final document pruning stages, after execution with a maximum document height and node width of respectively $(3, 1)$ and $(4, 3)$. We ran both configurations with a maximum of 4.000 iterations and pruning threshold of 30.000 query plans. Both executions halt after reaching the maximum number of iterations, and output candidate sets of respectively 26 and 36 documents. Among the overall set of document candidates, we observed a variety of nesting and width, within the specified dimensions of each execution.

In the final pruning steps and when comparing the different run configurations, both (a) and (b) lead to similar documents, and only documents of width

Table 1. Document ranking (low → high) during final pruning steps, with **X** signifying a removed document. The last step's final document ranks are underlined.

(a) MaxDim(H = 3,W = 1)

| Execution time | 142 s |
| Result size | 26 |

Documents	Rank				
Products|Bids	1	3	4	X	
Bids|Products	2	2	3	1	_2_
Products|Users	3	4	2	3	X
Users	4	5	X		
Products|Comments	5	1	1	2	_3_
Products|Users|Regions	6	6	5	4	_1_
Comments	7	X			

(b) MaxDim(H = 4, W = 3)

| Execution time | 166 s |
| Result size | 36 |

Documents	Rank					
Products|Comments	1	1	1	1	1	_2_
Products|Bids	2	5	5	X		
Products|Bids|Users	3	2	2	2	2	X
Products|Bids|Users|Regions	4	3	4	4	3	_1_
Users|Bids	5	4	3	3	X	
Products|Users	6	6	X			
Comments	7	X				

1 are remaining, though with run (b) having a document of height 4. In the final step (b) also prunes to a smaller minimum set of 2 documents rather than 3.

Whenever a document is pruned, for example in (a) when `Comments` is pruned, the rank of each document will be re-calculated. Subsequently, in that example, `Products|Comments` is the only document now containing `Comments` information and consequently, its rank shifts from 5 to 1. Similar events can be observed throughout the pruning process.

The pruner also skips essential documents when they are the only remaining option to answer a specific query. For example, `Regions` is only embedded in one document, and is essential to answer a query on a `User`'s `Region`.

Furthermore, altering the degree of pruning thresholds from a maximum query plan size of 30K to 80K only results in a minor change in (b), and yields `Bids|Products` over `Products|Bids`.

5.2   Performance Evaluation

We evaluate the quality of DBSR's schema recommendations in the document database MongoDB, selected for its widespread popularity and maturity.

The evaluation compares two schema recommendations from Table 1 (a), which feature respectively 3 and 5 document collections, to a normalized schema consisting of the 5 original tables (as shown in Fig. 1). The recommender's input workload is executed against these schemas and consists of 11 `JOIN` queries.

Evaluation Setup. In order to conduct the evaluation, we extended the YCSB NoSQL benchmark [9] with a custom data loader and workload model based on the online auction case (RUBiS benchmark [6])[2]. The MongoDB database is a 3-node cluster on Amazon AWS; the primary node serves as a query router, and two shards horizontally partition the data based on the primary key. Secondary indexing is implemented per document collection when required by a query plan.

---

[2] Benchmark repository: https://github.com/vreniers/YCSB-MongoDB-RUBiS.

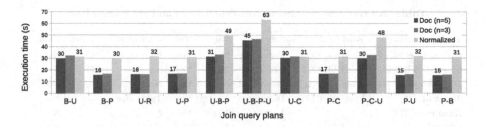

Fig. 5. Query join performance on recommended and normalized schemas.

Results. Figure 5 shows the execution time per join query, executed numerously, on three different schemas. For example, $QP_{P \rightarrow B}$ queries a `Product`'s information and all its `Bids`. The recommended schemas in most cases outperform the normalized schema, and in other cases, the baseline performance is similar. These performance gains stem from eliminating costly `JOIN` queries, in which the intermediate results are returned to the client at each step to formulate the follow-up query. Despite using only 3 document collections, many queries can be answered with a single look-up. In terms of the increase in data redundancy when compared to the normalized schema, mainly `Product` information is duplicated three times, and `User` with `Region` information in the document set $D_{P|U|R}$.

Using a slightly larger set of 5 documents yielded no discernible difference over using the minimal schema recommendation. This can be attributed to the manner in which the documents are ranked, namely they are sorted based on their global utility to all queries. It could be the case that a single document is highly effective for a single or few queries, but not globally. To take such cases into account, the relative weight of these queries can be increased which ranks their utilized documents higher, or by implementing a more local optima search.

6 Related Work

Table 2 shows an overview of all other existing schema tools for NoSQL databases, and we distinguish between (i) transformation tools that essentially apply transformation rules (e.g. heuristics) to a data model to result in a target schema, and (ii) generators, which enumerate multiple data structures.

Many tools shown in Table 2 simply apply a straightforward conversion from for example an ER-model guided by queries (e.g. Chebotko et al. [7]) and yield a somewhat optimal schema. While C. Lee et al. [15] enumerate all possible columnar structures by enumerating over foreign dependencies, it lacks a cost model and therefore does not provide a schema recommendation.

6.1 In-Depth Comparison

We provide an in-depth comparison between DBSR and the approaches of schema generators by Bermbach et al. [5] and Mior et al. (NoSE) [18], which provide schema recommenders for NoSQL columnar stores (e.g. Cassandra). Despite

Table 2. Overview of schema conversion tools and recommenders.

Transformation	Workload	Schema	Dupli.	Nest	Cost model	Index	Plans
Chebotko et al. [7]	Read (J, O, E)	Columnar	Yes	Yes*	No	C	No
Mortadelo [22]	Read (J, O, E)	Col/Doc	Yes	Yes	No	C	No
De Lima et al. [17]	Frequency(R)	Document	No	Yes	No	-	No
Jia et al. [13]	Freq(W/R(J))	Document	Yes	Yes	Table size	-	No
Zhao et al. [23]	-	Nested	Yes	Yes	No	-	No
QODM [16]	Read (J)	Generic	Yes	Yes	No	-	No
Banerjee et al. [4]	-	JSON	No	Yes	No	-	No
Schema Generators							
Lee et al. [15]	-	Columnar	Yes	Yes*	No	-	No
Bermbach et al.[5]	R(J, E), W	Columnar	Yes	Yes*	Schema rank	S	No
NoSE [18]	R(J, O, E), W	Columnar	Yes	Yes*	Query cost	C	Yes
DBSR	Read (J)	Document	Yes	Yes	Extensive	S	Yes

Abbreviations: Read (R), Write (W), Join (J), Ordering (O), Equality search (E), Clustering index (C), Secondary index (S), *Groups data together.

working on fundamentally different data structures, they follow a similar approach in enumerating data structures and cost-based elimination.

Candidate Generation. The initial process in Bermbach et al. [5] loops over each JOIN query and creates a single materialized view table, enabling a single lookup per query. NoSE [18] creates materialized views for each step in the JOIN query similar to our approach. In Bermbach et al. [5], multiple schemas are calculated as the cartesian product of singular materialized views. In each potential schema, it is then evaluated whether a data structure can be used for another query. In NoSE [18] candidate combinations are merged when they meet certain requirements: identical primary key, no clustering or secondary indexes, and have a different set of data attributes. In our approach, we can flexibly merge data structure candidates, at various points (e.g. overlap, or connection), and only when JOIN queries benefit from such a merge. In a second stage, NoSE [18] and Bermbach et al. [5] can add data structures (i.e. look-up tables) when required by write/update queries. A similar approach could also be implemented in DBSR.

Schema Assessment. In both approaches, every potential schema option is created as every possible combination of data structures that constitute a valid schema. In contrast, we calculate the optimal schema by pruning the least effective document structures using a non-linear utility heuristic. In Bermbach et al. [5], each schema is ranked in terms of a simple scoring function that builds on two metrics: (i) average number of secondary indexes and (ii) average amount of data duplication. In NoSE [18], a query cost model is implemented, and each schema is assessed by the total cost of executing all queries against this schema.

7   Conclusions

In this paper, we have presented a document-based schema recommender (DBSR) for NoSQL document-oriented databases. The DBSR framework provides several contributions as re-usable modules, namely (i) a workload-driven document generator, with (ii) cost-based pruning algorithms for query plans and document data structures. These modules, combined in the framework, can provide a schema recommendation for an ER data model and read workload. The schema recommendation features document structures, query plans and secondary indexing suggestions, along with a utility matrix that provides insights into the efficiency of involved documents and query costs.

Our evaluation provides (i) an analysis of the schema generation and pruning process, and (ii) an experimental performance evaluation of a recommended schema using an extension of YCSB in MongoDB. Significant performance benefits were shown for read queries, at the expense of data redundancy. The pruning approach eliminates documents based on their relative global utility.

In future work, we would like to investigate alternative pruning-based approaches (e.g. more local solution space exploration), as well as NoSQL benchmarks that evaluate NoSQL schema recommendations that function on ER models, rather than key-value pairs in YCSB. The further integration between databases, (micro-)benchmarking, and schema recommendation will allow evaluating candidates automatically, and subsequently calibration of the cost models used tailored to the selected use case, database technology and deployment.

Acknowledgments. This work has been funded by the KU Leuven Research Fund.

References

1. Entity relationships and document design. https://docs.couchbase.com/server/4.0/data-modeling/entity-relationship-doc-design.html. Accessed 25 May 2020
2. MongoDB: Data model design. https://docs.mongodb.com/manual/core/data-model-design/. Accessed 25 May 2020
3. Atzeni, P., Bugiotti, F., Cabibbo, L., Torlone, R.: Data modeling in the NoSQL world. Comput. Stand. Interfaces **67**, 103149 (2020)
4. Banerjee, S., Sarkar, A.: Logical level design of NOSQL databases. In: 2016 IEEE Region 10 Conference (TENCON), pp. 2360–2365 (2016)
5. Bermbach, D., Müller, S., Eberhardt, J., Tai, S.: Informed schema design for column store-based database services. In: 2015 IEEE 8th International Conference on Service-Oriented Computing and Applications (SOCA), pp. 163–172, October 2015
6. Cecchet, E., Marguerite, J., Zwaenepoel, W.: Performance and scalability of EJB applications. ACM SIGPLAN Not. **37**(11), 246–261 (2002)
7. Chebotko, A., Kashlev, A., Lu, S.: A big data modeling methodology for apache Cassandra. In: IEEE International Congress on Big Data (2015)
8. Cheng, Chun-Hung., Lee, Wing-Kin, Wong, Kam-Fai: A genetic algorithm-based clustering approach for database partitioning. IEEE Trans. Syst. Man Cybern. Part C (Appl. Rev.) **32**(3), 215–230 (2002)
9. Cooper, B.F., Silberstein, A., Tam, E., Ramakrishnan, R., Sears, R.: Benchmarking cloud serving systems with YCSB. In: Proceedings of the 1st ACM Symposium on Cloud Computing, pp. 143–154 (2010)

10. Gómez, P., Casallas, R., Roncancio, C.: Data schema does matter, even in NoSQL systems! In: IEEE Tenth International Conference on Research Challenges in Information Science (RCIS) (2016)
11. Gómez, P., Roncancio, C., Casallas, R.: Towards quality analysis for document oriented bases. In: International Conference on Conceptual Modeling (2018)
12. Grolinger, Katarina., Higashino, Wilson A., Tiwari, Abhinav, Capretz, Miriam A.M.: Data management in cloud environments: NoSQL and NewSQL data stores. J. Cloud Comput. Adv. Syst. Appl. **2**(1), 1–24 (2013). https://doi.org/10.1186/2192-113X-2-22
13. Jia, T., Zhao, X., Wang, Z., Gong, D., Ding, G.: Model transformation and data migration from relational database to MongoDB. In: IEEE International Congress on Big Data (BigData Congress) (2016)
14. Kanade, A., Gopal, A., Kanade, S.: A study of normalization and embedding in MongoDB. In: IEEE International Advance Computing Conference (IACC) (2014)
15. Lee, C., Zheng, Y.: Automatic SQL-to-NoSQL schema transformation over the MySQL and HBase databases. In: 2015 IEEE International Conference on Consumer Electronics - Taiwan (2015)
16. Li, X., Ma, Z., Chen, H.: QODM: a query-oriented data modeling approach for NoSQL databases. In: 2014 IEEE Workshop on Advanced Research and Technology in Industry Applications (WARTIA), pp. 338–345. IEEE (2014)
17. de Lima, C., dos Santos Mello, R.: A workload-driven logical design approach for NoSQL document databases. In: Proceedings of the 17th International Conference on Information Integration and Web-based Applications & Services (2015)
18. Mior, M.J., Salem, K., Aboulnaga, A., Liu, R.: NoSE: Schema Design for NoSQL Applications. IEEE Transactions on Knowledge and Data Engineering (Oct 2017)
19. Pasqualin, D., Souza, G., Buratti, E.L., de Almeida, E.C., Del Fabro, M.D., Weingaertner, D.: A case study of the aggregation query model in read-mostly NoSQL document stores. In: Proceedings of the 20th International Database Engineering & Applications Symposium (2016)
20. Reniers, V., Van Landuyt, D., Rafique, A., Joosen, W.: Schema design support for semi-structured data: Finding the sweet spot between NF and De-NF. In: 2017 IEEE International Conference on Big Data (Big Data), pp. 2921–2930 (2017)
21. Stonebraker, M.: SQL databases v. NoSQL databases. Commun. ACM **53**(4), 10–11 (2010). https://doi.org/10.1145/1721654.1721659
22. de la Vega, A., García-Saiz, D., Blanco, C., Zorrilla, M., Sánchez, P.: Mortadelo: automatic generation of NoSQL stores from platform-independent data models. Future Gener. Comput. Syst. **105**, 455–474 (2020)
23. Zhao, G., Lin, Q., Li, L., Li, Z.: Schema conversion model of SQL database to NoSQL. In: 2014 Ninth International Conference on P2P, Parallel, Grid, Cloud and Internet Computing, pp. 355–362, November 2014

Empirical Studies of Conceptual Modeling

Quantifying the Impact of EER Modeling on Relational Database Success: An Experimental Investigation

Yoram Timmerman$^{(\boxtimes)}$, Antoon Bronselaer , and Guy De Tré

Department of Telecommunications and Information Processing, Ghent University,
Sint-Pietersnieuwstraat 41, 9000 Ghent, Belgium
{yoram.timmerman,antoon.bronselaer,guy.detre}@ugent.be

Abstract. Despite the widespread idea in literature that the inclusion of EER modeling in the design process of a relational database is beneficial for the success of that database, almost no quantitative cost-benefit analyses of EER modeling exist today to support this statement. In order to fill this need, an empirical study is performed in which the success of a relational database of which the design process contains an EER modeling phase is compared to the success of a relational database in which only the minimally needed design effort was put. Hereby, database success is treated as originally proposed by the DeLone and McLean Information Systems Success Model, by specifically focusing on the information quality and system quality of both databases. To this end, respectively, the total amount of time that is needed by an end user to complete a set of tasks by using the database, and the total execution cost that is needed by the database system before a correct solution to each task is submitted, is analyzed. Moreover, the work accounts for the possible moderation of the technical competence of an end user in the relationship between EER modeling and the success of the eventual relational database. Preliminary results indicate that the inclusion of EER modeling in relational database design significantly highers the perceived information quality and system quality of that database. Moreover, there is statistical evidence that this result is independent of the competence profile of that user.

Keywords: Conceptual modeling · EER · Relational databases · SQL · Information Systems Success

1 Introduction

Since several decades, conceptual modeling is a central part of various kinds of information system (IS) development projects [10]. One area in which conceptual modeling plays an important role is relational database design. Indeed, it is generally assumed that in order to preserve the success of a relational database, its implementation should be preceded by the construction of a conceptual model [23]. An important conceptual grammar to this end is the Extended

© Springer Nature Switzerland AG 2020
G. Dobbie et al. (Eds.): ER 2020, LNCS 12400, pp. 487–500, 2020.
https://doi.org/10.1007/978-3-030-62522-1_36

Entity-Relationship (EER) grammar [6,9,10]. EER modeling allows the database designer to describe his/her data domain knowledge before actually implementing the database. It results in a diagram that visually represents the data that should be stored in the database and the behaviour that the database should support. This EER diagram is then translated into a corresponding relational database schema [15,23].

Literature provides several reasons on why EER modeling should be part of any relational database design process. First, it forces database designers to reason about the different pieces of data and their relationships before actually implementing the database. Second, it results in a visual and very intuitive representation of the data, ensuring smooth communication between database designers and domain experts. As such, the usage of EER modeling allows for the early detection of possible requirement errors [14]. Third, plenty of algorithms exist for the translation of EER models into corresponding relational database schemas, allowing for a fluent incorporation of EER models in the database design process [13,19].

However, despite the omnipresent recommendations regarding the usage of conceptual models, in practice conceptual design is often neglected during database design projects. Although EER is the most commonly used conceptual grammar in the context of database design, studies in Australia and Germany have illustrated that only 42% (Australia) to 52% (Germany) of the computer-science related employees come into contact with EER modeling on a regular basis [6,10]. Respectively 38% and 23% of the respondents have never used EER or have never heard about it. Some recent relational database research even questions the value of conceptual modeling [12].

A possible explanation for the limited adoption rate of conceptual grammars during database design is the lack of empirical evidence of the positive impact of conceptual modeling on databases. It is surprising that, although conceptual modeling is widely promoted in literature, almost no empirical research regarding its added value has been performed until now. Batra and Marakas state that "researchers have not attempted to conduct case or field studies to gauge the cost-benefits of enterprise-wide conceptual data modeling" [3]. This work tries to address this need by quantifying the impact that the construction of a conceptual model has on the success of relational databases by using an operational quality measurement procedure. Here, the definition of IS success by DeLone and McLean, which will be elaborated upon in Sect. 2, is used as a starting point [7]. An experiment is conducted in which the success of two relational databases, both containing the same information, is evaluated. However, for one database the design process of the database schema included the construction of an EER model, while for the other database only the minimally needed design effort was taken in order to construct the database.

The structure of the remainder of the paper is as follows. Section 2 describes the relevant literature. In Sect. 3, the research questions and hypotheses are formulated. Section 4 then describes the methodology, after which the results of the experiment are listed in Sect. 5. Section 6 discusses the obtained results. Finally, in Sect. 7 the conclusions of this work are written down.

2   Background

Regarding **IS success**, the most important theoretical framework is the DeLone and McLean model [7]. DeLone and McLean suggest six dimensions that are closely related to the success of an IS. Important to note in the context of this work are **Information Quality (IQ)** and **System Quality (SQ)**. IQ relates to the quality aspects of the data themselves: accuracy, completeness, meaningfulness ... Contrary, SQ relates to the characteristics of the system on which the IS runs (e.g. resource utilization, execution cost ...). An important characteristic of the model is that the different dimensions are strongly interrelated. Stated informally, the information and system quality have an influence on the way that users interact with the IS (Use) and the extent to which they are satisfied with the IS (User Satisfaction). This again has an impact on the extent to which individuals make decisions based on the IS (Individual Impact), in the end leading to an impact on the organization in which the IS is used (Organizational Impact). Empirical research has validated the existence of these relationships [8]. As such, IQ and SQ (in)directly influence each of the other dimensions in the model.

In the past decades, several procedures for the **measurement of the IQ and SQ of an IS** (and data quality in general) have been proposed. Most of these procedures rely on the construction of a set of criteria that should be fulfilled by a dataset or system in order for that dataset or system to be of high quality [4,20]. The more criteria that are satisfied by a given IS (or its content), the higher its associated quality.

Important to note here is that criteria based techniques typically look at quality as a purely intrinsic property, i.e. a property that does not depend on the context in which a dataset or system is used. However, one could argue that in order to be able to measure IQ or SQ, it is important to take into account the purposes for which one wants to use a dataset or system. Indeed, a given dataset may be very well-suited to complete a given task, while it may be totally useless with respect to another task. Criteria-based techniques typically do not take into account this context. In order to fill this gap, **operational procedures** were developed in which quality measurement is approached from a different angle [5]. The idea behind these procedures is that the quality of a dataset or system depends on the ease with which the tasks that should be performed with the help of that dataset/system can be completed. The easier it is to use a dataset/system for a given purpose, the higher its quality for that purpose.

In this work, the operational measurement procedure proposed by Bronselaer et al. [5] will be used. Here, the ease of completion of a task is expressed as an inverse function of the cost needed to complete the tasks. Typical cost units associated with tasks are time, resource utilization, computational cost ... Next to the fact that this procedure does not neglect the context in which the system or dataset is used, it also allows for a more objective way of measuring quality than criteria-based systems, as no human intervention is necessary in order to construct a set of criteria. Finally, as quality is measured in terms of a cost, the technique allows to measure IQ or SQ on a ratio scale, contrary to criteria-based procedures that produce values on an ordinal scale.

Regarding the **impact of EER modeling on relational database success**, until now, to our knowledge, only very limited research has been performed. The only relevant study that was found, performed by Turk et al., concludes that the usage of EER modeling has a statistically significant positive impact on the quality of relational database schemas [21]. Although this study forms a first attempt in order to assess the value of conceptual modeling, a few remarks should be made. First, the number of participants was fairly limited. Secondly, the quality has been assessed with the help of a grading schema. As such, the assessment of the relational database schema quality required human intervention, possibly limiting the objectivity of the evaluation. Finally, the study does not account for the impact of possible moderators in the relationship between EER modeling and eventual relational database quality, such as the competence of database users.

3   Research Questions and Hypotheses

As Sect. 2 illustrated that IQ and SQ (in)directly impact each of the other IS success dimensions, this paper exclusively focuses on the impact of EER modeling on the IQ and SQ of relational databases. Moreover, this work explicitly accounts for the possible moderation of the technical competence of relational database users in the relationship between the usage of EER modeling and relational database success. Indeed, it could be possible that the impact of conceptual modeling on relational database success is differently perceived (e.g. smaller) by end users with a stronger relational database knowledge compared to end users with only limited knowledge.

As such, the following two research questions can be formulated:

1. What is the impact of the inclusion of EER modeling in a relational database design process on the IQ and SQ of that database, compared to the situation in which only the minimally needed effort is taken to design a database that stores the same data?
2. What is the impact of the technical competence of end users on the relationship between the inclusion of EER modeling in the relational database design and the IQ and SQ of that database?

Based on these research questions, the following hypotheses were made:

1. Relational databases of which the design process includes an EER modeling phase have better IQ and SQ compared to relational databases for which only the minimally needed effort is taken to design the database.
2. The inclusion of EER modeling in the design process of a relational database is beneficial for both the IQ and SQ of the eventual relational database, independently of the technical competence of end users.

4   Methodology

To empirically test the hypotheses mentioned in Sect. 3, an experiment was conducted in December 2019. This section elaborates upon the design of that experiment. It should be noted however that additional information (including datasets, EER diagrams, database schemas and hand-outs) can be found on a dedicated link: https://osf.io/kasyg/.

4.1   Relational Databases

The basis for the experiment was the official IMDb (Internet Movie Database) dataset, which can be found online in the form of seven different tab-separated files together with its associated documentation [11]. This dataset was chosen for two different reasons. First, as the data domain consists of several entity types that are heavily interconnected, constructing a database for the IMDb dataset can be assumed to be a realistic example of a real-life design problem. Second, the subject of the dataset (the film industry) is assumed to be part of the general knowledge of people. This is important, as an unknown data domain would first require the participants to acknowledge themselves with the meaning of the data, possibly impacting the results of the experiment.

Starting from the IMDb dataset, two different PostgreSQL relational databases were constructed. The design process of the first relational database, which will be called the **minimal effort relational database (MEDB)** in the following, was kept as simple as possible: each .tsv-file was mapped to a corresponding table and each attribute to a corresponding column. Only information that was present in the online documentation offered by IMDb was translated into the corresponding relational database functionality. As such, no primary or foreign key constraints were defined for this database and all columns had the associated "varchar" datatype. As almost no design effort at all was put in the design of MEDB, it is not a completely realistic representation of what an everyday database design process in practice looks like. However, as the goal of this work is to quantify the total impact of including an EER modeling phase in the design process, the database serves as a perfect zero point. Contrary, the design process of the second relational database, the **EER-based relational database (EERDB)**, included an EER modeling phase. The EER model was constructed using the general knowledge of the authors about the data domain. Moreover, the recommended EER design principles that can be found in literature were adopted [2,23]. Finally, the mapping of the EER diagram to a relational database schema was performed by following default mapping algorithms [2,19].

The data that are stored in both databases are exactly the same, the structure of the data is known exactly before the start of the design process and the data does not change over time. This is not always the case in practice, as many real-life relational database schemas are regularly updated. However, the impact of EER on schema evolution was not taken into account in this work. The reason for this is that throughout the design of the experiment, it was chosen to minimize the possibility of any biases on the measured IQ and SQ of the relational databases during the experiment as much as possible. As such, we opted for a very narrow and easily controllable database use case.

4.2   IQ and SQ Measures

In order to assess relational database IQ and SQ, the operational measurement procedure introduced in Sect. 2 was used. As such, IQ and SQ can be measured by looking at the ease with which a set of tasks can be completed with the help of the dataset or system. In order to be able to adopt this procedure in the context of the proposed experiment, a task set consisting of analytical database questions was constructed. Each of the tasks was based on earlier analyses that have been made on IMDb data (e.g. [1, 18]). The task set could thus be assumed to be a realistic example of real-life analytical questions that are typically solved with the help of relational databases. Some of the questions were split up in multiple questions, each handling a specific subproblem. As such, in total eleven analytical questions were obtained.

Following Bronselaer et al. [5], the **Information Quality** of an IS can be measured as the inverse of the ease with which end users are capable to solve the tasks with the help of the data stored in the IS. In the current context, the ease with which tasks are solved can then be measured as the inverse of the total amount of time that an end user needed in order to formulate a SQL query that correctly solved the task. Similarly, the **System Quality** can be measured as the inverse of the ease with which the IS is capable of processing the SQL queries that the end users submit to solve the tasks. As a metric for this ease, the inverse of the query execution cost metric provided by PostgreSQL was chosen. This cost is a fixed value that is computed based on the query execution plan [16]. As such, in this study the total query execution cost that was needed by the relational database in order for an end user to solve a task was used as a measure for the SQ of the database. This total execution cost is equal to the sum of the execution costs of all queries that were submitted by an end user until a correct solution was found.

Important to note is that the presence of indices can have a large impact on the execution cost of a query. As the definition and creation of indices is not an inherent part of the EER grammar, for both MEDB and EERDB, no indices were explicitly created by the authors. However, PostgreSQL automatically defines an index for all existing primary key constraints. As such, the only indices that are present are those that are associated with an existing primary key constraint.

4.3   Participants

The participants were Bachelor students that had followed an introductory relational database course in the fall of 2019. In total, 202 students participated to the experiment. 103 students were randomly assigned to the group that had to perform the tasks with the help of MEDB, the other 99 students had to perform the tasks with the help of EERDB. The sample included students from different fields of expertise. However, the dominating group of students were informatics and computer science engineering students. Although the subjects only had limited experience with EER design and SQL at the time that the experiment was conducted, we believe that choosing students as subjects improved the reliability of the experiment. The main motivation for this is that each subject followed the same course on relational databases. As such, we were able to very closely control the SQL background knowledge of all participants. Situations were thus excluded in which subjects of one of database group would require SQL concepts that they had never encountered before in order to solve a given question, while this would not be the case for the other group. Contrary, our subject selection strategy made sure that all participants had the necessary background knowledge in order to be able to solve each of the tasks. In a context with industry professionals as subjects, this would be much more difficult to achieve.

4.4 Experimental Setup

Before conducting the experiment, a request for ethical advice was made to the Ethics Commission of the Faculty of Arts and Philosophy of Ghent University, as human participants were involved in the experiment. All procedures performed in the study were in accordance with the ethical standards of the institutional committee and with the 1964 Helsinki declaration and its later amendments or comparable ethical standards.

Participants were asked to solve as many tasks as possible during a session of 75 min. Separate sessions were provided for the MEDB and EERDB user groups. Before the start of the session, participants were offered an informed consent, explaining the procedure of the experiment, which was also orally explained in the classroom. All subjects were given the relational schema of the database of the group they belonged to, together with some general documentation regarding that database. No EER diagrams were handed out. The reason for this is that the goal of the experiment was to quantify the impact of EER modeling on the IQ and SQ of the eventual relational database. In order to be able to make an honest comparison between the IQ and SQ of both databases, it was chosen to only hand out information that was directly associated to the relational databases themselves and to not hand out additional information to the subjects belonging to the EERDB group. Finally, a summary of the SQL concepts taught during the year was handed out to each participant. Participants were not informed about the goal of the research, in order to prevent possible effects of this knowledge on the results. The tasks had to be solved via an in-house developed query exercise platform, called Q'exr [17]. This query tool allowed the participants to submit queries in order to find a solution to a given task, which are passed along to the underlying relational database (either MEDB or EERDB). Subsequently, the user receives feedback on the correctness of his/her solution. During the experiment, users were able to navigate between different questions, independently of which questions were already solved. As the Q'exr platform had already been used extensively during the introductory database course, it was assumed that the participants were familiar enough with the platform in order to be able to perform the experiment.

5   Results

Based on the measured values for the total amount of time and the total execution cost, statistical tests were performed in order to determine whether the difference in IQ and SQ between MEDB and EERDB can be considered to be statistically significant or not. Moreover, we accounted for the possibility that differences in SQL competence could influence the impact of EER modeling on the IQ and SQ of the database. Therefore, each participant was categorized into one out of four SQL competence categories ("Weak", "Moderate", "Good" and "Very good"), based on earlier evaluations of the SQL competences of the students that took place in the context of the introductory relational database course. The first quartile of students was categorized in the "Weak" group, the second in the "Moderate" group et cetera.

In order to test the statistical significance of the differences in IQ and SQ, two-way ANOVA (Analysis of Variance) tests were conducted with one dependent variable (total amount of time/total execution cost) and two independent variables (database and SQL competence) for each task [22]. Moreover, a two-way ANOVA test also allows for conclusions concerning whether an interaction effect (IE) exists between the used database and SQL competence. In case an IE exists, conclusions about statistically significant differences in IQ or SQ can only be drawn for each SQL competence group separately.

Datasets that are the subject of a two-way ANOVA analysis should fulfill a couple of requirements [22]. First, the residual data in every cell (i.e. participants using the same database and belonging to the same competence group) of the experiment design should be approximately normally distributed. This was verified for each test using a normal Q-Q plot. Second, homogeneity of variances (HOV) should apply, meaning that the variances between the different cells should not differ too much. In case normality or HOV did not apply to the data under analysis, one or more transformations have been applied to the dependent variable in order to correct for these deviations. If transformations were not satisfactory in order for the data to satisfy normality or HOV, a robust two-way ANOVA has been used, in which the statistical significance of the difference in the medians between different cells was tested, instead of the difference in the means. If this was still not satisfactory in order to comply with the assumptions, then no statistical test could be performed. Finally, outliers were removed from the dataset. Although this could affect the results obtained by the test, it was verified manually for every test that outlier removal did not alter the conclusions that could be drawn based on that test.

5.1   The IQ Dimension: Time Measurement

In order to detect the existence of an IE and/or statistically significant differences in the IQ of both databases, for each task two-way ANOVA tests were performed in which the dependent variable was the total amount of time needed in order to find the solution to that task. The results are summarized respectively in Tables 1 and 2. Results have been found to be statistically significant for $p < .05$.

Table 1. Results of the two-way ANOVA tests (p, df_{inter}, df_{error} and η^2) regarding the existence of an IE between SQL competence and database group for the total amount of time. The number of outliers for both database groups ($N_{o,M}$ and $N_{o,E}$), the result of the Levene's test for equality of variances (p_{HOV}), the used operator (mean or median) and the applied transformation (with $f^n(x) = f(f(\ldots f(x)\ldots)))$) are reported as well.

Task	$N_{o,M}$	$N_{o,E}$	Operator	Transformation	p_{HOV}	p	df_{inter}	df_{error}	η^2
1	5	3	Mean	None	.051	.014	3	138	.074
2	2	3	Mean	$f(x) = log(x)$	.230	.746	3	127	.010
3	2	7	Mean	$f(x) = log(log^3(x) + 1)$	.050	.952	3	158	.002
4	0	4	Mean	$f(x) = log(x)$	.141	.616	3	111	.016
5	1	4	Mean	None	.084	.072	3	86	.078
6	3	4	Mean	$f(x) = log(log^3(x) + 1)$	.061	.645	3	119	.014
7	1	4	Median	$f(x) = log(log^3(x) + 1)$	.096	.120	3	102	N.A.
8	0	5	Median	None	.234	.140	2	68	N.A.
9	0	2	Mean	None	.061	<.001	2	30	.041
10	0	1	Mean	$f(x) = log(x)$	.141	.008	3	31	.314
11	0	1	Mean	None	N.A.	N.A.	N.A.	N.A.	N.A.

Table 2. Results of the two-way ANOVA tests (p) regarding the existence of a statistically significant difference in (mean/median) total amount of time between MEDB and EERDB users (split up by SQL competence). The number of subjects (N_M and N_E), mean/median time values (T_M and T_E), and standard deviations (σ_M and σ_E) for both groups are reported as well.

Task	SQL comp.	N_M	N_E	T_M	T_E	p	σ_M	σ_E
1	Weak	10	14	1989.570	1431.130	.002	118.929	127.141
1	Moderate	22	18	1943.552	876.052	<.001	101.423	112.127
1	Good	22	17	1834.879	1231.673	<.001	101.423	115.378
1	Very good	10	27	1329.551	990.971	.057	150.435	91.552
2		64	71	2.664	2.642	.609	0.031	0.029
3		79	87	−0.217	−0.249	<.001	0.004	0.004
4		32	87	2.760	2.247	<.001	0.051	0.029
5		28	66	581.293	550.171	.555	46.055	25.110
6		45	83	−0.289	−0.341	<.001	0.009	0.007
7		32	78	−0.238	−0.305	.007	0.067	0.045
8		22	53	2.445	2.424	.010	0.311	0.231
9	Moderate	1	6	463.579	591.515	.280	191.811	78.307
9	Good	2	11	449.315	608.159	.290	135.631	57.833
9	Very good	2	11	1258.728	573.856	<.001	135.631	57.833
10	Weak	1	4	2.837	2.494	.071	0.164	0.082
10	Moderate	1	8	2.319	2.451	.453	0.164	0.058
10	Good	2	10	2.470	2.384	.460	0.116	0.052
10	Very good	1	12	3.022	2.303	<.001	0.164	0.047
11	Very good	1	12	424.789	174.273	.001	64.380	18.585

No interaction effect exists for tasks 2 until 8. As such, for these tasks conclusions for the group as a whole could be drawn. The results indicate that for tasks 3, 4, 6, 7 and 8, the mean/median total amount of time needed in order to solve the task was significantly higher for MEDB users compared to EERDB users. For tasks 2 and 5, the difference in mean total amount of time between both groups was not statistically significant. However, even for these tasks, the time needed by EERDB users was still smaller compared to MEDB users.

For tasks 1, 9 and 10, an interaction effect exists between the SQL competence group and the used database. As such, analysis was performed separately for each SQL competence group. For task 1, a significant result was found for the "weak", "moderate" and "good" group, while for task 9 and 10, only for the "very good" group, a significant difference was found. Finally, for task 11, only a test for the "very good" group could be performed (with a statistically significant result in favour of EERDB), as no "weak", "moderate" or "good" MEDB users were present in the data for this task.

5.2   The SQ Dimension: Execution Cost Measurement

In order to detect the existence of an IE and/or statistically significant differences in the SQ of both databases, two-way ANOVA tests were performed in which the dependent variable was the total execution cost needed by the database system in order to process each submitted query of a user, until finally a correct query was submitted. The results are summarized respectively in Tables 3 and 4.

No interaction effect exists for tasks 2, 5, 7, 8 and 10. For tasks 5, 7 and 10, a statistically significant difference exists between the total execution cost of MEDB and EERDB in favour of EERDB. Contrary, for tasks 2 and 8, the total execution cost was higher for the EERDB database compared to the MEDB database. However, these results were not statistically significant.

For tasks 1, 6 and 9 an interaction effect exists. For task 1, a significant difference was only found for the "moderate" users, in favour of EERDB. For task 6, an IE was found, although the difference in total execution cost is statistically significant for each of the different SQL competence groups. The reason for this is that the impact of EER modeling on the execution cost for this task is significantly stronger for "weak" users compared to the other competence groups. For task 9, a statistically significant difference was only found for the "very good" users.

For tasks 3 and 4, no two-way ANOVA results were performed, as the transformation of the dependent variable and the usage of robust operators was not satisfactory in order for the data to comply with two-way ANOVA assumptions. Nonetheless, the mean cost for MEDB and EERDB are reported in Table 4. It is clear that there is a large difference in mean cost between both groups in favour of EERDB. Taking into account both the large sample sizes and the large differences in mean cost, it could probably be assumed that this measured cost difference is in fact a real difference. Finally, for task 11, because of a lack of data, only a test for the "very good" group could be performed. For this group, a significant difference was found in favour of EERDB.

Table 3. Results of the two-way ANOVA tests $(p, df_{inter}, df_{error}$ and $\eta^2)$ regarding the existence of an IE between SQL competence and database group for the total execution cost. The number of outliers for both database groups $(N_{o,M}$ and $N_{o,E})$, the result of the Levene's test for equality of variances (p_{HOV}), the used operator (mean or median) and the applied transformation (with $f^n(x) = f(f(\ldots f(x)\ldots)))$ are reported as well.

Task	$N_{o,M}$	$N_{o,E}$	Operator	Transformation	p_{HOV}	p	df_{inter}	df_{error}	η^2
1	4	7	Mean	None	.145	**.004**	3	135	.095
2	3	2	Mean	None	.232	**.329**	3	127	.027
3	6	7	Mean	None	N.A.	N.A.	N.A.	N.A.	N.A.
4	3	10	Mean	None	N.A.	N.A.	N.A.	N.A.	N.A.
5	7	4	Mean	$f(x) = log^3(x)$	.050	**.140**	3	80	.066
6	5	10	Mean	$f(x) = log(x)$	.261	**.049**	3	112	.067
7	3	3	Mean	$f(x) = log^3(x)$	.083	**.992**	3	101	.001
8	1	5	Mean	$f(x) = log(x)$	.275	**.165**	2	66	.053
9	0	3	Mean	None	.140	**<.003**	2	29	.326
10	0	3	Mean	$f(x) = log(x)$	.319	**.057**	3	31	.213
11	0	0	Mean	$f(x) = log(x)$	N.A.	N.A.	N.A.	N.A.	N.A.

Table 4. Results of the two-way ANOVA tests (p) regarding the existence of a statistically significant difference in (mean/median) total execution cost between MEDB and EERDB users (split up by SQL competence). The number of subjects $(N_M$ and $N_E)$, mean/median cost values $(C_M$ and $C_E)$, and standard deviations $(\sigma_M$ and $\sigma_E)$ for both groups are reported as well.

Task	SQL comp.	N_M	N_E	C_M	C_E	p	σ_M	σ_E
1	Weak	14	13	130687.703	211078.194	**.065**	29943.599	31073.942
1	Moderate	23	17	273184.540	147465.145	**.001**	23361.682	27173.374
1	Good	21	16	216970.527	198836.016	**.627**	24448.846	28009.672
1	Very good	13	26	191554.862	130688.344	**.112**	31073.942	21972.595
2		63	72	97253.517	118259.548	**.053**	7770.498	7412.393
3		75	87	42575.235	21867.475	N.A.	3407.635	1706.201
4		29	81	151396.863	25434.414	N.A.	15379.584	2719.522
5		22	66	−0.146	−0.159	**<.001**	0.004	0.002
6	Weak	7	15	4.359	0.366	**<.001**	0.091	0.062
6	Moderate	8	18	3.991	3.467	**<.001**	0.085	0.057
6	Good	14	20	4.137	3.406	**<.001**	0.065	0.054
6	Very good	14	24	4.218	3.403	**<.001**	0.065	0.049
7		30	79	−0.192	−0.206	**.002**	0.004	0.025
8		21	53	4.830	4.875	**.568**	0.069	0.052
9	Moderate	1	5	64963.510	122889.512	**.272**	47197.310	21107.279
9	Good	2	11	100734.120	95714.692	**.891**	33373.538	14230.524
9	Very good	2	11	258036.585	104402.773	**<.001**	33373.538	14230.524
10		5	32	4.443	3.606	**<.001**	0.149	0.059
11	Very good	1	13	4.815	4.198	**.026**	0.253	0.070

6   Discussion

Although no statistically significant effect has been found for every single task and dimension, it is clear that a couple of conclusions can be drawn based on the obtained results. For IQ and SQ, respectively five out of seven and three out of five tasks that were evaluated globally were found to be significantly easier with EERDB compared to MEDB. Additionally, twelve SQL competence subgroup tests were performed for both dimensions, of which respectively six and seven again displayed a statistically significant result in favour of EERDB. Furthermore, even if no statistically significant result was obtained, the mean/median total searching time/total execution cost was often still lower for EERDB in comparison with MEDB. Moreover, it is important to note that for both IQ and SQ, not a single task was found for which the exclusion of EER modeling from the design process was statistically proven to be a better option. This is an even more remarkable result when taking into account the fact that in total 36 different two-way ANOVA tests were performed. It should be noted that for tasks 9 to 11, the obtained results are not as explicit as compared to most of the tasks positioned earlier in the experiment. However, this is probably due to the lack of available data for these tasks. In general, it can be concluded that the usage of EER modeling in the design of a relational database is beneficial, both for the IQ and SQ of the database. This is in line with the hypotheses formulated in Sect. 3. Moreover, we were able to quantify the exact impact of the inclusion of an EER modeling phase in the design process. Depending on the specific task, differences in IQ and SQ vary between a few percentages up to 90%.

For most tasks, no interaction effect was found between the used database and SQL competence. Most of the tasks for which analysis had to be split up between different SQL competence profiles are positioned at the end of the experiment. As such, the existence of an IE for these tasks could be explained again because of a lack of data. The only notable exception to this end is task 1, for which an IE was found for both the IQ and SQ dimension. A possible explanation for this could be that the query behaviour for this task was influenced by the fact that this was the first task that most participants tried to solve, implying that they still had to acknowledge themselves with the database. Nonetheless, even for task 1, for all SQL competence groups the measured values were in favour of EERDB. As such, the evidence provided by this work points in the direction of the fact that EER modeling is beneficial for the success of a relational database as perceived by the end users, independently of the competence of the end user with regards to relational databases. This again underwrites the hypotheses formulated earlier. The contributions of this work are twofold. First, to our knowledge, this is the first study that thoroughly quantifies the impact of conceptual modeling on the success of a relational database. Secondly, this study is also the first to account for the technical competence of the end user in estimating the impact of EER modeling on relational database success. Nonetheless, this exploratory study has several limitations and leaves open opportunities for further research. First, as a consequence of the limited duration of an experiment session, not much data are present for tasks 9, 10 and 11, especially for MEDB and for participants with limited relational database competences. Alternative experiment designs should therefore be examined. Second, the study performs a cost-benefit analysis of the inclusion of EER modeling in the database design process. In this analysis, only the impact on the final database is evaluated. However, in order to get a completely accurate view on the impact of EER modeling, the impact on the complexity and duration of the database design process itself should also be taken into account. Third, this study does not consider evolutions of the EER diagrams and relational database schemas. Finally, although the results of this work are quite clear, only one specific movie-related use case (IMDb), one specific conceptual grammar (EER) and one IS type (relational databases) were investigated. Based on the aforementioned limitations of this preliminary study, the authors have already made plans for further research, in order to get an even more accurate cost-benefit view on the impact of EER modeling in the context of relational database design, and of conceptual modeling in general.

7 Conclusions

In this study, the impact of the usage of EER modeling on the success of a relational database was quantified. An experiment was set up in which participants had to solve a predefined set of analytical tasks on a database. The participants were randomly divided into two groups, one in which the participants had to complete the tasks using a database of which the design process included an EER design, and one in which the participants had to complete the tasks using a database that was constructed with the least needed effort in order to store data. By measuring the total amount of time needed by the participants and the total execution cost needed by the system to resolve the different tasks, the impact of the inclusion of an EER design phase on the IQ and SQ of the resulting database was determined. Preliminary results indicate that the inclusion of EER modeling in the design of a relational database is beneficial for the success of that database. Compared to the situation in which no EER design is performed, huge gains in both information quality and system quality of the eventual relational database are obtained. Moreover, statistical evidence exists that this impact of EER modeling is independent of the SQL competence of end users.

References

1. Analyzing IMDb Data: Actors vs. Actresses. http://dangoldin.com/2016/05/22/analyzing-imdb-data-actors-vs-actresses/. Accessed 27 Mar 2020
2. Bagui, S., Earp, R.: Database Design using Entity-Relationship Diagrams, 2nd edn. Auerbach Publications, Boston (2011)
3. Batra, D., Marakas, G.M.: Conceptual data modelling in theory and practice. Eur. J. Inf. Syst. 4(3), 185–193 (1995). https://doi.org/10.1057/ejis.1995.21
4. Bronselaer, A., De Mol, R., De Tré, G.: A measure-theoretic foundation for data quality. IEEE Trans. Fuzzy Syst. 26(2), 627–639 (2017). https://doi.org/10.1109/TFUZZ.2017.2686807

5. Bronselaer, A., Nielandt, J., Boeckling, T., De Tré, G.: Operational measurement of data quality. In: Medina, J., Ojeda-Aciego, M., Verdegay, J.L., Perfilieva, I., Bouchon-Meunier, B., Yager, R.R. (eds.) IPMU 2018. CCIS, vol. 855, pp. 517–528. Springer, Cham (2018). https://doi.org/10.1007/978-3-319-91479-4_43
6. Davies, I., Green, P., Rosemann, M., Indulska, M., Gallo, S.: How do practitioners use conceptual modeling in practice? Data Knowl. Eng. **58**(3), 358–380 (2006). https://doi.org/10.1016/j.datak.2005.07.007
7. DeLone, W.H., McLean, E.R.: Information systems success: the quest for the dependent variable. Inf. Syst. Res. **3**(1), 60–95 (1992). https://doi.org/10.1287/isre.3.1.60
8. DeLone, W.H., McLean, E.R.: The DeLone and McLean model of information systems success: a ten-year update. J. Manag. Inf. Syst. **19**(4), 9–30 (2003). https://doi.org/10.1080/07421222.2003.11045748
9. Elmasri, R., Navathe, S.: Fundamentals of Database Systems, 7th edn. Pearson Education, Boston (2007)
10. Fettke, P.: How conceptual modeling is used. Commun. Assoc. Inf. Syst. **25**(1), 571–592 (2009). https://doi.org/10.17705/1CAIS.02543
11. IMDb Datasets. https://www.imdb.com/interfaces/. Accessed 17 Mar 2020
12. Lukyanenko, R., Parsons, J.: Is traditional conceptual modeling becoming obsolete? In: Ng, W., Storey, V.C., Trujillo, J.C. (eds.) ER 2013. LNCS, vol. 8217, pp. 61–73. Springer, Heidelberg (2013). https://doi.org/10.1007/978-3-642-41924-9_6
13. Markowitz, V.M., Shoshani, A.: Representing extended entity-relationship structures in relational databases: a modular approach. ACM Trans. Database Syst. **17**(3), 423–464 (1992). https://doi.org/10.1145/132271.132273
14. Moody, D.L.: Theoretical and practical issues in evaluating the quality of conceptual models: current state and future directions. Data Knowl. Eng. **55**(3), 243–276 (2005). https://doi.org/10.1016/j.datak.2004.12.005
15. Olivé, A.: Conceptual schema-centric development: a grand challenge for information systems research. In: Pastor, O., Falcão e Cunha, J. (eds.) CAiSE 2005. LNCS, vol. 3520, pp. 1–15. Springer, Heidelberg (2005). https://doi.org/10.1007/11431855_1
16. PostgreSQL: Documentation 9.0: using EXPLAIN. https://www.postgresql.org/docs/9.0/using-explain.html. Accessed 25 Mar 2020
17. Query Exerciser. https://qexr.ugent.be/welcome/login. Accessed 27 Mar 2020
18. Simple IMDb Data Analysis - Kaggle. https://www.kaggle.com/ajithpanner/simple-imdb-data-analysis. Accessed 27 Mar 2020
19. Teorey, T.J., Yang, D., Fry, J.P.: A logical design methodology for relational databases using the extended entity-relationship model. ACM Comput. Surv. **18**(2), 197–222 (1986). https://doi.org/10.1145/7474.7475
20. Timmerman, Y., Bronselaer, A.: Measuring data quality in information systems research. Decis. Support Syst. **126**, 113138 (2019). https://doi.org/10.1016/j.dss.2019.113138
21. Turk, D.E., Vijayasarathy, L.R., Clark, J.D.: The value of conceptual modeling in database development: an experimental investigation. In: Proceedings of the Evaluation of Modeling Methods in Systems Analysis and Design Conference (2003)
22. Two-Way ANOVA in SPSS Statistics. https://statistics.laerd.com/spss-tutorials/two-way-anova-using-spss-statistics.php. Accessed 31 Mar 2020
23. Ullman, J., Widom, J.: A First Course in Database Systems, 3rd edn. Pearson Education, India (2007)

Modeling Difficulties in Data Modeling
Similarities and Differences Between Experienced and Non-experienced Modelers

Kristina Rosenthal[1](✉)(iD), Stefan Strecker[1](iD), and Oscar Pastor[2](iD)

[1] Enterprise Modelling Research Group, University of Hagen, Hagen, Germany
{kristina.rosenthal,stefan.strecker}@fernuni-hagen.de
[2] ProS Research Center, Universitat Politécnica de Valencia, Valencia, Spain
opastor@dsic.upv.es

Abstract. We study modeling difficulties encountered by experienced modelers while performing a data modeling task and compare our observations with findings we obtained from studying modeling processes of non-experienced modelers. Using the concept of cognitive breakdowns, we analyze audio-visual protocols of the modelers' modeling processes, recordings of modelers' interactions with the employed modeling software tool and survey data of modelers about their own perceptions of modeling difficulties. Based on a mixed methods research design, we identify typical modeling difficulties modelers face when performing data modeling. The present findings suggest nine types of modeling difficulties related to modeling entity types, generalization hierarchies, relationship types, attributes, and cardinalities. Contrasting the identified modeling difficulties with difficulties encountered by non-experienced modelers contributes to a better and more complete understanding of modeling processes performed by modeling experts and novices—and to inform design science research on specific targeted tool support for overcoming these difficulties at different stages of modelers' mastering of data modeling.

Keywords: Data modeling · Modeling difficulty · Cognitive breakdown · Novice and expert problem-solving · Mixed methods research

1 Introduction

Viewed as an activity, conceptual modeling involves an intricate array of cognitive processes and performed actions including abstracting, conceptualizing, contextualizing, associating, visualizing, interpreting & sense-making, judging & evaluating [15,24]. Hence, conceptual modeling is construed as a complex task involving codified knowledge, e.g., on modeling language concepts and their semantics as well as tacit knowledge acquired through experience [22]. Expert modelers who have accumulated extensive modeling experience and internalized codified modeling knowledge are, hence, expected to exhibit individual modeling processes different from non-experienced, novice modelers in terms of the modeling difficulties faced [3,18].

© Springer Nature Switzerland AG 2020
G. Dobbie et al. (Eds.): ER 2020, LNCS 12400, pp. 501–511, 2020.
https://doi.org/10.1007/978-3-030-62522-1_37

In the presented research, we study modeling difficulties encountered by experienced modelers while performing a data modeling task and we investigate whether different (idealized) types of modeling difficulties relate to the modeler's level of modeling experience by contrasting findings with findings from an earlier study on individual modeling processes of novice modelers [15]. Eight experienced modelers are observed while performing a data modeling task using a modeling software tool [21]. We combine complementary modes of observation into a multi-modal data collection approach to obtain a rich(er) picture of the individual modeling processes under investigation and to attenuate the limitations of the used modes of observation (the approach is described in further detail in [14]). Following earlier research on modeling difficulties (e.g., [4]), we use the concept of cognitive breakdowns [10] for identifying modeling difficulties in audio-visual protocols of modeling processes, i.e., think aloud protocols [8]. Different from earlier studies on modeling difficulties, we also draw on visually inspecting recordings of modeler-tool interactions and on surveying the observed individuals about performing the modeling task to identify modeling difficulties.

Our primary research objective is to identify and classify modeling difficulties experienced modelers face. A subsequent research objective is to contribute to a better understanding of similarities and differences between non-experienced and experienced modelers—in the present study in terms of modeling difficulties faced by modelers during data modeling. Findings from the present study are intended to inform design science research on developing (tool) support for conceptual modeling aimed at mitigating modeling difficulties—providing modelers with support tailored to their stage of mastering conceptual modeling.

After introducing related work in Sect. 2, the mixed methods research design is explained in Sect. 3. Section 4 provides the findings that are discussed in Sect. 5, followed by a conclusion and an outlook on future research (Sect. 6).

2   Related Work

In their foundational study, Batra and Davis derive a process model of data modeling to identify similarities and difference between experts and novices and strategies followed by expert modelers. The process model distinguishes the enterprise, the recognition and the representation level as distinct levels of abstraction. It is concluded that experts focus on developing a holistic comprehension of the problem, whereas novices are largely unable to integrate parts of the problem description resulting in more errors in their models [3]. Venable develops a teaching strategy supporting novice data modelers to achieve a more advanced level of expertise [22]—building on findings by Batra and Davis. More recently, Wilmont et al. compare modeling approaches of novices and experts by investigating cognitive mechanisms of process modeling, especially collaborative modeling. Based on analyzing think aloud protocols of modelers creating concept maps, the study suggests that main differences between experts and novices relate to experts having a richer mental model of possible modeling concepts and being able to integrate the different actions of modeling, i.a., abstracting, generalizing and reflecting, in a purposeful way—in contrast to novices experiencing difficulties in integrating the actions and not finding the right level of abstraction [24]. Studying resulting data models, Shanks investigates differences between experts and novices along several dimensions to arrive at the insight that the data models constructed by expert modelers are more syntactically correct, complete, innovative, flexible and better understood than those of novices [18]. In an earlier study, Batra evaluates errors in novices' data models complemented with analyzing think aloud protocols to achieve insights into why the identified errors have been committed [1]. As main causes, the complexity of the modeling task in terms of the number of possible relationship types, misapplication of modeling heuristics, and a lack of knowledge about database design are identified.

Taking a different angle, prior work compares expert to novice modelers viewing conceptual modeling as ill-structured problem solving (cf. [10]), e.g., by examining applied problem-solving heuristics, i.e., strategies for controlling cognitive activities to overcome cognitive limitations [19]. Yet another perspective is taken viewing conceptual modeling as communication and the modeling process as a dialog (e.g., [9]). Modeling strategies taken by individuals are identified based on linguistics analyses [9]. Bera investigates how ontological modeling guidelines assist modelers in constructing conceptual models and suggests that modeling guidelines can be helpful but have to be used carefully [4].

Another stream of related research investigates the process of process modeling to better understand how individuals create process models, and how the process model as outcome of the modeling process is affected by different modeling styles (e.g., [6,12,13]). Individual modeling processes are observed by recording modeler-tool interactions that are analyzed using data mining techniques, cluster analysis and visualizations of modeling processes [6,12]. As future research direction, it is envisioned to complement the observations with think aloud protocols and eye movement tracking data and to develop an integrated visualization [13].

Updating prior work, the present study investigates individual modeling processes from complementary modes of observation including modeler-tool interactions and think aloud protocols to better understand difficulties of experienced modelers in comparison to non-experienced modelers when data modeling. Replays of modeler-tool interactions and the PPMCharts used in [6] for process modeling inspire the data analysis in the present work on data modeling.

3   Study Design

Mixed-Methods Research Design: This study follows a mixed methods research design [7,23] applying a recently conceived multi-modal observation and data generation approach [14] and a corresponding data analysis strategy supported by a modeling tool integrated with a modeling observatory [21]. Following a mixed methods design pursues the objective of diversity of views [23, p. 442], including two points of data integration: one during the observations and one during data analysis (see Fig. 1). At the first point of data integration, four modes of observation are combined to take different perspectives on the modeling processes: (a) Recording verbal protocols; (b) Videotaping modelers from an 'over-the-shoulder' perspective; (c) Recording modeler tool-interactions; (d) Surveying modelers. Please see [14] and Table 1 and Fig. 1 in the supplementary material [16] for a detailed description of the observation modes.

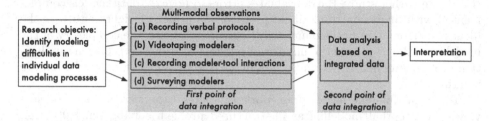

Fig. 1. Mixed methods research design (cf. [15, p. 6]).

Study Conduct: The study was conducted in May and June 2019 with eight subjects individually constructing a conceptual data model using a variant of the Entity-Relationship Model (ER model, [5]). To foster comparability, we ran a standardized data collection procedure for all participants (see Fig. 2) under observation by one of the researchers, taking place in rooms designed to ensure a quiet environment. The used main modeling task from the library domain is designed to reduce effects of varying prior domain knowledge (cf. [4]), i.e., we assume participating subjects have sufficient knowledge about the library domain to work on the modeling task, because all of them are academics. Furthermore, the modeling task is designed, so that an experienced modeler shall be able to complete the modeling in no more than 45 min. Please see the supplementary material for a detailed explanation of the data collection procedure (Table 2 in [16]), the main modeling task including a reference solution (Fig. 3 in [16]) and the pre- and post-modeling questionnaires (Fig. 5–9 in [16]).

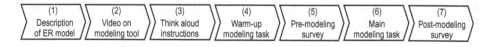

Fig. 2. Standardized data collection procedure.

Data Analysis: The data analysis strategy constitutes the second point of data integration including data transformation [7, pp. 224–226]. First, information on open- and closed-ended questions from the pre- and post-modeling surveys are integrated into a description characterizing the sample of subjects (discussed as "qualitizing" in literature on mixed methods research, e.g., [23, pp. 446f]). Second, different types of data are combined to identify modeling difficulties using the concept of cognitive breakdowns following problem-solving research and Cognitive Load Theory (CLT, e.g., [20]). Humans have limited cognitive capacity in performing complex tasks as, e.g., conceptual modeling—potentially leading to cognitive difficulties if the capacity of the cognitive resources is exceeded [20]. To add structure to the data, we coded audio-visual protocols of the modeling processes by systematically assigning codes to video segments (e.g., [7, pp. 213–215], cf. Fig. 2 in supplementary material [16]). We start with an explicit code "Cognitive breakdown" for segments in which a subject explicitly verbalizes a difficulty experienced during modeling or when the subject interrupts or terminates a modeling activity [4, p. 4]. This is complemented with codes generally anticipated in think aloud protocols, i.e., codes not directly relating to the modeling task, but which refer to actions and comments which are an indication of the level of the difficulty of a task ("General codes"), and with inductive codes and sub codes emerging during the coding process (see Table 3 in the supplementary material for the entire coding scheme [16]). In order to group the modeling difficulties inducing the observed breakdowns, sub codes for the code "Cognitive breakdown" are developed and iteratively refined. Coding audio-visual protocols is supplemented with inspecting visualizations of the recorded modeler-tool interactions [14] to identify or further explore unclear situations in the audio-visual protocols (cf. Fig. 4 in the supplementary material [16]), and with reviewing the post-modeling survey about perceived modeling difficulties serving as indication for closer inspecting segments of the protocols.

3.1   Participant Characteristics

We recruited eight academics (E1–E8) from the context of conceptual modeling, working in an academic context or studying in the final stage of their Master studies. The sample size is considered suitable as think aloud protocol and video analysis is recognized as labor-intensive approach to achieve in-depth insights accompanied by relatively small sample sizes [11]. Four subjects were female and four male with an age between 25 and 45 (with a median of 35 years and a mean of 35.125 years). As first language, five subjects stated Spanish, one Dutch, another one Portuguese and the other one German. Two subjects were Postdoctoral researchers holding a PhD, four were doctoral candidates with Masters degrees and two Master students with Bachelor degrees, holding their highest degree in Computer Science (7) or Business and Social Studies (1) and working or studying in subjects within the fields of Computer Science (7) or Information Science (1).

All subjects reported work experience of three years and four months to 25 years with a median of nine and a half years and prior experience in conceptual data modeling ranging from two years with constructing 30 conceptual models and reading 50 models to 20 years with constructing 100 conceptual models and reading 200 models (with a median experience of 10.5 years, a median of constructing 40 conceptual models and reading 75 models). Seven of the subjects had one to several completed courses on conceptual modeling during their studies. In the test on theoretical knowledge of conceptual data modeling with the ER model, the number of correct answers to the six yes/no questions ranged from four to six with a median of five. Altogether, the characteristics of the subjects suit the intention to study experienced modelers in an academic context—in alignment with conceptualizations of expert modelers in related studies (e.g., [3, p. 87], [18, p. 65]). Regarding knowledge of the library domain, all eight subjects stated to have visited a library at least once with the frequency of using the services of a library ranging from not at all to very often with a median of sometimes/often (on a scale: not at all – rarely – sometimes – often – very often). The subjects borrowed 0 to 100 books in a library (with a median of 45), and two subjects stated that they knew what the term shelfmark means in the library domain. After modeling, the participants were asked to self-assess the statement "I had difficulties understanding the modeling task" on a scale from 1 to 7 where 1 corresponds to "I do not agree at all" and 7 to "I agree entirely". The answers ranged only from 1 to 3 with a median of 2—indicating that the participants understood the modeling task well enough to perform the task.

4   Modeling Processes and Modeling Difficulties

As intended, we observe the modeling task to pose challenges on the experienced modelers: The lengths of the observed modeling processes range from 38 to 52 min with a median of 46 min and a mean of 45 min. Four modeling processes were terminated by the observer while three participants finished the task by themselves, and one participant (E7) accidentally terminated the modeling session after 38 min. We only observe two silent periods of 30 s in six total hours of audio-visual protocols and, therefore, conclude that the think aloud instructions were suitable to initiate the intended behavior.

We observe cognitive breakdowns as indication for modeling difficulties in all modeling processes with a wide range of numbers of breakdowns, ranging from one to seven (with a median of 4.5). However, only three participants explained encountered difficulties relating to the modeling task in the post-modeling questionnaire. The observed breakdowns split into nine types of modeling difficulties that are explained and exemplified in the following by providing transcribed examples from the think aloud protocols (see Table 1 for an overview).

Decide Between Attribute and Generalization: Two modelers encountered difficulties related to the decision whether to reconstruct a statement in the problem representation by adding an attribute to an entity type or by specifying a generalization hierarchy (with three occurrences). For example, E4 encountered a difficulty relating to the generalized entity type LIBRARYITEM: *"There is different kinds of items... um, so I will create... um... an entity to identify the different types, well... um, or maybe some, um... as there is, um, four different types, I prefer to separate them in, um, different entities, not one entity"*.

Choose Data Type of Attribute: Two participants faced difficulties in choosing a data type for an attribute that is adequate in the context of the modeling task. For example, E3 faced difficulties about the data type for the attribute YEAROFPUBLICATION: *"let's see, year of publication... um, now is it just a year...*

um, I will call it year, let's see how it works... year... and a year can be an integer type, because we don't need any decimals... or it can be a date".

Table 1. Completion times (in minutes) and numbers of breakdowns.

Participant	E1	E2	E3	E4	E5	E6	E7	E8	#
Completion time	41	52	47	49	46	46	38	41	360
Breakdowns	4	4	7	6	4	5	1	6	37
Decide between attribute and generalization				2	1				3
Choose data type of attribute				1				1	2
Specify generalization hierarchies		1	2					2	5
Decide between entity type and relationship type	1			1		2		1	5
Establish relationship types					1				1
Model recursive relationship types	1	1	1	1	1				5
Develop identifiers for relationship types	1	1	3	2		2	1	1	11
Determine cardinalities		1			1	1			3
Counteract compromising of model integrity	1							1	2

Specify Generalization Hierarchies: Encountered by three participants with five occurrences, this type of difficulty relates to specifying generalization relationships. For example, E2 faces difficulties relating to the generalized entity type LIBRARYITEM (*"Um... no... in DVD, the entity, I am going to erase the playable media, I am going to put the ICAA attribute inside of the DVD entity... because I do not need to specify the playable media as an entity"*) and terminates modeling the generalization relationship without solving the problem.

Decide Between Entity Type and Relationship Type: Four modelers encountered a difficulty related to modeling decisions as to whether to model an entity type or a relationship type to reconstruct a given statement of the problem representation (with five occurrences). For example, E4 has difficulties when modeling the entity type LOAN: *"Of course, there is a loan, um, users... this is, um... relationship between, um, library item, um... and, um, user... which is a loan... um... a loan, um, looks like a... of course, loan is an entity".*

Establish Relationship Types: One participant encountered severe problems in establishing relationship types between the entity types LOAN, USER and COPY. Remarkably, the difficulty caused a long period of uncertainty in the modeling process of E5 (about 12 min). However, the participant finally solved the problem and this type of difficulty could be observed only once.

Model Recursive Relationship Types: We could observe difficulties in modeling the recursive relationship type SUPERVISES in five modeling processes. A text passage from the think aloud protocol of E3 illustrates the uncertainty with regard to determining the role designators: *"I think that should be it... so, a* *supervisor... supervises a supervisee... oh, this should be the other way round then... I think... let's check... yes, that makes sense"*.

Develop Identifiers for Relationship Types: Seven modelers faced difficulties in finding identifiers for relationship types that are descriptive and sensible in the context of the modeling task—constituting the most frequent type in terms of the total number of occurrences (11). A passage from the think aloud protocol of E4 indicates this type of difficulty: *"This relationship must have another name... I will choose... so... um... this is borrow... so, a library user... borrows... um... make... um, make... um, the name is not ok"*. Please note that participants mentioned that modeling difficulties of this type may be related to problems with the English language.

Determine Cardinalities: We identified difficulties with regard to determining cardinalities for relationship types in three modeling processes as illustrated in the think aloud protocol of E2: *"One item copy is related with, no is found at one location, but one location can have several item copies ... um ... location is ... ok, um ... we can have the location could be, not have items, so I am going to put as minimum zero cardinalities, as maximum several item copies, exactly"*.

Counteract Compromising of Model Integrity: We identified two modelers experiencing difficulties relating to threats to the model's integrity. The modelers chose to counteract the situation with adding an integrity constraint (E1) or a comment (E8) to the model (*"ok, contract date ... and ... ok, I don't need the information with the year I think ... or ... um ... could be, added as a comment ... or a constraint ... ok, maybe lets add this, if it's in the requirements it should be added I guess"*, E8).

5   Discussion

Analyzing six hours of audio-visual protocols of experienced modelers constructing a data model combined with analyzing modeler-tool interactions and surveying modelers leads us to identify nine types of modeling difficulties these subjects faced while performing the modeling task. In the following, we compare these findings to modeling difficulties faced by non-experienced data modelers working on a related but much less complex modeling task also from the library domain [15], and discuss limitations of the present work.

Our analysis suggests that the experienced modelers encounter difficulties predominantly with respect to modeling relationship types, in particular when developing sensible identifiers for relationship types as most common type of difficulty by far. Both observations also applied for non-experienced modelers [15], and are in line with prior work on difficulties in data modeling suggesting that modeling problems are experienced mainly in modeling relationship types [2]. However, the experienced modelers faced only few difficulties in determining cardinalities for relationship types whereas the non-experienced modelers faced numerous difficulties of this type [15]. Also, difficulties with deciding whether a relationship type warrants modeling could be observed more frequently in the modeling processes of the non-experienced modelers but occur in the experts' modeling processes as well. A further difference pertains to experienced modelers recognizing threats to the model's integrity and encountering a difficulty in counteracting. However, this type of difficulty could be observed only twice for experienced modelers—but not at all for non-experienced modelers. In addition, the experienced modelers faced further difficulties with regard to modeling generalization hierarchies and a recursive relationship type—modeling concepts that the novices were not confronted with.

Principle limitations relate to analyzing think aloud protocols. Generally, it is assumed that thinking aloud does not interfere with thought processes—but as the modeling task includes a visual, non-verbal perceptual component, thinking aloud may slow down thought processes and/or modeling performance [8]. Differences in verbalization skills have long been discussed (e.g., [8]), and thus we included a think aloud training in the data collection procedure. Furthermore, all participants model and think aloud in English, not their first language. However, all participants work or study in a context characterized by the use of English. Please note that we recruited the participants solely from an academic context. Although several participants reported work experience outside an academic context, actual practitioners are not included in the study sample. We plan to complement the present study with follow-up studies observing subjects including practitioners with various backgrounds, e.g., regarding the first language.

6   Conclusion and Outlook

Integrating complementary modes of observation to identify types of modeling difficulties in eight data modeling processes of experienced modelers and contrasting our findings with difficulties encountered by non-experienced modelers indicates considerable overlaps in types of modeling difficulties experienced and non-experienced data modelers face, i.e., a majority of difficulties relating to modeling relationship types, besides clear differences in difficulties related to determining cardinalities and fostering model integrity.

As to the long-term objective of design science research on developing tailored support for modelers, the present results are intended as a starting point for further studies aiming to refine and extend the present findings (cf. [15]). Another potential path for future research lies in further integrating our preliminary findings on modeling difficulties with results from earlier work on expert-novice similarities and differences in conceptual modeling [3,22,24] and other problem-solving contexts [17]. Extending and integrating the present findings contributes to better understand difficulties in data modeling and modeling expertise in its genesis—and, hence, to contribute to a theoretical basis informing design science research on targeted modeler support at different levels of modeling experience.

References

1. Batra, D., Antony, S.R.: Novice errors in conceptual database design. Eur. J. Inf. Syst. **3**(1), 57–69 (1994)
2. Batra, D.: Cognitive complexity in data modeling: causes and recommendations. Requir. Eng. **12**(4), 231–244 (2007). https://doi.org/10.1007/s00766-006-0040-y
3. Batra, D., Davis, J.G.: Conceptual data modelling in database design: similarities and differences between expert and novice designers. Int. J. Man-Mach. Stud. **37**(1), 83–101 (1992)
4. Bera, P.: Situations that affect modelers' cognitive difficulties: an empirical assessment. In: 5th Americas Conference on Information Systems (AMCIS). Research Paper 254, Detroit, MI (2011)
5. Chen, P.P.S.: The entity-relationship model–toward a unified view of data. ACM Trans. Database Syst. **1**(1), 9–36 (1976)
6. Claes, J., Vanderfeesten, I., Gailly, F., Grefen, P., Poels, G.: The Structured Process Modeling Theory (SPMT) a cognitive view on why and how modelers benefit from structuring the process of process modeling. Inf. Syst. Front. **17**(6), 1401–1425 (2015). https://doi.org/10.1007/s10796-015-9585-y
7. Creswell, J.W., Plano Clark, V.L.: Designing and Conducting Mixed Methods Research, 3rd edn. Sage, Los Angeles (2018)
8. Ericsson, K.A., Simon, H.A.: Protocol Analysis: Verbal Reports as Data, 2nd edn. MIT Press, Cambridge (1993)
9. Hoppenbrouwers, S.J.B.A., Proper, H.A.E., van der Weide, T.P.: A fundamental view on the process of conceptual modeling. In: Delcambre, L., Kop, C., Mayr, H.C., Mylopoulos, J., Pastor, O. (eds.) ER 2005. LNCS, vol. 3716, pp. 128–143. Springer, Heidelberg (2005). https://doi.org/10.1007/11568322_9
10. Newell, A., Simon, H.A.: Human Problem Solving. Prentice-Hall, Englewood Cliffs (1972)
11. Nielsen, J.: Estimating the number of subjects needed for a thinking aloud test. Int. J. Hum.-Comput. Stud. **41**(3), 385–397 (1994)
12. Pinggera, J., et al.: Styles in business process modeling: an exploration and a model. Softw. Syst. Model. **14**(3), 1055–1080 (2015). https://doi.org/10.1007/s10270-013-0349-1
13. Pinggera, J., Zugal, S., Furtner, M., Sachse, P., Martini, M., Weber, B.: The modeling mind: behavior patterns in process modeling. In: Bider, I., et al. (eds.) BPMDS/EMMSAD -2014. LNBIP, vol. 175, pp. 1–16. Springer, Heidelberg (2014). https://doi.org/10.1007/978-3-662-43745-2_1
14. Rosenthal, K., Ternes, B., Strecker, S.: Understanding individual processes of conceptual modeling: a multi-modal observation and data generation approach. In: Modellierung 2020, Vienna, Austria, pp. 77–92 (2020)
15. Rosenthal, K., Strecker, S.: Toward a taxonomy of modeling difficulties: a multi-modal study on individual modeling processes. In: 40th International Conference on Information Systems (ICIS), Munich, Germany (2019)
16. Rosenthal, K., Strecker, S., Pastor, O.: Supplementary Material for "Modeling Difficulties in Data Modeling: Similarities and Differences Between Experienced and Non-experienced Modelers" (2020). https://doi.org/10.5281/zenodo.3992737
17. Schenk, K., Vitalari, N.P., Davis, K.S.: Differences between novice and expert systems analysts: what do we know and what do we do? J. Manag. Inf. Syst. **15**(1), 9–50 (1998)

18. Shanks, G.: Conceptual data modelling: an empirical study of expert and novice data modellers. Australas. J. Inf. Syst. **4**(2), 1–11 (1997)
19. Srinivasan, A., Te'eni, D.: Modeling as constrained problem solving: an empirical study of the data modeling process. Manag. Sci. **41**(3), 419–434 (1995)
20. Sweller, J.: Cognitive load during problem solving: effects on learning. Cogn. Sci. **12**(2), 257–285 (1988)
21. Ternes, B., Rosenthal, K., Barth, H., Strecker, S.: TOOL - modeling observatory & tool: an update. In: Short, Workshop and Tools & Demo Papers Modellierung 2020, Vienna, Austria, vol. 2542, pp. 198–202. CEUR-WS, Vienna (2020)
22. Venable, J.R.: Teaching novice conceptual data modellers to become experts. In: International Conference Software Engineering: Education and Practice, pp. 50–56. IEEE, Dunedin (1996)
23. Venkatesh, V., Brown, S.A., Sullivan, Y.W.: Guidelines for conducting mixed-methods research: an extension and illustration. Inf. Syst. **17**(7), 435–494 (2016)
24. Wilmont, I., Brinkkemper, S., van de Weerd, I., Hoppenbrouwers, S.: Exploring intuitive modelling behaviour. In: Bider, I., et al. (eds.) BPMDS/EMMSAD -2010. LNBIP, vol. 50, pp. 301–313. Springer, Heidelberg (2010). https://doi.org/10.1007/978-3-642-13051-9_25

Towards a Framework for Empirical Measurement of Conceptualization Qualities

Sotirios Liaskos[✉] and Ibrahim Jaouhar

School of Information Technology, York University, 4700 Keele St.,
Toronto M3J 1P3, Canada
{liaskos,jaouhar}@yorku.ca

Abstract. Conceptualization development is central in modeling language design. As one of their first design steps, language designers need to decide on a set of concepts on which the language will be based and which can be understood and used by a population of modelers for characterizing and representing relevant domain information. Thus, exposing candidate concept sets to future users may offer insights on how well the concepts of choice are understood and distinguished from each other by those who will be called to actually use the language. We propose an empirical measurement framework to allow just that. The framework consists of an instrumentation approach whereby participants sampled from the user population classify domain expressions to the corresponding concepts, and a set of measurement constructs for translating participant observed data into design insights. A small case study is conducted to explore the feasibility and limitations of the proposed approach.

Keywords: Conceptual modeling · Conceptualization quality · Experimental study · Goal models

1 Introduction

Developing conceptualizations lies at the heart of conceptual modeling language design. Such conceptualizations are sets of concepts and their definitions that the language designers think are useful for modeling a domain [12,26]. Once the main conceptualization is decided, designers can proceed with the definition of syntax, notation, modeling and reasoning procedures and mechanisms and other components needed to develop a fully-fledged modeling language. However, deciding why a particular candidate set of concepts is better than a competing one, all else being equal, seems to remain an art rather than a science. Designers seem to have little to rely on for knowing if and how end users would understand candidate conceptualizations that emerge in the design process.

We propose an empirical measurement framework to be used for assisting the evaluation of qualities of conceptualizations in the context of a language design

© Springer Nature Switzerland AG 2020
G. Dobbie et al. (Eds.): ER 2020, LNCS 12400, pp. 512–522, 2020.
https://doi.org/10.1007/978-3-030-62522-1_38

effort. The framework consists of a set of empirical constructs, operationalized on the basis of exposing untrained experimental participants to sets of concepts and then asking participants to classify expressions of the domain under the concept that best describes each. The resulting metrics reveal levels and patterns by which participants agree on how expressions should be classified, both within themselves and with the language designers. Subsequent descriptive analyses offer designers insight of how their conceptualization proposals are understood by prospective modelers. In an empirical study, we investigate whether consistencies exist among the metrics and between the metrics and our intuition.

The rest of the paper is organized as follows. In Sect. 2 we present our motivation and the experimental constructs we propose. In Sect. 3 we describe the empirical study we performed and in Sects. 4 and 5 we discuss our findings, limitations, future and related work.

2   Conceptualizations and Their Quality

2.1   Conceptual Modeling Languages and Conceptualizations

Conceptual modeling languages are based on the definition of a core set of concepts that modelers are to use in order to develop models according to the language. Such sets are called *conceptualizations* (henceforth also: *concept sets*), that is, *"concepts used to articulate abstractions of state[s] of affairs in a given domain"* [12]. Based on this foundation of concepts, a modeling language complete with syntax, notation, modeling procedures and mechanisms can be developed [4,17]. To facilitate the discussion that follows, we distinguish between the *concern domain* (henceforth *domain*), which describes the aspects of reality that we wish to focus on in our modeling (e.g. intention/motivation, process, structure, function etc.) and *application domain*, the actual problem that we wish to model (e.g. a travel agency or a flight booking system).

It is easy to observe that for the same or similar concern domain, different concept sets can emerge. Taking the intention domain for example, several *goal modeling* languages have been introduced: KAOS [10], *i** [33], URN/GRL [2,34], Tropos [30], iStar 2.0 [9] and their variants, as well as Archimate and its a motivation aspect [31]. These languages have similar but not the exact same concept sets. For instance, KAOS models intention using a set that includes *"agents"*, *"goals"*, *"constraints"* and *"actions"* [10], while iStar 2.0 includes *"actors"*, *"goals"*, *"qualities"* and *"tasks"* (the latter referred to as *"plans"* in some Tropos conceptualizations [30]) and Archimate's motivation aspect has *"goals"*, *"outcomes"*, *"drivers"* and *"requirements"* [31].

2.2   Conceptualization Quality

Given two candidate concept sets for a domain, examples can be devised in which it is obvious for some observer that one conceptualization is a better fit for the domain than the other. For example, the above mentioned iStar 2.0

concepts seem to be more suitable for modeling intention than the concepts *"account"*, *"credit"* and *"debit"*, which are probably better suited for, say, modeling economic transactions. However, more rigorous and systematic measures of fit would be useful when the candidate conceptualizations are not as semantically distant, and therefore which one should be preferred is not as "obvious" or a matter of strong agreement among designers.

Our proposed framework focusses on *empirical* measures of fit between a chosen conceptualization and its domain, i.e. measures coming from observing behaviors and attitudes of potential users of the conceptualizations (or proxies of such users). To devise such goodness-of-fit measures, and a theory thereof, we draw inspiration from well established methods from the area of qualitative content analysis [18]. At the heart of content analysis lies the effort to classify defined units of qualitative content (e.g. text, audiovisual) into a system of codes, a "data language". The latter contains data *variables*, each offering a set of semantically mutually exclusive *values* (also: *codes*), each of which is best suited for classifying specific *units* of content.

Our reference to the content analysis tradition is based on an analogy between conceptualizations and such variables. Given a unit of phenomena in the world – known indeed through consumption of content (interview responses, policy documents etc.), modelers choose one of the concepts of the conceptualization to model the unit as such. For example, an iStar 2.0 modeler confronted with the unit "Travel Office" has to choose a concept from the iStar 2.0 concept set we saw above to incorporate the unit within their model. In the iStar 2.0 diagram, the unit will most likely emerge in form of a circular visual element, signifying that the modeler has decided to model it (*code* it) as an *"actor"*, simultaneously excluding the possibility of modeling it as something else (e.g. *"task"*).

Continuing our analogy with content analysis, a variable and its set of codes can be seen as a measurement instrument that detects the presence or absence of specific kinds of meaning within content. For such an instrument to be useful it needs to be *reliable*, i.e. to result in the same coding outcome independent of the coding event and involved person(s) [18]. A similar expectation largely holds in modeling. We would not like "Travel Office" to be modelled as either an *"actor"*, a *"task"* or a *"quality"* in equal frequency depending on who does the modeling and when, the domain information being otherwise the same.

We propose three conditions for a conceptualization to be reliable – which by no means exhaust all such conditions. Firstly, the conceptualization allows for reproducible modeling: a group of different modelers in different times, when exposed to the exact same information about the application domain, they will choose the same concepts to model the same units of content. Thus, "Travel Office" is always modelled using the same concept independent on whom one asks and when. We will henceforth refer to this reliability construct as *agreement*, which can be intra-rater (compare answers of the same person at different times) and inter-rater (compare answers of different persons). Secondly, the way modelers classify domain information into concepts, should agree with standards set by conceptualization designers. We call this, *accuracy*. Thus, when the designers expect that "Travel Office" should be modelled as *"actor"* within a given application domain description and modelers actually do so in practice, this supports the belief that *"actor"* is a concept that will likely be used as intended. Finally, a conceptualization would tend to be more reliable if its constituent concepts have minimum or no *semantic overlap*, in a way that each concept partitions states of affairs within an application domain instance into classes with no or minimal intersection. For instance, all instances of *"goals"* and all instances of *"actors"* in the application domain are conceptualized as such, respectively, without a large class of instances being equally able to be classified either way based on the same application domain information.

These reliability features need not be seen as a pre-requisite for conceptual modeling language usefulness. However, they can be useful for supporting language design in terms of assessing how the concept set will be understood by the application community.

2.3   Metrics

Operationalizations of the qualities described above is based on observing how a group of human participants S uses a provided concept set O to model a description of a state of affairs. The group of participants is sampled from a population of potential users (modelers) of the language which will use O as its basis, or a proxy when a suitable sample is unattainable. The participants are trained to O using definitions and authoritative examples, such as those that accompany language guides and tutorials. Then the participants are offered a set L of *expressions* of states of affairs within some application domain and are asked to *classify* each to one of the concepts in O. Reliability qualities can then be explored through various aggregations and visualizations of such observational data, on the basis of the constructs discussed above: agreement, accuracy and overlap. We turn our focus to operationalizations of each of these.

Agreement is based on the measuring of the degree to which participants in S classify each item in L using the same concept from O. Given an item $l \in L$ the *agreement per expression* $(GpE(l))$ is any measure of concentration of classifications of l to specific subset of concepts by the participants. From the several available options, we here adopt the Herfindahl-Hirschman index – used in Economics to measure market concentration – normalized to [0,1] [6]. Specifically, let $f(l, o_i)$ be the proportion of classifications in which l is classified by $s \in S$ as $o_i \in O$. The GpE for l is then:

$$GpE(l) = \frac{\sum_{o_i \in O} f(l, o_i)^2 - 1/|O|}{1 - 1/|O|}$$

The closer the index is to 1, the more the concentration of responses to a specific concept, hence the more the agreement on the classification of l. GpE can be used as a building block for aggregated agreement measures such as the *total agreement* (GT) which is the average GpEs of all expressions in L. Note that although the above are for inter-rater analysis, analogous constructs can be envisioned for intra-rater agreement.

Accuracy measures are based on calculating the degree to which participants in S classify an item l in L in a way that agrees with how the designers would classify l. Analogously to agreement, *accuracy per expression* ($\boldsymbol{ApE(l)}$) is the proportion of classifications that are in agreement with the authoritative one for item l, normalized from the interval $[q, 1]$ to $[0, 1]$, where $q = 1/|O|$ is the proportion expected by random. Then, *accuracy per concept* ($\boldsymbol{ApC(o)}$) is aggregation of individual ApEs by the authoritative concept to which l is classified by the designers, $ApC(o) = mean_{l \in L_o}(ApE(l))$, where $L_o \subseteq L$ is the set of items that designers think should be classified as o. Finally *accuracy per participant* ($\boldsymbol{ApP(s)}$) measures each participant's $s \in S$ proportion of classifications that agree with the authoritative classification.

Overlap is based on measuring the degree to which participants in S classify each item in L on the same pair of concepts from O. One way to define *observed overlap per expression* ($\boldsymbol{VpE(l, o_1, o_2)}$) for two concepts o_1 and o_2 is:

$$VpE(l, o_1, o_2) = \frac{min\{f(l, o_1), f(l, o_2)\}}{max\{f(l, o_1), f(l, o_2)\}}[f(l, o_1) + f(l, o_2)]$$

where, again, $f(l, o)$ is the proportion of classifications in which l is classified as o. The observed overlap per pair is the average per expression for a specific pair $\boldsymbol{VpI(o_1, o_2)} = mean_{l \in L}(VpE(l, o_1, o_2))$ – noting that the average can be weighted per authoritative classification through the *overlap per concept* $\boldsymbol{VpC(o)} = mean_{o' \in O}(VpP(o, o'))$ metric.

3   Case Study

We now turn to an empirical study we performed to acquire initial feasibility evidence for some of the measures. Our goal is to examine whether acquisition of the measures is possible and whether they are consistent with each other and with intuitions we have about the qualities of the languages we put to test.

Two conceptualizations are studied: one constructed as a subset/derivative of iStar 2.0 and one from a made-up language we call *"intention models"*. The goal modeling language conceptualization contains the concepts {*goal, quality, task, belief*} the former three concepts adopted directly from the iStar 2.0 and *belief* added from GRL [34]. The intention modeling language conceptualization contains the concepts {*goal, objective, claim, assertion*}. The concepts are chosen in a way that the first two and the last two appear to be synonyms, so referring to the same kinds of phenomena in the application domain.

A number of sets of expressions are also prepared for each language: one featuring only a list of such without any additional context, one based on the main example from the iStar 2.0 guide contextualized within a description of a fictional character with goals, tasks, qualities copied as-is from the guide [9] and beliefs constructed from scratch, and a third constructed in the same way from Archimate's authoritative examples on motivation structures; the expressions are transferred as-is from concept instances in exemplar models [31]. For the intention models, an additional set of expressions and context description concerning a hypothetical grocery store owner are constructed from scratch.

The experimental units are initially placed in two separate instruments, one for goal models and one for the intention models. Each instrument starts with an instructional video presenting the concepts through the authoritative definitions and authoritative examples. Then, each expression set is presented in a separate screen, with its context description, wherever applicable, and participants are asked to classify each expression to one of the four concepts of the corresponding concept set. A total of 41 participants from the Mechanical Turk pool [7], 13 female and 28 male, ages 23 to 69 (median 40), majority (34) in Science, Technology and Engineering are recruited.

Results. For a first glimpse of how the two languages compare, we use a heatmap style visualization we call *concept overlap maps* to visually explore overlaps between concepts, as in Fig. 1. Starting from intention models, the categories within intentions and statements exhibit substantial overlap compared to other pairs, as strongly expected. Also in agreement with expectation, goal models show that *goals* overlap with *tasks* and, less so with *qualities*.

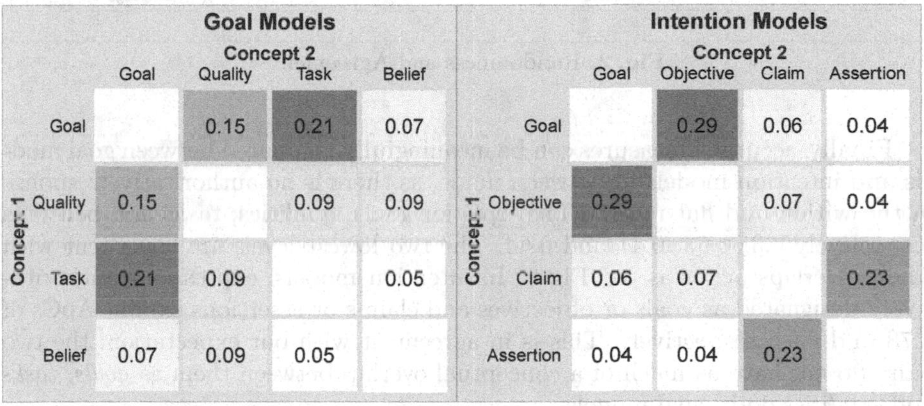

Goal Models					Intention Models			
Concept 2					Concept 2			
	Goal	Quality	Task	Belief		Goal	Objective	Claim	Assertion
Goal		0.15	0.21	0.07	Goal		0.29	0.06	0.04
Quality	0.15		0.09	0.09	Objective	0.29		0.07	0.04
Task	0.21	0.09		0.05	Claim	0.06	0.07		0.23
Belief	0.07	0.09	0.05		Assertion	0.04	0.04	0.23	

Fig. 1. Concept Overlap Maps

As a second exploratory step, we compare GpE with the p values of simple multinomial tests for each expression against the hypothesis that participants classify randomly, i.e. choose one of the four choices as if rolling a dice. Histograms of the results are seen in Fig. 2(A). For the analysis, intention models are considered in three modes: as introduced (*flat mode*, "Int. M. Flat"), with each pair of overlapping concepts (*goal-objective* and *claim-assertion*) merged to one (*between mode*, "Int. M. Between") and, conversely, focussing on the dominant overlapping pair in each expression and treating it as if it were a two-concept language (*within mode*, "Int. M. Within"). As expected, more frequent high levels of GpE are observed in the between mode of intention models. Goal models offer similar distributions of GpE as flat mode intention models. Comparison with the binomial result, however, which offers an indication of overall randomness, shows that patterns of agreement may exist within seemingly low GpEs; from Fig. 1 we see that in goal models this is probably due to the distance of belief from the three other concepts.

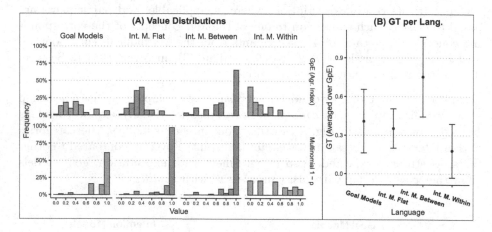

Fig. 2. Randomness and Agreement

Finally, accuracy measures can be meaningfully compared between goal models and intention models in between mode, as there is no authoritative response in the within and flat modes. The ApC for goals, qualities, tasks and beliefs is respectively 0.3, 0.63, 0.47 and 0.64. The two lowest levels are consistent with where overlaps occur as per Fig. 1. In intention models, expressions authoritatively designated as goals or objectives and claims or assertions exhibit ApCs of 0.78 and 0.93, respectively. This is in agreement with our expectation: the two pairs do not have as much of a conceptual overlap between them as *goals, tasks* and *qualities* do in goal models.

4   Validity Concerns and Future Work

We now discuss important validity threats and pitfalls that one must be mindful of when considering the proposed measurement approach. In terms of *external validity*, generalization of the findings is sensitive to the choice of expressions, the domain of origin thereof, and the participant sample. For an independent investigator, a first check can include expressions taken or derived from the authoritative examples most often provided by designers in language-defining publications, tutorials and guides. Such expressions can be assumed to be the best samples of: (a) expressions describing phenomena the designers destine their language to be used for, (b) associations between expressions and their authoritative classifications. The participant sample, on the other hand, is meant to be taken from a modeler population, i.e., persons who could be using the language in practice. From an *internal validity* viewpoint one can further observe that both the collected expressions and the training procedure can interfere with conclusions with respect to the conceptualization qualities. For example, an otherwise well-chosen conceptualization may yield low agreement measures or strange overlaps due to bad training or badly written expressions. This can be mitigated by observing the behavior of the measures over repeated studies on the same conceptualization whereby training and expression choices and formats vary. An additional *construct validity* threat is whether and how the way a participant classifies an expression to a concept is biased by the way it is written. For example, in iStar 2.0, the examples in the language guide [9] train modelers that if, e.g., bill payment is a task it is written as *"Pay Bills"* but if it is a goal it is written as *"Have Bills Paid"*. Using such cues, participants may accurately classify expressions according to language style rather than the domain information, revealed e.g. in the description context. Avoiding such effect is on the investigator's hands and interests, who can choose to tailor both training and expressions to specific needs.

Finally, the agreement, accuracy and overlap measures themselves are subject for further study and refinement from a variety of angles. One is their ability to compare concept sets of different sizes. While the proposed normalizations allow for rough qualitative comparisons, a theory of such comparisons is yet be developed. It would be specifically relevant to know if decrease in conceptual granularity (cf. [14]) is always (as a law) accompanied with increase in accuracy and agreement, and, if yes, how we control for this increase for a fair comparison. A second concern is the identification of statistical properties of the measures so to allow inferences to populations, when random sampling has been assumed.

Thirdly, a connection of these measures with existing conceptualizations of language quality can be investigated. Relevant here are the analytical constructs of *lucidity, laconicity, soundness* and *completeness* [32] as used for ontological analysis of conceptualization quality [12]. The constructs presented here appear to be coarser and do not clearly indicate the specific pathology of the conceptualization in those terms. For example, low agreement – they way we defined it – may not be an exclusive symptom of *construct redundancy* as it can also be caused by, e.g., *incompleteness*. It appears, nevertheless, that refinements of our constructs are possible to allow for some commensurability if not direct operationalization relationships with the four quality constructs. Regardless, empirical investigation does not compete with the need for ontological analysis. Likewise, more work will be required to position such metrics within established language quality attributes [19,23,25]. For example, *modeler appropriateness* and *participant appropriateness* [19] refer to the correspondence between the language constructs and the way producers and users of models perceive reality. From an empirical standpoint, however, any measurement of comprehensibility or domain appropriateness (i.e., lucidity, laconicity etc. [12,32]) is likely based on modeler and/or participant samples, requiring care in clarifying the precise object of measurement and the relevant influencing factors.

5   Related Work and Conclusions

Empirically studying conceptual modeling languages is not a new enterprise, with many efforts having been dedicated on firstly understanding the basic empirical constructs of quality [19,23,25] and then engaging in experimental or other empirical activity. A plethora of studies have been conducted focussing on various understandability conceptions of conceptual models in general. Houy et al. offer a comprehensive survey aimed at organizing our understanding of understandability [16]. Much of the work has focussed on process and entity or other domain structure models, e.g. [8,24]. Goal models, our example focus here, have also been the subject of empirical investigation in various instances, e.g., Hadar et al. [13], Horkoff and Yu [15], Santos et al. [27], Estrada et al. [11] or Liaskos et al. [1,20–22]. A strong appeal to the consensus of user populations has been put forth by Caire et al. [5], which we also espouse as a principle. Naturally, this line of work is complemented by several analytical and ontology-based efforts to explore qualities of intention conceptualizations, e.g., Bernabè et al. [3].

Our work is inspired by a vision of measurement *standardization* for systematizing empirical evaluation, as is commonly done in other disciplines. By using standard, reproducible and comparable quality assessment instruments, language designers are better equipped in their effort to demonstrate the qualify of their designs and increase the appeal of such to practitioners.

References

1. Alothman, Norah., Zhian, Mehrnaz, Liaskos, Sotirios: User perception of numeric contribution semantics for goal models: an exploratory experiment. In: Mayr, Heinrich C., Guizzardi, Giancarlo, Ma, Hui, Pastor, Oscar (eds.) ER 2017. LNCS, vol. 10650, pp. 451–465. Springer, Cham (2017). https://doi.org/10.1007/978-3-319-69904-2_34
2. Amyot, D., Mussbacher, G.: User requirements notation: the first ten years, the next ten years (Invited Paper). J. Software **6**(5), 747–768 (2011)
3. Bernabé, César Henrique., Silva Souza, Vítor E., Almeida Falbo, Ricardo de., Guizzardi, Renata S.S., Silva, Carla: GORO 2.0: evolving an ontology for goal-oriented requirements engineering. In: Guizzardi, Giancarlo, Gailly, Frederik, Suzana Pitangueira Maciel, Rita (eds.) ER 2019. LNCS, vol. 11787, pp. 169–179. Springer, Cham (2019). https://doi.org/10.1007/978-3-030-34146-6_15
4. Bork, D., Karagiannis, D., Pittl, B.: How are metamodels specified in practice? empirical insights and recommendations. In: Proceedings of the 24th Americas Conference on Information Systems (AMCIS 2018). New Orleans, LA (2018)
5. Caire, P., Genon, N., Heymans, P., Moody, D.L.: Visual notation design 2.0: towards user comprehensible requirements engineering notations. In: Proceedings of the 21st IEEE International Requirements Engineering Conference (RE 2013), pp. 115–124 (2013)
6. Cracau, D., Lima, J.E.D.: On the normalized herfindahl-hirschman index: a technical note. Int. J. Food Syst. Dyn. **4**(7), 382–386 (2016)
7. Crump, M.J.C., McDonnell, J.V., Gureckis, T.M.: Evaluating Amazon's mechanical turk as a tool for experimental behavioral research. PLoS ONE **8**(3), e57410 (2013)

8. Cruz-Lemus, J.A., Genero, M., Manso, M.E., Morasca, S., Piattini, M.: Assessing the understandability of UML statechart diagrams with composite states–a family of empirical studies. Empirical Software Eng. **14**(6), 685–719 (2009)
9. Dalpiaz, F., Franch, X., Horkoff, J.: iStar 2.0 Language Guide. The Computing Research Repository (CoRR) (2016). http://arxiv.org/abs/1605.07767
10. Dardenne, A., van Lamsweerde, A., Fickas, S.: Goal-directed requirements acquisition. Sci. Comput. Program. **20**, 3–50 (1993)
11. Estrada, H., Rebollar, A.M., Pastor, O., Mylopoulos, J.: An empirical evaluation of the i* framework in a model-based software generation environment. In: Proceedings of the 18th International Conference on Advanced Information Systems Engineering (CAiSE 2006), pp. 513–527. Luxembourg (2006)
12. Guizzardi, G.: Ontological foundations for structural conceptual models. Ph.D. thesis, University of Twente (2005)
13. Hadar, I., Reinhartz-Berger, I., Kuflik, T., Perini, A., Ricca, F., Susi, A.: Comparing the comprehensibility of requirements models expressed in Use Case and Tropos: results from a family of experiments. Inf. Software Technol. **55**(10), 1823–1843 (2013)
14. Henderson-Sellers, B., Gonzalez-Perez, C.: Granularity in conceptual modelling: application to metamodels. In: Proceedings of the 29th International Conference on Conceptual Modeling (ER 2010), pp. 219–232. Vancouver, Canada (2010)
15. Horkoff, Jennifer, Yu, Eric: Finding solutions in goal models: an interactive backward reasoning approach. In: Parsons, Jeffrey, Saeki, Motoshi, Shoval, Peretz, Woo, Carson, Wand, Yair (eds.) ER 2010. LNCS, vol. 6412, pp. 59–75. Springer, Heidelberg (2010). https://doi.org/10.1007/978-3-642-16373-9_5
16. Houy, C., Fettke, P., Loos, P.: Understanding understandability of conceptual models - What are we actually talking about? In: Proceedings of the 31st International Conference on Conceptual Modeling (ER 2012), pp. 64–77. Florence, Italy (2012)
17. Karagiannis, D., Kühn, H.: Metamodelling platforms. In: Proceedings of the 3rd International Conference on E-commerce and Web Technology, pp. 182–197. France (2002)
18. Krippendorff, K.: Content Analysis: An Introduction to its Methodology. SAGE (2004)
19. Krogstie, J.: Model-Based Development and Evolution of Information Systems: A Quality Approach. Springer, Heidelberg (2012). https://doi.org/10.1007/978-1-4471-2936-3
20. Liaskos, S., Dundjerovic, T., Gabriel, G.: Comparing alternative goal model visualizations for decision making: an exploratory experiment. In: Proceedings of the 33rd ACM Symposium on Applied Computing (SAC 2018). pp. 1272–1281. PAU, France (2018)
21. Liaskos, S., Ronse, A., Zhian, M.: Assessing the intuitiveness of qualitative contribution relationships in goal models: an exploratory experiment. In: Proceedings of the 11th ACM/IEEE International Symposium on Empirical Software Engineering and Measurement (ESEM 2017), pp. 466–471. Toronto, Ontario (2017)
22. Liaskos, Sotirios, Tambosi, Wisal: Factors affecting comprehension of contribution links in goal models: an experiment. In: Laender, Alberto H.F., Pernici, Barbara, Lim, Ee-Peng, de Oliveira, José Palazzo M. (eds.) ER 2019. LNCS, vol. 11788, pp. 525–539. Springer, Cham (2019). https://doi.org/10.1007/978-3-030-33223-5_43
23. Lindland, O.I., Sindre, G., Solvberg, A.: Understanding quality in conceptual modeling. IEEE Software **11**(2), 42–49 (1994)

24. Mendling, J., Strembeck, M.: Influence factors of understanding business process models. In: Proceedings of the 11th International Conference on Business Information Systems, pp. 142–153. Innsbruck, Austria (2008)
25. Nelson, H.J., Poels, G., Genero, M., Piattini, M.: A conceptual modeling quality framework. Softw. Quality J. **20**, 201–228 (2012)
26. Olivé, A.: Conceptual Modeling of Information Systems. Springer, Heidelberg (2007). https://doi.org/10.1007/978-3-540-72677-7
27. Santos, M., Gralha, C., Goulão, M., Araújo, J.: Increasing the semantic transparency of the KAOS goal model concrete syntax. In: Proceedings of the 37th International Conference on Conceptual Modeling (ER 2018), pp. 424–439. Xi'an, China (2018)
28. Stoet, G.: PsyToolkit: a software package for programming psychological experiments using Linux. Behav. Res. Methods **42**(4), 1096–1104 (2010)
29. Stoet, G.: PsyToolkit: a novel web-based method for running online questionnaires and reaction-time experiments. Teach. Psych. **44**(1), 24–31 (2017)
30. Susi, A., Perini, A., Mylopoulos, J.: The tropos metamodel and its use. Informatica **29**, 401–408 (2005)
31. The Open Group: ArchiMate® 3.1 Specification. Technical report (2019)
32. Wand, Y., Weber, R.: On the ontological expressiveness of information systems analysis and design grammars. Inf. Syst. J. **3**(4), 217–237 (1993)
33. Yu, E.S.K.: Towards modelling and reasoning support for early-phase requirements engineering. In: Proceedings of the 3rd IEEE International Symposium on Requirements Engineering (RE 1997). pp. 226–235. Annapolis, MD (1997)
34. Yu, E.S.: GRL - Goal-oriented Requirement Language. http://www.cs.toronto.edu/km/GRL/

Networks, Graphs and Conceptual Modeling

Deep Temporal Multi-Graph Convolutional Network for Crime Prediction

Yaqian Wang, Liang Ge$^{(\boxtimes)}$, Siyu Li, and Feng Chang

College of Computer Science, Chongqing University, Chongqing 400030, China
{wangyaqian,geliang,lisiyu,fengchang}@cqu.edu.cn

Abstract. Urban safety and security play a crucial role in improving life quality of citizen and the sustainable development of urban. In this paper, we propose a Deep Temporal Multi-Graph Convolutional Network (DT-MGCN) model which integrates graph generation component with spatial-temporal component to capture the dependencies between crime and various external factors. More specifically, in the graph generation component, we propose to encode the Euclidean and non-Euclidean correlations among regions into multiple graphs, which will reflect the heterogeneous relationships. The spatial-temporal component which simultaneously employs graph convolutional network (GCN) to capture the spatial patterns and encoder-decoder temporal convolutional network (EDTCN) to describe the temporal features. The experimental results on a real-world crime dataset collected from Chicago demonstrate the effectiveness of the proposed DT-MGCN model, which obtains high accuracy and outperforms the state-of-the-art baselines.

Keywords: Crime prediction · Spatial-temporal · Graph convolutional network · Encoder-decoder temporal convolutional network

1 Introduction

Crime rate (also known as the incidence of criminal cases) is an index of the frequency of certain criminal cases, and generally refers to the number of criminal cases per 100,000 population. Crime prediction plays a crucial role in improving public security and reducing the financial loss of crimes. The vast majority of traditional algorithms predict the crime by leveraging demographic data (official counts are collected by the U.S. Census Bureau every 10 years) [1], which could fail to capture the dynamics of crimes in urban.

An ever increasing volume of urban related data, with spatial and temporal attributes, from weather to air quality to economic activity, is available for public organizations, including police departments, to integrate with internal data. This offers the opportunity to apply data analytics methodologies to extract useful predictive models related to crime events, which can enable police departments to utilize their limited resources better and develop more effective strategies

© Springer Nature Switzerland AG 2020
G. Dobbie et al. (Eds.): ER 2020, LNCS 12400, pp. 525–538, 2020.
https://doi.org/10.1007/978-3-030-62522-1_39

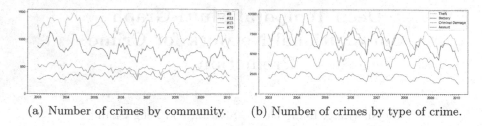

(a) Number of crimes by community.   (b) Number of crimes by type of crime.

Fig. 1. Number of crimes per month (2003–2010).

for crime prevention. In particular, extensive criminal justice studies show that the incidence of criminal events is not equally distributed within a city. In fact, crime rates can change with respect to the geographic location [17,18] of the area (there are low-risk and high-risk areas) and crime trends can vary (seasonal patterns, peaks, dips) with respect to the period of the year[6]. For this reason, an accurate predictive model must be able to automatically detect both which areas in the city are more affected by crime events and how the crime rate of each specific area varies with respect to the temporal period. This knowledge can enable police departments to efficiently allocate their resources to specific crime hot spots [10].

In our work, we introduce abundant external factors to enhance the spatio-temporal relationship to predict crime. The community area is used as our geographical unit of study, since it is well-defined, historically recognized and stable over time [2]. In total, there are 77 community areas in Chicago. As shown in Fig. 1, we can observe the incidence of crime varies greatly among different months, crime types and communities. We infer the crime rate of arbitrary crime categories in a community of Chicago, at different months of a year. We propose a DT-MGCN model which integrates graph generation component and spatial-temporal component to capture the dependencies between crime and various external factors. The main contribution of this paper can be summarized as follows:

- We propose the DT-MGCN model by combining the GCN and EDTCN. The GCN is used to capture the topological structure of the communities to model spatial dependence, EDTCN is used to capture the dynamic change of crime data to model temporal dependence. The DT-MGCN model can also be applied to other spatiotemporal forecasting tasks.
- We develop a encoder-decoder temporal module, which consists of multiple residual blocks stacked by dilated causal convolutions (DCC). It has a long receptive field and can capture dynamic temporal correlations effectively.
- Our method has smaller prediction error compared with other state-of-art approaches.

2   Related Work

Crime rate forecasting has a positive impact on social stablity and has drew much attention in academia. Related researchers have proposed many methods to solve crime prediction problem. Early statistical methods for crime prediction were simple time series models, containing Autoregressive Integrated Moving Average (ARIMA) [23] and its variant, Negative Binomial Regression (NB) [14], Geographically Weighted Negative Binomial Regression model (GWNBR) [19], etc. These methods depend on data stationary assumption, thus they have limited ability to model complex crime data.

Later, models based on traditional machine learning methods, such as Support Vector Regression (SVR) [20] and Support Vector Machine (SVM) [11] were applied to crime prediction to model more complex data. However, these methods cannot capture non-linearity in crime data effectively, and barely utilize spatial correlations. Moreover, they need more detailed feature engineering.

Recently, methods based on deep learning have been applied in many fields and achieved success, which has inspired the study of crime prediction to use deep-learning-based methods modeling the complex spatial-temporal dependencies of the crime data. Wawrzyniak et al. [21] proposed a method for short-term crime forecasting based on the Long Short Term Memory (LSTM). Mary et al. [15] used the Artificial Neural Networks (ANN), this model detects crime patterns from inferences collected from the crime scene. Chun et al. [5] applied Deep Neural Network (DNN) on the individual's criminal charge. Huang et al. [9] proposed a hierarchical recurrent networks framework, which has a three-level Gated Recurrent Units (GRU) architecture to capture the complex time evolving dependencies between the crime occurrences in different time slots. Yi et al. [24] proposed a Neural Network based Continuous Conditional Random Field (NN-CCRF) model to predict crime rate. However, the main limitation of the above models is that traditional convolution operations can only capture the spatial characteristics of regular grid structures but do not work for data points with irregular topologies. Therefore, they fail to make an effective use of the topological structure of the region network to capture complex spatial correlations.

In order to overcome the limitation of traditional convolution and capture more complex spatial-temporal dependencies, Li et al. [13] proposed a framework that combines the diffusion convolutional with the recurrent neural network(DCRNN) to forecast traffic conditions. Yu et al. [25] proposed the spatiotemporal GCN (ST-GCN), which uses a full convolution structure combining graph convolution with 1D convolution. In ST-GCN, the graph convolution is used to obtain the spatial correlation, and the 1D convolution is used to extract the temporal dependencies. STGCN is much more computationally efficiently than the above-mentioned models using RNNs. In addition, most existing spatiotemporal prediction methods ignore multiple spatial correlations between different regions in the geographical network, and they hardly utilize multiple temporal correlations and external factors.

3 Preliminary

3.1 Crime Rate Prediction Problem

The crime rate prediction problem can be regarded as a spatiotemporal prediction problem which predicts the future crime rate of the whole city using history observed crime rate from the N communities. The communities network can be defined as a weighted directed graph $\mathcal{G} = (\mathcal{V}, \mathcal{E}, W)$ where $\mathcal{V}$ is a defined set of $|\mathcal{V}| = N$ nodes, $\mathcal{E}$ is a set of edges and $W \in \mathbb{R}^{N \times N}$ is a weight matrix encoding the connection weight (e.g. distance, similarity) between two communities. We predict crime rate in the next Δ time steps using the previous M history observations. Given a time step t, we use x_t^i to represent the observed crime rate of community i at time step t. Then use $X_t = [x_t^1, ..., x_t^i, ..., x_t^N] \in \mathbb{R}^N$ to define the history crime rate of all communities at time step t. We can regard the observed crime rate at time step t as a graph signal $z \in \mathbb{R}^N$. Formally, the crime rate prediction model is any function $f : \mathcal{X} \to \hat{\mathcal{X}}$ that produces a mapping:

$$\hat{X}_{t+1}, \hat{X}_{t+2}, ..., \hat{X}_{t+\Delta} = f(X_{t-M+1}, X_{t-M+2}, ..., X_t; \Theta) \tag{1}$$

where Θ is the parameters to be learned; $\hat{X}_{t+1}$ is the predicted crime rate at time step $t + 1$.

3.2 Spectral Graph Convolution

Graph convolutional network has gained great attention in recent years since traditional convolutional network (CNN) couldn't handle the non-Euclidean structure data. The graph convolution [22] is a convolution operation implemented by using linear operators that diagonalize in the Fourier domain to replace the classical convolution operator [8]. In this paper, we utilized the graph convolution on spectral domain known as spectral graph convolution to capture the spatial correlations. For a graph signal $z : \mathcal{V} \to \mathbb{R}^N$, the spectral graph convolution between signal and kernel Θ can be written as:

$$\Theta *_\mathcal{G} z = U((U^T \Theta) \odot (U^T z)) = U\Theta(\Lambda)U^T z = \Theta(U \Lambda U^T)z = \Theta(L)z \tag{2}$$

where $\odot$ denotes the Hadamard product; $U = \{u_0, \cdots, u_{N-1}\} \in \mathbb{R}^{N \times N}$ is the Fourier basis and $L = D - W \in \mathbb{R}^{N \times N}$ is the combination Laplacian matrix with $D_{ii} = \sum_j W_{ij}$; $\Lambda = diag([\lambda_0, \cdots, \lambda_{N-1}]) \in \mathbb{R}^{N \times N}$ is the diagonal matrix of eigenvalues of L. U is the matrix of eigenvectors of L. Since the computation complexity of Eq. 2 is high for large graphs, Chebyshev polynomial approximation [7] can be used to reduce the complexity. The spectral graph convolution can be finally written as:

$$\Theta *_\mathcal{G} z = \Theta(L)z = \sum_{k=0}^{K-1} \theta_k T_k(\tilde{L})z \tag{3}$$

where $\tilde{L} = 2L/\lambda_{max} - I_N$ is the scaled Laplacian matrix, the Chebyshev polynomial can be computed as:

$$T_k(z) = 2z T_{k-1}(z) - T_{k-2}(z), T_0 = 1, T_1 = z \tag{4}$$

4   Framework

To solve the above problem, we propose a deep temporal multi-graph convolutional neural network model, the architecture of our model is shown in Fig. 2. In this section, we present the details of DT-MGCN architecture.

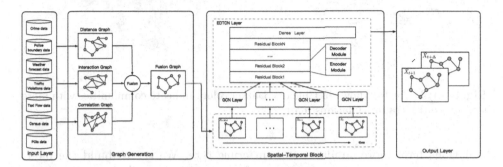

Fig. 2. DT-MGCN architecture.

4.1   Graph Generation Component

We propose to build inter-community graphs, where the links between communities reflect the spatial relationships. More specifically, the nodes in the graph are the communities, and the edges represent relationships between communities. We also encode weights on the edges as the relationship strength between communities can be different. Moreover, since there may be various relationships between communities that can help our prediction, we construct multiple graphs: distance graph, interaction graph and correlation graph.

Distance Graph: The distance graph can be defined as a weighted undirected graph $\mathcal{G}_D = (\mathcal{V}, \mathcal{E}, W_D)$, we denote $d_{i,j}$ as the distance between two communities i and j, and use the reciprocal of the distance $W_D = d_{i,j}^{-1}$ to mark the weight between two communities so that closer communities will be linked with higher weights.

Interaction Graph: The historical taxi flow can also provide plenty of information to construct the inter-community graphs. As shown in Fig. 3(a), we construct an interaction graph to indicate whether two communities are interacted with each other frequently according to the historical taxi flow records. We define the interaction graph as a weighted directed graph $\mathcal{G}_I = (\mathcal{V}, \mathcal{E}, W_I)$, denote $I_{i,j}$ as the number of taxi flow records between two communities i and j, we use $W_I = I_{i,j}$ to mark the weight between two communities so that two communities taxi flows are more frequent will be linked with higher weights.

Correlation Graph: The correlation between communities is not only related to distance but also related to similarity. Those communities with similar population composition, topographical distribution, building distribution and traffic

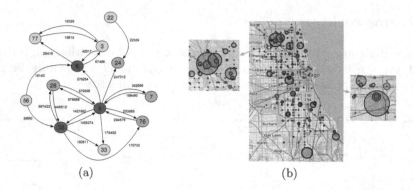

Fig. 3. (a) Major taxi flows in Chicago. Darker colors indicate communities with more taxi trips. (b) Traffic violations map.

violations have more similar trends in crime rate. We try to build the inter-community graph with the correlation of communities' population composition, POI and traffic violations data, and then compute the correlations between every two communities as the inter-community link weights in the graph. In this work, we define the correlation graph as a weighted undirected graph $\mathcal{G}_C = (\mathcal{V}, \mathcal{E}, W_C)$, and use the popular Pearson coefficient to calculate the correlation. Denote $p_{i,j}$ as the Pearson correlation between community i and community j, n is the number of communities, $W_C = p_{i,j}$ is the weight between two communities.

$$p_{i,j} = \frac{\sum\limits_{i=1}^{n}(X_i - \overline{X})(Y_i - \overline{Y})}{\sigma_i \sigma_j} \tag{5}$$

Fusion: The graph fusion step merges different graphs into one fused graph. We combine different graphs by weighted summing their adjacency matrices at the element level. Since the adjacency matrices' value of different graphs may vary a lot, we first normalize the adjacency matrix A for each graph, the resultant A^* is the normalized adjacency matrix.

$$A^* = D^{-1}A + I \tag{6}$$

$$D = \begin{pmatrix} \sum_{j=1}^{N-1} A_{0,j} & 0 & \cdots & 0 \\ 0 & \sum_{j=1}^{N-1} A_{1,j} & \cdots & 0 \\ \vdots & \vdots & \ddots & \vdots \\ 0 & \cdots & \cdots & \sum_{j=1}^{N-1} A_{N-1,j} \end{pmatrix} \tag{7}$$

To keep the fusion result normalized after the weighted sum operation, we further add a softmax operation to the weight matrix. Suppose we have N graphs to blend together, we can denote the graph fusion process as:

$$W_1', W_2', \ldots, W_N' = Softmax(W_1, W_2, \ldots, W_N) \tag{8}$$

$$X = \sum_{i=1}^{N} W_i' \circ A_i^* \tag{9}$$

where $\circ$ is the element-wise product, X is the graph fusion result, which will be used in the graph convolution part.

4.2   GCN Layer

In the spatial-temporal component, the input sequence $\mathcal{X} = \{X_{t-M+1}, ..., X_t\}$ is fed into the graph convolutional layer. For the cirme rate prediction problem, the input is a sequence of graph signal $\mathcal{X} \in \mathbb{R}^{N \times F \times M}$ where F is the number of features of the input graph signal. For the graph signal with F features $X \in \mathbb{R}^{N \times F}$, the spectral graph convolution can be generalized by Eq. 3 as:

$$y_j = \sum_{i=1}^{F} \Theta_{i,j}(\tilde{L})x_i \in \mathbb{R}^N, 1 \le j \le F' \tag{10}$$

where the $F \times F'$ vectors of Chebyshev coefficients $\Theta_{i,j} \in \mathbb{R}^K$ (F, F' are the size of input and output of the feature maps, respectively). Therefore, the graph convolution for 2-D variables is denoted as $\Theta *_g X$ with $\Theta \in \mathbb{R}^{F \times F' \times K}$ and the output is $Y = \{y_1, ..., y_{F'}\} \in \mathbb{R}^{N \times F'}$. For each frame of input sequence $X_t \in \mathbb{R}^{N \times F}$ ($F = 1$), we can use the same kernel Θ to do the 2-D spectral graph convolution. Thus the graph convolution on input sequence can be written as:

$$\mathcal{Y} = \Theta *_g \mathcal{X} \Leftrightarrow Y_j = \Theta *_g X_j \in \mathbb{R}^{N \times F'}, t - M + 1 \le j \le t \tag{11}$$

where $\mathcal{Y} = \{Y_{t-M+1}, ..., Y_t\} \in \mathbb{R}^{N \times F' \times M}$ is the output of graph convolution and M is the length of the input sequence. We take $\mathcal{Y}$ as convolution result, and then use $\mathcal{Y}$ as the input of the dynamic temporal decoder-encoder network.

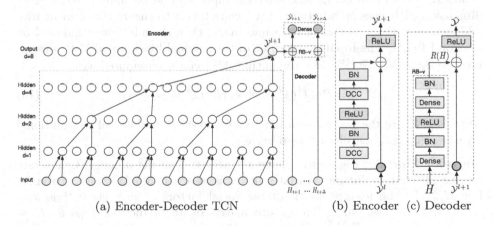

(a) Encoder-Decoder TCN   (b) Encoder   (c) Decoder

Fig. 4. Architecture of EDTCN

4.3 EDTCN Layer

The EDTCN architecture is similar to the classical Seq2Seq framework. In the encoder part, stacked dilated causal convolutions are constructed to capture the long-term temporal dependencies. In the decoder part, the decoder includes a variant of residual block (RB) (referred as RB-v) and an output dense layer. The module RB-v is designed to integrate output of stochastic process of historical observations and future covariates. Then the output dense layer is adopted to map the output of RB-v into our final forecasts.

Encoder Module: Dilated causal convolution allows the filter to be applied over an area larger than its length by skipping input values with a certain step. Figure 4(a) is an example of DCC with dilation factors $d = \{1, 2, 4, 8\}$, where the filter size $K = 2$ and a receptive field of size 16 is reached by staking four layers. The DCC layer is a 1-D fully convolution layer with a kernel which size is K. Formally, for a 1-D sequence input $x \in \mathbb{R}^M$ and a kernel $\phi \in \mathbb{R}^K$, the DCC operation S on element t of sequence is defined as:

$$S(t) = (x *_d \phi)(t) = \sum_{k=0}^{K-1} \phi(k) \cdot x(t - d \cdot k) \tag{12}$$

where d is the dilation factor. Stacking multiple dilated convolutions enable networks to have very large receptive fields, which can capture long-term temporal dependencies with a smaller number of layers.

Figure 4(b) shows the basic module for each layer of the encoder, where both of two dilated convolutions inside the module have the same kernel size K and dilation factor d. Each RB consists of two layers of DCC, first of which is followed by a batch normalization (BN) and rectified nonlinear unit (ReLU) and second of which is followed by another BN. The output of the second BN layer is added to the input of the RB, since the input and output may have different dimensions, RB uses an additional 1×1 convolution to ensure the element wise addition $\oplus$ receives tensors of the same shape, then the addition is followed by a second ReLU. The input and output of the residual block are all 3-D tensors. For the input $\mathcal{Y}^l \in \mathbb{R}^{M \times N \times F^l}$, the output $\mathcal{Y}^{l+1}$ can be computed as:

$$\mathcal{Y}^{l+1} = ReLU(\mathcal{Y}^l + \Phi_1^l *_d (ReLU(\Phi_0^l *_d \mathcal{Y}^l))) \tag{13}$$

where Φ_0^l, Φ_1^l are the two convolution kernels of two dilated causal convolutional layers within residual block l, respectively.

Decoder Module: Figure 4(c) shows the structure of the decoder. Crime rate can be affected by future covariates, such as weather, holidays and weekends. Let H_{t+1} be the feature vector of the social factors at prediction time step $t + 1$ and then we can get a feature matrix of all prediction steps as $H = [H_{t+1}, ..., H_{t+\Delta}]^T \in \mathbb{R}^{\Delta \times F_h}$ where $F_h = 13$ is the number of features we select (weather types, 10 dimensions; whether the day is weekend, 1 dimension; whether the day is weekday, 1 dimension; whether the day is holiday, 1 dimension). For the residual function $R(\cdot)$, we first apply a dense layer to extract important features and BN. Then a ReLU activation is applied followed by another dense layer and BN, another dense layer is used to map low to high dimensions to get $\mathcal{H} \in \mathbb{R}^{N \times F_H \times \Delta}$ (F_H is the number of units of first dense layer). The module RB-v allows for two inputs, H is the future covariates and $\mathcal{Y}^{l+1}$ is the output of the encoder. In order to capture the information of these two inputs, the spatio-temporal component output $\hat{\mathcal{Y}}$ can be written as:

$$\hat{\mathcal{Y}} = ReLU(\mathcal{Y}^{l+1} + R(H)) \tag{14}$$

The final output of the model is a sequence of crime rates $\hat{\mathcal{X}} = \{\hat{X}_{t+1}, ..., \hat{X}_{t+\Delta}\}$, which represent next Δ steps' crime rates for each node. $tanh$ is a hyperbolic tangent which ensures the output values are in the range of $(-1, 1)$.

$$\hat{\mathcal{X}} = tanh(\hat{\mathcal{Y}}) \in \mathbb{R}^{N \times 1 \times \Delta} \tag{15}$$

We use the L2 loss to measure the performance of our model and the loss function of our model can be defined as:

$$L(\hat{X}_{t+1}, ..., \hat{X}_{t+\Delta}; \Theta) = \sum_{t} \sum_{i=1}^{\Delta} ||\hat{X}_{t+i} - X_{t+i}||^2 \tag{16}$$

where Θ are all trainable parameters in the model; X_{t+i} is the ground truth and $\hat{X}_{t+i}$ is the model's prediction.

5 Experiment

5.1 Datasets

We evaluated our framework with seven datasets collected from Chicago City.

Crime Data: The crime data of Chicago are obtained from the City of Chicago data portal [3]. The crime data collected from Chicago has detailed information about the time and location (i.e., community area) of crime and the types of crime from Jan 1, 2001 to Dec 31, 2014. There are over five million recorded crime incidents in total over 14 years.

Other Related Data: (1) The census data of Chicago are obtained from the U.S. Census Bureau [1]. (2) Taxi flow data, traffic violations data and weather forecast data of Chicago are obtained from the City of Chicago data portal [3]. Traffic violations data including speed violations and red light traffic violations. In Fig. 3(b), the size of the circles represents the number of violations. Speed violations in blue and red light violations in red. Speed violations are much more concentrated in certain radars while red light traffic violations are more dispersed throughout the city of Chicago. (3) POI information for representing the characteristics of different community ares in a Chicago city. There are 10 major categories of POI defined by FourSquare[4]: *food, residence, travel, arts & entertainment, outdoors & recreation, college & education, nightlife, professional, shops and event.*

5.2   Setting of Hyperparameters

We use python deep learning framework Pytorch to construct the DT-MGCN model. The grid search method is used to find the best parameters on validations. We test the number of the terms of Chebyshev polynomial $K \in 1, 2, 3$. As K becomes larger, the forecasting performance improves slightly. Considering the computing efficiency and the degree of improvement of the forecasting performance, we set the kernel size K and filters' number of graph convolutional layer are set as 2 and 32, respectively. The kernel size K_d and filters' number of dilated casual convolution layers are set as 3 and 16, respectively. Dilation factor d of dilated casual convolutional layers is set as 2 and the number of residual blocks is set as 3. We use Adam algorithm [12] with learning rate of 0.001 to train the model. For the adjacency matrix construction, we set $W_1 = W_2 = W_3 = \frac{1}{3}$. The batch size is 32 and the number of epochs is 30. For all the tests, we use 12 history observed data points ($M = 12$) to predict crime rate in next 12 months.

5.3   Metrics and Baselines

To evaluate the performance of the proposed model, we use three evaluation metrics including mean absolute error (MAE), root mean square error (RMSE) and mean relative error (MRE). They are defined as:

$$RMSE = \sqrt{\frac{\sum_{i=1}^{n} |y_i - \hat{y}_i|^2}{n}} \tag{17}$$

$$MRE = \frac{\sum_{i=1}^{n} |y_i - \hat{y}_i|}{\sum_{i=1}^{n} y_i} \tag{18}$$

$$MAE = \frac{\sum_{i=1}^{n} |y_i - \hat{y}_i|}{n} \tag{19}$$

where $\hat{y}_i$ is an inference and y_i is the ground truth denoting the crime rate of a community; n is the number of community. We compare the DT-MGCN model with following models:

- GWNBR[19]: Geographically weighted negative binomial regression approach can capture the non-stationary property of crime.
- ConvLSTM[16]: ConvLSTM is a combination of CNN and long short term memory(LSTM), which can be used to solve spatiotemporal sequence forecasting problem.
- DCRNN[13]: Diffusion Convolutional Recurrent Neural Network is a model which integrates GCN and gated recurrent gate (GRU) for spatiotemporal forecasting.
- STGCN[25]:Spatio-Temporal Graph Convolutional Networks is a complete convolutional structure for spatiotemporal prediction.

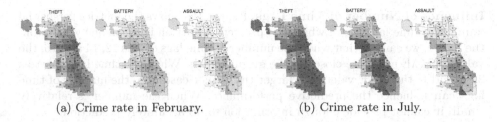

(a) Crime rate in February.   (b) Crime rate in July.

Fig. 5. Crime rates of overall and primary crime categories in Chicago by community areas in year 2014. Darker colors indicate higher values. (Color figure online)

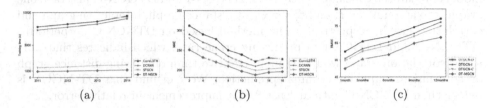

(a)   (b)   (c)

Fig. 6. (a) Training cost comparison of DT-MGCN and baseline models. (b) Influence of number of time lags. (c) Performance on different variants DT-MGCN models.

5.4 Results and Discussion

In this work, we focus on the crime categories whose average frequency of occurrence is top10 in Chicago per month. The top 10 categories are *theft, battery, criminal damage, narcotics, assault, other offense, burglary, motor vehicle theft, deceptive practice and robbery*. Theft is the largest among all the categories, and top-10 categories cover 91.70% of total crime incidents.

Predicting Results Visualization: Figure 5 shows the geographical distributions of different categories of crime occurrences in Chicago in February and July, respectively. From these visualization results, we can observe that

(1) different geographical regions have different crime occurrence distributions given a specific crime category; (2) crimes of different categories exhibit different occurrence patterns in the same district of a city; (3) crimes from different time periods show different geographical distribution patterns, the crime rate in July is generally higher than in February. Especially for theft, people wearing less in the summer, which makes theft easier.

Training Time of the Model: The training time of these four models are shown in Fig. 6(a). In this comparative experiment, the training time of DCRNN and ConvLSTM are very long since they use RNN to capture the time dependencies of crime and the training speed of RNN network is slower than CNN. The training speed of the DT-MGCN model proposed in this paper is the fastest. This is because the DT-MGCN model uses the EDTCN network to capture the temporal dependencies. The EDTCN network can obtain a large enough receptive field by using fewer layers, and can also adjust the dilation factor d of the dilated causal convolution to increase the receptive field of the EDTCN network.

Influence of Number of Time Lags: Figure 6(b) shows the metrics versus the number of time lags M, in which the prediction horizon is set to one year. From the figure, we can see that when the number of time lags equals 12, 14 and 16, the value of MAE are more closer to the ground truth. When the time lags is set as 2, 4, and 6, the MAE values are larger than other cases. So, the number of time lags can influence the predictive performance. When the number is relatively small, it cannot provide enough information to do accurately prediction.

Performance on Different Variants Models: We compare three variants of DT-MGCN with different graphs. Figure 6(c) shows comparison of variant models on dataset Chicago. DTGCN-D, DTGCN-I and DTGCN-C just take one graph into account. D, I, and C represent distance graph, interaction graph and correlation graph, respectively. The method based on DTGCN-C outperforms DTGCN-D and DTGCN-I in predicting crime rate, which indicates that only using correlation graph would be more effective than only using distance graph or correlation graph for criminal prediction. We can find that DT-MGCN is better than DTGCN-C with at least 8.81% improvement in relative error.

Table 1. Performance comparison of DT-MGCN and baseline models on dataset Chicago.

Models	2011		2012		2013		2014	
	MRE	MAE	MRE	MAE	MRE	MAE	MRE	MAE
GWNBR	0.214	275.61	0.267	330.51	0.278	316.34	0.268	272.51
ConvLSTM	0.145	221.41	0.171	302.87	0.183	263.46	0.174	229.75
DCRNN	0.129	209.65	0.154	290.33	0.165	248.37	0.159	220.23
STGCN	0.122	198.63	0.145	271.46	0.157	229.37	0.151	204.83
DT-MGCN	**0.114**	**188.63**	**0.137**	**262.72**	**0.146**	**213.63**	**0.140**	**196.54**

Prediction Performance: Our proposed DT-MGCN model performs the best on the dataset. Unlike GWNBR, ConvLSTM, DCRNN and STGCN, our proposed DT-MGCN model applies multiple graphs to learn the pairwise spatial correlation in a data-driven manner, and take advantage of EDTCN to capture the dynamic of temporal correlation under various situations. We can see that DT-MGCN is better than STGCN with at least 7.14% improvement in relative error (Table 1).

6   Conclusion

In this paper, a novel deep temporal multi-graph convolutional network model called DT-MGCN is proposed and successfully applied to forecasting crime rate. Our model combined multi-graph convolutions in the spatial dimension with deep temporal convolutions in the temporal dimension. Firstly, we construct multiple graphs: including distance graph, interaction graph and correlation graph in the spatial dimension to capture the Euclidean and non-Euclidean correlations among communities. And then, we fuse the multiple graphs and then apply the convolutional layer on the fused graph to predict community-level future crime rate. Secondly, we applied EDTCN to capture the dynamic temporal periodicity. We evaluate our model on a real-world dataset and the experiments show our model obtain the best performance against other baseline methods.

Actually, crime rate is affected by dynamic temporal periodic, like daily-periodic, weekly-periodic and monthly-periodic. In the future, we will take three independent components to respectively model three temporal properties of crimes into account to further improve the forecasting accuracy.

References

1. United States Census Bureau. http://www.census.gov
2. WIKIPEDIA. Community areas in Chicago, the free encyclopedia (2015)
3. Chicago Data Portal. https://data.cityofchicago.org
4. Foursquare Developers [EB/OL]. https://developer.foursquare.com
5. Chun, S.A., Paturu, V.A., Yuan, S., Pathak, R., Atluri, V., Adam, N.R.: Crime prediction model using deep neural networks. In: DG.O., pp. 512–514. ACM (2019)
6. Dash, S.K., Safro, I., Srinivasamurthy, R.S.: Spatio-temporal prediction of crimes using network analytic approach. In: IEEE International Conference on Big Data, pp. 1912–1917. IEEE (2018)
7. Defferrard, M., Bresson, X., Vandergheynst, P.: Convolutional neural networks on graphs with fast localized spectral filtering. In: Advances in Neural Information Processing Systems, pp. 3844–3852 (2016)
8. Henaff, M., Bruna, J., LeCun, Y.: Deep convolutional networks on graph-structured data. CoRR abs/1506.05163 (2015)
9. Huang, C., Zhang, J., Zheng, Y., Chawla, N.V.: Deepcrime: attentive hierarchical recurrent networks for crime prediction. In: CIKM, pp. 1423–1432. ACM (2018)
10. Ibrahim, N., Wang, S., Zhao, B.: Spatiotemporal crime hotspots analysis and crime occurrence prediction. In: Li, J., Wang, S., Qin, S., Li, X., Wang, S. (eds.) ADMA 2019. LNCS (LNAI), vol. 11888, pp. 579–588. Springer, Cham (2019). https://doi.org/10.1007/978-3-030-35231-8_42
11. Kianmehr, K., Alhajj, R.: Effectiveness of support vector machine for crime hotspots prediction. Appl. Artif. Intell. **22**(5), 433–458 (2008)
12. Kingma, D.P., Ba, J.: Adam: A method for stochastic optimization. arXiv preprint arXiv:1412.6980 (2014)
13. Li, Y., Yu, R., Shahabi, C., Liu, Y.: Diffusion convolutional recurrent neural network: data-driven traffic forecasting. In: International Conference on Learning Representations (ICLR 2018) (2018)
14. Rumi, S.K., Luong, P., Salim, F.D.: Crime rate prediction with region risk and movement patterns. CoRR abs/1908.02570 (2019)
15. Shermila, A., Bellarmine, A., Santiago, N.: Crime data analysis and prediction of perpetrator identity using machine learning approach, pp. 107–114, May 2018
16. Shi, X., Chen, Z., Wang, H., Yeung, D.Y., Wong, W.K., WOO, W.C.: Convolutional LSTM network: a machine learning approach for precipitation nowcasting. In: Advances in Neural Information Processing Systems, vol. 28, pp. 802–810 (2015)

17. Tang, Y., Zhu, X., Guo, W., Wu, L., Fan, Y.: Anisotropic diffusion for improved crime prediction in urban China. ISPRS Int. J. Geo-Inf. **8**(5), 234 (2019)
18. Wang, H., Kifer, D., Graif, C., Li, Z.: Crime rate inference with big data. In: KDD, pp. 635–644. ACM (2016)
19. Wang, H., Yao, H., Kifer, D., Graif, C., Li, Z.: Non-stationary model for crime rate inference using modern urban data. IEEE Trans. Big Data **5**(2), 180–194 (2019)
20. Wang, P., Mathieu, R., Ke, J., Cai, H.J.: Predicting criminal recidivism with support vector machine. In: 2010 International Conference on Management and Service Science, pp. 1–9, August 2010
21. Wawrzyniak, Z.M., et al.: Data-driven models in machine learning for crime prediction. In: 2018 26th International Conference on Systems Engineering (ICSEng), pp. 1–8, December 2018
22. Wu, Z., Pan, S., Chen, F., Long, G., Zhang, C., Yu, P.S.: A comprehensive survey on graph neural networks. CoRR abs/1901.00596 (2019)
23. Yadav, R., Kumari Sheoran, S.: Crime prediction using auto regression techniques for time series data. In: 2018 3rd International Conference and Workshops on Recent Advances and Innovations in Engineering (ICRAIE), pp. 1–5, November 2018
24. Yi, F., Yu, Z., Zhuang, F., Guo, B.: Neural network based continuous conditional random field for fine-grained crime prediction. In: IJCAI, pp. 4157–4163. ijcai.org (2019)
25. Yu, B., Yin, H., Zhu, Z.: Spatio-temporal graph convolutional neural network: a deep learning framework for traffic forecasting. In: Proceedings of the 27th International Joint Conference on Artificial Intelligence (IJCAI) (2018)

A Conceptual Framework for Dynamic Planning of Alternative Routes in Road Networks

Sven Hartmann[1]([⊠]), Jack Alshami[1], Hui Ma[2], and Dietrich Steinmetz[1]

[1] Clausthal University of Technology, Clausthal-Zellerfeld, Germany
{sven.hartmann,jack.alshami,dietrich.steinmetz}@tu-clausthal.de
[2] Victoria University of Wellington, Wellington, New Zealand
hui.ma@vuw.ac.nz

Abstract. We propose a conceptual framework to be utilized by developers of applications that require alternative routes in road networks. Our framework implements an efficient approach for dynamic alternative route planning that can respond to road network changes. With our framework, state-of-the-art algorithms for alternative route planning can be enabled to cope better with dynamic changes. We design a conceptual graph data model to reflect the semantic context of alternative route planning, and propose a dynamic index to store and reuse alternative routes. Our experiments with real-world road network data indicate that our framework can generate high-quality alternative routes in dynamic road networks efficiently.

Keywords: Geographic information · Data modelling · Graph database

1 Introduction

Route planning systems and online map services are popular to guide travelers to their destination. Road network data is used to compute min-cost paths and alternative routes. Road networks can be regarded as graphs, with nodes for intersections and edges for road segments. The cost associated with an edge may have different meanings, e.g., cost of traversing the road segment, distance, travel time, fuel consumption, carbon emission, or another attribute of interest.

Once a trip started, relevant *alternative routes* are computed in real-time (i.e., in milliseconds) taking into consideration the current road network information, so that they fulfill quality constraints [20], i.e., they should not be too similar, not cause much higher costs, and not have unnecessary detours. In the real world, road network information is time-dependent and stochastic. Road networks are subject to discrete changes. The costs associated with road segments may change dynamically due to several factors, e.g., weather conditions, traffic jams, and accidents. Due to changes, alternative routes computed at the origin of the trip may not be suitable anymore, and need to be re-computed dynamically.

© Springer Nature Switzerland AG 2020
G. Dobbie et al. (Eds.): ER 2020, LNCS 12400, pp. 539–554, 2020.
https://doi.org/10.1007/978-3-030-62522-1_40

Various real-world applications require dynamic alternative routes. Traffic flow optimization applications like [10, 21, 23] use dynamic alternative routes to forecast traffic congestion and improve traffic flow by redirecting vehicles to alternative routes. Application developers of all these applications face similar challenges when dealing with alternative routes, so there is good reason to support them such that alternative route planning does not become a computational bottleneck for their applications. To be successful, applications in the domain of transportation and logistics need to address new hurdles; just to name a few: 1) The transportation volume is steadily growing, and so do the number of vehicles and travelers. 2) Due to technological progress (e.g., road sensors, 5G, social networks, vehicular networks), more and new dynamic information become available and are taken into account in route planning. This makes it possible to react faster and more flexible to highly dynamic changes. 3) There is an increasing demand in more advanced route planning that can optimize multiple objectives simultaneously, thus making route planning even more elaborate and complex.

State-of-the-art algorithms for alternative routes planning, such as K* [2] and CSAR [20], were originally developed for static road networks. For a survey see [1, 4]. They can be applied for dynamic road networks, too. When changes occur, then these algorithms recompute alternative routes from scratch. This is very expensive and consumes a lot of resources, especially when road network changes occur frequently. This is not a smart approach, in particular, as road network changes might only affect very few alternative routes. Therefore smarter approaches are in demand. Dedicated approaches for *dynamic alternative route planning* (DARP) are required that can determine alternative routes efficiently in response to road network changes. To increase the efficiency and reduce resource consumption, the use of a suitable index is called for. Data structures used by existing static algorithms for alternative routes planning cannot easily be adapted to cope with dynamic changes. To avoid inefficient re-computations from scratch, a graph data model can serve as the basis for building an index.

The aim of this work is to propose a uniform conceptual framework for emerging applications that rely on dynamic alternative routes. We provide an abstraction of the computations and updates of alternative routes which can utilized when developing new applications. This simplifies the processing of various types of (spatial) queries on dynamic road networks, and can serve as building blocks for more complex queries involving dynamic alternative routes. Our conceptual framework can offer application developers a smart response to road network changes without computing paths from scratch. To make static algorithms work efficiently in dynamic road networks, we will investigate data structures that are suitable to build an efficient dynamic index. For this purpose, we will also propose a graph data model that gives the semantic context for building a suitable index. The following objectives will be achieved:

- propose a conceptual data model for dynamic alternative route planning;
- propose a conceptual framework for dynamic alternative route planning, including a dynamic index that is used in our framework to efficiently store and manage alternative routes;

– and conduct an initial experimental evaluation of our proposed conceptual framework using real-world datasets.

Organization. This paper is organized as follows. In Sect. 2, we provide preliminaries on dynamic alternative routes in road networks. In Sect. 3, we present our proposed conceptual framework and discuss our conceptual graph data model, our algorithms and our index structure. In Sect. 4, we describe the experiments conducted to investigate our framework and discuss the results. Section 5 summarizes related work. Section 6 concludes our paper.

2   Modeling Dynamic Alternative Routes

Our conceptual framework aims to implement an approach to dynamic alternative routes planning that offers a good balance between efficiency and effectiveness. To begin with, we discuss how to model information of dynamic road networks, i.e., time-dependent and stochastic road network changes.

A *road network* is a directed graph $G = (V, E)$ where V is a set of road points and E a set of road segments. Road points model intersections, terminal nodes and other points of interest, e.g., pickup and drop-off locations of travelers. Road segments model parts of roads. Each edge e is associated with a cost $c(e)$ that captures an attribute of interest, usually the travel time. The cost $c(p)$ of a path p is just the sum of the costs of its edges. We model road network changes as time-dependent changes of the cost of road segments. Let ΔG denote a list of road network changes.

Let p_s be a min-cost path from an origin s to a destination t. Other paths p with the same origin and destination as p_s are called *alternative routes*. For a traveler, alternative paths are functionally equivalent to the min-cost path, but often have some non-functional properties that are of particular interest for the traveler. We use $A(p_s)$ to denote a set of alternative routes of p_s.

For road segments, different attributes may be considered to define the associated cost, e.g., travel time, distance, travel cost, fuel consumption, risk of traffic jam, etc. The min-cost path is usually computed based on a single attribute. Often, this is the travel time. Alternative routes may offer a different compromise between these attributes.

Considering alternative routes is important for travelers in many situations. For example, in on-demand shuttle services, travel plans are computed to satisfy point-to-point travel requests, according to some quality of service constraints and/or objectives. While the path between the origin and the destination is often set as the min-time path, the traveler might prefer a cheaper itinerary in case time is not critical. If the traveler pays per distance (e.g., in taxis), avoiding fast but long-distance routes is of interest for the traveler.

Common quality criteria for alternative routes are established in [1,20]. Let p be a path and p_s the corresponding min-cost path. For simplicity, we assume here that the min-cost path is unique. We define the sharing ratio $share(p, p_s) := \frac{c(p \cap p_s)}{c(p_s)}$, and the stretching ratio $stretch(p, p_s) := \frac{c(p)}{c(p_s)}$, where γ, ϵ are fixed constants with $0 \leq \gamma$, $0 \leq \epsilon$. An alternative route is of *high-quality* if it is locally optimal, has limited sharing, i.e., $share(p, p_s) < \gamma$, and limited stretch, i.e., $stretch(p, p_s) < \epsilon$. A sufficient condition for local optimality is the absence of local detours.[1] This is generally desirable for high-quality alternative routes.

For a travel request from s to t on a road network G with dynamic changes ΔG, dynamic alternative routes planning aims to dynamically generate high-quality alternative routes from s to t.

3   Our Proposed Framework

In this section, we present our conceptual framework for dynamic alternative route planning which is illustrated in Fig. 1.

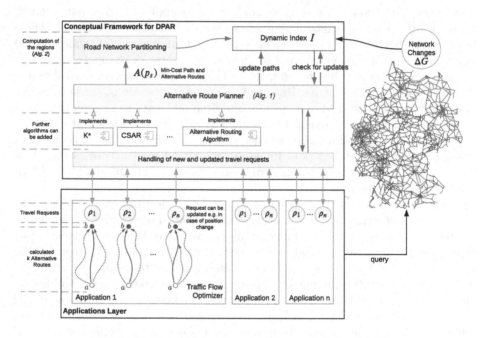

Fig. 1. Outline of our conceptual framework for DARP.

Initialization. When a travel request occurs, the min-cost path from the origin to the destination is determined and the initial set of alternative routes is computed. Then (the relevant part of) the road network is partitioned into disjoint regions, and the dynamic index is initialized. This index will be used to manage the regions, the paths and the relation between them.

---

[1] The exact definition of local optimality is technical. Let α be fixed. A path p is locally optimal if 1) every subpath p' with $c(p') < \alpha$ is a min-cost path, and 2) if p' is a subpath of p with $c(p') > \alpha$ and $c(p'') < \alpha$ where p'' is the path obtained by removing the end points of p', then p is a min-cost path.

Example 1. To illustrate this, consider the road network in Fig. 2 and suppose a traveler is going from origin s to destination t. The min-cost path is $s{\to}5{\to}6{\to}7{\to}8{\to}t$ of cost 22. Two alternative routes of interest are 1) $s{\to}1{\to}2{\to}7{\to}4{\to}t$ of cost 24, and 2) $s{\to}1{\to}2{\to}3{\to}4{\to}t$ of cost 26. Each of the paths from s to t is partitioned by three regions as illustrated in Fig. 2.

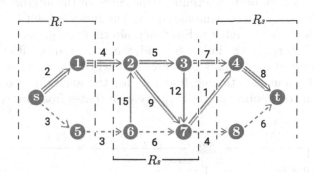

Fig. 2. Example of a road network G. The dashed edges form the min-cost path from the traveler's origin s to destination t. The green and red edges represent two alternative routes of interest for the traveler. R_1, R_2 and R_3 are regions used to partition the paths (Color figure online).

For each travel request, a suitable partition into regions is determined and fixed. The computation of new alternative routes is not performed immediately when a road network change occurs. Rather this is postponed until reaching the entry point of the region that contains the updated road segment. The intention behind this is to reduce the number of times that re-computations are initiated, and as a result the overall re-computation effort.

Algorithm 1 is central to our framework. Initially, the alternative routes are computed using a static algorithm, then the index is constructed using Algorithm 2. We propose to use a dynamic index to efficiently respond to road

---

Algorithm 1. Dynamic Alternative Route Planning

1: **Input:** road network G, min-cost path p_s, number of alternative routes k
2: $A(p_s) \leftarrow$ compute alternative routes from scratch(G, p_s, k).
3: $R, I \leftarrow$ road network partitioning$(G, p_s, A(p_s))$ *(Algorithm 2)*
4: **while** updates occurring on G and destination t has not yet been reached **do**
5:     $\Delta G \leftarrow$ get updates(G)
6:     update dynamic index$(I, \Delta G)$
7:     $r \leftarrow$ get current region(R)
8:     **if** ΔG affects the current region r **then**
9:         $A(p_s) \leftarrow$ compute alternative routes(G, I, r, R) *(Algorithm 3)*
10:    **end if**
11: **end while**

---

network changes, so that new alternative routes can be re-computed efficiently while traveling. When road network changes occur, it checks which regions are affected. If needed, Algorithm 1 calls Algorithm 3 to compute new alternative routes using the dynamic index, and continues waiting for road network changes.

Use of a Dynamic Index. Based on an idea in [14], the part of the road network containing the alternative routes is partitioned into multiple regions. Once the regions have been determined, the edges of the alternative routes are organized accordingly into a dynamic index. The index is built by Algorithm 2. The intention for this is as follows. First, new alternative routes can be computed using the edges stored in the index. Second, the computation effort is decreased since the number of road points is reduced, at which the checking for updates takes place. Without partitioning into regions, the algorithm would check for changes at each road point and build alternative routes from scratch each time.

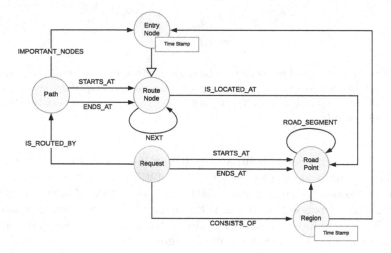

Fig. 3. Our conceptual graph data model for dynamic alternative route planning.

To provide the semantic context for the dynamic index, we design a conceptual graph data model for dynamic alternative route planning, see Fig. 3,[2].

Travel Time. Due to dynamic road network changes, the costs associated with road segments are time-dependent and stochastic. We regard the travel time as a random variable X. Hence, road segments are not associated with a fixed travel time, but with a probability distribution. Based on real-world data from travelers, [3] noted that lognormal distribution is the best fit to model travel time on road networks. That is, $X = e^{\mu + \sigma \cdot Z}$, where Z is a standard normal variable with parameters μ and σ. The mean and variance of X are the following:

$$Mean(X) = \exp(\mu + \sigma^2/2) \tag{1}$$

---

[2] For a better overview, we show the conceptual graph data model with its nodes and relationships, but only those properties that are crucial for our purpose.

$$Variance(X) = \exp(\sigma^2 - 1) * \exp(2\mu + \sigma^2) \qquad (2)$$

The parameters μ and σ can be obtained as follows:

$$\mu = (1/n) * \sum_{i=1}^{n} \ln(x_i). \qquad \sigma^2 = 1/n * \sum_{i=1}^{n} (\ln(x_i) - \mu)^2, \qquad (3)$$

where n is the number of edges in the sample group, and x_i represents a value in the sample. The sample group consists of all the edges on the min-cost path and the alternative routes.

Regions. The use of regions helps to reduce the cost of re-computing new alternative routes. While the traveler is traversing within a region, the paths are considered to be still valid and no re-computation is needed. To partition the road network into regions, one needs to decide how wide they should be. Different strategies can be used to choose the width. It is recommended to use the upper limit of the confidence interval of X to set the width:

$$Width = Mean(X) + t_{1-\alpha} * \sqrt{Variance(X)/n}. \qquad (4)$$

where α is the confidence level, and $t_{1-\alpha}$ the corresponding value of the t-table. Thus, a sufficiently high percentage of edges has a smaller cost than the width. Choosing a smaller width would result in more regions, and the re-computation would be started more often, thus causing an increase in the computation effort.

Example 2. For the paths in Fig. 2, the width is set to 5.9 using Eq. (4). Note that this results in three regions for partitioning the road network.

Entry Points of Regions and Timestamps. Many road network changes do not affect the traveler. Only updates that occur along the computed paths need to be handled. To determine if a path is subject to an update, we equip every region r with a timestamp $TS(r)$, see also Fig. 3. Similarly, we equip each entry point u in a region with a timestamp $TS(u)$.

The entry point is the first road point of a given path in a given region. Each path has multiple entry points, each belonging to a different region. Each region can have several entry points that belong to different paths. If a road segment that belongs to a path is subject to a change, the corresponding entry point of the region that contains the edge will get a new timestamp. While traversing the path, the timestamps of entry points and their corresponding regions are compared at each entry point on the path to decide whether an update occurred and new paths should be computed.

New Alternative Routes. Our framework computes the new min-cost path and new alternative routes from the current point c to destination t by reusing the previously computed paths. The current point is the current location of the traveler. The previously computed paths were computed when the traveler requested alternative routes and stored in the dynamic index.

Algorithm 2. Partition Road Network

1: **Input:** road network G, min-cost path p_s, alternative routes $A(p_s)$.
2: **Output:** regions R, dynamic index I.
3: $paths = \{p_s \cup A(p_s)\}$
4: $width \leftarrow$ calculate region width($paths$, mean (Eq. 1), variance (Eq. 2))
5: $R \leftarrow$ determine regions(G, $paths$, $width$)
6: **for each** region $r \in R$ **do**
7:     $TS(r) \leftarrow$ the current time of global clock
8: **end for**
9: **for each** edge $(u, v) \in paths$ **do**
10:     $r \leftarrow$ find appropriate region((u, v), $width$, R)
11:     assign edge to region((u, v), r)
12:     **if** (u, v) is the first edge of path $p_s \in r$ **then**
13:         mark u as a entry point of region r
14:         $TS(u) \leftarrow$ the current time of global clock
15:     **end if**
16: **end for**
17: $I \leftarrow$ construct dynamic index from R
18: return R, I

Algorithm 3. New Alternative Routes

1: **Input:** road network G, dynamic index I, current region r, regions R
2: **Output:** new alternative routes $A(p_s)$
3: $UpdatedEdge \leftarrow$ determine updated edge(G, $\Delta(G)$)
4: $c \leftarrow$ find entry node of current region(r)
5: $Neighbors \leftarrow$ get entry nodes and neighbor entry nodes of regions R
6: **for each** node u in $Neighbors$ **do**
7:     $MinCostPath \leftarrow$ compute min-cost path(c, u) (static algorithm like A*)
8:     $IndexPath \leftarrow \{ \}$
9:     **while** not reaching the destination **do**
10:         $IndexEdge \leftarrow$ extract next edge(I)
11:         $IndexPath$.add($IndexEdge$)
12:     **end while**
13:     $FinalPath \leftarrow$ merge paths($MinCostPath$, $IndexPath$.)
14:     $A(p_s)$.add($FinalPath$)
15: **end for**
16: return $A(p_s)$

Algorithm 3 recomputes new alternative routes after changes have occurred. For every changed edge, it determines the region (r_i), and updates the edge in the index. Then the neighboring points are searched for in the regions r_{i-1}, r_i and r_{i+1}. The neighboring point is an entry point that belongs to a region adjacent to the examining region. The reason behind checking points in region r_{i-1} is that it is sometimes better to go a step backward and compute paths at prior road points. The algorithm then determines min-cost paths to these points, explores the index to extract the appropriate edges, and groups them together to form the new alternative routes (Fig. 4).

Example 3. Figure 3 illustrates Algorithm 3. Suppose edge (6, 7) is deleted, i.e., its travel time is updated to ∞. When the traveler reaches the entry point 6, the algorithm determines the neighboring points 5, 2, 4, 8, then finds min-cost paths to them (using a static algorithm like A*) and computes the paths from the current point c to the destination t in a recursive way. The new alternative routes after the updates are 1) $6 \rightarrow 2 \rightarrow 7 \rightarrow 4 \rightarrow t$ with cost 33, 2) $6 \rightarrow 2 \rightarrow 7 \rightarrow 8 \rightarrow t$ with cost 34, and 3) $6 \rightarrow 2 \rightarrow 3 \rightarrow 4 \rightarrow t$ with cost 35.

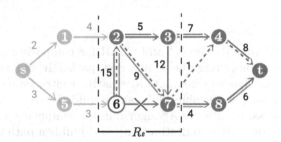

Fig. 4. The road network G after changes have occurred. The traveler's current location is at node 6. The dashed edges form the new min-cost path (based on the updated road network) from the current location to destination t. The green and red edges represent the new alternative routes. R_2 is the region that contains the updated edge (Color figure online).

Finally, we hasten to emphasize that the dynamic index used is a major difference between our framework and state-of-the-art static algorithms for alternative route planning, such as K* [2] and Candidate Sets for Alternative Routes (CSAR) [20]. Without the dynamic index, one would need to compute alternative routes from scratch whenever the road network changes. This is expensive as it requires exploring the road network completely and building the corresponding data structure each time an update occurs. K* (using a heap tree) and CSAR (using a via-nodes list) have to do that. This means extra effort for them, so that more time is needed to recompute the alternative routes. If we want to react to updates on road network in real time, computing alternative routes from scratch is not a feasible option.

4 Experimental Evaluation

We implemented our conceptual framework as a prototype using Neo4j and Java. In this section, we report on the experiments that we carried out to investigate the efficiency and effectiveness it can provide in generating dynamic alternative routes. All experiments were run on an Intel i7-4210@3.1 GHz with 8G RAM.

Datasets. We use three real-world road network datasets [7], see Table 1, of different sizes to assess scalability. To analyze the impact of different frequencies of road network changes, we consider three dynamicity levels (i.e., percentage of road segments updated per minute): low (6%), medium (30%), and high (60%).

Table 1. Size of datasets used in the experiments.

Dataset	#Road points	#Road segments	Path lengths used in tests
New York	264,346	733,846	39 and 78 and 141
Florida	1,070,376	2,712,798	40 and 74 and 119
Eastern USA	3,598,623	8,778,114	49 and 100 and 187

Baseline Algorithms. We use K* and CSAR for comparison. K* [2] is a fast static heuristic for computing the k min-cost paths. It can respond to road network changes, but has to recompute alternative routes from scratch without considering any quality constraints. K* can be guided with heuristics to speed up the search process. It calls the A* algorithm for computing shortest paths in forward manner (from origin to destination), and builds a path graph structure using a heap tree index. Alternative routes are obtained by calling Dijkstra's algorithm on the path graph structure in backward manner, from a new special node until reaching the desired number of alternative routes. CSAR [20] is a static heuristic for computing high-quality alternative routes that are guaranteed to fulfill three desired quality criteria (limited sharing, limited stretching, local optimality). To explore alternative routes, the road network is subdivided and a via-node list is maintained. All alternative routes go through via-nodes. In [17], CSAR was evaluated using different road network sizes and different sets of parameters. We use the same parameter settings.

Note the following for both baseline algorithms: If the traveler is at road point c and an update occurs on some edge, then new alternative routes are computed from the current road point c to the destination t, regardless of where the update occurred.

Experiments. Our experiments compare our framework to the two baseline algorithms. Each experiment is repeated 30 times using the same road network changes to isolate the affection of other processes running on the same machine. The observed standard deviation was always below 2%. Further, as road network changes are generated randomly, each experiment is repeated 30 times using different random changes to control the randomization and get reliable results.

Quality of Results. In this experiment, we investigate the quality of the generated alternative routes. Note that our framework and CSAR always generate alternative routes without detours, so that local optimality is achieved by design. On the contrary, K* does not guarantee local optimality.

Figure 5 shows the results obtained in terms of sharing and stretching. Similar to CSAR, our framework generates very good alternative routes that share

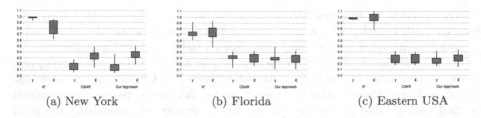

(a) New York   (b) Florida   (c) Eastern USA

Fig. 5. Quality of results. Sharing limit (γ) and stretching limit (ϵ) are shown for the generated alternative routes. (Smaller values are better.)

not much with the min-cost path, while K* generates alternative routes with a much higher share. Similar to CSAR, our framework finds alternative routes whose costs are not much higher than the min-cost path, while K* mainly finds alternative routes whose costs are considerably higher. Thus, our framework and CSAR find similar alternative routes that are near-optimal. Our framework outperforms K* and achieves better results with almost 60% increase on the quality of alternative routes in terms of sharing and stretching in comparison to the min-cost path.

Recall that, by design, K* computes alternative routes without considering the quality criteria. Therefore, alternative routes often have a huge share with the min-cost path as well with other alternative routes. Similar to CSAR, our framework satisfies the quality criteria, and build high-quality alternative routes, with a small share and slightly higher costs. Hence, in terms of quality, our framework is competitive to CSAR and superior to K*.

Effect of Path Length on Execution Time. In this experiment, we use paths of different lengths to study the effect of changing the path length on the performance. We compare the execution using three path lengths for each dataset. The results are shown in Fig. 6. Here low dynamicity level (6%) and $k = 3$ are used.

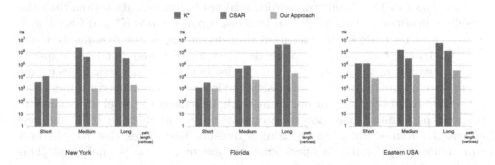

Fig. 6. Impact of the path length on the execution time. Three sets of path lengths are considered: short ($\leq$50 nodes), medium (50 to 100 nodes) and long ($\geq$100 nodes). The execution time is measured in ms. (Lower values are better.)

Our framework achieves better execution time than the baseline algorithms for any path length. As a result, it outperforms the baseline algorithms with almost 90% decrease on the execution time for paths with different lengths.

In K*, the heap tree grows exponentially in terms of the path length, and it takes more time to build the alternative paths. In CSAR, the via-node list becomes larger when paths have more nodes, and more paths are examined to find the suitable alternative routes. In our framework, increasing the path length requires performing more insertion operations. Our dynamic hash index has an excellent time complexity for insertions. Since the number of entries can be defined in advance, collisions can be avoided safely. This confirms the superiority of our proposed framework in terms of efficiency.

Effect of Dynamicity Level on Execution Time. In this experiment, we vary the dynamicity level to study the impact of the frequency of road network changes. We consider three levels: low (up to 6% of edges are updated per minute), medium (up to 30%) and high (up to 60%).

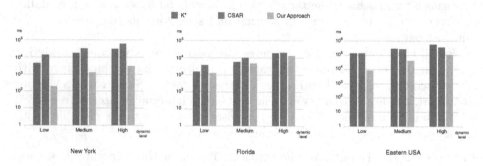

Fig. 7. Impact of the dynamicity level on the execution time. Three levels of dynamicity are considered: low (up to 6%), medium (up to 30%) and high (up to 60%). The execution time is measured in ms. (Lower values are better.)

As shown in Fig. 7, our framework achieves better execution time than the baseline algorithms. As a result, our framework outperforms K* and CSAR with 40% to 85% decrease in the execution time depending on the dynamicity level.

The baseline algorithms explore the road network and build the required data structure (heap tree in K*, via-nodes list in CSAR) from scratch each time an update occurs. Therefore, increasing the level of dynamicity consumes more resources and more time. In our framework, increasing the level of dynamicity requires performing more accessing operations to the index to build the new alternative routes. Since we are using a dynamic hash index that has the best time complexity for search operations, the execution time is minimized. This confirms the superiority of our framework in terms of efficiency.

Effect of Width of Regions on Execution Time. The width parameter is critical for efficiency. Choosing an inappropriate width may be harmful. In case of too narrow regions, the checking for road network updates may be performed more often than necessary, which increases the execution time. On the other hand, too wide regions may lead to missing out some road network changes and not responding to them, which reduces the efficiency of finding alternative routes. Hence, choosing the proper width is essential for the performance and quality that can be achieved.

Table 2. Possible choices for the width of regions

Width	$\frac{1}{2}$Upper limit	Upper limit	2*Upper limit	4*Upper limit
Execution time (ms)	10808.7	9465.9	11570.9	17876.6
Missed updates	0 out of 11	0 out of 11	1 out of 11	1 out of 11

In this experiment, we test several choices for the width to detect the best one in terms of execution time and number of road network changes to which our framework is able to respond. We use the NY dataset, a min-cost path with 74 nodes, and a list of 11 road network changes. We test four different choices for the width based on upper limit of the confidence interval, see Eq. (4). Table 2 shows the results. Hence, choosing the upper limit of the confidence interval as the width provides the best outcomes.

5 Related Work

Alternative route planning has attracted lots of research interest, cf. [1,4]. A conceptual graph data model and framework for dynamic alternative route planning, however, was not yet given. In the literature, some related problems in dynamic road networks and, more generally, dynamic graphs have been studied. These works use various interesting graph partitioning approaches and index structures, cf. [5]. An adaptation to alternative routes was not subject of these research works and appears hard. We mention some recent examples.

[16] discusses strategies for spatial graph clustering. Balanced partitions of edges are formed based on spatial proximity of nodes. An auxiliary data structure, however, is not used to store dynamic data or respond to dynamic updates. [18] studies spatial object search in road networks. Road networks are partitioned into a hierarchy of interconnected regional sub-networks. A B^+-tree is used, but consumes too much memory. [26] studies k-nearest neighbor search in road networks. Road networks are hierarchically partitioned into subgraphs. A balanced search tree index (G-tree) is used that outperforms [18]. [25] studies keyword-aware continuous k-nearest neighbor queries in road networks. A keyword-based 2-hop index is used to store node labels. The index size is kept small so that distance queries can be answered faster. The keywords' frequency is modeled using Zipf's distribution, which is suitable for keywords but not for travel time.

[19] studies shortest path queries in dynamic graphs. An adaptive shortest-path subgraph structure is used to decrease redundant efforts. The edges of the

shortest path are stored in this data structure and updates are applied directly to it. This approach performs well in graphs with up to 2000 nodes and low dynamicity. For more frequent updates, however, the performance is worse than recomputing from scratch. [24] studies constrained shortest path queries. Road networks are partitioned using an idea from [6]. An overlay graph is built on the top of it. An index structure based on the overlay graph is used, so that query processing becomes faster and cheaper. Such a data structure, however, does not avoid the reconstruction of indexes when system parameters change. [14] studies edge-constrained shortest path queries in dynamic graphs. Edge-disjoint partitioning (EDP) of graphs is used. A dynamic index is built with two components: a set of graph partitions and a set of lookup tables. While significant speedups are possible for this particular problem, EDP does not scale well when the size of the query label set or the frequency of graph updates increases. A drawback is that EDP is not tailored to road networks.

[15] studies real-time ride-sharing. A kinetic tree index is used to store travel requests and schedules. A drawback is the exponential explosion of the tree size for multiple close-by requests. Uncertainty due to road conditions is not studied.

To the best of our knowledge, the approaches above were not adapted to alternative routes in dynamic road networks. In our framework, we used a hierarchical hash table data structure to build a dynamic index that is tailored to road networks. It is based on a specific graph partitioning strategy and tailored to reduce the re-computation effort and compute alternative routes over dynamic road networks efficiently.

6   Conclusion and Future Work

In this paper, we presented initial research results towards a conceptual framework for dynamic alternative routes. We believe that our approach not only offers a common understanding of alternative route queries in road networks for application developers, but also contributes to demonstrate the practical usefulness of conceptual modeling techniques in the transportation and logistics domain.

We addressed the problem of dynamically generating alternative routes in road networks with low computation effort. In terms of efficiency, our framework improves K* and CSAR with almost 40% to 85% decrease in the execution time for different levels of dynamicity. In terms of quality of the generated alternative routes, our framework is comparable to CSAR and better than K* with almost 60% quality increase.

For the future, there are several ideas on our research agenda. We plan to conduct empirical studies with application developers to investigate comprehensibility and usage of our conceptual framework. We intend to extend our experiments to include other baseline algorithms and temporal road network datasets. We also plan to explore how our framework can be used for applications in other domains and with other types of networks that require alternative routes.

References

1. Abraham, I., Delling, D., Goldberg, A.V., Werneck, R.F.: Alternative routes in road networks. J. Exp. Algorithmics **18**, 1–17 (2013)
2. Aljazzar, H., Leue, S.: K^*: a heuristic search algorithm for finding the k shortest paths. Artif. Intell. **175**, 2129–2154 (2011)
3. Arroyo, S., Kornhauser, A.L.: Modeling travel time distributions on a road network. TRB (2005)
4. Bast, H., et al.: Route planning in transportation networks. In: Kliemann, L., Sanders, P. (eds.) Algorithm Engineering. LNCS, vol. 9220, pp. 19–80. Springer, Cham (2016). https://doi.org/10.1007/978-3-319-49487-6_2
5. Buluç, A., Meyerhenke, H., Safro, I., Sanders, P., Schulz, C.: Recent advances in graph partitioning. In: Kliemann, L., Sanders, P. (eds.) Algorithm Engineering. LNCS, vol. 9220, pp. 117–158. Springer, Cham (2016). https://doi.org/10.1007/978-3-319-49487-6_4
6. Delling, D., Goldberg, A.V., Razenshteyn, I., Werneck, R.F.: Graph partitioning with natural cuts. In: IEEE PDPS, pp. 1135–1146 (2011)
7. Demetrescu, C., Goldberg, A., Johnson, D.: 9th DIMACS implementation challenge. Shortest Path (2006). www.dis.uniroma1.it/challenge9/index.shtml
8. Eppstein, D.: Finding the k shortest paths. SIAM J. Comput. **28**, 652–673 (1998)
9. Eppstein, D., Galil, Z., Italiano, G.F., Nissenzweig, A.: Sparsification-a technique for speeding up dynamic graph algorithms. J. ACM **44**, 669–696 (1997)
10. Faro, A., Giordano, D.: Algorithms to find shortest and alternative paths in free flow and congested traffic regimes. Transp. Res. C **73**, 1–29 (2016)
11. Felner, A.: Finding optimal solutions to the graph partitioning problem with heuristic search. AMAI **45**, 293–322 (2005)
12. Frigioni, D., Marchetti-Spaccamela, F., Nanni, U.: Fully dynamic algorithms for maintaining shortest paths trees. J. Algorithms. **34**, 251–281 (2000)
13. Gonzalez, H., Han, J., Li, X., Myslinska, M., Sondag, J.P.: Adaptive fastest path computation on a road network: a traffic mining approach. PVLDB, pp. 794–805 (2007)
14. Hassan, M.S., Aref, W.G., Aly, A.M.: Graph indexing for shortest-path finding over dynamic sub-graphs. In: ACM SIGMOD, pp. 1183–1197 (2016)
15. Huang, B., Jin, W.: Large scale real-time ridesharing with service guarantee on road networks. PVLDB **7**, 2017–2028 (2014)
16. Huang, W., Jing, N., Rundensteiner, E.: Effective graph clustering for path queries in digital map databases. In: ACM CIKM, pp. 215–222 (1996)
17. Kroge: Comparing k Shortest Paths with reasonable alternative routes. Bachelor thesis, Clausthal University of Technology (2017)
18. Lee, L., Heng, T.: ROAD: a new spatial object search framework for road networks. IEEE TKDE **24**, 547–560 (2012)
19. Liu, X., Wang, H.: Dynamic graph shortest path algorithm. In: Gao, H., Lim, L., Wang, W., Li, C., Chen, L. (eds.) WAIM 2012. LNCS, vol. 7418, pp. 296–307. Springer, Heidelberg (2012). https://doi.org/10.1007/978-3-642-32281-5_29
20. Luxen, S.: Candidate sets for alternative routes in road networks. ACM J. Exp. Algorithm **19**, 2–7 (2015)
21. Neukart, F., Compostella, G., Seidel, S., von Dollen, D., Yarkoni, S., Parney, B.: Traffic flow optimization using a quantum Annealer. Front. ICT **4**, 29 (2017)
22. Ramalingam, G., Reps, T.: On the computational complexity of dynamic graph problems. TCS **158**, 233–277 (1996)

23. Rezaei, M., Noori, H., Mohammadkhani Razlighi, M., Nickray, M.: ReFOCUS+: multi-layers real-time intelligent route guidance system with congestion detection and avoidance. IEEE TITS **10**, 1109 (2019)
24. Wang, X., Yang, L.: Effective indexing for approximate constrained shortest path queries on large road networks. PVLDB **10**, 61–72 (2016)
25. Zheng, B., et al.: Keyword-aware continuous kNN queries on road networks. In: IEEE ICDE, pp. 871–882 (2016)
26. Zhong, R., Li, G., Tan, K.L. Zhou, L.: G-tree: an efficient index for kNN search on road networks. In: ACM CIKM, pp. 39–48 (2013)

EER→MLN: EER Approach for Modeling, Mapping, and Analyzing Complex Data Using Multilayer Networks (MLNs)

Kanthi Sannappa Komar[1], Abhishek Santra[1], Sanjukta Bhowmick[2], and Sharma Chakravarthy[1(✉)]

[1] Information Technology Laboratory and CSE Department, University of Texas at Arlington, Arlington, TX, USA
sharmac@cse.uta.edu

[2] Department of Computer Science, University of North Texas, Denton, TX, USA

Abstract. Extended Entity Relationship (or EER) modeling is an important step after application requirements for data analysis are gathered, and is critical for translating user requirements to a given executable data model (e.g., relational, or for this paper Multilayer Networks or MLNs.) EER modeling provides a more precise understanding of the application and data requirements and an unambiguous representation from which the data model (on which analysis is performed) can be generated algorithmically. EER has played a central role in the modeling of user-level requirements to relational, object oriented etc. UML, whose roots are in EER modeling, is extensively used in the industry.

Although big data analysis has warranted many new data models, not much attention has been paid to their modeling from requirements. Going straight from application requirements to data model and analysis, especially for complex data sets, is likely to be difficult, error prone, and not extensible to say the least. Hence for data models used in big data analysis, such as Multilayer Networks, there is a need to transform the user/application requirements using a modeling approach such as EER.

In this paper, we start with application requirements of complex data sets including analysis objectives and show how the EER approach can be leveraged for modeling given data to generate MLNs and appropriate analysis expressions on them. This is timely as MLNs are gaining popularity (and also subsume graphs) as a meaningful data representation for big data analysis.

For demonstrating the algorithm and applicability of the proposed approach, we demonstrate our approach on three data sets to generate MLNs, to map analysis requirements into expressions on MLNs. We also demonstrate it for three types of MLNs. The data sets are from DBLP (Database Bibliography-Computer Science Publications), IMDb, a large international movie data set, and US commercial airlines. Our experimental analysis validate modeling and mapping. We do not elaborate on

© Springer Nature Switzerland AG 2020
G. Dobbie et al. (Eds.): ER 2020, LNCS 12400, pp. 555–572, 2020.
https://doi.org/10.1007/978-3-030-62522-1_41

computations as it is a separate topic in itself. The correctness of results are verified using independently available ground truth.

Keywords: Multilayer networks · Network decoupling · EER Modeling

1   Introduction

Big data analytics is predicated upon our ability to model and analyze disparate, complex data sets and computation requirements. RDBMSs have served well for modeling and analyzing data sets that need to be managed over a long period of time and that are suited for relational representation. Data warehouses and OLAP came about to improve the analysis aspect of RDBMSs using more powerful queries (to provide multi-dimensional analysis) that could not be done earlier. This evolution has continued with NoSQL systems providing alternate data models and analysis for data that were difficult (or inefficient) to model using RDBMSs. Similarly, Map/Reduce have filled a niche not addressed by RDBMSs. We see the applicability of Multilayer Networks (or MLNs), its modeling, and analysis as another important step in the evolution of aggregate analysis of complex data sets.

In this paper, our focus is on data sets with diverse types of entities that are defined by multiple features and interact through varied and complex relationships. Although graph modeling is used, the analysis and computations are different from the ones addressed in either RDBMSs or recent NoSQL systems, such as Neo4J. Instead of a database, the data is transformed into MLN data structures using EER modeling and computations are performed on these using packages and libraries that are available. Just to give an idea, an analysis may need community detection, degree-centrality (or hubs) detection, and combine layers using Boolean operator (AND, OR, and NOT) or use weighted bipartite graph matching. We will not go into the details of the operators and computations as this paper is about modeling and mapping of analysis into appropriate computations. However, we present some results to convince the reader that this workflow has been completely defined.

Although EER modeling is widely used for relational and object-oriented data modeling, there is no modeling approach when it comes to complex, diverse data sets. This is likely to create problems for representation of such data sets to unambiguously match analysis objectives. We will exemplify this with user requirements below.

1.1   Data Set Descriptions with Analysis Objectives

We have chosen *three data sets for modeling and analysis* from different application domains to illustrate the broader applicability of our proposed framework. While larger data sets can be used, we selected these as reliable ground truth data from orthogonal sources were available. Although we have indicated many analysis objectives to show the capability of this approach, due to space constraints, we show a subset of them *in the experimental analysis section*. However, all of them have been computed.

1. Internet Movie Database (IMDb): This data set is publicly available and stores information about movies, TV episodes, actor, directors, ratings and genres of the movies, etc. [2]. Here the entities are of different types as they can be actors, directors, movies, etc. The features/relationships can be co-actors, similar-genre-acting, directed-a-movie, same movie ratings etc.

Analysis Objectives. Analysis requirements on this data sets can be diverse. As sample examples, one may want to analyse *actor-based relationships*:

(A1) Find co-actor groups that are *most popular* and *most versatile*
(A2) *Cluster* groups of co-actors who have worked in movies with high ratings
(A3) *Predict* new groups of actors who have not worked together before, but benefit from working together in future.

2. Database Bibliography (DBLP): As most researchers are familiar with, the DBLP dataset is publicly available and stores information about computer science publications in various conferences and journals. It captures the author names and institutions, years, conference/journal names and links to the papers [1]. Clearly, there are multiple entities that can be related based of different types of relationships.

Analysis Objectives. Again, our aim is to be able to perform analysis, such as:

(A4) Find *strongest* co-author groups who have collaborated on at least 3 papers
(A5) For each conference, find *most popular groups* of co-authors who publish frequently
(A6) For the *most popular* collaborators in each conference, find the 3-year period(s) when they were *most active*
(A7) For each conference that publishes maximum papers in each period, find the *most popular paper review score*.

3. Author-City Data Sets: Airline data set contains the flights between different cities. This information can be combined with the author information from the DBLP data set to indicate who lives in which city. It can also be used for actors and directors.

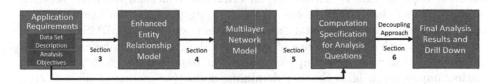

Fig. 1. EER→MLN Flow Chart: Application Requirements to Analysis and Drill Down

Analysis Objectives. For such a diverse data set, the analysis objectives can get complex. For example,

(**A8**) Find *strong* co-author groups who are also friends on Facebook (if Facebook information is available)
(**A9**) Find cities where the largest concentrations of authors reside
(**A10**) What is a good city to hold conferences of authors to maximize attendance?

We have selected the analysis objectives to be varied for the purpose of illustrating the need and effectiveness of the approach being proposed. They range from relatively easy analysis of finding clusters/communities of co-actors to more complicated predictions of potential future teaming of actors and potential city for holding a conference. All objectives have been computed even though we show only a subset in this paper.

Problem Statement. *For a given dataset with $\mathcal{F}$ features and $\mathcal{T}$ entity types and a set of analysis objectives ($\mathcal{O}$), develop: (i) an EER diagram for modeling the data set in conjunction with application requirements, (ii) develop an algorithm to convert the EER diagram into the data model (MLNs in this case in addition to Relations for drill down), (iii) map the analysis objectives ($\mathcal{O}$) into computable expressions on the generated data model, and finally (iv) compute the expressions using available/proposed techniques.*

Figure 1 shows the flow and contributions of the paper. Section 2 has related work. Section 3 shows mapping of user requirements to an EER diagram using the standard notations. In Sect. 4 we discuss the mapping of the EER diagram into homogeneous, heterogeneous, and hybrid MLNs using the proposed algorithm. In Sect. 5.1, we briefly introduce the *decoupling* approach used for big data analysis. In Sect. 5.2 we demonstrate with examples how the *analysis objectives are mapped* to expressions on the generated MLNs. In Sect. 6, we compute the expressions and *validate* our results independent *orthogonal* sources.

2   Related Work

ER and EER models have served as a methodology for database design by representing important semantic information about the real world [6] application. Relational database modeling has clearly benefited from this body of work and has motivated UML for OO design. A good EER diagram based on the user analysis requirements is critical for an error-free relational database schema. Numerous tools have been developed for creating the EER diagram and algorithmically mapping it into relations for different commercial DBMSs.

However, with the emergence of structured data sets with inherent relationships among entities and complex application requirements, such as shortest paths, important neighborhoods, dominant nodes (or groups of nodes), etc., [7,12], the relational data model was not the best choice for modeling as well as analyzing them [5]. This led to the evolution of NoSQL data models including the graph data model [3]. In many cases, like friendship (Facebook), collaborations (Movies) and follower-followee (Twitter) relationships, relationships needed to be modeled explicitly using graph model. This gave rise to computations over these data models. Recently, there has been some work in the area of graph modeling from EER diagrams, but is limited to simple attributed graphs only [6,17,18]. However, most of these works either do not handle recursive relationships [18], and weak entities [8] or are application-specific [11]. To the best of our knowledge, there has been no systematic approach to modeling MLNs using data sets and requirement objectives.

Multilayer networks were introduced when the data sets necessitated graph data models to capture multiple types of nodes and relationships, features and connections with a need to analyze the effect of different combinations of perspectives [14,23]. There is substantial work on analysing different types of multilayer networks based on meta-paths across graphs [23,25], community detection [13,15,19] and centrality measurements [20]. However, to the best of our knowledge *there is not any work that creates a EER model from the given requirements and provides an algorithm for the generation of a multilayer network given for the analysis of given objectives.*

3   Application Requirements to EER Model

Any analysis objective to be computed from data involving multiple entities, features and complex relationships has been shown to benefit from a multilayer network model [14]. EER diagrams [10] are well-established and have been used to model and design schema for relational databases. An EER diagram is crucial for creating a database that satisfies 2NF. In this section, we illustrate the first stage from Fig. 1 where requirements from three different sets of real-world analysis objectives (Sect. 1.1) are mapped to EER diagrams.

3.1   Internet Movie Database (IMDb) Analysis

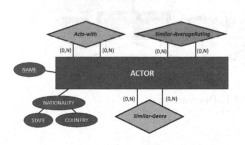

Fig. 2. IMDb EER Diagram

The data set consists of top 500 actors and their co-actors across all movies, giving a total of 9000+ actors. Based on the information in the IMDb data set **and** analysis objectives (**A1-A3**), one can build an EER diagram (shown in Fig. 2) as described below[1]:

– **Entities**: *Actor* with the key-attribute as name and nationality as a composite attribute comprising of the state and country.

---

[1] Note that the relationship details can change based on analysis objectives.

- **Recursive Relationships**:

  - *Acts-with*: Two actors are related if they have worked in at least one movie
  - *Similar-Genre*: *Genre* is a categorical variable, as it takes fixed, limited number of values, such as "comedy", "action", etc. Also an actor acts in multiple movies of the same genre – i.e., in 3 action movies, 1 comedy movie, etc. For every actor we generate a vector with *number of movies for each genre*. We then compute the Pearsons' Correlation Coefficient (PCC) between the genre vectors for each actor pair. Two actors are related if PCC is at least 0.9^2.
  - *similar-AverageRating*: The movie ratings are given from 0 to 10. Note, however, when we take the average of the ratings, the values become real numbers. To evaluate the similarity we created 10 ranges - [0–1), [1–2), ..., [9–10]. Two actors are related if their average ratings fall in the same range.

- **(Min, Max) Cardinality Ratios:** All relationships have *(0,N)..(0,N)* cardinality as an actor can be similar to none or multiple actors.

3.2 Database Bibliography (DBLP) Analysis

For DBLP, we have considered all publications from VLDB, SIGMOD, ICDM, KDD, DaWaK and DASFAA from the 2001–2018. Based on data set description and analysis objectives (**A4–A7**), the EER diagram shown in Fig. 3 has been discussed below

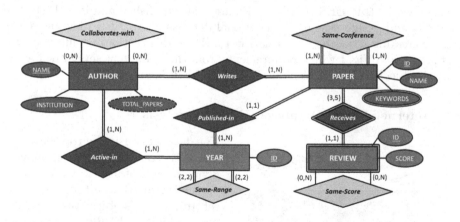

Fig. 3. DBLP EER Diagram

---

[2] Choice of coefficient reflects relationship quality and its value can be based on how actors are weighted against genres. We have chosen 0.9 for relating actors in their top genres.

– **Entities including Weak:**

- *Author* with attributes - name (key) and institution. *Total_Papers* is a derived attribute that can be calculated using *writes* binary relationship.
- *Paper* with attributes, Paper ID (key), name and keywords (multi-valued)
- *Year* with year ID as the key attribute
- *Review:* Existence of a review is dependent on the existence of a paper, thus it is a *weak entity*. It has ID (partial key) and score as the two attributes.

– **Recursive Relationships:**

- *Collaborates-with*: Two authors are related if they have worked together on at least 3 published papers
- *Same-Conference*: Two papers are related if they are published in same conference.
- *Same-Range*: 3-year periods are required for analysis. Thus, the period from 2001 to 2018 is divided into 6 disjoint 3-year periods, from [2001–2003] to [2016–2018]. Two years are related in they are in the same 3-year period.
- *Same-Score*: Typically, each review receives an overall score between 1 and 5 that can be rounded off. Thus, two reviews with the same score can be related.

– **Binary Relationships:**

- *Writes*: A relationship to indicate if an author has written a paper.
- *Active-in*: A binary relationship is created between author and year entities to denote whether an author was actively publishing in that year.
- *Published-in*: Similarly relationship between paper and year entities is established to show in which year a paper was published.
- *Receives*: Every paper published is related to all the reviews that it receives.

– **(Min, Max) Cardinality Ratios:**

- *Collaborates-with* recursive relationship has cardinality ratio as *(0,N)..(0,N)* as each author can work individually or with any number of authors. *Same-Conference* has cardinality *(1,N)..(1,N)* as many papers are published in the same conference, thus a paper is related to at least one paper. Cardinality of *Same-Range* is *(2,2)..(2,2)* as each year is related to the other 2 years in the 3-year period. *Same-Score* has *(0,N)..(0,N)* cardinality as a review may not be related to any other review.
- Binary relationship *Writes* between author and paper entity has *(1,N)..(1,N)* cardinality as an author can publish one or more papers and also paper can have one or more authors. Similarly, *Active-in* has *(1,N)..(1,N)* cardinality as an author is active in at least one year and in a given year many authors can be active. The *Published-in* relationship has *(1,1)..(1,N)* cardinality as paper is published only in one year but many papers can be published in a year. Finally, for *Receives* the cardinality is *(3,5)..(1,1)* as every paper receives 3 to 5 reviews, however each review is for exactly one paper.

3.3   Author-City Data Set Analysis

For final set of analysis objectives (**A8–A10**) based on author-city data set, the
EER diagram shown in Fig. 4 has been discussed below

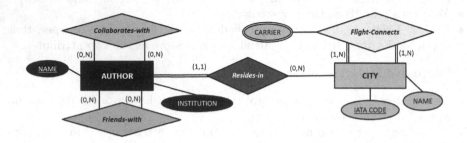

Fig. 4. Author-City EER Diagram

- **Entities:**

- *Author* with attributes - name (key) and institution
- *City* with attributes - IATA/Airport Code (key) and name

- **Recursive Relationships:**

- *Collaborates-with*: Two authors are related if they have worked together on
  at least 3 published papers.
- *Friends-with*: A relationship to signify if two authors are friends on Facebook.
- Flight-connects: Two cities are related if there is a flight connecting them
  with a multi-valued attribute to capture the operating *carriers*.

- **Binary Relationships:** A binary relationship, *Resides-in* exists between
  the author and city entity depicting the residence.

- **(Min, Max) Cardinality Ratios:**

- *Collaborates-with* and *Friends-with* recursive relationships have *(0,N)..(0,N)*
  cardinality, as an author may work individually and may not be friends with
  anyone on Facebook, respectively.
- Binary relationship *Resides-in* between author and city entity has
  (1,1)..(0,N) cardinality as an author can reside in only one city. However,
  a city may not be any author's residence or multiple authors can reside in it.

4   Generating MLNs from an EER Diagram (EER→MLN)

We provide an overview of the MLN models before discussing our algorithm to
convert an EER to MLN (Sect. 4.2 and 4.3). We use the algorithm to translate
EER diagrams discussed in Sect. 3.1, 3.2 and 3.3.

4.1   Multilayer Networks: An Overview of the Data Model

Multi-feature data comprises of multiple relationships among the same or different types of entities. Relationships among the entities can either be specified by explicit interactions (like flights, co-authors, and friends) or based on a similarity metric depending on the type of the feature like nominal, numeric, time, date, latitude-longitude values, text, audio, video or image. For flexible, loss-less, structure-preserving and efficient analysis of such data sets based on different combinations of features, multilayer networks (or MLNs) have been proposed in the literature to be an ideal choice [14, 21].

A multilayer network model is a *network of networks*. In this case, every layer represents a distinct relationship among entities with respect to a single feature. The sets of entities across layers, which may or may not be of the same type, can be related to each other too. Formally, a **multilayer network**, $MLN(G, X)$, is defined by two sets of graphs: i) The set $G = \{G_1, G_2, \ldots, G_N\}$ contains graphs of N individual layers, where $G_i(V_i, E_i)$ is defined by a set of vertices, V_i and a set of edges, E_i. An edge $e(v, u) \in E_i$, connects vertices v and u, where $v, u \in V_i$ and ii) A set $X = \{X_{1,2}, X_{1,3}, \ldots, X_{N-1,N}\}$ consists of bipartite graphs. Each graph $X_{i,j}(V_i, V_j, L_{i,j})$ is defined by two sets of vertices V_i and V_j, and a set of edges (also called links or inter-layer edges) $L_{i,j}$, such that for every link $l(a, b) \in L_{i,j}$, $a \in V_i$ and $b \in V_j$, where V_i (V_j) is the vertex set of graph G_i (G_j.)

Based on the type of relationships and entities, multilayer network are of different types. Layers of a **homogeneous MLN (or HoMLN)** are used to model the diverse relationships that exist among the **same type of entities** like movie actors who are linked based on if they act together or have similar average rating. Thus, $V_1 = V_2 = \ldots = V_n$ and inter-layer edge sets are empty as no relations across layers are necessary. Relationships among **different types of entities** like researchers (connected by co-authorship), research papers (connected if published in same conference) and year (related by pre-defined ranges/eras) are modeled through **heterogeneous MLN (or HeMLN)**. The inter-layer edges represent the relationship across layers like writes, published-in and active-in. In addition to being collaborators, researchers may be Facebook friends. Thus, to model multi-feature data that capture **multiple relationships within and across different types of entity sets**, a combination of homogeneous and heterogeneous MLNs is used, called **hybrid MLN (or HyMLN)**. Figure 5 shows an example of each generated from the algorithm below.

4.2   Algorithmic Steps for Translating an EER Diagram to MLNs

Below, we present our algorithm (8 steps) for generating an MLN (can be homogeneous, heterogeneous, or hybrid) from the EER diagram developed using the application requirements. These steps are somewhat different from the traditional EER diagram translation to a Database model. With each step, we explain the rationale and provide an example from the EER diagrams shown earlier.

A layer consists of nodes with a node id which is unique and a node label which need not be unique. An edge consists of an edge label which is not unique and connects two node ids. Typically, node ids are kept unique for the purposes of computation. Below, we assume node ids are generated as part of the translation process. In this paper, we do not show how additional information of nodes and edges that come out of the EER diagram are kept. They cab ne maintained as .csv files (or translated into relations) to be used for drill down analysis of results. EER model also helps in modeling only those attributes of nodes and edges that are relevant to the analysis objectives and drill down.

1. **Each binary relationship** in the EER diagram corresponds to either an individual layer or a bipartite graph (of inter-layer edges) between two layers. Typically, entity id is used as the label of nodes in the layer. Other attributes are not typically stored as part of MLN (to reduce storage), but are stored separately (for example, as a relation or as a .csv file) for drill-down of the results later. The relationship name is used as intra- or inter-edge label and again, other relationship attributes are stored separately for drill down of results. We show some drill down results in Sect. 6.
   For example, the relationship Acts-with in Fig. 2 is translated into a layer Actor with name as node label and acts-with as edge label. In contrast, the relationship writes in Fig. 3 becomes a bipartite graph between the layers Paper and Author.
2. **Each binary recursive relationship** translates to a separate homogeneous layer whose intra-layer connectivity is defined by the relationship.
   For example, the layer Actor(Acts-with) in Fig. 5 (a) is obtained by the binary recursive relationship Acts-with in Fig. 2 on the Actor entity.
3. **Each binary non-recursive relationship** translates to a bipartite graph between the layers corresponding to entities of the relationship.This assumes that the layers have been formed earlier by binary recursive relationships.
   For example, Author-Year inter-layer edges in Fig. 2 (b) are formed by the relationship active-in in Fig. 3 between Author and Year entities.
4. **Translation of the attributes** (of an entity or a relationship) other than the key is done in the same way as we do for a relational model. Atomic, component, and multi-valued attributes are handled in the same manner. Derived attributes are not stored but are computed.
5. Hence, relationships have to be translated **in a specific order**: binary recursive first, followed by binary non-recursive relationships.
6. **Super and Sub entities** can be present in the EER diagram. If an entity type is a **super class**, either a layer can be created for it or layers can be created for each of its sub-class entity types depending on characteristics such as disjoint, overlapping, partial and total. This is quite similar to the translation to the relational model. Relationships present on these entities dictate the translation. Mapping of the relationships will follow the above steps.
   For example, it is possible that the super class may become a separate layer for some analysis objectives and sub classes may become separate layers for other analysis objectives. Different MLNs can be created from the EER diagram to meet the analysis objectives. Person as a super entity may have overlapping

sub entities actors and directors. If there are separate recursive relationships for the Person entity, it will become a separate layer.

7. A **weak entity** and its non-recursive binary relationship is translated as follows. Unlike how it is done for the relational model, a **weak entity** is translated into a separate layer (using a binary recursive relationship on that entity) and the weak relationship is translated into a bipartite graph with edge labels indicating the dependence (combining the primary and the partial key).

    For example: The Review weak entity in Fig. 3 becomes a separate layer in addition to the Layer Paper (Fig. 5 (b)). The intra-layer edges are dictated by the Same-Score recursive relationship. This layer has a bipartite graph with the Paper layer with the inter-layer edge labels corresponding to the Paper ID and Review ID.

8. Currently, **n-ary relationships** that **cannot** be mapped to multiple binary relationships are not supported. If they can be mapped to multiple binary relationships, the above steps handle them. If not, such a relationship involves handling a **hyper-edge** across multiple layers of a MLN which is beyond the scope of this paper.

4.3   Summary of the Algorithm

The above algorithmic steps when applied translates an EER diagram to a MLN(s) along with drill down information in a form that is queryable and searchable. Below we make a few comments on the overall translation of the EER diagram. Note that the **same** EER diagram is used for generating relations or .csv files for drill down thereby enhancing the use of the EER modeling.

- Each entity with **multiple** binary recursive relationships gives rise to a **Homogeneous MLN.**
- **Multiple entites** with *both* binary recursive (one each) and binary non-recursive relationships give rise to a **Heterogeneous MLN.**
- If the EER diagram has both kinds of entities and relationships as indicated above (as in 4) and there is at least one relationship between entities that form the homogeneous and heterogeneous layers, a **Hybrid MLN** is obtained.
- **Strong entities** as well as **weak entities** are translated as described above and become separate layers.
- The **min-max cardinality information** will give an insight into the minimum and maximum associations (or edges) that a node can have. This can help to calculate the *minimum, maximum and average degree* of the corresponding layer or bipartite graph.
- A **partial participation of an entity** translates to a node that is not connected to any other node (i.e., no intra- or inter-edge). *For example, the author can work individually (Partial Collaborates-with relationship).* Whereas a **total participation** implies every node has at least one edge.
- The **direction** of the inter or intra layer edges has to be implied from the semantics of the relationship. This can also be specified as part of the relationship. *For example, co-authorship will be bi-directional, whereas a relationship*

like follows-on-Twitter will be a directional. This is typically specified as part of the application requirement and can be incorporated into the EER model relatively easily as part of the relationship using the (min, max) cardinality information.

4.4   Application of the Above Algorithmic Steps

For the 3 sets of analysis discussed in Sect. 3, the following MLNs, shown in Fig. 5, are generated by applying the above algorithmic steps. Node and edge labels have not been shown for simplicity.

IMDb Analysis: Based on the EER (Fig. 2), a **Homogeneous MLN** (Fig. 5 (a)) is obtained with 3 layers having every actor element as a separate node with intra-layer edges dictated by *Acts-with, Similar-AverageRating* and *Similar-Genre* recursive relationships (Using (**2**)). The node label is the actor name and intra-layer edge labels are the relationship names (Using (**1**)). Relationship semantics do not need a direction, thus edges are undirected.

DBLP Analysis: The EER in Fig. 3 gets translated into a **Heterogeneous MLN** (Fig. 5 (b)) with 4 layers - Author, Paper, Year and Review with intra-layer edges corresponding to *Collaborates-with, Same-Conference Same-Range* and *Same-Score* recursive relationships, respectively (Using (**2**), (**7**) for Weak Review Entity). The binary non-recursive relationships - *Writes, Active-in, Published-in, Reviews* generate 4 bipartite graphs between the layer pairs - Author-Paper, Author-Year, Paper-Year and Paper-Review, respectively (Using (**3**)). The node and edge labels are the key attributes and relationship names (Using (**1**), (**7**)). The relationships do not have an explicit requirement for direction, thus every intra/inter layer edge is *undirected*.

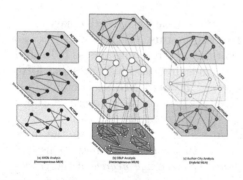

Fig. 5. MLN models for analysis set 1, 2 and 3

Author-City Analysis: The EER model in Fig. 4 leads to the generation of a **Hybrid MLN** (Fig. 5 (c)) with two Author Layers and a City Layer with intra-layer edges based on the *Collaborates-with, Friends-with* and *Flight-connects* recursive relationships (Using (**2**)). The binary non-recursive relationship *Resides-in* is used to introduce the inter-layer edges between the City layer and each of the Author layers (Using (**3**)). Node labels are name (Author layers) and IATA code (City layer), while the edge labels are relationship names (Using (**1**)). Collaboration, Residence and Friendship are bi-directional relationships. For the *Flight-connects* relationship it is assumed that if a flight exists from city a to city b, then a reverse flight also exists. Thus, every inter/intra layer edge is undirected in this HyMLN.

5   Analysis Objectives to Computation Specification

For the analysis of MLNs, a number of aggregate features are used for computation of objectives. They are: notions of community, centrality, and substructure. In this paper, we use community and centrality which are briefly summarized below.

Informally, a *community* is defined as a connected subgraph whose vertices are more connected to each other than to other vertices in the rest of the network (or layer). This objective is achieved by optimizing network parameters such as modularity or conductance in single layer graphs. Several algorithms are available for community detection of a graph [4]. A community is a weaker group of connected nodes than a clique. Since cliques of size greater than three are hard to find, community as a dense connected graph is used as a substitute.

Centrality Metrics are used for measuring the importance of vertices. They include degree centrality (number of neighbors), closeness centrality (mean distance of the vertex from other vertices), betweenness centrality (fraction of shortest paths passing through the vertex), and eigenvector centrality (the number of important neighbors of the vertex) [16].

It is also interesting to note that both community and centrality detection cannot be expressed in SQL (is an optimization problem).

5.1   Decoupling-Based Approach

Recently, a novel decoupling approach has been proposed for detecting communities and centralities in an efficient manner. This uses the equivalent of "divide and conquer" for MLNs [21, 26].

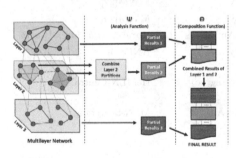

Fig. 6. Decoupling approach

Decoupling requires partitioning (derived from the MLN structure; individual layers as partitions - Fig. 6) and a way to compose partial (or intermediate) analysis results for community/centrality detection of MLNs. Substantial work has been done to identify the composition function (referred to as Θ, see Fig. 6) that is appropriate for efficient community/centrality detection (referred to as Ψ, see Fig. 6) on MLNs.

5.2   Computation Specification Mapping

Once the EER diagram is created based on the application requirements (data set description + analysis objectives) and translated into MLNs, the next step is to map each objective into an expression using Θ and Ψ on the MLNs generated. This step is relatively easier to identify once the operators to apply and the type of composition to perform is determined, This step is similar to writing SQL queries once the specific database schema is generated and populated.

We show below how aggregate feature computation is specified along with composition to be used. The challenge in successfully applying network decoupling is to match the analysis function, Ψ and the composition function, Θ. Table 1 gives the mapping of each analysis objective **A1** to **A10** to their computation specification (in *left* to *right* order), analysis function (Ψ) and composition function (Θ). For few analysis, the composition is defined, for others we provide a short description of composition process.

Table 1. MLN expression for each analysis objective

Analysis	Mapping		
	Computation specification	Ψ	Θ
IMDb (**HoMLN**): 3 Actor Layers: *Acts-with, Similar-Genre, Similar-AverageRating*			
A1	*Acts-with* Θ *Similar-Genre*	Degree-Centrality	AND[20]
A2	*Acts-with* Θ *Similar-AverageRating*	Community	AND[19]
A3	NOT(*Acts-with*) Θ *Similar-Genre* Θ *Similar-AverageRating*	Community	AND[19]
DBLP (**HeMLN**): Author (Au), Year (Y), Paper (P), Review (R)			
A4	Au	Community	
A5	P Θ Au	Community	MWM[22]
A6	P Θ Au Θ Y	Community	MWM[22]
A7	Y Θ P Θ R	Community	MWM[22]
Set 3: Author-City (**HyMLN**): City (C) and 2 Au Layers - *Collaborates-with, Friends-with*			
A8	*Collaborates-with* Θ *Friends-with*	Community	AND[19]
A9	C Θ *Collaborates-with*; C Θ *Friends-with*	Centrality (Degree)	HeMLN-Centrality
A10	*Collaborates-with* Θ *Friends-with* Θ C	Community(Au), Degree-Centrality(C)	MLN-Searching

IMDb Analysis: For **A1** using network decoupling, we first find the *high degree* nodes in *Acts-with* and *Similar-Genre* layers, separately to detect the popular co-actors and versatile actors. Using the AND composition (details in [20]) we find all those *popular co-actors who are also highly versatile*. For **A2**, the AND composition is applied on the communities from the *Acts-with* and *Similar-AverageRating* layers to generate and filter out the groups of co-actors who have high ratings. In **A3** aim is to find actors who have not acted together but act in the same genre and in movies of similar ratings – which increases their possibility of acting together in future. We apply the NOT operation on the Acts-with layer to find the complement graph of actors who have never acted together. In the first step of network decoupling, we take communities from each of the three layers; the Similar-Genre, Similar-AverageRating and the complement of the Acts-with layer. We then combine the resultant communities using the AND composition function to find *groups of actors who have a high chance of acting together in future*.

DBLP Analysis: For **A4**, the Author layer communities will give the desired result. For **A5**, **A6** and **A7** the communities from Author, Paper, Year and Review layer need to be paired up in the specified order to meet the analysis objectives. In [22], the HeMLN community detection has been proposed where for any two layers a bipartite graph is constructed using their communities. Each community is considered to be a meta-node. Two meta-nodes in two different layers are connected if there is at least one inter-layer edge between them. The weight of these edges (meta-edges) between the meta-nodes is given by the number of inter-layer edges between them. These meta nodes (communities) in the bipartite graph are uniquely paired using the composition function (Θ) Maximal Weighted Matching (MWM) that maximizes the overall meta-edge weight and is based on traditional matching proposed by Jack Edmonds [9]. For **A5**, the Author communities that get *matched* with Paper communities (corresponding to conferences) are the most popular. For **A6**, the matched Author communities from A5 are paired with Year communities to find their most active periods. For **A7**, first Paper communities are matched to Year communities to obtain the highly publishing conferences per period. Then, the matched Paper communities are matched to Review communities, to get the *most popular review score*.

Author-City Analysis: **A8** is computed by the AND composition on the communities from two Homogeneous Author layers. For **A9**, the cities having high inter-layer degree with any one of the author layers are the *cities with high author concentrations*. In **A10**, ideally a conference will get more attendance if it is organized in a city that is a) well-connected via flights, b) where large co-author communities reside and c) large sections of those co-author groups are friends in order to maximize the advertisement of the conference. Thus, using the decoupling approach the communities from the two author layers and high degree nodes from the City layer are composed (and filtered) in order to obtain the desired set of *probable venues for a conference*.

6   Experimental Analysis

Using the decoupling approach, we executed the mapped computation specifications (Sect. 5.2) on the generated IMDb HoMLN, DBLP HeMLN and Author-City HyMLN (Fig. 5). Different parts of composition functions (Θ) have been implemented in C++ and Python 3.7.3 and executed on a quad-core 8th generation Intel i7 processor machine with 8 GB RAM.

Due to space constraints, we are presenting few interesting results (and provide validation) from the HoMLN and HeMLN that have been built using real

Table 2. Left: IMDb HoMLN stats. **Right:** DBLP HeMLN stats

IMDb Actor	#Nodes	#Edges	DBLP	#Nodes	#Edges
Acts-with	9485	45,581	**Author**	16,918	2,483
Similar-Genre	9485	996,527	**Paper**	10,326	12,044,080
Similar-AverageRating	9485	13,945,912	**Year**	18	18

world data snapshots (Statistics shown in Table 2). *Also note that the drill down has been performed using the database created from the EER model while translating it into MLNs.*

A3 Analysis: Predicting new collaborations boils down to finding highly-rated actors who have worked in similar genres, but have not acted together. We detected 900 groups of actors with similar genre preferences and average rating *but most of whom have not worked together.* Table 3 shows few recognizable *actors* who have not acted together, obtained after drill-down analysis.

Table 3. (A5): Highly rated genre actors who have **not** co-acted.

Actors	Common prominent genres
Dafoe, Crowe	Action, Crime
Swank, Winslet	Drama
Hanks, Witherspoon, Diaz	Comedy, Romance
Depp, Cruise	Adventure, Action
DiCaprio, Gosling	Crime, Romance
Cage, Banderas	Action, Thriller
Grant, Hudson, Stone	Comedy, Romance

Out of these, as per reports in 2017, there had been **talks of casting Johnny Depp and Tom Cruise in pivotal roles in Universal Studios' cinematic universe titled Dark Universe** [24].

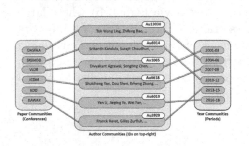

Fig. 7. (A6): Active Periods for Popular Co-authors

A6 Analysis: The **most popular unique co-author groups** for **each conference** are obtained by MWM (first composition). The matched 6 author communities are carried forward to find the *year periods* in which they were **most active** (second composition). Overall, 6 results are obtained (path shown by **bold blue lines** in Fig. 7.) Few prominent names are shown in the Fig. 7 based on citation count (from Google Scholar profiles.) For example, for *SIGMOD, VLDB and ICDM* the most popular researchers include **Srikanth Kandula (15188 citations), Divyakant Agrawal (23727 citations) and Shuicheng Yan (52294 citations)**, respectively who were active in different periods in the past 18 years.

7   Conclusions

In this paper, we have leveraged the EER modeling to generate MLNs and expressions for their analysis. *Ad hoc* big data analysis without a formal approach for generating models from application requirements is difficult and error-prone. In this paper, we have taken the first step towards modeling big data for analysis as well as drill down. We believe that this approach has broader implications.

Acknowledgments. For this work, Dr. Chakravarthy was partly supported by NSF Grant 1955798 and Dr. Bhowmick was partly supported by NSF grant 1916084.

References

1. DBLP dataset. http://dblp.uni-trier.de/xml/
2. The internet movie database. ftp://ftp.fu-berlin.de/pub/misc/movies/database/
3. Angles, R., Gutierrez, C.: Survey of graph database models. ACM Comput. Surv. (CSUR) **40**(1), 1–39 (2008)
4. Blondel, V.D., Guillaume, J., Lambiotte, R., Lefebvre, E.: Fast unfolding of community hierarchies in large networks. CoRR abs/0803.0476 (2008)
5. Chakravarthy, S., Beera, R., Balachandran, R.: DB-subdue: database approach to graph mining. In: Dai, H., Srikant, R., Zhang, C. (eds.) PAKDD 2004. LNCS (LNAI), vol. 3056, pp. 341–350. Springer, Heidelberg (2004). https://doi.org/10.1007/978-3-540-24775-3_42
6. Chen, P.P.S.: The entity-relationship model–toward a unified view of data. ACM Trans. Database Syst. (TODS) **1**(1), 9–36 (1976)
7. Das, S., Santra, A., Bodra, J., Chakravarthy, S.: Query processing on large graphs: approaches to scalability and response time trade offs. Data Knowl. Eng. **126**, 101736 (2020)
8. De Virgilio, R., Maccioni, A., Torlone, R.: Model-driven design of graph databases. In: Yu, E., Dobbie, G., Jarke, M., Purao, S. (eds.) ER 2014. LNCS, vol. 8824, pp. 172–185. Springer, Cham (2014). https://doi.org/10.1007/978-3-319-12206-9_14
9. Edmonds, J.: Maximum matching and a polyhedron with 0, 1-vertices. J. Res. Natl. Bureau Stand. B **69**(125–130), 55–56 (1965)
10. Elmasri, R.: Fundamentals of database systems. Pearson Education India (2008)
11. Graves, M., Bergeman, E.R., Lawrence, C.B.: Graph database systems. IEEE Eng. Med. Biol. Mag. **14**(6), 737–745 (1995)
12. Jayaram, N., Khan, A., Li, C., Yan, X., Elmasri, R.: Querying knowledge graphs by example entity tuples. IEEE Trans. Knowl. Data Eng. **27**, 2797–2811 (2015)
13. Kim, J., Lee, J.: Community detection in multi-layer graphs: a survey. SIGMOD Rec. **44**(3), 37–48 (2015)
14. Kivelä, M., Arenas, A., Barthelemy, M., Gleeson, J.P., Moreno, Y., Porter, M.A.: Multilayer networks. CoRR abs/1309.7233 (2013)
15. Melamed, D.: Community structures in bipartite networks: a dual-projection approach. PLoS ONE **9**(5), e97823 (2014)
16. Newman, M.: Networks: An Introduction. Oxford University Press Inc., New York (2010)
17. Pokorný, J.: Conceptual and database modelling of graph databases. In: Proceedings of the 20th International Database Engineering & Applications Symposium (2016)

18. Roy-Hubara, N., Rokach, L., Shapira, B., Shoval, P.: Modeling graph database schema. IT Professional **19**(6), 34–43 (2017)
19. Santra, A., Bhowmick, S., Chakravarthy, S.: Efficient community re-creation in multilayer networks using Boolean operations. In: International Conference on Computational Science (2017)
20. Santra, A., Bhowmick, S., Chakravarthy, S.: Hubify: efficient estimation of central entities across multiplex layer compositions. In: IEEE ICDM Workshops (2017)
21. Reddy, P.K., Sureka, A., Chakravarthy, S., Bhalla, S. (eds.): BDA 2017. LNCS, vol. 10721. Springer, Cham (2017). https://doi.org/10.1007/978-3-319-72413-3
22. Santra, A., Komar, K.S., Bhowmick, S., Chakravarthy, S.: A new community definition for multilayer networks and a novel approach for its efficient computation. arXiv preprint arXiv:2004.09625 (2020)
23. Shi, C., Li, Y., Zhang, J., Sun, Y., Philip, S.Y.: A survey of heterogeneous information network analysis. IEEE Trans. Knowl. Data Eng. **29**(1), 17–37 (2017)
24. Stolworthy, J.: Dark universe: Johnny Depp and Javier Bardem join tom cruise in universal's monster movie franchise (2017). https://www.independent.co.uk/us
25. Sun, Y., Han, J.: Mining heterogeneous information networks: a structural analysis approach. ACM SIGKDD Exp. Newslett. **14**(2), 20–28 (2013)
26. Vu, X.S., Santra, A., Chakravarthy, S., Jiang, L.: Generic multilayer network data analysis with the fusion of content and structure. In: CICLing 2019 (2019)

Conceptual Modeling of Complex
and Data-Rich Systems

Modeling and Analysis of Boundary Objects and Methodological Islands in Large-Scale Systems Development

Rebekka Wohlrab[1,2]([图]) [iD], Jennifer Horkoff[1] [iD], Rashidah Kasauli[1] [iD],
Salome Maro[1] [iD], Jan-Philipp Steghöfer[1] [iD], and Eric Knauss[1] [iD]

[1] Chalmers|University of Gothenburg, Gothenburg, Sweden
{wohlrab,jenho,rashida}@chalmers.se,
{salome.maro,jan-philipp.steghofer,eric.knauss}@cse.gu.se
[2] Systemite AB, Gothenburg, Sweden

Abstract. Large-scale systems development commonly faces the challenge of managing relevant knowledge between different organizational groups, particularly in increasingly agile contexts. In previous studies, we found the importance of analyzing methodological islands (i.e., groups using different development methods than the surrounding organization) and boundary objects between them. In this paper, we propose a metamodel to better capture and analyze coordination and knowledge management in practice. Such a metamodel can allow practitioners to describe current practices, analyze issues, and design better-suited coordination mechanisms. We evaluated the conceptual model together with four large-scale companies developing complex systems. In particular, we derived an initial list of bad smells that can be leveraged to detect issues and devise suitable improvement strategies for inter-team coordination in large-scale development. We present the model, smells, and our evaluation results.

Keywords: Boundary objects · Agile development · Empirical studies

1 Introduction

Large-scale systems engineering companies commonly face the challenge of coordination between multiple and multidisciplinary teams (e.g., software, systems, hardware). Especially in large-scale agile development, inter-team coordination is a recognized challenge [8]. In practice, ways of working are not universal in large companies. Teams are surrounded by other organizational parts that do not use the same methods—and thus become "*methodological islands*" [14]. For instance, in a large automotive company, more than 500 teams exist, using diverse practices (agile, waterfall), with complex interdependencies and multiple suppliers. Coordination is supported by various artifacts (e.g., written documents, models, backlogs, or code). Furthermore, phone calls, meetings in communities of practice, and other mechanisms are used to coordinate concerns around these

© Springer Nature Switzerland AG 2020
G. Dobbie et al. (Eds.): ER 2020, LNCS 12400, pp. 575–589, 2020.
https://doi.org/10.1007/978-3-030-62522-1_42

artifacts. In such a situation, it can be challenging to coordinate knowledge between different organizational groupings. Practitioners need to better understand the factors causing these groups (or islands) to cluster or form and the effectiveness of the current ways of supporting communication. For example, is a particular written document between two islands fit for coordination? Is it too flexible or too rigid? Is it both complex and changing frequently? Is it governed, and do those that govern the document understand its use? Can the current coordination situation be understood, made explicit, and improved?

In previous studies, we have aimed to characterize these coordination needs by focusing on methodological islands (MIs) and boundary objects (BOs) [14]. Boundary objects create a common understanding between groups and can facilitate inter-team coordination and knowledge management [27]. We have investigated the nature and use of these BOs in practice, but we have not yet created a method to systematically capture BOs and MIs (BOMIs) in a structured way. To the best of our knowledge, there is no modeling approach and conceptual model available to specifically address boundary objects and methodological islands.

In this paper, we address this gap by proposing a metamodel for boundary objects and methodological islands in large-scale systems development. This model is based on empirical data and accounts from ongoing projects [14,25,26]. By creating such a model, a complete picture of an organization's coordination needs and boundary objects can be established, analyzed, and used to identify and mitigate current issues in a more visual and structured way.

We evaluated the metamodel together with four large-scale systems companies and describe the corresponding instance models created. We present initial findings on how the model can be used to identify bad smells and issues.

This paper is organized as follows: Sect. 2 presents the background. Section 3 describes our metamodel, method and smell description, followed by the evaluation in Sect. 4. Section 5 briefly reviews related modeling approaches, Sect. 6 discusses our findings and describes threats to validity, while Sect. 7 concludes the paper.

2   Background

We describe background information to motivate this paper's contributions.

Boundary Objects. Boundary objects (BOs) are "*objects which are both plastic enough to adapt to local needs and the constraints of the several parties employing them, yet robust enough to maintain a common identity across sites*" [20]. The concept was initially coined in sociology and has proven to be useful in a variety of domains. Recently, BOs have increasingly been studied in software and systems engineering [19,27,29].

Over the last two years, we have engaged with four large-scale systems engineering companies to support them in adopting agile methods and managing important knowledge. We used the design science methodology [10] to investigate coordination in large-scale systems engineering, develop suitable *design artifacts* targeting practical problems, and evaluate them in several iterations.

We build upon the findings of this long-term project. In Sect. 4, we describe the participating companies in further detail.

As part of our work on BOs, we conducted several studies. We analyzed currently used artifacts and created guidelines to manage them in large-scale agile contexts, including concerns related to the level of detail and versioning of these artifacts [27]. We found that BOs can belong to several super types (e.g., Technology, Task, or Planning) [14] and should be managed in groups of representatives of several teams [27]. Moreover, we studied architecture descriptions and interfaces as BOs [24,25]. We found that important dimensions of interface change are stability, time to perform a change, criticality, level of abstraction, distance to affected parties, number of affected components, position in the interface's lifecycle, and maturity of affected functions. Moreover, many companies describe *information models* to capture artifact types and their relations. These information models also serve as BOs, change over time, and can be used to define the required degree of alignment of different teams' practices [26].

BOs are commonly used between individuals from several (sub-)disciplines, who refer to concepts with different terminologies [27]. The groups using BOs need to be properly understood to enable inter-team coordination.

Methodological Islands. The mix of methods in large-scale organizations is a recognized challenge [27]. In our empirical study on large-scale development, agile teams were described as *"agile islands in a waterfall"* [14]. This phenomenon is not limited to the discrepancy of agile and plan-driven methods, but a general issue. Therefore, we use the term *methodological islands* (MIs) for organizational groups using different development methods than the surrounding organization. We identified that MIs can be of different types, e.g., individual teams (e.g., component teams), groups of teams (e.g., departments), or entire organizations. MIs arise due to several *drivers* related to *business, process,* and *technology.*

Based on these studies, we got an understanding of BOs and MIs in large-scale systems engineering. These findings needed to be better instrumentalized to support practitioners, in particular, using a systematic approach to capture BOs and MIs [14]. Such an approach would constitute a formal treatment to describe and evaluate coordination needs.

3   BOMI Metamodel, Method, and Analysis

In the following, we present our main contributions, i.e., the BOMI metamodel, method, and analysis capabilities provided by the model. We continued our design science approach [10] but with a focus on developing a metamodel, modeling guidelines, and model smells. An overview of the input artifacts and steps of our method is shown in Fig. 1.

We went through several iterations designing an artifact (metamodel, method, and smells) and performing evaluations of the artifact both locally and with four companies. In the first round, we used our informal drawings and lists of collected BO and MIs in practice, along with our knowledge gathered from the companies, to come up with a first draft of the artifact. The paper authors

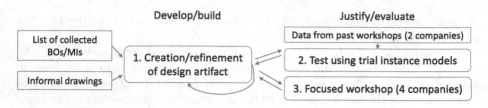

Fig. 1. Overview of steps of our research method

discussed the artifact and made local improvements. We then used historical data gathered from workshops with two of the companies to create trial models of their BOMI situation. After discussion, this caused further iteration over the artifact. Finally, we evaluated the design artifact in a focused workshop (see Sect. 4). The four companies we collaborated with are described in Table 1.

Table 1. Descriptions of participating companies.

Company A	Develops telecommunications products. Separate organizational units exist for sales, product management, and other purposes
Company B	Develops mechanical products, both for consumer markets and for industrial development and manufacturing. The systems are decomposed into several elements, which is also reflected in the organizational structure
Company C	Is an automotive Original Equipment Manufacturer (OEM). Traditionally, the company has been structured according to vehicle parts (e.g., powertrain, chassis, ...), but has undergone restructuring into agile teams
Company D	Develops high-tech solutions for vehicular systems. Software development teams are largely independent of hardware development

3.1 BOMI Metamodel

To capture our conceptual model, we use a UML class diagram. Other languages could work just as well, but we choose UML due to its familiarity. The latest version of the BOMI metamodel can be found in Fig. 2.

Based on our past findings, the most critical element of the metamodel is the BO itself (in dark gray). We label this class as an interface, given the nature of BOs as interfaces between methodological islands. We give this class a *SuperType* and *SubType*, based on our past classification findings [14]. The *SuperType* is an enumeration, with a set list of options, while we found an enumeration was too restrictive for the *SubType*, and leave this as free text (a String).

We use our experiences to identify a number of internal BO attributes, including the *Purpose*, *Level of detail*, *Frequency of change*, *Level of modularity* and

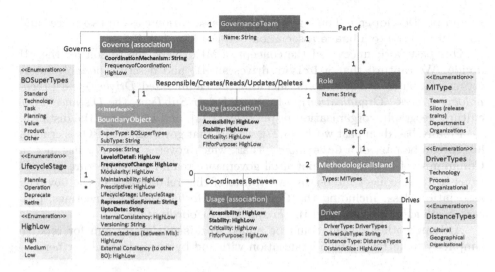

Fig. 2. Metamodel for Boundary Objects and Methodological Islands (BOMI)

Maintainability, whether the BO represents *Prescriptive* knowledge (as opposed to descriptive), which *Lifecycle* stage the BO is used in, with an enumeration of four options (*Planning, Operation, Deprecate, Retire*), *Representation Format* (e.g., free text, model, table), the level of *Internal Consistency*, and what sort of *Versioning* information it may have. The last two attributes describe the relationship between this BO and other classes in the model, in this case, *Connectedness* of the MIs using the BO, and how *Externally Consistent* it is with other BO instances. These attributes are either free text (String) or are described via a simple qualitative scale of *High*, *Medium*, and *Low* (the HighLow enumeration). We found that although this qualitative scale can be used for a quick summary, often a more complex description is needed. For example, for architecture descriptions, the level of detail of the BO changes depending on the *Lifecyle* stage. Thus, we find the need to accompany each attribute with a short explanation of the value. We omit this from the current metamodel for simplicity, but note that the instance models should be accompanied by some explanatory text.

A Methodological Island (in green) contains an enumeration of types based on our past findings (*Teams, Silos, Departments, Organizations*). For MIs, the relations to other elements are crucial. Organizational Roles, with role *names* are part of the MIs. A Role is responsible for, or has a CRUD relationship with a BO. The Usage association class between these classes captures how Roles use BOs. We can model a BO's accessibility for a Role, its *Stability*, *Criticality*, and whether it is *Fit for Purpose*. Ideally, a Role is part of a MI, and the Role's interaction with the BO is described in the Usage class. In some cases, practitioners were reluctant to explicitly model roles and only model BOs and MIs, either because the inclusion of Roles caused the model to drastically increase in size or because the Role and MI were similar (e.g., "Development Team" → Role should be "Developer"). Thus, we repeat this association class in two places and one can also create a `Usage` association between `BOs` and `MIs`.

Our past work uncovered the concept of MI drivers, the reason for the MI divide. We capture that a `Driver` drives an `MI`, and describe possibly interesting attributes of the drivers, including an enumerated *Driver Type* (*Technology, Process, Organization*), a free-text *Driver SubType*, the *Distance Type* culture/geography/organization inspired by [3,11], and the size of the distance.

Finally, based on past work [25,27], we find that governance of BOs is crucial. `Roles` can be part of a `Governance Team`, which governs a `BO`. For instance, a Community of Practice is a potential governance team for architecture descriptions [25]. We collect interesting attributes of this relationship in the `Governs` association class, including the *Coordination Mechanism* (e.g., meetings, processes, standards, tools), and the *Frequency of Coordination*.

Although other details could be added to this model, we aim for relative simplicity to better enable instantiation with and by our industrial partners.

3.2   BOMI Method

As part of our modeling workshops, we created a simple list of guiding questions based on our metamodel concepts and attributes, e.g., "Which BO would you like to focus on?", "What roles interact with the BO?", and "Which islands do the roles belong to?". The full list of questions can be found in our online appendix[1]. These questions are intended to guide in the creation of a BOMI instance model, either led by a modeling facilitator, or independently in a company.

3.3   Instance Example

To illustrate our model in action, we present an example derived from a workshop with our industrial partners in Fig. 3. More details about how this example was derived are provided in Sect. 4. For this example, we again use UML syntax. In developing a BOMI language, we could create a domain-specific visual language, using customized icons or different shapes. Although promising, we leave the exploration of a BOMI-specific visual syntax to future work, and instead use the visual syntax of UML, with the benefit of familiarity for our industrial partners.

In this example, Company A (more detail in Sect. 4) chose to focus on a `User Story` which is a `BO` that is used in planning, acting as a *Backlog Item*. Other attributes include the *Level of Detail, Frequency of Changes*, and *Representation Format*. In this example, we include extra explanatory text for the attributes in parentheses. Two `MIs`, the `Development Team` and the `Product Management Team`, use this `BO` for coordination. `Developers` and `Product Owner` roles are part of these `MIs`, respectively. `Usage` for the `Developer` is captured via an association class, the attributes indicating that the `User Story` is easily accessible, critical, but with low stability, amongst other things. A similar `Usage` class captures usage of the `BO` by the `Product Owner`. The `Product Owner` is part of a `Forum`

---

[1] https://doi.org/10.6084/m9.figshare.12363764.v1.

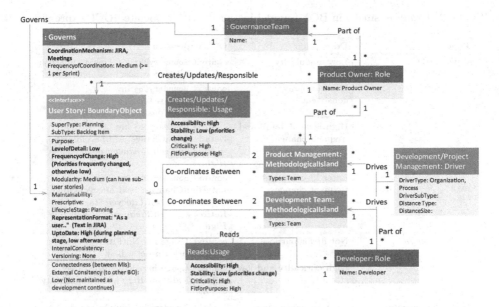

Fig. 3. Instance model of BOMI setup for user stories for company A

of **Product Owners** who make up the **Governance Team** for the **User Story**
BO. The **Governs** association class captures attributes of the governance process,
e.g., they coordinate using the JIRA tool and meetings, and coordinate at least
once per agile sprint. Note that due to time restrictions, this model is incomplete,
thus a blank value for some of the object attributes. We consider how an instance
model like this could be analyzed in the next section.

3.4 BOMI Analysis

Although the process of creating a BOMI instance model is useful to understand
BOs and MIs, one can go a step further and use the instance model created
to detect potential issues or "smells" in the BOMI configuration, similar to the
idea of smells in models or source code [2,22]. The idea is that these smells can
be detected and discussed, determining if there is an underlying problem. This
analysis and discussion would be conducted by those having a higher-level view
of an organization, e.g., team leaders, project managers. The overall aim is to
promote potential beneficial changes in the BOs, MIs, and ways of working.

We can detect these smells within a BO, or across relationships in the model.
For example, we can detect smells within individual attributes: low modularity,
high maintainability, not up to date, not internally consistent, or not externally
consistent. We can also detect possible smells between attributes, including: having a high level of detail but a high frequency of change, meaning that frequent
changes may be difficult and involve changing many elements; and being in an
early lifecycle stage (planning) yet being very infrequently changed, or being in
a later lifecycle change (deprecate, retire) yet having a high frequency of change.

Table 2. Example smells in BOMI model instances with associated OCL expressions.

Type	Description	OCL expression
Within BO	Low modularity	context BoundaryObj inv LowModularity: self.$Modularity = Low$
	Not internally consistent	context BoundaryObj inv InternalInconsistency: self.$InternalConsistency = Low$
	High level of detail and frequent change	context BoundaryObj inv DetailedHighChange: self.$LevelofDetail$ $= High$ and self.$FrequencyofChange =$ $High$
	Later lifecycle and frequent change	context BoundaryObj inv LateHighChanges: (self.$LifecycleStage =$ $Deprecate$ or self.$LifecycleStage =$ $Retire$) and self.$FrequencyofChange =$ $High$
Within Usage	Not fit for purpose	context Usage inv NotFit: self.$FitForPurpose = Low$
	High criticality and low stability	context Usage inv CriticalUnstable: self.$Criticality = High$ and self.$Stability$ $= Low$
Missing Elements/ Relationships	No governance team	context BoundaryObj inv Governed: self.$Governed \rightarrow$ size > 0
	No one responsible for BO	context BoundaryObj inv Responsible: self.$Responsible \rightarrow$ size > 0
	No one can update BO	context BoundaryObj inv Updated: self.$Updates \rightarrow$ size > 0
Across Elements	Governing roles should use BO	context BoundaryObj inv GovernsUses: self.$Governs \rightarrow$ forAll(g | g.$PartOf \rightarrow$ select(r | r.$Uses = $ self)$\rightarrow$size > 0)
	High frequency of change but low frequency of coordination	context BoundaryObj inv GovernsUses: self.$FrequencyofChange = High$ and self.$Governs \rightarrow$ select(g | g.$FrequencyofCoordination = Low) \rightarrow$size > 0

Similarly, with the Usage association class, smells include not being fit for purpose, or high criticality with low stability or low accessibility. For instance, in Fig. 3, usage of the BO by both the developer and product owner is critical but the stability is low. Is it acceptable for something so critical to change so frequently? Looking into the BO, we see the lifecycle stage is planning, so the organization may argue that high criticality and low stability is unavoidable for key artifacts like user stories in this early stage. If the artifact was instead in an operational stage, this situation may pose more of a problem.

We can also detect smells at a broader level, e.g., the BO has no governance team, or no one responsible for it. Our company partners suggest that those governing a BO should also use it, to ensure that they are aware of how the BO is used. It can also be checked whether there exists someone who can update and delete the BO. And, if the Usage is critical, or if the frequency of change is high, the Governs class should likely have a high frequency of coordination.

We summarize how automatic checking of some of these smells could look using OCL expressions [5] in Table 2. In our case, eventual tool support should allow the model to be drawn without necessarily following these expressions, capturing reality with smells. These expressions could be checked after a first version of an instance model is created. The output of such a check should be discussed within an organization, to determine if the smell is a problem in reality, and to discuss what sort of changes could be made.

4   Evaluation

The final step in our method was a 1.5-h online workshop in April 2020 to try out the metamodel, method, and smell ideas with seven representatives from four companies, described in Table 1. The participants included systems engineers, requirements specialists, and tooling specialists. During the workshop, we reserved 20 min for a review of BOMI concepts and to introduce the new metamodel using prepared material[2]. We then split off into four virtual breakout rooms for 30 min of modeling instance models in focused sessions. Each room had at least one researcher and the representatives from one company. The researchers went through the guiding method questions from Sect. 3.2 and drew an instance model based on the answers of the participants, sharing their screen.

Despite the short time-frame, we were able to get four relatively complete models (e.g., Fig. 3), with the statistics in terms of element type used shown in Table 3. We opted to focus on one BO at a time; thus, each model had only one BO. The modelers were also able to capture 2–5 MIs, 1–5 Usage association classes, 1–4 Drivers, and one Government Team and Governs association class per model. Some of the attribute information for each model was filled in, but many attributes were left blank due to time restrictions.

Table 3. Element count of four instance models from the workshop.

Model	BO	MI	Usage	Driver	Role	Governance team	Governs
C1	1	2	2	1	2	1	1
C2	1	3	1	1	5	1	1
C3	1	5	5	4	0	1	1
C4	1	3	1	2	2	1	1

The final 30 min (allowing for short breaks) was used to discuss our experiences and gain feedback, with several of the authors taking notes. The authors then met to share and review our notes, consolidating and discussing experiences. Feedback included that the current typing hierarchy for MIs was often hard to

---

[2] https://doi.org/10.6084/m9.figshare.12363764.v1.

apply, and MIs are often multi-dimensional. To deal with this, we allowed MIs to have more than one type in the updated metamodel. We also acknowledge that our current list of possible types (*MIType* in Fig. 2) may not be complete. Previously, instead of the `Driver` class, we had an Ocean association class between MIs with a driver attribute. We noted in our modeling exercises that MIs can have many drivers and can share drivers. Thus, we reworked the Ocean association class to the current `Drivers` class. We also made note that most of the attribute descriptions were hard to capture with enumerations (High/Medium/Low) and that we often needed free text descriptions to capture the subtleties, e.g., frequency of change varying depending on the lifecycle stage. Finally, we made many small improvements to the class attributes. We used all of this feedback to create the final version of the metamodel presented in Sect. 3. The previous three versions of the model can be found in our online appendix[3].

Our modeling sessions did not give us extensive time to apply the smell analysis examples as described in Sect. 3.4, and we were also hindered by the incompleteness of some of the instance model attributes. However, we presented some draft smells and asked for feedback from the participants. We generally asked "Can the current issues with the BO be captured in the model?" Although the participants were not opposed to automated checks as described in Sect. 3.4, they were more interested in human-centered manually-detected smells, e.g., "Can I draw this?" For them, the first and most important smell is whether the participants had the knowledge to instantiate the metamodel. Our participants also suggested a smell having to do with the complexity of the overall model: "I can draw it, but it is a mess", indicating that the overall design of their BOMI situation could be overly complex and poorly thought-out. Therefore, model complexity checks or basic checks such as for cohesion and coupling may be useful. Our participants also suggested the check that those responsible for governance should also be users, and that the governance team should consist of a diverse set of roles or islands, i.e., not just be made up by one type of user. Some of these smells could be expressed formally over the model, as in Sect. 3.4, but others can instead be included as points to consider in the methodology.

Overall, our company partners were positive about the experience. Based on their interest, we are currently arranging longer sessions for two out of four companies, inviting further internal participants knowledgeable about key BOs.

5   Related Work

A number of related conceptual modeling approaches have been proposed.

Knowledge Management. Our work bears similarities to approaches that focus on modeling for knowledge management, e.g., [1, 21]. Here the focus is often knowledge creation, distribution, representation, and retrieval. Our approach captures some of these elements in the BOMI metamodel, including the format of the BO, its purpose, and users. However, our focus is less about capturing

---

[3] https://doi.org/10.6084/m9.figshare.12363764.v1.

implicit knowledge through a global strategy and more about understanding the way that diverse organizational islands coordinate knowledge through artifacts.

Other related work uses patterns to detect potential problems in information flows, e.g., consecutive transformations, which are similar to our notion of smells [18]. Our focus is less on the flow of information but more on effective coordination, thus our specific smells are quite different compared to [18].

Agent-Orientation. Our work bears some similarity to agent-oriented or multi-agent system modeling which emphasizes the rational behavior of individual agents in a system, e.g., [9,13]. Most of this work has an exchange of resources by agents through some form of dependency. Although agent concepts could be used to capture MI, the islands are more like social groupings emerging due to various drivers, and often do not act together as a sentient and autonomous whole. Similarly, BO could be resource dependencies, but our concept of BO is richer, and we place more emphasis on the means of use and attributes of BO, compared to resources in agent-oriented modeling.

BOMI is in line with the Comakership organizational pattern [6], with our notion of smells fitting with the idea of continuous improvement. However, these patterns focus on inter-organizational coordination, while BOMI covers inter-team coordination, and BOMI does not make use of i* or intentions, with attributes such as "Purpose" in the BO fulfilling this role to a lesser degree.

Communication. Work in [17] introduces ontologies for collaboration, communication, and cooperation, with several elements and components echoed by our BOMI metamodel. However, their focus is not on supporting diverse groups as with our MI, or on the attributes and specifics of the boundary objects or artifacts. Some of the work which has focused on modeling communication focused on autonomous agents and their protocols, e.g., [7], while we focus on communication between MIs, always consisting of humans.

Coordination. Related work on coordination modeling focuses on coordination between information systems rather than human-oriented MIs [16]. In this view, coordination between systems can be captured via APIs, a type of BO. Previously, benefits and limitations of languages for capturing APIs have been investigated [12], e.g., i* and e^3 value modeling. Although the focus lay more on the use and value of APIs and less on coordination between methodologically diverse groups, BOMI may still be beneficial for API analysis.

Further work is more process-oriented. [23] applies e^3 value modeling, process modeling, and physical delivery modeling to support cross-organizational coordination. ActivityFlow focuses on supporting incremental and flexible workflow definitions, allowing for workflow coordination between organizations [15]. BOMI takes a static, rather than process-oriented view, as our partner companies, with an agile mindset, focus less on workflows and more on practices.

Ecosystems. Work in ecosystem modeling is also related (e.g., [4,28]), as our BOMI approach can be said to produce a type of ecosystem model; however, existing ecosystem models focus more on external coordination, where the internal methodologies of a partner are more opaque. Our BOMI models tend to have a mix of internal and external MIs and BOs, often with a particular focus on supporting diversity in internal ways of working.

6 Discussion and Future Work

We have presented a conceptual model for BOMI, described how we instantiated it together with four large-scale systems development companies, and derived example smells over the instances that can be checked with OCL constraints. Concretely, we have found that the BOMI model allowed us to create initial models with a rather low time effort (20 min of introduction of general concepts plus 30 min of modeling). Our participants were positive about the outcome of the session and the initial models allowed us to test our list of initial smells. We believe that the described findings are a good starting point to evaluate and tailor the BOMI metamodel further. For instance, tooling, access, and security information could be added to the model, e.g., to facilitate security analysis concerning boundary objects.

In this paper, we focused on BOMI-specific smells. General UML smells, e.g., related to the use of names, attributes, or "data clumps" [2], might also be applicable to BOMI models, and are an interesting area for future work.

Moreover, we propose to investigate the creation and use of an expressive domain-specific visual language and tool support to capture BOMI models. Currently, we rely on UML class diagrams due to the availability of general modeling tools and the existing familiarity with class diagrams. However, there might be stakeholders (e.g., project managers, sales representatives) that are not familiar with class diagrams and could benefit from a domain-specific language.

Finally, we plan to build on these findings to help companies proactively address coordination issues and facilitate the management of boundary objects in practice. Concretely, we aim to conceive a constructive method to continuously analyze the current situation with key stakeholders, propose actions for improvement, and mechanisms to assess the impact of implemented changes.

Threats to Validity. To improve *internal validity/credibility*, we used an interactive modeling process with open questions, triangulated the experiences of the participating companies, and aimed to provide detailed descriptions in this paper. A cross-company workshop was used to present the intermediate findings and perform member checking with the participants.

A threat to *construct validity* relates to the nature of the domain we model. The concepts of boundary objects and methodological islands can be misunderstood and interpreted in various ways. We intended to provide clear definitions and engaged in a long-term project with the participating companies to ensure a common understanding of the concepts.

Considering *external validity*, we used a sample of four large-scale companies that develop embedded systems. We believe this sample provides valuable insights, but acknowledge we may have different findings with a different sampling approach. We describe the companies' characteristics in this paper to facilitate the assessment of what findings might be transferable to other contexts.

With respect to *reliability*, the previously acquired knowledge of the participating companies in the project is a potential threat. As stated before, we have previously collaborated on boundary objects and methodological islands, which will not be the case for other researchers or research contexts. However, the general notation used in this paper is rather straight-forward and comprehensible for other modelers, which facilitates replication. Moreover, we have made the explanatory material and models available online.

7   Conclusions

In this paper, we have focused on the challenge of inter-team coordination and knowledge management in large-scale systems development using diverse development practices. While initial empirical studies existed, there has been a lack of systematic modeling approaches that can support practitioners in modeling their current and diverse coordination settings, and analyzing them to identify issues. To address this issue, we proposed a conceptual model that can be used to model methodological islands (i.e., groups that work with a different methodology than their surrounding organization) and boundary objects between them (i.e., artifacts that can be used to create a common understanding across sites and support inter-team coordination). We presented an initial list of bad smells that can be leveraged to detect issues and devise suitable strategies for inter-team coordination in large-scale development. We evaluated the conceptual model together with four large industrial companies developing complex systems and present our positive evaluation results.

We plan to build onto these findings to devise a constructive method supporting the analysis of coordination issues and suggesting improvement strategies, as well as mechanisms to continuously assess the effect of these strategies.

Acknowledgments. This work was partially supported by the Software Center Project 27 on Requirements Engineering for Large-Scale Agile System Development and the Wallenberg AI, Autonomous Systems and Software Program (WASP) funded by the Knut and Alice Wallenberg Foundation.

References

1. Ale, M.A., Toledo, C.M., Chiotti, O., Galli, M.R.: A conceptual model and technological support for organizational knowledge management. Sci. Comput. Program. **95**, 73–92 (2014). https://doi.org/10.1016/j.scico.2013.12.012
2. Arendt, T., Taentzer, G.: UML model smells and model refactorings in early software development phases. Results of the SPES 2020 Project, AP4, Universität Marburg (2010)
3. Bjarnason, E., Sharp, H.: The role of distances in requirements communication: a case study. Requirements Eng. **22**(1), 1–26 (2017). https://doi.org/10.1007/s00766-015-0233-3

4. Boucharas, V., Jansen, S., Brinkkemper, S.: Formalizing software ecosystem modeling. In: Proceedings of the 1st International Workshop on Open Component Ecosystems, pp. 41–50 (2009)
5. Cabot, J., Gogolla, M.: Object Constraint Language (OCL): a definitive guide. In: Bernardo, M., Cortellessa, V., Pierantonio, A. (eds.) SFM 2012. LNCS, vol. 7320, pp. 58–90. Springer, Heidelberg (2012). https://doi.org/10.1007/978-3-642-30982-3_3
6. Colombo, E., Mylopoulos, J.: A multi-perspective framework for organizational patterns. In: Embley, D.W., Olivé, A., Ram, S. (eds.) ER 2006. LNCS, vol. 4215, pp. 451–467. Springer, Heidelberg (2006). https://doi.org/10.1007/11901181_34
7. Dignum, F., Dietz, J., Verharen, E., Weigand, H.: Communication modeling-the language/action perspective. In: Proceedings of the 2nd International Workshop on Communication Modeling (LAP 1997) (1997)
8. Dingsøyr, T., Moe, N.B., Faegri, T.E., Seim, E.A.: Exploring software development at the very large-scale: a revelatory case study and research agenda for agile method adaptation. Empirical Software Engineering (2017)
9. Gonçalves, E., Araujo, J., Castro, J.: iStar4RationalAgents: modeling requirements of multi-agent systems with rational agents. In: Laender, A.H.F., Pernici, B., Lim, E.-P., de Oliveira, J.P.M. (eds.) ER 2019. LNCS, vol. 11788, pp. 558–566. Springer, Cham (2019). https://doi.org/10.1007/978-3-030-33223-5_46
10. Hevner, A.R., March, S.T., Park, J., Ram, S.: Design science in information systems research. MIS Q. **28**, 75–105 (2004). https://doi.org/10.2307/25148625
11. Holmström, H., Fitzgerald, B., et al.: Agile practices reduce distance in global software development. Inf. Syst. Manage. **23**(3), 7–18 (2006)
12. Horkoff, J., et al.: Modeling support for strategic API planning and analysis. In: Wnuk, K., Brinkkemper, S. (eds.) ICSOB 2018. LNBIP, vol. 336, pp. 10–26. Springer, Cham (2018). https://doi.org/10.1007/978-3-030-04840-2_2
13. Jureta, I., Faulkner, S.: An agent-oriented meta-model for enterprise modelling. In: Akoka, J., et al. (eds.) ER 2005. LNCS, vol. 3770, pp. 151–161. Springer, Heidelberg (2005). https://doi.org/10.1007/11568346_17
14. Kasauli, R., Wohlrab, R., Knauss, E., Steghöfer, J.P., Horkoff, J., Maro, S.: Charting coordination needs in large-scale agile organizations with boundary objects and methodological islands. In: Proceedings of the International Conference on Software and System Process (ICSSP 2020) (2020)
15. Liu, L., Pu, C.: Activity flow: towards incremental specification and flexible coordination of workflow activities. In: Embley, D.W., Goldstein, R.C. (eds.) ER 1997. LNCS, vol. 1331, pp. 169–182. Springer, Heidelberg (1997). https://doi.org/10.1007/3-540-63699-4_14
16. Norrie, M.C., Wunderli, M.: Coordination system modelling. In: Loucopoulos, P. (ed.) ER 1994. LNCS, vol. 881, pp. 474–490. Springer, Heidelberg (1994). https://doi.org/10.1007/3-540-58786-1_97
17. Oliveira, F.F., Antunes, J.C., Guizzardi, R.S.: Towards a collaboration ontology. In: Proceedings of the Brazilian Workshop on Ontologies and Metamodels for Software and Data Engineering. João Pessoa (2007)
18. Schneider, K., Lübke, D.: Modeling and improving information flows in the development of large business applications. In: Ali Babar, M., Dingsøyr, T., Lago P., van Vliet, H. (eds.) Software Architecture Knowledge Management, pp. 175–197. Springer, Heidelberg (2009). https://doi.org/10.1007/978-3-642-02374-3_10
19. Sedano, T., Ralph, P., Péraire, C.: The product backlog. In: Proceedings of the 41th International Conference on Software Engineering (ICSE 2019), pp. 200–211 (2019)

20. Star, S.L., Griesemer, J.R.: Institutional ecology, 'translations' and boundary objects: amateurs and professionals in Berkeley's museum of vertebrate zoology, 1907–39. Soc. Stud. Sci. **19**(3), 387–420 (1989)

21. Strohmaier, M., Yu, E., Horkoff, J., Aranda, J., Easterbrook, S.: Analyzing knowledge transfer effectiveness-an agent-oriented modeling approach. In: Proceedings of the 40th Annual Hawaii International Conference on System Sciences (HICSS 2007), pp. 188b–188b. IEEE (2007)

22. Van Emden, E., Moonen, L.: Java quality assurance by detecting code smells. In: Proceedings of the Working Conference on Reverse Engineering, pp. 97–106 (2002)

23. Wieringa, R., Pijpers, V., Bodenstaff, L., Gordijn, J.: Value-driven coordination process design using physical delivery models. In: Li, Q., Spaccapietra, S., Yu, E., Olivé, A. (eds.) ER 2008. LNCS, vol. 5231, pp. 216–231. Springer, Heidelberg (2008). https://doi.org/10.1007/978-3-540-87877-3_17

24. Wohlrab, R., Pelliccione, P., Knauss, E., Heldal, R.: On interfaces to support agile architecting in automotive: an exploratory case study. In: Proceedings of the International Conference on Software Architecture (ICSA), pp. 161–170 (2019)

25. Wohlrab, R., Eliasson, U., Pelliccione, P., Heldal, R.: Improving the consistency and usefulness of architecture descriptions: Guidelines for architects. In: Proceedings of the International Conference on Software Architecture (ICSA), pp. 151–160 (2019)

26. Wohlrab, R., Knauss, E., Pelliccione, P.: Why and how to balance alignment and diversity of requirements engineering practices in automotive. J. Syst. Softw. **162**, 110516 (2020)

27. Wohlrab, R., Pelliccione, P., Knauss, E., Larsson, M.: Boundary objects and their use in agile systems engineering. J. Softw. Evol. Process **31**(5) (2019)

28. Yu, E., Deng, S.: Understanding software ecosystems: a strategic modeling approach. In: Proceedings of the 3rd International Workshop on Software Ecosystems, pp. 65–76 (2011)

29. Zaitsev, A., Tan, B., Gal, U.: Collaboration amidst volatility: the evolving nature of boundary objects in agile software development. In: Proceedings of the European Conference on Information Systems, vol. 24 (2016)

Structural and Computational Properties of Possibilistic Armstrong Databases

Seyeong Jeong, Haoming Ma, Ziheng Wei, and Sebastian Link[✉]

School of Computer Science, The University of Auckland,
Auckland 1010, New Zealand
s.link@auckland.ac.nz

Abstract. We investigate structural and computational properties of Armstrong databases for a new class of possibilistic functional dependencies. We establish sufficient and necessary conditions for a given possibilistic relation to be Armstrong for a given set of possibilistic functional dependencies. We then use the characterization to compute Armstrong databases for any given set of these dependencies. The problem of finding an Armstrong database is precisely exponential in the input, but our algorithm computes an output whose size is always guaranteed to be at most quadratic in a minimum-sized output. Extensive experiments indicate that our algorithm shows good computational behavior on average. As our possibilistic functional dependencies have important applications in database design, our results indicate that Armstrong databases can effectively support business analysts during the acquisition of functional dependencies that are meaningful in a given application domain.

Keywords: Sample data · Functional dependency · Possibility theory

1 Introduction

Background. Functional dependencies (FDs) are fundamental for understanding the structure and semantics of data, and have a fruitful history in database theory and practice. In a formal sense, FDs are to database constraints what Horn clauses are to logic [8]. An FD expresses that the values on some attributes uniquely determine the values on some other attributes. For example, every person has only one mother. Due to their ability to express desirable properties of many application domains, FDs have been used successfully for core data management tasks, including cleaning [16], design [10,11], integration [5], exchange [15], modeling [14,17], querying [9], and updating [21].

Motivation. Relational databases were developed for applications with certain data, including accounting, inventory and payroll [6]. Modern applications, such as information extraction, sensors, and data integration produce large volumes of uncertain data [4,18]. As an example application, sufficiently simple to motive our research and explain our findings, we consider an employee who extracts

© Springer Nature Switzerland AG 2020
G. Dobbie et al. (Eds.): ER 2020, LNCS 12400, pp. 590–603, 2020.
https://doi.org/10.1007/978-3-030-62522-1_43

information from web-sites about weekly project meetings in her company. This is a typical case where information about the confidence of objects is useful, but probability distributions are unavailable. In such cases, qualitative approaches are attractive, for example possibility theory [2,7].

Figure 1 shows a possibilistic relation (p-relation) where each object is
associated with a possibility degree
(p-degree) from a finite scale: $\alpha_1 >$
$\dots > \alpha_{k+1}$. The top degree α_1 is
reserved for objects that are 'fully
possible', the bottom degree α_{k+1}
for objects that are 'impossible' to
occur. Intermediate degrees and their
linguistic interpretations are used as
preferred. Attributes involve *Project*,
storing projects with unique names,
Time, for the weekday and start time,
Manager, for the managers of the

Proj	Time	Mgr	Room	p-deg.
Eagle	Mon, 9am	Ann	Aqua	α_1
Hippo	Mon, 1pm	Ann	Aqua	α_1
Kiwi	Mon, 1pm	Pete	Buff	α_1
Kiwi	Tue, 2pm	Pete	Buff	α_1
Lion	Tue, 4pm	Gill	Buff	α_1
Lion	Wed, 9am	Gill	Cyan	α_1
Lion	Wed, 11am	Bob	Cyan	α_2
Lion	Wed, 11am	Jack	Cyan	α_3
Lion	Wed, 11am	Pam	Lava	α_3
Tiger	Wed, 11am	Pam	Lava	α_4

Fig. 1. Running example of a p-relation

project that attend, and *Room*, for the unique name of a room. The employee classifies the possibility with which tuples occur in the relation according to their source. Tuples from the official web-site are assigned p-degree α_1, indicating they are fully possible, tuples from a project manager's web-site are assigned α_2, tuples from a project member's web-site get degree α_3, and tuples that originate from rumors are assigned p-degree α_4. Implicitly, any other tuple has p-degree α_5, indicating that it is impossible to occur. A different interpretation may result from already held, confirmed, requested, planned, and all other meetings. The p-degrees may have numerical interpretations, e.g. $1 > 0.75 > 0.5 > 0.25 > 0$. Either way, the employee has chosen 5 p-degrees to assign qualitative levels of uncertainty to tuples, with top degree α_1 and bottom degree α_5.

Naturally, the assignment of p-degrees results in a linearly ordered chain of possible worlds: For $i = 1, \dots, 4$, the relation r_i consists of tuples with p-degree α_i or higher, i.e. α_j with $j \leq i$. The p-degree of world r_i is α_i. In particular, fully possible tuples occur in every possible world, and are therefore also fully certain to occur. The possible worlds of the p-relation in Fig. 1 are illustrated in Fig. 2. Interestingly, p-degrees enable us to express classical FDs with different degrees of certainty (c-degree). For example, the FD $\sigma_1 = Manager, Time \rightarrow Room$ is satisfied by the world r_4, and thus holds in every possible world. Consequently, it is assigned the top c-degree, denoted by β_1. The smallest relation that violates $\sigma_2 = Room, Time \rightarrow Project$ is r_4, that is, the FD is assigned the second highest c-degree, β_2. The smallest relation that violates $\sigma_3 = Project, Time \rightarrow Manager$ is r_3, that is, the FD is assigned the third highest c-degree, β_3. The smallest relation that violates $\sigma_4 = Project \rightarrow Manager$ is r_2, and the FD thus holds with c-degree β_4. The FD $Manager, Room \rightarrow Time$ is violated even by the smallest possible world r_1, and is thus assigned the bottom c-degree $\beta_5 = \beta_{k+1}$.

Hence, the p-degree α_i of the smallest possible world r_i in which the FD is violated, determines the c-degree β_{k+2-i} with which the FD holds. A classical FD together with a c-degree was introduced as a possibilistic FD (pFD) in [12]. In the article, the possibilistic grounding of the pFDs was developed in depth and their difference in expressivity to previous work was explained. In addition, pFDs of this kind correspond to possibilistic Horn clauses, covering the classical equivalence between classical FDs and Horn clauses as the special case where only two p-degrees are present. The main motivation for pFDs is schema normalization [13].

In a nutshell, the possibilistic model [12] enables one to assign different degrees to the classical notion of data redundancy [22]. This makes it possible to define and compute different degrees of classical normal forms (Boyce-Codd and Third Normal Forms [1]), each eliminating/minimizing different degrees of data redundancy [13]. For example, to eliminate redundant data value occurrences in $r_4 - r_3$ (e.g. **Lava**), it suffices to normalize with pFDs of c-degree β_1. In contrast, to eliminate redundant data value occurrences in r_1 (e.g. **Pete**), one must normalize with pFDs of any c-degree. However, input to such normalization algorithms are sets of meaningful pFDs, as identified by teams of business analysts and database designers.

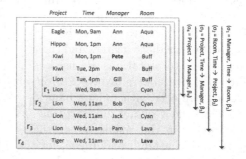

Fig. 2. Worlds of p-relation and scope of pFDs

The Problem and Armstrong Models. A challenging problem for design teams of the target database is therefore to identify the set of pFDs that are meaningful within the given application domain. For this purpose, the design team communicates with domain experts, and have to overcome a mismatch in expertise: The design team knows database concepts but not the domain, while domain experts know the domain but not database concepts. As humans learn a lot from good examples, it is likely that examples constitute an effective tool in helping design teams to identify more of the meaningful pFDs. Similar to the case of classical FDs, we view Armstrong databases as perfect examples [3,11,14]. In fact, an Armstrong database for a given set of constraints from a fixed class is a single database that satisfies all given constraints and violates all those constraints from the class that are not implied by the given set. As such, an Armstrong database satisfies all the constraints currently perceived to be meaningful by the design team and explicitly violates every constraint not perceived to be meaningful. In particular, an Armstrong database for a given set of pFDs has the astonishing property that every pFD holds with the highest c-degree in the Armstrong database with which it is implied by the given pFD set. For example, the p-relation in Fig. 1 is Armstrong for the four given pFDs shown in Fig. 2. The FD *Manager, Time → Project* has c-degree β_2, as the smallest world which violates it is r_4. If this FD were to hold with full certainty in the application domain, i.e. c-degree β_1, domain experts would simply notice such violation in the Armstrong database. More generally, domain experts would notice when a meaningful constraint is violated by the Armstrong database (namely whenever it is incorrectly perceived as meaningless by the design team) and point this out to the design team. Our aim is to investigate structural and computational properties of Armstrong databases for pFDs, both in theory and in implementations and experiments. Our overarching goal is to improve the acquisition of requirements, i.e., to increase the number of meaningful pFDs that are recognized as such. This would generalize known results from the pure relational model of data [11], subsumed as the special case of our possibilistic model with two available p-degrees.

Contributions. Our contributions can be summarized as follows. (1) We establish sufficient and necessary conditions for a given p-relation to be Armstrong for a given set of pFDs, subsuming the characterization of classical Armstrong relations for FDs in terms of maximal, agree, and closed sets as a special case [3,14]. (2) While the problem of computing an Armstrong p-relation for a given set of p-FDs in precisely exponential in the input, we establish an algorithm that is guaranteed to compute an Armstrong p-relation whose size is always guaranteed to be at most quadratic in the size of a minimum-sized Armstrong p-relation, again generalizing classical results [3,14]. (3) Our algorithm is transferred into practice by an implementation. (4) Extensive experiments with our implementation show two extreme cases where output of exponential and logarithmic size in the input are produced, respectively. For randomly created inputs and fixed schema sizes, output sizes display logarithmic growth and output times display constant behavior in the number of available p-degrees, and for fixed numbers of available p-degrees, output sizes and times both display low-degree polynomial growth in the size of the schema. Our results provide a technical platform for using Armstrong databases during the requirements acquisition of pFDs.

Organization. Section 2 discusses background from the relational model. Our possibilistic model is defined in Sect. 3. In Sect. 4 we characterize Armstrong p-relations for pFDs, and show how to compute them. Our tool is briefly discussed in Sect. 5. Section 6 presents the results of our experiments. Finally, we conclude in Sect. 7 and briefly discuss future work. Most proofs have been omitted to meet space requirements.

2 Armstrong Relations for Functional Dependencies

FDs are probably the most studied class of constraints, due to their expressivity, computational behavior, and impact on practice. This applies to most of the existing data models, ranging over conceptual, relational, object-relational, Web, graph, and uncertain models. FDs were already introduced in Codd's seminal paper [6]. In this section we give a concise summary about the structural and computational properties of Armstrong relations for classical FDs from the relational model. Subsequently, these will be extended to our possibilistic model.

A relation schema, denoted by R, is a finite non-empty set of *attributes*. Each attribute $A \in R$ has a *domain* $dom(A)$ of values. A *tuple* t over R is an element of the Cartesian product $\prod_{A \in R} dom(A)$. For $X \subseteq R$ we denote by $t(X)$ the *projection* of t on X. An *relation* over R is a finite set r of tuples over R. In our example, $R = \text{WEB}$ has attributes *Project, Time, Manager*, and *Room*. Figure 2 shows examples of relations and their tuples. For attribute subsets X, Y we write XY for their set union, and identify singletons with their element.

A *functional dependency* (FD) over R is an expression $X \rightarrow Y$ where $X, Y \subseteq R$. A relation r *satisfies* $X \rightarrow Y$ iff for all $t, t' \in r$, $t(X) = t'(X)$ implies that $t(Y) = t'(Y)$. In Fig. 2, relation r_3 satisfies the FDs *Manager, Time* $\rightarrow$ *Room* and *Room, Time* $\rightarrow$ *Project*, but not the FD *Project, Time* $\rightarrow$ *Manager*. A relation r satisfies a given FD set Σ iff r satisfies all $\sigma \in \Sigma$. For a set $\Sigma \cup \{\varphi\}$ of FDs, Σ *implies* φ iff every relation that satisfies Σ also satisfies φ. If $\Sigma = \{\sigma_1, \sigma_2, \sigma_3, \sigma_4$ from Fig. 2, then Σ implies the FD *Manager, Time* $\rightarrow$ *Project*, but Σ does not imply the FD *Manager, Room* $\rightarrow$ *Time*.

A relation r is *Armstrong* for Σ iff r satisfies Σ and for every FD φ not implied by Σ, r does not satisfy φ. Consequently, an Armstrong relation for Σ satisfies an FD φ if and only if φ is implied by Σ. In Fig. 2, the relation r_1 is Armstrong for the FD set $\Sigma = \{\sigma_1, \sigma_2, \sigma_3, \sigma_4\}$. As r_1 satisfies the FD *Manager, Time* $\rightarrow$ *Project*, this FD is implied by Σ; and as r_1 violates *Manager, Room* $\rightarrow$ *Time*, this FD is not implied by Σ. The left of Fig. 3 shows also an Armstrong relation for Σ. In fact, up to renaming, it is the same relation as r_1.

We are now introducing further concepts that will allow us to summarize the characterization of Armstrong relations for classical FDs. For a given relation r and distinct tuples $t, t' \in r$, the *agree set* $ag(t, t')$ of t, t' is the set of attributes $A \in R$ such that $t(A) = t'(A)$ holds. The *agree set* of r is the set of agree sets for all pairs of distinct tuples $t, t' \in r$. For example, the agree set of the first two tuples in relation r_1 of Fig. 2 is $\{Manager, Room\}$, and the agree set of r_1 consists of the following attribute sets: $\{Manager, Room\}$, $\emptyset$, $\{Time\}$, $\{Project, Manager, Room\}$, $\{Room\}$, and $\{Project, Manager\}$.

A set X of attributes is *closed* under Σ iff $X = \{A \in R \mid \Sigma \text{ implies } X \rightarrow A\}$. For R, Σ, $cl_\Sigma(R)$ is the set of attribute sets closed under Σ. For example, if $\Sigma = \{\sigma_1, \sigma_2, \sigma_3, \sigma_4\}$ from Fig. 2, then the following attribute sets are closed: $\emptyset$, $\{Time\}$, $\{Manager\}$, $\{Room\}$, $\{Project, Manager\}$, $\{Manager, Room\}$, $\{Project, Manager, Room\}$, and $\{Project, Time, Manager, Room\}$ itself.

A set X of attributes is *maximal* for an attribute A under Σ iff Σ does not imply $X \rightarrow A$, but for all $B \in R - (XA)$, Σ implies $XB \rightarrow A$. That is, X is maximal for A with the property that X does not functionally determine A. The maximal sets for R under Σ is the union of the maximal sets for each attribute of R under Σ. For example, if $\Sigma = \{\sigma_1, \sigma_2, \sigma_3, \sigma_4\}$ from Fig. 2, then the maximal sets for *Project* are $\{Manager, Room\}$ and $\{Time\}$, for *Time* it is $\{Project, Manager, Room\}$, for *Manager* they are $\{Time\}$ and $\{Room\}$, and for *Room* they are $\{Project, Manager\}$ and $\{Time\}$.

The significance of these concepts is embodied in the following theorem. The second subset relationship actually ensures that r satisfies Σ, while the first subset relationship ensures that r does not satisfy any FD not implied by Σ.

Theorem 1 *[3,14]. A relation r over relation schema R is Armstrong for an FD set Σ over R if and only if $max_\Sigma(R) \subseteq ag(r) \subseteq cl_\Sigma(R)$.*

Based on our examples before and Theorem 1 it follows immediately that the relation r_1 is Armstrong for the set $\Sigma = \{\sigma_1, \sigma_2, \sigma_3, \sigma_4\}$ from Fig. 2. The problem of computing an Armstrong relation for a given FD set is precisely exponential in the input [3]. However, as every maximal attribute set is also closed [14], Theorem 1 can be used to construct an Armstrong relation for a given set Σ of FDs by i) computing the set of maximal sets for R under Σ, and ii) creating a relation that starts with a single tuple t and then inserts for each maximal set X for R under Σ a new tuple t' that has agree set X with the previous tuple. Following this construction for the set $\Sigma = \{\sigma_1, \sigma_2, \sigma_3, \sigma_4\}$ from Fig. 2, we could introduce tuples which have agree set with the previous tuple in the following sequence of maximal sets: $\{Manager, Room\}$, $\{Time\}$, $\{Project, Manager, Room\}$, $\{Room\}$, and $\{Project, Manager\}$. Up to renaming, this would lead to the relation r_1 shown in Fig. 2.

It has been shown that this algorithm produces an Armstrong relation that is always guaranteed to have a number of tuples that is at most quadratic in that of a minimum-sized Armstrong relation [3]. The main complexity concerns the computation of the maximal sets. Mannila and Räihä have established an iterative algorithm MAXFAM [14] which takes as input a relation schema R and FD set Σ over R and computes for each $A \in R$ the set $max_\Sigma(A)$. In fact, MAXFAM refines the set of maximal sets for R by adding one FD of the input at a time. That is, if R has n attributes, the set $max_\emptyset(R)$ consists of all $n-1$ element subsets of R, and the algorithm then refines these sets by computing $max_{\Sigma' \cup \{\sigma\}}(R)$ in one iteration from $max_{\Sigma'}(R)$ until $\Sigma' \cup \{\sigma\} = \Sigma$. The details are given in [14] but not of importance to the current article.

3 Possibilistic Functional Dependencies

We summarize briefly the definition of the possibilistic model from [12].

Uncertain relations are modeled by assigning to each tuple some degree of possibility with which the tuple occurs in the relation. Formally, we have a *possibility scale*, or p-scale, that is, a strict linear order $\mathcal{S} = (S, <)$ with $k+1$ elements. We write $\mathcal{S} = \{\alpha_1, \ldots, \alpha_{k+1}\}$ to declare that $\alpha_1 > \cdots > \alpha_k > \alpha_{k+1}$. The elements $\alpha_i \in S$ are called *possibility degrees*, or p-degrees. Here, α_1 is reserved for tuples that are 'fully possible' while α_{k+1} is reserved for tuples that are 'impossible' to occur in a relation. Humans like to use simple scales in everyday life to communicate, compare, or rank. Here, the word "simple" means that items are classified qualitatively rather than quantitatively by putting precise values on them. Classical relations use two p-degrees, i.e., $k = 1$.

A *possibilistic relation schema* $(R, \mathcal{S})$, or p-relation schema, consists of a relation schema R and a p-scale $\mathcal{S}$. A *possibilistic relation*, or p-relation, over $(R, \mathcal{S})$ consists of a relation r over R, and a function $Poss$ that assigns to each tuple $t \in r$ a p-degree $Poss(t) \in \mathcal{S} - \{\alpha_{k+1}\}$. We sometimes omit $Poss$ when denoting a p-relation. Figure 1 shows a p-relation over $(\text{WEB}, \mathcal{S} = \{\alpha_1, \alpha_2, \alpha_3, \alpha_4, \alpha_5\})$, where WEB consists of the four attributes *Project, Time, Manager* and *Room*.

P-relations enjoy a possible world semantics. For $i = 1, \ldots, k$, let r_i consist of all tuples in r that have p-degree at least α_i, that is, $r_i = \{t \in r \mid Poss(t) \geq \alpha_i\}$. Indeed, we have $r_1 \subseteq r_2 \subseteq \cdots \subseteq r_k$. If $t \notin r_k$, then $Poss(t) = \alpha_{k+1}$. Every tuple that is 'fully possible' occurs in every possible world, and is therefore also 'fully certain'. Hence, relations are a special case of p-relations. Figure 2 shows the possible worlds $r_1 \subsetneq r_2 \subsetneq r_3 \subsetneq r_4$ of the p-relation of Fig. 1.

Similar to the scale $\mathcal{S}$ of p-degrees α_i for tuples, we use a scale $\mathcal{S}^T$ of certainty degrees β_j, or c-degrees, for FDs. Formally, the correspondence between p-degrees in $\mathcal{S}$ and the c-degrees in $\mathcal{S}^T$ is defined by the mapping $\alpha_i \mapsto \beta_{k+2-i}$ for $i = 1, \ldots, k+1$. Hence, the *marginal certainty* $c_r(\sigma)$ by which the FD $\sigma = X \to Y$ holds on the p-relation r is either the top degree β_1 if σ is satisfied by r_k, or the minimum amongst the c-degrees β_{k+2-i} that correspond to possible worlds r_i in which σ is violated, that is,

$$c_r(\sigma) = \begin{cases} \beta_1 & , \text{ if } \models_{r_k} \sigma \\ \min\{\beta_{k+2-i} \mid \not\models_{r_i} \sigma\} & , \text{ otherwise} \end{cases}.$$

We can now define the semantics of pFDs. Let $(R, \mathcal{S})$ denote a p-relation schema. A *possibilistic functional dependency* (pFD) over $(R, \mathcal{S})$ is an expression $(X \to Y, \beta)$ where $X \to Y$ denotes an FD over R and $\beta \in \mathcal{S}^T$. A p-relation $(r, Poss)$ over $(R, \mathcal{S})$ satisfies the pFD $(X \to Y, \beta)$ if and only if $c_r(X \to Y) \geq \beta$.

For example, the p-relation r from Fig. 1 satisfies the pFDs (σ_i, β_i) from Fig. 2 for $i = 1, \ldots, 4$. In fact, it is true for r that $c_r(\sigma_i) = \beta_i$ for $i = 1, \ldots, k$.

4　Possibilistic Armstrong Relations

We establish structural and computational properties of Armstrong p-relations for pFDs. In particular, we will first generalize Theorem 1 from classical FDs to pFDs, and then utilize the characterization to develop an algorithm that computes an Armstrong p-relation for any given set of pFDs. While the problem of finding an Armstrong p-relation remains precisely exponential in the input, our algorithm always produces an output of a size that is at most quadratic in that of a minimum-sized Armstrong p-relation for the input.

4.1　Structural Characterization

Similar to the elegant classical characterization of Theorem 1 we would like to have sufficient and necessary conditions to decide when a given p-relation is Armstrong for a given set of pFDs.

By definition, a p-relation $(r, Poss)$ over $(R, \{\alpha_1, \ldots, \alpha_{k+1}\})$ is Armstrong for the pFD set Σ if and only if for all $i = 1, \ldots, k$, and for all $X \rightarrow Y$ over R,

$(r, Poss)$ satisfies $(X \rightarrow Y, \beta_i)$ if and only if Σ implies $(X \rightarrow Y, \beta_i)$.

Now, the definition of satisfaction means that $(r, Poss)$ satisfies $(X \rightarrow Y, \beta_i)$ if and only if the world r_{k+1-i} satisfies the FD $X \rightarrow Y$. For $i = 1, \ldots, k$, and the pFD set Σ, the β_i-cut of Σ is the FD set $\Sigma_i = \{X \rightarrow Y \mid \exists j \leq i (X \rightarrow Y, \beta_j) \in \Sigma\}$. It has been shown that Σ implies the pFD $(X \rightarrow Y, \beta_i)$ if and only if the FD set Σ_i implies the FD $X \rightarrow Y$ [12].

Consequently, $(r, Poss)$ is Armstrong for Σ if and only if for all $i = 1, \ldots, k$, the world r_{k+1-i} is an Armstrong relation for the FD set Σ_i. Using the characterization from Theorem 1, we arrive at the following result.

Theorem 2. *Let Σ be a set of pFDs over p-relation schema $(R, \mathcal{S})$ with $|\mathcal{S}| = k + 1$. A p-relation $(r, Poss)$ over $(R, \mathcal{S})$ is Armstrong for Σ if and only if for all $i = 1, \ldots, k$, the world r_{k+1-i} is an Armstrong relation for the β_i-cut Σ_i of Σ. That is, if $max_{\Sigma_i}(R) \subseteq ag(r_{k+1-i}) \subseteq cl_{\Sigma_i}(R)$ holds for all $i = 1, \ldots, k$.* □

For our running example, we can verify with Theorem 2 that the p-relation in Fig. 1 is Armstrong for the pFD set Σ shown in Fig. 2. We have already seen that r_1 is an Armstrong relation for $\Sigma_4 = \{\sigma_1, \sigma_2, \sigma_3, \sigma_4\}$. The following table shows the maximal sets $max_{\Sigma_i}(A)$ for all $i = 1, \ldots, 4$. Instead of writing $max_{\Sigma_i}(A)$, we simply write $max_i(A)$ to ease notation, and we use the leading characters to denote our attributes.

A	$max_1(A)$	$max_2(A)$	$max_3(A)$	$max_4(A)$
Project	$\{MTR\}$	$\{MR, T\}$	$\{MR, T\}$	$\{MR, T\}$
Time	$\{MRP\}$	$\{MRP\}$	$\{MRP\}$	$\{MRP\}$
Manager	$\{PTR\}$	$\{PTR\}$	$\{PR, T\}$	$\{R, T\}$
Room	$\{MP, PT\}$	$\{MP, PT\}$	$\{MP, T\}$	$\{MP, T\}$

Knowing these maximal sets, we can verify by Theorem 2 that r_2 is Armstrong for $\Sigma_3 = \{\sigma_1, \sigma_2, \sigma_3\}$, r_3 is Armstrong for $\Sigma_2 = \{\sigma_1, \sigma_2\}$, and r_4 is Armstrong for $\Sigma_1 = \{\sigma_1\}$. Note that only the maximal sets in red font are realized by the relations. This is a consequence of the chain of possible worlds, since the maximal sets realized in some world are also realized in every world that contains it. In fact, the tuple in $r_2 - r_1$ realizes the maximal set PR for Σ_3 together with the previous tuple, the two tuples in $r_3 - r_2$ realize the maximal sets PTR and PT for Σ_2 together with their corresponding previous tuples, and the tuple in $r_4 - r_3$ realizes the maximal set MR for Σ_1.

4.2   Computational Characterization

We establish an algorithm that computes an Armstrong p-relation for any given set of pFDs. By Theorem 2 we compute the maximal set families $\{max_i(A)\}_{A \in R}$,

---

Algorithm 1. Armstrong p-relation

Require: Set Σ of pFDs over p-schema $(R, \{\beta_1, \ldots, \beta_k\})$
Ensure: Armstrong p-relation for Σ
1: $\Sigma_0 \leftarrow \emptyset$;
2: **for all** $A \in R$ **do** $\max_0(A) \leftarrow \{R - \{A\}\}$;▷ Maximal set families for empty FD set
3: **for** $i = 1$ to k **do** $\{\max_i(A)\}_{A \in R} \leftarrow \text{MAXFAM}(R, \Sigma_i - \Sigma_{i-1}, \{\max_{i-1}(A)\}_{A \in R})$
                                                      ▷ Max set families for next β-cut
4: **for all** $A \in R$ **do** $t_0(A) \leftarrow c_{A,0}$;   ▷ Initial tuple
5: $j \leftarrow 0$; $r \leftarrow \{t_0\}$; $Poss_r(t_0) = \alpha_1$; $\max(R) \leftarrow \emptyset$;   ▷ Some initializations
6: **for** $i = k$ downto 1 **do**
7:      $\max_i(R) \leftarrow \max_i(R) - \max(R)$ ▷ Remove already realized max sets
8:      **for all** $W \in \max_i(R)$ **do**   ▷ Realize next max set as agree set
9:          $j \leftarrow j + 1$;
10:         **for all** $A \in R$ **do**
11:             **if** $A \in W$ **then** $t_j(A) \leftarrow t_{j-1}(A)$;   ▷ t_j and t_{j-1} agree on A
12:             **else** $t_j(A) \leftarrow c_{A,j}$;   ▷ Unique value for t_j on A
13:         $Poss_r(t_j) \leftarrow \alpha_{k+1-i}$ ▷ t_j gets possibility α_{k+1-i}
14:         $r \leftarrow r \cup \{t_j\}$;
15:     $\max(R) \leftarrow \max(R) \cup \max_i(R)$ ▷ Mark elements from $\max_i(R)$ as realized
16: **return**(r);

---

and realize them with tuples of p-degrees α_{k+1-i}, for $i = 1, \ldots, k$. Algorithm 1 is a high-level description of this strategy.

We start with the maximal set families under the empty FD set in line (2). Since the β_i-cuts form a chain $\Sigma_1 \subseteq \Sigma_2 \cdots \subseteq \Sigma_k$ of classical FD sets, and the classical algorithm for computing maximal sets is iterative, we can compute the maximal set families $\{\max_i(A)\}_{A \in R}$ by refining the maximal set families $\{\max_{i-1}(A)\}_{A \in R}$ based on the "new" FDs in $\Sigma_i - \Sigma_{i-1}$. This is achieved by line (3). The call $\text{MAXFAM}(R, \Sigma_i - \Sigma_{i-1}, \{\max_{i-1}(A)\}_{A \in R})$ invokes the classical procedure [14], but fetches the maximal set families for each p-degree.

We then begin to realize the maximal sets as agree sets, starting with a base tuple of p-degree α_1 in lines (4, 5). The for-loop between lines (6) and (15) realizes the maximal sets from lower to higher c-degrees β_i (line 6) by inserting a single new tuple (line 14) for each unrealized maximal set, lines (7, 8). The new tuple has agree set with its predecessor tuple on the current maximal agree set, lines (8–12) and is assigned p-degree α_{k+1-i} in line (13). Line (15) marks the maximal set as realized.

As every maximal set $X \in max_i(R)$ is also closed under Σ_i [14], Theorem 2 shows that Algorithm 1 is correct.

Theorem 3. *On input* $((R, \{\beta_1, \ldots, \beta_k\}), \Sigma)$, *Algorithm 1 computes a p-relation that is Armstrong for* Σ. $\qquad\qquad\qquad\qquad\qquad\qquad\qquad\qquad\square$

If we apply Algorithm 1 to our p-relation schema $(\text{WEB}, \{\alpha_1, \ldots, \alpha_5\})$ and the pFD set Σ from Fig. 2, it will compute an Armstrong p-relation such as the one shown in Fig. 1, up to renaming.

4.3   Complexity Results

We recall what we mean by precisely exponential [3]. Firstly, it means that there is an algorithm for computing an Armstrong p-relation, given a set Σ of pFDs, where the running time of the algorithm is exponential in Σ. Secondly, it means that there is a set Σ of pFDs in which the number of tuples in each minimum-sized Armstrong p-relation for Σ is exponential - thus, an exponential amount of time is required in this case simply to write down the p-relation. The exponential lower bound is retained from the special case where $k = 1$, and the input family would be $exp_n := ((R_n = \{A_1, \ldots, A_{2n}, B\}, \{\alpha_1, \alpha_2\}), \Sigma_n^{exp})$ where $\Sigma_n^{exp} := \bigcup_{i=1}^{n} \{\{(A_{2i-1}, A_{2i}\} \to B, \beta_1)\}$. The upper bound follows immediately from the fact that we are able to apply the classical exponential-time algorithm for the maximal set computation.

Theorem 4. *The complexity of finding an Armstrong p-relation, given a set Σ of pFDs, is precisely exponential in Σ.*   □

The case exp_n shows a negative extreme case in which the number of tuples in the output is exponential in the input size. However, there are also positive extreme cases in which the number of tuples in the output is logarithmic in the input size. Such a case is given by $log_n := ((R_n, \{\alpha_1, \alpha_2\}), \Sigma_n^{log})$ where $\Sigma_n^{log} := \bigcup_{i=1}^{n} \{(\{X_1, \ldots, X_n\} \to B, \beta_1) \mid \forall i = 1, \ldots, n, X_i \in \{A_{2i-1}, A_{2i}\}\}$.

Despite the worst-case exponential time complexity, our algorithm makes conservative use of resources. An Armstrong p-relation for Σ is minimum-sized if there is no Armstrong p-relation for Σ with a fewer number of tuples. Let $max_\Sigma(R)$ denote the maximal sets that need to be realized in any Armstrong p-relation r for a pFD set Σ. Due to Theorem 2 it follows that $|max_\Sigma(R)|$ is bounded by $|ag(r) = ag(r_k)|$, and that $|ag(r)|$ is bounded by $\binom{|r|}{2}$. From $|ag(r)| \leq \binom{|r|}{2}$ follows that $\sqrt{(1 + 8 \cdot |max_\Sigma(R)|)/2} \leq |r|$, and Algorithm 1 shows that $|r = r_k| \leq |max_\Sigma(R)| + 1$. If the size of a p-relation is the number of its tuples, we thus obtain the following result.

Theorem 5. *Algorithm 1 returns an Armstrong p-relation for Σ whose size is at most quadratic in that of a minimum-sized Armstrong p-relation for Σ.*   □

5   The Tool

We have transferred our findings into a prototype implementation[1] that design teams can use to compute Armstrong p-relations for any given set of pFDs. Figure 3 shows the graphical user interface for the tool. Users can declare the input in the form of an attribute set, and choose whether they want to compute a classical or a possibilistic Armstrong database. In the former case, they can simply enter an FD set. In the latter case, they can define how many p-degrees

---

[1] https://www.dropbox.com/s/fciy01597tgxnfu/Possibilistic-Armstrong-Calculator.exe.

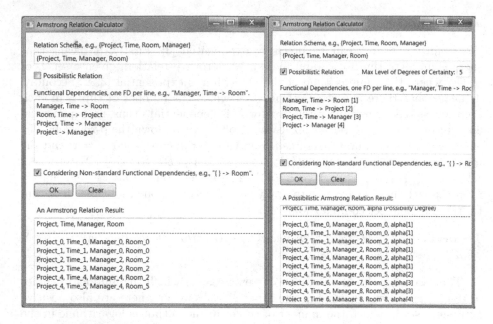

Fig. 3. GUI for classical and possibilistic case of running example

are available, i.e., specify k, and then enter a pFD set. Finally, users can choose whether to consider non-standard (p)FDs, whose left-hand attribute set is empty. The screenshots in Fig. 3 show the GUI for our running example (right), and for the running example after "forgetting" the possibilistic information (left).

6   Experiments

We report on some experiments that illustrate the extreme cases exp_n and log_n, as well as the average case performance of Algorithm 1.

Extreme Cases. Figures 4 and 5 illustrate the experiments for the extreme cases of exponential and logarithmic output size, respectively. It shows, in particular, that even under extreme circumstances the algorithm performs well. For example, Fig. 4 shows that even an Armstrong p-relation with 65,000 tuples can be computed in less than 90 s, while Fig. 5 shows that even with huge input sizes, the algorithm still returns a result within 2hrs. However, applying the algorithm to instances of exp_n beyond $n = 25$ is not feasible.

Average Cases. We studied average behavior by applying Algorithm 1 to random input. For each fixed number $n = 5, \ldots, 15$ of attributes, and each fixed number $k = 1, \ldots, 10$ of c-degrees, we generated 250 input sets Σ, each of which had between n and $n^2/2$ pFDs with three attributes on average, and a randomly assigned p-degree between 1 and k. With n and k as the x- and y-axes, respectively, the z-axis was then either the average number of tuples in the output, or the time it took to compute it.

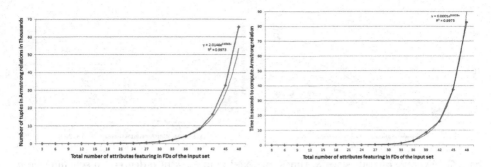

Fig. 4. Output sizes & times for exponential case

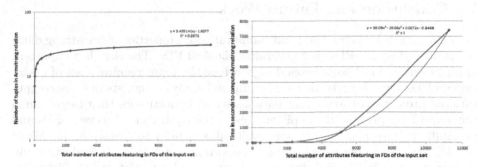

Fig. 5. Output sizes & times for logarithmic case

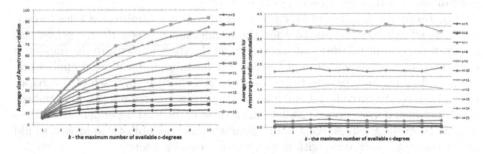

Fig. 6. Average output sizes & times for fixed schema sizes n in number k of p-degrees

Figure 6 shows the average output size and time in the number k of p-degrees, parameterized by the schema size n. For fixed n, there is logarithmic growth of the output size and constant time in k. The size growth results from a significant number of maximal sets being realized by a small k. The computation time is agnostic to k because each FD is visited once, irrespective of its p-degree.

Figure 7 shows the average output size and time in the schema size n, parameterized by k. For fixed k, the output size and times are both low-degree polynomial in n. Extreme cases are therefore considered to be the exception.

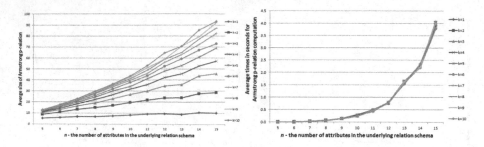

Fig. 7. Average output sizes & times for fixed number k of p-degrees in schema size n

7   Conclusion and Future Work

We have established structural and computational properties of Armstrong data-bases for a class of pFDs that generalize classical FDs. The class has important applications in database schema design, where the input requires a set of mean-ingful pFDs. Our theoretical and experimental analysis suggests that the compu-tational properties of Armstrong databases are supportive for their target use in the acquisition process of the pFDs. Due to the equivalence between pFDs and possibilistic Horn clauses [12], our results also transfer to Armstrong models of possibilistic Horn clauses, which have important applications in abductive and deductive reasoning, knowledge approximation and compilation [20]. Note that the results of this article have been extended to the combined class of pFDs and possibilistic cardinality constraints [19].

For future work it would be interesting to conduct empirical studies to con-firm the effectiveness of our tool for the acquisition process. Here, we may use our tool to compute Armstrong databases on the fly, and measure the impact of their use on recognizing those pFDs that are meaningful for a given application domain. It is also interesting to combine the possibilistic approach of this paper with the recently introduced embedded uniqueness constraints [24] and embed-ded functional dependencies [23,25]. Since these embedded dependencies address data with missing values, combining them with our possibilistic approach would mean that uncertain data with missing values can be addressed.

References

1. Arenas, M.: Normalization theory for XML. SIGMOD Rec. **35**(4), 57–64 (2006)
2. Balamuralikrishna, N., Jiang, Y., Koehler, H., Leck, U., Link, S., Prade, H.: Pos-sibilistic keys. Fuzzy Sets Syst. **376**, 1–36 (2019)
3. Beeri, C., Dowd, M., Fagin, R., Statman, R.: On the structure of Armstrong rela-tions for functional dependencies. J. ACM **31**(1), 30–46 (1984)
4. Brown, P., Link, S.: Probabilistic keys. IEEE Trans. Knowl. Data Eng. **29**(3), 670–682 (2017)
5. Calì, A., Calvanese, D., Lenzerini, M.: Data integration under integrity constraints. In: Seminal Contributions to Information Systems Engineering, 25 Years of CAiSE, pp. 335–352 (2013)

6. Codd, E.F.: A relational model of data for large shared data banks. Commun. ACM **13**(6), 377–387 (1970)
7. Dubois, D., Prade, H.: Possibility theory and its applications: where do we stand? In: Kacprzyk, J., Pedrycz, W. (eds.) Springer Handbook of Computational Intelligence, pp. 31–60. Springer, Heidelberg (2015). https://doi.org/10.1007/978-3-662-43505-2_3
8. Fagin, R.: Horn clauses and database dependencies. J. ACM **29**(4), 952–985 (1982)
9. Johnson, D.S., Klug, A.C.: Testing containment of conjunctive queries under functional and inclusion dependencies. J. Comput. Syst. Sci. **28**(1), 167–189 (1984)
10. Köhler, H., Link, S.: SQL schema design: foundations, normal forms, and normalization. Inf. Syst. **76**, 88–113 (2018)
11. Langeveldt, W.D., Link, S.: Empirical evidence for the usefulness of Armstrong relations in the acquisition of meaningful functional dependencies. Inf. Syst. **35**(3), 352–374 (2010)
12. Link, S., Prade, H.: Possibilistic functional dependencies and their relationship to possibility theory. IEEE Trans. Fuzzy Syst. **24**, 1–7 (2016)
13. Link, S., Prade, H.: Relational database schema design for uncertain data. Inf. Syst. **84**, 88–110 (2019)
14. Mannila, H., Räihä, K.J.: Design by example: an application of Armstrong relations. J. Comput. Syst. Sci. **33**(2), 126–141 (1986)
15. Marnette, B., Mecca, G., Papotti, P.: Scalable data exchange with functional dependencies. Proc. VLDB Endow. **3**(1), 105–116 (2010)
16. Prokoshyna, N., Szlichta, J., Chiang, F., Miller, R.J., Srivastava, D.: Combining quantitative and logical data cleaning. Proc. VLDB Endow. **9**(4), 300–311 (2015)
17. Ram, S.: Deriving functional dependencies from the entity-relationship model. Commun. ACM **38**(9), 95–107 (1995)
18. Roblot, T., Hannula, M., Link, S.: Probabilistic cardinality constraints - validation, reasoning, and semantic summaries. VLDB J. **27**(6), 771–795 (2018)
19. Roblot, T., Link, S.: Cardinality constraints and functional dependencies over possibilistic data. Data Knowl. Eng. **117**, 339–358 (2018)
20. Selman, B., Kautz, H.A.: Knowledge compilation and theory approximation. J. ACM **43**(2), 193–224 (1996)
21. Tan, H.B.K., Zhao, Y.: Automated elicitation of functional dependencies from source codes of database transactions. Inf. Software Technol. **46**(2), 109–117 (2004)
22. Vincent, M.: Semantic foundations of 4NF in relational database design. Acta Inf. **36**(3), 173–213 (1999)
23. Wei, Z., Hartmann, S., Link, S.: Discovery algorithms for embedded functional dependencies. In: Maier, D., Pottinger, R., Doan, A., Tan, W., Alawini, A., Ngo, H.Q. (eds.) Proceedings of the 2020 International Conference on Management of Data, SIGMOD Conference 2020, Online Conference [Portland, OR, USA], June 14–19, 2020. pp. 833–843. ACM (2020)
24. Wei, Z., Leck, U., Link, S.: Discovery and ranking of embedded uniqueness constraints. Proc. VLDB Endow. **12**(13), 2339–2352 (2019)
25. Wei, Z., Link, S.: Embedded functional dependencies and data-completeness tailored database design. Proc. VLDB Endow. **12**(11), 1458–1470 (2019)

Trust-Aware Curation of Linked Open Data Logs

Dihia Lanasri[1]([✉])(ID), Selma Khouri[1](ID), and Ladjel Bellatreche[2](ID)

[1] ESI, Algiers, Algeria
{ad_lanasri,s_khouri}@esi.dz
[2] LIAS/ISAE-ENSMA, Poitiers, France
bellatreche@ensma.fr

Abstract. Trust was widely discussed and formalized in the literature. In the context of Big Data and Connected World, it becomes crucial for developing data-driven solutions. Trusted data increase the quality of decision support systems. Recently, companies are racing towards Linked Open Data (LOD) and Knowledge Bases (KB) to improve their added value, but ignore their SPARQL query-logs. If well cured, these logs can present an asset for analysts. A naive and direct use of these logs is too risky because their provenance and quality are highly questionable. Users of these logs in a trusted way have to be assisted by providing them with in-depth knowledge of the whole LOD environment and tools to cure these logs. In this paper, we propose an ontology-based model inspired by the recent developments in $< trust, risk, value >$-ontology engineering. Then, a trust-aware curation approach is presented, composed of enriched ETL-like operators integrating trust metrics that keep only trustworthy queries. Finally, experiments are conducted to study the effectiveness and efficiency of our proposal.

Keywords: Trust · Risk · Linked open data logs · Data curation

1 Introduction

LOD/KB become a key source for different companies, organizations, and governments to create knowledge and increase the added value. Beneficial exploitation of this data is not an easy task because it requires an understanding of the LOD ecosystem composed mainly of *data-sets* in RDF format and *query-logs*[1] collected from SPARQL endpoints and published by some initiatives like LSQ[2].

Recently, the complexity of LOD/KB sources encourages the exploitation of their query-logs in decision support systems for different purposes such as statistical analysis [8] and multidimensional models exploration [19]. However, these sources are sometimes published by less credible providers who may provide inaccurate data. This fact makes their use more risky. Consequently, using LOD/KB

---

[1] For simplicity, we use query-logs to refer to LOD query-logs.
[2] https://aksw.github.io/LSQ/.

© Springer Nature Switzerland AG 2020
G. Dobbie et al. (Eds.): ER 2020, LNCS 12400, pp. 604–614, 2020.
https://doi.org/10.1007/978-3-030-62522-1_44

data, especially the LOD query-logs, has to be controlled by integrating the trust dimension.

Trust has been studied in many fields like psychology, economy, social networks, and so on. A reference definition of Trust is provided by [15]: "Trust is the subjective probability with which an agent expects that another agent or group of agents will perform a particular action on which its welfare depends" [3]. Trust is a complex concept linked to other crucial concepts such as <u>risk</u> [3], <u>quality</u> [10], <u>provenance</u> [25] and value [23]. The importance of trust and its surrounding concepts motivates the ontology engineering community to propose reference ontologies covering the triplet $< Risk, Value, Trust >$. These ontologies have been published in ER'2018 [23], and CoopIS'2019 [3]. *These findings represent a great opportunity for the LOD community to either ensure an a priori integration of trust into both their datasets and query-logs or a posteriori annotation by trust degrees.*

By examining the literature, we find that several LOD/KB integrate the trust in the construction level. This gives rise to uncertain LOD/KB [12] such as YAGO, NELL, and Knowledge Vault. The Web of data is missing a uniform way to assess trustworthiness of information which could affect knowledge bases [17]. This augments the risk of exploiting such data and their query-logs. To deal with the trust requirement in uncertain LOD/KB, some studies extending the RDF model were proposed to annotate triples by a trust value and query them with tSparql(trust-aware SPARQL) language [17].

However, even if the LOD triples are annotated with a level of trust, their query-logs may contain many issues that can affect their trustworthiness because they are provided by unknown users or agents, who may have malicious intentions. Moreover, the expertise level of providers may affect strongly the quality of these queries. All these issues make the direct exploitation of these query-logs risky. In this context, trust is an imperative requirement to be considered and query-logs have to be carefully <u>curated</u> before using them by decision-support systems.

In traditional warehouses, the Extract-Transform-Load (ETL) mechanism is responsible for achieving the curation of data by filtering, transforming, and cleaning undesired data. In contemporary data-driven decision support systems using published data such as crowdsourcing [14] and review analysis, data curation infrastructures play a key role in data preparation by leveraging traditional ETL operators and considering other related to the trust. In this paper, we adopt the same vision by considering the adaptation of ETL operators for the curation of query-logs by considering the trust aspects related to their structure, quality, and provenance. We achieve this task using modeling and meta-modeling efforts.

In this paper, we propose an ontology-based Meta-Model, based on the reference trust ontology [3], to formalize the definition of Trust in LOD query-logs, explicit the main dimensions of risks affecting their trust and define the actions to be executed to ensure trust. Based on this meta-model, a trust-based data curation approach for LOD query-logs is described. A profiling technique is used to understand the structures of these logs and to identify their quality and provenance. This technique is followed by the definition of ETL-Like operators adapted to the trust context.

This paper is organized as follows: Sect. 2 describes our related work. Section 3 presents in detail our approach. Section 4 reviews our experiments. Section 5 concludes the paper.

2   Related Work

1- Trust in Data Field. In our context, we relate trust to: **i) Trust in *LOD* datasets:** Some studies proposed systems for analyzing trust in *LOD* data sources [16] and estimate the trustworthiness of their data [13]. [11] defined an adapted RDF algebra for semantic web sources to identify their provider and data trustworthiness. *tSPARQL*, a trust-aware SPARQL is used for trust weighted RDF graphs where every triple is associated with a trust value [17]. When trust is related to quality [10], many approaches [22] and measures [6] are defined to evaluate *LOD* quality. **ii) Trust in *LOD* query-logs:** A couple of research dealt with SPARQL logs by statistically analyzing their structure, for: (a) detecting *robotic* and *organic* queries [21]; (b) analyzing their graphic representation [7,8]; and (c) improving source selection by keeping only those that respond to a given request using Query Log Mining model [26].

2- Data Curation Solutions. In the big data era, many challenges faced data quality and provenance, which required different curating solutions [9]. Consequently, many data curation services [4,5], ETL-like [20] tools were proposed.

The absence of works expliciting the concept of trust and defining trust-aware curation approach in the context of LOD query-logs motivates our proposal.

3   Trust-Aware Curation Approach for *LOD* Query-Logs

To formalize our curation problem, we consider a set of query logs $SL = \{QL_1, QL_2, \ldots QL_m\}$ extracted from various SPARQL endpoints. Each query log QL is associated with a provenance denoted by *prov* (e.g., a log from DBpedia). QL is a set of SPARQL (trusted and untrusted) queries $QL = \{Q_1, Q_2, \ldots Q_k\}$, where Q is a SPARQL query. A BGP (Basic graph pattern) is the main part of the query. It is a set of triple patterns <S P O> containing query variables at the subject(S), predicate(P), or object(O) position.

The **objective** of our study is to curate the *LOD* query logs and identify trusted queries that can be used for decision support systems. This requires: (i) a definition of ETL operators based on the profiling of queries and (ii) a proposition of an ETL-log pipeline orchestrating the ETL operators.

As **Output**, we will have for each query log QL: (i) a set of *curated queries* $CQ = TrustQ \cup UTrustQ$ where $(TrustQ)$ is trusted queries, while $(UTrustQ)$ is untrusted rejected queries. A curated query is a query Q parsed by trust-aware ETL operators and annotated by a TrustDegree value.

$$\textbf{TrustDegree} = \begin{cases} Boolean\ value: \ 0 \ \Leftrightarrow \ Q \in UTrustQ \ ; 1 \ \Leftrightarrow \ Q \in TrustQ \\ Categorical\ value \end{cases}$$

The categorical value is an additional annotation that depends on the operator. For example, the operator 'Expertise filter' evaluates the expertise level (expert; intermediate; beginner) of the query. The analyst can consider only expert queries as trusted. And (ii) *Rate of Trust*: at the end of each curation operation, we compute the global trust rate for each source SL as follows:

$$\textbf{RateOfTrust} = \frac{QL - ||TrustQ||}{QL}$$

where QL and $||TrustQ||$ represent respectively the number of all queries extracted from the logs of the source SL, and the number of trusted queries.

3.1   Meta-Model of Trust for *LOD* Query-Logs

In their Reference Ontology of Trust, Amaral et al. [3] state that the conceptualization of trust should refer to (i) agents and their goals; (ii) agents' beliefs; (iii) possibly executable actions of a given type; and (iv) risk.

We consider this ontology as a foundation for defining our trust meta-model related to LOD query-logs sources. In the proposed reference ontology of [3], *Trust* is modeled as a complex mental state of a *Trustor* agent, composed of a set of *Beliefs* about a *Trustee* and her *behavior*. Trust is about an Intention of the Trustor (a cognitive agent) regarding a goal, for the achievement of which she counts upon the Trustee. Figure 1(c) illustrates the fragment of their ontology that we used in our meta-model. Based on this definition, in our context, the Trustor is the data analyst who wants to exploit the LOD sources and the Trustee is the LOD environment (we focus on the query-logs component of LOD, Fig. 1(b)).

Trust is a complex model composed of a set of *Beliefs* that inheres in the Trustor. These beliefs include:(i) the Belief that the Trustee has the capability to perform the desired action (Capability Belief); and (ii) the belief that the Trustee's Vulnerabilities will not prevent him from performing the desired action (Vulnerability Belief). Vulnerability is manifested by risk events [3].

In our context, the *CapabilityBelief* entity is related to the set of queries generated in the logs, and the *VulnerabilityBelief* entity is related to two sources of risks: Veracity issues and Quality issues. *TrustDegree* represents the quantitative perspective of trust in the proposed Ontology. In our context, the *TrustDegree* is the *RateOfTrust* of the logs which is based on the TrustDegree of the queries (following last formula in *cf.* Sect. 3). In our experiments, each risk dimension is detailed in next section, and an ETL operator will be defined as a curation action for each risk (Fig. 1(a)).

3.2   Trust-Aware Log Profiling and ETL for *LOD* Logs

In order to analyze the trust of *LOD* logs and identify their risks, we propose a profiling approach inspired from data profiling field [1]. We propose to adapt and extend their classification to *LOD* logs. As defined in our meta-model, two main dimensions of risk are identified:

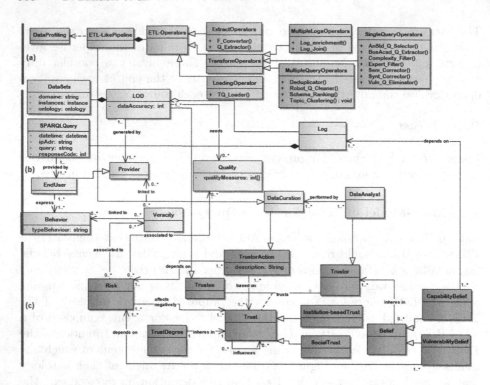

Fig. 1. Meta-Model of trust for *LOD*. (a) Our Meta-Model for data curation. (b) Our Trust Meta-Model for LOD Logs. (c) Meta-Model of trust extracted from [3]

Logs Veracity Analysis. In order to encourage analysts to trust external *LOD* logs, their veracity (provenance) should be deeply analyzed: **1. Provenance analysis:** verifies these two aspects: *a) Provenance of logs:* checks the credibility of log provider. *b) Provenance of queries:* identifies information linked to the agent providing the query by analyzing query's metadata. Users writing queries may have good intentions like learning SPARQL, exploring *LOD* sources. They may be experts or beginners, but they could sometimes have bad intentions. To identify risky ones: i) *Trusted or vulnerable provider* detects malicious IPs, ii) *Provenance profiling* identifies the Expertise level of users writing the queries and the Provenance organisms (company, academic institution or private user). However, IP address is not sufficient to discover user's profile. Consequently, **2. Behavior analysis** is proposed to identify organic and bot malicious queries.

Log Quality Analysis. When trust is related to quality [10], three types of analysis are distinguished: **1- Single query analysis:** queries are analyzed one by one to detect: a) *Syntactic errors*; b) *Semantic errors* c) *Query type:* analytic or standard queries and d) *Query complexity:* Complex queries indicate generally an expert profile behind, which is more trusted. **2- analysis of queries interactions:** the interactions between queries help to understand their behavior. This consists to detect a) *Duplicate queries*, b) *Schema overlap* and c) *Topic overlap:* to get an idea about the main domains of interest in a LOD log. **3-Analysis of logs interactions.** the interaction between LOD logs of different sources is considered to identify: a) *Semantic overlap* and b) *Sources overlap*.

In what follows, we consider each risk dimension discussed and we propose an ETL operator that curates queries according to this dimension. Some proposed operators are adapted from traditional ETL [24] and new ones specific to our context are introduced. They can be orchestrated to form an ETL-pipeline to be used as a service by analysts. We define three main categories of operators (Extract-Transform and Load) as illustrated in our meta-model(Fig. 1(a)), and we detail each operator by providing its signature and semantic.

Extract Operators: used for extracting queries and their metadata from logs.

- *Query extractor:* $(Q\_Extractor(QL) : Queries)$ reads each raw log file line by line where each line represents a SPARQL query with its metadata. It may also carry POST/GET queries. To get value from LOD logs, we focus on SPARQL queries of type "select and construct" that represent an analytic purpose. This operator extracts query metadata: *IP address, execution dateTime* and *response code.*
- *Format converter*$(F\_Converter(Queries,' UTF - 8') : Queries)$: queries contain special characters (like blank represented by "%20"). This operator parses each extracted query using 'UTF-8' decoder for human-readable format.

Transformation Operators: organized into three main categories (Fig. 1(a)):

- *Business/Academic query extractor* $(BusAcad\_Q\_Extractor(Queries, Type) : (TrustQ, UTrustQ, RateOfTrust))$: Based on the IP address of each SPARQL query, WHOSIP API is used to get details about each IP address like: *issuer* (company, university or private user), location, etc. This allows classifying business queries and academic ones. The analyst can decide what to consider according to her goals.
- *Vulnerable query eliminator* $(Vuln\_Q\_Eliminator(Queries) : (TrustQ, UTrustQ, RateOfTrust))$: It deletes the queries coming from untrusted provider with bad intention. To eliminate vulnerable IPs, a provided database of blacklisted IPs[3] is used, which contains more than 30 publicly updated lists of malicious IPs.
- *Complexity filter* $(Complexity\_Filter(Queries, shape, depth) : (TrustQ, UTrustQ, RateOfTrust))$: defines the complexity of queries basing on their depth and shape (star, flower,...) using [7] classification and data analysts decide what to keep.
- *Syntactic corrector* $(Synt\_Corrector(Queries, REGEX) : (TrustQ, UTrustQ, Rate OfTrust))$: Syntactically wrong queries have Response code $\in$ (4xx, 5xx). Regular expressions $(REGEX)$ are used to correct wrong queries respecting the SPARQL1.1 syntax. Some curation actions are: (i) Add declared variables in the BGP into the SELECT clause; (ii) Put declared variables between parenthesis '()', and (iii) Add missed prefixes using a predefined list of prefixes[4].

---

[3] https://github.com/stamparm/ipsum.

[4] http://www.scholarlydata.org/ontology/doc/alignments/.

– *Semantic corrector* (*Sem_Corrector(Queries, LOD_DS)* : (*TrustQ, UTrustQ, RateOfTrust*)): successful queries (Response code = 200) with empty result may be semantically wrong. Wrong data type is an example of these errors. In the statement: *(?x :age 'Peter')*, 'age' cannot be a string. Based on the *LOD* ontology, the algorithm proposed in [2] is used to fix semantic errors.

– *Analytic/standard query selector* (*AnStd_Q_Selector(Queries, Type)* : (*TrustQ, UTrustQ, RateOfTrust*)): Data analyst may decide to select one *Type* of queries. Standard queries are construct or select queries without aggregate functions (*Sum, Count, Avg, Min, Max*) contrary to Analytic ones [18] containing them.

– *Robot query cleaner* (*Robot_Q_Cleaner(Queries)* : (*TrustQ, UTrustQ, RateOfTrust*)): Each group of queries with the same IP address is studied at once time. According to our tests, if an important number of queries (Queries Number > 100) is executed in a small lapse of time (Execution Time < 10 s) and their execution succeeds, a malicious behavior is suspected and they could falsify the decisions. This operator deletes the robot queries and keeps only organic ones.

– *Expertise filter* (*Expert_Filter(Queries, ExpertLevels)* : (*TrustQ, UTrustQ, RateOfTrust*)): it identifies approximately if a query is written by an expert, intermediate or beginner user. For each set of queries grouped by user session (same IP during 30 min) and based on the results of complexity analysis of each query, the operator analyzes the behavior of the user to enhance her query. If complex [5] queries with few attempts (<5 attempts) the profile can be about an expert. If many attempts (>10 attempts) and simple [6] queries, it may be a beginner. Otherwise, it can be an intermediate. The analyst can decide what to consider.

– *Deduplicator* (*Deduplicator(Queries)* : (*TrustQ, UTrustQ, RateOfTrust*)): deletes all blanks in queries and detects similar queries. Duplicate queries are rejected.

– *Topic clustering* (*Topic_Clustering(Queries, Topics)* : (< *TrustQ, Topic* > , *RateOfTrust*)): It detects the topic of each query based on the *LOD* ontology. Each main superclass (*SupCl*) of the ontology is associated manually to a topic (t_x). Then, for each query (*Q*), the operator identifies the *SupCl* of its prefixes and triples' URIs, by executing the query *(select SupCl where URI rdfs:subClassOf SupCl)*. The output of the operator is a set of groups of queries {$Group_x$:< Q, t_x >}, each group assigns a set of queries *Q* to a topic t_x.

– *Schema ranking* (*Schema_Ranking(Group_x* < Q, t_x >) : (*TrustQ, UTrustQ, RateOfTrust*)): For each group $Group_x$ < Q, t_x >, the operator finds the similarities between queries' graph patterns (*BGP*). The operator starts by sorting queries by depth ($depth(Q_1) < \cdots < depth(Q_m) < depth(Q_m)$) where $depth(Q_x)$ is the number of distinct Triples in a BGP. If $Triples(Q_m) \subseteq Triples(Q_n)$, Q_m will be discarded because it does not provide any added value.

– *Logs join*(*Log_Join({TL})* : (*JL, RateOfTrust*)): It allows integrating many logs according to their semantic similarities. Let's assume TL_1, TL_2 are curated

---

[5] Complex query: query with complex shapes like Forrest, Bouquet and depth > 7.
[6] Simple query: query with simple/ chain shapes and depth <3.

logs, both have a set of topics, $Topics_1 = \{t1, ..., tn\}$ and $Topics_2 = \{t1, ..., tm\}$. Based on entity matching(scify) and semantic similarities(ws4j), the operator identifies st where st is set of semantically similar topics of $Topics_1$ and $Topics_2$. Joining logs returns new log $JL = \{Q_j\}$ where $topic(Q_j) \in st$ and $Q_j \in (TL_1 \cup TL_2)$.

- *Logs enrichment*$(Log\_enrichment(QL_x; QL_y) : (QL_x, RateOfTrust))$: log QL_x contains queries executed in order to query its associated LOD source DS_x. However, it often happens that QL_x contains some queries that use other LOD sources DS_y. E.g. in scholarly data log, we can find queries executed against DBpedia knowledge base. This operator annotates each query of QL_y with its KB source based on its Prefixes and URIs. Then, it moves queries with DS_x annotation into QL_x.

Loader Operator: - *Trusted query loader*$(TQ\_Loader(queries, Target) : void)$: loads the curated trusted queries generated from previous steps into a database/file.

4   Experiments and Results

Our motivation for the experiments is guided by a real application of a leading company in the field of Home appliances. Its R&D division; in collaboration with some universities wants to analyze the impact of the *relationships between companies and research institutions to highlight common interests*. This analysis can be performed by using relevant internal sources and external ones (e.g., DBpedia, Scholarly Data). An analysis of LOD data by an analyst is a very tedious task due to the complex connections between these data. A strategy inspired by *Query-By-Example* principle, widely developed in relational databases, is adopted in which our analyst first explores the LOD query-logs. Direct use of these logs represents a serious risk, and a curation approach has to be executed. Our experiments are performed on the scholarly data and DBpedia logs. Our solution is developed with JAVA, Scala and JENA for SPARQL data.

Scholarly data (SChD) log contains 5.499.797 queries (SPARQL and GET/SET queries) and DBpedia (Dbp) log contains 3.193.672 SPARQL queries. In order to improve the trust of SPARQL logs and extract accurate results, we execute our trust-aware curation approach on these logs. The process starts by executing the proposed log profiling techniques. We propose the Trust-aware ETL pipeline (T-ETL) that orchestrates the ETL operators proposed in *cf.* Sect. 3.1 in the same order illustrated in Fig. 2. To evaluate the effectiveness of our approach, we use the metrics proposed in Sect. 3. The pipeline starts by extracting <u>select and construct</u> queries than reformat them. The T-ETL process detects 139.932 select and construct queries among the whole scholarly data log and 6.680 in DBpedia (we filtered queries related to research topic). Figure 2 summarizes the obtained results after each step of T-ETL.

As shown in Fig. 2(a), the number of risky queries declines after each step of the T-ETL pipeline to reach at the end *515 accurate queries for SChD* and *192 for Dbp*. An important number of queries (79% = 111.240 SChD, 43% = 3.790

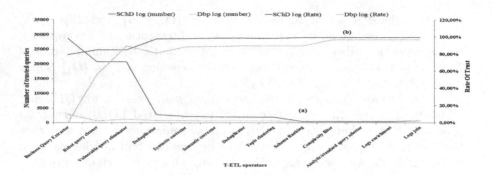

Fig. 2. Experiments' results (a) Number of trusted queries (b) Rate of Trust

Dbp) is executed from universities which *may reflect the intention of students or teachers to learn SPARQL.* According to our motivating example, academic queries may interest the analyst. If she is only interested by business context, she will keep the business queries (21% = 28.692 SChD, 57% = 2.890 Dbp).

Among more enhancement, the T-ETL discards all robot queries representing (27% = 7.911(SChD), 56% = 1.633 (Dbp)) from business queries. They are launched from private IP addresses and from companies. The analysis of the users' behavior shows that we can keep 20.781 (SChD) and 1.257 (Dbp) organic queries. A small number of vulnerable IPs (21 IPs) based on the blacklisted IPs(stamparm/ipsum) is detected, which leaves 20.724 (SChD) and 1.245 (Dbp) of invulnerable queries. After that, T-ETL starts the deduplication and keeps 2.810 (SChD), 751 (Dbp) of unique queries. Then, it corrects them syntactically and semantically to get the best quality and gain the confidence of the analyst. 2.008 (SChD), 698 (Dbp) of correct queries are obtained. The most topics tackled in the treated queries are agent, academic events, documents, etc. The last operation consists to enrich the two obtained logs where we found just 6 queries of scholarly data in DBpedia, then we move them to SChD log. The execution of topic clustering and then schema ranking (which eliminates queries included in other queries) reduces the number of total queries into 515 (SChD) and 192 (Dbp) reflecting the most trusted and interesting ones among the whole logs.

Then, the complexity-filter operator shows that most queries are either simple or with a star shape indicating an intermediate users behind. Most probably, a large part of complex forest and tree queries are written by experts(11,65%) or intermediate users(73,6%). Most queries written by beginner users(14,75%)are simple or with chain shape. Most of queries are 'standard' (98,83%) while few ones (1,17%) are 'analytic'. The last step consists to join these two logs based on semantic similarities of their topics, this gives a total number of 623 queries.

In Fig. 2(a), the number of queries declines keeping more trusted ones after each operation of the T-ETL, implying the enhancement of the confidence rate after each step of the trust-based ETL process. The graph in Fig. 2(b) indicates that this metric is improved from 79% to achieve 99% (SChD) and from 56% to 97% (Dbp). There is an inverse relationship between these two metrics.

5 Conclusion

Today, Many companies turned to *LOD* logs which are a real worth. However, these logs suffer from many risks due to the users behind which are of different profiles and with plenty of intentions. In this paper, we proposed an ontology-based Meta-model to conceptualize the concept of trust in *LOD* environment. Then, we detailed a trust-based data curation approach to discard the vulnerabilities present in LOD logs remaining to keep queries from trusted provenance with high quality. The experiments conducted on DBpedia and scholarly data show that our approach participates strongly in keeping just queries with the best quality from a credible issuer. Currently, we are developing a curation suite tool supporting our proposal. Another issue that needs more attention is the integration of AI techniques to assign trust to query logs (learned trust).

Acknowledgements. We would like to thank Prof. Giancarlo Guizzardi for his valuable comments on risk, value, and trust ontologies.

References

1. Abedjan, Z., Golab, L., Naumann, F.: Data profiling: a tutorial. In: ICDE, pp. 1747–1751 (2017)
2. Almendros Jiménez, J.M., Becerra Terón, A., Cuzzocrea, A.M.: Detecting and diagnosing syntactic and semantic errors in SPARQL queries. In: EDBT/ICDT Workshops (2017)
3. Amaral, G., Sales, T.P., Guizzardi, G., Porello, D.: Towards a reference ontology of trust. In: OTM Conferences, pp. 3–21 (2019)
4. Beheshti, A., Benatallah, B., Nouri, R., Tabebordbar, A.: CoreKG: a knowledge lake service. Proc. VLDB Endow. **11**(12), 1942–1945 (2018)
5. Beheshti, A., Benatallah, B., Tabebordbar, A., Motahari-Nezhad, H.R., Barukh, M.C., Nouri, R.: DataSynapse: a social data curation foundry. Distrib. Parallel Databases **37**(3), 351–384 (2019)
6. Behkamal, B., Kahani, M., Bagheri, E.: Quality metrics for linked open data. In: DEXA, pp. 144–152 (2015)
7. Bonifati, A., Martens, W., Timm, T.: DARQL: Deep analysis of SPARQL queries. In: WWW, pp. 187–190 (2018)
8. Bonifati, A., Martens, W., Timm, T.: An analytical study of large SPARQL query logs. VLDB J. 1–25 (2019)
9. Cai, L., Zhu, Y.: The challenges of data quality and data quality assessment in the big data era. Data Sci. J. **14** (2015)
10. Ceolin, D., Maccatrozzo, V., Aroyo, L., De-Nies, T.: Linking trust to data quality. In: METHOD Workshop (2015)
11. Dividino, R., Sizov, S., Staab, S., Schueler, B.: Querying for provenance, trust, uncertainty and other meta knowledge in RDF. JWS **7**(3), 204–219 (2009)
12. Djebri, A.E.A., Tettamanzi, A.G.B., Gandon, F.: Linking and negotiating uncertainty theories over linked data. In: Companion of WWW, pp. 859–865 (2019)
13. Dong, X.L., et al.: Knowledge-based trust: estimating the trustworthiness of web sources. arXiv preprint arXiv:1502.03519 (2015)

14. Dumitrache, A., et al.: Crowdtruth 2.0: quality metrics for crowdsourcing with disagreement. arXiv preprint arXiv:1808.06080 (2018)
15. Gambetta, D., et al.: Can we trust trust? Br. J. Sociol. **13**, 213–237 (2000)
16. Gaona-García, P.A., et al.: A fuzzy logic system to evaluate levels of trust on linked open data resources. Revista Facultad de Ingeniería Universidad de Antioquia **86**, 40–53 (2018)
17. Hartig, O.: Querying trust in RDF data with TSPARQL. In: ESWC, pp. 5–20 (2009)
18. Hung, E., Deng, Y., Subrahmanian, V.S.: RDF aggregate queries and views. In: ICDE, pp. 717–728 (2005)
19. Khouri, S., Lanasri, D., Saidoune, R., Boudoukha, K., Bellatreche, L.: Loglinc: log queries of linked open data investigator for cube design. In: DEXA, pp. 352–367 (2019)
20. Llave, M.R.: Data lakes in business intelligence: reporting from the trenches. Procedia Comput. Sci. **138**, 516–524 (2018)
21. Malyshev, S., Krötzsch, M., González, L., Gonsior, J., Bielefeldt, A.: Getting the most out of Wikidata: semantic technology usage in Wikipedia's knowledge graph. In: Vrandečić, D., et al. (eds.) ISWC 2018. LNCS, vol. 11137, pp. 376–394. Springer, Cham (2018). https://doi.org/10.1007/978-3-030-00668-6_23
22. Sales, T.P., Almeida, J.P.A., Santini, S., Baião, F., Guizzardi, G.: Ontological analysis and redesign of risk modeling in archimate. In: EDOC, pp. 154–163 (2018)
23. Sales, T.P., Baião, F., Guizzardi, G., Almeida, J.P.A., Guarino, N., Mylopoulos, J.: The common ontology of value and risk. In: ER, pp. 121–135 (2018)
24. Skoutas, D., Simitsis, A.: Ontology-based conceptual design of ETL processes for both structured and semi-structured data. IJSWIS **3**(4), 1–24 (2007)
25. Suriarachchi, I., Plale, B.: Crossing analytics systems: a case for integrated provenance in data lakes. In: e-Science, pp. 349–354 (2016)
26. Tian, Y., Umbrich, J., Yu, Y.: Enhancing source selection for live queries over linked data via query log mining. In: JIST, pp. 176–191 (2011)

Author Index